The Cambridge History of English Literature

Edited by

A. W. WARD, Litt.D., F.B.A.,
Master of Peterhouse

and

A. R. WALLER, M.A., Peterhouse

14 volumes, and two volumes supplementary to the History, 8vo. Price per volume $2.50 net. Subscriptions received for the complete work at $36.00 net, payable at the rate of $2.25 on the notification of the publication of each volume.

Send for complete descriptive circular

G. P. PUTNAM'S SONS

New York   London

THE CAMBRIDGE HISTORY

OF

ENGLISH LITERATURE

VOLUME IX

FROM STEELE AND ADDISON
TO POPE AND SWIFT

The Cambridge History

of

English Literature

Edited by

A. W. Ward, Litt.D., P.B.A.

Master of Peterhouse

and

A. R. Waller, M.A.

Peterhouse

Volume IX

From Steele and Addison
To Pope and Swift

New York: G. P. Putnam's Sons
Cambridge, England: University Press
1913

The Knickerbocker Press, New York

PREFATORY NOTE

THE present volume, we hope, will shortly be followed by the tenth, dealing with the age of Johnson. As the canvas grows more crowded, we must ask our readers to take note that the grouping of writers, on the principles which we have endeavoured to follow in this work, makes it impossible, even were it desirable, to maintain a strict chronological order as to the inclusion of particular names in particular volumes. Thus, in the present volume, notices of several divines, and, again, of several dramatists, together with the mention of other names, have had to be reserved for its successor.

Mr. H. G. Aldis has been good enough to contribute to this volume a full and retrospective bibliography of Scottish literature, from the beginning of the seventeenth century onwards, which, though covering wider ground than the chapter to which it is attached, will, we believe, be welcome to students. We have also to thank Mr. A. T. Bartholomew for much bibliographical and other assistance, and Mr. J. B. Williams for some valuable notes on the history of English journalism.

A. W. W.
A. R. W.

September, 1912

CONTENTS

CHAPTER I

DEFOE—THE NEWSPAPER AND THE NOVEL

By W. P. TRENT, LL.D., D.C.L., Professor of English Literature in Columbia University, New York

CHAPTER II

STEELE AND ADDISON

By HAROLD ROUTH, M.A., Peterhouse, Lecturer in English Literature in the Goldsmiths' College, University of London

CHAPTER III

POPE

By EDWARD BENSLY, M.A., Trinity College, Professor of Latin, University College of Wales, Aberystwyth

CHAPTER IV

SWIFT

By GEORGE ATHERTON AITKEN, M.V.O.

CHAPTER V

ARBUTHNOT AND LESSER PROSE WRITERS

By G. A. AITKEN, M.V.O.

CHAPTER VI

LESSER VERSE WRITERS

I

By THOMAS SECCOMBE, M.A., Balliol College, Oxford

II

By GEORGE SAINTSBURY, LL.D., D.Litt., F.B.A., Merton College, Oxford, Professor of Rhetoric and English Literature in the University of Edinburgh

CHAPTER VII

HISTORICAL AND POLITICAL WRITERS

I. BURNET

By A. W. WARD, Litt.D., P.B.A., Master of Peterhouse

Contents

Contents

CHAPTER XI

BERKELEY AND CONTEMPORARY PHILOSOPHY

By W. R. SORLEY, Litt.D., F.B.A., Fellow of King's College, Knightbridge Professor of Moral Philosophy

PAGE

CHAPTER XII

WILLIAM LAW AND THE MYSTICS

By CAROLINE F. E. SPURGEON, Dr. of the University of Paris, Fellow of King's College for Women and Lecturer in English Literature at Bedford College, University of London

CHAPTER XIII

SCHOLARS AND ANTIQUARIES

I. BENTLEY AND CLASSICAL SCHOLARSHIP

By JAMES DUFF DUFF, M.A., Fellow and Lecturer in Classics
of Trinity College

II. ANTIQUARIES

By H. G. ALDIS, M.A., Peterhouse; Secretary of the University
Library

CHAPTER XIV

SCOTTISH POPULAR POETRY BEFORE BURNS

By T. F. HENDERSON

Contents

CHAPTER XV

EDUCATION

By J. W. ADAMSON, Fellow of King's College, London, and
Professor of Education in the University of London

ADDENDUM

VOL. VII

p. 468

Daniel, George, of Beswick (1616–57). Poems, from the original MSS. Ed. Grosart, A. B. 4 vols. 1878.

Fisher, Payne (1616–93). Marston Moor, Eboracense carmen. 1650. [Payne Fisher wrote much verse (chiefly Latin) in praise of Oliver Cromwell, after whose death he spent several years in the Fleet, and wrote as a royalist.]

CORRIGENDA

VOL. VIII

p. 7, footnote, line 2, *for* Royal Exchange *read* New Exchange, Strand

p. 31, footnote 2 at end, *read*: to the researches, conducted independently in each case, of W. J. Lawrence and Sir Ernest Clarke

p. 34, l. 4, and elsewhere, *for* St. Évremond *read* Saint-Évremond

p. 244. The verses, '*Why dost thou shade thy lovely face,*' here ascribed to Rochester, are the work of Quarles, and were first published in his *Emblems*. They have been printed in many editions of Rochester's poems, but whether they were claimed by him in jest, or falsely attributed to him by his editors, we have no means of knowing.

p. 423, l. 2, from foot, *for* 1655 *read* 1665

p. 425, l. 23. *Read as follows in lieu of the next two sentences of the text:* English imitations also appeared; Lord Broghill (Orrery)'s *Parthenissa* (first part) in 1654, with which, in spite of its "handsome language," Dorothy Osborne was not very much taken, and Sir George Mackenzie's *Aretina or the Serious Romance* in 1661. A complete edition of *Parthenissa* in three volumes was published in 1665 and 1667.

p. 430, l. 6, *insert* the *before* chevalier

p. 478, l. 34, Howard, James *should be inserted before* All Mistaken. (This and the subsequent play were by him, not by Edward Howard.)

p. 479, l. 24, *the entry Cibber should read*:

Cibber, *Theophilus.* An Account of the Lives of the Poets of Great Britain and Ireland, 5 vols. 1753.

p. 503, l. 8, *for* Grammont. Des *read* Grammont; des

p. 537, ll. 1, 2, *transfer entries* Gray, G. J. and Elton, O. *to heading* Sir Isaac Newton

VOL. IX

p. 355, footnote 1, for *The City of Gods,* read *The City of God.*

Defoe—The Newspaper and the Novel

CHAPTER I

Defoe—The Newspaper and the Novel

DEFOE is known to our day chiefly as the author of *Robinson Crusoe*, a pioneer novelist of adventure and low life. Students, indeed, remember that he was also a prolific pamphleteer of unenviable character and many vicissitudes. To his early biographers, he was not merely a great novelist and journalist, but a martyr to liberal principles and a man of exalted probity. His contemporaries, on the contrary, inclined to regard him as an ignorant scribbler, a political and social outcast, a journalist whose effrontery was equalled only by his astonishing energy. There is, probably, a measure of truth in all these views; it is certainly true that the novelist we remember was evolved out of the journalist we have forgotten.

When Defoe established his most important periodical, *The Review*, in February, 1704, the English newspaper, in a technical sense, was not quite fifty years old. There had been weekly *Corantos*, or pamphlets of foreign news, from 1622 to 1641, and, throughout the period of the civil war and the commonwealth, there had been weekly "newsbooks" designed to spread domestic news, official or unofficial, parliamentary or royalist; but there existed no real newspaper, no news periodical, not a pamphlet or a newsletter, until the appearance of *The Oxford Gazette* in November, 1665.[1] The intrigues that led to the founding of this paper, which soon became *The London Gazette* and, for many years, meagre and jejune though it was, possessed a monopoly of the printed news, are of abundant interest, but have already been noticed in this work.[2] It must suffice to say that such predecessors in journalism as Defoe had before

---

[1] See Williams, J. B., *History of English Journalism*, etc., p. 7.
[2] See *ante*, Vol. VII, Chap. xv, pp. 411–414.

he was of an age to be influenced by what he read were, in the main, purveyors of news through pamphlets and written news-letters—interesting and able men, many of them; generally staunch partisans; sometimes, as in the case of Marchamont Nedham, whom one regrets to encounter in Milton's company, shameless turncoats. From their rather sorry ranks, two figures of special importance stand out: Henry Muddiman, the best news disseminator of his day, who has been mentioned previously,[1] and Roger L'Estrange, who was worsted by Muddiman as an editor of "newsbooks," but in whom, as political journalist, indefatigable pamphleteer and competent man of letters, we discover Defoe's most significant prototype.

L'Estrange was born, of good Norfolk stock, on 17 December, 1616. He received an education befitting his station and, on reaching his majority, became a zealous supporter of the king. Betrayed in a plot for the recapture of Lynn, he was seized, unfairly condemned to death, reprieved, left languishing for a few years in Newgate and, finally, suffered to escape. During his imprisonment, he made a small beginning as a pamphleteer, and it is to the exasperating treatment accorded him that we may partly attribute the dogmatic partisanship which is the most striking characteristic of his political and ecclesiastical writings. His adventures on the continent and his experiences in England from his return in 1653 to the death of Cromwell may be passed over. Late in 1659, he came forward as a writer of pamphlets and broadsides designed to promote the restoration of Charles II. Many of them may be read in the tract entitled *L'Estrange his Apology*, but his only production of the period that possesses any general interest is his scurrilous attack on Milton bearing the inhuman title *No Blinde Guides*. After the restoration, L'Estrange felt that his services were not duly recognised; but he did not, on that account, neglect his assumed duties as castigator of all persons whom he deemed factious—particularly presbyterians. His tracts of this period often contain important information about their author and throw light on the times; but, save for occasional passages of quaint homeliness, they make dismal reading.

In the summer of 1663, he published his stringent *Considerations and Proposals in order to the Regulation of the Press*, and

[1] See *ante*, Vol. VII, pp. 396, 411 ff.

he soon had his reward in his appointment as one of the licensers, and as surveyor of printing presses. He was also granted a monopoly of the news; but his two weekly newsbooks caused dissatisfaction, and *The Gazette* finally drove him from the field. He was more successful as a suppressor of seditious publications —witness the notorious case of John Twyn—but such sinister success as he had has cast upon his name, whether fully merited or not, a reproach from which it will never be freed. For about fifteen years, his official duties seem to have checked his fluent pen; but, during this period, he began, probably with his version of the *Visions* of Quevedo, in 1667, the long series of his translations, and he published, in 1674, a sensible *Discourse of the Fishery*, thus anticipating Defoe in the character of promoter.

In 1679, he assailed Shaftesbury and the exclusionists in pamphlets which won him the royal regard. During the next year, he was in the thick of the controversy about the popish plot, labouring to allay the popular fury against Roman Catholics. His denunciations of Oates and other informers led to machinations against himself. He was falsely accused of endeavouring by bribery to secure the defamation of Oates, and he was charged with being a papist. He was acquitted by the council; but public opinion ran so high against him that he fled, for a short time, to Holland. To employ a phrase in the title of one of his tracts, "a whole Litter of Libellers" assailed him at this season; but "the Dog Towzer" was not to be thus daunted. He returned in February, 1681, and kept the press busy, not only with apologetic pamphlets, but with bitter assaults upon the dissenters and with one of the most important of his works, his political newspaper *The Observator: In Question and Answer.*

This journal, of two double-columned folio pages, began its career on 13 April, 1681, and ran to 9 March, 1686/7. After no. 5, readers could not be sure how many issues they would receive a week; but, as a rule, the tireless editor supplied them with three or four numbers devoted to abuse of dissenters, whigs, trimmers and Titus Oates. Throughout, he employed a device, which he had not originated, but which his example made popular for a generation—the trick of casting each number in the form of a dialogue. It is needless to attempt to chronicle the changes in the form of title and in the persons of his interlocutors, since, in order to avoid the mistakes already made by bibliographers, one would need to examine every page of the periodical—an appalling task. It is enough to say that L'Estrange had a large share in the final discrediting of Oates; that, until it suited the king's purpose to issue the declaration of indulgence, clerical and royal favour crowned his ecclesiastical and political zeal; and that his many critics had abundant excuse for the diatribes they continued to issue against him. Defoe, who was probably in London during the larger part of *The Observator's* life, may thus early have determined that, if ever he should edit a paper of his own, he would avoid the awkward dialogue form and an extravagance that defeated its own ends.

The date of his knighting by James II, April, 1685, may be held to mark the zenith of L'Estrange's career. In 1686, he was sent on a mission to Scotland; in 1687, in his answer to Halifax's famous *Letter to a Dissenter*, he supported the king's claim to the dispensing power; in 1688, he received from James a reward in money that may have made him feel less keenly the suppression of *The Observator*. At the revolution, he was dismissed from his post of licenser and imprisoned. For several years after his release, he led a troubled life. He was more than once rearrested; his health declined; his wife died ruined by gambling; he was disappointed in his children; and, long before his death, on 11 December, 1704, he had lost all his influence and become a bookseller's hack. Yet it is to this period that we owe his most important literary work, *The Fables of Æsop and other Eminent Mythologists: with Moral Reflections*, which appeared as a folio in 1692, and was followed, in 1699, by a second part, *Fables and Storyes Moralized*. His long series of translations, many of them from the French and the Spanish,[1] is noted elsewhere. Defoe did not follow far in his steps as a translator; but it is not improbable that, when, in his old age, he found himself cut off from journalism, he remembered the example set him by L'Estrange and displayed an even more remarkable general literary fecundity. It is almost needless to add that, whether as journalist, pamphleteer, or miscellaneous writer, Defoe, in comparison with his predecessor, profited from the general advance made by the late seventeenth century toward a less cumbrous prose.

[1] Cf. as to these, *post*, Chap. x.

There was another journalist contemporary with L'Estrange to whom Defoe was indebted. This was Henry Care, whose opposition to the church party made him a special object of *The Observator's* vituperations. He edited, in 1678–9, a quarto *Pacquet of Advice from Rome*, which soon added to its title the word *Weekly* and continued its existence, through five volumes, to 13 July, 1683. Later, he supported James and the Roman Catholics. If we may trust Defoe, there is no doubt that Care's early death was brought on by bad habits. He is chiefly important to us because it was from him that Defoe borrowed the general idea of the department in *The Review* known as the proceedings of "the Scandalous Club."

Space is wanting for a full discussion of the evolution of journalism between the fall of *The Observator* and the founding of *The Review*. A few meagre newspapers sprang up to rival *The Gazette* so soon as James had fled the kingdom, and, between 1690 and 1696, John Dunton, the eccentric bookseller, later famous for his *Life and Errors* and for his absurd political pamphlets, published his *Athenian Gazette*, afterwards *The Athenian Mercury*, as an organ for those curious in philosophical and recondite matters. From Dunton, Defoe borrowed some of the topics discussed in the miscellaneous portion of his paper. In 1695, the Licensing Act, which had for some years been administered with moderation, was allowed to lapse, and several new journals were at once begun, some of which were destined to have important careers. Chief among these were *The Flying Post*, a triweekly whig organ, edited by the Scot George Ridpath, for many years a bitter opponent of Defoe, and the tory *Post Boy*, which was published by Abel Roper, a special object of whig detestation, and, for some time, edited by Abel Boyer, who, later, changed his politics. These and *The Post Man*, as well as the printed newsletter of Ichabod Dawks and the written newsletter of John Dyer, notorious for his partisan mendacity, were primarily disseminators of news. They were supplemented, in March, 1702, by the first of the dailies, *The Daily Courant*, which, like the weekly *Corantos* of eighty years before, consisted of translations from foreign papers. It soon fell into the hands of Samuel Buckley, a versatile man with whom Defoe was often at odds. On 1 April, 1702, the most important strictly political organ of the whigs was begun by

John Tutchin, a small poet and pamphleteer, who had suffered under Jeffreys and was still to endure persecution for his advanced liberal opinions. He took L'Estrange's old title, *The Observator*, and continued the dialogue form. Two years later, Tutchin's form and his extreme partisanship were imitated by the famous non-juror and opponent of the deists, Charles Leslie, whose short-lived *Rehearsal* became the chief organ of the high churchmen. Meanwhile, a few months before Leslie's paper appeared, Defoe, not without Harley's connivance, had begun his *Review* as an organ of moderation, ecclesiastical and political, and of broad commercial interests. Although his satirical discussions of current topics may have given useful hints to Steele and Addison, it seems clear that Defoe's chief contribution to journalism at this period is to be found in his abandonment of the dialogue form and of the partisan tone of his predecessors and immediate contemporaries. He adopted a straightforward style, cultivated moderation and aimed at accuracy, because, more completely than any other contemporary journalist, he made it his purpose to secure acquiescence rather than to strengthen prejudice. But, in what follows, we must confine ourselves to his own varied career.

Defoe is usually said to have been born in London in 1661, the date being derived from a reference to his age made in the preface to one of his tracts. That this is an error seems clear from his marriage license allegation. He must have been born in London, the son of James Foe, a butcher of the parish of St. Giles, Cripplegate, at the end of 1659 or early in 1660. His father came of Northamptonshire stock; but the name of his mother's family has not been ascertained. Beyond the fact that his parents were presbyterians, who early set him apart for the ministry, we know little concerning his childhood. When he was about fourteen, he entered a dissenters' school kept at Stoke Newington by Charles Morton, a somewhat distinguished scholar and minister, and he probably remained there three or four years, by which time he had given up the idea of becoming a preacher. He has left some account of his education, which appears to have been practical and well adapted to the needs of his journalistic career, since emphasis was laid on history, geography and politics, the modern languages and proficiency in the vernacular.

Scarcely anything is known of his life between 1677 or 1678, when he may be presumed to have left school, and January, 1683–4, the date of his marriage, when he was a merchant in Cornhill, probably a wholesale dealer in hosiery. There is evidence from his writings that, at one time, he held some commercial position in Spain, and it is clear that his biographers have not collected all the passages that tend to show his acquaintance with Italy, southern Germany and France. As it is difficult to place any long continued absence from England after his marriage, it seems plausible to hold that he may have been sent to Spain as an apprentice in the commission business and have taken the opportunity, when returning, to see more of Europe. His "wander-years," if he had them, must be placed between 1678, the year of the popish plot and the murder of Godfrey, and 1683, the year of the repulse of the Turks from Vienna, since it is practically certain that he was in London at each of these periods.

Not much more is known of his early life as a married man. His wife, Mary Tuffley, who survived him, was of a well-to-do family, bore him seven children and, from all we can gather, proved a good helpmeet. That he soon left her to take some share in Monmouth's rebellion seems highly probable; but that, between 1684 and 1688, he became an embryo sociologist and was engaged in the systematic travelling about England that has been attributed to him is very doubtful. How he escaped Jeffreys, whether he ever was a presbyterian minister at Tooting, what precisely he wrote and published against James II— these and other similar matters are still mysteries. It seems plain that he joined William's army late in 1688; that he took great interest in the establishment of the new government; that his standing in the city among his fellow dissenters was outwardly high; and that he cherished literary aspirations. His first definitely ascertained publication is a satire in verse of 1691. In the following year he became a bankrupt, with a deficit of about £17,000.

It is usual to attribute his failure to unbusinesslike habits, and to pay little attention to the charges of fraud brought against him later. As a matter of fact, this period of his life is so dark that positive conclusions of any kind are rash. It would seem, however, that he suffered unavoidable losses through the war with France, that he was involved in too many kinds of enterprises, some of them speculative, and that his partial success in paying off his creditors warrants leniency toward him.   Some friends appear to have stood by him to the extent of offering him a situation in Spain, which he could afford to reject because of better opportunities at home.   Within four years, he was doing well as secretary and manager of a tile factory near Tilbury.   He also served as accountant to the commissioners of the glass duty, and there is no good reason to dispute his claim that he remained in fairly prosperous circumstances until he was ruined, in 1703, by his imprisonment for writing *The Shortest Way with the Dissenters.*

Shortly after his bankruptcy, Defoe, full of the speculative spirit of the age, was engaged in composing his *Essay upon Projects*, which did not appear until 1697.   Of all his early productions, this is much the most interesting to the general reader, who is left wondering at the man's versatility and modernity, particularly in matters relating to education, insurance and the treatment of seamen.   At the end of 1697, he plunged, on the king's side, into the controversy with regard to the maintenance of a standing army, and he continued to publish on the subject, though some of his tracts have escaped his biographers.   In 1698, he began writing against occasional conformity in a manner which lost him much favour with his fellow dissenters, and he also made an effective contribution to the propaganda of the societies for the reformation of manners. His duties as head of a tile factory and as government accountant clearly did not occupy all his time, save for the single year 1699, to which not one work by him is plausibly assigned.   It was not until the end of 1700, however, that out of the small poet and occasional pamphleteer was evolved a prolific professional writer.   The occasion was the will of Charles II of Spain and the upsetting of William's plans for the partition of the Spanish monarchy.   Defoe supported his sovereign in several tracts, and he pleaded for the return of a parliament uncontrolled by moneyed interests.   But it was a sprawling satire in favour of the king, not homely tracts addressed to plain freeholders, that gave the middle-aged journalist his first taste of literary popularity.

This satire was *The True-Born Englishman*, which appeared

in January, 1701, and, both in authorised and in pirated editions, had an enormous sale. It was a reply to a poem by Tutchin, in which that journalist had voiced the popular prejudice against the foreign-born king. Defoe's vigorous verses turned the tables on his own hybrid people, and were good journalism, whatever one may think of them as poetry. They seem to have been the occasion of his introduction to the king, an honour which, much to the disgust of less favoured editors and pamphleteers, was not left unchronicled in his writings. We know little of his relations with William; but, at the time of his arrest for *The Shortest Way*, it was suspected that these had been close, and he himself dropped hints which cause one to believe that occasionally he served the king as an election agent much as, later, he served Harley.

"The Author of *The True-Born Englishman*," as Defoe for many years delighted to style himself, did not rest on his laurels as a writer during the short period before the death of his hero William. He published numerous tracts in which he dealt with occasional conformity, foreign affairs, particularly the inevitable war with France, the misdeeds of stock-jobbers and the rights of the people as opposed to the high-handed independence claimed by tories in parliament. The most weighty of these pamphlets is *The Original Power of the Collective Body of the People of England*, which is worthy of Somers; but we get a better idea of the character of Defoe himself through his attitude in the affair of the Kentish petitioners. There is something of the demagogue in the famous *Legion's Address*, which he wrote on this occasion; but, in his bold delivery of the document to Harley, the speaker, there is something of the uncalculating love of liberty that marks the true tribune of the people. Although he was probably still under a cloud on account of his bankruptcy, and although fellow-dissenters detected treason in his utterances on occasional conformity, he was, doubtless, at the zenith of his reputation among his contemporaries when he sat by the side of the Kentish worthies at the banquet given them on their release from prison.

The two most important pamphlets of 1702 were both concerned with ecclesiastical affairs—the acute *New Test of the Church of England's Loyalty* and the notorious *Shortest Way with the Dissenters*. The latter may have been designed both to serve the whigs and to reassure those dissenters who had not liked or understood Defoe's attitude on the now burning question of occasional conformity. Whatever his purpose, he overshot the mark by assuming the character of an intolerant "high-flyer" and by arguing for the suppression of dissent at all costs, no matter how cruel the means. It was no time for irony, especially for irony that demanded more power to read between the lines than either dissenters or extreme church-men possessed. The former were alarmed; the latter were en-raged when they discovered that they had been hoaxed into accepting as the pure gospel of conformity a tract written by a nonconformist for the purpose of reducing ecclesiastical intoler-ance to an absurdity. In January, 1703, the tory Nottingham issued a warrant for Defoe's arrest, but he was not apprehended until the latter part of May. Where he hid himself is uncer-tain; but there is evidence in his own hand that the prospect of a prison had completely unnerved him. After he was lodged in Newgate, he managed to resist all attempts to worm out of him whatever secrets of state he might possess. At his trial in July, he was misled into pleading guilty, and he received a sentence out of all proportion to his offence. The fine and the imprisonment during the queen's pleasure were less terrible in his eyes than the three public exposures in the pillory, and he used all the means in his power, including a promise through William Penn to make important revelations, in order to escape the more degrading part of his punishment. His efforts proving of no avail, he plucked up his courage and wrote against his persecutors his spirited *Hymn to the Pillory*. When he was pilloried at the end of July, the temper of the fickle populace had changed, and, instead of being hooted and pelted, he was hailed as a hero. Neither he nor the mob knew that the ex-perience marked a turning point in the career of one of the most variously, though not nobly, gifted men England has ever produced. Before his persecution, Defoe may have been somewhat shifty as a man of affairs and, perhaps, as a writer; but, on the whole, he had been courageous in facing disaster, and he had been more or less consistent and high-minded in his attitude toward public matters. After he was pilloried, the sense that he had been unjustly punished rankled in him, and he soon became dependent upon the bounty of Harley; to insure the continuance of that bounty, he sacrificed some, at least, of his convictions; in revenge, he began to betray his employer; and, in the end, he stood before the public as the most discredited and mercenary journalist of the day. Such was not the view of his early biographers, who found in him, as we have seen, only a maligned patriot and man of genius; but it seems impossible for the close student of Defoe's political writings, despite the sympathy he must feel for a kindly, brilliant and hardly used man, not to agree, in the main, with the contemporaries who denounced him.

It was held until recently that Defoe remained in Newgate until August, 1704, although more careful examination of *The Review* would have led to a different conclusion. Research in other newspapers and the publication of his correspondence with Harley have now made it clear that he was released, through Harley's good offices, about 1 November, 1703. This disposes of the story that *The Review* was founded while its editor was in prison, and it also absolves us from the necessity of supposing that, when, in his volume on the great storm, Defoe described devastations of which he had been an eye-witness, he was drawing on his imagination. The fact that, in this matter and in not a few others, research has tended to strengthen belief in his ability to tell the truth about himself ought to make it less possible for critics to treat him as totally untrustworthy. Such criticism has never been based upon adequate psychological study of the man, and it is not warranted by a minute examination even of his most discreditable writings. Instead of becoming a shameless and wholesale liar, Defoe, in all probability, developed into a consummate casuist who was often his own chief dupe. His experience of the pillory was ever before his eyes, and it seemed to him necessary and even meritorious to avoid the pitfalls that lay in those days before all journalists. For more than twenty years, he practised every sort of subterfuge to preserve his anonymity, and he soon grew sufficiently callous to write, presumably for pay, on all sides of any given subject. Within the arena of journalism, he was a treacherous mercenary who fought all comers with any weapon and stratagem he could command. Outside that arena, he was a pious, philanthropical, fairly accurate and trustworthy man and citizen.

Space fails us for a discussion of the pamphlets and poems of this period, the stream of which not even imprisonment or his employment as a busy agent for Harley could check. Mention should be made, however, of the two volumes of his collected writings—the only collection made by himself—which appeared in 1703 and 1705, as well as of controversial pamphlets against the eccentric John Asgill, the publicist Dr. Davenant, the tory politician and promoter Sir Humphrey Mackworth and the fanatic Charles Leslie. Only one tract of them all possesses permanent interest, the famous *Giving Alms no Charity*, of November, 1704, and even that is probably less of an economic classic than some have thought it. Defoe's real achievement of the time was his establishment of *The Review*, the importance of which as an organ of political moderation has already been pointed out. It was equally important as a model of straight-forward journalistic prose, and, in its department of miscellanea, its editorial correspondence when Defoe was away from London and other features, it probably exerted an influence out of proportion to its circulation, which was never large. In its small four-paged numbers, in the main triweekly, the student of contemporary France, of English ecclesiastical history, of the union with Scotland, of the war of the Spanish succession, of the movements of the Jacobites, of the trial of Sacheverell, of British commerce and of manners and customs in general finds abundant materials to his hand. Why its eight large volumes and incomplete ninth supplementary volume (17 February, 1704, to 11 June, 1713) have never been reprinted from the unique set in the British Museum it is hard to say. Even as the record of one man's enterprise and pertinacity (Defoe wrote it practically unaided and kept it going with extraordinary regularity during the years he was serving as a government agent in Scotland), it would be worthy of a place on our shelves— much more so when that man is the author of *Robinson Crusoe*. Such republication would not be equivalent to the erection of a monument of shame, since, on the whole, the Defoe of *The Review* is liberal and consistent in his politics and far-sighted in commercial and economic matters. In a sense, too, a reissue of these rare volumes would be a monument to the prescience of that enigmatical, underestimated politician Robert Harley, who clearly perceived the political importance of the press.

Not even the briefest description can be given of Defoe's
horseback rides through England in 1704 and 1705 as an election
agent for Harley. Highhanded tories and creditors set on by
his enemies tried to stop him; but he eluded them and continued
both to send Harley reports which prove him to have been a
journalist of the first order, and to make observations which
stood him in good stead in his later sociological and economic
writings. He also found time to compose and publish his dull
political allegory *The Consolidator* and to labour on his still
more ponderous satire in verse *Jure Divino*, which appeared the
next year, 1706, in folio, adorned with a full-wigged portrait of
the self-complacent author. These, as well as his impudent
satire *The Dyet of Poland*, his excellent pamphlets against
religious intolerance in South Carolina, his indiscreet support,
in a tract called *The Experiment*, of the clerical impostor Abraham Gill, his spirited answers to Lord Haversham, who had
taunted him with poverty and writing for hire, are all, more or
less, forgotten; but, so long as the literature of the supernatural
finds favour, there will be interested readers of the one classic
production of this stage of his career, *A True Relation of the
Apparition of one Mrs. Veal, the next Day after her Death, to one
Mrs. Bargrave at Canterbury, the 8th of September, 1705*. Even
this convincingly realistic narrative is, thanks to the researches
of George A. Aitken, no longer to be credited, as Sir Walter
Scott and many others have thought, to Defoe the master of
verisimilitude in fiction. It is now seen to be the circumstantial account of a ghost story current at the time, a product of
Defoe's genius for reporting, not a clever hoax designed to sell
Drelincourt's pious manual.

From the autumn of 1706 to the spring of 1710, Scotland is
the main scene of Defoe's activity, and Scottish affairs are the
main subject of his pen. His movements and whereabouts are
not always certain; but it is evident that none of his biographers
has realised how large a portion of his time he spent out of
London as the agent, first of Harley, then of Godolphin. He
was in Scotland from October, 1706, to December, 1707, for-
warding the union in every way in his power and, after that
was secured, labouring to allay popular discontent. He kept
the press busy with pamphlets, the full tale of which will
doubtless never be known. He wrote Harley long and inter-

esting letters; he attended parliamentary committees; he furnished statistics on matters of trade; he wormed himself into the confidence of men in all positions—in short, to use his own phrase, he played the part of a perfect spy, developing his powers of duplicity at every turn.   Few agents have ever more thoroughly earned their hire, or have served more niggardly masters than was Harley.   When, at last, Defoe, almost reduced to penury, was allowed to return without the place in the customs for which he hoped, he found his patron tottering to his fall.   He was graciously permitted to transfer his services to Godolphin and, early in 1708, was sent back to Scotland.   Of his labours for his new chief, we have no full account; but there was probably no decline in his faithfulness and efficiency.   There was some decline in his literary activity, for the main work of 1708–9 is his huge, dull, but apparently accurate *History of the Union*, a volume which shows that Defoe had not a little of the methodical patience characteristic of latter-day historians, but, as yet, little of the skill in book-making which he was afterwards conspicuously to display.

In the early months of 1710, Defoe, although he saw clearly the folly of impeaching Sacheverell, made that noisy clergyman the subject of several tracts.   Later, he transferred his services to Harley, not, however, without allowing himself free criticism of the extreme tories.   In the autumn, he was sent to Scotland to watch the Jacobites, and it is a letter written to Harley at this time which first causes us to suspect that he was betraying his employer.   Some years ago, William Lee attributed to Defoe, on strong internal evidence, a satirical pamphlet of 1711, entitled *Atalantis Major;* but no one would suspect, from the way in which Defoe refers to his efforts to suppress this tract, that he was its unblushing author.   There is no absolute proof that he was; but, when, a little later, we find him charged with writing against Harley in *The Protestant Post Boy*, and, later still, encounter attacks upon that minister in pamphlets full of the characteristics of Defoe's style, our faith in the journalist's fidelity is greatly shaken.

Whether the inscrutable Harley, now earl of Oxford, had entire faith in his agent does not appear.   Certain it is, however, that, for the next two or three years, Defoe was continually making surreptitious visits to the prime minister and sending him letters, which not infrequently contained requests for money. That he was as well paid by Oxford as enemies asserted may be doubted; but there is no doubt that his advice was sought on many matters and that he was employed by outsiders to secure the minister's countenance for various schemes. Meanwhile, the stream of pamphlets flowed una-bated, and the tone of *The Review* was adroitly changed in favour of peace with France. As a result, Defoe was despised and distrusted by whigs and tories alike. The modern student, making allowance for the factiousness of the times, for the undeveloped state of party government, for Defoe's pecuniary embarrassments and his social ostracism after the pillorying, finds it possible to extenuate his conduct and is impelled to admire his dexterity and his resourcefulness. There is ground, too, for maintaining that, in some important respects, he was consistent, and a better counsellor than Oxford deserved. He opposed the passage of the obnoxious schism bill, and he seems never to have wavered in his support of the Hanoverian suc-cession.

As luck would have it, his second imprisonment was the direct result of his activity against the Jacobites. During a visit to Scotland in the autumn of 1712, he was much alarmed at the progress Jacobitism seemed to be making, and he wrote several tracts on the subject, in some of which he made an unfortunate use of his favourite weapon, irony. Such a title as *Reasons against the Succession of the House of Hanover* should have deceived no one; but this tract and others furnished cer-tain whigs with an occasion for bringing an action against him for treason. Their object was twofold—to crush Defoe and to besmirch Oxford, if the latter took any overt measures to protect his unacknowledged agent. The scheme was clever, but Defoe's measures to counteract it—too intricate to be described here—were cleverer. He would doubtless have come off scot-free, had he not made the tactical mistake of reflecting in *The Review* upon chief justice Parker. This con-tempt of court led to his being confined, for a few days, in the queen's bench prison in May, 1713. Immediately upon his release, he began to edit a new trade journal *Mercator*, in the interest of Bolingbroke's treaty of commerce, suffering *The Review* to expire quietly. There is some, though, perhaps, not sufficient, evidence to show that, at this time, his services were controlled by Bolingbroke rather than by Oxford; but, towards the end of 1713, he was again in frequent communication with the latter, through whose favour he secured a pardon under the great seal for all past offences, thus effectually stopping, for the time, the schemes of his whig enemies.

The year 1714 was a turning point for him, as well as for his tory employers.   He continued *Mercator*[1] almost to the time of the queen's death.   The paper, together with numerous pamphlets of the period, including the four which form *A General History of Trade*, gives abundant proof of the liberality of his commercial views, although it scarcely justifies his modern admirers in styling him the father of free trade.   He also wrote voluminously in opposition to the schism bill; and he entered into obscure intrigues against his old enemy George Ridpath, which resulted in his forming a connection with a rival *Flying Post*.   In this, he published a glowing eulogy of the new king and an indiscreet attack upon one of the lords regent, which led to his indictment for libel and, in the following year, to his trial and conviction.   How he escaped punishment will soon appear.   Meanwhile, apparently with Oxford's connivance, he published the first of the three parts of his notorious apology for the administration of that statesman, *The Secret History of the White Staff*.   This was the signal for a swarm of acrimonious whig tracts, which made much capital out of Defoe's careless admissions with regard to his patron's intrigues with the Scottish Jacobites.   A second part, in which Bolingbroke was treated more leniently, speedily followed, and then, at the end of the year 1714, Defoe's health

[1] Perhaps it may not be amiss to give a concrete illustration of Defoe's casuistry.   This is furnished by a comparison of the evasive language he used in his *Appeal* (1715) with regard to his editorship of *Mercator*, and the frank language about his share in that journal which he permitted himself to use in a short-lived trade paper of 1719, *The Manufacturer*, which has escaped his bibliographers but was attributed to him by his contemporaries and is certainly his.   Moreover, in the *Appeal*, he stated categorically that he had "never had any payment or reward for writing any part" of *Mercator;* but in his letter to Oxford of 21 May, 1714, he wrote that Arthur Moore, who undertook to support the paper, had "declined any consideration for it ever since Lady Day last."   There is little reason to doubt that Defoe was a poorly paid editor; but it is very certain that his relations with *Mercator* were much closer than he wished readers of that periodical to believe.

broke down—or else he deemed it expedient to pose as an apoplectic who had not long to live.

A full discussion of this tangled matter would be tedious. Lee, who did not know the date of publication of Defoe's *Appeal to Honour and Justice, tho' it be of his worst enemies*, the masterly account of the journalist's career which closed with a pathetic note to the effect that he had been ill for six weeks and was still in grave peril, seems, by assigning the tract to January, 1715, to have fixed the date of his hero's illness in November and December, 1714, thus managing to make the bibliography of Defoe square not only with these dates but with high conceptions of his probity. Unfortunately, it has been discovered that the *Appeal* was published on 24 February, 1715. This brings the period of the illness into the early weeks of 1715, that is, into a time when, according to Lee, Crossley and a contemporary of Defoe, the pamphleteer William Pittis, our journalist was actively plying his trade. It does not follow that Defoe may not have been out of health about this time— his situation, with an expensive family, no fixed source of income, a worse than doubtful reputation and an indictment for libel hanging over him, might well have undermined an even stronger constitution than his; but it does seem to be clear that, on Oxford's repudiating the *White Staff* tracts, Defoe published several others designed to throw dust round the whole controversy and to minimise his own part in it, and that, these attempts failing, he wrote his *Appeal*, upon which he expended all the resources of his genius for casuistry, without succeeding in changing the opinions of his contemporaries one iota. It is a proof of his literary skill, however, that this adroit and moving pamphlet has misled many a confiding biographer and uninformed modern reader.

Belief in a serious breakdown of Defoe's health is rendered almost ridiculous by an examination of his bibliography, certain and plausible, for the year 1715. It contains at least thirty pamphlets and two thick volumes, the first instalments of *The Family Instructor* and of a *History of the Wars of Charles XII of Sweden*. No newspaper now taxed his pen for regular contributions, he had to support his family and, perhaps, drown his apprehensions as to the trial awaiting him, and he had every inducement to display his loyalty. Hence, a multitude of certain and suspected tracts on nearly every phase of affairs, especially on the rebellion of the autumn. Meanwhile, in July, he had been convicted of libel; but sentence had not been passed. It never was passed, probably because Defoe managed, through an appealing letter and by pointing to numerous loyal pamphlets, to secure the favour of that very chief justice Parker whom he had offended in 1713. Parker introduced him, as a valuable secret agent and journalist, to Lord Townshend, the principal secretary of state. A bargain was soon struck, the gist of which was that Defoe should continue to pass as a tory journalist still labouring under the displeasure of the government, and that, as such, he should edit mildly tory periodicals and secure employment with more rabid Jacobite organs, in order that he might be able to tone down or suppress treasonable articles and keep the administration posted upon what was going on in Jacobite circles. The arrangement seems to have lasted for some ten years, 1716–26, and, by his discovery of the letters attesting it, Lee succeeded, not only in showing that the older biographers were in error in supposing that Defoe's activity as a political journalist had ceased with Queen Anne's death, but, also, in disinterring from the newspapers of the time, particularly from the weeklies published by Mist and Applebee, a mass of articles surely from Defoe's pen and illustrative of his not inconsiderable powers as an essayist. His chief activity as a spy dates from 1716 to 1720 and is mainly connected with the office of the Jacobite publisher, Nathaniel Mist. Whether he was Mist's good or evil genius, whether, as Lee opined, Mist tried to kill Defoe on discovering his treachery and pursued him maliciously for many years, whether, on the other hand, Defoe's gradual abandonment of journalism was not due to advancing years and the competition of younger men, are questions we cannot discuss here. It seems enough to say that, prior to, and throughout, his short career as a writer of fiction, Defoe was almost preternaturally active as a journalist and pamphleteer.

His tracts for the year 1717 alone are sufficiently numerous and discreditable to warrant all that his contemporaries said of him as a mercenary scribbler. To this bad year, that of his exemplary *Memoirs of the Church of Scotland*, belong his forged *Minutes of Mesnager*, his unprincipled tracts against Toland, his impertinent and, in the main, overlooked contributions to the Bangorian controversy. As remarkable, however, as his industry, his versatility, his unscrupulousness and his impudence, is the confidence some modern students, notably Lee, have been able to maintain in him. Many of his tracts belonging to this period have been rejected because of the assumption that Defoe was too virtuous or too dignified to have written them, or that no mortal man could have written so much. It may be safely held that Defoe was capable of writing almost anything, and that few pens have ever filled with greater facility a larger number of sheets. On the other hand, no condemnation of Defoe the spy and scribbler is just that does not also include statesmen who, like Townshend and Stanhope, employed him, rivals, who, like Toland and Abel Boyer, were for ever hounding him, religious controversialists who set him a bad example and partisan publishers and public who suffered themselves to be exploited by him. With all his faults, he was probably the most liberal and versatile writer of his age; with his comparative freedom from rancour, he seems a larger and more humane figure than any of the more aristocratic men of letters that looked down on him, including Pope and Swift; though an Ishmael, he managed to secure comfort for his family and a partial amnesty for himself in his old age; and he wrote the most authentic and widely read classic of his generation.

Our reference to *Robinson Crusoe* brings us to 25 April, 1719, the date of the publication of the first part of that immortal story. Defoe was nearly sixty years old, but he had hitherto written almost nothing that would have preserved his name for the general public. During the next five years, most of his fiction was to be composed, and, during the ensuing six, he was to become perhaps the most extraordinarily prolific old man in the history of English literature. Although he never ceased to be a journalist and pamphleteer, he became, for the last eleven years of his life, primarily a writer of books, and especially of fiction. The change has surprised many, and a word or two must be given to an attempt to describe in outline his evolution.

Although there is evidence that Defoe was rather widely read in English *belles lettres*, particularly in Rochester and other authors of the restoration, there is little or no direct evidence that he was a wide reader of fiction.   It would be rash, however, to assume that he had not dipped into some of the reprinted Elizabethan romances; that he had not tried to read one or more of the interminable heroic romances, whether in the original French or in English versions or imitations; that he was ignorant of the comic and the satiric anti-romances, or that he had not read with some enjoyment the novels of his own time—the stories of intrigue by Aphra Behn, the highly coloured pictures of the court and of the aristocracy by Mrs. Manley, and the attempts at domestic fiction by Mrs. Eliza Haywood and other more or less forgotten women.   If some bibliographers are right, we must hold that he wrote more than one tract which shows the influence of Mrs. Manley's *New Atalantis*, and that he translated at least one picaresque story, abbé Olivier's *Life and Adventures of Signior Rozelli* (1709, 1713).   It is much more certain, however, that he must have been familiar with lives of criminals, with chapbooks and compilations such as those of Nathaniel Crouch ("R. Burton"), with the work of Bunyan and with *The Tatler* and *The Spectator*.   In other words, it is chiefly to the popular narratives of his day and to contributory forms like the essay and biography that Defoe owes whatever in his fiction is not due to his own genius and experience as a writer.

As a matter of fact—setting aside the possibility that he translated the story of Rozelli and even added a somewhat questionable appendix to the edition of 1713 and a *Continuation* in 1724—one can find in Defoe's writings, prior to 1719, grounds for believing that he may have evolved into a novelist of adventure and of low life with comparatively little indebtedness to previous writers of fiction.   He had had great practice in writing straightforward prose since 1697; and, by 1706—witness *Mrs. Veal*—he had learned how to make his reporting vivid and credible by a skilful use of circumstantial detail.   In his political allegory *The Consolidator*, he had begun, though crudely, to use his imagination on an extended scale, and he had already, in *The Shortest Way*, displayed only too well his gifts as an impersonator.   In some of the tracts written between 1710 and 1714, notably in the two parts of *The Secret History of the October Club*, he had shown great ability in satiric portraiture and considerable skill in reporting speeches and dialogue.   In

1715, he had introduced some mild religious fiction into *The Family Instructor*, and, three years later, in the second part of this book, he had made still greater use of this element of interest. In the same year, 1715, he had assumed the character of a quaker in some of his tracts; and, since 1711, he had been publishing predictions supposed to be made by a second-sighted highlander. Again, in 1715, he had described the career of Charles XII of Sweden as though he himself were "A Scots Gentleman in the Swedish Service"; and there is reason to believe that, in the following year, he wrote, as "A Rebel," a tract dealing with the rebellion in Scotland. In 1717, he skilfully assumed the character of a Turk who was shocked by the intolerance displayed by English Christians in the Bangorian controversy, and it seems almost certain that, in 1718, he wrote for Taylor, the publisher of *Robinson Crusoe*, a continuation of the *Letters* of the famous *Turkish Spy*. Finally, when it is remembered that, in 1718, he was contributing to *Mist's*, week by week, letters from fictitious correspondents, that his wide reading in geography had given him a knowledge of foreign countries, particularly of Africa and both Americas, and that he had long since shown himself to be a skilful purveyor of instruction and an adept at understanding the character of the average man, we begin to see that, given an incident like the experiences of Alexander Selkirk and an increasing desire to make money through his pen in order to portion his daughters, we have a plausible explanation of the evolution of Defoe the novelist out of Defoe the journalist and miscellaneous writer.

The immediate and permanent popularity of *Robinson Crusoe* is a commonplace of literary history. Defoe, who had a keen eye for his market, produced, in about four months, *The Farther Adventures* of his hero, which had some, though less, *vogue*, and, a year later, *Serious Reflections during the Life and Surprizing Adventures of Robinson Crusoe*, a volume of essays which had no *vogue* at all. The original part, *The Strange and Surprizing Adventures*, at once stirred up acrimonious critics, but, also, attracted many imitators and, in the course of years, became the occasion of legends and fantastic theories. All these—for example, the story that Harley was the real author of the book—may be dismissed without hesitation. Almost equally without foundation, despite his own statements, is the

notion that *Robinson Crusoe* is an allegory of Defoe's life.   It
may even be doubted whether he ever hawked his manuscript
about in order to secure a publisher.   Some things, however,
may be considered certain with regard to this classic.   Defoe
wrote it primarily for the edification, rather than for the delectation, of his readers, although he did not evade giving them
pleasure and although, assuredly, he took pleasure himself in
his own creation.   It is equally clear that, in many of its pages,
Defoe the writer of pious manuals is to be discovered; in others,
Defoe the student of geography and of volumes of voyages;
in others, Defoe the minute observer and reporter.   The book
is a product that might have been expected from the journalist
we know, save only for the central portion of the story, the
part that makes it a world classic, the account of Crusoe alone
on his island.   Here, to use a phrase applied by Brunetière to
Balzac, Defoe displays a power of which he had given but few
indications, the power to make alive.   This power to make
alive is not to be explained by emphasis upon Defoe's command
of convincing details or by any other stock phrase of criticism.
It is a gift of genius, denied to preceding English writers of
prose fiction, displayed by Defoe himself for a few years in a
small number of books, and rarely equalled since, although
after him the secret of writing an interesting and well-constructed tale of adventure was more or less an open one.   The
form of his story could be imitated, but not its soul.   The
universal appeal implied in the realistic account of the successful struggle of one man against the pitiless forces of nature was
something no one else could impart to a book of adventure,
something Defoe himself never caught again.   It is this that
links *Robinson Crusoe* with the great poems of the world and
makes it perhaps the most indisputable English classic of
modern times, however little of a poet, in a true sense, its author
may have been.

   That *Robinson Crusoe* was written "all in the day's work"
is clear to the student of Defoe's bibliography for 1719, which
includes, in addition, an attack on Bishop Hoadly, a biography
of baron de Goertz, a tract on stock-jobbing—precursor of
many pamphlets on the South Sea Bubble,—a life of captain
Avery, introducing the long series of tracts devoted to pirates
and other criminals, an account of that extraordinary prodigy

Dickory Cronke, otherwise known as "the Dumb Philosopher," contributions to *Mercurius Politicus*, *Mist's*, *The Whitehall Evening Post*, and a new paper founded by Defoe, *The Daily Post*—but the list seems endless. There is little reason, however, for believing that he kept his copy by him and poured it forth at specially favourable times, or that he had a "double" whose style is undistinguishable from his. He was, rather, the most practised and versatile journalist and hack writer of the day, known to publishers as willing to turn every penny, unhampered by regular official or commercial employment, and obliged to keep up his income in order that he might continue, as during the past five or six years, to live at Stoke Newington in a condition approaching affluence. One change, however, as has been noted, is apparent in Defoe's literary habits during the last twelve years of his life. Throughout his early career, the pamphlet was the form of composition best adapted to his genius, and the books he attempted were somewhat laboured and amorphous. During his later period, while he still wrote pamphlets freely, he tended more and more to the production of elaborate books, in the construction of which, despite continual lapses into garrulity, he displayed remarkable skill. Except for the summer journeys, which, from 1722 to 1725, may be presumed to have furnished him with materials for that delightful and invaluable guidebook in three volumes, *A Tour thro' the Whole Island of Great Britain*, and for short periods when he was disabled by the stone, Defoe's old age, up to the autumn of 1729, must have been that of an animated writing machine. Was he seeking to dull the pangs of conscience, or to live down a scandalous past? Probably the latter, and, more probably still, to lay by money for his daughter Hannah, who was certain to be an old maid.

The next book of importance after the two parts of *Robinson Crusoe* was *The History of the Life and Adventures of Mr. Duncan Campbell*, the deaf and dumb conjurer, which appeared at the end of April, 1720. A bibliographical mystery hangs over this curious production as well as over other books and tracts relating to Campbell. That Defoe is the main author of the original *History* and of a pamphlet entitled *The Friendly Demon* (1726) seems clear: that he may have been aided in the first of these either by William Bond or by Mrs. Eliza Haywood is probable, and that he had nothing to do with the other works relating to Campbell, save, possibly, the posthumous *Secret Memoirs* of 1732, is likely.   In May, 1720, came the book, which, together with *A Journal of the Plague Year* (1722), shows that Defoe possessed, not only a genius for producing effects of verisimilitude, but, also, a considerable share of something which it is hard to distinguish from historical imagination. This is, of course, *The Memoirs of a Cavalier*, the absorbing story of the wars in Germany and England, for the accuracy of which so many untrained persons have been willing to vouch that some critics have assumed for it a superfluous manuscript source.   A month later appeared that fine example of the fiction of adventure, *The Life, Adventures and Piracies of the Famous Captain Singleton*, which is a proof at once of Defoe's extensive knowledge of geography and of his power to extend his imagination, not only back into the past, as in *The Memoirs of a Cavalier*, but out into the regions of the far away and the strange. *Singleton* also holds attention by that interest in criminals which Defoe naturally began to display in greater degree so soon as he formed his six years' editorial connection with John Applebee, the chosen publisher of the confessions and biographies of noted malefactors.   It has, moreover, another link with Defoe's next great book, *The Fortunes and Misfortunes of the Famous Moll Flanders* (January, 1722), for, in *Singleton*, we find Defoe beginning to display a power of characterisation which is seen in very respectable measure in *Moll Flanders* and, also, in *Colonel Jacque* and *Roxana*.   It is, however, as a realistic picture of low life in the large that *Moll Flanders* is supreme, just as the book of the next month, *Religious Courtship*, is the unapproachable classic of middle class smugness and piety.   It is pious middle class folk that figure in the two books devoted to the great plague; but it is the pestilence itself that dominates our imagination and fills us with unstinted admiration for Defoe's realistic power.   That power is seen to a less extent in *The Impartial History of Peter Alexowitz the Present Czar of Muscovy* and in *The History and Remarkable Life of the truly Honourable Colonel Jacque;* but, so long as the latter book has readers, Charles Lamb's praise of the affecting picture of the little thief will command grateful assent.   If Lamb had gone farther and asserted that the year 1722, the year of *Moll Flanders*, of

Religious Courtship, of the *Due Preparations* and *A Journal of the Plague Year*, of *The History of Peter the Great*, and of *Colonel Jacque*, was the greatest *annus mirabilis* in the career of any English writer, who would have been rash enough to say him nay?

The next year is almost a blank unless we accept indecorous contributions to a controversy about the use of cold water as a specific in fevers—and an undignified Defoe is a person of whom some credulous students will form no conception. By March, 1724, however, we have our prolific and masterly writer once more, for that is the date of *The Fortunate Mistress*, better known as *Roxana*, the story in which Defoe makes his greatest advance, not a very great one after all, toward the construction of a well ordered plot. This, also, is the year of one of the best of his sociological works, his treatise on the servant question, *The Great Law of Subordination Considered*, as well as of the first volume of the *Tour*. Before the year closed, he had written his popular tracts on Jack Sheppard, and the last of his generally accepted works of fiction, *A New Voyage round the World*, notable for its description of the lower parts of South America and for the proof it affords that its author's powers of narration and description were on the wane. From 1725 to his death, Defoe is a writer of books of miscellaneous information rather than a pioneer novelist, yet there is reason to believe that he did not abandon the field of narration so entirely as has been generally held. *The Four Years Voyages of Capt. George Roberts* (1726) may be, in considerable measure, the dull record of the experiences of a real seaman, but it bears almost certain traces of Defoe's hand. The far more interesting *Memoirs of Captain George Carleton* (1728) has for its nominal hero a man who is known to have existed, and who may have taken a direct or indirect share in its composition; but it is now clear, almost beyond dispute, that the shaper of Carleton's book, the writer who has vitiated many of the accounts given of the career of Peterborough in Spain, is not dean Swift, as has been acutely argued, but our protean scribbler Daniel Defoe. It is less certain, perhaps, that Defoe, in 1729, performed for Robert Drury's entertaining *Journal* of his captivity in Madagascar precisely the services he had rendered to Carleton's *Memoirs;* but there is very strong evidence to support this view, which is that of Pasfield Oliver, the latest editor of the book.

But, apparently, there was no limit, save death, to Defoe's productiveness. Accordingly, we must pass over, with scarcely a word, the numerous pamphlets and volumes of the years 1725–31. The most important of the tracts are those of a sociological character, for example, the astonishingly suggestive *Augusta Triumphans: or the Way to make London the Most Flourishing City in the Universe*. The most interesting and important of the books is, most surely, *The Complete English Tradesman*, which, for variety of information, shrewd practical wisdom, engaging garrulousness and sheer carrying power of easy vernacular style, is nothing short of a masterpiece. Charles Lamb seems to have been rather fantastic in discovering in it a source of corruption for its author's countrymen. The book has probably corrupted just as many promising young men as *Roxana*—see the exemplary pages of Lee's biography of Defoe— has reclaimed wayward young women. Next to *The Tradesman* in interest, some would place the curious group of books dealing in a half sceptical, half credulous and altogether gossiping, fashion with occult subjects—*The Political History of the Devil*, *A System of Magic* and *An Essay on the History and Reality of Apparitions*. Others, with quite as much reason, will prefer *A Plan of the English Commerce*, or that sound and well written treatise *The Complete English Gentleman*, which, ironically enough, was left incomplete and was not published until about twenty years ago. The wiser lover of quaint and homely books will read, or, at least, glance over, all the productions of Defoe's last years on which he can lay his hands, will wish that the world might see a collected edition of them and will not allow the biographers to persuade him that there was any marked falling off in the old man's productivity, save for a mysterious period which stretched from the autumn of 1729 to the midsummer of 1730.

What happened to Defoe during these months we do not know and probably shall not know unless new documents unexpectedly come to light. In the spring of 1729, he had married his favourite daughter Sophia to the naturalist Henry Baker; in the autumn, he had been taken ill, just as the opening pages of *The Complete English Gentleman* were going through the press. In August, 1730, he was writing from Kent to his son-in-law Baker a letter full of complaints about his own bad health, his sufferings at the hands of a wicked enemy and his betrayal by one of his sons. It seems likely that he had transferred some property to his eldest son, Daniel, on condition that the latter would provide for his mother and her unmarried daughters, but that the shifty son of a shifty father had not lived up to his obligations. It is certain that, for some reason or other, the home at Newington, a pleasant one according to Baker's description, had been broken up after Defoe's recovery from his illness in the autumn of 1729. It seems probable that he believed it necessary to separate from his family and to take refuge in London and, later, in Kent. Was he the victim of hallucinations—had he any real enemy whose malice he must avoid—was he trying, as he had tried before the marriage, to elude certain financial demands made by the canny Baker— had he reverted to the practices of his early manhood and engaged in hazardous speculations? Who can tell? All that we now seem to know definitely is that, during the autumn of 1730 and the early winter of 1731, he was writing pamphlets and revising books in a way that indicates little falling off of energy and absolutely no decay of mental powers, and that, on 26 April, 1731, he died of a lethargy at his lodgings in Ropemaker's alley, Moorfields, not far from where he was born.

He was buried in what is now Bunhill fields. The newspapers of the day took slight, but not unfavourable, notice of his death; his library was sold in due course; his reputation as a writer went into a partial eclipse which lasted until the close of the century; and then, *mirabile dictu*, he was hailed by admiring biographers and critics, not merely as a great writer, but as a consistent patriot and a Christian hero. Of late, it has become impossible to view him, as a man, in any such favourable light; but it seems probable that he was more sinned against than sinning, and it is coming to be more and more admitted that, as a writer and an important figure of his age, he is second only to Swift, if even to him. Some incline to regard him as the most wonderfully endowed man of his times, seeing in him a master journalist, an adroit and influential politician with not a few of the traits of a statesman, an economist of sound and advanced views, a purveyor of miscellaneous information vast in its range and practical in its bearings, an unequalled novelist of adventure and low life and, last but not

least, a writer whose homely raciness has not been surpassed
and a man the fascinating mystery of whose personality cannot
be exhausted.   It is impossible to sum him up, but those who
are not satisfied with calling him "the author of *Robinson
Crusoe*" may content themselves with affirming that he is the
greatest of plebeian geniuses.

CHAPTER II

Steele and Addison

STEELE and Addison are writers of talent who rose almost to genius because they intuitively collaborated with the spirit of their age. They came to London at a time when, quite apart from politics, society was divided into two classes, apparently so irreconcilable that they seemed like two nations. On the one side was the remnant of the old order, which still cherished the renascence ideals of self-assertion and irresponsibility and had regained prominence at the restoration. They followed the old fashion of ostentation and self-abandonment, fighting duels on points of honour, vying with each other in quips and raillery, posing as atheists and jeering at sacred things, love-making with extravagant odes and compliments, applauding immoral plays, while the more violent, the "gulls" and "roarers," roamed through the town in search of victims to outrage or assault. The women, in these higher circles, read and thought of little but erotic French romances, wore false eyebrows and patches, painted themselves, gesticulated with their fans and eyes, intrigued in politics and passed the time in dalliance. But, on the other hand, the citizens of London, who, since Tudor times, had stood aloof from culture and corruption, were now no longer the unconsidered masses. Each new expansion of trade gave them a fresh hold on society, while the civil war, which had decimated or ruined the nobility, conferred on the middle class a political importance of which their fathers had never dreamt. As a rule, members of the citizen class who have risen in the social scale intermarry with the aristocracy and imitate the manners, and especially the vices, of the class into which they enter. But, in the great political revolution of the seventeenth century, merchants and traders had triumphed through their moral character even more than by their material prosperity. The time had come when England was weary of all the medieval fanaticism, brutality and prejudice which had risen to the surface in the civil war, and it was the citizen class, apart from the zealots on both sides, which had first upheld moderation. The feud which Greene, a century before, had symbolised as *a quaint dispute between the velvet breeches and cloth breeches* had entered upon its last phase. Votaries of Caroline elegance and dissipation had become a set apart. They still had all the glamour of wealth and fashion; but they had lost their influence on the civilisation of the country. The middle class had broken away from their leadership and had pressed forward to the front rank of national progress. It has already been shown[1] how they had trodden down the relics of a less humane and less reasonable age, reforming the laws for debt and the administration of prisons, refuting the superstition of witchcraft, attacking scholasticism in the universities and founding the Royal Society—nay, more, how the more enlightened had pleaded for a purer and simpler morality, for gentler manners, for a more modest yet dignified self-respect. To the superficial observer, these protests and appeals must have sounded like isolated voices in a confused multitude. In reality, they were indications of a new civilisation which was already fermenting underneath. A new London had sprung up since the great fire and, with it, a generation of Londoners whose temperament and occupations led them to form a standard of culture, honour and religion peculiar to themselves. Such progress is the work of a whole class. It is never initiated by individuals, though one or two thinkers are generally needed to give form and expression to the tendencies of the rest. In this case, the victory of "cloth breeches" was not complete until Steele and Addison had discovered in what quarter to look for the movement and in what form to reveal to men their own ideas. These writers saw further and deeper than their contemporaries, because each, according to his own character, had first been born again.

It was Steele who led the way. Nature had endowed him

[1] Ante, Vol. VII, Chap. xvi., pp. 437–451.

with the instincts and temperament of one of king Charles I's cavaliers. He had the same generosity, love of pleasure, restlessness, chivalry and tincture of classical culture. Like many others of this class, he was extremely impressionable; but, unlike his prototypes, he lived in an age when recklessness and self-indulgence, though still fashionable in some circles, ran counter to the better tendencies of the time. Thus, the conviviality and gallantry which were popular in the guardroom caused him many searchings of heart, when confronted by the disapproval of scholars and moralists. In such moments of inward discontent, the gay life of the capital lost its glamour; the puritan spirit came over him, and he perceived that the dissipation of the young man-about-town was, at best, a pose and the moral teaching of the ancients a lamentable protection against the temptation of the senses. Cicero, Seneca and Plutarch had proved persuasive monitors to many a Jacobean and Caroline essayist, because the renascence had endowed the classics with almost scriptural authority. But, though Steele belonged to the class which still clung to these guides from respect for the old times, he also came daily into contact with the new enlightened religion of the middle class. He committed to paper the thoughts which passed through his mind in these moments of reflection and published them in 1701 for the edification of others under the title *The Christian Hero*.

This booklet is an attempt to persuade educated men into accepting the Bible as a moral counsellor. Steele describes how Cato, Caesar, Brutus and Cassius died, and argues that heathen philosophy failed each in the great crisis of his life. He then tells over again the story of the creation of Adam and Eve, and how, after their fall, men became corrupt and so a prey to ambition and the love of ostentation. This dependence on the applause of the world is, to Steele, the root of all evil; even the tales which young fellows tell of debauches and seductions are prompted by "fame"; even "heathen virtues, which were little else but disguised or artificial passions (since the good was in fame) must rise or fall with disappointment or success." Christ, and then St. Paul, by their labours and death, first brought men help, teaching them that the true guide in conduct is conscience. Man sins or suffers through dependence on the world; he is saved by the inwardness and self-effacement of Christianity. In the spiritual distress which drove Steele to write this pamphlet, he had learnt to think for himself. The description of Eve's creation[1] shows that he had studied Milton, then an unfashionable author; the passage on chivalrous respect for women's virtue was a defiance to the conventionality which regarded immorality as a sign of high spirits; the advice that a man should do a kindness as if he would "rather have his generosity appear an enlarged self-love than a diffusive bounty" was a new ideal for good taste; in his contention that the false ideals of society led men to err, he touched the true weakness of his times.

Thus, *The Christian Hero* is important because it foreshadows Steele's message to his age. But, though the book passed through a second edition within the same year and continued to be popular with readers of a certain religious temperament, it was not otherwise a success. The prosperous middle class, busy with the peaceful round of city life, did not need to be warned against choosing Caesar or Brutus for their model or Seneca for their spiritual pastor. Nor, again, if they ever opened this little manual of meditations, would they find it clearly explained how the self-sacrifice of St. Paul and the divinity of Christ could guide them amid the thousand little perplexities of their growing social system. Steele sermonised on heroism to readers who were interested in manners, and deserved the fate "that from being thought no undelightful companion, he was soon reckoned a disagreeable fellow."[2]

This missionary spirit, when roused, impelled him to other forms of expression. Having not yet found his peculiar bent, he was inevitably attracted to the drama. During a century, comedy and tragedy, with intervals of repression, had been one of the most popular outlets for an author and must have seemed exactly the medium for a man with Steele's sense of humour and knowledge of character. Besides, the moral movement among the people, which had been influencing Steele, had also caught the theatre. Sir Richard Blackmore and Jeremy Collier[3] were calling for a pure and reformed drama,

[1] Chap. II.
[2] *Mr. Steele's Apology for Himself and his Writings*, 1714.
[3] Cf. *ante*, Vol. VIII, pp. 185 ff.

and so Steele's conscience, as well as his tastes, urged him to put his ideas on the stage. Since the restoration, writers of comedies had aimed at brilliance and cleverness. As the court was amused at cuckoldry, they represented seducers and seduced as endowed with all the wit, ingenuity, or beauty which society admired, while intrigues leading to adultery could always be rounded off into a well-constructed, if somewhat unoriginal, plot. Steele went over the same ground—love, courtship, married life, intrigue; his purpose, however, was avowedly to paint virtue and vice in their true colours. Following the example of Molière, from whom he borrowed freely, he covered his bad characters with ridicule and confusion. But he was not content to let them occupy the front of the stage, as Molière had done. He wished to champion virtue; so his villains, for the most part, are minor characters, dismissed with humiliation at the *dénouement*, while his leading figures are quite ordinary people, whose careers begin and end in the triumph of homely virtues. Such characters, however desirable in a book of devotions, lack true comic interest, and Steele was obliged to lead his heroes and heroines through a series of domestic calamities and surprises, in order to sustain sympathy. In *The Funeral, or Grief-à-la-mode* (1701), his first and best constructed comedy, the defunct Lord Brumpton has to be kept secretly alive all through the play, in order to shame his worldly widow's enjoyment of affluence and freedom, and to reward his daughters' two suitors. In *The Lying Lover* (1703), copied from Corneille's *Menteur*, young Bookwit becomes drunk, then fights and appears to kill his rival, is arrested, suffers all the pangs of remorse and the horrors of Newgate and, after this gruesome lesson against intemperance and duelling, learns that his victim still lives and ends by marrying the sweetheart whom he had courted with a fidelity rare on the stage. In *The Tender Husband* (1705), the third and last of Steele's plays at this period of his career, he rises to one of Molière's leading ideas, in the conception that a son tyrannised till manhood in a boorish home will end by deceiving his father and contracting a foolish marriage, and that a girl, left to the companionship of French romances, will become a "Quixote in petticoats." But, when the elder Clerimont is presented as despatching his mistress, disguised as a gallant, to tempt the virtue of his wife and then, on the failure of the seducer, tearfully seeking a reconciliation, all dramatic propriety is sacrificed, in order to give a by no means convincing picture of conjugal tenderness. Such was the tone which the moral movement of queen Anne's reign introduced into the theatre, and, since succeeding dramatists came under this influence, Steele may be regarded as the founder of sentimental comedy.[1] Unhappily, as in the case of most comedies with a purpose, plots are sacrificed to the moral, and, apart from improbability of incident, Steele's plays show but little of that correctness of construction which the age exacted.

If Steele's dramatic work added scant laurels to his reputation, it was of the first importance in forming his mind. He had come to his task with the same stock of ideas as had served him in composing *The Christian Hero*. But, as a playwright, he had to make these ideas talk and act. He had to penetrate beneath the surface of life, and to show how often a profession or training degrades a man; how servants inevitably become mimics of their masters' excesses and frivolities; how women, who are untrained in the serious responsibilities of life, fall victims to fulsome adulation and often end in a marriage of convenience; how the best of them, for lack of moral sense, become tyrannical and fastidious before wedlock, and how others prey like vampires on their deluded husbands. Thus, Steele had learnt to look inside the domestic circle and to note how fashion and conventionality were warping the natural goodness of his fellow-creatures. Here and there, he hints at the conception of the purer and simpler, though rather emotional, family life which he was afterwards to depict. But, as we have seen, comedy was not a suitable medium for teaching of this nature. Although an atmosphere of earnest inquiry and reflection had formed itself in London, and had reached the stage, the public of the playhouse was not yet in a mood for social and moral speculation. It still expected wit and amusement. Steele had yet to discover where the world of thought that embodied the qualities which he had in mind was to be found, and how he was to approach it.

He discovered it five years later in the coffee-houses. Here

---

[1] Ward, A. W., *A History of English Dramatic Literature*, revised ed. 1899, vol. III, p. 493.

could be met serious-minded, progressive citizens, who were steadily outnumbering and overbearing the votaries of the old social régime. Matthew Arnold has said that, when "England entered the prison of Puritanism," it "turned the key on its intellectual progress for two hundred years." In reality, it was precisely this class, made up of inheritors of puritan narrowness and perseverance, which created a new culture for England out of its coffee-houses. It has already been shown[1] how Londoners, as early as the protectorate, began to assemble in these rendezvous and how, by daily intercourse, they learned to feel interest in each other's manners and habits of thought. As they cared little for the more frivolous diversions of the capital, they tended more and more to seek the pleasures of news and conversation, until, by the beginning of the eighteenth century, coffee-houses had become the most striking feature of London life.[2] Men who gathered day after day in these resorts were not only interested in their companions' ideas and demeanour; they cultivated an eye for trivial actions and utterances, a gift for investigating other people's prejudices and partialities, and they realised the pleasure of winning their way into the intricacies of another man's mind. Hence, they acquired a new attitude towards their fellow-creatures. Characters which would formerly have been ridiculed or despised were now valued as intellectual puzzles, eccentricities attracted sympathetic attention, and it became the note of intelligent men to be tolerant. Besides this sentiment of friendliness, the mere conditions of clublife imposed a new code of manners. If men were to enjoy daily intercourse, they had to respect each other's opinions and to cultivate self-suppression. Thus, consideration for others became the fashion, and the middle class, besides studying character, came to regard courtesy as a part of civilisation.[3]

---

[1] *Ante*, Vol. VII, Chap. XVI, pp. 441–443.

[2] Macaulay, *History of England*, chap. III.

[3] It is true that one has only to read *The Dunciad* (though not written by a coffee-house *habitué*) to be convinced that St. Grobian still had votaries no less ardent than Nashe or Harvey. "Flytings" continued as a literary tradition, and their existence does not disprove the taste for gentler manners, which grew up in coffee-houses and influenced literature. Compare *The Coffee Scuffle* (1662) or *A Coffee-House Dialogue* (1679) (see *ante*, Vol. VII, p. 443) with any scene from *The Tatler* or *The Spectator*.

Men learned other things in coffee-houses besides the amenities of social intercourse. Clubland had taken so universal a hold on London that nearly every man of intelligence frequented some resort of this kind. Now, these were just the people who read and wrote books; they created thought and taste; the future of literature depended on their ideas and ways of expression. Until the time of the restoration, neither writers nor readers had practised the studied simplicity of true conversation. Even pamphleteers like Nashe, Dekker or Rowlands, whose one aim was to follow popular taste, had never broken away from book knowledge, despite their slipshod style, and the literary cliques which handed round manuscript essays and characters had reproduced in their writings only such conversation as might be a vehicle for their clinches and conceits. Men had confined their literary interests to the library and, as a consequence, their style was either ponderous or precious. The Royal Society had already started a movement against redundance of phrase; but it may well be doubted whether the protests of Spratt, Evelyn and South[1] would have had lasting effect without the influence of coffee-houses. It was here that, besides practising benevolence in small things, men learnt to unravel literary ideas in a style that was colloquial as well as cultured. Conversation has a mysterious power of awakening thought. Commonplaces and trifles appear in a new light, and fresh notions are continually struck off like sparks. The man who has formed his mind by intercourse is more versatile and alert than he whose intellect has grown by reading, and he has learnt to speak in short simple sentences, because the ear cannot, like the eye, follow long periods. Moreover, he must abandon the phraseology of books, because the written word had long assumed a formal, almost impersonal, air, and must borrow turns and phrases from daily parlance to give an individual touch to his theories.

Thus, the middle classes were accomplishing their own education. They were becoming thinkers with a culture and a standard of manners born of conversation and free from pedantry of thought or expression. Coffee-houses had given them a kind of organisation; a means of exchanging ideas and forming the public opinion of their class. But this spirit was

[1] *Ante*, Vol. VIII, chap. XVI.

at present manifest only in the atmosphere where it had been formed. It was not found in theatres, universities or *salons*. Coffee-houses had unconsciously become fraternities for the propagation of a new humanism, and a writer could come into touch with the ideas and sentiments of the age only in those centres.

This movement was so inchoate that the middle classes themselves were hardly conscious of it. Steele certainly did not perceive into what a world of thought and sentiment he was penetrating when he ventured, in *The Tatler*, to appeal to coffee-houses. After writing *The Tender Husband*, he seems to have relinquished the theatre for the more lucrative career of a court favourite. He, probably, never lived within his income and, after losing, in 1708, his position of gentleman-waiter to prince George of Denmark and failing to obtain two other posts, he returned to literature in order to meet his debts. Since the censorship had been removed from the press, journalism had become a profitable enterprise, and Steele's chief motive in starting *The Tatler* on 12 April, 1709, was, undoubtedly, the fear of bankruptcy. However, the desire to improve his fellow-creatures was as strong as in the days of *The Christian Hero*. Steele was himself a frequenter of coffee-houses. He knew how confused and misguided their political discussions often were, thanks to the irresponsible news-sheets which flooded London; and he also realised how many other topics were wrongly or superficially canvassed in those daily and nightly gatherings. So, he set himself to enlighten, as well as to entertain, his fellow-talkers. As gazetteer, he could give the most trustworthy foreign news, and, as a man of culture and society, he could tell them what to think concerning other matters which occupied a discursive and critical generation. The paper came out three times a week, and each issue (unlike *The Spectator*) contained several essays, dated, according to their subjects, from particular coffee-houses[1].

Thus, in its original conception, *The Tatler* was hardly more

---

[1] "All accounts of gallantry, pleasure, and entertainment, shall be under the article of White's Chocolate house; poetry, under that of Will's coffee-house; learning, under the title of Grecian; foreign and domestic news, you will have from St. James's coffee-house; and what else I shall on any other subject offer, shall be dated from my own apartment." *The Tatler*, no. 1.

than an improved imitation of Defoe's *Review*[1] and *The Athenian Mercury*. From the first, Steele aimed at making his paper more comprehensive. He perceived that different coffee-houses stood for widely different interests, and he laid them all under contribution. He persevered in finding instruction or amusement for every taste, till *The Tatler* became almost as diversified as the opinions of its readers. In the hands of most editors, so undiscriminating a policy would soon have reduced a journal to a periodical miscellany, and Steele the essayist is certainly not free from charges of inconsistency and confusion. But it must be remembered that his long struggle after a sober, scholarly existence, though hardly successful in his personal life, had rendered him keenly responsive to kindred influences around him, and enabled him to discover and give expression to the spirit of humanised puritanism which existed beneath the babel of coffee-houses. Like all originators, he had to feel his way. He began by making a feature of foreign intelligence and theatrical news[2] and, full of middle-class disgust at frivolity and incompetence, exposed the vagaries of prominent social characters, apparently convinced that offenders would mend, if pilloried under a pseudonym.[3] Inspired by the same respect for order and regularity, he gave expression, in some rather commonplace articles,[4] to the public antipathy against gambling, and argued, in a series of papers,[5] that duelling was a senseless, guilty practice, observed by exquisites as an affectation of bravery but secretly condemned by level-headed burghers. He warned his readers against swindlers, pointing at certain well-known sharpers as dogs, but without a touch of the old English amusement at roguery. Indeed, except for two jestbook stories,[6] a mock testament[7] and a few sentimental extravagances in the style of seventeenth century romances,[8] his earlier attempts in a lighter vein consist of coffee-house discussions on literary

[1] See *ante*, Chap. I.
[2] Nos. 3, 4, 5, 7, 8, 14, 20, 21, 59 and 66 (by Swift), 191, 203 (Swift and Steele).
[3] *E. g.* Colonel Pickel and Florimel, no. 7; Florimel and Prudentia at Bath, no. 16; Lord Hinchinbroke, nos. 22, 58, 85; Tom Colson, no. 46; Dr. John Radcliffe, no. 44; Henry Cromwell, no. 47; Beau Feilding, nos. 50, 51; Duke of Ormond, no. 54.   [4] Nos. 13, 14, 15, 56.   [5] Nos. 25, 26, 28, 29, 31, 38, 39.
[6] Nos. 2, 42.   [7] No. 7.
[8] *E. g.* Unnion and Valentine, no. 5.

questions[1] and talks on current topics of city life such as changes in slang[2] and the abuse of the title esquire.[3]

These and similar performances were half-hearted, because Steele was finding his true level in the alleged lucubrations of Isaac Bickerstaff. He had borrowed this pseudonym from Swift's famous pamphlet, as being the best known type of intellectual detective and watchman. Soon, coffee-houses began to make their influence felt, and, as he gradually marked out as his province the intimate world of conduct and courtesy, he tended more and more to invest his figurehead with a new personality. The literature of coffee-houses must be as light and informal as their discussions;[4] so, he puts his moral counsels into the mouth of Bickerstaff, in order to preserve a conversational style and an air of persuasive authority quite acceptable to men who looked up to a self-constituted oracle in all their debates.[5] As his readers were interested in eccentricity, Bickerstaff becomes an aged recluse living a lonely and mysterious life, surrounded, as Swift had suggested, by the old-fashioned paraphernalia of astrology and attended by his familiar Pacolet,[6] like the now discredited magicians of the previous century. And yet this atmosphere of unreality gives effectiveness to Bickerstaff's character. His isolation enables him to study his fellow creatures dispassionately, and Pacolet, like the *diable boiteux* of Lesage, reveals to him the inaccessible secrets of other people. As the numbers of *The Tatler* increased, he developed into the first, and rather roughdrawn, portrait of eighteenth-century civilisation. He has the reasonableness and insight of coffee-houses, a sympathy with common things, out of which the domestic novel was to come, and a spirit of independent thought, coupled with respect for order and religion, such as the seventeenth century never knew.

In this thin disguise, Steele touched on all those questions

---

[1] Nos. 6, 17, 43.   [2] No. 12.   [3] No. 19.

[4] See no. 62, on the propriety of words and thoughts, in which it is maintained that conversation "is not to savour in the least of study" and that literary style "is to admit of something like the freedom of discourse."

[5] See *The Character of a Coffee-house*, 1673, *The Spectator*, no. 24.

[6] The name appears to have been taken from a character in the romance of *Valentine and Orson*, whose horse was enchanted. Sir Philip Sidney alludes to the horse in *An Apologie for Poetrie* (1581).

of breeding, good taste, courtesy and chivalry where the middle class had discarded old aristocratic ideals, without having yet learnt to trust entirely to their own. No wonder *The
Tatler* became immensely popular when its readers found
their half-formed notions confirmed and proclaimed. One of
their perplexities centred round the ideal of what they called
a gentleman. In aristocratic circles, men still emulated the
type set forth by Jacobean essayists[1] and affected "warmth
of imagination, quick relish of pleasure and the manner of
becoming it."[2] Such lubricity and self-assertion would be
intolerable where friendly intercourse was the foundation of
culture, and Steele points out that the first quality of a gentleman is not brilliance but forbearance and the art of accommo-
dating another's susceptibilities without sacrificing one's own.
Many recognise this ideal, but have not the tact to combine
compliance with self-respect, and become "pretty fellows"[3]
or even "very pretty fellows,"[4] or, again, affect an unwar-
rantable familiarity and merely succeed in becoming "whis-
perers without business and laughers without occasion."[5]
Society being now a mosaic of different units, all of them seeking
some common ground of intellectual fellowship, men of one
interest, such as are many scholars and soldiers,[6] are shown to
be as superficial as those who think that boisterous good humour
will make up for a lack of ideas.[7] But, again and again,
Steele insists that a man's first duty is to please his hearers,
showing how often the "wag" and the "wit" of the old school
still abuse the privileges of acquaintanceship merely to gain
a reputation for smartness and satire.[8]

The puritan desire to see the seriousness of life in every
word and deed was now being humanised into a standard of
good taste, and, if Londoners refused to admire cleverness
devoid of charity, they were even more ready to be warned
against coarser methods of self-advertisement. Affectation
in dress and manner, such as the manipulation of the snuff-
box or the wearing a cane on the fifth button, is mercilessly
ridiculed;[9] the man who uses expletives to make his conversa-

---

[1] *Ante*, Vol. IV, Chap. XVI.   [2] *The Tatler*, no. 21.
[3] No. 21.   [4] No. 24.
[5] No. 38.   [6] No. 61, nicknamed by Steele "men of fire."
[7] No. 63.   [8] Nos. 184, 219, 225, 244, 264.   [9] Nos. 27, 35, 96.

tion forcible is declared to be merely empty-headed;[1] the whole fraternity of fops is characterised as "the order of the insipids";[2] but the severest strictures are passed on the pretence of viciousness which was part of the dandies' pose.[3] Thus, the two nations pass before us. On the one hand, the degenerate imitators of Jacobean cavaliers and restoration courtiers, with the underworld of sharpers and gamesters; on the other, the middle-class coffee-houses, where citizens learnt to become urbane without ceasing to be pious. Steele belonged to both classes and traces the conflict between them. In many of his papers, after gibbeting the false ideal, he presents the true model, and it is not surprising that his own moral struggle, which gave him this insight, is sometimes recorded. In one paper, he pleads for the rake, claiming that he sins, repents and sins again only because his natural passions are too strong for him.[4] Later, in a fit of self-humiliation, he confesses that good nature is often laziness,[5] and, towards the end of *The Tatler*,[6] he denounces his own besetting sin, declaring that the drunkard cannot be either a friend, a gentleman, a master or a subject, and is especially dastardly when he has a virtuous wife.

If, however, the middle classes had much to reform in the manners of men, they had far more to criticise in the social position of women. When Madame de Rambouillet brought together in her *salon* the most cultured men and the most beautiful women in France, she created a new standard of social refinement for Europe. The management of intimate relations between the two sexes became a proof of good breeding, and the civilisation of any court could almost be measured by the influence which ladies enjoyed in it. In the earlier Stewart times, the English aristocracy readily adopted this cult, and all people of quality practised the art of inspiring or suffering the passion of love. But, so soon as this accomplishment became a fashion, it was perverted to most ignoble uses. The coarser types of the restoration gained caste by affecting the same delicacy of sentiment and purity of devo-

---

[1] No. 137.   [2] No. 166.
[3] Nos. 77, 191 and 213 in which Tom Springly pretends to be preparing for an assignation with a married woman at Rosamond's Pond, when he is really going to evening prayers.   [4] No. 27.   [5] No. 76.   [6] No. 241.

tion, while they really gratified their lusts. Immorality was invested with a ritual of compliments, odes, assignations and addresses, and, when the rising middle class came into touch with the *beau monde*, many well-intentioned young people were too inexperienced to detect the baseness which underlay this glitter and polish. Steele had primarily designed *The Tatler* to be an organ of the coffee-houses, and his first few papers on women are hardly anything but what one might expect from the gossip of the smoking-room.[1] But, in the stage of social evolution thus reached, the follies of men and women were so inextricable that Steele could not satirise rakes and fops without penetrating into the lives of their victims or deceivers. So far back as the protectorate, moralists had begun to abandon the savage invective which Elizabethan and Jacobean misogynists had affected, and filled pamphlets with more humane, but none the less searching, ridicule of female frivolities.[2] Steele is continuing a puritan tradition as well as breaking new ground, when he allows us to catch sight of the treachery and dishonour hidden beneath these hypocritical observances; sometimes, dwelling on the persecutions and outrages to which girls unwittingly exposed themselves and, at other times, revealing the jealousies and intrigues of more experienced matrons who looked on marriage, for all its euphemisms, as a game of skill or a masque of vanity.[3] Now and then, he gives us glimpses of the amours of those who shrink from matrimony or dwells upon the more horrible tedium and disillusionment of marriages made without love.[4] Had Steele lived in an age of decadence, he would, like most satirists in such periods, have confined himself to invective. But, if he helped to push one social order into the grave, he also helped to bring another to the light. As in his papers on men's manners, so now, after exposing vice, he holds up to admiration virtue, especially in his well-known portrait of Lady Elizabeth Hastings, whose passion is so high-souled and graceful that "to love her is a liberal education."[5]

[1] E. g. nos. 10, 20, 23.   [2] *Ante*, Vol. VII, Chap. XVI, p. 440.
[3] Nos. 33, 139, 198, 248; 22, 91, 98, 107, 200, 212, 245, 247, 248.
[4] Nos. 49, 53, 149, 199.
[5] No. 49. Congreve had already described her under the name of Aspasia, no 42. Other models of conjugal virtue will be found in the translation of Pliny's letters to his wife, no. 149, and the story of Antioohus and Stratonice, no. 185.

Such portraits would have had but little effect if Steele had not also pointed out the change which must inevitably befall the moral training of youth. While showing that vice was often concealed under a veil of refinement and liberality, he argued that the young give way to its allurements from a false idea of manliness or by way of revolt against parental tyranny. The old puritan methods of education had to be softened and humanised. He argued that children could be kept from extravagance and sensuality only by a sense of self-respect and by awakening in them tender memories of a father or mother whom they had learnt to love.[1] He then explains how the parent or guardian must be their companion, and encourage their confidence if he is to understand their characters, ending with the portrait of a perfect father, Dr. Lancelot Addison, the one man "among all my acquaintances, whom I have thought to live with his children with equanimity and good grace."[2]

In his charming papers on childhood, as well as in his moral essays on men and women, Steele writes like a man at one with his audience. He does not feel the need to argue or convince; it is enough to appeal to the sense of right and wrong. As he said himself, when exposing the tyranny of husbands,[3] "touching upon the malady tenderly is half way to the cure; and there are some faults which need only to be observed, to be amended." His business was not so much to create sentiments as to awaken them by a vivid description, and teach his readers to recognise their own principles in some poignant situation. As civilisation became complex and peaceful, the affairs of daily life assumed greater importance; men concerned themselves with little things, and Steele found himself enabled to play on the deeper springs of thought and emotion, by describing an everyday episode. In this way, he discovered the modern "short story," that is to say, a tale which suggests fundamental ideas or convictions.[4] Among

[1] Nos. 9, 60, 61, 83, 185. [2] Nos. 30, 189, 207, 235. [3] No. 149.

[4] Compare, in this connection, the best tales of earlier times, from the story of Rhampsinitus's Treasure Chamber (Herodotus, bk. II, chap. 121) to Jean de Bove's *Des Trois Larrons* or no. 16 of *A C. Mery Talys*, with such productions as Balzac's *Chef d'Œuvre inconnu*, or Turgenev's *The Jew*. Even when old stories are retold with all the art of a modern *raconteur* (e.g. *Li Amitiez de Ami et Amile* and *Aucassin et Nicolette*, by Pater, W., in *Renaissance Studies* (last ed.), 1910, and *La Légende de*

the problems of social life which he thus illumined with
imagination or even with emotion, none lay nearer Steele's
own heart than questions of family life. To heighten and
illustrate such reflections, he invented a lady editor, Jenny
Distaff, Bickerstaff's half-sister, a typical middle class girl,
who, from time to time, gives her views on women's affairs.[1]
But, as he returned again and again to this congenial theme,
Jenny's personality grew upon him till she became the heroine
of his domestic sketches. When reminding his female readers
that matrimony is not a flight of romance, but a resolve to
stake one's happiness on union with a partial stranger, he
makes Jenny's marriage with Tranquillus the occasion for
counsels based on this view, and gives a lively description of
the wedding festivities.[2] From time to time, the young couple
reappeared to illustrate the experiences of married life. We
have the first inevitable passing cloud which is happily smoothed
over and forgotten.[3] Like sensible *bourgeois*, they learn to
understand one another, and Steele gives a picture of the
lady's character maturing in wedlock. She and her husband
dine with her half-brother, and she enters the room "with a
decent and matronlike behaviour."[4] The household thrives,
and the perils of prosperity are dwelt on. Jenny calls on the
astrologer, and, this time, he notices "in her manner and air,
something . . . a little below that of the women of first
breeding and quality but at the same time above the simplicity
and familiarity of her usual deportment."[5] Bickerstaff then
discovers that his sister had fallen a victim to the love of
display and writes to warn her husband of the folly of aiming
above their station in life. Thus, besides discovering the
short story, Steele might well have invented the serial domestic
novel, if only the conditions of his work had permitted more
continuity of application. For, in his writing, we find, for
the first time, the temperament which is drawn to the pathos,
and even the tragedy, of family life. He gave up one paper[6]
to a picture of perfect domestic happiness, describing it as

St. Julien l' Hospitalier, by Flaubert, G., in *Trois Contes* (last ed.), 1908), the
difference is still apparent.   The story of Philippus (Horace, *Epist.* 1, 7) resembles
the modern type, because the Romans of the empire had learned to see a whole
background of philosophy and sentiment behind the affairs of daily life.

[1] Nos. 10, 33, 36, 37.   [2] No. 79.   [3] No. 85.
[4] No. 104.   [5] No. 143.   [6] No. 95.

"a complication of all the pleasures of life and a retreat from its inquietudes"; and, five weeks later,[1] he introduces us to the same family plunged in the deepest woe as they gather round the death-bed of their mother. In these and other fugitive papers of like nature, we may notice the rise of that sentimentality which dominated the taste of the mid-eighteenth century and survives so late as Thackeray's novels. Steele, thanks to his double character, was one of the first to find that he could combat his own wayward, bohemian nature by cultivating a tenderness for home affections. The next generation either followed his example or discovered the same secret, fleeing from the crudity of their own civilisation by exaggerating the softer side of life, till lachrymose sensibility became the mark of refinement. He tells us himself how he was often driven to seek a steadying force in solemn and melancholy thoughts, and admits that he reserved certain times "to revive the old places of grief in our memory and ponder step by step on past life."[2] Thus, out of distant memories, Steele recalled many intimate and pathetic scenes which a less effusive writer would have shielded from public gaze. Had it occurred to him to weave such incidents as the oft-quoted description[3] of his father's death and of his mother's passionate grief into the history of Jenny Distaff, the domestic novel would, in a rudimentary form, have been invented. As it was, he ended the story with a sequel in which an unexpected hamper of wine vanishes among boon companions.

Steele touched on many more topics. As was to be expected from the mouthpiece of the coffee-houses and from the self-appointed "Censor of Great Britain," he is full of contempt for feudal prejudices and the arrogance of the rich.[4] He sided with Hoadly, bishop of Winchester, against Blackall, bishop of Exeter, on the doctrine of passive obedience.[5] He worked up Roger Grant's supposed healing of a blind boy into an enthusiastic description not unlike a broadside.[6] He criticised

---

[1] No. 114.   [2] No. 181.   [3] *Ibid.*

[4] Nos. 66, 144, 180, 181, 196. In the same spirit, he gave some striking sketches of character in low life—the ungraciously humorous account of Guardeloop the French tailor's wedding (no. 7), with its picture of "low gallantry," being succeeded by sergeant Hall's letter to sergeant Cabe (no. 87), full of cheerful and unaffected heroism, and the escapades of the imperturbable Will Rosin (no. 105), "a man of tranquillity without reading Seneca."   [5] Nos. 44, 50.   [6] No. 55.

the lack of pulpit eloquence.[1] He composed, or published, some charming letters on the pleasures of country life.[2] Just as John Dunton[3] had constituted himself an oracle for all questioners in *The Athenian Mercury*, so Steele, sometimes, filled whole numbers with the correspondence he received or pretended to receive. In his constant endeavour to "extirpate . . . all such as are either prejudicial or insignificant to society,"[4] his characterisation is often onesided and becomes caricature. But, now and then, he pierced beneath the superficiality almost inseparable from satire, and hinted at the profound complexity of the civilised mind, showing, in several papers,[5] how the ordinary human character is inextricably interwoven with the social fabric to which it belongs and becomes as particoloured as the woof itself. While society grows more heterogeneous, conflicting principles exist side by side, and, as men are bound, in some measure, to think according to their environment, they misunderstand each other on the commonest topics, fluctuate between opposite ideals and often end by distrusting their own instincts and mistaking their own emotions. These more complex and impressionable personalities are distinguished from simpler types: first, society nonentities, subordinate characters of men such as Tim Dapper, who are "like pegs in a building, they make no figure in it but hold the structure together,"[6] and, then, the vast workaday world, which steadfastly performs the tasks of its rulers, and "cannot find out that they are doing nothing."[7]

These reflections are accidental and were probably shared by many another coffee-house critic of men and manners. Steele had neither the talent nor the opportunity to work them up into a philosophy. The same lack of system impairs his interpretation of literature. At a time when the most enlightened critics admired a poet for his rhetoric, Steele discovered in Shakespeare and Milton the sublime moralists of middle-class life, quoting from their pages to show where the everyday virtues of fidelity, pity and conjugal love have

---

[1] Nos. 66, 72.   [2] Nos. 112, 169, 203.
[3] See preceding chap. of this volume.   [4] No. 186.
[5] Nos. 25 (influenced by Molière's *Le Mariage forcé*), 57, 83, 138, 186, 206, 227.
[6] No. 85.   It is worth noting that Addison used the same simile in *Spec.* no. 495.   [7] No. 203.

found their purest and noblest expression.[1] He does not, however, seek to impress this view on his public. Beyond retelling the Bible story of Joseph and his brethren,[2] to illustrate how, in moments of despondency, he "turns his thoughts to the adversities of persons of higher consideration in virtue and merit to regain tranquillity," he never taught his readers how to look for moral and spiritual guidance in literature. They are left to glean what they can from chance utterances. Had it been otherwise, these papers would have been the most remarkable critical production of Steele's generation.

The Tatler continued to appear three times a week until 2 January, 1711, and then ceased abruptly. The loss of his gazetteership, though it deprived Steele of access to first-hand news, can hardly have influenced him, since foreign intelligence in *The Tatler* had long dwindled into an occasional and perfunctory paragraph. Possibly, he was allowed to retain his commissionership of stamps under the new government only on the understanding that a paper connected with the whig party should be discontinued. He may really have feared that the secret of authorship was now widely divulged, and that the association of his not unblemished name with moral counsels might revive the ridicule which had greeted *The Christian Hero*. But, besides this, he was suffering the discouragement of a man who wades beyond his depth. The self-imposed task of censor had led him deeper and deeper into the complex questions of his day, while his journalistic methods allowed of only fleeting and superficial glimpses at truth. Had he been fully conscious of his inability, he would probably, with characteristic candour, have freely confessed it. As it was, he sank under a temporary attack of weariness,[3] all the more irresistible because another writer, who had been intermittently associated with him in the paper, seemed to have acquired without effort that art of expression which Steele himself lacked.

This collaborator was Addison.[4] In reality, his achieve-

---

[1] Nos. 40, 47, 53, 68, 102, 104, 188, 237.   [2] No. 234.

[3] See no. 271. Swift (*Journal to Stella*) says "he grew cruel, dull, and dry. To my knowledge, he had several good hints to go upon; but he was so lazy and weary of the work, that he would not improve them."

[4] "That paper was advanced indeed! for it was raised to a greater thing than I

ment was the fruit of a mental readjustment more laborious
and fundamental than Steele's, though of a different character.
Like the creator of *The Tatler*, Addison had to put new wine
into old bottles. He was a man of scholarly habits and unusual ability, but taciturn and lacking in initiative. When
Steele plunged into London life, Addison was studying at
Magdalen, where he peacefully won academic distinction
and stored his mind with the wit and wisdom of antiquity.
At this time, the universities were far removed from the outer
world, and, if Oxford made him a distinguished Latinist,[1]
it also made him a recluse more competent to imitate Vergilian
hexameters than to lead the thought of his generation. He
left the university in 1699; but four years' travel among the
chief centres of European culture did not draw his mind out
of the academic mould into which it had been cast. There
were still patrons to reward the man of scholarly attainments; and Addison, who had to make his own fortunes,
seems to have been content to revive his university reputation
among the few, by some work of graceful and recondite learning. A boyish interest in the writing on London signposts
had been developed by his academic training into a taste for
numismatics,[2] and, of all the resources of Europe, nothing
seems to have left so deep an impression on his mind as collections of coins. As a result, one of the first fruits of his
travels, printed posthumously, was *Dialogues upon the Usefulness of Ancient Medals*, a treatise which shows an intimate familiarity with Latin poets and singular ingenuity in
elucidating obscure passages by the light of legends and de-
vices, but touches no other human interest except curiosity
in Roman dress. About the same time, he prepared for pub-

---

intended it! For the elegance, purity and correctness which appeared in his
writings were not so much my purpose, as (in any intelligible manner as I could)
to rally all those singularities of human life through the different professions and
characters in it, which obstruct anything that was truly good and great." Steele,
in preface to *The Drummer* (1721).

[1] A glance at Addison's early successes will show how enduringly academic
were the influences which shaped his mind. He was elected demy of Magdalen
1689 and published vol. I of *Musae Anglicanae* in 1691; composed *Dissertatio de
Romanorum poetis* in 1692; delivered *Oratio de nova philosophia* in 1693; engaged in
translating Herodotus in 1696; was elected to a fellowship, 1698; published vol. II
of *Musae Anglicanae* (containing his own Latin poems) in 1699.

[2] *The Tatler*, no. 18.

lication a diary of travel, recording faithfully his impressions of the customs, character and polity of the people, on the model of Bacon's *Essays*.[1] Even these notes, which appeared in 1705 as *Remarks on Italy*, show little enthusiasm, except where his wanderings lead him directly on the track of ancient literature.

The year before, he made a name for himself throughout London, and thus assured his future, by producing *The Campaign*. The origin of this celebrated piece was political. The whigs had just vindicated their policy by the victory of Blenheim, and Godolphin was looking for a party poet who should give voice to the wave of triumph and patriotism which was passing over the nation. Halifax suggested the distinguished writer of Latin verse who had already produced a few scholarly verse translations and some complimentary addresses to patrons in the courtly style. To most writers, a theme such as the battle of Blenheim would naturally have suggested an elegy or a pindaric ode. But Addison, with characteristic judgment, cast his effusion into the form of an epic; for, in this poetic form, a store of poetic imagery and poetic exaggeration presented itself ready-made, and the author of *The Campaign* found that his task was to select and apply expressions such as would shed heroic grandeur on the achievements of the British arms. In fact, he treated his subject as if it were an academic exercise in rhetoric; and, although the versification is often prosaic and the vigorous passages[2] are balanced by lapses into platitude, he acquitted himself with remarkable ingenuity and tact. While paying extravagant tributes to "Anna's royal cares" and to "Marlborough's mighty soul," he succeeded in addressing the nation at large. He flattered their most cherished boasts—their pride in British freedom, their hero-worship, their love of fighting—in phrases consecrated by Homer, Vergil, Lucan, Statius, Silius Italicus, while the exigencies of the heroic couplet almost necessarily involved "turns" and "points" such as the polite age admired. The pamphlet in verse[3]

---

[1] *Essay on Travel.*

[2] *E.g.* the celebrated simile in ll. 272–92.

[3] It was followed, in 1707, by an anonymous pamphlet in prose, *The Present State of the War.*

took the town by storm, and the author, who had been given
a commissionership of appeals as a retaining fee, was now
rewarded with an undersecretaryship of state.

From this time forth, Addison was one of the elect. In
1706, he became undersecretary of state to Lord Sunderland;
in 1707, he accompanied Lord Halifax to Hanover; in 1709,
he became chief secretary to the marquis of Wharton, lord
lieutenant of Ireland, and, besides these experiences in administration, he held a seat in parliament from 1708 till his
death. So, he was never again in want, and at no time
passed through the stormy and varied experiences which bring
sympathy with human nature and insight into character.
Even during the lean years, he had been too reticent and polite
to become a bohemian, and, in the years of plenty, it seemed
inevitable that he should settle down to the leisurely discharge
of his public functions and keep up his literary studies merely
as a polite and elegant pastime. And yet, it was during this
period of his life that Addison immeasurably enlarged his
intellectual outlook. He made the acquaintance of Pope and
Swift, renewed his school and college friendship with Steele
and, like other men of culture, frequented the coffee-houses.
Gradually, he came under the full influence of the great social
movement, and, as his thoughts centred round questions of
morals and manners, he achieved the feat of bringing his vast
classical learning to shed light on these modern problems.
Instead of using ancient literature to illustrate medals, he
discovered how to make it illustrate the weaknesses and
peculiarities of his contemporaries. He learned to refer the
perplexities and doubts of his own day to the wisdom and
experience of antiquity. His scholarly instincts, instead of
drawing him into the library, sharpened his natural gift of
silent observation and provided unlimited material for his
sense of humour.

The Tatler gave him just the opportunity which he needed.
After discovering, by a remark on Vergil,[1] that Steele was the
author of the paper, Addison became an occasional contributor

---

[1] See *The Tatler*, no. 6, on Vergil's choice of words, in which it is pointed out
that, whereas Aeneas, at other times, is called *Pius* or *Bonus*, he is termed *Dux
Trojanus* when about to seduce Dido. Addison had suggested this idea to Steele
at Charterhouse.

and, despite the distractions of his official life, began to adapt his talents to the new literary art. Like Steele, he had to feel his way, and seems to have gradually realised what was in his mind, by the process of writing. His first paper[1] bids good-bye to pedantry by declaring that

men of wit do so much employ their thoughts upon fine speculations, that things useful to mankind are wholly neglected: and they are busy in making emendations upon some enclitics in a Greek author, while obvious things, that every man may have use for, are wholly overlooked;

and then, as if dissatisfied with the recondite studies of his manhood, he reverts to his boyish interest in signposts and writes an essay on the inconveniences arising from their misspellings. But his own habits of thought had been formed by the great teachers of antiquity, and, the more he watched Bickerstaff's attempts at sugaring the didactic pill, the more their arts suggested themselves to him. Steele did, indeed, carelessly try his hand at allegory;[2] and Addison, acting on a hint from Swift, revived the classical myth, taking Plato and Ovid for his chief models. These visions and dreams point very commonplace morals, but they astonish by their boldness of fancy and compel belief by their realism of detail.[3] Steele had drawn realistic pictures of Grobianism and immorality; Addison, by nature, was averse to anything primitive, but had learnt from Theophrastus, Terence and Horace to expect proportion in the most trivial details of conduct. Accordingly, the more he studied men, the more he cultivated an eye for the little inconsistencies and perversions of his fellow creatures. This acquired appreciation of "the golden mean" blended with a natural gift for genial caricature. Wherever his abnormally keen sense for proportion had detected some eccentric or unreasonable *penchant*, he pictured a man completely under its domination, gravely worked out the irrational tendency to its logical conclusion and then left his reader to laugh

---

[1] *The Tatler*, no. 18. [2] *The Tatler*, no. 48.

[3] Swift had suggested, in no. 67, that the most famous characters of all time might be represented as seated at a banquet. Addison produced his first allegorical masterpiece on this theme in collaboration with Steele in no. 81 and followed it up with others, nos. 97, 100, 120, 123, 146, 147, 161.

at the result.   The wellworn theme of bucolic self-importance is developed into the delightful portrait of Sir Harry Quickset;[1] the self-absorption of the half-educated appears in the comical account of the dancing-master who made the house shake while he studied "orchesography";[2] women's passion for pets is illustrated by the admirable story of the maidservant (really "an arch baggage") sent to consult the astrologer on the health of Cupid, her mistress's lap-dog[3]; pedants are defined as "all men of deep learning without common-sense," and their absurdities are exposed in the vagaries of Tom Folio[4] and the entomologist's will.[5]   The Londoner's passion for news is caricatured in the person of the political upholsterer.[6]

Addison indulged in many other graceful flights of fancy, which gave his satire[7] a charm of its own; but he showed little originality of thought.   And yet, though he was content to follow Bickerstaff or, rather, the public opinion of coffee-houses, his few contributions[8] are a turning point in the history of the essay.   These familiar topics became full of a new vitality under his pen.   His work, if anything, is less vigorous and less searching than Steele's; but it has the other eloquence of form which turns human utterance into literature.   Until now, the essay had not completely established itself as a literary type.   In the hands of Bacon, it was little more than a string of meditations, while the inventiveness of popular writers had been lavished on character sketches, epigrams, satires and revivals of medieval thought.   Cowley, and, after him, Temple, had, largely under the influence of Montaigne, given a new turn to the essay, which had thus come to exercise an important effect upon the transformation of English prose.[9] Steele and Addison entered into an inheritance which increased

---

[1] No. 86. [2] No. 88. [3] No. 121.
[4] No. 158 [5] Nos. 216, 221. [6] Nos. 155, 160.

[7] E.g. a court "for examining the pretensions of several who had applied to me for canes, perspective glasses, snuff-boxes, orange-flower waters and the like ornaments of life," nos. 103, 110, 116; talkers differentiated as musical instruments, no. 153; inconstancy of life symbolised by a coach journey in which the occupants unaccountably lose their tempers, no. 192; the ecclesiastical thermometer which should register excess, even in the virtues of churchmanship, no. 220; frozen words, no. 254; the court of honour, a picturesque way of discussing points of etiquette and good manners, nos. 250, 253, 256, 259, 262, 265.

[8] Forty-one papers contributed by Addison independently; thirty-four in conjunction with Steele. [9] Cf. ante, Vol. VIII, Chap. XVI.

and multiplied in their hands. With the first few numbers of
The Tatler, pre-restoration humour had been abandoned
after a few attempts, and Steele addressed himself to the
intellect of the middle class in the unliterary guise of a news-
sheet, though his ideas had long outgrown so restricted a
compass. As has been shown, his material was unmistakably
leading him towards the novel of domestic life. Addison probably retarded the transition, by giving to an irresponsible and
inadequate medium a completeness and dignity which satisfied
the intellectual and artistic needs of his generation. For
Addison not only endowed the essay with the airs and graces
of cultured writing—he discovered the prose style which suits
the genre. Steele had rightly conceived that *The Tatler*
must be written in a colloquial vein, and had dashed off his
papers with the freedom and effusiveness of his own conversation. Addison was too reserved ever to be a voluble talker;
he never became communicative except in a small circle of
kindred spirits. Thus, the riches of his mind had found
expression only in polished and confidential intercourse, and
when, following the example of Steele, he began to talk on
paper, his subtle and unaffected personality found free play
with his pen as in conversation. And so, he created a perfect
style for detached literature—lucid, colloquial, full of individuality and yet chastened by that careful choice of words
which, like other scholars, he had already cultivated in writing
Latin verse.

Addison had completely mastered the art of essay writing
when Steele discontinued *The Tatler*. The fall of the whig
ministry in the previous year, deprived both writers of lucrative
positions. But the reasons for resuming the interrupted
work were not merely financial. The production of *The
Tatler* had brought with it experiences such as no other contemporary writer had been privileged to enjoy. While
ransacking society, clubland and literature for "copy," Steele
and Addison had discovered, partly in themselves and partly
in others, a moral and intellectual tone purer and more humane
than the spirit which they had breathed into their own paper.
Greatly as that periodical had developed, it could not altogether
escape from the desultory and superficial character which it
had assumed at its origin. Yet a new journal offered boundless

possibilities, and the artist's instinct, as well as the moralist's zeal, played a part in founding *The Spectator*.

Thus, the new enterprise was not a mere sequel to *The Tatler*—a pennyworth of diversion containing something to suit all tastes. The old paper, in its primary conception, had been too much like a medley in which social scandal, city gossip and foreign news emulously claimed the reader's attention. Its successor was to be a series of literary pamphlets, concerned only with morals and manners, each number being confined to a single theme and bearing a distinct message from the world of religion, thought or humour. Though its appeals were narrowed in scope, they were to be more often repeated. The paper appeared every day and, by sheer frequency, grew into the life of its readers like an intimate counsellor or a constant friend. Above all, the periodical was to have the persuasiveness of personality. As the editors could not write in their own names, they profited by the example of Isaac Bickerstaff and published their reflections under a fictitious character. While, however, the astrologer of *The Tatler* had been merely an ingenious embellishment, a suggestive curiosity introducing its readers to truths which they could have appreciated without him, Mr. Spectator both gave his name to the paper and typified the spirit in which it was written. The first number, on 1 March, 1711, was given up to a sketch of his mind and this portrayal marks an epoch in the history of English culture. Addison, who drew the picture and is, indeed, the inspiring genius of the whole periodical, here really describes his own mental attitude since he left "academic bowers," taking with him all his classical learning, to join the observers of modern life. His ideas were largely due to the new atmosphere in which he now found himself; but, as his intellectual emancipation had cost him much, he realised his purpose more intensely than did his fellows. For Mr. Spectator is the type of a new culture which grew out of puritanism. Men of profound learning had, under the old civilisation, been specialists—theologians, demonographers, jurists, philosophers or university scholars. Mr. Spectator is also profoundly learned; he is acquainted with all celebrated books in ancient and modern tongues. Nay, more, he is a traveller, and, like the great renascence scholars, has visited every accessible country in search of knowledge. Yet he has no profession; he does not belong to a school of thought. He has simply stored his mind with the wisdom, wit and humour of other countries and ages, and he spends his life in observing his contemporaries and, consciously or unconsciously, comparing their manners, customs and ideas with those of which he has read. He visits "The Exchange," theatres, coffee-houses; wherever men gather he is to be found, until, as Addison says, "he has made himself a speculative statesman, soldier, merchant or artisan without ever meddling with any practical part in life." Such Addison had learnt to be, and such, also, without the concluding qualification, was the ideal of the protestant middle class of this century. Now that the great disputes as to religion and government had been settled, the descendants of the puritans were free, fifty years before Voltaire, "to cultivate their garden." They brought to the task of self-education an ever growing knowledge of books and the same seriousness and humanity which began to guide the more enlightened so far back as the civil war.[1] Such a generation might reform and, on occasion, take an interest in the theatre or even cultivate *belles lettres;* but their true sphere was found in the routine of daily life. Conversation and study made them thoughtful; yet it was a practical thoughtfulness centring round their institutions, manners and intellectual development. Steele, and especially Addison, while writing for *The Tatler*, had hinted that the wisdom and integrity of other ages were the best guides towards the improvement of their own; but it was one of the distinguishing marks of the new journal that both essayists avowedly adopted this principle.

After Addison had portrayed Mr. Spectator, it was inevitable in the day of cliques and coffee-houses that he should be made a member of a club. Steele undertook this task, as he had performed it for Mr. Bickerstaff. But "the Trumpet Club,"[2] like nearly all the creations of *The Tatler*, had been hardly more than an afterthought: an incidental piece of monitory satire, conceived with insight and humour, warning us against the consequence of an ill-spent youth by the portraits of five

[1] *Ante,* Vol. VII, Chap. XVI, pp. 436–441, 445–451.
[2] *The Tatler,* no. 132.

tedious and futile old men. Steele had learnt much by the time he came to sketch the Spectator's club.[1] He appears to have derived the idea from the numerous classical dialogues then fashionable, in which each interlocutor is intended to have a character of his own and represent a point of view. He pictured five men who moved in different spheres of life and could uphold different opinions on social and moral questions. Yet, from their first appearance, Mr. Spectator's friends did more than lend dramatic or dialectical interest to their discussions. The new journal was conceived in a spirit of restrained idealism, and its types were intended, each in his own character, to be an object lesson to his class. They are not introduced to us merely as men who hold theories. Just as Mr. Spectator is the perfected student of humanity, so his companions retain a certain mellowness and suavity of disposition, though, like other ordinary people, they are cramped and misdirected by their petty destinies. It is significant that three, at least, of these creations are represented as triumphing just where their prototypes in *The Tatler* failed. The first is Sir Roger de Coverly, a man of naturally strong intelligence and physical vigour, whose enthusiasm for life has been temporarily blasted by a rather mysterious love affair. But he did not become listless, like Cynthio[2] after Clarissa had broken his heart, nor futile, like the old man brought up before the court of honour who talked only of Madame Frances.[3] He has, indeed, resigned himself to an inglorious existence among his bucolic and admiring tenants; but he has not fallen a victim to a sense of self-importance like the pompous and empty-headed Sir Harry Quickset.[4] He overflows with loving kindness, and his long career of feudal autocracy has only added a touch of independence and eccentricity to his benevolence. There is captain Sentry, a man of unquestioned energy, ability and personal courage, who has retired from the army, because he lacks the gift of self-advertisement. Yet he does not spend his time in detracting from the success of other soldiers, like the major of whom Bickerstaff had heard,[5] but has withdrawn to the social pleasures of London and resigned himself good-humouredly to a life of

---

[1] *The Spectator*, no. 2. [2] *The Tatler*, no. 58. [3] *Ibid.* no. 110.
[4] *Ibid.* no. 86. [5] *The Tatler*, no. 202.

leisurely obscurity.   There is a lawyer, who has no taste for
his profession and resides at the Inner Temple "to obey the
direction of an old humoursome father."   Yet, instead of
wasting his life, he devotes his ample leisure to Aristotle,
Longinus and the theatre, until he has cultivated much of
The Spectator's own character, since "his familiarity with the
customs, manners, actions and writings of the Antients makes
him a very delicate observer of what occurs to him in the
present world."   Another member, Will Honeycomb the fop,
had been for centuries a butt in comedy and satire.   Tudor
moralists[1] had denounced the man of fashion as guilty of
deadly sins.   Jacobean free-lances,[2] again and again, had
depicted him as ignorant, indolent and insolent.   During the
civil war, this antipathy against the type had grown into
hatred through association with cavaliers, and, even after the
revolution, many regarded the man of fashion as vicious and
ridiculous.   Steele, who had followed the puritan tradition
in several numbers of *The Tatler*, still retained the old standpoint.   But the satire has gone.   Will is portrayed as vain and
worldly—so a fop must always seem to the serious middle class
—but not as depraved.   He is the best of his type, a brilliant
talker, with a kind heart and an irresistible charm of manner.
The spirit of *The Spectator* is most clearly seen in the figure
of Sir Andrew Freeport the merchant.   For more than a
century, traders had been characterised as dishonest and
avaricious, because playwrights and pamphleteers generally
wrote for the leisured classes and were themselves too poor
to have any but unpleasant relations with men of business.
Commerce was, however, now a great power in society and
politics.   Merchants were ambassadors of civilisation, and
had developed intellect so as to control distant, and, as it
seemed, mysterious, sources of wealth by a stroke of the pen.[3]
Thanks to coffee-houses, merchants now had the opportunity
of coming to understand their own importance through
mutual discussion, and Steele had already, in *The Tatler*,
given glimpses of their prudence or dignity and claimed that

---

[1] *E.g.* Tottel's *Dice Play*, 1532; W. de Worde's *A Treatise of a Gallant*, n.d.;
Robin Conscience, 1550, and Crowley's *Tracts*.   See *ante*, Vol. III, Chap. v.

[2] *E. g.* Greene, Nashe, Dekker, Rowlands, etc. Cf. *ante*, Vol. IV, Chap. xvi.

[3] See *The Spectator*, no. 174.

they had as much right to the title of gentlemen as courtiers and scholars had.[1] Still, it was something new in literature to show how a man trained in a counting-house could be the intellectual equal of the Spectator and his friends. Sir Andrew is not a wit; his conversation abounds in homely phrases; his mind is not stored with the wisdom of books; yet he has made himself an original thinker, with ideas not fettered by tradition, but derived from experience in trade and expressed with the lucidity of conviction.

When Steele sat down to sketch this group, he probably intended each to be little more than a figurehead, enlivened with a few touches of individuality. Yet, so introspective was the age in which he wrote, that, as if unconsciously, he has made them, in this his first description, hardly less than studies of social environment and character. After this brilliant beginning, it is disappointing to find that, though the characters frequently reappear, they are afterwards employed only to maintain an argument or give information about the world which each represents or, again, in imitation of dramatic technique, merely as confidants of Mr. Spectator and foils to throw into relief his views and peculiarities. They are interwoven with lines of thought which run through the periodical only by way of embroidery; at the most, they are used as living examples of some habit or quality which defies ordinary description. We are not vouchsafed any glimpse of their progress through the world or of the development of their minds. Even the Coverly papers are not really an exception to this. Steele first showed what was the knight's true function when he depicted Sir Roger as protesting against the over-civilisation of city life and declaring himself to be "so whimsical in a corrupt age as to act according to nature and reason."[2] Henceforth, the country baronet became the type of Arcadian simplicity. From the days of Tudor jest-books,[3] the city man had laughed at the backwardness of the provincial, and the sense of urban superiority is not missing

---

[1] "That tradesman who deals with me in a commodity which I do not understand with uprightness, has much more right to that character (*i.e.* of a gentleman), than the courtier who gives me false hopes, or the scholar who laughs at my ignorance." *The Tatler*, no. 207.

[2] *The Spectator*, no. 6.   [3] Cf. *ante*, Vol. III, Chap. v.

in the Coverly papers. It is most significant that Addison, with an idealist's instinct, endowed Sir Roger with all the guilelessness and piety which London society lacked, and lovingly returned again and again to the theme, as if he found in it a refuge from the artificiality of his own life. In his enthusiasm for the golden age, which he pictured among the villages and manors of old England, Addison created a whole society round Sir Roger—including Will Wimble, the cadet of an ancient family, too brainless for a liberal profession, too proud to enter business, really of the same class as the odious Mr. Thomas Gules,[1] but portrayed as gentle and lovable, like all the other inhabitants of the smiling land. And yet the Coverly papers are only a series of sketches. The Spectator spends a month in the country, and Sir Roger makes a few visits to town. Nothing else is recorded until the knight's unexpected death, except smalltalk. It is true that his most trifling utterance has an irresistible charm, because it contributes towards the picture of ideal simplicity, godliness and nobleness of heart. Even his little weaknesses and touches of vanity, recorded with exquisite humour are the defects of his qualities. In truth, these essays are the first masterpiece of humanised puritanism; though, as regards the history of the novel, they do not mark an advance on the story of Jenny Distaff.

In any case, Steele and Addison could hardly have created the novel, after creating Mr. Spectator as their ideal of editorship. That taciturn and contemplative investigator[2] has intellectual curiosity, but little sympathy. He ranges over a field so incredibly wide that he is forced to see life from a distance. Steele and Addison do not always stand aloof. They had shown, in occasional papers, that they understood the human heart and the pathos of unrecorded destiny; but they never, for long, escape from their own conception of sporadic and dispassionate observation. It was no small effort of creativeness to unify in one clear-cut character vague tendencies towards critical contemplation, though the spectacle of a half-formed and half-humanised democracy was too engrossing in its outlines to leave room for the intensive study of a novelist. So, the personalities of the Spectator's club tend to fade out of importance, and the journal confined its

---

[1] *The Tatler*, no. 256.   [2] Cf. *The Spectator*, nos. 4, 270, 454.

development to the lines which Addison had already marked out. It covered practically the same ground as *The Tatler*, ridiculing or inveighing against old-fashioned ideals of gallantry and self-indulgence,[1] urging that kindness is better than cleverness,[2] that self-suppression is the essence of good breeding;[3] penetrating the secrets of home life and exposing the humiliations of citizens who affect aristocratic immorality,[4] the stupidity of husbands who tyrannise over their wives[5] or fathers over their children,[6] the folly of women who marry for money[7] or think that the pleasures of society are preferable to the duties of the household. As Steele took the responsibility of seeing that "copy" was forthcoming day by day, a few of his papers are still written with that hurried diffuseness which has lost *The Tatler* many readers. In his best work, he conforms to the studied simplicity and artistic concentration which Addison had developed in *The Tatler* and was continuing to cultivate with great success.

But, if *The Spectator* surpassed its predecessor in style, it achieved an even greater advance in thought. The moralists of the seventeenth century had drawn their wisdom from books, Bickerstaff had drawn his from experience; while Addison showed how to draw from both sources. It is surprising how much quaint and curious lore is introduced into the pages of *The Spectator* merely to give point or freshness to an uninspiring theme,[8] as where the buyers of lottery tickets suggest the legend of Mahomet's coffin suspended in mid-air by the force of two magnets,[9] or the curiosity of the town concerning the letter with which each essay was signed is mocked by means of a dissertation on cabalism.[10] It is, however, when these writers continue Bickerstaff's more serious duties of censorship that the full influence of literature becomes most marked. *The Tatler* had criticised the follies and foibles of society by the light of common sense; *The Spectator* never fails in its higher criterion—the mellow and dignified experience of antiquity. Sometimes, the petulant efforts of modern writers are compared

---

[1] See, especially, *The Spectator*, nos. 158, 182, 261, 244, 318.
[2] *Ibid.* nos. 23, 151, 169, 172, 177, 348.   [3] *Ibid.* nos. 24, 286, 422, 438.
[4] *Ibid.*, nos. 33, 91, 41, 45, 89, 260, 288, 298, 299, 342.
[5] No. 236.   [6] No. 431.   [7] Nos. 149, 268, 311, 320.
[8] Nos. 94, 191, 211, 221, 343, 439.   [9] No. 191.   [10] No. 221.

with the noble simplicity of ancient literature.[1] Sometimes, the pettiness or malice of the writers themselves is reproved on the authority of Simonides,[2] Cicero,[3] Epictetus,[4] or by a description of the Augustan circle.[5] In these respects, Addison differed only in method and thoroughness from Jacobean essayists, who quoted Roman or Italian authors whenever their reading rendered them discontented with the worn-out traditions of their own society. But Mr. Spectator went far deeper than this. Not only did he quote the judgments and counsels of the ancients on questions common to all moralists of all ages; but, when straying from the beaten track, and counselling his contemporaries on their peculiarities and eccentricities, he was still guided by a Roman sense of self-respect and reasonableness. His exquisite portrait of the valetudinarian who took his meals in a weighing chair is really inspired by Martial's contempt for those who are more anxious to live than to live rightly.[6] The sense of solemnity which comes over Mr. Spectator in Westminster abbey descends on him from Lucretius,[7] and Seneca would have approved of the diary of an idle man and of that of a woman of fashion.[8]

Steele, as usual, followed his master's lead and introduced copious quotations and allusions into his more serious papers. But, at best, he was an indifferent scholar, and, except in the Pharamond papers,[9] he never approached Addison's tact and felicity. Much as he admired Mr. Spectator's cultured and contemplative mind, his own experience was leading him to work out a philosophy of life on different lines. As, in *The Tatler*, he had taken refuge in sentimentality, so now, in *The Spectator*, he still fought against his own inborn unconventionality by advocating a regularity of conduct which he could not practise. The puritans had always disliked what was unusual or self-willed, and Steele brought Cicero and the Stoics to their help, showing how the recklessness of the spendthrift, the capriciousness of the man who varies his greetings according to his mood, or even the impertinence

---

[1] Nos. 223, 229, 249, 446.   [2] No. 209.
[3] No. 243.   [4] No. 355.   [5] No. 253.
[6] No. 25.   [7] No. 26.   [8] Nos. 317, 323.
[9] Nos. 76, 84, 97, 480. Pharamond was borrowed from La Calprenède's novel.

of fops who affect hurry or indolence, are really offences against "decency" and "decorum." [1] Such observances, which had formerly been the creed of the middle class, began to have a universal binding force, now that they were backed by the authority of culture. It is significant that some of his leading ideas on education, [2] on the evils of vanity in dress and on the reading of romances, [3] had already been fully put forward by Ascham in *The Scholemaster*. This strengthening of public opinion was undoubtedly important in a half-formed society, but it was soon to grow into the narrow British insistence on respectability, bitterly satirised by Victorian writers. Even at this early stage, the appearance of a girl riding in man's clothes, after the French fashion, suggests to Steele the reflection that eccentricity of dress is nothing less than an offence against virtue. [4] Sometimes, Steele breaks away from the social formulae which he helped to codify and gives free play to his gift of seeing things in a natural, almost a primitive, light. Returning to one of the favourite themes of *The Tatler*, he has independence enough to show how there existed among traders a whole world of romance and destiny undreamt of by the politer classes. [5] His sympathies led him deeper into human nature. As the amusements of polite society became more costly and artificial, a new class of lackeys had grown up beneath the glittering surface, very different from the servingmen of the Elizabethan drama. Steele was one of the first to discover not only the humour but the pathos of their lives. First, we have a glimpse of high life below stairs, in which the frivolities of the rich are absurdly aped by their servants; and, then, the tragedy of the attendant's life, who earns his daily bread as the silent confederate of his master's viciousness and the victim of his caprice. [6] Steele, again, was one of the first to champion women of the lower class. Since the Middle Ages, female character had been one of the favourite butts of popular satire, and, all through the sixteenth and seventeenth centuries, savage invective against prostitution had been common. To Steele, all women are distressed heroines. He shows how shopgirls and barmaids,

[1] Nos. 222, 259, 284.
[2] Nos. 157, 168, 230.
[3] See Steele's comedies.
[4] No. 104.
[5] Nos. 174, 218, 248.
[6] Nos. 88, 96, 137.

so far from being naturally bad, are often, by the nature of their employment, forced to submit to the loose talk and familiarity of men; and, when he comes to describe the most abandoned, instead of inveighing against harlotry, he reveals, for the first time, the "white-slave traffic" of his age, with all its fiendish stratagems for sapping the virtue of its dupes and its secret patrons among high society.[1]

Many of these glimpses of life are given us in the form of letters, and, as *The Spectator* always welcomed correspondence, and, on two occasions, publicly asked for it,[2] there is often danger of taking genuine communications for a device of the editors.[3] Steele, in fact, posed as the "courier of Love,"[4] starting a kind of "agony column," in which lovers could communicate with each other, and in at least one paper he printed some of his own love-letters. Some of the epistles, however, are unmistakably inventions. It must be remembered that, for more than a century,[5] the epistle had become a recognised literary type, and that *The Spectator* would naturally avail itself of "the gentler art" to lend variety and grace to its papers. But, while letter-writers, from Seneca to Loveday,[6] had used this form of composition to convey ideas, Steele and his associates went further. To them belongs the credit of discovering that the epistle could become a picturesque type of character-sketch. Among others, Thomas Hearne is said to have portrayed Arthur Charlett as Abraham Froth, who describes the discussions of his futile club with prolix self-satisfaction,[7] and John Hughes composed the two admirably characteristic letters on the education of a girl, one from Célimène, who despairs of breaking in her charge to all the artificialities of polite society, and the other from a self-styled "rough man" who fears that "the young girl is in a fair way to be spoilt."[8] Steele is certainly the author of the footman's love-letter couched, like *The Yellowplush Papers* of a later day, in language which he can neither understand nor spell, with that inimitable touch of nature, suggestive of *The Conscious Lovers*, "Oh! dear Betty, must the nightingales sing to those

---

[1] Nos. 155, 182, 190, 266, 274, 437.   [2] Nos. 428, 442.
[3] C. Lillie (1725) published two vols. of letters which had been sent to *The Tatler* and *The Spectator* but not printed.
[4] No. 204.   [5] *Ante*, Vol. VII, Chap. XVI, pp. 443–444.
[6] Cf., as to Robert Loveday, *ante*, Vol. VII, p. 495.   [7] No. 43.   [8] No. 66.

who marry for money and not to us true lovers?"[1] Besides
revealing character, letters were admirably adapted to disclose
the secrets of private life. In the guise of a correspondent,
Steele found new scope for the gift of storytelling which he
had developed in *The Tatler*. Some of the communications
contained glimpses into the comic side of domestic history—
such as the account of Anthony Freeman's device for escaping
from the over-affectionate attentions of his wife;[2] while others
are fragments torn from sordid reality, like the "unhappy
story in low life" telling how the drunken weaver unwittingly
sells a successful lottery ticket which his wife had pinched herself
to buy.[3] In some numbers, Steele goes further and narrates a
sequence of events by an interchange of letters. One of his
noblest efforts in this style is a correspondence by which a widow
wins back her petulant and wasteful son from the dissipations
of London,[4] and one of his wittiest is the series of letters which
release Cynthio from Flavia's inconvenient affection.[5]

Thus, Steele was on the verge of inventing the epistolary
novel; but, as in *The Tatler*, so, now, he had neither the perseverance nor the self-confidence necessary to create a literary
type. He was more inclined to follow his illustrious contemplative collaborator, who, in the meantime, had created
the serial treatise. Addison began with a succession of rather
fugitive but witty attacks on the staging of the Italian opera,[6]
in which his own scholarly love of simplicity, inspired by
Terence and Horace, blended with the inherited middle-class
dislike of all that was un-English. These early papers are
hardly more than outbursts of Addisonian irony, such as he
might have vented on any other of society's laughable weaknesses. But material prosperity and the discussions of
coffee-houses had brought the middle class to a stage at which
they felt the need of culture and eagerly read anything on
taste or style. In this way, Addison found himself leading a
reaction in literature, just as Steele had led a reaction in
manners. The drama was the natural field for a critic nur-
tured at the university; so, Addison began to discuss tragedy
in a didactic spirit, not without sallies of characteristic irony
insisting on what he calls "the moral part of the perform-

---

[1] No. 71.   [2] Nos. 212, 216.   [3] No. 242.
[4] No. 263.   [5] No. 398.   [6] Nos. 5, 13, 18, 29, 31.

ance," showing how the *technique* of playwriting contributes to dramatic effect, and how false art may be detected by comparison with the great masters.[1] As he warmed to his work, he perceived that the coffee-house public would never take more than a passing interest in the stage. There was a danger that, in literary taste as in morality, the inexperienced, for sheer lack of proper models, might accept as their standard of poetry the precious and artificial style of versifying with which fashionable society still amused itself. What the citizens of London really needed was a literature as serious as themselves. Accordingly, Addison gave up a whole week's issues to the criticism of conceits and mere verbal dexterity, condemning acrostics, lipograms, rebuses, anagrams, chronograms, *bouts rimés*, puns and paragrams; and, after dismissing all these kinds of false wit,[2] he shows his unacademic readers in what true wit consists. It is illustrative of the middle-class reaction in literature that he should base his definition on the reasoning of so modern and independent a thinker as Locke,[3] and should follow up Dryden's preface to *The State of Innocence* by restricting the meaning of wit to "the resemblance of ideas . . . that give delight and surprise to the reader," always supposing the resemblance to be founded on truth and common-sense.[4] Addison, indeed, was teaching his fellow citizens to expect far more than wit or art from literature. His aim was to find "the precepts of morality" which should underlie every work of inspiration; and, with this end in view, he endeavoured to explain the universal charm of such artless compositions as *Chevy Chace* and *The Children in the Wood*. Among the middle class, the love of medieval ballads had survived the renascence and was probably not yet dead; but Addison essayed a task beyond the learning of his age when he attempted to subject folklore to the canons of criticism. In his day, men could judge poetry only under the shadow of the classics, and *The Spectator* is still pedantic enough to praise the old minstrelsy because it finds therein a few parallels to Vergil and Horace.[5]

---

[1] Nos. 39, 40, 42, 44, 51.   [2] Nos. 58–61.

[3] *Essay concerning the Human Understanding*, ed. 1690, chap. XI, p. 68.

[4] No. 62. See also no. 63, which sums up his view of false wit in a delightful allegory.   [5] Nos. 70, 74, 85.

Steele had loyally supplemented these more scholarly papers, whenever Addison gave him an opening for a humorous contribution[1] and even succeeded in showing how Raphael's cartoons[2] are studies in the grandeur of human emotions. But his spontaneous and erratic genius quite failed to keep pace with the dogmatism of Addison's next and greatest critical effort. This was the series of Saturday papers[3] in which he criticises *Paradise Lost* by the canons of Aristotle, Longinus and Le Bossu and, though finding faults in Milton, judges him to be equal if not superior, to Homer or Vergil. From the eighteenth century point of view, he was right. The middle classes who read books were not themselves subjected to the great emotions of life, but were bent on methodically building up their own culture. Hence, they could not appreciate the mystery, the passion, the wildness or the pathos of ancient epic, and it is significant that these qualities are not conspicuous in the great translations of the period, which charmed by their rhetoric and polish. The average eighteenth-century reader had somewhat the same point of view as the Italian critics of the renascence and valued what had passed through the crucible of the intellect and smelt of the lamp. When people at this stage of culture consider a work of imagination, they are too prosaic to comprehend the romance of human activity. They want projected shadows of life, which are vaster than reality and bolder in outline, though less searching. Milton met these intellectual requirements more fully than his forerunners, and Addison, in interpreting his poet, seems to have followed Minturno's line of argument when he championed the epic against the *romanzi*. Addison contended that Milton dealt with the destiny of the whole world, they but with that of a single nation. His characters, though fewer in number, appear more varied and less earthbound than theirs. The conception of sin and death contains "a beautiful allegory" affecting all humanity. Adam and Eve typify different beings before and after their fall. Their "conferences" are less mundane than the "loves" of Dido and Aeneas; Satan is more wily and more travelled than Ulysses.[4]

---

[1] Nos. 22, 36, 65.　　[2] No. 226.　See no. 244 for an answer to this paper.
[3] Nos. 267, 273, 279, 285, 291, 297, 303, 309, 315, 321, 327, 333, 339, 345, 351, 357, 363, 369.　　　　　　　　　　　　　　　　　[4] No. 297.

Besides, *Paradise Lost* was originally conceived as a tragedy, and, though the dramatic atmosphere which pervades its final form is rightly judged to be a blemish,[1] it is, for this reason, more easily reducible to Aristotle's rules. After taking a bird's-eye view of the action, the actors, the sentiments and the language,[2] Addison proceeds to consider each book separately. No greater service could have been rendered to the unformed taste of his time than to point out where Milton is to be admired, and Addison has the wisdom to illustrate his criticisms so copiously that these papers almost constitute a book of selected "beauties." Much that he praises is of permanent value, such as grandeur of style and loftiness of conception; but, in much again, his literary judgment is unconsciously biassed by a spirit of propaganda. In reality, *The Spectator* was continuing, after nearly two generations, the same reaction against restoration ideals which Milton had begun in his old age. Thus, *Paradise Lost* had a hold on Addison's admiration quite apart from its intrinsic merits. Milton's tumultuous and overburdened similes seemed perfect, in contrast with the artifices of the little wits.[3] Eve's purity and modesty exercised an exaggerated charm in view of contemporary looseness,[4] and it was regarded as specially appropriate that her dream, inspired by Satan, should be full of pride and conceits.[5] Moreover, the age saw that learning was its salvation and, in *Paradise Lost*, enjoyed the quite artificial pleasures of research. Addison no longer holds to Lionardi's, Fracastor's and Scaliger's[6] creed that all erudition is an ornament to poetry; but he experiences a subtle delight in tracing obscure parallels in inspiration—comparing the sword of Michael with the sword of Aeneas, or the golden compasses of the Creator with the Minerva's aegis, or the repentance of Adam and Eve with the grief of Oedipus. And, finally, *The Spectator* was furthering a religious revival under the auspices of culture and, therefore, found in *Paradise Lost* the same kind of superiority that Harington[7] had claimed for *Orlando Furioso*. Addison

---

[1] *L'Arte Poetica*, 1564.   [2] Nos. 267, 273, 279, 285.
[3] No. 303.   [4] Nos. 321, 345.   [5] No. 327.
[6] See Lionardi, *Dialogi della Inventione Poetica*, 1554; Fracastor, *Opera*, 1555; Scaliger, *Poetices Libri Septem*, 5th ed. 1617. See Spingarn, J. E., *Literary Criticism in the Renaissance*, 1908.   [7] *An Apologie of Poetrie*, Pt. 2.

reconciles himself even to the speeches of the Almighty, though they are not "so proper to fill the mind with sentiments of grandeur, as with thoughts of devotion";[1] while the morning and evening hymns, and the use of scriptural phraseology throughout the poem, seemed like a touch of inspiratiòn higher than any of which a pagan could boast.

These Milton papers met with an enthusiastic reception. They exercised an influence throughout the eighteenth century and only became obsolete when Sainte-Beuve had taught Europe that the critic should be less of a judge than a reconstructor—almost an artist who creates a picture of the author's mind and of the atmosphere in which he wrote. In any case, Addison never attempted to enlarge the bounds of thought. His aim was to gather up the best ideas of his time and put them within reach of the ordinary reader. The same is true of his successive papers on æsthetics, or, as he calls them, "On the Pleasures of the Imagination."[2] He wanted to show how the emotions can be raised and purified by what men see and read. So, he discussed the intellectual pleasure to be found, first, in landscapes and gardens, then, in statues, pictures and architecture, and, then, in the mirrored views of life which a descriptive writer can call up before the mind's eye. This difficult and intricate subject involved an inquiry into the psychology of the imagination and a scientific discrimination of the functions and limits of the different arts. Granted his limitations, Addison is more than equal to the task. He draws on his own travels and experiences, he applies the wisdom of the ancients and the more recent discoveries of Descartes, Locke and Berkeley;[3] yet his exposition is lucid and complete within the compass of eleven short essays. But, though he popularises admirably the ideas of his time, he cannot investigate for himself. The thoughts of his contemporaries lead him to the very brink of Lessing's discovery concerning the relation of poetry to sculpture,[4] but he does not take a

[1] No. 315.

[2] Nos. 411–421, originally written as a single essay years before. See *Some portions of Essays contributed to the Spectator by Mr. Joseph Addison*, Glasgow, 1864.   [3] *New Theory of Vision*, 1709.

[4] Nos. 416, 418; Addison was probably aware of Varchi's comparison of poetry with painting in *Lezzioni, lette nell' Accademia Fiorentina*, 1590; see Spingarn, *ibid.* Lessing's *Laokoon, oder Über die Grenzen der Mahlerey und Poesie*, appeared in 1766.

step further when his guides leave him. Nevertheless, these papers must have awakened in many a new sense of aesthetic enjoyment.[1] Among other things, he protests against the artificiality of *rococo* gardens, and shows what a mine of wonder and reflection had been opened up by natural philosophy.[2]

Although Addison varied these dissertations with humorous and satirical essays,[3] the tone of *The Spectator* became more and more serious as the numbers continued to appear. At the outset, he had declared, in two papers,[4] that his practice was to put his thoughts together without premeditation; but, towards the close, he admitted the need of methodical discourses.[5] He had other things to teach besides the appreciation of literature and art. In the latter half of the seventeenth century, England had exchanged a civilisation of war for a civilisation of peace and needed a religion to match. Martial patriotism, of course, still ran high; but the typical man of culture was a peaceful Londoner, busy with his family and his profession, and the only battles which he fought were those with himself. As has been shown, the votaries of the old *régime* continued the tradition of atheism. But the middle classes were still devout and only needed to bring into their worship that cult of urbanity at which they aimed in their daily lives. No one could be more susceptible to this tendency than a man of Addison's character, and, when he set himself to lead a social reform, it was inevitable that he should write on religion. He is no more original on this theme than on others. Humanised Christianity is to be found, in all its sweetness, in Jeremy Taylor and had already proved itself in John Webster's great book[6] of sufficient power to end the witch persecution. But, though Addison was not the first to proclaim the gospel of peace and goodwill, he was the first who could bring it into the hearts and homes of London citizens. Like the earlier puritans, he held that religion should govern every thought and action, but not to

---

[1] *E.g.* Akenside's *Pleasures of the Imagination*, 1764.   [2] Nos. 414, 420.

[3] *E.g.* nos. 81 (party patches), 102 (the use of the fan), 205 (the woman of fashion in church), 247 (women as talkers), 265 (the head dress), 275 (a beau's head), 281 (a coquette's heart), 343 (the Pythagorean monkey), 361 (catcalls), 377 (bill of mortality through love).   [4] Nos. 46, 124.   [5] No. 476.

[6] *The Displaying of supposed Witchcraft*, 1677. See *ante*, Vol. VII, Chap. XVI, pp. 449–451.

the exclusion of the world. His creed was one of acquiescence and inward piety. Zeal was often a cloak for pride, self-interest or ill-nature; enthusiasm led to bigotry and superstition. A Christian's devotion should be self-contained, with just enough fervour to prevent religion from becoming a mere philosophy.[1] Addison held, also, to the need of self-examination, but not of despondency or self-contempt. To him, everything was under the direction of a Supreme Being,[2] who, as the Stoics and Juvenal had long before taught, knew better than man what was good for him.[3] The duty of human beings was to be reconciled to their lot, to forget the differences and humiliations of this life in the expectation of eternity, and to seek a sober happiness in a sense of doing right.[4] These lay sermons are accompanied by a few verse paraphrases of the *Psalms*, rendered with polished simplicity, and are varied by allegories, among which *The First Vision of Mirza* is justly celebrated for its tranquil, lofty style.

The Spectator's last number appeared on 6 December, 1712. Both writers had cultivated to a surprising degree the art of the *flâneur* and knew how to turn innumerable and generally unnoticed episodes of city life into charming sketches. Such things as a sensation in a coffee-house, a fencing-match, an argument in a bookshop, an old beggar, or a man who applauds with a stick in a theatre gallery, are among their best studies of character.[5] But, apparently, both editors had written themselves out. Addison, at the instigation of his friends, set to work on *Cato*, the first four acts of which had been written before the beginning of *The Tatler*, perhaps as early as 1703. With many misgivings, he allowed the tragedy to be produced at Drury Lane on 14 April, 1713. It was a time of great political excitement; and, when so prominent a public man as Addison produced a drama on Cato's last stand for liberty, against the usurpation of Caesar, both parties turned the situation against their opponents and applauded furiously. In any event, the play was bound to have been a success. It pictures the last of the Roman republicans, a statuesque

[1] Nos. 185, 201, 483.
[2] Nos. 120, 121, 387, 489, 494, 495, 531, 543.   [3] Nos. 207, 237, 391, 441.
[4] Nos. 186, 213, 219, 381, 483.
[5] See respectively nos. 403 and 481, 436, 438, 376, 235.

outline magnanimous and unmoved, surrounded by a treachery which is baffled by the loyalty of his sons and Juba, accepting death rather than dishonour and, in his last moments, taking thought for those around him. The plot is twofold. Side by side with the study in public virtue and high politics, a drama of the tender passion occupies the stage. When Cato's son Marcius dies gallantly fighting against the traitor Syphax, his brother wins the hand of Lucia, for which they had both been honourable rivals, and Juba, the once rejected suitor of Marcia, Cato's daughter, romantically rescues her from the clutches of Sempronius in disguise and finds that she has loved him all the time. Thus, in the consecrated form of a Roman tragedy, the public enjoyed that grandiose, if unsubstantial, projection of character which they admired in Milton, together with the sentimental chivalry of a French romance. To modern taste, the diction is hopelessly declamatory, and the plot full of absurdities. But the ordinary reader of the eighteenth century would almost regard such artificiality as inevitable in a play which has strictly observed the unities, contains a "reversal of intention" and a "recognition"[1] and abounds in crisp and quotable epigrams.

Meanwhile, Steele plunged into politics and, after much pamphleteering, was expelled from the House of Commons for uttering seditious libels. In 1714, he returned to literature and started several periodicals, especially *The Guardian*, to which Addison contributed fifty-one papers; and, in 1722, he produced his last complete comedy, *The Conscious Lovers*. Though the plot is largely borrowed from Terence's *Andria* and, where original, abounds in more glaring improbabilities than his earlier work, the play is remarkable because it resumes in brief all Steele's best ideas on life and character. We have the sketch of servants whose natural freshness is being gradually tainted by the corrupt and contagious air of lackeydom;[2] we have satire on marriages of convenience, duelling and the chicanery of the law; a glance at the opposition between the hereditary gentry and the rising commercial class; while, in

---

[1] The περιπέτεια and ἀναγνώρισις of Aristotle; see *Politics*, ed. Butcher, S. H., 3rd ed. 1902.

[2] Besides the scenes in which Tom and Phillis appear, see the episode of the footboy newly arrived in London, act v, sc. 2.

Bevil junior, Steele portrays his ideal of a gentleman, chivalrous and honourable to women, considerate to men, respectful to his father and self-controlled amid the riotous pleasures of the capital.

Steele and Addison produced other work[1] separately. But, when they ceased to collaborate in *The Spectator*, which was subsequently continued by one of their circle, both became authors of secondary importance. Their task was already done. The peculiar circumstances of their lives gave them an unrivalled opportunity of observing the movement of their time. Thanks to a certain conventionality of intellect, coupled with amazing cleverness, they became the heart of this movement, and made it literature. In this sense, they collaborated with their age. As a comparison between the two writers is almost inevitable, it may be said, in conclusion, that Steele was the more original and Addison the more effective. Steele conceived the periodical essay, but never perfected it; he accidentally discovered the short story and verged upon the domestic novel, without substantially influencing the development of either genre. This ineffectiveness was partly due to his volatile nature and somewhat unstable life, but it was also largely due to the presence of Addison. That successful and self-contained mentor seems to have unconsciously restrained Steele's initiative. But, while he curbed his companion's talents, he displayed the utmost efficiency in the use of his own and, without any deep fund of ideas or sympathy, raised Steele's conception of an essay to a degree of perfection never since surpassed. The Londoners of queen Anne's reign chiefly valued *The Spectator* for Addison's humorous papers and religious dissertations. The modern student most admires its accuracy and penetration, and the true and long-enduring picture which it gives of middle-class culture and character.

[1] See bibliography.

CHAPTER III

Pope

THE great writer of whom this chapter treats was a man of real poetic genius, the growth and direction of which were powerfully affected by his physical constitution, his circumstances and the character of the age. None of his achievements belong to the very highest forms of poetry. Where he excelled, his pre-eminence is beyond dispute; yet his deficiency in qualities more prized by a later generation has imperilled his very right to be regarded as a poet. On certain points, all are practically agreed. Pope is a memorable example of a conscious literary artist, the type in our country of the classical spirit; rarely has a poet shown himself a truer or more delicate representative of his own time. Even did his work no longer appeal to us by its enduring merit, he must escape neglect because of his part in England's literary development.

Pope's true position has not always been recognised. He has been viewed from the standpoint of periods out of sympathy with his excellences and impatient of his defects, and his influence has been regarded as a monstrous barrier restraining all deep and natural emotion until swept away by the torrent of the romantic revival. He has figured as one who left the free air of heaven for the atmosphere of the coffee-house, as the first to introduce a mechanical standard of poetry, owing its acceptance to the prosaic tone of his day. Attention to the historic side of literature has brought sounder views. It is urged that, far from making nature give way to art, he shared the reaction, not confined to England, against an artificial mode, and stood in a real sense for a return to nature. Rather than having been the originator of a movement, he represents its climax, as he carried to completion a work already begun.

Pope's attitude was not one of revolt. His poetry did not disgust on its first appearance by deserting accepted models. His immediate success proves how closely he was in touch with his contemporaries. In the directness and lucidity of his style, he improved his inheritance from Waller, Denham and Dryden. In the skill with which he elaborated the heroic couplet, he was indebted to these poets, above all to Dryden, as well as to the translations of Sandys. In the striving after simplicity, in the rejection of the extravagance of the so-called metaphysical poets, he instinctively followed an existing movement, precisely as the justness of thought and clarity of expression in Swift and Addison had an immediate ancestry. But, in prose and poetry alike, the qualities greatly admired in that period, and valuable in any, were won at the cost of others whose loss must be deplored, and poetry suffered most.

Alexander Pope was born in London on 21 May, 1688, of parents past middle age. They were devout Roman catholics; their son's adherence to this creed seems to have been prompted by filial affection. The accident of belonging to a proscribed church decided the course of his education. It is curious to reflect that, displaying such affinity for polish and precision, he should have missed a classical training. After brief schooling, he was taken home to Binfield, in Windsor forest, where his father had settled on retiring from his linendraper's business, and from about the age of twelve was largely self-taught. He grew up undersized, delicate and deformed, though we have testimony to the beauty of his voice and the brilliance of his eye. The presence of a fiery soul within this frail tenement was proved when, in an unliterary home, amid the languor of sickness and the lack of mental discipline, he developed a poetic genius, not fitful and uneven but inspired by a continual endeavour after the highest attainable in the form and music of his verse. Pope's own account of these early studies was:

When I had done with my priests, I took to reading by myself, for which I had a very great eagerness and enthusiasm, especially for poetry: and in a few years I had dipped into a great number

of the English, French, Italian, Latin and Greek poets. This I
did without any design but that of pleasing myself: and got the
languages by hunting after the stories in the several poets I read.[1]

Of his knowledge of Italian, there is little trace. His Greek
was, certainly, not strong. In spite of some acquaintance with
French literature, he never seems to have had any real familiarity with the language. With regard to scholarship, he was
doubtless "shady in Latin"; but he was profoundly affected
by the Roman poets, with whose style and ways of thought
he showed a remarkable affinity. We everywhere feel the
influence of the finish, dignity and sonorousness of Latin poetry.

Of his own countrymen, Waller, Spenser and Dryden were
his favourites. While yet a child, he began to "lisp in
numbers." At his first school, he was punished for lampooning
his master; at the next, he tacked together speeches from
Ogilby's *Iliad* to be acted by his companions. Shortly after,
as he told Spence, he began an epic, *Alcander Prince of Rhodes*,
and completed four books. This he destroyed in mature life.
We hear, also, of a tragedy on St. Geneviève. The satirical
lines on the author of *Successio* (1712) were said by Pope to
have been written at fourteen; but the earliest poem that has
a place in his works is the *Ode on Solitude*, sent to Henry Cromwell in a letter of 1709, and there stated to have been composed
when the author was not yet twelve; the lines, however, were
retouched after transcription and further improved before
their publication in 1735. The boy soon recognised the
weakness of his own efforts and turned to translation. He
was already familiar with attempts by others. In after years,
he still spoke with rapture of the pleasure he had received as a
boy from Ogilby's rendering of Homer. His own translation
of the first book of Statius's *Thebais* was professedly made
"almost in his childhood," but corrected before publication.
He also tried his hand on part of the *Metamorphoses* and began to submit Chaucer to a similar process. His half-sister
remarked of these early years, "I believe nobody ever studied
so hard as my brother did. He did nothing else but write and
read." But Pope's literary judgment was not based solely
on books. At a susceptible age, he formed a friendship with

[1] Spence's *Anecdotes*, ed. Singer, S. W., 1820, p. 193.

more than one man of mature years, knowledge of the world
and taste for letters. Among the earliest of these was Sir
William Trumbull, a retired diplomatist living near Binfield.
Others were Wycherley, Henry Cromwell, a literary man about
town, and William Walsh, styled by Dryden the best critic
of our nation. Pope corresponded with these, sought their
advice and submitted his verses. His *Pastorals* went from
hand to hand and were complimented in flattering terms.
Tonson offered to publish them, and, after some delay, they
appeared in the sixth volume of his *Miscellany*, on 2 May, 1709.

If we take Pope's own word, they had been composed when
he was sixteen. Parts, at least, had been written a year or two
later, and none assumed their final form until both numbers
and language had been assiduously polished. The paper is
still extant, containing a list of passages drawn up by Pope,
with which he was dissatisfied, and alternatives appended for
Walsh's choice. But the pastoral was a dying form of poetry
into which fresh blood could not now be infused. Writing
among country sights and sounds, Pope has, at the utmost,
two or three descriptive touches from his own observation.
In his ironical criticism in *The Guardian*, Pope remarked that
Philips, in his *Pastorals*, gave "manifest proof of his knowledge
of books"; his own amply deserve this praise. He had gleaned,
not from Theocritus and Vergil alone, but from Spenser,
Sidney, Drummond, Milton, Waller, Dryden, Congreve,
Walsh and Sannazaro. The real merit of the *Pastorals* lay in
the versification. The new poet was clearly possessed of a
quite exceptional metrical skill.

Windsor Forest (1713) belongs, in great part, to the period
of the *Pastorals*. It is no longer a purely literary exercise,
but an attempt to apply observation and reading to a larger
theme. The design, for which Pope was indebted to Denham's
Cooper's Hill, was to combine a description of the countryside
and field-sports with the historical and literary associations
of the district. He was induced to add after l. 290 the lines
by Lord Lansdowne (George Granville), who was anxious that
he should praise the peace of Utrecht. It must be confessed
that Pope is not strong in the appreciation of natural scenery,
although Wordsworth was pleased to allow that a passage
or two in *Windsor Forest* contained new images of external

nature. Pope's treatment is largely conventional, and the atmosphere is spoilt by one of the worst faults of pseudo-classicism—the Mars-Bacchus-Apollo element. The plumage of the dying pheasant may be over-elaborated; still, it is distinctly pleasing to find a recognition that other of God's creatures besides man have a right to enjoy themselves on this earth. But, in his pastoral and sylvan efforts, Pope had now clearly shown that, as a nature poet, he was not in advance of his age. Thomson was yet to come.

The sacred eclogue *Messiah* was printed in *The Spectator* for 14 May, 1712. In his attempt to pour the Messianic prophecies of Isaiah into the mould of a Vergilian eclogue, Pope, in spite of an undeniable impressiveness, lowered their majesty by artificial epithet and paraphrase. It is curious to note how gradually the false attitude came home to critics. Warton and Bowles use very guarded language when suggesting that, in a few passages, Pope had weakened the sublimity of Isaiah. It was Wordsworth who cited the poem as an illustration of artificial poetic diction.

An Essay on Criticism, which appeared in 1711, was, apparently, written in 1709, though Pope attempted afterwards to assign its composition to an earlier date. It was natural that, being studiously careful of his form, with the examples of Horace, Vida and Boileau before him (not to mention Roscommon and Buckinghamshire), he should try to discuss the principles of his art. He gave his poem, indeed, the title *An Essay on Criticism;* but it is clear that he is addressing not so much the ingenuous reader as the intending writer. He once said that he had digested all the matter in prose before he began it in verse; but, according to Jonathan Richardson, he often spoke of the *Essay* as "an irregular collection of thoughts, thrown together as they offered themselves, as Horace's *Art of Poetry* was." And this would seem a true description, for Pope was not a pioneer. He did not aim at leading his generation along new ways, but at recalling them to paths trodden by the ancients. Originality, even from the point of view of his own days, is not to be expected from him. But, though he inevitably insisted on truths which may now appear obvious, his genius for conciseness and epigram has stamped many a truth of this nature with the form that it must wear for all time. With the *Essay*, Pope became famous.

Young Lord Petre, by snipping a lock of Miss Fermor's hair, had caused ill-feeling between the families. Pope was invited by his friend Caryll to allay this by taking the theme for a playful poem. *The Rape of the Lock*, in its first form, was written within a fortnight and published anonymously in Lintot's *Miscellany*, 1712. For the genre, Pope was indebted to Boileau's *Lutrin*, as Boileau had been to Tassoni's *Secchia Rapita;* but, in its blending of mock-heroic, satire and delicate fancy, this exquisite specimen of filigree work, as Hazlitt called it, remains unmatched. Pope's hand was never happier than in adding to the original sketch his machinery of sylphs and gnomes. But his genius for touching appears throughout. Nothing could better illustrate Pope's methods of working than to turn to the earlier version of the six lines beginning canto 1, 13, and to watch how vastly each one has been improved. The parody of Sarpedon's speech in the fifth canto was not introduced till the edition of 1717. In Germany, *The Rape* gave rise to a long series of imitations.

Two poems, of uncertain date, appear first in the volume of 1717: *Eloisa to Abelard* and the *Elegy to the Memory of an Unfortunate Lady*. In these, Pope made a sustained attempt to present pathos and passion. To modern taste, his emotion is too rhetorical. The lady's personality and fate are vague. Pope's puzzling note darkened the mystery. Research has shown that, while the death and details were imaginary, his warm sympathy for Mrs. Weston was the basis on which the poem was built. But, the gleaning of phrases, the dexterous piecing together of parts of a poem, are hardly suited for the expression of deep and spontaneous feeling. It is possible that a poet may brood for long over a cruel bereavement and yet not destroy the impression of sincerity by the elaborate treatment of his grief. Such genuine emotion, however, as is embodied in Pope's poem seems hardly deep or definite enough to give warmth to the whole. The feeling has been fondled for a literary purpose.

The material for *Eloisa* was taken from John Hughes's translation of a French paraphrase of the Latin epistles that passed under the names of Abelard and Eloisa. The motive is the struggle in her heart between her human passion for Abelard and her dedication to the service of God. In the background of the poem, the convent of the Paraclete and its surroundings, there are touches which anticipate the romantic feeling for natural scenery and architecture. A writer of our own time can still say of the poem, *Ce n' est pas seulement une des expressions les plus fortes de la passion qui aient été données, c' est la seule qui existe de l' amour absolu.*[1] But it may be doubted whether, in Pope's fervid tones, we are listening to the voice of nature and passion and not rather to a piece of superb declamation.

Whatever exception may be taken to his attempts in the higher sphere of passion, Pope's sense of friendship, and something further which it is not easy to define, are expressed with singular charm in his *Epistles to Mr. Jervas, to a Young Lady with the works of Voiture* and *to the Same on her leaving the Town after the Coronation.* It is characteristic that the last two *Epistles* were written, in the first instance, for Teresa Blount, and transferred afterwards to her younger sister Martha. At this time, Pope seems to have been specially susceptible to female influence. How much genuine feeling and how much conventional gallantry made up his attitude to Lady Mary Wortley Montagu, it might be hard to determine. The most likely explanation of the bitterness with which he assailed her in after years is to be found in her own statement, that a declaration of passionate love provoked on her side an immoderate fit of laughter. On the other hand, it was his fondness of thirty years for Martha Blount, at times misunderstood, that helped him through the long disease of his life.

Pope's literary activity in this first stretch of his career was singularly varied. Any dramatic work was confined to a share in Gay and Arbuthnot's *Three Hours after Marriage.* His *Ode for Music on Saint Cecilia's Day* marks the absence of the lyrical gift. His other attempts to sing were of the slightest; but there is enough variety in the rest to show the directions in which he could turn his extraordinary technical skill. We miss any indication of what was to be the main subject of his

[1] Montégut, Émile, "Heures de Lecture d' un Critique: Pope," *Revue des deux Mondes,* 15 March, 1888.

matured art. And, just when we might have expected him to plan a great original work, he binds himself to years of translation, and, this task over, we find him in a new field. Pope has been described,[1] at this stage, as a potential romanticist, and we are conscious, in more than one of his poems, of feelings that faded away and a promise that was never fulfilled. Something must be allowed to the spirit of the times, something to his long term of hard labour on his *Homer*, something to advancing years. For Pope aged early: to his gayer youth succeeded a more or less invalid middle age, which might itself account for a change of tone and a restriction in his choice of subject. The psychology of poetic creation is a perilous topic; but it would seem that his fervour was frequently kindled, not so much by the theme itself as by the consciousness of literary effort in treating it; that, in short, his inspiration grew in the course of composition. The main features of his style were now formed. Change of taste has done its worst with them; but it is unfair to construct an idea of the essential from the accidents of his art. At his best, he is signally direct, free from artificial balance, otiose epithets and pseudo-classical periphrasis. The nature of many of his winged words is responsible for the belief that Pope's qualities were hard and prosaic. But the exact matching of thought with speech, making any other mode of expression inconceivable, is not less remarkable in passages where the idea is more poetical. Pope did not restrict himself to conversational language: his style is exceptionally rich in apt reminiscences of other writers. But his acquaintance with men of the world, at a time when literature held little aloof from everyday life, made him sensitively aware what his audience demanded. In this respect, the age of Anne may be called Augustan. Its chief men wrote primarily for the few. Pope has been compared to Horace, from whom he widely differs in much else. But the *curiosa felicitas* of both was connected with the same instinct. One of the conditions of Pope's correctness was that no extravagance or solecism should offend his reader's taste. His early devotion to books has been described. "I had rather," he confided to Spence, "be employed in reading than in the most agreeable conversation"; and, in all that he read, his tenacious

[1] Montégut, Émile, *op. cit.*

memory and sense for apt expression never slumbered. Individual as his style remains, his fabric is many a time woven with threads drawn from another's web. But he was no plagiarist. The form of words is borrowed or adapted to fit a thought of his own that already asked for utterance. We are reminded again and again of the advantage to which he had studied Milton and Waller and Dryden, and many another predecessor, besides taking hints from contemporaries. Many passages of this kind were noted by Warton and Wakefield and later editors, and a closer search will bring more to light. Pope is not one of those writers who are never at a loss for a word, still less for ten. His style rests on his oriental patience in elaborating his art. "I corrected," he observes in his preface of 1717, "because it was as pleasant to me to correct as to write," and a study of their gradual growth proves that, in many of his lines, the finest touches are due to second intentions. Thus

> And strike to dust th' imperial tow'rs of Troy[1]

owes its full effectiveness to an afterthought, and the inevitable couplet that tells of fit instruments of ill[2] is an improvement on an earlier attempt. Autographs, proof-sheets and revised editions all attest his passion for retouching. "I will make my enemy do me a kindness when he meant an injury," he writes to Caryll, "and so serve instead of a friend"; and he blotted lines that Dennis had condemned. In minute care of workmanship, he has not been outdone by Tennyson. The sense of the supreme importance of polish was a legacy from Augustan Rome. The endeavour for compactness makes Pope, at times, ungrammatical or obscure. Austin Dobson has characterised his age:

> When Phoebus touch'd the Poet's trembling ear
> With one supreme commandment, *Be thou Clear.*[3]

But, in *An Essay on Criticism*, where there is need above all to be lucid, Pope, more than once, sins by ambiguity, as, again, in *An Essay on Man*. The metrical principles which

---

[1] *The Rape of the Lock*, canto III, l. 174.   [2] *Ibid.* ll. 125–6.
[3] *A Dialogue to the memory of Mr. Alexander Pope; Collected Poems*, 1897, p. 304.

he followed from an early period were expounded in a letter
to Cromwell. He excepts against hiatus, the use of expletives,
monosyllabic lines—unless very artfully managed—the repetition of the same rimes within four or six lines and the too
frequent use of alexandrines; and recommends that the same
pause in the verse should not to be continued for more than
three lines in succession.

Pope has been charged with monotony in his management
of the heroic couplet. The surprising thing is that he should
have achieved so much variety. He was extraordinarily
dexterous in varying the music of his verse within the limits
he had set himself. The effect is due to change in pause and
beat, a judicious attention to the number of syllables in his
words, with an unobtrusive employment of every degree of
alliteration and of what may be called the opposite of alliteration, as in

> Eyes the calm sunset of the various days.[1]

The charge that, with Pope, the couplet is almost exclusively
the unit of composition requires qualification. At his best,
we find him working with the larger unit of the paragraph.
As the ideas of a prose-writer using short independent sentences
are not necessarily less consecutive than those developed in
lengthy periods, so Pope, by avoiding *enjambement*, is not
compelled to express a series of disconnected thoughts. A
study of his more careful paragraphs shows, too, with what
art he extended alliteration over the boundaries of the couplet
and studied the music of the larger division. The most serious
fault which can be detected is that his ear for rime was not so
delicate as his sense of rhythm. When all allowance has been
made for the pronunciation of his day, there still remain a
large number of unsatisfactory rimes. Weakness, too, is
shown in the repetition of the same set of rimes after too
short an interval, and the employment of others too close
in sound to those immediately preceding.

Before the end of the period whose productions are contained in the *Works* of 1717, he had already published the first
instalment of his most laborious enterprise. He once observed

---

[1] *Epistle to Robert Earl of Oxford, and Earl Mortimer*, l. 38.

that, had he not undertaken his translation of the *Iliad*, he would certainly have written an epic poem. Towards the close of his life, he formed a plan for one on Brutus of Troy; but Conington has well remarked that Pope's sympathy with epic grandeur was the sympathy of art, not of kindred inspiration. So far back as 9 April, 1708, we find Trumbull, in a letter to Pope, acknowledging the receipt of the Sarpedon episode in the *Iliad*, afterwards published in Tonson's *Miscellany*, and renewing a request that he would translate "that incomparable poet" and "make him speak good English." In his preface to the *Iliad*, while mentioning the encouragement received from Steele, Swift, Garth, Congreve, Rowe and Parnell, Pope states that Addison was the first whose advice determined him to undertake this task.

By his own confession, it was gain as much as glory that "winged his flight." His father's fortune was not large. Catholics were double-taxed. His own health required indulgence. In short, without exactly writing for money, he went where money was. The work was to be published by subscription, and the eagerness of his friends secured a long list of names. Yet the difficulties in his path might have appalled a less stout heart. To engage one's activity for a long way ahead would seem to demand a robuster constitution than he possessed. Further, Pope had no sound knowledge of Greek. But he set resolutely to work. The linguistic difficulties were surmounted by a comparison of previous translators, Latin, English and French. Parnell wrote *An Essay on the Life, Writings and Learning of Homer* (in vol. I of the *Miscellany*), while, in the compilation of the notes from Eustathius and other sources, help was given by Parnell, Broome and Jortin. The first four volumes appeared in 1715, 1716, 1717, 1718, and the last two, with a dedication to Congreve, in 1720. The harvest-home was sung by Gay in *Mr. Pope's Welcome from Greece*. Tickell, a member of Addison's circle, published a translation of the first *Iliad* on the same day as Pope's first volume. It was supposed, in some quarters, that Addison had inspired it as a rival venture and even had a principal hand in the performance. Pope, naturally, was suspicious and the incident was one cause of his estrangement from Addison. As a translation in the narrower sense, his rendering has very obvious shortcomings. Of this, no proof was needed. Wakefield, in his edition (1795), has shown in detail how largely Pope's inaccuracy was due to his having taken the sense of the text of Homer from Chapman, Hobbes, Ogilby, Dacier and others. Not only did he often miss the meaning of the original; but he followed his predecessors in additions which had no warrant in the Greek. All this, however, in a sense, is beside the mark. Pope, for all his defects in scholarship, approached Homer with reverence and confessed himself incapable of doing justice to him. But he was right when he asserted that it ought to be the endeavour of anyone who translates Homer "above all things to keep alive that spirit and fire which makes his chief character." Others have produced translations; but Pope's work is a poem. The style and taste of his time more closely suited the character of Latin poetry.[1] He has artificial turns which are as far removed as can be from the directness of his original; but the reader who cannot, or will not, view these accidents in their true proportion, and who is impervious to the beauty of the work, must, at the same time, be impervious to much in Homer.

It has been said that Pope's *Iliad* was the cause of the vicious poetic style prevalent in the latter part of the eighteenth century. A certain periphrastic pomp was found easy of imitation, and became a marked feature in the verse of men who were without a touch of his poetic power. The popularity of his *Iliad* has lasted for long; but there are signs that the attraction it exercised on several generations is waning. A critic who has shown unsurpassed insight and sympathy in his estimate of Pope wrote, in 1881, "No one will venture to say Pope's *Iliad* has gone, or is likely to go, out of fashion."[2] One would be glad to feel that this judgment and forecast were not unduly optimistic.

Shortly after the long labour of the *Iliad* was over, Pope was engaged in two fresh enterprises. The translation of the *Odyssey* was shared with two Cambridge men, Elijah Fenton

[1] In 1740, J. and P. Knapton brought out in two volumes, *Selecta Poemata Italorum Qui Latine Scripserunt. Accurante A. Pope*, based on an anonymous selection by Atterbury (1684). There are several traces in Pope's works of his indebtedness to renascence Latin verse.

[2] Courthope, W. J., *The Works of Alexander Pope*, vol. III, p. 35.

and William Broome, to whom half the books were allotted,
Fenton taking I, IV, XIX and XX, and his colleague II, VI, VIII,
XI, XII, XVI, XVIII and XXIII, while Pope translated the rest
and assumed, in addition, the office of revision. The first
three volumes were published in 1725, and the remaining two
in the next year. Pope's general supervision of the translation,
and the skill with which his subordinates assumed his style,
prevented any obvious contrast between the parts. The
correspondence between Pope, Broome and Fenton throws
light on one of the least honourable incidents in Pope's career.
He received by subscription £4500, out of which he allowed
Broome £570 and Fenton £200. He was entitled to demand
the lion's share; but, after vainly endeavouring to suppress
the details of the collaboration, he induced Broome to allow
a statement to appear under his name which led the public
to suppose the chief partner to be responsible for all but five
books. The weariness that had come over Pope told on his
execution, nor was the *Odyssey* so congenial a subject to him.
He had been at his best in the speeches of the *Iliad* and groaned
most heavily over the homely scenes in Ithaca.

Pope's treatment of his coadjutors figured prominently
henceforward in the personalities of his opponents. But the
Odyssey was also the occasion of his friendship with Joseph
Spence, through the latter's *Essay on Pope's Odyssey* (1726–7).
During this time, Pope had been engaged on his edition of
Shakespeare, undertaken at Tonson's invitation and published
in March, 1725. His main disqualifications are patent. He
had no intimate knowledge of the Elizabethan period and lacked
some of the qualities—above all the patience—requisite for
a thorough editing of the text. But a man of his genius could
hardly devote himself to a literary subject without leaving
some result. "Proofs of the time and toil he spent upon the
text can be found on nearly every page."[1] His preface has,
at least, the merit of a sincere recognition of Shakespeare's
greatness. The task of pointing out the errors in Pope's
edition was undertaken by Lewis Theobald, a man memorable
for his high deserts among Shakespearean critics.[2] This was

[1] Cf. *ante*, Vol. V, pp. 300–301; and see Lounsbury, T. R., *The first editors of
Shakespeare*, p. 100.

[2] Cf. *ante*, Vol. V, pp. 301–302.

the offence that gained him the laurel in *The Dunciad*. Pope's labours as translator and commentator left him little leisure for original verse. Among the shorter pieces of this period is the *Epistle to Robert Earl of Oxford, and Earl Mortimer* (1721), dedicating Parnell's *Poems* to him. Pope excels all other men, even Dryden, in the compliments he pays his friends; and, for variety of music and dignity of style, this *Epistle* is unsurpassed. Admirable, too, is the skill with which Harley's indolence is elevated to the rank of a rare virtue. Whatever may be the historical verdict on Harley as a politician, Pope has cast an unfading halo about the memory of the man.

Thanks to Homer, Pope had thriven; he had settled in his Twickenham villa in 1719 and associated on equal terms with the first men of his day. But, though he had a heart capable of strong affection and generosity, he was apt to brood over injuries real and imaginary, and employ to the full his "proper power to hurt." He had provoked Dennis, in *An Essay on Criticism*, and avenged himself on Dennis's *Reflections* by *The Narrative of Dr. Robert Norris* (1713), ostensibly in reply to the criticisms on *Cato*. Addison's dissociation of himself from this attack, probably, contributed to the estrangement between them. Two years later, Pope, who sent several papers to *The Guardian*, resented a eulogy there of Ambrose Philips's *Pastorals*, and wrote a paper (15 April, 1713) contrasting his own *Pastorals* with Philips's and giving the preference to the latter. In 1716, he retorted on Curll for having published *Court Poems*, ascribing them to "the laudible translator of Homer," by *A Full and True Account of a Horrid and Barbarous Revenge by Poison on the Body of Edmund Curll*. Towards the end of queen Anne's reign, Pope, Swift, Gay, Parnell and others had been in the habit of meeting at Arbuthnot's rooms in St. James's palace. Nights with these gatherings had closed Harley's toilsome days. A literary scheme with which this informal club dallied was a satire on various forms of pedantry in the person of an imaginary Martinus Scriblerus.[1] In 1726, Swift had revisited England after twelve years' absence, and stayed for part of his time at Twickenham, Gay being a fellow-guest. He repeated the visit in the following year. In June, 1727, appeared the first two volumes of *Miscellanies*.

[1] Cf. *post*, Chap. v.

The preface was signed jointly by Swift and Pope. *Miscellanies, the last volume*, 1728, contained the character of Addison which had first appeared in *Cytherea: or poems upon Love and Intrigue*, 1723, and now received new additions. *A fragment of a Satire* corresponds to lines 151–214 of the *Epistle to Dr. Arbuthnot*, though, in its latest form, quite half the lines have undergone change. But the exercise in the "gentle art" which made most stir was the opening piece of the volume, Pope's *Martinus Scriblerus ΠΕΡΙ ΒΑΘΟΥΣ: or the Art of Sinking in Poetry*. In this, "the Bathos or Profund, the Natural Taste of Man and in particular the present age" was discussed and illustrated by quotations from Blackmore (who had rebuked Pope for an unseemly parody of the first *Psalm*), Ambrose Philips, Theobald, Dennis, Welsted, Thomas Cooke and others. In chapter VI, the several kinds of geniuses in the "Profund" are classified as ostriches, parrots, porpoises and so forth, and three or four sets of initials are given in each class. Pope's intention, apparently, was to draw down attacks from the offended authors so that he might have a pretext for the publication of *The Dunciad*, which he was now preparing to bring out. In the preface to the 1728 edition of this work, the reader is told that

every week for these last two months past the town has been persecuted with pamphlets, advertisements, and weekly essays, not only against the wit and writings, but against the character and person of Mr. Pope.

But it has been shown[1] that, when the provocation is considered, the attacks made upon Pope were extremely few, and did not include a single pamphlet, while four of them, if not Pope's own handiwork, were inspired by him. It was evident, too, that the composition of the poem had preceded the attacks. It seems to have been on the stocks, in some form or other, for several years. What determined its plan and hastened its completion was, undoubtedly, the pain given him by Theobald's *Shakespeare Restored*, which must have been all the keener because he could not fail to perceive the justice of the criticism. In the preface to the 1729 edition of *The Dunciad*, the dedication

[1] Lounsbury, *u. s.* p. 207.

to Swift is said to have been due to the fact that the latter had snatched the first draft of the poem from the fire and urged the author to proceed with it. Pope was certainly engaged on *The Dunciad* when Swift was his guest, and the latter claimed some credit for the work on the ground that his deafness had prevented conversation. But it has never been shown that he had any actual share in the composition of the work. The story of its publication reveals one of the most intricate series of manoeuvres in which Pope was ever implicated. Evidently, he felt anxious at the thought of putting before the public the whole mass of his personalities, and of acknowledging them under his own name. *The Dunciad* appeared, anonymously, in May, 1728. It bore on the title "Dublin Printed, London Re-printed for A. Dodd," and was advertised as the second edition. Its success was immediate, and several further issues followed. Pope was emboldened to bring out a more elaborate form in 1729. Names, with a very few exceptions, were now printed in full, whereas, in the previous edition, initial and final letters, or initial only, had been the rule. The dedicatory lines to Swift, which had been purposely omitted, were restored and the poem was garnished with "Notes Variorum and the Prolegomena of Scriblerus." An elaborate piece of caution on Pope's part was to assign the copyright to Lords Bathurst, Burlington and Oxford, who afterwards assigned it to Lawton Gilliver. Its authorship was not openly acknowledged till 1735. The main idea of *The Dunciad* was taken from *Mac Flecknoe*, and, in emulating his master's vigorous satire, Pope must have felt that he was put upon his mettle. *The Dunciad*, even in its earlier form, is four times the length of *Mac Flecknoe*, and, while Dryden's assault is almost exclusively upon Shadwell, Pope, though aiming principally at Theobald, attacked, at the same time, whole battalions of his enemies. There are two sides to *The Dunciad*. Though Pope's claim that the lash was lifted in the interests of all honest men must be rejected, he was not merely indulging in an outburst of personal malice. In places, especially in the book added later, there is effective chastisement of literary vices, without an undue admixture of the personal element. But his treating *The Dunciad* like a large open grave into which fresh bodies of his victims could be flung, has impaired the value of his general satire. The tremendous energy with which he "dealt damnation round the land" has had a result which would have astounded himself. Though our protests are challenged by the presence of some names, such as Bentley and Defoe, yet, with regard to the bulk of his victims, the reader is apt to feel even more than acquiescence in Pope's verdict. Perhaps it is thought that his dunces must have been exceptionally dull, as dullards of the eighteenth century. Of course, Pope was unjust, but an element of injustice enters into all satire. If he chose to attack individuals by name, we can hardly complain that he did not select nonentities for the purpose. In allowing his personal resentment to make choice of Theobald as a hero, Pope was particularly unjust. Theobald had produced his share of unsuccessful work; yet it was plain that Pope was not provoked by his dramatic failures but by his immeasurable superiority in Shakespearean criticism. Again, he committed the error of insisting that literary inefficiency must be accompanied by moral degradation. Though dulness never dies, he tried to spread the belief that he had annihilated her particular representatives whom he attacked. To judge from the warfare that ensued, they showed an intolerable unwillingness to be extinguished. The legend that no man branded in *The Dunciad* could obtain employment from booksellers is incredible.

The coarseness of a great part of the second book suggests that, if Swift had no more immediate share in it, Pope had, at least, been encouraged by his example. But it is impossible to dispute the brutal vigour of these Rabelaisian $\mathring{a}\theta\lambda a$. In the development of its plot and action, *The Dunciad* is inferior to Pope's earlier and lighter mock-heroic. The chief space is occupied by what are really episodes in a main narrative that is barely more than introduced. In recalling it as a whole, we are apt to think of passages which had no place in the three-book form.

In the warfare arising out of *The Dunciad*, a considerable part was played for some years by *The Grub-Street Journal*, which virulently assailed Pope's adversaries and praised those who appeared in his defence. It is certain that Pope had a large hand in this paper; but his subterranean methods have, apparently, made it impossible now to determine his precise share.

His poetical energy during the next few years was deeply influenced by a friend for whom he felt the warmest admiration. Bolingbroke had been known to Pope before he fled to France. Their acquaintance had been renewed on his visit to England in 1723. During his residence at Dawley, 1725–35, their intercourse was frequent. When in exile, Bolingbroke had become interested in philosophical and ethical questions, and drew Pope to take some of these as subjects for his verse. The first result was the *Epistle to the Earl of Burlington, Of Taste* (1731), afterwards altered to *Of False Taste*, and ultimately, under the sub-title *Of the Use of Riches*, placed fourth of his *Moral Essays*. It is a finished specimen of Pope's art and attitude. The denunciation of extravagant expense, the appeal to good sense and nature, are alike characteristic. The sketches or touches of character in the first part, Villario, Sabinus, Visto, Virro (the precursor of the dean who had much taste, and all very bad) yield to the description of Timon's villa which fills half the poem. Trouble came of this last. Pope had to learn, as the creator of Harold Skimpole learned later, that, when prominent traits are taken from life, the public will insist on complete identity. There seems to be no ground for supposing ingratitude, but he had no doubt been thinking of Canons and the duke of Chandos. The next *Epistle* was that *To Lord Bathurst* (III), also entitled *Of the Use of Riches* (1732). Pope professed that this was one of his most laboured works; yet his fondness for retouching led him, at the end of his life, to transpose parts and to convert it into a dialogue. He starts with the thought that the miser and spendthrift are divinely appointed to secure a due circulation of wealth; but the merits of the *Epistle* lie in passages, such as the end of Buckingham and the rise and fall of Sir Balaam. We see how Pope is being drawn into the opposition fomented by Bolingbroke, the lines in which he dwells on the facilities given to corruption by paper credit being an attack on Walpole.

The *Epistle* now placed first among the *Moral Essays*, that *Of the Knowledge and Characters of Men*, came out in the same year (1732). The difficulties in attempting to judge a man's character are set forth, and the solution is found to lie in the discovery of the ruling passion, to which reference had already been made in the fourth *Epistle*, and which is dealt with at some length in *Epistle* II of *An Essay on Man*. This theory of the predominant passion is used to explain the career of the duke of Wharton, and its presence in the hour of death is shown by two illustrations in Pope's best style, that of Narcissa (Mrs. Oldfield) and Euclio. One of Pope's most brilliant similes occurs in *Epistle* I.[1] Later, at Warburton's suggestion, extensive alterations were made in the order of parts, to give the poem "all the charm of method and force of connected reasoning"; but it cannot be said to have gained by his interference. *Epistle* II, *Of the Characters of Women*, though finished by February, 1733, was kept back till 1735. The "lady" to whom it was addressed was Martha Blount. Her name, as Pope tells Caryll, was suppressed at her own desire. An advertisement to the first edition declares upon the author's "Honour that no one Character is drawn from the Life." As Warton pointed out, the imaginary Rufa, Silia, Papilia and others are in the style of the portraits in Young's fifth *Satire* (1725). The characters of Philomede, Atossa and Chloe were withheld until Warburton's edition (1751). Chloe is understood to be Lady Suffolk; Philomede, Henrietta, duchess of Marlborough. In the case of Atossa, scandal and controversy have raged. A report was early spread that Pope had taken £1000 from Sarah, duchess of Marlborough, for a promise to suppress these lines in which her character was drawn, and broke his promise. This story, inherently improbable, has never been proved. The character, as it stands, has details that cannot apply to her, and it seems not unlikely that Pope drew traits from the duchess of Buckinghamshire also. During this same time, he had been busy with his *Essay on Man*, *Epistle* I of which appeared in February, 1733, II and III following in the course of the year. These were anonymous, as he was diffident of their reception. IV appeared under his name in January, 1734. He hoped, at one time, to extend the work and to fit into its frame his *Moral Epistles*, from material on false learning and education which found a place in the fourth *Dunciad*.

In the account of his design, given in the second volume of his *Works* (1735), he hopes that, if the *Essay* has any merit,

it is in steering betwixt the extremes of doctrines seemingly opposite

[1] Ll. 41–50 (the last waking image).

. . . and in forming out of all a temperate, yet not inconsistent, and a short, yet not imperfect, system of Ethics.

Epistle I treats of the nature and state of man with respect to the universe; II of man with respect to himself; III of man with respect to society; IV of man with respect to happiness. The intention running through the whole is expressed in the couplet:

> Laugh where we must, be candid where we can,
> But vindicate the ways of God to man.[1]

Pope's methods of composition, his want of philosophical training and his inability to conduct a sustained argument made it impossible for him to produce a great philosophical poem. It must be granted that he has no harmonious and clearly developed system, and often fails to recognise the logical results of his beliefs. But it does not follow that, because he was a loose thinker, he is not, in the main, expressing his genuine feelings or what he fancies to be such. While recognising that he is no metaphysician, we should not lose sight of the exquisite workmanship of separate passages or of the interest of the whole as an expression of contemporary thought. Bolingbroke, in one sense, was the begetter of the poem. The legend that Pope merely versified a prose sketch by Bolingbroke is absurd; that the poet was deeply indebted to him is certain. There are passages in Bolingbroke's philosophical fragments that must have been known to Pope when he was composing the *Essay*, and, as the poet's own philosophical reading was superficial, it is probable that, in many cases, the thoughts of others had come to him through Bolingbroke's mind. At the time when Pope wrote, newer and more liberal modes of thought were not yet generally accepted or assimilated, or their relation to orthodoxy clearly defined, nor was Pope the only man whose religious views hovered between unsectarian Christianity and something that could barely be distinguished from deism. It is easy to show that Pope, in one place, is pantheistic, in another a fatalist, in yet another deistical, though he repudiated the charge; that his theory of self-love and reason will not stand examination; that his conception of the historical development of political and re-

[1] *Epistle* I, ll. 15–16.

ligious organisations is vague in the extreme. But the fact
that the *Essay* is still read with pleasure is a proof of the consummate power of the style. It attracted a wider attention
than any other of Pope's works. A Swiss professor, Jean-Pierre
de Crousaz, proceeded to demolish its philosophy, and it
inspired Voltaire to write *La Loi Naturelle* (1756). Pope,
dismayed at Crousaz's onslaught, was overjoyed when
Warburton came to his aid in a set of letters appearing in
The Works of the Learned (1738–9). "You understand me,"
he wrote, "as well as I do myself; but you express me better
than I can express myself." During the remainder of Pope's
life, Warburton was one of his chief intimates. He became
the authorised commentator on Pope's poems and was left
by will the copyright of all his published works.

In 1735, a collection of Pope's letters was published by
Curll. Many years before, Cromwell had given a number of
letters from Pope to a Mrs. Thomas: she sold them to Curll,
who printed them in 1726. Pope, who had long ceased to
pride himself on his acquaintance with Cromwell, was genuinely annoyed. Soon, he began to beg various friends to return
his letters; and, seeing in how favourable a light they would
show his character, to the discomfiture of his enemies, he conceived the idea of getting them published. In 1729, on the plea
that his own and Wycherley's reputation had been injured
by Theobald's edition of Wycherley's literary remains, he induced Oxford to allow some letters and papers which would
clear their reputation to be deposited in his library, and to let the
publishers acknowledge his permission to obtain copies. He
then published the correspondence between Wycherley and himself as a supplement to Theobald's volume, but the book did
not sell. The curious history of the 1735 collection has been
elaborately traced by Charles Wentworth, Dilke and Elwin.
Curll received an offer in writing from "P. T." of a large collection of Pope's letters. After negotiations, printed copies of
Pope's correspondence from 1704 to 1734 were delivered to him
by an unknown person. Apparently at Pope's instigation,
Curll was summoned before the House of Lords, as the advertisement spoke of letters from peers, the publication of which,
without their consent, was a breach of privilege. None such
being forthcoming, Curll escaped. It seems fairly certain that

Pope engineered the whole business, in order to provide an excuse for publishing his own edition in 1737. More remarkable than the device for publication was the way in which he had manipulated the correspondence. Besides numerous alterations, additions and omissions, parts of different letters were combined, dates altered, and letters to one correspondent addressed to another. The fact that Caryll took copies of letters before returning them was a main cause of the laying bare of Pope's tricky methods. By a strange fate, his attempts to set his moral character right with his contemporaries have seriously damaged his reputation with posterity. For several years, Pope urged Swift to return his letters, on the ground, at first, that he was afraid of their getting into Curll's hands, later, that he might wish to print some himself. Swift, at last, consented to hand over all he could find. Pope appears to have arranged that they should be printed and a copy sent to Swift, who consented to their being published in Dublin. Pope included them in vol. II of his *Works in Prose* (1741), where they are stated to be copied from an impression sent from Dublin, and to have been printed "by the Dean's direction," and complained to friends that Swift had published them without his consent. The letters to Cromwell are interesting as illustrating Pope's early tastes and ambitions; but his elaborate way of doctoring the correspondence for whose publication he was himself responsible makes it of very little worth as biographical evidence, unless the originals or genuine copies, as in Caryll's case, have survived. As a whole, the letters are disappointing; they are wanting in naturalness and charm, and, too often, are a mere string of moral reflections.

The year 1733 was, perhaps, the most prolific in Pope's life. About the beginning of the year, when he had for the moment laid aside *An Essay on Man* on account of ill-health, Bolingbroke observed to him how well the first satire of Horace's second book would "hit his case" if he were to imitate it in English. On this hint, Pope "translated it in a morning or two and sent it to the press in a week or fortnight after." The suggestion of a friend, and the framework of Horace, had given him one of the greatest opportunities of his literary life. The brilliance and conciseness of his style, his command alike over a lofty and over a conversational tone, the power of pungent epigram with which he stung his enemies, the affectionate enthusiasm with which he praised his friends, the fondness with which he lingered over the subject of himself—all here found expression. Horace's rambling method lent itself to his purpose, and the original text, while sparing him the task of constructing his own scheme, enabled him to display his skill in adaptation and parallel. While, in one part, adopting a tone of proud superiority as the conscious champion of virtue, he does not deny the presence of a personal animus:

> Whoe'er offends, at some unlucky time
> Slides into verse, and hitches in a rhyme.[1]

The most savage blow was aimed at "furious Sappho." Lady Mary had been attacked in "The Capon's Tale" in Pope and Swift's *Miscellany*, and, again, in *The Dunciad*. Pope suspected her of being, at least part, author of *A Pop upon Pope*, which gave an imaginary account of his whipping by two of his victims in *The Dunciad*. In March, 1733, appeared *Verses addressed to the Imitator of Horace: By a Lady*, in which Pope's body, soul, and muse were mercilessly reviled. Of this piece, Lady Mary, it would seem, was the chief author, helped, perhaps, by Lord Hervey, smarting from the reference to himself as "Lord Fanny" in the first *Imitation of Horace*.[2] Hervey replied, on his own account, in the feeble *Letter from a Nobleman at Hampton Court* (1733). Pope's rejoinder was the prose *Letter to a Noble Lord* (printed, but not published, in 1733); but his most conclusive reply to the attacks he had provoked was in his *Epistle to Dr. Arbuthnot* (1735), misnamed by Warburton *The Prologue to the Satires*. This magnificent outburst of autobiography, self-laudation, satire and invective contains some of Pope's most finished and brilliant work. He professed that, feeling the awkward necessity to say something of himself, he had merely put the last hand to a desultory piece which he had had no thoughts of publishing. Parts, it is true, such as Addison's character and the lines on his own mother, were of earlier date; but the bulk of the composition is, obviously, written for an immediate end. Beginning with lively complaints of the persecution from friend and foe which his fame has brought on him, he sketches his career as a man

[1] Ll. 77–78.　　　　　　　　　　[2] *Sat.* II, i, 6.

of letters, the encouragement received by him, all that he has endured from critics, his shrinking from literary coteries, his own lofty aims and his promptness to attack vice high or low. He closes by dwelling on his father's character and his own devotion to his mother's declining years. His pride in the approval and love bestowed by the fittest on his studies and himself is seen in those lines which Lamb could not repeat without emotion; but, in general, the blame is more thickly sown than the praise. Gildon, Dennis, Colley Cibber, Philips, Curll, Budgell, Welsted, Moore, Bentley, Theobald, all are made to feel his lash. A satiric portrait of Bubb Dodington was transferred in later editions to Halifax; but the two most famous full-lengths are those of Lord Hervey[1] and Addison.[2] Both are essentially unjust, and the latter is a masterpiece of plausible misinterpretation. No less remarkable than the number of passages of high excellence is the art with which they are introduced into the context and the supreme ease that throughout distinguishes the style.

Pope soon followed up the success of his first imitation of Horace. *Satire* II, ii, appeared in 1734, I, ii, "Sober advice from Horace," anonymously in the same year. *Epistle* I, vi, in January, II, ii, in April, II, i, in June and I, i, at the end of 1737. They have been called perfect translations, "the persons and things being transferred as well as the words." They are, however, something less and something more than translations. Horace's point of view is not always caught. In places, adherence to the Latin produces a train of thought not perfectly natural in English; but, for the most part, the imitations give keen pleasure as originals, and the pleasure is made more various by comparison with the model. There is a wide difference between the two satirists. Pope has less of the mellow wisdom of Horace's maturity and more of the fiery temper of his youth. The lofty and declamatory moral tone is in the manner, rather, of Juvenal. Full use is made of the chances for personal reference. It cannot be said that Pope administers justice impartially. When there is an opportunity for an example of vice, his personal enemies have the first claim, while supporters of the opposition in arms against Walpole

[1] Ll. 305–333.   [2] Ll. 193–214.

are treated with leniency. Of his compliments to his friends,
Hazlitt has well said "they are equal in value to a house or
an estate." His use of irony is extraordinarily skilful. It is
seen at its best in his treatment of George II in *Epistle* II, i;
his frequent hits, elsewhere, at king George II and his consort
are due to his having adopted wholesale the opinions of the
opposition. Pope's style in the *Satires* is at its very highest.
In such lines as

> And goad the prelate slumb'ring in his stall[1]

or

> Bare the mean heart that lurks beneath a star,[2]

the thought is expressed to perfection and acquires a further
atmosphere from the words chosen. The *Imitations* of *Epistle*
I, vii, and the latter part of *Satire* II, v, in octosyllabic verse
are of a totally different character, being attempts to copy
Swift's manner. The *Satires* (II and IV) *of Dr. Donne Versified*
were included in the collection of 1735; the latter had appeared,
anonymously, in 1733. If Pope is to be believed, they were
composed at the request of Lords Oxford and Shrewsbury;
but, if written earlier, they were largely revised in the reign of
George II, when many of the modern instances were added.
Pope had thought of dealing, after the same fashion, with the
Satires of Joseph Hall[3] whom he has imitated in more than one
place, but Hall's versification invited less change. The two
Dialogues of 1738 were treated by Warburton as an epilogue to
the *Satires*. They appeared at a time when the opposition
to Walpole was exceptionally active, and are full of evidence of
Pope's sympathy with that side. In one of these, a friend
contrasts Pope's severity with Horace's "sly, polite, insinuating
style," and presses him to take safe subjects for his satire.
Pope ironically agrees:

> Come, harmless characters, that no one hit.[4]

He laments, that, though virtue is an empty boast, the dignity
of vice should be lost, and ends with a picture of universal

---

[1] *Epilogue to the Satires, written in* 1738, *Dial.* II, l. 219.
[2] *Imitations of Horace, Sat.* II, i, l. 108.
[3] Cf. *ante*, Vol. IV, pp. 377 ff.   [4] *Epilogue, etc.* (1738), *Dial.* I, l. 65.

corruption. In *Dialogue* II, the poet defends his practice of
personal satire, showing that he can appreciate merit, that it is
not friendship only which prompts his lays and that he praises
virtue in whatever party. He ends by dwelling on his proud
consciousness of his office as a satirist. It is difficult at first
to reconcile this boast with the elaborate party purpose of the
two poems. But, often as Pope perverted his powers for
personal ends, capable as we know him to have been of in-
sincere professions, it is difficult not to feel, when reading his
lofty claim, that, at the moment, he believed his satire to be
an instrument for righteousness. The unfinished *1740* found
among Pope's papers is of interest in showing the feeling of a
section of the opposition to their nominal leaders, Pulteney
and Carteret.

The new *Dunciad* (1742) embodied materials on the mis-
application of learning, science and wit originally designed
for another poem. Its appearance seems due to Pope's irritation against the university of Oxford for declining to offer
Warburton the degree of D.D. While gratifying many
personal grudges, as in the notorious lines on Bentley,[1] the
satire was, to a large extent, general, falling on the Italian opera,
the abuses of education at school and college, antiquaries,
naturalists and freethinkers. The lines describing the final
consummation of the power of dulness have won deserved
praise; those on the fashionable tour, though less elevated,
are almost equally brilliant.

Pope had frequently directed his satire at Colley Cibber.
His most offensive line was in the *Epistle to Arbuthnot* (l. 97).
In the new *Dunciad*, Cibber was introduced as "Dulness's
Laureate Son." Cibber, in reply, published a letter in which
he suggested that, if "Sawney" had been substituted for
"Cibber" in the *Epistle*, the satire would have been equally
just. To prove this, he told how, having met Pope in very
doubtful company in years gone by, he would take credit
for Homer in having saved his translator from serious harm.
Cibber's good-humoured patronage was sufficiently exasperating, and, to Pope, who was ambitious of fame as a moralist,
this full-flavoured anecdote, with the derisive engravings
which it occasioned, must have been particularly galling.

[1] Ll. 203–274.

In revenge, he installed Cibber in Theobald's place as hero of *The Dunciad* in the new edition which incorporated the fourth book (1743). Pope has been reproached for allowing his rancour to inflict irreparable injury on his original design. Certainly, the change of the opening is ludicrously inapposite, but the hero's personality is little to the fore in the later books. Cibber was no dullard, but neither were many of the other "dunces"; and he undoubtedly had much of the bad taste and folly that is apt to attend on cleverness. A man of his character was not so hopelessly unsuited for the throne.

Warburton was now on terms of growing intimacy with Pope. He had contributed "Aristarchus on the Hero of the Poem" and notes to the latest edition of the *Dunciad*, and his influence is felt in parts of the fourth book. He had written commentaries on *An Essay on Man* and on *An Essay on Criticism* and was engaged on the *Ethic Epistles*. This edition, completed in time for Pope to present to some of his friends, was suppressed by Warburton at Bolingbroke's suggestion in consequence of its containing the character of Atossa.

Pope, who had been for some time in failing health, died on 30 May, 1744.

With Pope, the classical spirit in English poetry reached its acme. That the life of so supreme a genius for style coincided with the period when the social interest in man had dwarfed the feeling for nature, and when knowledge of the town was more prized than romance or pathos, gave double strength to the reaction when it came. His immediate influence, however, was immense and extended across the sea to Germany, France and other parts of Europe. Before his death, the first traces of the coming change were seen; but the effect of his language and numbers prevailed for long when the tone and subject of poetry were changing. When the dust of the long controversy had been laid that raged during the first quarter of the next century, it came to be recognised that Pope's claim to rank among the very greatest poets could no longer be allowed; but that, in his own class and kind, he need not yield to any one. He has suffered most, in general repute, from a distaste for the period which he faithfully reflected, from the narrowness of devotees of nature and from the comparative rarity of a true sense of form in the average reader of poetry.

With the professional student, his permanence is secure; but heaven forbid that Pope should ever become a mere subject for research! Important for the history of English poetry and taste, he is important, also, as the writer of lines that live. Critics may attempt to define his limitations and point him to his place in the great company of poets; but, within the pale of literary orthodoxy, there is room for difference. The survival of poets other than the very highest must depend not on their historical value, but on their finding in each generation a body of admirers. It has been said that admiration for Pope comes with years. If so, it is among the kindliest provisions of Providence against old age. The question is essentially one of temperament. Those who, while not responding readily to violent emotions, are keenly interested in men and manners, with but a chastened passion for green fields, who can appreciate satire and epigram and have a nice sense of finish, will, in every age, enjoy the poetry of Pope for its own sake.

CHAPTER IV

Swift

SWIFT'S writings are so closely connected with the man that they cannot be understood properly without reference to the circumstances under which they were produced. The best way, therefore, of arriving at Swift's views and methods will be to set out briefly the chief events of his life, and, afterwards, to consider the more important of his writings.

Jonathan Swift's royalist grandfather, Thomas Swift, of a Yorkshire family, was vicar of Goodrich, and married Elizabeth Dryden, niece of Sir Erasmus Dryden, the poet's grandfather. The eldest of his large family, Godwin, a barrister, went to Ireland, where he became wealthy; and some of his brothers followed him. One of them, Jonathan, who had married Abigail Erick, was made steward of the king's inns, Dublin, but he did not live long, and, seven months after his death, on 30 November, 1667, his only son, Jonathan, was born. The widow was left dependent mainly on her husband's brother, Godwin. A nurse took the child to Whitehaven, and kept him there three years; and, not long after his return to Dublin, his mother returned to her relatives in England, leaving the boy in his uncle's care. He was sent to Kilkenny school, where he met Congreve; and, when he was fourteen, he was entered as a pensioner at Trinity College, Dublin. Why he afterwards felt so much resentment against his relatives is not clear; for his uncle gave him, not "the education of a dog," but the best obtainable in Ireland. Swift was often at war with the college authorities; but he got his degree in 1685.

In 1688, Swift's uncle Godwin died, having lost his fortune, and Swift realised that he must not depend on any one but himself. The revolution brought trouble for Ireland, and the young man joined his mother at Leicester and looked about for employment. After a time, an opportunity came from Sir William Temple, who was now living in retirement at Moor park, near Farnham. Temple's father had been a friend of Godwin Swift; he had himself known the Swifts in Ireland; and Lady Temple was a connection of Swift's mother. A man of cultivation and refinement, and a renowned diplomatist, Temple was in need of someone to assist him in his literary work, and Swift was chosen. Temple is said to have treated him entirely as a dependent; but it must be remembered that, at this time, Swift was an untrained youth of twenty-two, and the distance between him and "a person of quality" like Temple would inevitably be great, especially in those days.

In later years, Swift spoke somewhat disparagingly of Temple, saying that he had felt too much what it was to be treated like a schoolboy. Temple sometimes seemed out of humour for three or four days, while Swift suspected a hundred reasons. In 1690, his patron sent Swift with a letter of introduction to Sir Robert Southwell, secretary of state in Ireland, in the hope that he would find Swift a post or procure for him a fellowship at Trinity college. The letter said that Swift knew Latin and Greek and a little French; that he wrote a good hand, and was honest and intelligent. Nothing came of this recommendation, and Swift was soon back at Moor park. Temple procured for him the M.A. degree at Oxford and recommended him to William III. "He thinks me a little necessary to him," wrote Swift. In 1693, he was sent by Temple to represent to the king the necessity of triennial parliaments; but the king was not convinced.[1] The first publication of anything by Swift appears to have been in February, 1691-2, when he printed in the fifth supplement to *The Athenian Mercury*, a curious forerunner of *Notes and Queries*, a "Letter to the Athenian Society," enclosing a Pindaric ode, in which he referred to his "young and almost vergin muse." In 1694, Swift parted from Temple, disappointed at the failure of his patron to make any definite

---

[1] "I have sent him [the secretary] with another complaint from Papa to the King, where I fancy he is not displeased with finding opportunities of going." *Martha, Lady Giffard, Her Life and Correspondence*, ed. Longe, J. S., 1911, p. 216.

provision for him; and, in October, he was ordained deacon, and priest in the following January. He found it necessary to ask Temple for testimonials, and Temple went further than he was asked, and obtained for Swift the prebend of Kilroot. Swift, however, soon tired of Ireland; and, in 1696, he was once more at Moor park. In the meantime, he had had a love affair with a Miss Jane Waring, whom he addressed as Varina; but he represented to her that he was not in a position to marry. He remained with Temple until that statesman's death in 1699. Lady Temple had died in 1694, and Temple found his secretary more and more useful. Swift was learning much in many directions. He read classical and historical works in the library; he heard of public affairs and of the experiences of his patron; he had opportunities of studying the way of servants in great houses; and he formed the lasting affection of his life. Lady Giffard, Temple's sister, who kept house for him after his wife's death, had as a companion or servant Mrs. Johnson, widow of a merchant of good position; and this Mrs. Johnson had two daughters, one of whom, Esther, a bright child of eight when Swift first met her, was a great favourite with the family, and received a legacy under Temple's will. Swift acted as tutor to the girl, and, by the time of his last sojourn at Moor park, she had, he says, grown into perfect health and was looked upon as one of the most beautiful and graceful young women in London.

Temple took part in the controversy on ancient and modern learning, and in an essay he quoted the spurious "*Epistles of Phalaris*" as evidence of the superiority of the ancients. He was answered by William Wotton, and, in 1697, Swift wrote his contribution to the controversy, the clever *Battle of the Books*, which, however, was not published till 1704. By his will, Temple had left Swift £100 and any profit that was to be made by the publication of his posthumous works. Unfortunately, this task led to a protracted quarrel with Lady Giffard. Swift was "as far to seek as ever." An application to the king came to nothing, and he thought it well to accept an invitation to be chaplain and secretary to Lord Berkeley, one of the lords justices in Ireland; but a rival persuaded Lord Berkeley that the post was not fit for a clergyman, and Swift departed in dudgeon. He was, however, presented to the living of Laracor, near Trim, with two other small livings, together with the prebend of Durlaven, in St. Patrick's, and these brought in an income of some £230 a year. Laracor had a congregation of about fifteen persons; but he was often in Dublin and, through his friendship with Lady Berkeley and her daughters, soon became well known there. He suggested to Esther Johnson that she and her friend Rebecca Dingley, who, in some way, was related to the Temple family, might, with advantage, live in Ireland, and the ladies took his advice. Swift was now thirty-four, Esther Johnson a young woman of twenty. Everything was done to avoid any occasion of scandal. When Swift was absent, the ladies used his rooms in Dublin; when he was there, they took separate lodgings, and he was never with Esther Johnson except in the presence of a third person.

Swift was soon back in England. He had already written one of his most amusing poems, the burlesque *Petition of Mrs. Frances Harris;* and, in 1701, he wrote the pamphlet *A Discourse on the Dissensions in Athens and Rome*, which was attributed by some to Somers and by others to Burnet. He was evidently well known in London society by the time that *A Tale of a Tub* appeared in 1704, after lying in manuscript for seven or eight years. He became a friend of Addison, who sent him a copy of his *Travels in Italy* with an inscription: "To Jonathan Swift, the most agreeable of companions, the truest friend, and the greatest genius of his age this work is presented by his most humble servant the author." Of one of his poems, *Baucis and Philemon*, Swift said that Addison made him blot out fourscore lines, add fourscore and alter fourscore. Steele, too, at this time, was among his friends; but he spoke with some contempt of the ordinary coffee-house wits. He took part in the attack on the almanac written by the astrologer John Partridge, producing a parody, *Predictions for the ensuing year by Isaac Bickerstaff*, in which he foretold that, on 29 March, Partridge would die of fever; and, on 30 March, he printed a letter giving an account of Partridge's end. Partridge protested that he was alive; but Swift represented that he was really dead, inasmuch as his credit was gone. Other wits joined in the fray, and Steele, on starting *The Tatler* in 1709, adopted the name Bickerstaff as that of the supposed author.

At the same time, Swift was engaged in more serious work. In 1708–9, he produced important pamphlets on church questions, which show that he was beginning to understand that the interests of the whig party could not be reconciled with those of his order, and was busily engaged in representing to the government the claims of the Irish clergy to the first fruits and twentieths, which had already been granted to the clergy in England.

An attempt to lessen the power of the duke of Marlborough had come to nothing. Harley, just when he seemed to have attained success, lost his office; Marlborough and Godolphin joined the whigs, and, by the end of 1708, Somers was lord president of the council and Wharton lord lieutenant of Ireland. Swift was hoping for preferment for himself; but he informed correspondents that no promise of making his fortune would prevail on him to go against what became a man of conscience and truth and an entire friend to the established church. Hopes that had been held out to him came to nothing, and Swift retired to Ireland. A great change, however, was not far distant. The prosecution of Sacheverell gave the high church party its chance. The whigs were turned out of office: Harley became chancellor of the exchequer, and the new parliament of November, 1710, had a great tory majority. In September, Swift was again in London, and the events of the three following years, with all Swift's thoughts and hopes, are set out before us in his letters to Esther Johnson and Mrs. Dingley, afterwards to be published as the *Journal to Stella*. In a very short time, Swift was in company with Harley and St. John. The whigs, he said, had clutched at him like a drowning man at a twig, but he minded them not. Harley listened to the proposals as to first fruits, showed familiarity with Swift's Christian name and, in general, was excessively obliging. Swift confessed that he was willing to revenge himself upon his old friends, who had neglected him. "I will make them repent their ill-usage before I leave this place," he said. But we must not forget that, in joining the tories, he was only rallying to the side with which he was really in sympathy. The interests of the church were paramount with him; and he had come to see that tories were the church's natural guardians. In October, he attacked Godolphin in

The Virtues of Sid Hamet the Magician's Rod, and published a pamphlet against Wharton, charging him with nearly every crime. In the following month, he took in charge a weekly paper, *The Examiner*, which had just been started by St. John,[1] and he wrote for it regularly until June, 1711. St. John afterwards said, "We were determined to have you: you were the only one we were afraid of."

An attempt to assassinate Harley, in March, 1711, greatly increased the popularity of that minister. Swift was much alarmed while Harley's life was in danger. He had, Swift said, always treated him with the tenderness of a parent, and never refused him any favour as a friend. The efforts of the party were now devoted to bringing the war with France to an end. Harley was created earl of Oxford, and became lord treasurer. The whigs, opposed to a peace, formed an alliance with Nottingham, previously an extreme tory. Swift, who had given up his connection with *The Examiner*, composed, in November and December, 1711, two pamphlets in favour of peace: *The Conduct of the Allies and of the late Ministry in beginning and carrying on the present war*, and *Some Remarks on the Barrier Treaty*. He also attacked the duchess of Somerset in *The W—ds—r Prophecy*, and assisted the government by *A Letter to the October Club*, which consisted of the more extreme tories. The danger threatening the government from the House of Lords was removed, in December, by the creation of twelve new peers, and by the dismissal of the duke of Marlborough from his employments.

Swift had now attained a position of great importance, and the authority he possessed and the respect shown him gave him much pleasure. He often used his power in the service of humble friends as well as of persons of more social consequence. "This, I think, I am bound to do, in honour to my conscience," he says, "to use of my little credit toward helping forward men of worth in the world." To literary men, he was specially helpful. The Brothers' club, which had been founded in 1711, to advance conversation and friendship, included St. John and other ministers, Swift, Arbuthnot and Prior. The club does not seem to have lasted beyond 1713, but its members frequently called each other "brother" in

[1] See *post*, Chap. VIII.

later years. With regard to his own promotion, Swift felt
that he should be asked rather than ask.[1] Recognition of
his services was, no doubt, to some extent, delayed by the wish
of ministers to keep him at hand to assist them; but the main
difficulty was the suspicion as to his orthodoxy, an argument
which had considerable weight with the queen. Oxford was
kind to him; "mighty kind," says Swift; "less of civility
but more of interest!" At last, in April, 1713, he was given
the vacant deanery of St. Patrick's—a somewhat disappointing
end to his hopes, inasmuch as it involved banishment to Ireland,
and the payment of heavy expenses on the deanery. His
health was bad; he was subject to attacks of giddiness; and his
reception in Dublin was anything but friendly. In October,
Swift returned to London. Peace had now been secured,
and the question before the country was that of the succession
to the crown. Oxford was not above suspicion; St. John
(now Viscount Bolingbroke) was involved in Jacobite plots.
Swift was not aware of these schemings, although there was
widespread suspicion which led to much uneasiness in the
country. The queen was in ill-health, and it was known that
her life was very precarious.

Swift's efforts to repair the growing breach between Oxford
and Bolingbroke came to nothing. In many respects, his
sympathies were with Bolingbroke; but his friendship for
Oxford made it impossible for him to desert that minister.
He refused, therefore, to join with the men now in power.
Oxford was deprived of office on 27 July, 1714; but Bolingbroke's
triumph was short-lived, for, on 1 August, queen Anne died.
Swift retired to Dublin, where he lived "in the corner of a
vast unfurnished house."

In Dublin, of course, Swift was in constant intercourse
with Esther Johnson; but his relations with Stella, as she has
come to be known, were complicated by his friendship for
Hester Vanhomrigh, the daughter of a widow with whom he
had become acquainted in 1708. In 1710, when Swift went

[1] He did not, however, always leave it to others to make the suggestion. On
5 January, 1712/3, he wrote to Oxford: "I must humbly take leave to inform your
Lordship that the Dean of Wells died this morning at one o'clock. I entirely
submit my small fortunes to your Lordship." *Marquis of Bath's Papers*, Hist.
MSS. Comm., 1904, I, 228.

to London, he had taken lodgings near the family, and he was frequently with them.

Hester Vanhomrigh was then nineteen. By 1713, she was known to him as Vanessa, and he wrote a poem, *Cadenus and Vanessa*, to explain the relations between them. This curious piece was not meant for publication, but, rather, as a self-justification, to explain how it was that a girl felt admiration for a man who had grown old in politics and wit and had lost the arts that would charm a lady. He regarded her as might a father or a tutor; but, when he offered friendship, she said that she would be the tutor and would teach him what love is. Vanessa was passionately in love; and, on the death of her mother, she and her sister retired to Ireland, a step which, no doubt, was very embarrassing to Swift. He told her that he could see her very seldom, for everything that happened there would be known in a week. Her fragmentary letters are filled with reproaches, which Swift endeavoured to meet by temporising and by good advice as to diverting her mind by exercise and by amusing books. We cannot discuss here the theories that have been advanced as to the reason why Swift had not married Stella. It is alleged that a form of marriage was gone through in 1716; but the evidence in favour of this is quite insufficient, and, in any case, it was merely a form. It was at this time, according to Delany, that archbishop King, after parting from Swift, said, "You have just met the most unhappy man on earth; but on the subject of his wretchedness you must never ask a question." About 1723, a crisis occurred. One of the stories is that Vanessa, who had then lost all her near relatives, wrote to Stella asking her whether she was Swift's wife; whereupon Stella replied that she was and sent the letter to Swift. Swift, we are told, went at once to Vanessa, threw the letter on the table, and rode off. If this were true, Swift's conduct would be put in a very bad light; but the evidence is slight, and, according to another version, it was to Swift that Vanessa wrote. It is certain that Vanessa died soon afterwards, leaving a request that *Cadenus and Vanessa* and her correspondence with Swift might be published. Whatever interpretation be put upon them, the letters are very unpleasant reading.

In the meantime, Swift had become an Irish patriot, though

he viewed Ireland and the native population with contempt.
His hatred of injustice was, no doubt, strengthened by pleasure
in attacking the government in power; but he was certainly
sincere in his convictions. More will be said below of *A proposal
for the universal use of Irish manufacture*, published by him
in 1720, in which he urged the Irish not to use English goods,
and of the famous *Drapier's Letters*, written between April
and December, 1724, on the occasion of the granting of a patent
to William Wood to supply Ireland with a copper coinage.
In the former case, the printer was prosecuted, but no jury
could be found to convict, and the prosecution was dropped.
In the latter, amidst the greatest popular excitement, a crown
jury in Dublin represented that Wood's halfpence were a nui-
sance, and the government was beaten.

Before the Drapier's letters appeared, Swift was engaged
on his most famous work, *Gulliver's Travels:* but the book was
not finished until early in 1726, when Swift brought the manuscript to London, where it was published in October. Its
success was great and immediate. Arbuthnot said that he
thought it would have as long a run as John Bunyan, and Gay
states that the duchess of Marlborough was in raptures with it
on account of the satire on human nature with which it was
filled. During Swift's visit to England he had, however, received the troubling news of Stella's illness. To one friend
in Dublin he wrote, "We have been perfect friends these thirty-
five years; on my advice they both came to Ireland, and have
been ever since my constant companions, and the remainder
of my life will be a very melancholy scene." To another
friend he said:

This was a person of my own rearing and instruction from childhood, who excelled in every good quality that can possibly
accomplish a human creature. . . . Violent friendship is much
more lasting and as much engaging as violent love.

He returned to Ireland in August; but Stella's health improved,
and, in 1727, he paid another visit to London;[1] but in September
she was worse, and again he hurried back to Dublin. On the

---

[1] Swift may have contributed to Bolingbroke's *Craftsman* in 1726 and following
years. See *post*, Chap. VIII; and cf. Sichel, W., *Bolingbroke and his Times*, vol. II,
pp. 251–2.

way, he had been delayed at Holyhead, and, in a diary which he kept "to divert thinking," he speaks of the suspense he was in about his "dearest friend." Stella died in January, 1728, after making a will which describes her as "spinster." In the *Character of Mrs. Johnson* which Swift began to write on the night of her death, he calls her "the truest, most virtuous and valuable friend that I or perhaps any other person was ever blessed with." After his death, a lock of her hair was found in his desk in a paper marked "Only a woman's hair." Swift was himself so troubled with noises in the ear and deafness that he had no spirit for anything and avoided everybody. He had, as already noticed, been subject to giddiness for many years.

Swift was now a popular hero in Ireland, and there had been some hope that, during his visits to London, he would obtain preferment in England; but none was given him. In Ireland, he found the people would not do anything to help themselves. His growing misanthropy was shown in the terrible satire called *A Modest Proposal for preventing the children of poor people from being a burden to their parents or the country.* Ireland, he said, was a mass of beggars, thieves, oppressors, fools and knaves; but he must be content to die there: with such a people, it was better to die than live.[1] Elsewhere, he compared Ireland to a coalpit: a man who had been bred in a pit might live there all his life contented; but, if sent back to it after a few months in the open air, he could not be contented. Yet, notwithstanding his feelings, Swift did his work at St. Patrick's efficiently, and improved the lot of many by his charity. To Mrs. Dingley, he gave an annuity of fifty guineas a year, allowing her to believe that the money came from a fund of which he was trustee. He had various friends with whom, in his later years, he bandied riddles and other trifles; but, from time to time, he still produced admirable pieces, such as *A Complete Collection of genteel and ingenious Conversation, Directions to Servants, On Poetry: a Rhapsody* and *The Legion Club.* Gradually, his correspondence with friends in England fell off. In 1738, he wrote to Edward Harley, earl of Oxford:

I am now good for nothing, very deaf, very old, and very much

---

[1] *Welbeck Papers*, Hist. MSS. Comm., 1901, VI, 57. Swift's private affairs were, in 1730–3, in a bad condition, embroiled in law (*ibid.* 28, 47).

out of favour with those in power. My dear lord, I have a thousand things to say, but I can remember none of them.[1]

And, in 1740, he wrote to his cousin, Mrs. Whiteway,

I have been very miserable all night, and to-day extremely deaf and full of pain. I am so stupid and confounded that I cannot express the mortification I am under both in body and mind. All I can say is, that I am not in torture: but I daily and hourly expect it. I hardly understand one word I write. I am sure my days will be very few, few and miserable they must be.

The brain trouble, which had threatened him all his life, became worse, and there were violent fits of temper, with considerable physical pain. In 1742, it was necessary to appoint guardians, and Swift fell into a condition of dementia. The end came, at last, on 7 October, 1745. He left his fortune to found a hospital for idiots and lunatics, and was interred at St. Patrick's by the side of Stella. In an epitaph which he wrote for himself, he said he was *Ubi saeva indignatio cor ulterius lacerare nequit.*

One of the greatest and most characteristic of Swift's general satires is *A Tale of a Tub, written for the universal improvement of mankind,* an early work, composed about 1696, and published, with *The Battle of the Books,* in 1704. In his later years, when his powers were failing, we are told that Swift was seen looking at this volume and was heard to say, "Good God, what a genius I had when I wrote that book." A considerable, but by no means the largest or ablest, portion of the work is occupied by an account of the quarrels of the churches, told in the famous story of three brothers, Peter, Martin and Jack, representing Roman catholics, Anglicans and puritans; of the coat bequeathed to them by their father, whose will, explaining the proper mode of wearing it, they first interpreted each in his own way, and then, after many ingenious evasions of it, locked up in a strong box; and of their subsequent quarrels concerning the will and its significance. Throughout, the brothers act in accordance with the doctrine that beings which the world calls clothes are, in reality, rational creatures or men, and that, in short, we see nothing

[1] *Marquis of Bath's Papers,* Hist. MSS. Comm., I, 254.

but the clothes and hear nothing but them—a doctrine which Carlyle had in mind when he wrote his *Sartor Resartus*.

The manner in which Swift dealt with religious questions in this book led to suspicions as to the genuineness of his Christianity—a suggestion which Swift regarded as a great wrong. He said that he had attacked only Peter (who insisted, in turn, on being called "Mr. Peter," "Father Peter" and "Lord Peter") and Jack (who called his hatred of Peter zeal, and was much annoyed by Martin's patience), and that he had not made any reflections on Martin. What he satirised was not religion, but the abuse of religion. This defence is not very convincing; though we need not doubt Swift's orthodoxy, we cannot but feel that a scoffer would read the book with greater relish than a believer. The contempt poured on Roman catholics and dissenters is often in the worst taste, and touches upon doctrines and beliefs which an earnest member of the church of England would think it dangerous to ridicule. Such attacks on important doctrines may easily be treated as attacks on Christianity itself.

But *A Tale of a Tub* is far more than an account of the wrangles of the churches. It is a skilful and merciless dissection of the whole of human nature. To the satire on vanity and pride, on pedantry and on the search for fame, in the introductory dedication to Somers and the delightful dedication to prince Posterity, is added an attack on bad writing, which is continued, again and again, throughout the work. In conclusion, Swift observed that he was trying an experiment very frequent among modern authors, which is to write upon nothing: the knowledge when to have done was possessed by few. The work contains entertaining digressions, in one of which the author satirises critics. In former times it had been held that critics were persons who drew up rules by which careful writers might pronounce upon the productions of the learned and form a proper judgment of the sublime and the contemptible. At other times, "critic" had meant the restorer of ancient learning from the dust of manuscripts; but the third and noblest sort was the "true critic" who had bestowed many benefits on the world. A true critic was the discoverer and collector of writers' faults. The custom of authors was to point out with great pains their own excellences and other men's defects. The modern way of using books was either to learn their titles and then brag of acquaintance with them, or to get a thorough insight into the indexes. To enter the palace of learning at the great gate took much time; therefore, men with haste and little ceremony use the back door. In another digression, Swift treats of the origin, use and importance of madness in a commonwealth. He defined happiness as "a perpetual *possession of being well deceived*." The serene and peaceful state was to be a fool among knaves. Delusion was necessary for peace of mind. Elsewhere, Swift confesses to a longing for fame, a blessing which usually comes only after death.

In wit and brilliancy of thought, Swift never surpassed *A Tale of a Tub;* and the style is as nearly perfect as it could well be. Swift here allows himself more colour than is to be found in his later writings. In spite of discursiveness and lack of dramatic interest, the book remains the greatest of English satires.

The famous *Full and true Account of the Battle fought last Friday between the Ancient and the Modern Books in Saint James's Library*, generally known as *The Battle of the Books*, had its origin, as has been said, in the controversy respecting the relative superiority of ancient and modern learning, in which Sir William Temple had taken part. The controversy has now lost its interest, and Temple's ill-judged defence of the genuineness of the "*Epistles* of Phalaris" does not concern us. Swift assumes the genuineness of the letters; but the merit of the work lies in its satirical power. It may be that Swift had read *Le Combat des Livres* of François de Callières (1688); but, if so, he owed little to it. Among Swift's satires, the fragmentary *Battle of the Books* is relatively so little remembered, that its main features may be here recalled.

The piece is mainly an attack on pedantry, in which it is argued that invention may be weakened by overmuch learning. There were two tops to the hill Parnassus, the highest and largest of which had been time out of mind in the possession of the ancients, while the other was held by the moderns. The moderns desired to bring about a reduction in the height of the point held by the ancients. The ancients replied that the better course would be for the moderns to raise their own side of the hill. To such a step they would not only agree but would largely contribute. Negotiations came to nothing, and there was a great battle. But, first, we are told the story of the Bee and the Spider. A bee had become entangled in a spider's web; the two insects quarrelled and Aesop was called in as arbitrator. The bee, who is to be taken as typifying the ancients, went straight to nature, gathering his support from the flowers of the field and the garden, without any damage to them. The spider, like the moderns, boasted of not being obliged to any other creature, but of drawing and spinning out all from himself. The moderns, says Swift, produced nothing but wrangling and satire, much of the nature of the spider's poison. The ancients, ranging through every corner of nature, had produced honey and wax and furnished mankind with "the two noblest of things, which are sweetness and light." In the great battle between the books that followed, the moderns appealed for aid to the malignant deity Criticism, who had dwelt in a den at the top of snowy mountains, where there were spoils of numberless half-devoured volumes. With her were Ignorance, Pride, Opinion, Noise and Impudence, Dulness and Vanity, Positiveness, Pedantry and Ill-manners. She could change herself "into an octavo compass," when she was indistinguishable in shape and dress from "the divine Bentley," in person the most deformed of all the moderns. The piece ends abruptly with the meeting of Bentley and Wotton with Boyle, who transfixes the pair with his lance. We need not imagine that Swift held too seriously the views on the subject of the controversy expressed in this fragment: Temple, we are told, received a slight graze; and, says the publisher, the manuscript, "being in several places imperfect, we cannot learn to which side the victory fell." The piece was largely inspired by the desire to assist his patron; but, besides being a brilliant attack on his opponents, it abounds in satire of a more general nature, and its interest for us is not affected by the fact that Temple was on the wrong side.

The most famous of all Swift's works is *Gulliver's Travels*. The inception of the book has been traced to the celebrated Scriblerus club, which came into existence in the last months of queen Anne's reign, when Swift joined with Arbuthnot, Pope, Gay and other members in a scheme to ridicule all false tastes in learning. The *Memoirs of Scriblerus* by Arbuthnot were not published until 1741; but Pope said that Swift took the first hints for *Gulliver's Travels* from them. The connection of the *Travels* with the original scheme, however, is very slight, and appears chiefly in the third part of the work. Swift's book underwent discussion between him and his friends several years before it appeared. In September, 1725, he told Pope that he was correcting and finishing the work.

I hate and detest that animal called man, although I heartily love John, Peter, Thomas, and so forth. Upon this great foundation of misanthropy (though not in Timon's manner) the whole building of my Travels is erected, and I never will have peace of mind till all honest men are of that opinion.

Travels into several remote Nations of the World, by Lemuel Gulliver, first a surgeon, and then a captain of several ships, was published anonymously at the end of October, 1726, negotiations with the publishers having been carried on by Swift's friends, Charles Ford and Erasmus Lewis. In November, Arbuthnot wrote that the book was in everybody's hands, and that many were led by its verisimilitude to believe that the incidents told really occurred. One Irish bishop said that it was full of improbable lies, and, for his part, he hardly believed a word of it.

The scheme of the book has been known to us all from our childhood. In the first part, Gulliver describes, in simple language suited to a seaman, his shipwreck in Lilliput, where the tallest people were six inches high. The emperor believed himself to be, and was considered, the delight and terror of the universe; but, how absurd it all appeared to one twelve times as tall as any Lilliputian! In his account of the two parties in the country, distinguished by the use of high and low heels, Swift satirises English political parties, and the intrigues that centred around the prince of Wales. Religious feuds were laughed at in an account of a problem which was dividing the people: "Should eggs be broken at the big end or the little end?" One party alleged that those on the other side were schismatics:

This, however, is thought to be a mere strain upon the text, for the words are these, that all true believers shall break their eggs at the convenient end. And which is the convenient end seems, in my humble opinion, to be left to every man's conscience, or at least in the power of the Chief Magistrate to determine.

This part is full of references to current politics; but the satire is free from bitterness.

In the second part, the voyage to Brobdingnag, the author's contempt for mankind is emphasised. Gulliver now found himself a dwarf among men sixty feet in height. The king, who regarded Europe as if it were an anthill, said, after many questions, "How contemptible a thing was human grandeur, which could be mimicked by such diminutive insects" as Gulliver, and Gulliver himself, after living among a great race distinguished for calmness and common-sense, could not but feel tempted to laugh at the strutting and bowing of English lords and ladies as much as the king did at him. The king could not understand secrets of state, for he confined the knowledge of governing to good common-sense and reason, justice and lenity. Finally, he said: "I cannot but conclude the bulk of your natives to be the most pernicious race of little odious vermin that Nature ever suffered to crawl upon the surface of the earth." But Gulliver remarks that allowances must be made for a king living apart from the rest of the world.

The third part of the book is, in many ways, less interesting, partly because it is less plausible, partly because the story is interrupted more often by personal attacks. The satire is chiefly on philosophers, projectors and inventors, men who are given to dwelling in the air, like the inhabitants of the Flying Island. If it be said that the attacks on the learned were unfair, it must be remembered that the country had recently gone through the experience of the South Sea Bubble, when no project was too absurd to be brought before the public. Unfortunately, Swift does not properly distinguish between pretenders to learning and those who were entitled to respect. In the Island of Sorcerers, Gulliver was able to call up famous men of ancient times and question them, with the result that he found the world to have been misled by prostitute writers to ascribe the greatest exploits in war to cowards, the wisest counsels to fools, sincerity to flatterers, piety to atheists. He saw, too, by looking at an old yeoman, how the race had gradually deteriorated, through vice and corruption. He found that the race of Struldbrugs or Immortals, so far from being happy, were the most miserable of all, enduring an endless dotage, and hated by their neighbours. We cannot but recall the sad closing years of Swift's own life; but the misery of his own end was due to mental disease and not to old age.

In the last part of *Gulliver's Travels*, the voyage to the country of the Houyhnhnms, Swift's satire is of the bitterest. Gulliver was now in a country where horses were possessed of reason, and were the governing class, while the Yahoos, though in the shape of men, were brute beasts, without reason and conscience. In endeavouring to persuade the Houyhnhnms that he was not a Yahoo, Gulliver is made to show how little a man is removed from the brute. Gulliver's account of warfare, given with no little pride, caused only disgust. Satire of the law and lawyers, and of the lust for gold, is emphasised by praise of the virtues of the Houyhnhnms, and of their learning. They were governed only by reason, love and courtship being unknown to them. Gulliver dreaded leaving a country for whose rulers he felt gratitude and respect, and, when he returned home, his family filled him with such disgust that he swooned when his wife kissed him. But what made him most impatient was to see "a lump of deformity, and diseases both in body and mind," filled with pride, a vice wholly unknown to the Houyhnhnms.

It is a terrible conclusion. All that can be said in reply to those who condemn Swift for writing it is that it was the result of disappointment, wounded pride, growing ill-health and sorrow caused by the sickness of the one whom he loved best in the world. There is nothing bitter in the first half of the work, and most readers find only amusement in it; everything is in harmony, and follows at once when the first premises are granted. But, in the attacks on the Yahoos, consistency is dropped; the Houyhnhnms are often prejudiced and unreasonable,[1] and everything gives way to savage denunciation of mankind. It is only a cynic or a misanthrope who will find anything convincing in Swift's views.

Much has been written, in Germany and elsewhere,[2] on

---

[1] For Coleridge's criticism of the inconsistencies, see *The Athenæum*, August 15, 1896.

[2] See, especially, a paper by Borkowsky in *Anglia*, vol. xv, pp. 354–389.

the subject of Swift's indebtedness to previous writers. Rabelais's method is very different from Swift's, though Swift may have had in mind the kingdom of queen Quintessence when describing the academy of Lagado. The capture of Gulliver by the eagle and other incidents recall details in *The Arabian Nights*, then recently published in England. Swift had also read Lucian, *The Voyage of Domingo Gonsalez* and Cyrano de Bergerac's *Histoires comiques* and *Voyage à la Lune*. Whether he had also seen the *History of Savarambes* (1677), or Foigny's *Journey of Jacques Sadeur to Australia* (1693), is more doubtful. The account of the storm in the second part was made up of phrases in Surmy's *Mariners' Magazine*. Gulliver says that he was cousin of William Dampier, and Swift, of course, had studied *Robinson Crusoe*.

In *Hints towards an Essay on Conversation*, written about 1709, Swift commented humorously on people who monopolise conversation, or talk of themselves, or turn raillery all into repartee. These, and other remarks on the degeneracy of conversation, occur again in the witty and good-natured book published in Swift's later years, under the title *A Complete Collection of genteel and ingenious Conversation, according to the most polite mode and method now used at Court, and in the best Companies of England.* By Simon Wagstaff, Esq. This entertaining volume was given to his friend Mrs. Barber in 1738, when she was in need of money; but reference is made to it in a letter to Gay as early as 1731. Swift had noticed carefully the talk of people at fashionable gatherings, and, in conversations here put into the mouths of Miss Notable, Tom Neverout, Lady Smart, Lady Answerall, colonel Atwit and the rest, he satirises—but without bitterness—the banality, rudeness, coarseness and false wit of so-called "smart" society. But the best thing in the volume is the ironical introduction, in which Swift explains that he had often, with grief, observed ladies and gentlemen at a loss for questions, answers, replies and rejoinders, and now proposed to provide an infallible remedy. He had always kept a table-book in his pocket, and, when he left the company at the house of a polite family, he at once entered the choicest expressions that had passed. These he now published, after waiting some years to see if there were more to be gathered in. Anyone who aspired to being witty and smart must learn every sentence in the book and know, also, the appropriate motion or gesture. Polite persons smooth and polish various syllables of the words they utter, and, when they write, they vary the orthography: "we are infinitely better judges of what will please a distinguishing ear than those who call themselves scholars can possibly be." It might be objected that the book would prostitute the noble art to mean and vulgar people; but it was not an easy acquirement. A footman may swear, but he cannot swear like a lord, unless he be a lad of superior parts. A waiting-woman might acquire some small politeness, and, in some years, make a sufficient figure to draw in the young chaplain or the old steward; but how could she master the hundred graces and motions necessary to real success? Miss Notable and Mr. Neverout were described with special care; for they were intended to be patterns for all young bachelors and single ladies. Sir John Linger, the Derbyshire knight, was made to speak in his own rude dialect, to show what should be avoided. The labour of the work had been great; the author could not doubt that the country would come to realise how much it owed to him for his diligence and care.

Directions to Servants, published after Swift's death, was in hand in 1731, and we know that further progress had been made with it by the following year. It was, however, left incomplete. From some of his verses—*The Petition of Mrs. Frances Harris*, a chambermaid who had lost her purse, and *May the Cook-maid's Letter*—it is clear that Swift took special interest in the ways of servants. We know that he was good to the members of his own household, but insisted on their following strict rules. *Directions to Servants* is a good specimen of irony; it is, however, disfigured to an exceptional extent by coarseness. The ex-footman who is supposed to be the writer of the piece furnishes his friends with a set of rules to enable them to cheat and rob their masters in every set of circumstances. Servants, in general, must be loyal to each other; never do anything except what they are hired for; be out as much as possible; secure all the "tips" they can, and be rude to guests who do not pay. The cook is to "scrape the bottom of the pots and kettles with a silver spoon, for fear of giving them a taste of copper." The children's maid is to throw physic out of the window: "the child will love you the better; but bid it not tell." The waiting-maid must extort everything she can from her master, if he likes her, and, at the end, should secure a husband from among the chaplain, the steward and my lord's gentleman. It must be confessed that, after a few pages, this pitiless cynicism becomes depressing and a little tedious.

In 1708, Swift began a brilliant series of pamphlets on church questions. The first piece—a masterpiece of irony—was *An Argument against abolishing Christianity*, in which he banters very wittily writers who had attacked religion; but the banter is freely mixed with the irony which is never absent from his works. He begins by saying that no reader will, of course, imagine that he is attempting to defend real Christianity, such as, in primitive times, had an influence upon men's beliefs and actions. That would be a wild project: it would be to destroy at once all the wit and half the learning of the kingdom; to ruin trade and to extinguish arts and sciences. All he aimed at was to defend nominal Christianity; the other having been laid aside by general consent. He deals with the arguments that the abolishing of Christianity would be a gain of one day in seven; that it would remove the absurd custom by which a set of men were employed to denounce on Sundays what is the constant practice of all men on the other six; that, if the system of the Gospel were discarded, all religion would be affected and, consequently, those prejudices of education called virtue, conscience, honour and justice. If Christianity were abolished, the only topic left for the wits would be taken away. The spirit of opposition is ineradicable in mankind: if sectaries could not occupy themselves with religion, they would do worse, by contravening the law of the land, and disturbing the public peace. If Christianity is to be repealed, let us abolish religion in general; for, of what use is freedom of thought, if it will not conduce to freedom of action? Swift's moral, of course, is that we should both keep and improve our Christianity.

Another pamphlet, *The Sentiments of a Church of England Man with respect to Religion and Government*, was written in a more serious strain, and contained a warning to both parties. Swift found himself unable to join the extremists of either without offering violence to his integrity and understanding; and he decided that the truest service he could render to his country was by "endeavouring to moderate between the rival powers." "I believe I am no bigot in religion, and I am sure I am none in government." All positions of trust or dignity should, he felt, be given only to those whose principles directed them to preserve the constitution in all its parts. He could not feel any sympathy for non-conformists.

One simple compliance with the national form of receiving the sacrament is all we require to qualify any sectary among us for the greatest employments in the state, after which he is at liberty to rejoin his own assemblies for the rest of his life.

An unlimited liberty in publishing books against Christian doctrines was a scandal to government. Party feuds had been carried to excess. The church was not so narrowly calculated that it could not fall in with any regular species of government; but, though every species of government was equally lawful, they were not equally expedient, or for every country indifferently. A church of England man might properly approve the plans of one party more than those of the other, according as he thought they best promoted the good of church and state; but he would never be swayed by passion or interest to denounce an opinion merely because it was not of the party he himself approved. "To enter into a party as into an order of friars with so resigned an obedience to superiors, is very unsuitable both with the civil and religious liberties we so zealously assert." Whoever has a true value for church and state will avoid the extremes of whig, for the sake of the former, and the extremes of tory, for the sake of the latter. Swift's great object was to maintain the established constitution in both church and state.

Another piece, *A Project for the advancement of Religion and the Reformation of Manners* (1709), highly praised by Steele in *The Tatler*, contained a good many interesting suggestions, some excellent, others impracticable. Swift said that divines were justified in their complaint against the wickedness of the age; hardly one in a hundred people of quality or gentry appeared to act on any principle of religion, and great numbers of them entirely discarded it. Among men were to be found cheating, quarrels and blasphemies; among women, immorality and neglect of household affairs. In particular, there was fraud and cozenage in the law, injustice and oppression. Among the clergy, there was much ignorance, servility and pragmatism. It was in the power of the prince to cause piety and virtue to become the fashion, if he would make them the necessary qualifications for favour. It should be every man's interest to cultivate religion and virtue. Of course, it might be urged that, to make religion a necessary step for interest and favour, would increase hypocrisy; but, says Swift, if one in twenty were brought home to true piety and the nineteen were only hypocrites, the advantage would still be great. Hypocrisy at least wears the livery of religion, and most men would leave off vices out of mere weariness rather than undergo the risk and expense of practising them in private. "I believe it is often with religion as it is with love, which by much dissembling at last grows real." The clergy should not shut themselves up in their own clubs, but should mix with the laity and gain their esteem. "No man values the best medicine if administered by a physician whose person he hates or despises." More churches should be provided in growing towns: the printing of pernicious books should be stopped: taverns and alehouses should be closed at midnight, and no woman should be suffered to enter any tavern. In brief, it is the business of everyone to maintain appearances, if nothing more; and this should be enforced by the magistrates.

The question of the sacramental test, for the repeal of which there was an agitation in Ireland, was discussed in several pieces. The first of them, the able *Letter concerning the Sacramental Test* (1708), purported to be written by a member of the Irish parliament, and contained a contemptuous reference to Defoe: "One of these authors (the fellow that was pilloried, I have forgot his name) is indeed so grave, sententious, dogmatical a rogue that there is no enduring him." The whole body of clergy, says Swift, were against repealing the test, and, in Ireland, the clergy were generally loved and esteemed —and rightly so. It was said that popish interest was so formidable that all should join together to keep it under, and that the abolishing of the test was the only way of uniting all protestants; but there was not any real ground for fear of papists in Ireland.   The same views were repeated many years afterwards in *The Advantages proposed by repealing the Sacramental Test impartially examined* (1732), and in *Reasons humbly offered to the Parliament of Ireland for repealing the Sacramental Test, &c. in favour of the Catholics* (1733), in which are set out satirically the arguments that could be advanced by Roman catholics, the object being to show that they could urge as good reasons as could their brothers the dissenters.

In 1713, bishop Burnet published an introduction which was to preface the third part of his *History of the Reformation of the Church of England*.   He was an extreme party man and freely accused his opponents of sympathy with the pope, the Jacobites and the French.   In *A Preface to the B——p of S—r—m's Introduction*, Swift attacked him with a mixture of drollery and irony which must have had a very damning effect.   He was hated, says Swift, by everyone who wore the habit or followed the profession of a clergyman.   It would be well if he would sometimes hear what Truth said: he should not charge the opinion of one or two (and those, probably, non-jurors) upon the whole portion of the nation that differed from him, and he should not be so outrageous upon the memory of the dead, for it was highly probable he would soon be one of the number.   In another pamphlet, also published in 1713, *Mr. C—ns's Discourse on Free Thinking, put into plain English, by way of Abstract, for the use of the Poor*, Swift attacked deists by parodying the work of one of their body.   The piece purports to be written by a friend of Collins, and the object was to represent—very unfairly—that the views of deists were accepted by the whig party.   It seemed to him desirable, he says, that Collins's valuable work should be brought down to the understanding of the youth of quality and of members of whig clubs, who might be discouraged by the show of logic and the numerous quotations in the original.

A Letter to a Young Gentleman, lately entered into Holy Orders (1721) illustrates Swift's humour when undisturbed by passion, and its serious portions throw considerable light on his views.   He regrets that his friend had not remained longer at the university, and that he had not applied himself more to the study of the English language; the clergy were too fond of obscure terms, borrowed from ecclesiastical writers. He had no sympathy with the "moving manner of preaching," for it was of little use in directing men in the conduct of their lives.

Reason and good advice will be your safest guides; but beware of letting the pathetic part swallow up the rational. . . . The two principal branches of preaching are first to tell the people what is their duty, and then to convince them that it is so. The topics for both these, we know, are brought from Scripture and reason.

It was not necessary to attempt to explain the mysteries of the Christian religion; "indeed, since Providence intended there should be mysteries, I do not see how it can be agreeable to piety, orthodoxy or good sense, to go about such a work." The proper course was to deliver the doctrine as the church holds it, and to confirm it by Scripture.

I think the clergy have almost given over perplexing themselves and their hearers with abstruse points of Predestination, Election, and the like; at least it is time they should.

These views are exemplified in Swift's own *Sermons*, which contain little rhetoric, and, for the most part, are confined to straightforward reasoning. The appeal was to the head rather than to the heart; but it was marked by great common sense, force and directness. There is no reason for thinking that Swift did not honestly accept the doctrines of Christianity; Bolingbroke called him "a hypocrite reversed." We know that he concealed his religious observances; he had family prayers with his servants without telling his guests, and, in London, he rose early to attend worship without the knowledge of his friends. His sincerity was never doubted by those who knew him: when they were ill, they asked him to pray with them. In his last years, when his mind had given way, he was seen to pursue his devotions with great regularity. Outwardly, he performed, in an exemplary manner, the duties of his deanship, and was a loyal supporter of his church.

"I am not answerable to God," he says, "for the doubts that arise in my own breast, since they are the consequence of that reason which He hath planted in me, if I take care to conceal those doubts from others, if I use my best endeavours to subdue them, and if they have no influence on the conduct of my life."

He suspected those who made much profession of zeal; but, within his limits, he had a very real sense of his responsibilities.

"I look upon myself," he said, "in the capacity of a clergyman, to be one appointed by Providence for defending a post assigned me, and for gaining over as many enemies as I can. Although I think my cause is just, yet one great motive is my submitting to the pleasure of Providence, and to the laws of my country."

The series of writings on English politics begins with *A Discourse of the Contests and Dissensions between the Nobles and the Commons in Athens and Rome* (1701), written in defence of Lord Somers, who had been attacked by a tory House of Commons on account of the Partition treaty. The feuds between Lords and Commons were bitter, and, in this soberly written and weighty pamphlet, Swift showed the dangers of the quarrel for both parties, and the need of a due balance of power in the country. If a House of Commons, already possessing more than its share of power, cramped the hand that held the balance, and aimed at more power by attacking the nobles, then, said Swift, the same causes would produce the same consequences among us as they did in Greece and Rome. Party government, he pointed out, tends to destroy all individuality. Some said that this piece was by Somers himself, others that it was by Burnet; but, before long, Swift admitted that he was the author, and his services naturally earned the gratitude of the whigs.

The political pamphlets which Swift wrote during the closing years of queen Anne's reign are of interest rather to the historian than to the student of literature; for, in the main, they are concerned with questions of temporary interest or with personal quarrels. One of the ablest and most successful was *The Conduct of the Allies and of the late Ministry in beginning and carrying on the present war*, which went through many editions and had a great effect on public opinion. Swift's object was to show the burden of war on the nation; that submission had been made to these impositions for the advancement of private wealth and power or in order to forward the dangerous designs of a faction; so, the side of the war which would have been beneficial to us had been neglected; our allies had broken their promises; and the wiser course was to conclude peace. This carefully thought-out pamphlet was followed by *Some Remarks on the Barrier Treaty* (1712), which forms a supplement to it, and, in the same year, by *Some Advice humbly offered to the members of the October Club*, intended to appease extreme tories, who were dissatisfied with Harley.

During the months that followed the death of queen Anne, Swift wrote several pieces in which he put on record the defence of the late ministry, and, especially, of Oxford; denied the existence of intrigues with Jacobites, of the existence of which he clearly knew nothing, and explained his own connection with tories. One of these pieces was entitled *Memoirs relating to that change which happened to the Queen's ministry in the year* 1710; another, *Some free thoughts upon the present state of affairs;* and another, *An inquiry into the behaviour of the Queen's last Ministry*, in which he said that

among the contending parties in England, the general interest of Church and State is more the private interest of one side than the other; so that, whoever professeth to act upon a principle of observing the laws of his country, may have a safe rule to follow, by discovering whose particular advantage it chiefly is that the Constitution should be preserved entire in all its parts.

Other pamphlets dealt largely in personalities. One of the most violent is *A short character of Thomas Earl of Wharton* (1711), in which the lord lieutenant of Ireland is charged with every form of vice. He had, says Swift, three predominant passions, seldom united in the same man: love of power, love of money, love of pleasure, which rode him sometimes by turns, sometimes all together. If there were not any visible effects of old age, either in body or mind, it was "in spite of a continual prostitution to those vices which usually wear out both." *The Importance of the Guardian considered* (1713), and *The Public Spirit of the Whigs* (1714), had their origin in Swift's quarrel with Steele. However much Steele may be to blame for his part in the quarrel, Swift's personalities cannot be defended. Swift says that Steele, being the most imprudent man alive, never followed the advice of his friends, but was wholly at the mercy of fools or knaves or hurried away by his own caprices. After reading what he said of his sovereign, one asked, not whether Steele was (as he alleged) "a gentleman born," but whether he was a human creature.

The pamphlets relating to Ireland form a very important part of Swift's works. His feeling of the intolerable wrongs of the country in which he was compelled to live grew from year to year. He saw around him poverty and vice, due, as he held, partly to the apathy of the people, but mainly to the selfishness of the English government, which took whatever it could get from Ireland and gave little in return. Swift's concern was mainly with the English in Ireland; he had little sympathy for the "savage old Irish" or with the Scottish presbyterians in the north. But his pity for cottagers increased as he understood the situation more clearly and saw that they were so oppressed by charges which they had to bear that hardly any, even farmers, could afford to provide shoes or stockings for their children or to eat flesh or to drink anything better than sour milk and water. The manufactures and commerce of the country were ruined by the laws, and agriculture was crippled by prohibition of exportation of cattle or wool to foreign countries. No doubt, Swift was influenced by a feeling of hatred towards the whig government; but he was certainly sincere in the long series of pamphlets in which he denounced the treatment of Ireland by the English. This series began in 1720 with *A proposal for the universal use of Irish manufacture*, in which Swift puts forth a scheme for rejecting everything wearable that came from England. Someone had said that Ireland would never be happy till a law was made for burning everything received from England, except their people and their coals: "Nor am I even yet for lessening the number of those exceptions." Swift quoted the fable of Arachne and Pallas. Pallas, jealous of a rival who excelled in the art of spinning and weaving, turned Arachne into a spider, ordering her to spin and weave for ever out of her own bowels in a very narrow compass.

"I confess," says Swift, "I always pitied poor Arachne, and could never heartily love the goddess on account of so cruel and unjust a sentence; which, however, is fully executed upon us by

England, with further additions of rigour and severity, for the greatest part of our bowels and vitals are extracted, without allowing us the liberty of spinning and weaving them."

Before long, the want of small change in the coinage of Ireland began to be felt acutely, and, in 1722, a new patent was issued to an English merchant, William Wood; but Wood had to pay £10,000 to the duchess of Kendal for the job, and the Irish parliament, which had not been consulted, passed resolutions protesting against the loss that would be sustained by Ireland. A committee was appointed to enquire into complaints; while it was sitting, Swift published the first of the brilliant series of pamphlets known as *Drapier's Letters*. It was called *A Letter to the shopkeepers, tradesmen, farmers and the common people of Ireland concerning the brass half-pence coined by Mr. Woods*, and purported to be by "M. B. Drapier." It was written in the simplest language, which could be understood by all, and the arguments were such as would appeal to the people. From motives of prudence, Wood, and not the government, was attacked, and the main argument was that the coins were deficient in value and weight. Many of the allegations are baseless, while the reasoning is sophistical, but they served the purpose of stirring up the people to a sense of ill-treatment. Swift foretold that the country would be ruined; that tenants would not be able to pay their rents; and, alluding to Phalaris, he said that it might be found that the brass which Wood contrived as a trouble to the kingdom would prove his own torment and destruction. The committee of enquiry recommended a reduction in the amount of coin that Wood was to issue, and Walpole obtained a report from Sir Isaac Newton, master of the mint, to the effect that the coins were correct both as to weight and quality. Swift, feeling that any compromise would amount to defeat, brought out another pamphlet, *A Letter to Mr. Harding the printer*, in which he urged that the people should refuse to take the coins: the nation did not want them; there was no reason why an Englishman should enjoy the profit. It was not dishonourable to submit to the lion, but who "with the figure of a man can think with patience of being devoured alive by a rat?" Swift now openly widened the field of the controversy: the grievance of the patent became subordinated to the question of the servitude of the Irish people. He was afraid that concessions made by the government might result in the return of the people to their wonted indifference. The third letter was called *Some Observations upon a paper called the Report of the Committee of the most honourable the Privy Council in England relating to Wood's halfpence.* "Am I," he asked, "a free man in England and do I become a slave in six hours by crossing the Channel?" The country was now deluged with pamphlets and ballads, some of which were certainly by Swift, and no jury could be persuaded to convict the printers. At this point, Swift produced his *Letter to the whole People of Ireland*, which was intended to refresh and keep alive the spirit which he had raised, and to show the Irish that, alike by the laws of God and man, they were and ought to be as free a people as their brothers in England. The affair ended in a triumph for Swift. Bonfires were lit in his honour and towns gave him their freedom. It is not necessary to refer in detail to subsequent pamphlets: Wood's patent was cancelled, and he received a pension.

Swift wrote many other pieces about Irish grievances. In one of these, *The Swearers Bank* (1720), he dealt with a proposal to start a bank to assist small tradesmen. He argued that the scheme was not needed in a country so cursed with poverty as Ireland, and his satire was fatal to the project. In *The Story of the injured lady*,[1] he again poured forth his wrath against English misgovernment, and, in the *Answer* to this pamphlet, he told Ireland that she ought not to have any dependence on England, beyond being subject to the same government; that she should regulate her household by methods to be agreed upon by the two countries; and that she should show a proper spirit and insist on freedom to send her goods where she pleased. In *A short view of the state of Ireland* (1728), he gives a touching account of the condition of the country: though it was favoured by nature with a fruitful soil and a temperate climate, there was general desolation in most parts of the island. England drew revenues from

---

[1] This is not known to have been published before 1746, when it appeared in a collection entitled *The Story of the Injured Lady . . . with letters and poems never before printed. By the Rev. Dr. Swift.*

Ireland without giving in return one farthing value. "How long we shall be able to continue the payment I am not in the least certain: one thing I know, that when the hen is starved to death there will be no more golden eggs." In another piece, *On the present miserable state of Ireland*, he said,

We are apt to charge the Irish with laziness because we seldom find them employed: but then we do not consider that they have nothing to do: the want of trade is owing to cruel restrictions, rather than to any disqualification of the people.

The series reached its climax in *A Modest Proposal for preventing the children of poor people from being a burden to their parents or the country, and for making them beneficial to the public* (1729), in which, with terrible irony and bitterness, Swift suggested, in a spirit of despair at the helplessness of Ireland, that the poverty of the people should be relieved by the sale of their children as food for the rich. With the utmost gravity, he sets out statistics to show the revenue that would accrue if this idea were adopted. It would give the people something valuable of their own, and thus help to pay their landlord's rent; it would save the cost of maintaining very many children; it would lead to a lessening of the number of papists; it would be a great inducement to marriage. The remedy, Swift took care to point out, was only for the kingdom of Ireland, "and for no other that ever was, is, or, I think, ever can be upon earth"; and it did not involve any danger of disobliging England, "for this kind of commodity will not bear exportation." The suggestion was quite disinterested. "I have no children by which I can propose to get a single penny, the youngest being nine years old, and my wife past child-bearing."

In *An Examination of certain Abuses, Corruptions and Enormities in the City of Dublin* (1732), Swift, writing as a whig, burlesqued the fashion of charging tories with being in sympathy with papists and Jacobites, and of finding cause for suspecting disaffection in the most unexpected quarters. Under the guise of an attack on the earl of Oxford, he charged Walpole with avarice, obscurity of birth and profligacy.

One more pamphlet was published in 1733, *A serious and useful scheme to make a hospital for Incurables*, in which Swift dwelt on the necessity of dealing with the number of fools, knaves, scolds, scribblers, infidels and liars, not to mention the incurably vain, proud, affected and ten thousand others beyond cure. He hoped that he would himself be admitted on the foundation as one of the scribbling incurables; he was happy to feel that no person would be offended by his scheme, "because it is natural to apply ridiculous characters to all the world, except ourselves."

On literary subjects, Swift wrote little. In 1712, he published his *Proposal for correcting, improving and ascertaining the English Tongue*, in the form of a letter to Harley. In this tract, to which he allowed his name to be affixed, he urged the formation of an academy, which was to fix a standard for the language. New words, abbreviations, slang, affectation, phonetic spelling—of all these Swift complained, and he thought that an academy could stop improprieties, and find a way for "ascertaining and fixing our language for ever." Some time before, he had written to the same effect in no. 230 of *The Tatler*, "by the hands," as he says, "of an ingenious gentleman [Steele], who, for a long time, did thrice a week direct or instruct the kingdom by his papers." There, he pleaded for the observance in our style of "that simplicity which is the best and truest ornament of most things in life." He ended his *Proposal* by urging that, in England, as in France, the endowments of the mind should occasionally be rewarded, either by a pension or, where that was unnecessary, by some mark of distinction.

Nine years later, Swift published in Dublin an amusing satire, *A Letter of Advice to a young Poet; together with a Proposal for the encouragement of Poetry in this Kingdom* (1721). The professional poet, he says, would be embarrassed if he had any religion, for poetry, of late, had been "altogether disengaged from the narrow notions of virtue and piety." But the poet must be conversant with the Scriptures, in order to be "witty upon them or out of them." Scholarship was now quite unnecessary to the poet; and, if we look back, Shakespeare "was no scholar, yet was an excellent poet." Swift was for every man's working upon his own materials, and producing only what he can find within himself. Taking part in games will often suggest similes, images or rimes: and coffee-house and theatre must be frequented. The profession was in a sorry plight in Dublin, though poetic wit abounded. The city had no Grub street, set apart as a safe repository for poetry, and there was much need for a playhouse, where the young could get rid of the natural prejudices of religion and modesty, great restraints to a free people.

In the rather patronising *Letter to a very young Lady on her Marriage* (1727), Swift advises his friend to listen to the talk of men of learning; it is a shame for an English lady not to be able to relish such discourses, but few gentlemen's daughters could be brought to read or understand their own native tongue; they could not even be brought to spell correctly. Elsewhere, Swift combated the general view that it was not prudent to choose a wife with some taste of wit and humour, able to relish history and to be a tolerable judge of the beauties of poetry. There were, however, so few women of this kind that half the well educated nobility and gentry must, if they married, take a wife for whom they could not possibly have any esteem.

Swift's poetry has the merits of his prose, but not many other merits. He began by writing frigid "Pindaric" odes, after the fashion of Cowley, and, from his letters, we know that he set considerable value on them, and that they underwent much revision.[1] But Dryden was right when, after perusing some of these verses, he said, "Cousin Swift, you will never be a poet." This comment caused much annoyance to Swift, as we may conclude from the hostile references to Dryden in several of his writings. It was, however, taken to heart; for he produced no more stilted odes, but, in future, confined himself to lighter verse, modelled on Butler, and generally of a satirical nature. One of the earliest and most attractive of his playful pieces, the graceful *Baucis and Philemon*, was published, with the pretty verses *On Mrs. Biddy Floyd*, in the last volume of Tonson's *Miscellany* (1709). In other pieces, *A Description of a City Shower* and *A Description of the Morning*, published in *The Tatler*, the subject is treated purely from a humorous and satirical point of view. Among his later works, *The Grand Question debated* (1729), with its studies of Lady Acheson and of her maid, Hannah, is altogether delightful.

[1] Hist. MSS. Comm., *Seventh Report*, p. 680.

In two pieces written in imitation of Horace (1713–14), Swift described, in felicitous words, his friendship with Harley, and gave some account of his own feelings before and after he was appointed to the deanery of St. Patrick's. Harley saw Swift "cheapening old authors on a stall":

> A clergyman of special note
> For shunning those of his own coat;
> Which made his brethren of the gown
> Take care betimes to run him down:
> No libertine, nor over nice,
> Addicted to no sort of vice;
> Went where he pleased, said what he thought;
> Not rich, but owed no man a groat.

Harley adopted him as a humble friend, and said that Swift must be a dean: he need but cross the Irish sea to have power and ease. Swift had often wished that he had "for life, six hundred pounds a year," with a garden, and a good house for a friend. Now he had all this and more, and would have been content, could he have lived nearer London.

The famous *Cadenus and Vanessa* (1713) gives, in a mock classical setting, Swift's account of his acquaintance with Hester Vanhomrigh, and of his surprise and distress at finding her in love with him. Vanessa scorned fops and fine ladies; at length, she met the dean,

> Grown old in politics and wit,
> Caress'd by ministers of state,
> Of half mankind the dread and hate.

His fame led her to forget his age; but he did not understand what love was; his feelings were those of a father and a tutor. After a time, he found that her thoughts wandered, and, at length, she confessed that his lessons had

> found the weakest part,
> Aimed at the head, but reached the heart.

Cadenus was ashamed and surprised. He knew that the world would blame him, especially as she had "five thousand guineas in her purse." But Vanessa argued well, and, to his grief and shame, Cadenus could scarce oppose her. After all, it was flattering to be preferred to a crowd of beaux. He told her it was too late for him to love, but he offered friendship, gratitude, esteem. Vanessa took him at his word, and said she would now be the tutor. What success she had was yet a secret; whether he descended to "less seraphic ends" or whether they decided "to temper love and books together" must not be told.

As this poem was preserved by Hester Vanhomrigh, we may assume that she did not think Swift had done her injustice in the clever apology for his own conduct. As in the case of the correspondence, it is pleasant to turn from the verses about Vanessa to the pieces which Swift wrote year by year on Stella's birthday. With laughing allusions to her advancing years (when she was thirty-eight, he wrote "Stella this day is thirty-four (We shan't dispute a year or more)"), he dwells on her wit and the lustre of her eyes. Hers was "an angel's face a little cracked," with an angel's mind. He "ne'er admitted Love a guest"; having Stella for his friend, he sought no more. She nursed him in his illness, coming to his relief "with cheerful face and inward grief."

> When out my brutish passions break,
> With gall in every word I speak,
> She with soft speech my anguish cheers,
> Or melts my passions down with tears.

If her locks were turning grey, his eyes were becoming dim, and he would not believe in wrinkles which he could not see. On her last birthday, when she was sick and Swift grown old, he wrote that, though they could form no more long schemes of life, she could look with joy on what was past. Her life had been well spent, and virtue would guide her to a better state. Swift would gladly share her suffering,

> Or give my scrap of life to you,
> And think it far beneath your due;
> You, to whose care so oft I owe
> That I'm alive to tell you so.

Swift is at his best in these pieces of sincere affection for the woman whom he loved throughout her life.

It is strange to pass to some of his satires on woman,

which are among the bitterest and most savage of his verses,
and exhibit a physical loathing which suggests mental defect.
In *The Progress of Beauty*, he dwells on physical decay; in
The Progress of Marriage, he describes a union where "the
swain is old, the nymph coquette." In *The Journal of a
Modern Lady*, he satirises the woman whose life is given to
cards. In *The Lady's Dressing Room, Strephon and Chloe*,
and other pieces written about 1730–1, we see the increasing
disease of mind which could find nothing but what was loath-
some. It is unnecessary to dwell on these melancholy and
savage things, or on the coarse or foolish trifles which Swift
and the cronies of his later years bandied to and fro. They
had their origin in an attempt to escape from the deepening
gloom. Nor need we do more than glance at the political
ballads and skits—*Sid Hamet's Rod, The W—ds—r Prophecy,
The Fable of Midas, Dennis's Invitation to Steele* and the like—
in which Swift attacked his opponents while engaged in the
political warfare of 1710–13; or at those of later years relating
to Ireland. The *Epistle to Mr. Gay* contains a violent attack
on Walpole. It is enough to mention the inhuman onslaught
on Lord Allen in *Traulus* (1730), and *The Last Judgment* and
The Legion Club (1736), two of his last pieces, where savage
wrath has the fullest sway. In *The Legion Club*, an attack
on the Irish parliament, he pictures it as a madhouse, and
gives us the keeper's description of the various members.
If he could destroy the harpies' nest with thunder, how would
Ireland be blessed! They sold the nation, they raved of making
laws and they scribbled senseless heads of bills:

> See, the Muse unbars the gate;
> Hark, the monkeys, how they prate!

Would Hogarth were there, so that every monster might be
painted! At length, he could not bear any more of it:

> Keeper, I have seen enough.
> Taking then a pinch of snuff,
> I concluded, looking round them,
> May their god, the devil, confound them!

In the fable called *The Beasts Confession to the Priest*

(1732), Swift dwells on "the universal folly of mankind of mistaking their talents." When the land was struck with plague, their king ordered the beasts to confess their sins. The ass confessed that he was a wag; the ape claimed strict virtue, but said his zeal was sometimes indiscreet; the swine said his shape and beauty made him proud, but gluttony was never his vice. Similarly, the knave declares he failed because he could not flatter; the chaplain vows he cannot fawn; the statesman says, with a sneer, that his fault is to be too sincere. Swift's conclusion is that he had libelled the four-footed race, since

> Creatures of ev'ry kind but ours
> Well comprehend their nat'ral powers

though

> now and then
> Beasts may degen'rate into men.

On Poetry: a Rhapsody (1733) was thought by Swift to be his best satire. In this very powerful piece, he describes the difficulty of the poet's art, and the wane of public encouragement. After much satirical advice, he tells the writer who has had to put aside all thoughts of fame to seek support from a party:

> A pamphlet in Sir Bob's defence
> Will never fail to bring in pence.

Praise of a king will always be acceptable, and, with change of names, will serve again in the following reign. Or, the poet may live by being a puny judge of wit at Will's: he must read Rymer and Dennis, and Dryden's prefaces, now much valued,

> Though merely writ at first for filling,
> To raise the volume's price a shilling.

Jobbers in the poet's art were to be found in every alley, generally at war with each other. As naturalists have observed, a flea

> Has smaller fleas that on him prey;
> And these have smaller still to bite 'em,
> And so proceed *ad infinitum*.

Who can reach the worst in Grub street?

> the height we know;
> 'T is only infinite below.

And then the piece ends with satirical adulation of king and minister, such as poetasters loved.

The poem *On the Death of Dr. Swift* (1731), with its mixture of humour, egotism and pathos, is, in many respects, the best and most interesting of Swift's verse. An incomplete pirated version appeared in 1733, and an authorised copy in 1739; the poem was finally revised before its issue by Faulkner in 1743. Swift begins with comments on our dislike to be excelled by our friends, and then pictures his own coming death and what his acquaintances would say of him—his vertigo, loss of memory, oft told stories, which could be borne only by younger folk, for the sake of his wine. At last, their prognostications came true: the dean was dead. Who was his heir? When it was known he had left all to public uses, people said that this was mere envy, avarice and pride. The town was cloyed with elegies, and Curll prepared to

> treat me as he does my betters,
> Publish my will, my life, my letters,
> Revive the libels, born to die,
> Which Pope must bear, as well as I.

Friends shrugged their shoulders, and said, " I 'm sorry—but we all must die." Ladies received the news, over their cards, in doleful dumps:

> The Dean is dead (pray what are trumps?)
> Then Lord have mercy on his soul.
> (Ladies; I'll venture for the *vole*.)

In a year, he was forgotten; his wit was out of date. But, sometimes, men at a club would refer to him and discuss his character. This gives Swift the opportunity for a defence of himself. He had aimed at curing the vices of mankind by grave irony: "What he writ was all his own." He never courted men of rank, nor was he afraid of the great. He helped those in distress, and chose only the good and wise for friends. "Fair Liberty was all his cry." He valued neither power nor wealth. He laboured in vain to reconcile his friends in power, and, finally, left the court in despair. In Ireland, he defeated Wood;

> Taught fools their interest how to know
> And gave them arms to ward the blow.

Perhaps the dean had too much satire in his veins:

> Yet malice never was his aim,
> He lashed the vice, but spared the name.
>
> . . . . .
>
> True genuine dulness moved his pity
> Unless it offered to be witty.
>
> . . . . .
>
> He gave the little wealth he had
> To build a house for fools and mad,
> And showed by one satiric touch
> No nation needed it so much.

It will be seen, from what has been said, that Swift's verse has very little imagination or sentiment. It is merely witty prose put into fluent verse, with clever rimes. There is no chivalry, no real emotion, except the fierce passion of indignation. If "poet" connotes the love of beauty, the search after ideals, the preaching of what is ennobling, then Swift is not a poet. But his verse is an admirable vehicle for the expression of his passion and irony; and it is excellent of its kind, simple, sincere, direct, pointed, without any poetic ornament or show of learning.

Of Swift's correspondence, by far the most interesting, of course, is that with Esther Johnson, afterwards to be known as the *Journal to Stella*. The latter part of these journal-letters were first printed in Hawkesworth's 1766 edition of Swift; but Hawkesworth suppressed most of the "little language," and made other changes in the text. The publishers, however, presented the manuscript, with the exception of one letter, to the British Museum, and we now can read the letters as they were written, subject to difficulties due to deciphering and to numerous abbreviations, and to the fact that Swift, in later years, ruled out many words and sentences. The remainder of the *Journal*, consisting of the first forty letters, was published by Deane Swift in 1768. Unfortunately, the originals, with one exception, have been lost; but it is clear that Deane Swift took even greater liberties than Hawkesworth.

The *Journal to Stella* affords the most intimate picture of Swift that we possess, while, at the same time, it is an historical document of the greatest value. It throws much light on the relations between the pair, and it brings vividly before us Swift's fears and hopes during the two years and a half covered by the letters. His style, always simple and straightforward, is never more so than in this most intimate correspondence. He mentions casually the detailed incidents of his life and alludes to the people he met; he never describes anyone at length, but constantly summarises in a sentence the main characteristics of the man, or, at least, his estimate of his character. Bolingbroke, the "thorough rake"; Oxford, the "pure trifler"; Marlborough, "as covetous as hell and as ambitious as a prince of it"; Congreve, now nearly blind; the lovable Arbuthnot; Steele, who hardly ever kept an appointment; queen Anne, who found very little to say to those around her; Mrs. Masham, and other ladies of the court—of all these we are allowed a glance which seems to furnish us with a real knowledge of them.

Mr. Addison and I are as different as black and white, and I believe our friendship will go off, by this damned business of party . . . but I love him still as well as ever, though we seldom meet.

Day by day, we are told of party intrigues and of promises held out to Swift: "The Tories drily tell me I may make my fortune if I please," he noted in 1710, "but I do not understand them, or rather I do understand them." A few weeks later, he wrote,

To say the truth, the present ministry have a difficult task, and want me. Perhaps they may be as grateful as others: but, according to the best judgment I have, they are pursuing the true interest of the public; and therefore "I am glad to contribute what is in my power."

And, in February, 1711,

> They call me nothing but Jonathan, and I said I believed they would leave me Jonathan, as they have found me; and that I never knew a ministry do anything for those whom they make companions of their pleasures; and I believe you will find it so; but I care not.

Swift's financial troubles constantly come to light in these letters. "People have so left town," he says, "that I am at a loss for a dinner . . . it cost me eighteenpence in coach-hire before I could find a place to dine in." When he first came to London, he took rooms at eight shillings a week: "Plaguy dear, but I spend nothing for eating, never go to a tavern, and very seldom in a coach." In another place, he says, "This rain ruins me in coach hire." How much exaggeration there was in these protests against expense, it is not easy to say. The *Journal* abounds in arrogant references to great ladies and others; but the arrogance was partly affected and partly the result of a fear of being patronised. Once, when he was to have supped with Lady Ashburnham, he says: "The drab did not call for me in her coach as she promised but sent for us, and so I sent my excuses." When the duchess of Shrewsbury expostulated with him for not dining with her, Swift said he expected more advances from ladies, especially duchesses. Swift's genuine kindness to, and love of, those who were his friends is constantly appearing. When William Harrison, whom he had assisted to start a continuation of *The Tatler*, was ill, Swift was afraid to knock at the door; when he found that Harrison was dead, he comforted the mother. When Lady Ashburnham died, he wrote,

> She was my greatest favourite and I am in excessive concern for her loss. . . . I hate life when I think it exposed to such accidents; and to see so many thousand wretches burdening the earth, while such as her die, makes me think God did never intend life for a blessing.

Swift took much interest in a small poet called Diaper, a young fellow who had written some *Eclogues:* "I hate to have any new wits rise, but when they do rise I will encourage them: but they tread on our heels and thrust us off the stage." When his friend Mrs. Anne Long died, Swift said he was never more afflicted. Mrs. Long had "all sorts of amiable qualities and no ill ones, except but the indiscretion of too much neglecting her own affairs." For his servant, Patrick, to whom there are constant references, he showed the greatest forbearance. Patrick had good points, but he drank, and sometimes stopped out at night; he was, however, a favourite both of Swift and Mrs. Vanhomrigh.

The "little language" which Swift employed in writing to Stella had probably been used between them ever since they were at Moor park together. He constantly addressed Stella and Mrs. Dingley as "sirrahs," "girls," "dearest lives," and so on; but we can generally distinguish references intended for Stella only. There are frequent references to Stella's weak eyes. "What shall we do to cure them, poor dear life?" "It is the grief of my soul to think you are out of order." "I will write plainer for Dingley to read from, henceforth, though my pen is apt to ramble when I think who I am writing to." Nothing gave him any sort of dream of happiness, but a letter now and then from

his own dearest M. D. . . . Yes, faith, and when I write to M. D., I am happy too; it is just as if methinks you were here, and I prating to you, and telling you where I have been.

In another place, he says to Stella:

I can hardly imagine you absent when I am reading your letter or writing to you: No, faith, you are just here upon this little paper, and therefore I see and talk with you every evening constantly, and sometimes in the morning.

Besides the personal interest, the *Journal* throws valuable light on the social life of the day, both in Dublin and in London. There are constant allusions to Stella's life in Ireland and to the friends with whom she mixed. There was a club, with ombre, claret and toasted oranges; there are descriptions of Stella's rides and walks; of dinners at three or four o'clock; of London sights; of the Mohocks and other terrors; of the polite ways of society, and of snuff taken by ladies and of jokes which they indulged in. We hear, too, of the dangers of robbers at night across the fields of Chelsea and of the risk of French privateers in the Irish channel. The *Journal* is a mine of information for the historian and the student of manners, and of absorbing interest as a picture of character.

Swift's general correspondence is remarkable, like his other writings, for the ease with which he could always find apt words to express the exact meaning which he wished to convey. He also has the merit, essential in a good correspondent, that he can adapt himself readily to the character and point of view of the person to whom he is writing. In his letters, we have not only a graphic picture of Swift's own feelings and character, but clear indications of the nature of the men with whom he was in communication. In the letters to Pope, there is something of the artificiality of the poet; in those to King, the dignity and stateliness befitting a dignitary of the church; and, in those to Arbuthnot, the sincere affection which was a marked charm in the doctor. Unfortunately, when Swift wrote to the companions who occupied too much of his time in the period of his decay, he condescended to jests unworthy of him. In writing to his friends, he "never leaned on his elbow to consider what he should write." There is evidence that letters of importance were often carefully revised and considered before they were despatched; but, ordinarily, he wrote "nothing but nature and friendship," as he said to Pope, without any eye to the public.

Various interpretations have been placed on Swift's life and work. Much has been written in his defence since the unsympathetic studies of Macaulay, Jeffrey and Thackeray appeared; but he remains somewhat of a mystery. It is not easy to reconcile his contempt for mankind with his affection for his friends and their affection for him; or his attacks on woman with his love for one, and the love which two women felt for him. It is, again, difficult, in view of the decorum of his own life and his real, if formal, religion, to explain the offensiveness of some of his writings. Probably, this was due to a distorted imagination, the result of physical or mental defect; and it must be remembered that it is only here and there that coarseness appears. Sterne remarked, "Swift has said a thousand things I durst not say." But there is no lewdness in Swift's work, and no persistent strain of indecency, as in Sterne.

Some have suggested that Swift's avoidance of the common

ties of human life was due to fears of approaching madness; others have supposed that the explanation was physical infirmity; others, again, have found the key in his coldness of temperament or in his strong desire for independence. He appears to have hungered for human sympathy, but to have wanted nothing more. From the passion of love, he seems to have turned with disgust. The early years of poverty and dependence left an indelible mark on him, and he became a disappointed and embittered man. His mind, possessed by a spirit of scorn, turned in upon itself, and his egotism grew with advancing years. Cursed with inordinate pride and arrogance, he became like a suppressed volcano. His keenness of vision caused him to see with painful clearness all that was contemptible and degrading in his fellow men; but he had little appreciation for what was good and great in them. The pains and giddiness to which Swift was subject left their impression upon his work; "at best," he said, "I have an ill head, and an aching heart." His misanthropy was really a disease, and his life of loneliness and disappointment was a tragedy, calling for pity and awe, rather than for blame.

Swift's style is very near perfection. Clear, pointed, precise, he seems to have no difficulty in finding words to express exactly the impression which he wishes to convey. The sentences are not always grammatically correct, but they come home to the reader, like the words of a great orator or advocate, with convincing force. He realises so clearly what he is describing that the reader is, of necessity, interested and impressed. There are no tricks of style, no recurring phrases; no ornaments, no studied effects; the object is attained without apparent effort, with an outward gravity marking the underlying satire or cynicism, and an apparent calmness concealing bitter invective. There is never any doubt of his earnestness, whatever may be the mockery on the surface. For the metaphysical and the speculative, he had no sympathy.

Swift was a master satirist, and his irony was deadly. He was the greatest among the writers of his time, if we judge them by the standard of sheer power of mind; yet, with some few exceptions, his works are now little read. Order, rule, sobriety —these are the principles he set before him when he wrote, and they form the basis of his views on life, politics and religion.

Sincerity is never wanting, however much it is cloaked with humour; but we look in vain for lofty ideals or for the prophetic touch which has marked the bearers of the greatest names in our literature.   That which is spiritual was strangely absent in Swift.   He inveighs against folly and evil; but he seems to have no hope for the world.   He is too often found scorning the pettiness of his fellow-creatures, as in Lilliput, or describing with loathing the coarseness of human nature, as in Brobdingnag.   Satire and denunciation alone are unsatisfying, and the satirist must, in the end, take a lower place than the creative writer.

CHAPTER V

Arbuthnot and Lesser Prose Writers

ARBUTHNOT'S name is familiar to all readers of the literature of the early portion of the eighteenth century; but, to most people, he is known only by the references to him in the correspondence of Pope and Swift, and what he wrote is now little read. This is due, in part, to the nature of the topics which he chose, but chiefly to the fact that he was lavish in the assistance which he gave to his friends and took little trouble to preserve his work or to ensure its receiving recognition.

John Arbuthnot was born in 1667 at Arbuthnott, where his father had become parson in 1665. The village is near Arbuthnott castle in Kincardineshire; but whether the Arbuthnots were connected with the patron of the living, Viscount Arbuthnott, is not certain. After the revolution, Arbuthnot's father refused to conform to the General Assembly and was deprived of his living. He retired to a small property in the neighbourhood, and died in 1696. His sons left their old home; John—who had studied at Marischal college, Aberdeen, from 1681 to 1685—going to London, where he earned a living by teaching mathematics. In 1692, he published a translation of a book by Huygens on the laws of chance, and, two years later, he entered University college, Oxford, as a fellow-commoner, and acted as private tutor to a young man admitted to the college on the same day. In the summer of 1696, Arbuthnot decided to try some other course of life, and, in September, he took his doctor's degree in medicine at St. Andrews, where, we are told, he acquitted himself extraordinarily well in both his public and private trials. He seems to have returned to London to practise, and, at the end of 1697, he published *An Examination of Dr. Woodward's Account of the Deluge, etc.*, in which he pointed out the difficulties which made it impossible to accept Woodward's theory. Arbuthnot was now on friendly terms with many well-known literary and scientific men, including Pepys. In 1701, he published at Oxford an admirable essay *On the Usefulness of Mathematical Learning.* In 1704, he was elected a fellow of the Royal Society and, in 1705, was created an M.D. of Cambridge. In this latter year, he had the good fortune to be at Epsom when prince George of Denmark was taken ill, and he was always afterwards employed by the prince as his physician. In the summer, he dedicated to the prince a little volume, *Tables of the Grecian, Roman and Jewish Measures, Weights and Coins*, and was appointed physician extraordinary to the queen, a post which gave him considerable influence at court. In 1709, he became physician in ordinary to the queen.

When the negotiations for the union of England and Scotland were in progress, in 1706, Arbuthnot assisted in removing the prejudices of his countrymen by publishing at Edinburgh *A Sermon preached to the People at the Mercat Cross of Edinburgh on the subject of the Union*, and, before long, he was in close touch with Robert Harley, who had begun to plot against the duke and duchess of Marlborough. Abigail Hill, Harley's cousin, became bedchamber-woman and was secretly married, in Arbuthnot's lodgings in the palace, to Samuel Masham, of prince George's household. In 1710, Arbuthnot's position was still further secured both in his profession and at court: he was made a fellow of the college of physicians and was constantly with the queen. The downfall of the whigs followed the impeachment of Dr. Sacheverell, and Peter Wentworth expressed his belief that Arbuthnot was "as much heard as any that give advice now." In September, Swift came to London from Ireland, and undertook the management of the tory periodical *The Examiner;* but it is not until the following year that we find references to Arbuthnot in Swift's *Journal to Stella.* The acquaintance of Swift and Arbuthnot soon ripened into intimacy, and allusions to meetings between them, practical jokes which they perpetrated, and to the patronage which lay in Arbuthnot's way, become frequent. Arbuthnot, like Swift, may have had a hand in the attack on the Marlboroughs called *The Story of the St. Alb-n's Ghost;* but, however that may be, we know he was responsible for a series of pamphlets published, in 1712, with the object of convincing the public of the desirability of bringing to a close the war with France. The first of these pamphlets, published on 6 March, was called *Law is a Bottomless Pit, exemplified in the case of the Lord Strutt, John Bull, Nicholas Frog, and Lewis Baboon, who spent all they had in a Law Suit.* Other pamphlets, published between March and July, were called *John Bull in his Senses, John Bull still in his Senses, An Appendix to John Bull still in his Senses* and *Lewis Baboon turned Honest, and John Bull Politician.* Afterwards, these pieces were rearranged and printed in Pope and Swift's *Miscellanies* of 1727 as *The History of John Bull.* These pamphlets carried on, in their own way, the work done by Swift in his *Conduct of the Allies* and *The Examiner;* but it would appear that Arbuthnot was alone responsible for them. Arbuthnot, Pope told Spence, "was the sole writer of John Bull."

In October, Arbuthnot published an amusing pamphlet entitled *The Art of Political Lying,* and he was one of the society of tory statesmen and writers who called each other "brother" and had weekly meetings. At a dinner in April, 1713, George Berkeley, a young Irishman recently come to London, was present; afterwards, he wrote:

Dr. Arbuthnot is the first proselyte I have made of the Treatise[1] I came over to print: his wit you have an instance of in the Art of Political Lying, and in the Tracts of John Bull, of which he is the author. He is the Queen's domestic physician, and in great esteem with the whole Court, a great philosopher, and reckoned the first mathematician of the age, and has the character of uncommon virtue and probity.

Pope was introduced to Arbuthnot by Swift, in 1713, and, soon afterwards, we hear of the Scriblerus club, of which Pope, Swift and Arbuthnot, Gay, Parnell, Congreve, Lord Oxford and Atterbury were members. The wits decided to publish the *Memoirs of Scriblerus* and other pieces intended to ridicule, as Pope says, "all the false tastes in learning, under the character of a man of capacity enough, that had dipped into every art

---

[1] *Dialogue between Hylas and Philonous,* 1713.

and science, but injudiciously in each." The *Memoirs of Scriblerus* were not published until 1741; but other pieces connected with the scheme were included in the *Miscellanies* of 1727 and in *The Dunciad*.

From time to time, there were serious reports of the queen's health, and Gay, in his *Shepherd's Week*, referred to Arbuthnot as a skilful leech who had saved the queen's life. There were now serious dissensions in the ministry, Oxford struggling hard against his enemies; but, by July, Bolingbroke's friends felt sure of triumph. Oxford's fall came on 27 July, 1714; but the cabinet council which was to have met on the 29th was postponed owing to the illness of the queen. Everything that was possible was done by Arbuthnot and other doctors; but it was clear that she was sinking, and steps were taken to secure the peaceful succession of the elector of Hanover. *Fuimus tories,* was Arbuthnot's witty comment on the fall of the party. On the queen's death, he removed to Chelsea and, soon after, paid a visit to a brother in France. On his return, he took a house in Dover street, which became, as he called it, Martin's office, where old friends were always welcome.

An unmerciful attack, in 1715, on Gilbert Burnet, called *Notes and Memorandums of the six days preceding the Death of a late Right Reverend . . .* , has been attributed to Arbuthnot; but it has nothing of his characteristic style. Arbuthnot printed, in 1716, *The Humble Petition of the Colliers, Cooks, Cook-Maids, . . . and others*, and, in 1717, he had a hand in the play called *Three Hours after Marriage*, for which, however, Gay was chiefly responsible.[1] He may or may not be the author of a pamphlet called *An Account of the sickness and death of Dr. Woodward* (1719). Probably, he wrote a piece, printed in 1724, entitled *Reasons humbly offered by the Company exercising the trade and mystery of Upholders against part of the Bill for the better viewing, searching and examining of drugs, medicines, etc.* Two pieces relating to a wild boy named Peter, who had been brought to England and committed to Arbuthnot's care, are of doubtful authenticity. They are called *It cannot rain but it pours* (1725), and *The most wonderful wonder that ever appeared to the wonder of the British Nation* (1726). Arbuthnot was seriously ill in September, 1725, when Swift wrote, "If the world

[1] Cf. *ante*, p. 79.

had but a dozen Arbuthnots I would burn my Travels." Swift's visit to London, in 1726, to arrange for the publication of *Gulliver's Travels*, enabled him to see his friends, and he was introduced by Arbuthnot to the princess of Wales, shortly afterwards to become queen Caroline. After Swift's return to Ireland, Arbuthnot, who was very musical, recommended singers for the choir at St. Patrick's. In the following year, he published *Tables of Ancient Coins, Weights and Measures*, a larger version of the little book of 1705; and he was named an elect by the college of physicians, and delivered the Harveian oration. He may have contributed to *The Craftsman* in 1726–8.[1] There is no doubt he contributed to *The Variorum Dunciad* (1729); but his share cannot be identified. He may be the author of an attack on Bentley called *An account of the state of learning in the Empire of Lilliput*, and of *Critical Remarks on Capt. Gulliver's Travels, by Doctor Bantley*.

Arbuthnot's wife died in 1730, and his own health was bad; but Pope told Swift that he was unalterable in friendship and quadrille. In February, 1731, he published *A Brief Account of Mr. John Ginglicutt's Treatise, concerning the Altercation or Scolding of the Ancients*, and, later in the year, he printed a valuable medical work called *An Essay concerning the nature of Aliments*. This was followed, in 1733, by *An Essay concerning the effects of Air on Human Bodies*, and by a poem called *Know Yourself* (1734). His friends were now much troubled by his ill-health, which caused him to move to Hampstead for the sake of the air; but recovery was impossible. Pope visited his friend, and we have touching letters between Arbuthnot and Pope and Swift. In January, 1735, Pope published his *Epistle to Dr. Arbuthnot*, to whom he referred as the friend who had helped him "through this long disease, my life." Arbuthnot died on 27 February, in Cork street. Swift wrote that the death of "his friends, Gay and the Doctor, had been terrible wounds near his heart." Afterwards, Lord Chesterfield wrote of him as both his physician and his friend, entirely confided in by him in both capacities.[2] Johnson said of him, "I think Dr. Arbuthnot

---

[1] *Bolingbroke and his Times* (*The Sequel*) by Sichel, W., 1902, pp. 248 ff.; and cf. *post*, Chap. VIII.

[2] *Letters of the Earl of Chesterfield*, 1845, vol. II, p. 446.

the first man among them. He was the most universal genius, being an excellent physician, a man of deep learning and a man of much humour." Thackeray called him "one of the wisest, wittiest, most accomplished, gentlest of mankind."

A collection entitled *Miscellaneous Works of the Late Dr. Arbuthnot*, in two volumes, was published at Glasgow in 1750. Arbuthnot's son, George, inserted an advertisement in the papers, declaring that the contents "are not the works of my late father, Dr. Arbuthnot, but an imposition on the public." Some of the pieces are certainly not Arbuthnot's, and others are of doubtful authenticity; but a considerable portion are genuine, and the advertisement must be taken to mean only that the collection was unauthorised and untrustworthy. Fortunately, there is no doubt as to Arbuthnot's claim to the best of the work attributed to him, and the remainder may very well be neglected.

The History of John Bull will probably be found, nowadays, to be the most interesting of Arbuthnot's works. To enjoy it, some knowledge of the history of the time is necessary; but the allegory, as the brief sketch that follows will show, is, for the most part, transparent, and the humour is well kept up. The book begins with an account of the quarrels since the death of Charles II of Spain (Lord Strutt), who settled his estate upon his cousin Philip Baboon, to the great disappointment of his cousin Esquire South (archduke Charles of Austria). John Bull and Nicholas Frog (the Dutch) were afraid that Lord Strutt would give all his custom to his grandfather Lewis Baboon, and they threatened Lord Strutt that, if he continued to deal with his grandfather, they would go to law with him; while there were other tradesmen who were glad to join against Lewis Baboon if Bull and Frog would bear the charges of the suit. The case was put into the hands of Hocus, the attorney (the duke of Marlborough), and the decision went in favour of John Bull and his friends; but repeated promises that the next verdict would be the final determination were not fulfilled, and new trials and new difficulties continued to present themselves. Hocus proved himself superior to most of his profession:

He kept always good clerks, he loved money, was smooth tongued, gave good words, and seldom lost his temper; he was not worse than an infidel, for he provided plentifully for his family; but he loved himself better than them all. The neighbours reported that he was henpecked, which was most impossible with such a mild-spirited woman as his wife was.

John Bull was so pleased with his success that he thought of leaving off his trade and turning lawyer. John, in the main, was

an honest, plain-dealing fellow, choleric, bold, and of a very inconstant temper. . . . He was very apt to quarrel with his best friends, especially if they pretended to govern him. If you flattered him you might lead him like a child. John's temper depended very much upon the air; his spirits rose and fell with the weather-glass. John was quick and understood his business very well: but no man alive was more careless in looking into his accounts, or more cheated by partners, apprentices and servants. This was occasioned by his being a boon companion, loving his bottle and his diversion; for, to say truth, no man kept a better house than John, nor spent his money more generously.

His mania for the law was checked by his discovery of an intrigue between Hocus and Mrs. Bull, his first wife (the late whig parliament). Violent scenes ensued and, at last, Mrs. Bull was maltreated and died, leaving three daughters, Polemia, Discordia and Usuria. John at once married again (the new tory parliament). This wife was a sober country gentlewoman, who gave him good advice, urging him to bring the litigation to an end. When he looked through his attorney's bill, he was shocked at its length, and discovered that he had been egregiously cheated, and that the whole burden of the lawsuit had been thrown upon his shoulders. The other tradesmen abused Mrs. Bull, and said that their interests were sacrificed.

The second of the series of pamphlets begins with the discovery of a paper by the first Mrs. Bull containing a vindication of the duty of unfaithfulness incumbent upon wives in cases of infidelity of their husbands. This, of course, is a satire on the disloyalty of whigs. Then, Diego (earl of Nottingham) had an interview with the second Mrs. Bull, in the hope of satisfying her that John must not desert his friends; but she showed that Nick Frog had been deceiving John and endeavouring to make a private arrangement with Lewis Baboon. The guardians of

Bull's three daughters (the whig leaders) came to John and urged that the lawsuit should be continued; but John told them that he knew when he was ill-used; that he was aware how his family were apt to throw away their money in their cups; but that it was an unfair thing to take advantage of his weakness and make him set his hand to papers when he could hardly hold his pen.

The third pamphlet relates to John Bull's mother (the church of England), and his sister Peg (the Scottish church) and her love affair with Jack (presbyterianism). The mother was of a meek spirit, and strictly virtuous. She always put the best construction on the words and actions of her neighbours; she was neither a prude nor a fantastic old belle. John's sister was a poor girl who had been starved as nurse. John had all the good bits: his sister had only a little oatmeal or a dry crust; he had lain in the best apartments with his bedchamber towards the south; she had lodged in a garret exposed to the north wind; but she had life and spirit in abundance and knew when she was ill-used. The pamphlet ends with a letter from Nick Frog to John Bull urging him to mortgage his estate, and with an account of a conference between Bull, Frog, South and Lewis Baboon at the Salutation tavern (congress of Utrecht). The fourth part of *John Bull* is concerned, to some extent, with Jack and the bill against occasional conformity; and the fifth and last part refers to the meetings at the Salutation inn and the intrigues of the various tradesmen. John had interviews, with Nick Frog and Lewis Baboon about Ecclesdown castle (Dunkirk) and other matters, and the lawsuit was brought to an end with John in possession of Ecclesdown, to his great satisfaction.

Arbuthnot's masterpiece owed something to Swift's *Tale of a Tub*, published eight years earlier; but the plot in Swift's book is very slight, and there was nothing in the past history of satire to correspond to the clearly drawn characters and the well developed story designed to promote certain views on public policy in the minds of the people, which are to be found in *John Bull*.

The Art of Political Lying is a delightful skit, "like those pamphlets called 'The Works of the Learned.'" Political lying is the "art of convincing the people of salutary falsehoods, for some good end." A lie, it is suggested, is best contradicted by another lie; if it be said that a great person is dying, the answer should be, not that he is in perfect health, but that he is slowly recovering. One chapter of the promised treatise was to be an enquiry, which of the two parties are the greatest political liars. In both are to be found great geniuses; but they are prone to glut the market with lies. Heads of parties are warned against believing their own lies; all parties have been subject to this misfortune, due to too great a zeal in the practice of the art. There are many forms of political lies: the additory, the detractory, the translatory, which transfers the merit of a man's good action, or the demerit of a man's bad action, to another.

When one ascribes anything to a person which does not belong to him, the lie ought to be calculated not quite contradictory to his known quality. For example, one would not make the French king present at a Protestant conventicle, nor the Dutch paying more than their quota.

The wit of this *jeu d'esprit* is worthy of Swift at his best, and the method of gravely asserting impossible things and arguing from those assertions is often to be found in Swift's work. The style, too, has the vigorous and idiomatic character of Swift's, and there is abundance of humour.

The *Memoirs of Martinus Scriblerus*, of which we have only the first book, is a curious collection of satires on the learned; it contains much wit, but a good deal of the satire cannot be understood without considerable knowledge of metaphysics and medicine. The earlier part of the work, which relates to the parentage and bringing-up of Scriblerus, gave many hints to Sterne for his account of Tristram Shandy and his father. Martin was born at Münster, the son of a learned gentleman, Cornelius, by profession an antiquary. When the child was born, his father remembered that the cradle of Hercules was a shield, and, finding an antique buckler, he determined that the child should be laid on it and brought into the study and shown to learned men; but the maid-servant, having regard to her reputation for cleanliness, scoured the shield and, in so doing, showed that a certain prominency, on which the antiquaries had speculated, was nothing but the head of a nail. The nurse was indignant at the father's views about the proper food for the

infant and about its early education.   He found an assistant
in a boy called Crambe, who had a great store of words and
composed a treatise on syllogisms.   Martin had the Greek
alphabet stamped on his gingerbread, played games after the
manner of the ancients and wore a geographical suit of clothes.
Afterwards, he became a critic, practised medicine, studied the
diseases of the mind, and endeavoured to find out the seat of
the soul.   Then, he went on his travels, and visited the countries mentioned in *Gulliver's Travels*.

The *Memoirs of Scriblerus* were printed in the second volume
of Pope's prose works (1741), with a note from the booksellers
to the reader which stated that the *Memoirs*, and all the tracts
in the same name, were written by Pope and Arbuthnot,
"except the *Essay on the Origin of Sciences*, in which Parnell
had some hand, as had Gay in the *Memoirs of a Parish Clerk*,
while the rest were Pope's."   There cannot, however, be any
doubt that the *Memoirs* are wholly, or almost wholly, by
Arbuthnot, though suggestions were probably made by his
friends; Pope's earlier editors admitted that the knowledge of
medicine and philosophy displayed marked many of the chapters as the work of "the Doctor."   "To talk of Martin," wrote
Swift to Arbuthnot, "in any hands but yours is folly.   For you
every day give us better hints than all of us together could do in
a twelvemonth."

The *Memoirs* abound in wit, and are written with delightful
gravity; but some modern readers will find an element of truth
in Johnson's judgment that the absence of more of the *Memoirs*
need not be lamented, for the follies ridiculed were hardly
practised: "It has been little read, or when read has been forgotten, as no man could be wiser, better or merrier by remem-
bering it."   Arbuthnot's work was at its best when (as in *John
Bull*) he was dealing with matters of the world of action.   In
the *Memoirs of Scriblerus*, he attacked follies which, for the
most part, though not wholly, were obsolete; and, though this
criticism applies, also, to some of the matter in Sterne's*Tristram
Shandy*, yet the later humorist dealt with a wider field, which
embraced much besides Mr. Shandy's peculiarities, and he had
a love for his characters which makes them live, and prevented
him from allowing them to become grotesque.

Of the minor pieces connected with the Scriblerus scheme,

the chief is *An Essay concerning the Origin of Sciences* (1732), in which Pope claimed some share.   In this humorous piece, the inhabitants of India, Greece and Italy are said to have derived their knowledge from men-monkeys, the descendants of the original Ethiopians, with whom the gods conversed.   The design, wrote Pope, was "to ridicule such as build general assertions upon two or three loose quotations from the ancients." *Virgilius Restauratus* contains some amusing emendations in ridicule of Bentley, probably contributed by various members of the club, but chiefly by Arbuthnot.   *A Brief Account of Mr. John Ginglicutt's Treatise concerning the Altercation or Scolding of the Ancients* (1731), as Pope said, is of little value; its object was to satirise the practice of political opponents in applying to each other the language of Billingsgate, by showing that this sort of altercation is ancient and classical, while what is commonly considered polite is barbarous.

Arbuthnot's principal medical works are *An Essay concerning the nature of Aliments* (1731) and *An Essay concerning the effect of Air on Human Bodies* (1733).   In the first of these books, both of which may be read with interest by laymen, he argued that all that is done by medicine might be done equally well by diet.   Sir Benjamin Richardson, who has called the second work "one of the most remarkable books in the literature of medicine," says that Arbuthnot was far in advance of his age in medical science, and made some remarkable discoveries.   *An Essay on the Usefulness of Mathematical Learning* (1701) is an admirable and well reasoned paper, with some good suggestions respecting the study of mathematics.

Two other serious writings may be mentioned briefly.   *A Sermon preached to the People at the Mercat Cross of Edinburgh* (1706) was in defence of the union with England, then under discussion.   The text was "Better is he that laboureth and aboundeth in all things, than he that boasteth himself and wanteth bread."   Arbuthnot's countrymen were urged, in this wise and moderate paper, to pocket their pride, and take the benefits that the union offered to them.   "I have set before you to-day, on one hand, industry and riches; on the other, pride and poverty"; it was the interest of all classes in Scotland to accept the offer of a partnership in the great blessings

which England could bestow. The other piece, ΓΝΩΘΙ
ΣΕΑΥΤΟΝ *Know Yourself* (1734), is Arbuthnot's sole poem.
In this earnest study, probably his last work, he described the
principles of his own life.   Divine truth made clear his way,
encouraging him with the revelation of his high descent.

> In vain thou hop'st for bliss on this poor clod,
> Return, and seek thy father, and thy God:
> Yet think not to regain thy native sky,
> Borne on the wings of vain philosophy;
> Mysterious passage! hid from human eyes;
> Soaring you 'll sink, and sinking you will rise;
> Let humble thoughts thy wary footsteps guide,
> Regain by meekness what you lost by pride.

There seems to be no evidence that Arbuthnot knew William
King; but King was a tory, used his wit in the interests of the
party and was acquainted with Swift and Gay.   If Arbuthnot
and King met, they must have had a good deal in common,
besides easy-going temperaments.   King was born in 1663,
and was educated at Westminster and Christ Church, Oxford,
where he took his degree of D.C.L. in 1692.   (He should not be
confused either with Dr. William King, archbishop of Dublin,
or with Dr. William King, of St. Mary hall, Oxford, who wrote
The Toast.)   His first noticeable piece was an amusing *Dialogue
showing the way to Modern Preferment* (1690).   He became an
advocate at Doctors' Commons and secretary to princess Anne,
and joined Charles Boyle in the campaign against Bentley, in
the very clever *Dialogues of the Dead*, and other pieces.   Other
amusing works were *A Journey to London in the year* 1698, in
which King burlesqued a book on Paris written by Martin
Lister, and *The Transactioner, with some of his philosophical
Fancies* (1700), in which he ridiculed Sir Hans Sloane, editor
of the *Transactions of the Royal Society*.   King was given several posts in Ireland, where he wrote a poem, *Molly of Mountown*, on a cow whose milk he used; but he returned to England
about 1707, with straitened means.   He had already issued a
volume of *Miscellanies in Prose and Verse*, dedicated to the
members of the Beef-Steak club, which contains much of his
best work.   A clever poem was published, in 1708, under the
title *The Art of Cookery, in imitation of Horace's Art of Poetry,*

and, in 1709, he printed three parts of *Useful Transactions in Philosophy and other sorts of Learning*, a skit on the *Philosophical Transactions* and on Sloane, which may have furnished hints to Arbuthnot when writing the *Memoirs of Scriblerus*.

King wrote on the side of the high church party in the Sacheverell controversy, and attacked Marlborough in *Rufinus* (1712). He seems to have been an inmate of the Fleet prison; but Swift obtained for the "poor starving wit" the post of gazetteer, an office which he resigned in six months because, apparently, it required too much work, and regular hours. His last piece of importance was *Useful Miscellanies, Part the First* (1712), a curious but amusing compilation. A few months later, he died. His writings, which were edited by the indefatigable John Nichols in 1776, deserve to be better known than they now are.

Literary criticism at the end of the seventeenth century owed much to Boileau and Rapin, who pleaded for "good sense" and urged the wisdom of following classical models. Thomas Rymer, born in 1641, the son of a Yorkshire roundhead, published, in 1674, a translation of Rapin's *Reflections on Aristotle's Treatise of Poesie*, and wrote a play, *Edgar, or the English Monarch* (1678), in accordance with classical laws. But his principal literary work was *The Tragedies of the Last Age considered and examined by the Practice of the Ancients, and by the Common Sense of all Ages* (1678), in which he examined three of Beaumont and Fletcher's plays, and *Paradise Lost*. These pieces he found to be "as rude as our architecture." Both the poetry and Gothic architecture were condemned because they were not based on classical models. Rime he defended against the "slender sophistry" in *Paradise Lost*, "which some are pleased to call a poem." Dryden, in the preface to *All for Love* (1678), said that he had here endeavoured to follow the practice of the ancients, "who, as Mr. Rymer has judiciously observed, are, and ought to be, our masters." In order, however, to imitate Shakespeare in his style, he disencumbered himself of rime: "Not that I condemn my former way, but that this is more proper to my present purpose." In 1692, Rymer published (with the date 1693 on the title-page), *A short View of Tragedy: Its original excellency and corruption, with some reflections on Shakespeare and other practitioners for the stage;* in which he proved his incompetence as a critic by expressing contempt for Shakespeare's tragedies.   Dryden's criticism, said Johnson, "has the majesty of a queen; Rymer's has the ferocity of a tyrant."   In a letter to Dennis,[1] Dryden said that our comedy was far beyond anything of the ancients;

and notwithstanding our irregularities, so is our Tragedy.   Shakespeare had a genius for it; and we know (in spite of Mr. Rymer) that genius alone is a greater virtue (if I may so call it) than all other qualifications put together. . . . Who will read Mr. Rymer, or not read Shakespeare?   For my own part, I reverence Mr. Rymer's learning, but I detest his ill-nature and his arrogance.

But the preaching of "common sense" and of the need of laws in writing was a useful work, and, if Rymer is full of extravagances, he was at least qualified by his learning to discuss the practice of the ancients.   Spence says that Pope thought him generally right, though unduly severe on some of the plays he criticised.[2]   Rymer devoted the later years of his life to historical work, and we owe him a great debt for *Foedera*, fifteen volumes of which appeared before his death in 1713.

Gerard Langbaine, son of the provost of Queen's college, Oxford, of the same name, is known chiefly by his *Account of the English Dramatic Poets*, 1691.   Langbaine frequented the theatre and collected plays, and had already published, in 1687–8, catalogues of plays, with notes concerning the sources of the plots.   His passion for discovering plagiarisms annoyed Dryden and others, but his work was scholarly and is still sometimes useful.   A new edition of his book was brought out by Charles Gildon in 1699, under the title *The Lives and Characters of the English Dramatic Poets*.   The name Gildon, a hack writer on the whig side, is familiar to posterity because Pope wrote of his "venal quill."   He is described by a contemporary as of "great literature and mean genius."   Neither his critical nor his dramatic work is of value; but he wrote an entertaining book, *A Comparison between the Two Stages* (1702), in which, in dialogue forms, he discussed the plays and players of the day.

---

[1] *Select Works of Mr. John Dennis*, 1718, vol. ii., p. 504.
[2] Cf., as to Rymer, *ante*, Vol. VIII., p. 220, and, as to him and Jeremy Collier, see *ibid.*, p. 186.

Some interesting critical views are expressed in a letter to Prior (1721) on one of his tragedies, in which Gildon says that to move the passions is the chief excellence in that way of writing, and so allowed to be by all ages but the present, when critics had arisen who made diction or language the chief mark of a good or bad tragedy, and such a diction as, though correct, was scarcely tolerable in this way of writing; "for tragedy, consisting of the representation of different passions, must, of necessity, vary its style according to the nature of each passion which it brings on the stage."[1]   Gildon's *Life and Strange Surprizing Adventures of Mr. D— De F—, of London, Hosier,* "who has lived above fifty years by himself, in the kingdoms of North and South Britain" (1719) is an interesting pamphlet on the new romance of *Robinson Crusoe,* which shows that the authorship of that work was no secret to some, at least, of Defoe's contemporaries.   Gildon's charges of inconsistencies in *Robinson Crusoe* are sometimes without foundation.

One of the best known critics of his time was the redoubtable John Dennis.   Dennis had the advantage of an education at Harrow and Cambridge, of early travel in France and Italy and of the company, in his earlier days, of many men of culture. His plays are noticed elsewhere,[2] and it is not necessary to give details of his quarrels with Pope, Steele, Addison and others. His later criticisms are marred by pedantry and abuse, but there is often real merit in his work.[3]   He answered Collier's attack on the stage with two pamphlets, intended to be "a vindication of the stage, and not of the corruptions or the abuses of it," and, in 1701, published *The Advancement and Reformation of Modern Poetry: a Critical Discourse,* which was followed, in 1704, by *The Grounds of Criticism in Poetry.   An Essay on the Operas after the Italian Manner* (1706), was directed against the growth of effeminacy.   *An Essay on the Genius and Writings of Shakespeare* (1712), contains some excellent passages, but, for the most part, shows the writer's inability to understand or appreciate his subject.   Shakespeare, he says, had great qualities by nature, but he made gross mistakes: "If he had had

---

[1] *Calendar of Manuscripts of the Marquis of Bath,* Hist. MSS. Comm., 1908, vol. iii., p. 496.

[2] *Ante,* Vol. VIII, p. 219.

[3] See *John Dennis.   His Life and Criticism,* by Paul, H. G., New York, 1911.

the advantage of art and learning, he would have surpassed the very best and strongest of the Ancients." The poetical justice of which he was so fond he often missed in Shakespeare, and he regretted that the crowd in *Julius Cæsar* showed "want of art." His favourite views are indicated on the title-page of *The Advancement and Reformation of Modern Poetry* (1701), which is in two parts,

the first, showing that the principal reason why the Ancients excelled the Moderns in the greater poetry, was because they mixed religion with poetry. The second, proving that by joining poetry with the religion revealed to us in Sacred Writ, the modern poets might come to equal the Ancients.

The answer to the question why he preferred *Oedipus* to *Julius Cæsar*, is, says Dennis, "first, the *Oedipus* is exactly just and regular, and the *Julius Cæsar* is very extravagant and irregular: secondly, the *Oedipus* is very religious, and the *Julius Cæsar* is irreligious."

"Every tragedy," he adds, "ought to be a very solemn lecture, inculcating a particular Providence, and showing it plainly protecting the good, and chastizing the bad, or at least the violent. . . . If it is otherwise, it is either an empty amusement, or a scandalous and pernicious libel upon the government of the world."[1]

The same views are repeated in *The Grounds of Criticism in Poetry*. Poetry, he says, had fallen to a low level, because of ignorance of the rules by which poets ought to proceed.

If the end of poetry be to instruct and reform the world, that is, to bring mankind from irregularity, extravagance and confusion, to rule and order, how this should be done by a thing that is in itself irregular and extravagant is difficult to be conceived.[2]

One of the most entertaining as well as useful books of the first half of the eighteenth century is *An Apology for the Life of Mr. Colley Cibber, Comedian*, 1740; but of this mention has already been made in a previous chapter, in connection with Cibber's earlier plays.[3] In 1730, Cibber was made poet

---

[1] See "Epistle dedicatory" to *The Advancement*, etc.
[2] As to Dennis's own plays, see *ante*. Vol. VIII, p. 219.
[3] See *ibid.*, pp. 200–201.

laureate, an appointment which furnished material for the wits who attacked him.   From the time that Pope substituted Cibber for Theobald as hero of the *Dunciad*, Cibber has been constantly misrepresented as being a dunce, whereas his plays are amusing, and he is an admirable dramatic critic.   His worst fault was inordinate vanity; but this, to some extent, was carried off by the liveliness of his disposition.   Johnson was not friendly to Cibber, but he admitted that *An Apology* was "very well done," and Horace Walpole calls it "inimitable."   The book is admirable as an autobiography, because it displays the whole character of the writer; the criticism is intelligent and well informed; and the style is bright and amusing.

John Hughes, born in 1677, collected materials for the first two volumes of a *History of England* (1706), which is generally known as White Kennett's, who wrote the third volume.   He translated Fontenelle's *Dialogues of the Dead* and wrote an opera; and, in 1715, he published *The Works of Mr. Edmund Spenser . . . with a glossary explaining the old and obscure words*.   This, the first attempt at a critical edition of Spenser, appeared at a time when there was some wish in the air for relief from the rimed couplet.   Prior, in the preface to *Solomon*, said, "He that writes in rhymes, dances in fetters"; and he had real respect for Spenser, though he considered the verse of the older writers "too dissolute and wild."   But, to Spenser's first editor, his stanza seemed "defective" and his general composition "monstrous."   Hughes's own verse is of no importance; reference has been already made to his one tragedy, *The Siege of Damascus* (1720), which has some merit, and was very successful;[1] but the author died on the night of its production.   Johnson says that Hughes was "not only an honest but a pious man."   Swift and Pope agreed that he was among the mediocrities in prose as well as verse, and that he was too grave for them.   Hughes had written for *The Tatler* and *The Spectator*, and Steele, in *The Theatre*, said that his pen was always engaged in raising the mind to what was noble and virtuous.

A word must be added here as to several other editors of English classics, to some of whom reference is made also in other chapters of this work.   Nicholas Rowe has been previously treated, both as a dramatist[2] and as the producer, in

[1] See *ante*, Vol. VIII, p. 220.   [2] See *ibid.*, pp. 221–223.

1709, of the first edition of Shakespeare that can in any way be called critical.[1]   His chief service in the latter capacity lay in his preserving, in the "Life" which he prefixed to the plays, information, derived largely from Betterton, which might otherwise have been forgotten.   To subsequent editions of Shakespeare belonging to this period, it is unnecessary again to refer.[2]

To Warburton's edition (1747), Thomas Edwards, a barrister who devoted most of his time to literature, published a *Supplement*, which, in the third edition (1748), was called *The Canons of Criticism, and a Glossary*, "being a supplement to Mr. Warburton's edition of Shakespeare, collected from the notes in that celebrated work, and proper to be bound up with it." *The Canons* are satirical, with illustrations from Edwards's victim; *e.g.*, a critic "has a right to alter any passage which he does not understand"; "He may explain a difficult passage by words absolutely unintelligible." Johnson compared Edwards's attack to a fly stinging a stately horse; but, as Warton says, the attack was allowed "by all impartial critics to have been decisive and judicious." Warburton retorted in notes to *The Dunciad*.   Edwards died in 1757, at Samuel Richardson's house.   His *Canons of Criticism* went through many editions.

Benjamin Heath, a town clerk of Exeter, with literary tastes, published notes on the Greek dramatists, and, in 1765, *A Revisal of Shakespeare's Text*, "wherein the alterations introduced into it by the more modern editors and critics are particularly considered." Heath attacked Pope, Hanmer and Warburton, but agreed that the public was under real obligations to Theobald.   He himself was not so fortunate as to be furnished with the Shakespeare folios, still less the quartos; but he concluded that all readings deserving of attention were given by Pope or Theobald.   Some of his annotations were included in a collection published in 1819.   Among the manuscripts which he left unpublished on his death, in 1766, were notes (used by Dyce) on Beaumont and Fletcher's plays.

John Upton, rector of Great Rissington and prebendary of Rochester, edited Epictetus and Spenser's *Faerie Queene* (1758), and published *Critical Observations on Shakespeare* (1746).   In the Spenser, old spelling was preserved, and the notes were

---

numerous and learned. There had been a preliminary *Letter concerning a new edition of Spenser's Faerie Queene* (1751), in which Upton spoke contemptuously of Hughes and Pope as editors, and said that his edition of Spenser had been undertaken at Gilbert West's advice. In a preface to the second edition of *Critical Observations on Shakespeare*, Upton replied to and attacked Warburton.

Another clergyman of literary tastes, Zachary Grey, rector of Houghton Conquest, Bedfordshire, wrote much on church questions, but is mentioned here because of his edition of *Hudibras*, "with large annotations and a preface," which appeared in 1744, with illustrations by Hogarth. The text was explained by plentiful quotations from puritan and other contemporaries. Warburton rendered some help, which he apparently thought was not sufficiently acknowledged; for, in his *Shakespeare*, he said that he doubted whether "so execrable a heap of nonsense had ever appeared in any learned language as Grey's commentaries on *Hudibras*." A *Supplement* to Grey's valuable work, with further notes, appeared in 1752. Grey attacked Warburton in several pamphlets, and charged his antagonist with passing off Hanmer's work as his own. In 1754, Grey published *Critical, Historical and Explanatory Notes on Shakespeare*. He died in 1766.

The notice of the criticisms which followed on the work of the first editors of Shakespeare has taken us rather far into the eighteenth century; and later critics must be left to another volume.

CHAPTER VI

Lesser Verse Writers

I

JOHNSON, who seems to have disliked Prior for more reasons than one, spoke of his "obscure original." The poet's father, George Prior, was a joiner at Eastbrook in Wimborne, Dorset, where Matthew was born on 21 July, 1664. His parents were presbyterians who, in 1662, became nonconformists. Wimborne is famed for its collection of chained books, and one of these, Ralegh's *History of the World*, has a circular hole burned with a heated skewer through a hundred pages or so. Some local worthy invented the incredible tale that the damage was caused by a spark from a taper used by young Matthew while diligently reading this monumental work. The elder Prior came to London when his son was a boy, attracted by the prosperity of his brother Samuel, host first of the Rhenish tavern, Channel row, and afterwards (by 1688 at latest), of the Rummer tavern in Charing Cross. Another kinsman, Arthur Prior, who died in 1687, and left the poet £100, seems also to have been a vintner and may have succeeded Samuel at the Rhenish tavern. At one of these houses of resort, Matthew appears to have been apprentice, probably at the last mentioned. There, he was by chance found reading Horace by the earl of Dorset, of whom he always retained the most grateful remembrance.[1] His skill in verse rendering attracted the attention of the Dorset circle. At the earl's suggestion, he was sent to Westminster in 1680; next year, he

[1] Prior's *Dedication* of his *Poems* (1718) to Dorset's son and successor contains a character of the father which, though written in a panegyrical strain, may be described as one of the happiest tributes of the kind extant.

became a king's scholar, and passed under the immediate care of Busby, who, his "little birch" in hand, had fostered the juvenile talent of Dryden and Locke, as well as of South, Atterbury and a score of other bishops. At Westminster, his chief friends were Charles Montague, afterwards earl of Halifax, and his brother, James Montague; objecting to be separated from these confederates, Prior incurred the disapproval of his patron by refusing to go to Christ Church and entering, instead, as a scholar at St. John's college, Cambridge, in April, 1683. To his school and college, and to his university, he always remained conspicuously loyal.[1] In 1686, he took his bachelor's degree, and in the following year joined with Charles Montague in writing *The Hind and the Panther Transvers'd to the Story of the Country and the City Mouse*.[2] The form of this slight piece is copied from Buckingham's *Rehearsal*, which contains the originals of the poet Bayes and those "languishing gentlemen" Smith and Johnson. In *The Rehearsal*, Bayes takes them to the repetition of his latest rimed tragedy. Here, he makes them listen to as much as they can bear of his new poem in defence of the church of Rome. Some of the incongruities in Dryden's fable, and one or two incidental mistakes, are effectively twitted, and Dryden's method of argument (which abhors "knotty reasonings" as "too barbarous for my stile") is rather happily hit off. But the point of the jest— that Dryden's moral change will not always keep pace with his formal conversion—

Such was I—such, by nature still I am—

is but a sorry kind of personality. Prior seems to have indulged a *pique* against Dryden, which does not sit well on the lesser poet.[3] While Dryden left this attack without any effective retort, Pope avenged his injured fellow Catholics on Montague in his *Epistle to Arbuthnot* (where Montague figures as Bufo).

[1] His poems contain more than one recognition of the fact that
                    St. John's was founded in a Woman's Name.
Cf. especially, vol. ii, of Waller's edition of *The Writings of Matthew Prior* (Cambridge English Classics, 1905–7). For Prior's active interest in the university and its press, when he was in the midst of public affairs, see *The History of His Own Time*, p. 167 *et ai.* As to Westminster school, cf. *Longleat Papers.*
[2] Cf. *ante*, Vol. VIII, p. 53.
[3] Cf. *A Satire on the Modern Translators* (pp. 48–9) and *A Session of the Poets* (p. 299), in vol. ii, of Waller's edn., p. 278.

In 1688, Prior was chosen a fellow of St. John's, and blossomed forth in *An Ode*, written as a college "exercise" on the text "I am that I am." The poem, which, in accordance with custom, was sent to the earl of Exeter, in acknowledgment of a benefaction bestowed upon the college by one of his ancestors, seems to have recommended Prior to the notice of the family, as his verses in the Strephon vein *To the Countess of Exeter, Playing on the Lute*, and his lines *Picture* (at Burleigh House) *of Seneca dying in a Bath*, indicate.

Some recently discovered verses by Prior show that, in the reign of James II, he adhered to the side of the court, without suggesting that there was much depth in his loyalty.[1] At the revolution, he was thrown upon his own resources, and, not unnaturally, appealed to his earliest patron, Dorset, by sending *An Epistle to Fleetwood Shephard*, the *fidus Achates* of that nobleman. His reputation as a satirist would appear to have served him in good stead, for, although the other mouse was advanced first, Prior had not to wait long. During the winter of 1690–91, he obtained an appointment in the English embassy at the Hague, the meeting place of the coalition against Louis XIV organised by William of Orange. Prior was secretary to Lord Dursley, envoy extraordinary and plenipotentiary (in whose wife's copy of Milton he inscribed an extravagant compliment, repeated from one which he had previously paid to Lady Dorset[2]); and the envoy's gout gave the young attaché many opportunities of personal converse with William. His readiness caused the king to bestow on him, besides the half-serious nickname "*Secrétaire du Roy*," the appointment of gentleman of the king's bedchamber. He began to send contributions to Dryden's *Miscellanies*, taking care to publish loyal poems both in pindaric style and in a lighter vein. In 1693, he prepared, for the music of Purcell and the delectation of their majesties, a new year's *Hymn to the Sun*, and, in 1695, he was persuaded to take a conspicuous place in the group of bards who, in a black-framed folio, mourned "Dread Maria's Universal Fall." His diplomatic *Ode Presented to the King on his*

---

[1] See *Advice to the Painter, upon the defeat of the Rebels in the West*, etc., and *To the Bishop of Rochester* (Sprat) *upon his Account of the Rye-house Plot* (Waller, vol. ii, pp. 289–93). The queer stanzas *Orange* (*ibid.* 310–11) illustrate his transition.

[2] Waller, vol. i, pp. 15–16.

Majesty's Arrival in Holland after The Queen's death is in ballad-metre of eight and eight. In the same metre, he cast, also in 1695, *An English Ballad On the Taking of Namur By the King of Great Britain*, a sufficient taking off and down of the *Ode sur la Prise De Namur* by the Boileau *gloriosus* of 1692. A solemn congratulation in heroic couplets *To the King, at his Arrival in Holland, after the Discovery of the Conspiracy*, followed in 1696. On the other hand, in *The Secretary*, written at the Hague in the same year, we get the first real touch of the true quality of Prior's muse, describing, in the anapaestic metre which he may be said to have perfected, the jocund progress of the *"Englischen Heer Secretaris"* to a week-end holiday:

> In a little Dutch-chaise on a Saturday night,
> On my left hand my Horace, a Nymph on my right . . .
> For her, neither visits, nor parties of tea,
> Nor the long-winded cant of a dull refugee.

In 1697, came peace with the treaty of Ryswyk. Prior acted as secretary during the negotiations, and, for a long time, in consequence of intervals between the plenipotentiaryships of Portland, Jersey and Manchester, was virtually in charge. Sir William Trumbull complimented him on his happy blend of poetry and business; but he was not compensated by this for his lack of pay and definite prospect. He felt aggrieved that he was not sent envoy to Nancy on the occasion of the duke of Lorraine's marriage, and would have now been glad to get back to London; but he was kept until November, 1699, at Paris, where he did useful service and whence he wrote highly diverting letters, mixing *persiflage* with politics.[1]

[1] The Hague congress of 1690 is the actual starting-point of a volume published in 1740 by Prior's former secretary and executor Adrian Drift, under the title *The History of His Own Time by Matthew Prior*, and professing to be compiled from his own manuscripts. It is a piece of book-making extraordinary, containing, with a few original letters to and from Prior (which become rather more numerous in the last part of the book), a few state-papers that may, at the time, have been otherwise inaccessible, and more that were already public property. Prior's *Journal at the Court of France from* 31 *August to* 23 *October,* 1714, is a mere official diary kept by Drift for his chief; on the other hand, the *Account of* (Prior's) *Examination before the Committee of Council* (1713) is graphic and clear, and full of lively personal touches, illustrating the foolish and passionate behaviour of some members of the committee (including Lord Coningsby), who were angered by Prior's mingled freedom and reticence, and the annoyance of Walpole and

In 1699, Prior was made an under-secretary of state, and, during the latter part of this year, carried on an arduous series of services, including journeys to and from Paris, in connection with the second partition treaty. In December,[1] he produced his most elaborate "pindaric" ode, *Carmen Seculare for the year 1700, "To the King,"* eulogising William III through forty-two wearisome stanzas, and comparing him to the sun whose sacred light the poet contrasts with the arbitrary blaze of comets and meteors. Honours accumulated upon the poetic official. The university of Cambridge made him an honorary M.A., and he succeeded Locke as a commissioner of trade and plantations. Later in this year, the earl of Manchester was transferred from Venice to Paris, and Prior returned home with Jersey (who had been named one of the secretaries of state and whose *protégé* Prior now was), to serve under him. In the earlier part of 1701, before Louis XIV irritated the national pride by his recognition of James III and alarmed the city by his plain bid for Spanish trade, a parliamentary storm burst over the partition treaties and culminated in the impeachment of the whig lords, Portland and Oxford, Somers and Halifax, who had been in power during the negotiations. Prior, who was now, for a brief space (February to June, 1701), member for East Grinstead voted for the impeachment. Naturally enough, he was accused of treachery; but he was already showing himself a prerogative and high church man; and, under Anne, he gradually detached himself from his old whig allies in order to act with the tory chiefs Harley and St. John. During the early part of Anne's reign, we hear little of him save occasional poems and celebrations of English victories and an appeal to Godolphin to settle his debts (£500) and procure him employment abroad. But, meanwhile, he was cultivating his gift of trifling in verse, and producing, among short *fabliaux*, epigrams and multifarious matter, such little gems as the stanzas, Sir Walter Scott's

---

Stanhope, conveyed by telegraphic frowns. Prior's *Answer to the Report of the Committee of Secresy, appointed by Order of the House of Commons* contains an important argument in support of the conduct of the first stage of the peace negotiations without the cognisance of the allies; but is a fragment only. Some of the early events of the war are narrated at length by Drift, on the plea that Prior wrote poems about them. The whole compilation has small historical or biographical, and less literary, value.

[1] Cf. Drift, *u.s.* p. 144.

favourite, *Written in the Beginning of Mezeray's History of France*:

> Yet for the fame of all these Deeds,
> What Beggar in the *Invalides*
>   With Lameness broke, with Blindness smitten,
> Wished ever decently to die,
> To have been either Mezeray,
>   Or any Monarch He has written?

He writes formal odes to the queen, twits, not very worthily, his fellow panegyrist Boileau with the victory of Blenheim—

> Since, hir'd for Life, Thy servile Muse must sing
> Successive conquests, and a glorious King—

and gains increasing mastery over the heroic couplet, as may be seen by *An Ode Inscribed to the Memory of the Honourable Colonel George Villiers*, accidentally drowned in a river near Friuli in 1703—which contains some of his finest lines, beginning:

> Some from the stranded Vessel force their **Way**:
> Fearful of Fate, they meet it in the Sea:
> Some who escape the Fury of the Wave,
> Sicken on Earth, and sink into a Grave.

After Blenheim came Ramillies, to which, in *An Ode Humbly Subscrib'd to the Queen*, Prior, as he says, went out of his way to pay the tribute of some—not very successful—Spenserian stanzas. But, in 1707, he was compelled by the whig leaders to give up his public employment, and was imperfectly consoled by a secretaryship to the bishop of Winchester. In 1709, he published a first collection of his verse writings, which he describes as the product of his leisure hours, as he was only a poet by accident. Next year, upon the fall of the whigs, he joined Swift, Freind and others, under the *aegis* of St. John, in setting up *The Examiner*, in which he wrote an early paper.[1] His *Fable from Phaedrus* also appeared here. He soon came into

---

[1] No. 6, ridiculing some verses by Garth to Godolphin. Addison answered him in *The Whig Examiner*. Both pieces are printed by Drift, p. 318, and with Prior's *Two Riddles* and Addison's *Solution*, leave a feeble impression.

frequent contact with Swift, of not a few of whose lampoons he
had the first credit among their friends. Prior, who had been
expelled from the Kitcat club in 1707, was now hailed as one
of the seventeen "brothers," who formed an intimate tory club
under that name. A more substantial recognition soon followed, when, his unusual proficiency in languages having been
noted by St. John, he was made a commissioner of customs.
In March, 1711, he celebrated Harley's escape from the knife
of the assassin, and before and afterwards eulogised the minister
in various strains of verse.[1] In June of this year, he was sent
across the water to notify England's preliminary demands. On
his return, accompanied by the two French agents, Mesnager
and Gaultier, he was arrested at Canterbury by mistake. In
September, Swift brought out a fanciful relation of Prior's
journey by which the plenipotentiary's vanity was much
incensed. Frequent secret conferences about the conditions
of peace now took place—the first at Prior's house on 20 September. He was nominated plenipotentiary in November;
but, to appease the offended pride of Lord Strafford, another
of the plenipotentiaries, the appointment was cancelled. In
August, 1712, however, Prior went to France with Bolingbroke,
and was raised to the position of ambassador, though he did
not assume the title until Shrewsbury's return in the following
year. He was equally popular with Anne and Louis and
managed a personal correspondence between them.[2] The
peace was signed in April, 1713, and Prior lingered on in Paris, a
prey to intense uneasiness as to the future of his party, and as
to his own. He was in the midst of an ode imploring a gift of
Anne's portrait when the news of her death reached him. He
was at once deprived of his commissionership. In due course,
the earl of Stair, who had been appointed ambassador in Prior's
place, arrived and impounded such of his papers as he had not
previously secured. When, after his salary (as plenipotentiary)
and debts had been paid, he returned to England, in March,
1715, he was arrested by order of the Commons, and, in June,
impeached and handed over to the custody of the serjeant at
arms. Nothing incriminating either Bolingbroke or Oxford
could be extracted from him, and, after two years of detention,

[1] *Erle Robert's Mice*, "in Chaucer's Stile," is not the happiest of these.
[2] Drift, *u.s.* p. 377.

he was released in 1717. During his confinement, he wrote his second-longest poem, called *Alma: or, the Progress of the Mind.* To ease his pecuniary difficulties, his friends Arbuthnot, Gay and others, but especially Lords Harley and Bathurst, devised the plan of printing his poems in a sumptuous folio, three feet by one. All the notabilities subscribed to this edition, which appeared in 1718. Swift collected many guineas (four thousand were obtained in all) and took five copies himself. Lord Harley added another four thousand, for the purchase of Down hall in Essex. He paid several visits to this house, for the purpose of superintending alterations; but most of the time remaining to him he spent at the houses of friends, especially at Lord Harley's seat, Wimpole, with an occasional visit to St. John's college. He was harassed by his confinement at the messenger's house, and by the thought that the manœuvres of his enemies might end in some betrayal by him of his friends. Yet, during this period, he touched some of the lightest strings in *Alma* (the more didactic *Solomon on the Vanity of the World* had been originally composed at an earlier date); and, after his release, he could break forth into almost buoyant gaiety in the ballad *Down-Hall*, in which he describes his search for his future residence as

> A Place where to Bait, 'twixt the Court and the Grave;
> Where joyful to Live, not unwilling to Die.

Swift was but one of the friends of Prior's earlier days who were devoted to him. His old fellow-diplomatists in Paris, Torcy and abbé Gaultier, assure him of their regard: the duke of Buckingham compliments his *Solomon;* Bathurst is reluctant to return *Alma*, with whom he owns himself in love; Chesterfield testifies to admiration for Prior's *Nut-brown Maid;* the conversation of Smalridge is a great comfort to him and a compensation for the loss of Atterbury's, with whom he had a sharp quarrel. Harley's grand-daughter "little Peggy" or "mistress Margaretta" was a great favourite with Prior, and to her he first addressed his dainty and charming little *Letter*, afterwards expanded, 29 March, 1720.[1] The "little pretty lady" seems to

---

[1] **Waller**, vol. ii., p. 131.

have reciprocated his fondness, for she said that Prior made himself loved by every living thing in the house—master, child, servant, creature or animal. Prior was not insensible to the charms of Down hall, a typical Essex lath and plaster manor-farm. With the aid of Harley's factotum and land surveyor, honest John Morley of Harlow, he burlesqued the pride of Louis XIV in the improvements at Marly and Versailles. Yet some letters represent him toping in London taverns, a disappointed man, and Voltaire describes him dying in poverty as an English philosopher must learn to die. In his will, however, of which Harley and Adrian Drift were executors, he devoted £500 to that last of human vanities, a costly monument, to be sur-mounted by Coysevox's bust of himself—a gift of the *Grand Monarque*, with a long inscription from Freind. His death took place, on 18 September, 1721, during a visit to Wimpole, where he had contracted a lingering fever. He was duly buried in Westminster abbey. The best of his books, including Mezeray (but without the inscription), went to St. John's college.

Prior's versatility as a writer is greater than is always recognised. In addition to the lyrical verse of various kinds contained in the successive editions of his poems, or left behind him in manuscript,[1] he wrote three longer poems which, though none of them commends itself to modern taste, call for separate mention.

Henry and Emma, a Poem, *Upon the Model of The Nut-brown Maid* is dedicated *To Cloe* in some lines of the ordinary hu-morous type, and concludes with a sort of *envoi* by Venus, in approved *rococo* style. The pagan deities and their associates, indeed, disport themselves through the dialogue between the lovers which forms the substance of the poem, and which, as has been well said,[2] is "a futile attempt to apply the external classical style to what is in its essence romantic." With the style of the beautiful early sixteenth century ballad *The Nut-brown Maid* its charm disappears; but, though not professing oneself, with Cowper, "bewitched" by "this enchanting piece," one may allow that it paraphrases its original with an extra-

---

[1] It is now printed, together with *Essays* and *Dialogues of the Dead*, from Prior's literary papers preserved at Longleat, in vol. ii., of Waller's edition.

[2] Courthope, *History of English Poetry*, vol. v., p. 117.

ordinary profusion of elegant expressions.[1] Of course, a point in the argument is reached where elegance itself can no longer hold out; but, artificial as the treatment is, a vein of pathos, of the Griselda sort, runs through it to the last—so powerful is the effect of the main motive of the old ballad.

Alma, or The Progress of the Mind, treats in the form of a dialogue, extending over three cantos, the practically inexhaustible subject of the vanity of the world and of what it contains, the folly of the human thoughts which busy themselves with its changing phenomena. Apart from the management of the metre (of which immediately), there is little in this poem to enchain the interest of the reader. In its theme as well as in its form, it approaches *Hudibras;* but its superior urbanity cannot conceal its positive, as well as relative, lack of force. So much pleasure, however, did Prior take in the subject, which had the fluidity harmonising with his own mind when in a mood of relaxation, that he returned to it, in more methodical fashion, and in the heroic couplet, in *Solomon on the Vanity of the World, a Poem in Three Books*. These take the form of a long soliloquy by "the Hero and the Author,"

> Whose serious Muse inspires him to explain
> That all we Act, and all we think is Vain.

In the first, he treats of knowledge (indulging in a brief digression on the prospects of Britannia, "the great glorious Pow'r," which, though it cannot escape the universal doom, shall die last); in the second, of pleasure and the love of women; in the last, of power. All, alike, are vanity; but, in the final book, an angel comforts the pessimist philosopher with the promise of the Redeemer who, after "a Series of perpetual Woe," shall come forth from the royal race. Prior certainly took pains with the poem, and was rather proud of it; but, after being applauded by Cowper, Wesley, Crabbe and Scott, it has gone the way of *Alma*, or had, perhaps, preceded it into oblivion.

It was inevitable that a poet who rejoiced when he could turn to verse-writing from his political work at home and abroad should have transferred much of its spirit into his

---

[1] The usually misquoted line
> Fine by Degrees and beautifully less
occurs in this poem, as a compliment paid by Henry to Emma's figure!

poetry, and contributed his share to the pindaric odes and other panegyrical writing of his age. But, though *Carmen Seculare* may, from the point of view of length, be singled out among his pieces in praise of William or of Anne, no part of it can claim enduring remembrance for its own sake: it varies from the outrageous to the insipid.[1] His genius for *persiflage* suggested to him the notion, when the tide of success had turned, of turning with it upon Boileau, who had sung the earlier success of the French arms, and made him repeat the experiment after Blenheim.[2]

Of satires in verse, properly so called, no complete examples are to be found among his poems, though he seems in his early days to have thought of attempting this form of composition and left one or two fragmentary pieces of the kind behind him.[3] On the other hand, he was fertile in a wide variety of light satirical narrative in verse, from the familiar *fabliau* to the humorous ballad or character-sketch, and to epigrammatic sallies and *vers de société* of all sorts.[4] In many of these pieces, his lightness of touch, combined with a singular gift of saying, in language as clear and simple as prose, and yet rarely devoid of wit, and still more rarely without grace, exactly what he wanted to say, brought him much nearer to classical examples, above all to that of his favourite Horace, than the more elaborate didactic or semi-didactic efforts mentioned above. The best instances of Prior's success in the *fabliau* are *An English Padlock* and *Hans Carvel*, both of which are seasoned with the *gros sel* characteristic of the species; but they do not stand alone. To the humorous character-sketch, there are some admirable approaches in *Down-Hall, a Ballad*, where the figure of the landlady at the Bull in Hendon, bent on business, first, and the sorrows of memory, afterwards, stands forth for all time,[5] and the still more famous *Secretary*, an autobiographical reminiscence. But by far the best example of this class,

---

[1] Among the former may be reckoned the lines *Seeing the Duke of Ormond's Picture;* among the latter, some of the Harley series.

[2] *An English Ballad on the Taking of Namur* (1695). *A Letter to Monsieur Boileau Despréaux, Occasion'd by the Victory at Blenheim* (1704).

[3] *Advice to the Painter; A Session of the Poets; Epistle to Lord ——.* The last-named, which is printed by Waller (vol. ii, pp. 305–8), is conceived on an exceptionally large scale.

[4] Waller, vol. ii, p. 360. [5] See note 1 on next page.

a masterpiece in its way, is the poem which A. R. Waller was
fortunate enough to discover among the Longleat MSS., and to
which, in his edition,[1] he has given the name *Jinny the Just*.
The insight into character here displayed is equalled by the
nicety of *nuance* with which it is expressed; and the twinkle of
humour which animates the life-like portrait is absolutely
irresistible. Almost equally good is the earlier epitaph on
"Saunt'ring Jack and Idle Joan"—which, indeed, reaches a
higher plane in its scorn of the mental or moral apathy it depicts:

> Without Love, Hatred, Joy, or Fear,
> They led—a kind of—as it were;
> Nor wish'd, nor lov'd, nor Cough'd, nor Coy'd;
> But so They liv'd; and so They dy'd.

Among Prior's *vers de société* proper, in which the wit is always
playful and the flattery kept within the bounds of actual life, a
high place has always been assigned to his verses to children,
or concerned with them. The cult, it must be allowed, is not
one that makes for sincerity, though Prior was a genuine child-
lover.[2] His songs are rarely of high excellence; but in an inter-
mediate kind of lyric, half song, half poesy, he remains unsurpassed, with an inimitable—albeit, at times, a kind of wax
flower—prettiness. *Cloe Hunting*, *To Cloe Weeping* and many
another example of this style might be cited; but its acme is
reached in *A Better Answer to Cloe Jealous*, which ends with the
most exquisite grammatical *faux-pas*:

> Then finish, Dear Cloe, this Pastoral War;
> Now let us like Horace and Lydia agree;
> For Thou art a Girl as much brighter than Her,
> As He was a Poet Sublimer than Me.

Prior's epigrams are not uniformly good and, occasionally,
wanting in restraint; perhaps, his genius as a writer lacked the
concentration necessary for the epigram proper; his happiest
effort in this direction, the celebrated lines *Written in the Beginning of Mezeray's History of France*, part cited above, is, after

---

[1] Cf. with this the short *Journey to Copt-hall*, one of the Longleat MSS.

[2] See *A Letter to the Honourable Lady Miss Margaret-Cavendish-Holles-Harley*
("My noble, lovely, little Peggy"), already mentioned, and *To a Child of Quality,
five years old, the Author Forty*.

all, less an epigram than a train of thought suggested by the subject. As a whole, Prior's shorter poems, of which the entire series seems at last to be in our hands, mark him as the earliest, as he was one of the most consummate, masters of English familiar verse. In his own age, he had no rival in this kind of composition but Swift; that his success in it was more rapid and more widespread than Swift's may be attributed to his greater sympathy with the ordinary moods of the human mind, though it was primarily due to his more diversified skill in the management of metre and to his originality in the use of it.

In his *History of English Prosody*,[1] Saintsbury has entered very fully into this aspect of Prior's poetic genius, which, though it had of course not escaped the attention of critics, had hardly before received full consideration. He has directed attention to the fact that, though Prior wrote, not only his *Henry and Emma* and not a little of his other amorous poetry, but, also, his *Solomon*, which he esteemed his masterpiece, in the heroic couplet, he was far from entertaining a preference for the metre to which Dryden had assured its prerogative position.[2] In the *Preface* to *Solomon*, he goes out of his way to dwell on its shortcomings. He explains how the "Heroic with continued Rhime," as used by Donne and his contemporaries "carrying the Sense of one Verse most commonly into another, was found too dissolute and wild, and came very often too near Prose." On the other hand, the same couplet "as Davenant and Waller corrected, and Dryden perfected it," appears to him "too confined" for the freedom, and "too broken and weak" for the grandeur, of epic, as well as tedious in a poem of any considerable length. These objections he endeavoured, in his own practice, to meet in various ways. Like most of the poets of his own age and of that immediately preceding it, he sought refuge in the wide haven of pindarics, not without a certain amount of success, but without leaving his mark upon this measure, of which the day was on the wane in English poetry. In the conviction that he who "writes in Rhimes, dances in Fetters," he also essayed blank verse; but his efforts in this

[1] Vol. ii, pp. 423–5.
[2] See above as to Prior's feeling towards Dryden, which it would be absurd to describe as jealousy, but which was certainly, in a measure, antipathetic.

metre cannot be called successful; they comprise his translations of *The First and Second Hymns of Calliomachus*, as well as the *Prelude to a Tale from Boccace* and another fragment from *The Georgics*.[1] The characteristic mark of his blank verse in the longer pieces is an excessive use of double-endings, which arrest, rather than promote, its flow. Of more significance is his endeavour to employ, and to improve, the Spenserian stanza, for which, in the preface to his *Ode to the Queen*, he expresses high admiration, however imperfect may be the parallel which he draws between the genius of Spenser and that of Horace. The change introduced by him into the scheme of rimes cannot be said to contribute to sustain the rise of the stanza towards its close; but the comparative failure of the attempt was mainly owing to Prior's inability to rise, even with the help of an occasional archaism, to the grand manner of Spenser.[2]

It was neither in the heroic couplet nor in these substituted that Prior achieved eminence, or, as Saintsbury puts it, "the combination of that ease, variety and fluency for which his soul longed." In a delightful passage of *An Essay upon Learning*, after observing that those bred at Westminster school (like himself) grew "used very young to what Dr. Sprat calls the Genius of the place which is to Verses made Extempore, and Declamations composed in a very few hours," he goes on to say that

"As to Poetry, I mean the writing of Verses. . . . I would advise no Man to attempt it except he cannot help it, and if he cannot it is in Vain to diswade him from it. . . . Cowley felt it at Ten Years old, and Waller could not get rid of it at Sixty. . . . As to my own part I found This impulse very soon, and shal continue to feel it as long as I can think, I can remember nothing further in my life than that I made Verses." But, he continues, "I had Two Accidents in Youth which hindered me from being quite possessed with the Muse: I was bred in a College where Prose was more in fashion than Verse, and as soon as I had taken my first Degree was sent the King's Secretary to the Hague. . . . So that Poetry which by the bent of my Mind might have become the Business of my life, was by the happyness of my Education only the Amusement of it. . . ."

---

[1] Waller, vol. ii, pp. 339 and 537.

[2] Over his attempt to imitate Chaucer, it is better to draw a veil. It may be worth noting that his *Translation of an Epitaph upon Glanville, Bishop of Rochester* (*ibid.*, vol. ii, p. 356) is an amusing effort in English hexameters.

Here, in a nutshell, we have the history both of his poetry and, more especially, that of his versification. The metres which he chose, because they were congenial to him and to his easy, familiar style of poetic composition, were the octosyllabic couplet and various forms of couplet or stanza in which a large use was made of the anapaest. As to the former, both Swift and Prior, of course, originally modelled their verse on that of *Hudibras;* but they avoided (Prior perhaps not quite at the outset) what Saintsbury calls "the roughness, the curvets, the extravagances" intentionally introduced by Butler, and aimed at ease and naturalness—a verse as near prose as good verse can be—rather than at sudden and surprising effects. The frequent use of the anapaest in light measures and familiar verse was, apparently, an innovation of Prior's own designing; certainly, he domesticated it in English verse, and thus definitely enriched English poetry by providing its metrical instrument with a new variety of effect. Prior's use of this variety was virtually confined to occasions

When a man 's in a humour too merry for prose,

but not in an exaltation of spirit very far above it. English poetry, however, dealt freely with the gift, and the use of the anapaestic measure, which he had admirably fitted to his description of the secretary's *délassements*, the tribulations of Cloe and the golden mediocrity of Jinny the just, was employed for strains of a very different intensity by the poets of the romantic school. But, though it might be diverted from the use to which he had put it, the best examples of light and inspiriting versification which he produced with its aid must continue to be acknowledged as masterpieces of their kind.

As a prose writer, Prior might have attained to a high rank, had he cared to cultivate a form of composition which he reserved for the service of the state and for familiar correspondence with his friends. Apart from his share in *The Hind and Panther Transvers'd*, of which mention has been made above, he is now known to have been the author of prose compositions which, though few in number, are of high merit. They include, besides *An Essay upon Learning* already cited—which contains some sensible remarks on misapplied and superfluous learning, and some apt remarks on the art of quotation and on conversational wit—a more striking companion *Essay upon Opinion*. The tone of this essay, half gay, half cynical, is very characteristic of its author: most men, he argues, have no opinion of their own, but, as childless fathers did in ancient Rome, adopt that of the first man they like; others use the simple criterion of success or failure, as in the case (which might be illustrated from Prior's own verse) of Orange and Monmouth. Together with these essays are preserved *Four Dialogues of the Dead*, which deserve to be reckoned among the brightest examples of a device which maintained its popularity from Lucian down to Lyttelton, and from Lyttelton up to Landor. The first, *between Charles the Emperor and Clenard the Grammarian*, is a novel treatment of the old theme that greatness—and happiness with it—is relative only; the second, *between Mr. John Lock and Seigneur de Montaigne,* is an amusing and extremely voluble reproduction of Montaigne's concrete though discursive way of thinking, but can hardly have been intended as a serious criticism.[1] In the third *Dialogue, between the Vicar of Bray and Sir Thomas Moor*, Prior, as he had done in the first, displays considerable historical knowledge; but the talk of More, though it displays the main features of his noble character, lacks playfulness of touch. The fourth, *between Oliver Cromwell and his Porter*, which turns on the prophet-porter's contention that the master was ten times madder than the man, is hardly equal to its predecessors.

The spoiled child of the queen Anne fraternity of poets was the pliant fabulist John Gay. The younger son of William Gay, John was baptised at Barnstaple old church on 16 September, 1685. The family was impoverished, and, when his mother and father died, respectively, in 1694 and 1695, the boy was left to the care of his uncle Thomas Gay of Barnstaple, by whom, after being educated at the free grammar school of the town, the lad was apprenticed to a silk mercer in London. In London, after leaving the shop and spending some months in lounging unprofitably in his old home, Gay found an abettor in his old school-mate Aaron Hill, and another in a Westminster

[1] The first Lord Lyttelton, as to whose *History of the Life of Henry the Second* see Vol. X, Chap. XII, *post*, published the first series of *Dialogues of the Dead* in 1760, and the second in 1765.

hall bookseller, who, in May, 1708, brought out his first experiment in verse, an indifferent poem, in blank verse, with the title *Wine*, suggested by the *Cyder* of John Philips. This was followed by *A Tragical Comical Farce*, said (rather doubtfully) to have been acted in 1712 near the watch house in Covent garden, and detecting the "dudes" or "nuts" of the time in those dread aversions of Swift's, the Mohocks. In May, 1712, Gay contributed a translation of the story of Arachne in Ovid's *Metamorphoses* to *The Rape of the Lock* volume of Lintot's *Miscellaneous Poems and Translations;* and, five months later, he became secretary or domestic steward in the house of the high-minded widow of the duke of Monmouth beheaded in 1685. In January, 1713, he inscribed to Pope, as the first of contemporary poets, his trim georgic called *Rural Sports*. It is a smooth reflection of Pope's own pastoral, saturated with the false sentiment and poetic diction, so-called, of the period, and replete with "feather'd choirs" and "finny broods" (it contains, indeed, a minute and rather grotesque description of fly-fishing). Swift laughed at the modern Theocritus, who knew more about kine than Pope did, but yet could not distinguish rye from barley. In poetic taste, Pope was accepted by Gay as an unfailing mentor, and it was by Pope's express encouragement that, in December, he went on to supply the world with another heroic poem in three books on that "agreeable machine" *The Fan*. After a poor and unsuccessful comedy, *The Wife of Bath*, Gay's next work of any importance was his pleasing poem *The Shepherd's Week* (15 April, 1714), in six pastorals, with a prologue addressed to Bolingbroke, containing familiar flattering allusions to some of the greatest ladies of the day who might be tempted into becoming his patronesses. These pastorals of actual, as opposed to fashionable, rusticity, were written originally to cast ridicule upon those of Ambrose ("Namby-Pamby") Philips; for Gay was a born parodist. But they were so full of comic humour and droll portraiture of country life that they were soon popular on their own merits as rural poems. The grotesque passages (like those of Greene's pastorals[1]) helped to conceal the flimsiness of the texture, and the scheme thus serves as a link between the *Calender* of Spenser

---

[1] Cf. *ante*, Vol. III, pp. 405–406; as to the general characteristics of Elizabethan pastoral, cf. *ante*, Vol. IV, pp. 141–142.

and *The Gentle Shepherd* of Allan Ramsay, while the historical method adopted specially approved itself to Crabbe. Gay was an occasional contributor to Steele's *Guardian;* but his versatility in letters did not make up to the duchess of Monmouth for his deficiencies as domestic steward: in the summer of 1714 his position in her household came to an end, and he would have been in a bad case but for the kindness of literary friends. Swift procured him a secretaryship to Lord Clarendon envoy extraordinary at Hanover; and there is a curious rhymed petition to Lord Oxford, in which Gay solicits funds to enable him to set out on his journey. When, a few months later, queen Anne died, the embassage was at an end, and Gay was called to find a brief anchorage with Pope at Binfield. While there, he wrote, with a hint or two from Pope and Arbuthnot, a satirical tragi-comi-pastoral farce *The What D'ye Call it*, which gives us a distinct foretaste of his clever light librettist vein, and of his happy knack for a ballad (*Black-eyed Susan* and *'Twas when the Seas were roaring* were both his). It ridiculed, after the manner of *The Rehearsal*, a number of plays in vogue; and, in one of the offended dramatists, Steele, Gay lost a friend. His profits amounted to £100. In the following year, he composed, what is probably his best remembered poem, *Trivia, or The Art of Walking the Streets of London*, in three books, an elaborate imitation and expansion of Swift's *Tatler* poems *The City Shower* and the photographic *Morning*. The idea is good, the versification neat, and the mock heroic style admirable, while nearly every couplet is of historic interest to the antiquary and the student of eighteenth century street humours. This was published by Lintot 26 January, 1716, during part of which year Gay found a temporary home with Lord Burlington in Devonshire. A year later, Pulteney took him in his train to Aix, and, in 1718, he was at Nuneham with Lord Harcourt. The number of his patrons justified his collecting and publishing his poems in 1720 in two large quarto subscription volumes, brought out jointly by Lintot and Tonson. He realised £1000 by the venture, which he invested in South Sea stock. For the moment, he was the nominal holder of £20,000 worth; but it vanished in the crash, while he was deliberating what to do with it. Soon afterwards, his hopes of advancement in the new reign were dashed, while his dignity was offended by his nomination as gentleman usher to the princess Louisa, a child under three. In the meantime, he had brought out his *Fables* (1727) in octosyllabic verse, wherein he surveys mankind for the benefit of the youthful duke of Cumberland. Gay had now become a more or less regular inmate in the household of the duchess of Queensberry, Bolingbroke's "*Sa Singularité*" and Prior's Kitty, younger sister of Lady Jane Hyde, the "blooming Hyde with Eyes so Rare" of his own prologue to *The Shepherd's Week*. Gay had spent a great deal of time in polishing his *Fables*, elaborate trifles, the publication of which by Tonson had been still further delayed by costly expenditure on plates after Kent and Wootton. Ambling, colloquial and, occasionally, slipshod, like the bard himself, it cannot be said Gay's *Fables* maintain an inordinately high standard; yet their novelty and glossy ease won them an assured success which lasted for a hundred years before it began to wane. Apart from one or two later fables by Cowper and by Northcote, they are still, probably, the best that have been written in English verse: nor would it be easy for any fabulist to better the narrative of

> The hare who in a civil way
> Complied with everything like Gay,

a charming *fabliau* with a touch of personal application—disillusion, for the most part—quite in the manner of the early masters. Gay's *Fables* suffer, it is true, from juxtaposition with the terse masterpieces of La Fontaine. Compared with the immortal *bonhomme*, Gay took but little trouble with his work. The fables were applauded; but the draftsman of the illustrations, it is said, had the lion's share of the profit. A second set, adding sixteen to the original fifty, appeared in 1738.

Whenever he was off duty with the Queensberrys, Gay—always "inoffensive"—sought the society of Congreve, Prior, Arbuthnot and, above all, of Swift. To Swift's visit to England in 1736 was, in part, due Gay's next venture, *The Beggar's Opera*, which—unless an exception be made in favour of Lillo's *London Merchant* (1731)—may be described as the first popular success of the modern English stage.[1] It ran for the unprecedented, though not uninterrupted, space of sixty-two days,

[1] For a retrospective account of the progress of the drama in England, and the place occupied in it by *The Beggar's Opera*, see Vol. XI, *post*.

beginning 29 January, 1728, and continued a triumphant career in Bath, Bristol and other towns in the country, and even in the colonies. Like not a few *jeux d'esprit* of the day, it sprang from a saying of Swift, who observed to Gay that a Newgate pastoral might make "an odd pretty sort of thing"; and Gay wrote most of it at Twickenham when in the same house with Pope and Swift, whose opinion was that it was either very bad or very good. As often in comic opera, it was one of the numbers,

O ponder well! be not severe

that turned the scale and made the play an irresistible success, out of which Gay gleaned about £800.

Polly became the town darling, her songs were painted on fans and the actress who performed the part captured a duke for life. The factions of the day recognised Walpole (who led the applause on the first night) and Townshend in Peachum and Lockit. *The Beggar's Opera*, it was said, made Gay rich, and Rich (the manager) gay. Its literary value is very small, except historically as a link between the masque and the vaudeville. For the time, it superseded French and Italian opera, and made a new opening for English lyric on the stage. A sequel was prohibited by the lord chamberlain, and was promptly printed, the fortunate author making £1200 by *Polly* (as it was called), to which the duchess of Marlborough contributed £100 for a single copy.

Gay's later years were uneventfully spent in the house of his faithful patrons the duke and duchess of Queensberry, at Amesbury and at Burlington gardens. The duchess and Gay wrote some amusing joint letters to Swift, who entered into the correspondence with zest, beginning his reply low on the page as a mark of respect—receiving her grace, as it were, at the bottom of the stairs. Yet Swift's fondness for Gay himself was genuine, as may be discerned in more than one touching letter. The duchess looked after the gentle parasite's little comforts, and kept his money under lock and key, while the duke invested his savings for him, so that when he died, intestate, about £6000, or thereabouts, was left to be divided between his sisters. After an idle life which, on the whole, notwithstanding his unmanly repining, was one in which good fortune preponderated, Gay died suddenly, of inflammatory fever, on 4 December, 1732. He was interred with much pomp in Westminster abbey, where an imposing monument, erected by the unwearying duke and duchess, bears, together with Pope's, the light-minded poet's own characteristic epitaph:

> Life is a jest, and all things show it;
> I thought so once, and now I know it.

His easy-going, affectionate disposition made Gay a general favourite, even though, as Johnson observed, the wits regarded him rather as a playfellow than a partner. He was utterly devoid of energy; and though, in complaining of his treatment by the court, he laments "My hard fate! I must get nothing, write for or against," it is very far from clear what duties he would have been fit to discharge, had they been imposed upon him. He was, in truth, predestined on every account, in Pope's phrase, to "die unpension'd with a hundred friends."

Gay's longer poems, with the exception of *The Shepherd's Week* and *Trivia*, are dead. Of the shorter, some of the eclogues, such as *The Birth of the Squire, The Toilette, The Tea-Table* and *The Funeral*, contain many witty passages; and the epistles are all interesting, especially *Mr. Pope's Welcome from Greece*, the *ottava rima* of which has a spontaneous flash and felicity. Written on the completion of Pope's translation of *The Iliad*, it represents all the poet's friends as gathering to meet him on his return to town, each being characterised in one or two apt lines, or by a brief pert epithet, in the happiest possible manner. Among the miscellaneous pieces which deserve to escape neglect is the sprightly *Ladies' Petition to the Honourable the House of Commons*, in which the maids of Exeter protest against their loss of the chance of marriage through the interloping competition of widows.[1]

Gay's parodies of Ambrose Philips in *The Shepherd's Week* (which pleased by the very quality they were intended to ridicule) were suborned by Pope, and the quarrel was accentu-

---

[1] G. F. Underhill calls this poem "the least doubtful piece" in the collection known as *Gay's Chair*, a little volume published in 1820, with a life of Gay, by his nephew, Joseph Baller. There seems good reason to doubt the authenticity of some of the pieces there attributed to Gay; though the chair, in whose secret drawer they were found, has a well-authenticated history.

ated by the fact that Ambrose not only belonged to the rival or whig faction (he was secretary of the Hanover club in 1714) but was also a friend and adherent of Addison. A native of the midlands, Ambrose Philips (born in 1675) was educated at Shrewsbury and St. John's college, Cambridge (1693–6), of which he was fellow from 1699 to 1708. At Cambridge, he began writing English verse. In 1709, he abridged Hacket's well-known *Life of Archbishop Williams*. On 9 March of the same year, he addressed, from Copenhagen, his *Epistle to the Earl of Dorset*, Prior's early patron. It was published by Steele in *The Tatler* and praised as a great "winter-piece." His *Pastorals* appeared in the following autumn in Tonson's *Miscellany*, his being the first, and Pope's the last, in this same volume. In *The Guardian*,[1] Ambrose was thoughtlessly praised by Thomas Tickell as the only worthy successor of Spenser, Pope being completely ignored. Philips had also been cordially applauded in *The Spectator* for his artless type of eclogue. Pretending to criticise the rival pastorals and compare them, Pope, in an anonymous contribution to *The Guardian*,[2] gave the preference to Philips, but quoted all his worst passages as his best, and placed by the side of them his own finest lines, which, he says, want rusticity, and often deviate into downright poetry. The satire stung, as was intended, and Philips bought a rod and hung it up at a popular coffee-house (Button's) in order to carry out his threatened chastisement of Pope in public. The encounter was averted by Pope's prudence. To keep up the "reciprocation of malevolence," Pope scoffed at Philips in *The Dunciad* and elsewhere as one of Curll's authors, "a Pindaric writer in red stockings." Philips played his cards sufficiently well to extract some very fair Irish sinecures from the dominant whig party, but he did not live to "enjoy them." The poems of Philips which please best, says Johnson, are "those which from Pope or Pope's adherents procured him the name of Namby-Pamby, the poems of short lines by which he paid his court to all ages and characters, from Walpole, the steerer of the realm, to Miss Pulteney in the nursery." Henry Carey, the author of *Sally in our Ally*, mocked Philips under this name, and Swift called his pretty waxworks "little flams."

[1] Nos. 22, 23, 30, and 32.   [2] No. 40.

But the machinations of Pope managed to raise a perfect storm of ridicule, which, in numberless parodies and broadsides, broke over the "new versification," as it was called. The line generally consists of three trochees, followed by an extra-stressed monosyllabic foot. Many critics have pronounced these sweetmeats delightful, though cloying; and, it must be granted, in spite of ridicule, that Philips had a genuine sensibility and a kindness for the elder music in English poetry which is to his credit and which his age, for the most part, ignored. In 1723, he brought out *A Collection of Old Ballads*, including *Robin Hood*, *Johnny Armstrong* and the famous *Children in the Wood*, much belauded by Addison. The ballads are, in the main, bad versions derived from current broadsides; but the collection, such as it was, was one of the earliest of its kind. His only play of any note, *The Distressed Mother*, was derived immediately from Racine's *Andromaque*. He died in Hanson street, London, on 18 June, 1749. His poems, with a dedication to the duke of Newcastle, had been published in the year before his death.

Thomas Parnell is, probably, now less remembered for his verse than because of the fact that his life was written by Goldsmith and Johnson, and that from his younger brother was descended Charles Stewart Parnell. The son of a commonwealth's man, who, at the restoration, left Congleton in Cheshire, where the family had been long established and, settling in Ireland, purchased an estate which, together with his land in Cheshire, was afterwards owned by the poet, Thomas Parnell was born at Dublin in 1679. In 1693, he was admitted at Trinity college, Dublin, where in 1700 he proceeded M. A., and was ordained deacon under an episcopal dispensation on the score of age. Swift's friend Ashe, bishop of Clogher, named him archdeacon of that see in 1706, an appointment followed by his marriage to Anne, daughter of Thomas Minchin of Tipperary. Her death in 1711 seems to have unsteadied the young archdeacon's mind. Swift and Stella conceived a friendliness for the bereaved poet, who was taken to sup with Bolingbroke and was introduced to the lord treasurer (Oxford). By this time, he had changed his political vesture, and, in April, 1713, he wrote a *Poem on Queen Anne's Peace*. About this time, he became an intimate of the Scriblerus club and of Pope, who designed him to be one of "the children of Homer." Swift whipped up his Irish friends to procure Parnell a prebend. In May, 1716, archbishop King presented the poet with the vicarage of Finglass, worth over £100 a year. Meanwhile, he had become inseparable from Pope at Binfield and the Bath, and he retained his position in the Scriblerus circle to the last. He died suddenly at Chester (his end being hastened by habitual intemperance)[1] on his way to Ireland in October, 1718. His publications during his lifetime had been in periodicals; but he left many unprinted compositions, of which those which Pope thought best were selected by him and dedicated to the earl of Oxford, who wrote appreciatively of the *Noctes* he had spent in the company of Pope, Swift, Parnell and the doctor. Johnson, in conversation, deplored that Goldsmith's *Life* of the poet was so thin; but he made his own sketch an opportunity for a most splendid eulogy of Goldsmith's ease and versatility. Goldsmith wrote a fair epitaph, which was eclipsed by Johnson's.[2]

Goldsmith, Collins and Blair show signs of having studied Parnell, whose own work, apart from the manifest impress of Pope and Swift, was influenced, it is thought, to some extent, by Milton. Apart from his contribution to Pope's *Homer*, which took the form of a learned essay in the taste of the time on "The Life, Writings and Learnings of Homer," and a few imitative poems, Parnell did not write anything of importance. Pope was glad of his aid at the time, but, after Parnell's death, expressed a hope that his essay might be made "less defective." His poems, generally in heroic measure, run smoothly. *The Flies, an Eclogue*, has merit as a picture. *An Elegy to an old Beauty* enjoys an adventitious fame. After ridiculing the lady's strenuous efforts at resisting the ravages of time, Parnell goes on to explain how the daughter Fanny has acquired her mother's old artifices, with interest:

> And all that's madly wild, or oddly gay
> We call it only pretty Fanny's way.

[1] Hearne says he was undoubtedly killed by the immoderate drinking of "mild ale."

[2] *Qui sacerdos pariter et poeta, utrasque partes ita implevit, ut neque sacerdoti suavitas poetae, nec poetae sacerdotis sanctitas, deesset.*

A Nightpiece on Death is an early example of a convention which reached its acme with Gray's *Elegy*.[1]   *A Hymn to Contentment* is another fashionable exercise on the theme of Plantin, Desportes, Wotton and Pomfret, written in easy flowing octosyllabics.   All these copies of verse—the last and most meritorious of which as a model, and greatly admired during the age of Johnson, is *The Hermit*—were published posthumously in *Poems on Several Occasions*, issued by the poet's friend, corrector and patron, Pope, in December, 1721.   The only separate volume issued previously by Parnell was his *Homer's Battle of the Frogs and Mice with the Remarks of Zoilus* (May, 1717), satirising two objects of Pope's aversion, Theobald and Dennis. His scholarship had been of material service to Pope as translator, apart from his *Introductory Essay* on Homer (1715), which Pope, as usual, exalted in public and deplored in private.

Anne, daughter of Sir William Kingsmill of Sidmonton, was born in April, 1661, became maid of honour to queen Mary of Modena and was a friend of Anne Killigrew, who had kindred tastes; but, in 1684, she abandoned her court position and married colonel Heneage Finch, afterwards earl of Winchilsea. In 1690, Ardelia (her name as authoress) settled at beautiful Eastwell and began to write verses for circulation among her friends, the Thynnes, Tuftons, Twysdens and other Kentish people of distinction.   She died in Cleveland row and was buried at Eastwell in August, 1720.   She had adopted the practice of writing,

> Betray'd by solitude to try
> Amusements which the prosperous fly,

and soon showed that she had an eye for observing country scenes and that she loved them for their own sake.   She began by translations from French and Italian, and went on with blank verse dramas after the model of the virtuous and matchless Orinda; she wrote songs after Prior, pindarics after Cowley and fables after La Fontaine.   In 1713, she was persuaded to publish a selection of her poems.   She left a large number of

---

[1] Prompted by contrariness of his own or by Johnson's dislike of Gray, Goldsmith used to say that he preferred Parnell's *Nightpiece* greatly to the *Elegy*.

further poems in two manuscript volumes, one folio, the other octavo; these were edited by Myra Reynolds in 1903 and cannot fairly be said to have enhanced Lady Winchilsea's reputation. It had hitherto mainly depended on the discovery by Wordsworth that there were affinities with his own predominant mood in a few of her poems of 1713, especially the sentimental and meditative soliloquy entitled *A Nocturnal Reverie*, an enunciation of rural charms in which almost every other line begins with the word "when," while the last fifty verses conclude with the following two couplets:

> In such a *Night* let Me abroad remain,
> Till Morning breaks, and All's confus'd again;
> Our Cares, our Toils, our Clamours are renew'd,
> Or Pleasures, seldom reach'd, again pursu'd.

A few other poems, such as an ode *To the Nightingale*, sustain the same kind of impression, which gained indefinitely from the twilight of Eastwell as well as from the rarity of Ardelia's slim volume. Wordsworth's discovery was taken up with enthusiasm by Matthew Arnold, Edmund Gosse and others, and Lady Winchilsea was cited as a *rara avis*, a woodlark among those town sparrows, the best accredited poets of the days of queen Anne. To Pope, Gray and Prior, she had just seemed a female wit, with a stray predilection, and some genuine taste, for riming. The appearance of her poems in bulk certainly strengthens the idea that her *forte* was in gay and complimentary verse of the occasional order, and that she ought to rank not as a rival of Dyer and Collins, but as an imitator of Prior and a precursor of Gay, Cowper and Northcote. Her light verse, upon which she bestowed much pains, was based upon the miscellany poems of Dorset, Sedley and their queen Anne successors. Her verses *To Mr. F. now Earl of W.*, written in 1689, in an 886886 stanza, are among the best of their kind at that date. Her *Fanscombe Barn*, with its jolly beggars, is a tolerable parody of the Miltonic (written a few years after *The Splendid Shilling*); but her "Pindaricks," including *The Spleen*, issued separately in a miscellany of 1701, as well as in the volume of 1713, are unbearable. *The Spleen* contains the lines

> Now the jonquille o'ercomes the feeble brain,
> We faint beneath the Aromatick Pain.

The adjective was borrowed from Dryden's *Annus Mirabilis;* the phrase was appropriated by Pope in his *Essay on Man,* and the association of the odour of the jonquil with delicious pain by Shelley (*Epipsychidion*). Two of Lady Winchilsea's poems, *The Sigh* and *To Mr. Jervas* (the famous portrait painter and translator of *Don Quixote*), were printed in Steele's *Miscellany* (1714), her *Lines to Prior* in Prior's *Miscellaneous Works: To Mr. Pope* in the early collected editions of Pope.

A writer similar in calibre to Lady Winchilsea and, like her, destined to be raised too high by disproportioned praise, is John Pomfret, son of a vicar of Luton, whose studies were carried on at Bedford and at Queens' college, Cambridge (where he graduated M.A. in 1688). His elegy upon the death of queen Mary was the prelude to his taking orders and was soon rewarded by two considerable Bedfordshire rectories. He was a good early example of the cultivated, poetising, arch-aeologising, chess-playing divines of the eighteenth century. In 1699, he gave to the world his *Poems on Several Occasions,* the sale of which was stimulated next year when he issued anonymously *The Choice: A Poem written by a Person of Quality.* The poem obtained adventitious fame. At first, it was held to have been composed by a personage of distinction. Then, it was said to have been modelled upon a study of Sir William Temple's philosophic retirement among his peaches at Sheen. And the public was still more interested when it learned that the poet's frankly expressed aspiration to "have no wife" had displeased the bishop of London (Compton), to whom he had been recommended for preferment. As a matter of fact, he married and had a son, shortly before his death, at thirty-five, in 1702. *The Choice* was no more and no less than a familiar exercise, adapted to the taste of the time, of the old *Bonheur de ce Monde* theme, sung to death by the French poets, and best known to us in the poems of Wotton and Samuel Rogers ("Mine be a cot"). The versification will strike no one to-day as being (that which the theme demands) exceptionally neat; and the best modern anthologists ignore the poem. But, when the scheme for the *Lives of the Poets* was submitted by the book-sellers to Johnson, the name of Pomfret (together with three others) was added by his advice, chiefly, it seems, on the ground of Pomfret's ineradicable popularity (half a century later, Robert Southey is found solemnly asking "Why is Pomfret's 'Choice' the most popular poem in the language?"). Johnson said that probably no composition in our language had been so often perused and that it was the favourite of readers who, without vanity or criticism, seek only their own amusement. That Pomfret pleased many, surely argued some merit. Now, however, he pleases few, or is quite forgotten.

Thomas Tickell was born in 1688, at his father's vicarage, Bridekirk, in Cumberland, and, in April, 1701, entered Queen's college, Oxford, of which he became a fellow in November, 1700—a poetaster preferred over better men, according to the relentless tory, Thomas Hearne. In 1711, he acted as deputy professor at Oxford, where, according to the same authority, he delivered a "silly" course on bucolics, in which what was good was taken from Scaliger. Tickell, who was not "one of these scholars who wear away their lives in closets," found a stepping-stone into the outer world through the patronage of Addison. While still at Oxford, he had expressed his admiration of Addison (*To Mr. Addison on his Opera of Rosamond*) in extravagant terms. On arriving in London, he made Addison's acquaintance. Tickell was an accomplished poetiser and man of letters, and a graceful, though not profound, scholar, by no means the vain conceited coxcomb of Hearne's imagining. Addison was pleased with a homage that was worth accepting. In October, 1712, Tickell published his *Poem to his Excellency the Lord Privy Seal on the Prospect of Peace*, and, though the piece supported the tory peace of Utrecht, Addison, in *The Spectator*,[1] spoke warmly of its "noble performance." Pope praised its poetical images and fine painting—now undecipherable. Tickell repaid these compliments with compound interest. Verses by him were prefixed to Addison's *Cato*, and, as Addison rose, his admirer rose with him. Addison, as is well known, incurred Pope's enmity mainly in his *protégé's* behalf. In October, 1714, he asked to be excused reading the first two books of Pope's *Iliad*, on the ground that his interest in an English version of *The Iliad* had been forestalled by Tickell, whose first book he had "corrected." (He consented,

[1] No. 523.

however, according to Pope, to read the second book.) In June, 1715, Pope's first volume and Tickell's first book of *The Iliad* in English appeared almost simultaneously. Addison described Tickell's version as the best ever done in any language.[1] Pope wrote bitterly of Cato's "little senate" at Button's coffee-house. Meanwhile, Pope's own like senate unmasked their batteries. Parnell and Arbuthnot criticised the scholarship, Jervas and Berkeley the verse, of Tickell's translation. Pope himself, in his *Art of Sinking in Poetry*, cites illustrative passages from Tickell's version. Apart from this quarrel, the chief interest attaching to Tickell in literary history is in his character as satellite, executor and panegyrist of Addison, and as supplanter of Steele in Addison's estimation. In 1717, upon his appointment as chief secretary in Ireland, Addison took Tickell with him. When he became secretary of state, he appointed Tickell under-secretary; and, shortly before his death, made him his literary executor, instructing him to collect his writings in a final and authentic edition. Tickell addressed himself to this most difficult and delicate task with so much loyalty and assiduity that, by 3 October, 1721, the collective edition of Addison's works was ready for the public, in four sumptuous quarto volumes. It was prefaced by an unpretending notice, to which was appended the noble and pathetic elegy (characterised by Johnson as "sublime and elegant") *To the Earl of Warwick on the Death of Mr. Addison*, which furnishes Tickell's sole but sufficient title-deed to the poetical estate. Of its thirty-two lines, the most familiar, though not entirely the best, are, perhaps, the following:

> Can I forget the dismal night that gave
> My soul's best part for ever to the grave!
> How silent did his old companions tread
> By midnight lamps, the mansions of the dead
> Through breathing statues, then unheeded things,
> Through rows of warriors, and through walks of kings!

---

[1]
> "Who, when two wits on rival themes contest,
> Approves them both, but likes the worst the best."

Pope's *Epistle to Arbuthnot* (Longleat Version), see Elwin and Courthope's edn., vol. iii, p. 537.

What awe did the slow solemn knell inspire;
The pealing organ, and the pausing choir;
The duties by the lawn-rob'd prelate paid;
And the last words, that dust to dust conveyed!

Tickell did fair and, some think, ample justice to Steele in his references to him.   There can, however, be little doubt that Steele had been distressed and grievously hurt by the rupture; while the fact that Tickell should have taken his place in Addison's affections must have been inexpressibly galling.   His natural irritation had, no doubt, been intensified by Addison appointing Tickell under-secretary, and, still more, by his making Tickell his literary executor, offices which Steele might, naturally, have expected, had all gone well, to fill himself.   The omission of *The Drummer* from Addison's works gave him the opening he desired.   Steele objected to Addison's essays being separately printed, while some of their joint work was ignored. It seems certain that Addison contemplated a collective edition of his writings, in which his own personal contributions could be identified.   Steele's ambition, we must infer, was that he and his friend should go down to posterity together.   This hope was dashed to the ground by the appointment, in his place, of Tickell as Addison's literary executor.

Tickell followed up the Irish career which Addison had opened for him.   In May, 1724, he was appointed secretary to the lord justices, and Carteret testifies to the ability with which he performed the duties of his office.   *"Whiggissimus"* though he was, he managed to conciliate Swift.   He seems to have retained no ill-feeling against his detractors, and he died at peace at Bath on St. George's day, 1740.   Johnson described his poem *The Prospect of Peace*, beginning "The Haughty Gaul in ten campaigns o'erthrown," as a poem to be approved rather than admired; and this distinction applies to all his verses, more or less (with the exception of the elegy on Addison), including those in his favourite heroic measure, *On Queen Caroline's rebuilding of the Lodgings of the Black Prince and Henry V at Queen's College, The Royal Progress, An Epistle from a Lady in England to a Gentleman in Avignon* (an anti-jacobite piece, which ran to a fifth edition), a *Fragment of a Poem on Hunting, Part of the Fourth Book of Lucan,* complimentary poems *To Mr. Addison* and *To Sir Godfrey Kneller*, two formal poems entitled *Oxford*, and *Kensington Gardens*, and *The First Book of the Iliad*.

Johnson denounced him for confusing Grecian deities and Gothic fairies; both species were regarded by the critic as contemptible even when apart, but, in conjunction, positively ridiculous. Outside the range of his correct pentameters, Tickell essayed a wooden ballad in eight and six, entitled *Colin and Lucy*, which was translated into Latin by Vincent Bourne, and pronounced by Gray and Goldsmith (himself an offender in this respect) to be one of the best ballads in English. Gray, at any rate, ought to have known better. Tickell had very few poetical notes at his command, and none of them were "wood-notes wild" suitable to ballad or octosyllabic measure. His elegy rings true, as a sincere commemoration of a notable literary friendship.

II

The minor versifiers of the eighteenth century, among whom may be included some of the younger of Dryden's contemporaries, cannot be said to enjoy, or to have enjoyed for some generations, anything that approaches, even in the furthest degree, to what may be called popularity. From circumstances which, to avoid repetition, will be more fully noticed in dealing with the second group of them, they obtained a certain hold not merely on the standard "collections," but on books of anthology with an educational purpose. This lasted far into the nineteenth, and has not been entirely relaxed in the twentieth, century. They, and their somewhat more interesting successors, furnished mottoes and quotations to at least three generations of prose writers greater than themselves, and even to the vague, floating treasury from which common speech borrows things that, when the actual authors are read for the first time, strike the reader if not with "a wild surprise" at any rate with an amused one. Very few are those who, except for a special purpose, read many or any of these poets now; and fewer still those who derive much enjoyment from the reading. Yet they cannot be wholly neglected in such a work as this, though it would be an exceedingly rash critic who entered upon the task of dealing with them unconscious of its difficulties and dangers. Even in the separation of the two groups, there must be something that may well seem arbitrary; and there is the further difficulty that, while the treatment accorded to a few—rather in the later group than in this, but here, perhaps, also, in some cases—may seem inadequate, objection may be taken in others to what may appear too like a mere catalogue with ticket-comments. But no possible arrangement could satisfy everybody: and, in the present case, the adventure has been undertaken not lightly, and assisted at least by an old familiarity with the subjects.

We must, of course, begin with the group which, as has been said—though all its members lived into Pope's time, and two of them were specially singled out by him as patrons, and, in a way, patterns—represent, in actual historic relation, the younger contemporaries of Dryden.[1] First come the pair just referred to, and known now chiefly, if not wholly, by Pope's own words, "Granville the polite [George Granville, first baron Lansdowne] and knowing Walsh [William Walsh]." With them may be grouped four others less known to even second-hand fame: Richard Duke, George Stepney, William King (1663–1712) and Thomas Yalden, who linger, mummy fashion, in the collections of British poets, while two of them enjoy certain adventitious aids to personal remembrance. For Stepney, a notable diplomatist in his day, represented Marlborough in the taking-over of the principality of Mindelheim, and King is constantly confused with his twenty years younger namesake (1685–1763), the clever but venomous jacobite principal of St. Mary hall.

Granville, Lord Lansdowne, does not quite deserve, even from a literary point of view, the neglect which has betaken him, and, to all who can appreciate the genealogy of poetry— a thing which has attractions far other than those affecting Dryasdust—is by no means negligible. In him, we have, per- haps, the last remnant, though only an imperfect one, of Caro- line character, before we come to the wholly, or almost wholly, "Augustan" lyric. That strange fire which still burns, and occasionally even blazes, in Sedley and Rochester and Aphra Behn, only glimmers in him; but it has not quite gone out. It

[1] As to Dryden's relations with Granville, see *ante*, Vol. VIII, p. 61.

was, possibly, the presence of it, joined, as an acute reader aware of the circumstances may suspect, to the disapprobation, which he not obscurely hints, of the later character of "Myra," which makes Johnson unjust to Lansdowne. This grandson of Sir Bevil Granville, a descendant of the hero of the Azores, could not, so far as he was personally concerned, have been distasteful to the censor. He "endeavoured to be true at once to the King [James II] and the Church," which exceedingly difficult task Johnson would himself certainly have essayed. He was the author of a sentence which has frequently expressed the wishes of good Englishmen before and since, "Everybody wishes well to the King: but they would be glad if his ministers were hanged." He abstained from public life during the whole reign of William, but was an active tory member of parliament under Anne, became one of the two famous "panel" of peers, and was sent to the Tower by the Hanoverian government; though afterwards, like others, he was, in a way, reconciled by the good manners and good judgment of queen Caroline. But Johnson thought him "profane," which, perhaps, he was sometimes, and decided that his verses to "Myra" were "commonly feeble and unaffecting or forced and extravagant," while his other little pieces were "seldom either sprightly or elegant, either keen or weighty." They were "trifles written in idleness and published by vanity." These are neat antitheses; but, if any one will look dispassionately at the song "Love is by Fancy led about" or at "Thoughtful nights and restless waking," he will, with due historic allowance, hardly think the judgment just in the present case. Granville came at an unfortunate time in the history of the evolution of poetic species. His wings had dwindled, and he could not quite fly; nor was he content merely to walk gracefully. But his lyre has not forgotten that, in Joubert's famous phrase, it ought to be a "winged instrument."

Walsh was somewhat luckier: for his inheritance of the older time was in the lighter vein, and, perhaps, the critical power attributed to him, both by Dryden and by Pope, told him what not to attempt, and not to attempt too much. His work in verse (to which Johnson is somewhat kinder than he is to Lansdowne's) is very small, but there are several pieces in it which are not anybody's work. His couplets are distinctly good; except Garth's, they are, perhaps, the best between Dryden and Pope. The poem entitled *Jealousy*, in a rather elaborate stanza not ineffectively composed of a decasyllabic quatrain, an octosyllabic couplet and two "fourteeners," is far from contemptible. "Caelia, too late you would repent," in Caroline common measure, has kept much of the soar and swoop of that extraordinary example of anything "common"; and, what is perhaps his best known and most praised thing, *The Despairing Lover*, deserves all the praise and much wider knowledge. The quaintness of its expression and of its metre— a sort of regularised Skeltonic—is as crisp as it is quaint. And when it is remembered that *The Antidote*, which begins

When I see the bright nymph who my heart does enthrall,

was probably written as early as anything by Prior, and, per- haps, earlier still, it is difficult to be chary of applause. Walsh, a country squire, a county member and, for a time, a placeman at court—a man, too, who died in no very advanced middle age—can only have written for his amusement; but he might have amused himself very much worse.

A single paragraph must suffice for the quartette whom we subjoin to these two. In Duke, Johnson found little to be praised, and, in searches made at different times, the present writer has found still less. The bulk of his work is translation, in which, as elsewhere, he shows a certain ease. The absurd and, in fact, almost meaningless commendation of Stepney, that his work "made grey authors blush"—which Johnson quotes without assigning its author, but which he had printed elsewhere in its original context—is the chief thing memorable about him. Yalden, as stout a tory as Lansdowne, and a sus- pect about the time of Atterbury's fall, wrote pindarics which are not the worst of that too generally bad kind, and fables which, though unequal, are sometimes quite light and good. Luckily for him, he did not, like Lansdowne, lay himself open to the charge of "profanity," and Lansdowne's censor has given him high and detailed praise for a *Hymn to Darkness*, apparently written in emulation of Cowley's *Hymn to Light*. It is, fortunately, not in pindarics; though its stanza—a deca- syllable, two octosyllables and an alexandrine—is not very graceful. But the present writer is quite unable to discover how and why

> Thou dost thy smiles impartially bestow,
>   And knowest no difference here below;
>   All things appear the same by thee;
>   Though Light distinction makes, thou giv'st equality

is "exquisitely beautiful." The last of the four, Dr. William King, though a rambling and unequal writer, is, perhaps, the most readable. He wrote, in mixed verse and prose, *The Art of Cookery*, which is quite interesting; one piece of his *Orpheus and Eurydice*, beginning

> A roasted ant that's nicely done,

is familiar to all who were brought up on the old-fashioned *Speakers* and *Readers;* humour and good-humour abound in his work; he could turn little songs with a great deal of neatness; and he contrives almost everywhere neither to offend nor to bore.

A second, and very much larger, division, which may, indeed, perhaps with some sub-groupings, be made to include all the rest of the poets to be dealt with in this section, consists of those verse-writers who, though older than Pope, did not, for the most part, publish poetry before the close of the seventeenth century, and who represent the direct influence of Dryden, felt and exercised in parallel measure with that felt by Pope himself; so that, in their most characteristic work, they are of the queen Anne, or of the earliest Georgian, division. These, for the most part, though they may sometimes write pindarics, gravitate towards the couplet, and occasionally towards blank verse; confine themselves, though they do not abstain from lyric, to a few rather conventional forms of it; and, when they are not attempting large, and generally ill-selected, themes, approach very nearly to that "paper of verses" which had been contemptuously described in the generation before them. Not a few of the later born of them, as well as many of those who will be noticed in a subsequent chapter,[1] make their appearance, if not their first or only

[1] See Vol. X, Chap. VII, *post.*

appearance, in that remarkable collection of Dodsley, to which, accordingly, we must devote some direct attention as a whole. Some, such as Watts, have an abiding memory for parts of their work, while the rest is absolutely forgotten. Some, like Garth, have a place in the formal history of poetry which ought to preserve them long after their theme has lost whatever interest it may once have possessed. Others, like Blackmore, live in those "singing flames" of satire which at least ensure an uncomfortable immortality. With the three just named, we may begin.

The batch of writers previously reviewed, more or less, deserve the politely contemptuous French epithet "canary"; they seldom attempted major themes, and, when they did, still more seldom attacked them with the "horse, foot and artillery" of the long poem. With the trio just mentioned, the case is altered. The individual scale of Watts's pieces is, indeed, generally small; but their tone is always serious. Garth's best known, or singly known, work is, in design, burlesque; but the scale is considerable and the plan involves stretches of treatment which are not burlesque at all. Whatever may be said about Blackmore, two charges could never be brought against him: that the manner of his versifications was frivolous or that their bulk was insignificant.

Sir Richard Blackmore, though his exact birth year does not seem to be known, took his M.A. degree at Oxford in 1676, and, therefore—at the very earliest age of matriculation likely, even at that time—must have been born nearer 1650 than 1660; so that he may have been ten years older than Sir Samuel Garth, who was born in 1661, and can hardly have been much less than twenty the senior of Isaac Watts, the date of whose birth was 1674. But the order of their poetical merit must, on almost any conceivable system of criticism, be reversed.

Very few people, it may be suspected, are nowadays in a position to give offhand any opinion based on knowledge of Watts's actual quality as a poet. "Watts's Hymns" (as *Divine Songs for Children* and *Moral Songs* are commonly, but incorrectly, called) early excluded his other work from notice, in accordance with the curious doom which literary reputations often have to undergo: and, while they themselves are probably little known now, their old familiarity has left behind it a sort of good-humoured contempt to rest on the sluggard, and the little busy bee and the everlastingly misquoted "Let dogs delight."

But, though there are some very pretty things among these faded *immortelles*, and though Watts's quite exceptional command of flexible and original metre is often shown in them, they are by no means the only or the chief poetical documents of his productivity. Whether against them, as against nearly all Watts's work, Johnson's well-known objection to sacred poetry will lie, must be left to individual opinion. It might, perhaps, be argued, without much danger of refutation, that the paucity of successes ought to be set against the extravagant multitude of attempts by quite unqualified hands, and that the existence of any successes at all—hardly to be denied in the face of a chain of verse from *Dies Irae* to not a few of Christina Rossetti's pieces—bars too sweeping a condemnation. Undoubtedly, the bulk, if not the whole body, of Watts's *Horae Lyricae* comes under the censure, whether it be just or unjust. Too much of this collection is in the perilous form of "pindaric," and too much of this, again, succumbs to the special dangers of turgidity and frigidity which beset that form. For strictly impertinent and hopelessly disproportionate bombast, Watts's *Elegy on Mr. Thomas Gouge*, which Southey has justly ridiculed, is hardly outstripped by anything in the English language. Yet, even here, amid the bombast and the bathos, occur phrases, and even passages, which, by themselves, dissociated from their subject, are unquestionable poetry.

Elsewhere, the faults are less and the merits more continuous. The sapphics "When the fierce north wind with his airy forces," like nearly all English attempts at the metre before the last half century, balance and pivot the rhythm wrongly; but there is, at least, something grandiose about them, and, like Watts's other things, they show a healthy reaction against the chilling uniformity of the couplet. Watts was one of the earliest to try blank verse; and few will think his "essays without rhyme," as he himself called them, an item on the wrong side of his account. He was sometimes very happy in the dangerous "short measure"—the old "poulters' measure" split into four; and, in whatever form he writes, we shall not accompany him far without (though, perhaps, in a rather different sense) agreeing with Johnson himself that "his ear was well tuned and his diction elegant and copious." Inferior as he may be to Collins,[1] he shows the same combat of time and man: while the time is even more against him. And one cannot help speculating on what he might have done if his *floruit* had coincided, not with the junction of the seventeenth and eighteenth centuries but with that of the eighteenth and nineteenth.

There need be no such speculation in considering the cheerful, craftsmanlike and, on its own schemes, almost fully adequate, verse of Garth—during the whole of his life, it would seem, a "prosperous gentleman," in the full meaning of both adjective and noun, though, perhaps, a little unlucky after his death. For Pope's well-known compliment of his being "the best good Christian without knowing it" shows the risk of having an epigrammatist for a friend. His few minor pieces, *Claremont*, a poem of a place in the *Cooper's Hill* style, some prologues, epilogues, dedications, Kit-cat glass-pieces, and so forth, are well enough, but unimportant. *The Dispensary*, Garth's *magnum opus* (or *opusculum majus*) obtains for him the description above awarded to his muse. It is a burlesque, not so much in the manner of *Macflecknoe* (to which Garth could not rise) as in the manner of Boileau's *Lutrin;* and its subject is a quarrel between members of the college of physicians about the supply of medicines to a dispensary established some years before. The poem was very popular, and was frequently reprinted during the author's life, always in a revised and enlarged form; the alterations, as is not always the case, being, almost invariably, improvements. Like all pieces of the kind, it requires, perhaps, on the part of posterity, a rather trying effort to understand its personal and temporal allusions, situations and parodies. But, even as supplying a sidelight on the ways of so exceptionally interesting a time as that of William III and Anne may surely be called, it is valuable. To the student of English literature and English poetry, however, it has a far more cogent appeal. It represents, as a sort of practical *Ars Poetica* or object lesson, the stage between Dryden and Pope, and, without exaggeration, may be said to be the first draft—and not a very rough first draft—of the couplet versification and the poetic diction which were to dominate the

[1] See Vol. X, Chap. VII, *post.*

whole eighteenth century. There was nothing in Garth even distantly approaching the genius of Dryden or the genius of Pope; but he had learnt from Dryden all that Dryden could teach to a younger contemporary of more than ordinary talent, and he anticipated Pope in most things that did not require Pope's special gifts. The smooth running couplets with a clinching stamp at the close; the well-marked pause in the centre of each line; the balanced epithets in the respective halves, sometimes achieving epigram, but too frequently tempting to "pad"—all these things appear. And, in some passages, such as Horoscope's flight to Teneriffe and the descent of Hygeia to the shades, the method is shown almost within reach of its best, though its defects, too, already appear.

There is, thus, no need of the courage or the callousness of a "Swiss of Heaven" in making out a case for Watts or for Garth; but what shall be said of Blackmore? The present writer has read a great deal of Blackmore at different times, has recently re-read some and believes that his knowledge, if not exhaustive, is, at least, adequate. So far as it goes (and it extends even to *Eliza*, in part), it certainly does not support Johnson's contention that Blackmore has been exposed to worse treatment than he deserved; nor does it—and, on this head, it is pretty complete—enable him to accept the other dictum that *Creation*, if the poet had written nothing else, would have transmitted him to posterity among the first favourites of the English muse. Dismiss (most readers will not have much difficulty in doing so) all thoughts of *Arthur* ("*Prince*" and "*King*"), *Eliza*, *Alfred* and the rest; allow nothing on the score that Blackmore's diploma-piece, which the respectable Mr. Molyneux and the great Mr. Locke esteemed highly, consists of verses like

> He spread the airy ocean without shores
> Where birds are wafted by their feathered oars;

let *Creation*, which is easily accessible, count alone, with no bias, for or against it, from the fact that the praises of Addison and Johnson, if not those of Molyneux and Locke, were evidently secured by its decent orthodoxy—and in this work will be noticed an absence of the positive absurdities with which Blackmore's other poems abound; so that it will seem as if there were some foundation for the curious story that Blackmore submitted the piece to a club of wits, surely more complacent and more patient than wits usually are, who corrected it almost line by line. It displays some argumentative power: and the verse is not entirely devoid of vigour. But the whole is a flat expanse of bare didactic; while its constant attempt to cope directly with Lucretius adds exasperation to the disappointed expectance of something even distantly approaching the *furor arduus* of the enemy. The conclusion is that one must alter Johnson's final verdict slightly. He says that "whoever judges of this by any other of Blackmore's performances will do it injury." We should say that, in order to enjoy or endure *Creation*, at least one, and, if possible, more, of Blackmore's other performances ought to have been mastered. The reader would then, at least, feel how much worse *Creation* might have been.

Among the remaining verse-writers, a convenient sub-section may be formed of those who belong more particularly to what may be called the *Spectator* division—not that they were in all cases contributors to that periodical, though some were— the two Philipses, Edmund (or "Rag") Smith, William Broome, Elijah Fenton, John Hughes and Laurence Eusden.[1] All these were in, more or less, close connection with Addison, or Pope, or both; while, to them, we may add, though they were outliers in this respect, Joseph Trapp, who was born nearly as far back in the seventeenth century as Addison, and much earlier than Pope, outlived even the latter, and nearly reached the middle of the eighteenth; together with Henry Brooke, author of *The Fool of Quality*, who was a poet before he was a novelist, and David Mallet, who, to one doubtful, adds another certain, claim for something more than catalogue rank. It is in this group that we reach what we may call full eighteenth-century character, with little or nothing of "the last age" in them. Yet it is most noticeable, and to be missed only at the risk of missing, with it, the continuity of English verse, that, in them, we find two notes of the future which, in some degree, recall that last age itself. John Philips, long before Thomson, and with hardly any predecessors except Roscommon, reintroduced blank verse, the very Trojan horse of the citadel of the couplet. Ambrose

[1] As to Tickell see *ante*, pp. 191–194.

Philips, "Namby-Pamby"—the poet of society verse far below
Prior, of pastorals pastoralised to the most artificial-trivial
extent possible, of pale translations and second-hand things in
various *rococo* styles—introduces a second *fatalis machina*, a
machine more fatal than the former, in the shape of the three
volumes of *Ballads* published in 1723.[1]   And Mallet, in *William
and Margaret*, gives the first remarkable and influential example
of that ballad *pastiche* which has been disdained or abused for a
century past, but which, perhaps, was very much more effective
as a shoe-horn to draw on the romantic revival than, to that age,
would have been the genuine antiquities themselves.

John Philips, almost exactly a contemporary of Ambrose so
far as birth went, was an Oxford man of the Christ Church
set noteworthy at the junction of the centuries, and a tory;
while Ambrose was of St. John's college, Cambridge, and a
whig.   Although there does not seem to have been any personal
enmity between John Philips and Addison—indeed they had a
common intimacy through "Rag" Smith, and Addison praised
The Splendid Shilling highly—Philips, rather unluckily for
himself, was chosen to be pitted against Addison in celebrating
Blenheim.   The burlesque of Milton in *The Splendid Shilling*
is good-humoured, not in the least offensive, amusing and by no
means critically unjust; while the credit of the serious blank
verse of *Cyder* (for John Philips was the first well-known writer
after Milton to make this metre his chief vehicle) need not
depend on the certificate received by Johnson from "the great
gardener and botanist" Miller, to the effect that there was
more truth in it than in many prose treatises on the same subject.   *Blenheim* is that most terrible of failures, an unconscious
burlesque.   But it must be remembered, in Philips's excuse,
first, that Milton's description of the battles in Heaven is not
exactly the finest art of *Paradise Lost* and, secondly, that
"Rag" Smith's regret at its not having been written in Latin
means more than it directly conveys.   Undoubtedly, Philips
thought the poem more in the way of a prize composition in a
learned language than as anything original and vernacular;
and, had he written it thus, it would probably, to retort and
enlarge Macaulay's sneering comparison, have been quite as
good as most of Silius Italicus, and perhaps not so very much

[1] As to Ambrose Philips, see *ante*, pp. 184–186.

worse than parts of Lucan.   As it is, the other two poems set
men on the recovery of one of the greatest instruments of
English versification; and, if he was the author of the "Baccha-
nalian song" printed with them, he gave some hints to the
latest, and almost the best, of our practitioners in that cheerful
kind—Thomas Love Peacock.

Why Pope, in commiserating his own "ten whole years" of
collaborative translation, should have been more unkind to
William Broome than to Elijah Fenton, when both were his
collaborators, has not, I believe, been discovered: for jealousy of
superior scholarship, the commonly imputed cause, would have
applied to both.   Possibly there is no other reason than that
one presents a convenient, the other a very unlikely, rime.
There is, indeed, said to have been a contrast in temper—
Broome being rough, in that respect, and Fenton easy-going.
But, what might hardly have been expected, even had both
been of amiable dispositions, the pair of lieutenants were perfectly good friends.   It is curious that both of them attempted
blank verse translations of Homer, though the only permanent
fame that either was to achieve was as coadjutors in Pope's
couplet-manufactory, and as "hands" so "skilled" that, from
the first, it was difficult to isolate the work of any of the three
by mere reading.   Except for this connection with Pope and
for this early demonstration of the fatal facility of, at least, part
of his method, neither deserves much notice here.   Both
"pindarised"; both, in their lighter moods, tried the licensed
levities of octosyllabic tale and of lyric, more or less prim or
arch.   Both, but especially Broome, exhibit, in their blank
verse, that fatal tendency to stiff and stopped central pauses
which was to reach its height in Glover.   Johnson perceived,
though admitting that he could not define, a peculiarity in
Fenton's versification; but the present writer, though somewhat to this manner used, has neither discovered the secret—
nor, indeed, the fact.

Edmund or "Rag" Smith and John Hughes were both
friends of Addison.   The first, whose *Phaedra and Hippolitus*
bears about the same relation to *Phèdre* as Philips's *Distressed
Mother* does to *Andromaque*, was a typical example of the ne'er-
do-well scholar.   His work has smuggled itself into the *British
Poets;* but the assistance of his friends and the long suffering of

his college could not profit him, and his loose living carried him off before he experienced actual want. He must have had real humour—his Latin analysis of Pocock is one of the best things of the kind; and Addison's reply to his objection "What am I to do with Lord Sunderland?" (Smith being asked to write a whig *History of the Revolution*) "When were you drunk last, Rag?" is singularly defective in moral logic. The absurd panegyric of Oldisworth (in his memoir of Smith), cited by Johnson, ought not to be reckoned against wits which everyone seems to have acknowledged. But he has left us hardly any material for deciding whether he could have been a poet had he chosen. John Hughes put in more documents. That he edited, and showed some, though no complete, appreciation of Spenser, does not bring him within our range, but near it. It is noteworthy that Addison actually thought of him as a collaborator in *Cato;* and his own selection of the subject of his *Siege of Damascus* from so unusual a quarter as the early history of Islam argues a really poetical taste.[1] Nor is it absolutely necessary to accept Swift's decision that Hughes was "among the *mediocrists*," and Pope's that he "wanted genius." They were not altogether in the wrong; but this chapter is a chapter of "mediocrists," and there are things in Hughes's verse which neither Pope nor Swift was very well qualified to recognise. The "contents" of it would read not unlike those of Broome's and Fenton's; but the quality is sometimes superior. He seems to have been a special admirer and follower of Dryden's lyrical work, which he was even unwise enough sometimes to refashion, and he has succeeded in catching something, if not much, of that touch of the older magic which Dryden's lyre could give forth.

The members of a trio also named above, if not exactly great in themselves, belong to *gentes paullo majores* in poetry. Joseph Trapp was not only the first professor of poetry at Oxford, and, thus, possibly, the first professor of English literature in England, as well as the author of discourses on the subject which have solid critical merit; but he was a practical craftsman, if not exactly an artist in verses, and the author of one member of a most famous pair of epigrams; concerning which it is, perhaps, not improper to remark that, as he was actually incorporated

---

[1] As to Hughes's dramatic work, cf. *ante*, Vol. VIII, p. 220.

at Cambridge, mere inter-university jealousy could have nothing to do with the matter.　The eccentric author of *The Fool of Quality*, Henry Brooke, was a poet long before he published that strange compound of genius and dulness.　There were full thirty years between it and *Universal Beauty*—his longest and best known, though by no means his earliest or his best, work, in verse.　This philosophical poem is of a kind of which More and his group had set the fashion in the seventeenth century, and which was taken up in its own modes by the eighteenth.　It has only to be compared with Blackmore's much more belauded *Creation*—to which, in subject, it is partly akin—in order to see the immense improvement of form which Pope, who is said to have actually bestowed on it some revision, had brought about, as well as the fine talents of the younger writer.　It is more scientific than theological, though by no means atheistic or even deistic.　Indeed, Brooke, in his latter days, was reputed a "methodist."[1]　An attempt to translate Tasso, also in couplet, is but ineffectual, and a condensation of Chaucer's *Man of Law's Tale* sinks far below the comparative inadequacy of Dryden in such things, while it has nothing of his positive excellence.　Brooke also wrote *Fables*, in which he exhibits a fair knack at using the easy octosyllables in whose undress the century at large took refuge from the panoply of the heroic. A very curious piece called *Conrade*, purporting to be an ancient Irish legend, can hardly be without obligations to Macpherson —unless, indeed, it is the other way.　But Brooke has confined himself, so far as form goes, to constantly redundant heroic lines.　And the songs interspersed in his play are more than fairly successful when they are light, and not always a failure when they are serious.　Over all his work—verse and prose— there is, indeed, a curious atmosphere of frittered and wasted talent, sometimes approaching genius.　But, in his later days, he was, at least partially, insane: and whether he had been wholly sane at any time may, perhaps, be doubted.

On the other hand, though very harsh things have been said of David Malloch, who, for prudential reasons, changed his name to Mallet, just as his father, a Macgregor, had already changed his to Malloch during the outlawry of the clan, there never has been the slightest doubt about his sanity.　The

[1] As to his relation to the mystical movement see Chap. XII, *post*.

transactions of his life which made him most notorious, his reception of Sarah duchess of Marlborough's legacy for writing the life of her husband, and his neglect to perform the duty imposed; his still more famous acceptance of hire from Bolingbroke to libel Pope after his death; and his much more defensible share in the attack on Byng—these do not concern us here. But, to say, as Johnson says, that "there is no species of composition in which he was eminent" is merely to exclude, as Johnson doubtless did, the one species in which he was very eminent indeed. *William and Margaret*, written as early as 1723 is, of course, to some extent, a *pastiche* of older ballads and of snatches of Elizabethan song. But the older ballads themselves were always, more or less, *pastiches* of each other. And, if the piece had some creditors, it had many more debtors; nor does any single copy of verses deserve so much credit for setting the eighteenth century back on the road of true romantic poetry by an easy path, suited to its own tastes and powers. As to *Rule, Britannia*, modern criticism has usually been inclined to assign it rather to Thomson than to Mallet, though the two undoubtedly collaborated in the play wherein it appeared. But, to tell the truth, the merit of the piece lies rather in the music and the sentiment than in the poetry. Mallet's more ambitious poems *Amyntor and Theodora, The Excursion*, etc. are of little value; but the song gift of *William and Margaret* reappears in *The Birks of Endermay* (better known as *Invermay*). *Edwin and Emma*, once as well known as either and, perhaps, also possessing some schoolmaster virtue, is vastly inferior to *William and Margaret*.

Before turning to the *numerus numeri*—the tail of the list of these things seldom rich or rare, but, somehow, ambered in literary history—we must deal with one who, at some times, and to not a few persons, would have seemed worthy of a much more dignified place in the story. But, to the present writer, Richard Savage is as mediocre a mediocrist as Swift could possibly have found among his own contemporaries. The famous romance of his birth and maltreatment seems to be now almost unanimously disbelieved by historical critics: and, though his memory must always retain the great and inalienable privilege of Johnson's friendship, and of the *Life* which that friendship prompted, these can add nothing to his individual and intrinsic literary value. On the other hand, neither is it affected by the circumstance that, apart from Johnson's testimony to his friend, and even from some dropped hints in that testimony, we should be apt to think him an impostor, a libeller and something of a ruffian. We have only to do with the works and, when we turn to them, what do we find? *The Wanderer* may not be the worst of the descriptive didactic verse-tractates of its century; but, to the usual inquiry whether, as poems, they have any particular reason for existence, and the usual answer in the negative, there has to be added, in this case, the discovery that it has really no plan at all, and (the words are Johnson's own, and the sentiment is not denied by him) is a "heap of shining materials thrown together by accident." But we must ask, further, "Do the materials really shine?" and, if so, "with what sort of lustre?" The answer, one fears, must be, "With that of tinsel at best." *The Bastard* has a false air of pathos and indignation which will not survive careful reading. Neither passion nor poetry, but merely rhetoric, supplies the phrasing; and, long before you reach the end of the poem, you have been prepared to find it turn into a begging letter to queen Caroline. The *Volunteer Laureat* odes to the same royal personage are fully exposed to the stock satire on the regularly commissioned utterances of that kind of muse; and the lesser pieces are quite insignificant. One famous line of *The Bastard*,

> No tenth transmitter of a foolish face,

is not uncommonly attributed to Pope; and, perhaps, ignorance has here hit upon the truth, for Pope was very good to Savage. But it might well be a "windfall of the Muses" to anyone who, with his wits about him—and Savage certainly had his—had read either Pope himself, or, better still, Dryden.

We must now, with more excuse than the rash Frenchman in *Henry V*, "to the throng." Stephen Duck, queen Caroline's laureate *en titre*, and, as such, a special object not merely of Savage's jealousy but of Pope's, was a "silly shepherd," who, in his own life, showed forth a truer and a sadder moral than is to be found in all the fables and pastorals which have dealt with his kind. There was no more harm in Duck himself than there was good in the verses because of which they took him from the Wiltshire downs and made him a shepherd of souls. But he knew, if others did not, that he was in the wrong place, and committed suicide when barely fifty. His poems were dead before him; and nobody has ever attempted to revive them. Aaron Hill—a busy poetaster, playwright[1] and projector, whose work received hospitality from Anderson though not from Chalmers, who was a friend, and, so far as his means allowed, a patron to many poets of his time, and, coming in for Pope's satire, "took it fighting" and maintained an honourable reputation— was far above Duck but never got much beyond fair sprightliness. It is difficult to pardon him when one finds him, "on a *hint*," as he coolly says, "from Sir Henry Wotton," helping himself to almost every word and to whole lines of "You meaner beauties of the night" but mixing and watering them with his own feeble verbiage till there results one of the veriest smudges of paraphrase to be met with anywhere. And his pindarics have all the turgidity and all the frigidity of that luckless and misused form. But he is sometimes not undeserving of the compliment which Pope tacked to his sarcasm, and, if not quite a swan, is not wholly a goose, of Thames. In sprightliness itself, Hill nowhere approaches the justly famed *Pipe of Tobacco* of Isaac Hawkins Browne, a series of parodies which is one of the pleasantest items of *Dodsley* and which deserves a very respectable place among the many imitations of it which have appeared. David Lewis, who published two collections of poems by various hands many years before *Dodsley* itself, is, at least probably, responsible for the charming piece *My Winifreda*, which appears there as well as in Percy's *Reliques*, and has no other known author. To the names of Laurence Eusden, once poet laureate, Hildebrand Jacob and others it is difficult to attach the mention of any diploma-piece: but Anthony Hammond and his son James show, by comparison with their ancestor William[2] in the seventeenth century, that poetry, or at least verse-making, does run in families. Johnson was severe on James; but his amorousness will, perhaps, stand proof as well as Yalden's sublimity.

Two writers who, in the busy part of their lives, were nearly

---

[1] As to his dramatic labours, see Vol. X, Chap. IV, *post.*
[2] See *ante* Vol. VII. pp. 94, 100.

contemporary, who belong, one by attraction and the other by repulsion, to the circle of Pope, were active practitioners of verse as translators and otherwise, but, perhaps, derive their chief importance from connection with the criticism of poetry rather than with its production. Leonard Welsted, a Westminster and Cambridge man, wrote a good deal of verse and, indeed, hardly deserved, though he had provoked it, his place in the *inferno* of *The Dunciad*, even as a versifier. But his translation of Longinus does not show any mark of dulness, while the original remarks connected with it show that, if he could not exactly produce poetry, he could appreciate it in Spenser and Shakespeare to a degree not common in his day. Christopher Pitt, who was of Winchester and Oxford, and who could be intimate with Dodington and yet not lose some favour with Pope, throws a longer and larger shadow in this skiagraphy. His translation of Vergil, in a measure, ousted Dryden's in the his own words and lines, he will lose very little of him in those of Pitt.

The imitation of Spenser which has just been glanced at, and which, despite some recent attempts to contest the fact, was certainly a very important feature in the history of eighteenth century poetry, is, perhaps, not the only thing that need keep alive the memory of Gilbert West (to be distinguished from Richard West, the friend of Gray). He would otherwise be "only an excellent person," as, indeed, he seems also to have been. In his translations from Pindar and others, it is impossible to take any interest, and his occasional poems are very few and very slight. But his Spenserian *pastiches*, *The Abuse of Travelling* and *Education*, are not mere sketches or mere parodies, and deserve a little study. Johnson who, more than once, protested against the practice of which West seems to have furnished some of the earliest examples, yet allowed them contemporary, who belong, one by attraction and the other by repulsion, to the circle of Pope, were active practitioners of verse as translators and otherwise, but, perhaps, derive their chief importance from connection with the criticism of poetry rather than with its production. Leonard Welsted, a Westminster and Cambridge man, wrote a good deal of verse and, indeed, hardly deserved, though he had provoked it, his place in the *inferno* of *The Dunciad*, even as a versifier. But his translation of Longinus does not show any mark of dulness, while the original remarks connected with it show that, if he could not exactly produce poetry, he could appreciate it in Spenser and Shakespeare to a degree not common in his day. Christopher Pitt, who was of Winchester and Oxford, and who could be intimate with Dodington and yet not lose some favour with Pope, throws a longer and larger shadow in this skiagraphy. His translation of Vergil, in a measure, ousted Dryden's in the favour of the eighteenth century; though, to the possibly more impartial judgment of a posterity almost equally remote from either, it has not much, if anything, more of Vergil and a good deal less of poetry. His miscellaneous poems—which include many minor translations, one of the absolutely un-Spenserian imitations of the time, addresses to Young, Spence, Dodington and others, and some trifles—require no comment. But his other chief translation, earlier in date than *The Æneid*, that of Vida's *Art of Poetry*, is one of those things which, whatever their comparative merit and value as to kind, have a very high position in the kind to which they belong. Vida himself is open to plentiful censure. But, earlier than anyone else and in Latin verse of remarkable ease and finish, he had put the very theory of poetry which was held for much more than two centuries after his death in almost every country of Europe. And Pitt, holding that view still, and helped in testifying to it by the methodic achievements of Dryden and Pope, besides being possessed, too, of adequate scholarship and a competent faculty of verse, produced that rarest of things—a verse translation which really represents the original. For once, the translator is no traitor: the substance and the manner of his author are reproduced with extraordinary felicity. No real student of the history and criticism of poetry should fail to read Vida: and if (most unfortunately) he cannot read him in his own words and lines, he will lose very little of him in those of Pitt.

The imitation of Spenser which has just been glanced at, and which, despite some recent attempts to contest the fact, was certainly a very important feature in the history of eighteenth century poetry, is, perhaps, not the only thing that need keep alive the memory of Gilbert West (to be distinguished from Richard West, the friend of Gray). He would otherwise be "only an excellent person," as, indeed, he seems also to have been. In his translations from Pindar and others, it is impossible to take any interest, and his occasional poems are very few and very slight. But his Spenserian *pastiches*, *The Abuse of Travelling* and *Education*, are not mere sketches or mere parodies, and deserve a little study. Johnson who, more than once, protested against the practice of which West seems to have furnished some of the earliest examples, yet allowed them to be successful as regards "the metre, the language and fiction"; but a single line, taken at random,

> And all the arts that cultivate the mind

will, perhaps, induce readers to doubt the critic's praise as much as his blame. West, it is true, is not always so utterly un-Spenserian as this; but his choice of subjects is, in itself, fatal, and his intention is generally defeated by his execution itself.

The verses of James Bramston, some of which are to be found in *Dodsley*, are fair specimens of the easiest eighteenth century "verse of society"; but the honour of bringing up the rear in this procession of individuals must be reserved for one who, mere hack of letters as he was, and little as is positively known about him, accumulates an unusual assemblage of interesting details round his personality and his work. Reputed son of the great marquis of Halifax, ancestor, it seems, of Edmund Kean; creator, in the farce-burlesque of *Chrononhotonthologos*, of many quaint names and some actual lines of verse which have stuck in literary memory; inventor of Ambrose Philips's nickname, and of a rare set of skittish verses attached to it; musician, playwright and (it would seem, almost as much in gaiety of heart as on any other occasion in his life) suicide—Henry Carey will live for ever, if not in any of the above capacities, as author of the delightful words, and the almost more delightful music, of *Sally in Our Alley.*

More than one or two of these poets and versifiers, as well as several to be mentioned later, and some who must be merely catalogued or left altogether to silence, owed, if not (as in some cases they did) actual first publication, at any rate notoriety and even popularity, to a member of the maligned order of "booksellers"—Robert Dodsley, footman, verse-writer, playwright and publisher. Nearly all testimonies to "the good-natured author of *The Muse in Livery*" (as Thackeray calls him, in one of those invented touches which have almost the value of historical anecdotes) are favourable; and, if not a man of remarkable taste himself, he must have had a faculty very close thereto, that of catching at good suggestions from others. That he published much good work by many great men—Pope, Gray, Johnson—and others not far short of great—Young, Akenside, Chesterfield, Walpole—may have been partly matter of luck. But the publisher of the two collections of *Old Plays*, and of *Poems by Several Hands*, must, necessarily, have been a man of enterprise, and, almost as necessarily, one who knew a good thing when the idea occurred or was suggested to him. His own verse, which may be found in Chalmers, is by no means contemptible, and displays that peculiar ease—conventional to a certain extent, but with a conventionality differing from affectation—which, it may almost be said, came in and went out with the eighteenth century itself. But he had far too much good sense to make his *Collection* a means of publishing or republishing his own work. At first (1748), it consisted of three volumes only; the fourth, fifth and sixth appeared later, and the set was not completed till 1758. But it was very frequently reprinted; and, in 1775, more than a decade after Dodsley's death, it was revised by Pearch, with a continuation of four volumes more, in which many of the contributors to *Dodsley* reappear in company with some younger writers. The complete collection will supply something like a companion or chrestomathy to any review, like the present, of lesser eighteenth century poets.

W. P. Courtney, in a privately published book on the *Collection*, invaluable to all students of it, quotes, from *The*

Gentleman's Magazine for 1845, a diatribe (originally dated August, 1819, and extracted from *The Portfolio of a Man of the World*), the author of which does not seem to be known, against *Dodsley* as something than which "a more piteous farrago of flatness never was seen." This Aristarch proceeds to denounce its "paltry page of dilettante rhymes," "its namby-pamby rhyming"; wonders "how there could have been so many men in England who could write such stuff," finds in it "a littleness, an utter dulness which would be disheartening if it were not so gloriously contrasted by our present race" and remarks "what giants we appear in comparison to our fathers." Yet this censor, though he did admit "some redeeming pieces of the preceding generation," forgot that the best of them were not older but strictly contemporary. Gray was but just over thirty when *Dodsley* appeared first; Collins was but seven-and-twenty. If it was a day of small things generally in poetry; yet, but for Dodsley and his continuator, the proper estimation of that day would be very much more difficult than it is. And the censor might, to his advantage, have remembered that no period was ever more cheerfully convinced of the satisfactory appearance which it presented "in comparison with its fathers" than the very age which he was denouncing.

At the same time, if there was a great deal of ineptitude in attacking, there would, perhaps, be some in defending too ostentatiously and apologetically a collection which enshrines most of the best things of Gray, and some of not the worst things of Collins; *The Spleen* and *Grongar Hill* and *The Schoolmistress* and the *Hymn to the Naiads;* the inimitable mischief of Lady Mary's satire on society, and the stately rhetoric of Johnson's *Vanity of Human Wishes;* besides scores of pleasant trifles, like Browne's *Pipe of Tobacco* and Byrom's celebration of the Figg and Sutton battle, Warton's *Progress of Discontent* and James Merrick's *Cameleon*. Of the many mansions of poetry this may not be the most magnificent; but there are worse places for at least occasional residence than a comfortable Georgian house, with now and then a prospect from the windows into things not merely contemporary.

CHAPTER VII

Historical and Political Writers

I

BURNET

THE historical writers of the period covered by this volume may be grouped round two who, in the greater part of their literary activity, belong respectively to two different ages of English history. But Burnet survived the accomplishment of the Hanoverian succession, and Bolingbroke's most important literary activity connects itself with the early Georgian age.

Among the already numerous writings of Gilbert Burnet,[1] while he was still resident in Scotland and wholly occupied with the affairs—more especially, of course, the ecclesiastical affairs —of that kingdom, the following seem to call for special mention. In 1665 was printed anonymously *A Discourse on the Memory of that rare and truly virtuous Person Sir Robert Fletcher of Saltoun, written by a gentleman of his acquaintance,*[2] which is, in fact, only the reproduction of an inflated funeral sermon. His *Thoughts on Education*, on the other hand, though not printed till 1761, was written in 1668; designed as a series of suggestions for the training of a Scottish nobleman or gentleman's son, it does not make any reference to a university course, and is chiefly remarkable for the general breadth and liberality of the author's educational ideas. Burnet rightly

---

[1] Concerning Burnet as a divine, see Vol. VIII, Chap. XI.

[2] It appears to contain little or nothing about either Sir Robert or, of course, his more celebrated son, Burnet's pupil, who, at the time, was about twelve years of age.

deprecated the choice of a governor or tutor who was "a man of one study only"; and his ideas on religious instruction were in accordance with the latitudinarian tendencies of his later years, and with the dictates of common-sense. In the following year, he put forth, in the then popular dialogue form, *A Modest and Free Conference betwixt a Conformist and a Non-conformist, about the present distempers of Scotland*—a plea for "peace" from the moderate episcopalian point of view, which ends with an explanation of the oath of supremacy, not unfairly characterised by the (otherwise rather ineffective) nonconformist of the dialogue as "clearly making way for Erastianism." The announcement prefatory to these dialogues makes a great to-do of secrecy in connection with their publication. In the same year, Burnet moved to Glasgow, where he had been appointed professor of divinity, and where the failure of the accommodation scheme promoted by archbishop Leighton and himself rendered him impatient of episcopalian, and, still more, of presbyterian, modes of action. His attention was thus diverted from theology to history, and it was while still at Glasgow, that, by 1673, he completed his earliest historical work, though, in consequence of numerous changes which fear of Lauderdale, and consideration for even more exalted personages, made it advisable to introduce into the work, he did not publish it till four years later.

The Memoires of the Lives and Actions of James and William Dukes of Hamilton and Castleherald grew out of a series of visits to Hamilton, where Anne, the gifted wife of the third, and daughter of the first, duke, gave the eager young professor access to her father's, and her husband's, papers. Thus, it naturally suggested itself to him to compose a work on the lines which had already been followed in numerous French memoirs, although, to quote Burnet's preface, "there is but one in this country that hath hitherto written in that Method, and his Collections are so well received that it gives great encouragement to anyone who will follow him in it." In other words, Rushworth[1] was Burnet's exemplar; and, in an interesting disquisition in this preface, he argues in favour of the change of plan which, in accordance with the advice of Sir Robert Moray, esteemed by Burnet the wisest and worthiest man of the age,

---

[1] See, as to his *Collections*, Vol. VII, p. 213, *ante*.

he had adopted, in substituting for a historical relation a series of original documents, connected with one another by a narrative thread. Some of these links (the account, for instance, of Scottish church affairs from the reformation; the summary of Montrose's chances; the story of James duke of Hamilton's escape from Windsor; and the character of the duke following on the long account of his trial, with farewell letters, dying speech and prayer) are clear and impressive pieces of writing; but the interest of the work, as a whole, lies in the documents, as to which we have Gardiner's assurance that "the general accuracy of the book bears the test of a comparison" with the Hamilton papers examined by himself.[1] Burnet's work, by reason, rather than in spite, of its pragmatic character, has a place of its own in English historical literature. Whether its purpose of vindicating the character of the first duke of Hamilton from the reflections freely cast upon it was successfully accomplished is not a question which calls for discussion here.[2] Failure was the result of practically every undertaking in which he engaged, from his expedition in support of Gustavus Adolphus to his invasion of England at the head of a Scottish army; and his conciliatory spirit in public, as well as in private, affairs (he was a chief supporter of Dury's scheme for the union of the protestant churches) is no set-off against his repeated lack of insight as well as of resolution. His brother William, the second duke, of whose experiences up to his death at Worcester Burnet treats in a short concluding seventh book, was of a quicker, brisker and more determined nature; but there is a touch of pathos in the story of his "good end."

When, in May, 1679, Burnet brought out the first portion of his second historical work, which may be said to have established his importance in both English politics and in English historical literature, he had been a resident in London for about five years. His position there long had in it an element of uncertainty. Charles II, who, in 1673, had received him kindly as a visitor from Scotland, and had shown himself pleased with

---

[1] Burnet himself states: "The Vouchers of this whole Work lie at Hamilton."

[2] At least, it thoroughly refutes "one of the most bloody and pernicious of all the hellish slanders" to which the duke's name was subjected—the charge that he confused Scottish affairs in order to fish a crown for himself out of the troubled waters.

what he had read in manuscript of *The Memoires of the Hamil-tons*, he found considerably cooled towards him at a second audience in the following year.   Lauderdale, to whom, in the same year, Burnet had dedicated, in fulsome terms, his *Vindi-cation of the Authority, Constitution, and Laws of the Church of Scotland* (a series of dialogues composed from the point of view of a moderate episcopalian, staunch, however, to the principle of non-resistance), was now his enemy; and, in April, 1675, Burnet actually appeared before a committee of the House of Commons in support of charges brought against the duke. For the rest, though, in a sense, cast upon the world, Burnet never more signally displayed his buoyancy of spirit.   His acquaint-ance, the veteran Lord Holles,[1] now a leader of the opposition, induced Sir Harbottle Grimston, formerly speaker of the con-vention parliament, and now master of the rolls, a bitter foe of Rome, to appoint him preacher at the Rolls chapel, to which post was soon added the Thursday lectureship at St. Clement Danes; and his efforts in the pulpit—perhaps of all spheres of his activity the most congenial to him[2]—were seconded by those of his pen.   In London, he came into constant contact with Tillotson, Stillingfleet, Tenison and other representatives of the latitudinarianism under the influence of which, well read as he was in patristic literature, he had already fallen during an early visit to Cambridge (1663).   By far the most important of his productions in these London years (in which, it should be remembered, fell the so-called discovery of the popish plot and the ensuing agitation) was *The History of the Reformation of the Church of England*.   The first volume of this work, on which he had been busy during a large part of the years 1677 and 1678, was published in the summer of 1679.   No historical work was ever more fortunate in the time of its appearance; a pro-testant terror was sweeping the country; and the opposition, with which his relations had become very friendly, at last seemed to have the game in its own hands.   So late as December, 1680, he preached before the Commons on the occasion of a public fast for the prevention of all popish plots, and was thanked by the House for his sermon and for his *History*, the Lords join-ing in the latter acknowledgment.   And so much importance

[1] As to Denzil, Lord Holles, cf. *ante*, Vol. VII, Chap. IX, pp. 255 and bibl., **507** and 513, 514.   [2] Cf. *ante*, Vol. VIII, Chap. XI.

was attached to his ability and address, that, a year or two earlier (1678–9), he was repeatedly summoned to a secret audience with the king, when, however (as was not unfrequently the case with him), his indiscretions completely ruined the situation.

Quite apart, however, from the circumstances which made *The History of the Reformation* a book of the moment, there are considerations which go far to justify the opinion of Burnet's most recent biographer that this work "forms an epoch in our historical literature."[1] This tribute is its due, not so much because of the style of the book, which, besides being far more readable than any historical work proper which had preceded it, has the great merit of sincerity and clearly reflects the reasoned convictions of its author, a protestant and an erastian to the core. But the distinctive excellence of *The History* lies in its combination of these qualities with a sustained endeavour on the part of the author to base his narrative upon a personal investigation of the original documents at his command. In other words, he seeks, however imperfectly, to apply to the exposition of his subject the principles underlying a scientific treatment of history; in yet other words, he desires to reproduce so much of the truth concerning that subject as has become visible to his eye. These ideas, as has been seen, had been present to his mind when he set out to write *The Hamilton Memoirs;* and now he undertook to carry them out on a much larger scale and in reference to a body of events and transactions of the highest historical significance. Indeed, he seems to have contemplated the execution of the still more comprehensive design of a history of England, suggested to him by Sir William Jones, when he was diverted from this by the appearance, in 1676, of a new French translation, by F. de Mancroix, of Nicholas Sanders's *De Origine ac Progressu Schismatis Anglicani*, first printed in 1585, and first translated into French in the following year. The collection of materials, which Burnet was resolved upon obtaining, so far as possible, at first hand, proved a matter of great difficulty; for, though he had the encouragement and the advice of Stillingfleet and Lloyd[2] (to

---

[1] Foxcroft, H. C., *A Life of Gilbert Burnet, Bishop of Salisbury*, p. 151.

[2] As to Stillingfleet, bishop of Worcester, see Vol. VIII, Chapters XI and XVI *ante;* as to William Lloyd, successively bishop of St. Asaph, Lichfield and Coventry and Worcester, see *ib.*, Chap. XII.

whom, with Tillotson, the first draft of the work was submitted), as well as that of Sir John Marsham and William Petyt, he confesses to have had little experience in the very first requisite of the modern historian's task, the search for materials; and, to the chief storehouse of them, in the present case, Sir John Cotton's library, he and his amanuensis had only surreptitious access for a few days during the absence of the owner. In addition to Burnet's inexperience in the work of transcription, and the haste in which much of it had to be performed, the natural impatience of his disposition, and an inborn readiness to overleap difficulties in the way of conclusions, could not but affect the actual result of his labours. A great deal of fault has been found—and, no doubt, justly—with the inaccuracy and general imperfection of the transcripts on which his work was largely founded and which gave rise to endless blunders, although, of the myriad which his conscientious editor declares himself to have corrected,[1] a large proportion must have been excusable, and many, of course, are trivial. Some, however, were prompted by the strong opinions which Burnet never made any pretence of concealing. But, as he spared no pains—he is said to have read over Paolo Sarpi's *History of the Council of Trent* four or five times in order to master the historian's method—so he was certainly not intentionally incorrect. Notwithstanding the mistakes which he continued to commit, even after the success of his first volume had opened to him the Paper office, with Cotton's library and other invaluable collections of documents, his work, which was not published in its complete form till 1715,[2] remains an achievement worthy of the love of research which inspired it. Nor is the book without other merits. The story, as here given, of the renunciation of the Roman obedience by the church of England, and the conjunct story of Henry VIII's divorce from Catharine and of the imposition by him of the Acts of Succession and Supremacy, are

[1] See the elaborate preface in the concluding (seventh) volume of N. Pocock's edition (Oxford, 1865); where the critical and controversial literature connected with Burnet's work is examined at length. For the controversy with Atterbury see pp. 187 f.

[2] Part I had covered the reign of Henry VIII. Part II, dealing with the reign of Edward VI, and said to have been written in six weeks, appeared in 1681 ; part III (supplement) in 1715, when an unsatisfactory edition of the two earlier parts was also published. The records, throughout, were kept separate from the narrative.

told with force as well as with clearness, and without obvious suppression of any element in the tale. The author does not make any attempt to disguise his thoroughly protestant convictions; indeed, as against the Jesuits, he lets himself lapse into invective. But, in general, the dispassionateness of his narrative is almost as striking as its straightforwardness—the catastrophe of More and Fisher, for instance, seems related without partiality.

Of the principal controversial writings to which *The History of the English Reformation* gave rise, at a time when polemics between the church of Rome and her opponents could not but be at their height, a bibliographical list must suffice. To a French historian's, Joachim Legrand, elaborate "refutation" of the first two books of the work (1688), Burnet wrote a reply, which his adversary immediately published in a French translation, with his own counter-blast. Burnet himself was not one of those *rarae aves*, in any branch of literature, who hold that criticisms are best left to answer themselves, and few challenges found him unready. He quickly (1688) retorted in the *Oxford Theses Relating to the English Reformation* attributed to Obadiah Walker. On the other hand, in the case of the first two volumes of the popular Antoine Varillas's long-expected history of heresies, Burnet himself assumed the offensive, and, in two pamphlets printed at Amsterdam in the year of the appearance of this portion of Varillas's work (1686) and in the following year respectively, contributed to the overthrow of its author's reputation. Varillas had avowedly attacked the protestant reformation from the political side; and Burnet was well qualified to carry the war into the enemy's camp, and to show that the new *History* was "nothing but Sanders drest up in another Method." That method was the assumption of great documentary learning, and an audacious use of the imagination in the handling of such materials as the writer possessed. Burnet's pamphlets are in the perennial style of a "smashing" review, with an infusion of the personal element hardly in excess of what contemporary readers expected; and they served their purpose.

Finally, he took up Bossuet's gauntlet, flung down by the greatest catholic controversialist of his age in his famous *Histoire des Variations*, where *The History of the English Refor-*

mation had been treated "as the authoritative text-book of English Protestantism,"[1] in *A Censure of M. de Meaux' History* (1688), which sought to turn the tables on his august adversary.

Before the second volume of *The History* had been actually issued, Burnet had produced the interesting monograph on the last phase in the life of Rochester, who had read the first volume with real interest. To this pamphlet, which reveals a power of sympathy more valuable than the ordinary tact in which Burnet was signally deficient, reference has already been made.[2] To a slightly later date (1682) belongs the publication of *The Life and Death of Sir Matthew Hale, sometime Lord Chief Justice of His Majesty's Court of King's Bench*, an admirable little biography. Though Hale habitually heard Burnet preach at the Rolls, they were not personally acquainted, and the book was chiefly founded on the notes of a confidential clerk of the great lawyer, who was an incorruptible but successful judge, a powerful thinker and a man of lofty spirit and godliness of life. Burnet deprecates his *History* being set down as a "Panegyrick," and it merits preservation as the record of a man who, whatever his failings, in a factious age strove consistently to remain outside party.[3] Soon afterwards (1683), as if the personal history of one great lawyer had inspired him with interest in the more or less remote speculations of another, Burnet beguiled his leisure with a translation of *Utopia*, published in 1685, with a preface containing some verdicts on English contemporary and Elizabethan literature.

In the last years of Charles II's reign, Burnet, from fairmindedness rather than from caution, declined to throw in his lot with the extreme protestant faction, though he was always more or less in touch with them. On the discovery of the Rye house plot (1683)—early in which year Burnet seems first to have set hand to *The Memoirs*, or *Secret History*, which were ultimately to become *The History of My Own Time*[4]—he, after a passing moment of ignoble fear, courageously devoted himself

---

[1] Foxcroft, H. C., *u.s.*, p. 247.   [2] See *ante*, Vol. VIII, Chap. VIII, p. 237.

[3] Sir Matthew Hale proposed to himself as a model T. Pomponius Atticus, of whose *Life* by Cornelius Nepos he published a translation (1667), described as "very inaccurate." He is taken to task for his leaning to the popular side in Roger North's *Life of Lord Guilford*, pp. 79 ff. (Jessopp's edn.).

[4] Foxcroft, H. C., *u.s.*, p. 187.

to the interests of Lord Russell, and addressed to him two discourses not published till 1713, besides composing for Lady Russell a journal of the last five years of her husband's life,[1] which has justly attained imperishable renown. The connection of Burnet with the Russell family inevitably brought him into worse odour with the court, although the belief which the king seems to have entertained that Burnet wrote Lord Russell's dying speech was not founded on fact; and, after he had been deprived of both his lectureship and his preachership, he, in 1685, thought it safest to leave the country. Of the travels with which he occupied nine months, an account, as a matter of course both intelligent and lively, remains in *Some Letters* (to Robert Boyle), printed at Amsterdam in the following year. The accession of James II had made the prolongation of his exile more necessary than ever. In 1686, he settled down at the Hague, where, after a time, he became the confidential adviser of the princess of Orange, and, in a more restricted measure, of her wary consort. Burnet's activity as a political writer was now at its height, and, of the *Eighteen Papers relating to the Affairs of Church and State, during the reign of King James the Second,* all but one were written during his residence in Holland. It must suffice to note among these *A Letter*, written some little time before, *Containing some Remarks on the two Papers writ by King Charles II, concerning Religion* (1686), which contributed to the stir created by their publication and the comments from opposite points of view of Stillingfleet and Dryden;[2] *Vindication* from the two *Letters containing some Reflections on His Majesty's Proclamation for Liberty of Conscience*, dated, respectively, 12 February and 4 April, 1687; *Reflections* on the pamphlet entitled *Parliamentum Pacificum*, and charges contained in it (1688); the important and anonymous *Enquiry* into the measures of submission to the supreme authority (1688), which, by allowing restrictions upon the duty of non-resistance, practically rendered it futile. William's army of invasion was supplied with copies of this pamphlet (for gratuitous circulation), which completes the orbit of its author's political tenets.

[1] Printed in Lord (John) Russell's *Life of William Lord Russell* (1819).

[2] This, with the *Reflections on the Declaration for Liberty of Conscience*, had been previously printed among the *Six Papers* published in 1687.

A Review of the Reflections on the Prince's Declaration (1688), printed in the course of the march upon London, cut Burnet loose for ever from the cause of James II and the prince whom he persisted in treating as supposititious.[1] Other pamphlets accompanied the successive steps in the consummation of the revolution which established William and Mary on the throne and Burnet as bishop of Salisbury; but, with a few exceptions, of which we proceed to mention only the more important, and, above all, with the exception of his *Memoirs*, the pulpit now absorbed the indefatigable activity of his pen.

Besides part III of *The History of the Reformation* and a work which may be regarded as supplementary to it, the celebrated *Exposition of the Thirty-Nine Articles* (1699), in which the historical element is at least of as great value as the theological, Burnet produced, in the concluding period of his career, *An Essay on the Memory of the late Queen* (Mary II) (1695), which should find a place among the *éloges* of which the age was peculiarly prolific, rather than among critical disquisitions. There cannot be any doubt either that it was the result of profound grief, or that this feeling was warranted alike by the pure and noble character of Mary, and by Burnet's personal loss in the death of a princess whose trust in him was among the most cherished experiences of his life. With her sister, he was not on similar terms of intimacy; nor was it at all to Anne's liking that (in 1698) he was appointed preceptor to her son the duke of Gloucester, afterwards heir-apparent. He was, however, on good terms with the duke and duchess of Marlborough, his relations with queen Anne herself improved, and it was only in her last years that he found himself in steady opposition to her government. What he had most at heart, as a politician, was the succession of the house of Hanover, for which he had laboured hard in the critical season of the Act of Settlement (1701). For some time previously, he had been in correspondence with the electress Sophia and with her trusted counsellor Leibniz, between whom and Burnet there was much sympathy on religious, as well as on political, subjects, though, as in the case of the problem of a reunion of the protestant churches,

[1] Printed in *A second Collection of Several Tracts and Discourses, written in the years 1686–9, by Gilbert Burnet (consecrated Bishop of Sarum, Easter Day,* 1689), 1689.

these aspects could not be kept asunder. But the most interesting of Burnet's communications with Hanover is *A Memorial* offered to the electress by him in 1703, *containing a Delineation of the Constitution and Policy of England: with Anecdotes concerning remarkable Persons of that Time*, first published, from the original in the Hanover archives, in 1815. The electress, who was not a friend of long or tedious discourses, could not have objected to Burnet's treatise on either ground; though she may not have altogether relished the free criticism of the system of government pursued by her uncle Charles I and her cousin Charles II, and the assumption as to the "pretended" birth of her young living kinsman, whom the Jacobites called James III. To us, the interest of this characteristic manual lies not so much in the historical exposition of the reasons of the weakness of crown and nobility and the suggestion of "remedies" designed to strengthen the stability of the throne, as in the plea for a generous treatment by the church of England, with a view to future reunion, of presbyterians and even of other nonconformists. For the rest, though the treatise has not any particular value as a sketch of parties or persons, its anecdotes and general style make it very readable; and it was probably unnecessary for the artful prelate to forward for perusal, with his own manuscript, copies of *Hudibras* and *The Snake in the Grass*. Burnet's fear of being dull was, of all the fears which, from time to time, interfered with his self-confidence, the least well-grounded. The protest against the reprinting of the political works of Harrington and Milton is, however, unworthy of him.

Finally, we come to the work which, during the greater part of his life of ceaseless effort, Burnet must have regarded as that upon which his reputation as a writer would, in the end, mainly rest. It is true that he declared *A Discourse of the Pastoral Care*[1] to be of all his writings the one which pleased himself best[2]—a preference well according with the fine ironical tribute paid by Halifax to his "ill-natured" fondness for "degrading himself into the lowest and most painful duties of his calling."[3] But, though the spiritual element in Burnet's activity was

---

[1] Cf. *ante*, Vol. VIII, p. 343.

[2] *See* his "Autobiography" in *A Supplement to Burnet's History of My Own Time*, by Foxcroft, H. C. (Oxford, 1902), p. 506.

[3] Cf. Lady Russell's *Letters* (edition 1772), p. 201 note.

never quenched, "his times" and the world absorbed his most continuous literary effort; and something must here be said, in the first instance, concerning the genesis and evolution of one of the best-abused books in historical literature.

The two folio volumes of which the original edition of Burnet's *History of My Own Time* consists appeared in 1724 and 1734 respectively—in both cases, therefore, posthumously, as Burnet died in 1715. The first volume, however, which ends with the close of the reign of James II and the ensuing *interregnum*, and so much of the second volume as covers the reign of William III and the first two years, or thereabouts, of the reign of Anne, had, in their original form, been intended to constitute part of a work, designed on a somewhat different and looser plan, as "Memoirs" or a "Secret History" of the period which they covered. It will, therefore, be most convenient to trace this earlier production to its beginnings, before passing on to the published work in which it was ultimately merged.

Burnet's biographer, Miss Foxcroft,[1] assigns to the spring of 1683 the inception of the aforesaid "Memoirs" or "Secret History." At this date, Burnet was residing in London, having, since his estrangement from Lauderdale, practically ceased to take any active part in Scottish affairs, and already held a conspicuous position in the English political world; although, in consonance with the course of affairs, as well as with the logical evolution of his opinions, he had not yet definitively thrown in his lot with the whigs. It was, therefore, before the discovery of the Rye house plot, of which event the consequences reacted upon his career, that he may be concluded to have written the earliest section of his memoirs, which came to form, in substance, book I of *The History of My Own Time*, and comprises a summary of affairs, in England and Scotland, before the restoration. This section is written with a clearness and vivacity sufficient to arrest attention in what often proves the dullest portion of a memoir, its opening; but, already here, when partisanship was, of course, in abeyance, there are evident inaccuracies of statement about foreign and English affairs—for

---

[1] *A Life of Gilbert Burnet, Bishop of Salisbury.* I. *Scotland,* 1643–1674. By Clarke, T. E. S. II. *England,* 1674–1715. By Foxcroft, H. C., with an introduction by Firth, C. H. (Cambridge, 1907), p. 187.

instance, as to James I's supposed intention of a reconciliation with Somerset. Early in the narrative, the writer turns to the affairs of Scotland, which, he says, "are but little known." "Nor worth knowing" was the annotation added by Swift, who, by way of a sneer at the entire work, interlined its title as *The History of* (Scotland in) *His Own Times*.[1] It must be allowed that the method of Burnet's narrative, which frequently passes from England to Scotland, and back again, like a play with a main and a bye plot, though more or less unavoidable, is trying. Moreover, in the earlier part of the work, there is a marked contrast between the grasp which the writer possesses over Scottish affairs, and the less strenuous texture of the English sections of the narrative. In book I, the struggle between resolutioners and protesters is related with a thorough command of the subject, while the ensuing chapter on Cromwell, though highly entertaining, manifestly rests on evidence of a very doubtful character.

After, in July, 1683, sentence had been passed on Lord Russell, Burnet, unmanned, for the moment, by the terrible catastrophe, wrote a letter to his friend John Brisbane, secretary of the admiralty, who was cognisant of at least the plan of the memoirs, containing an abject attempt to conciliate the king by promising favourable treatment of him in the narrative which the writer was preparing.[2] On the other hand, the character of Charles II, which is the first of a series of characters with which the next division of the memoirs opened, conveyed a hint that a more complete treatment of the subject would follow "when it would be more safe."[3] When that time arrived, Burnet was a refugee in Holland; but he had taken his memoirs with him, and was busily engaged upon them while abroad. This appears from the threat which, in May, 1687, he contrived to convey to James II through the secretary of state, when informing him of his nationalisation in Holland, that, if he were condemned, in his absence, on a charge of intercourse with traitors in Scotland, he would have to publish what might

---

[1] *The History of My Own Time*, ed. Airy, O., vol. I, p. 29 and note.
[2] See *Life*, by Foxcroft, H. C., p. 192. Charles II is said to have, more philosophically, told Buckingham, who had advised conciliating Burnet, that the latter would not dare to malign him while he was alive, and that, after his death, it would not hurt him. [3] *Ib.*, p. 196.

be disagreeable to the king—to wit, his memoirs. Before he set sail with the expedition of William of Orange, in 1688, Burnet had brought them up to date, and he carried them on through the busy next period of his life; the last extant fragment of them deals with the dismissal, in 1696, of his kinsman, James Johnston, from the Scottish secretaryship.

Nothing remains of Burnet's original memoirs which treats of events or transactions dating from the period between February, 1696, and April, 1708; and, some years before the latter date, he had resolved upon recasting his memoirs in a different form— that in which they were ultimately given to the world. It is supposed that the appearance, in 1702–4, of the first edition of Clarendon's *History of the Rebellion* inspired Burnet with the thought of emulating his great predecessor in his own field;[1] while a more direct model was, together with a title, supplied to him in the *Historiae sui Temporis* of de Thou, for whom Burnet had a great admiration and whose general method of treatment he sought to follow, avoiding, like him, any attempt to deal at length with military operations or even to enter into a full discussion of foreign affairs, but falling far short of him by omitting to furnish either a general survey of the progress of European politics or any adequate notice of great literary personalities.[2] It was, as he states, likewise the example of de Thou, which induced Burnet to compose, in November, 1710, a short autobiography, which, however, he never revised and which was not published till our own day.[3] This "rough draught" deserved to become a permanent possession of English biographical literature, and could hardly fail to achieve popularity were it more widely known. For, apart from its lucid and perfectly trustworthy statement of the data of an enlightened and single-minded man's remarkable career, it

---

[1] It is curious to find the third earl of Shaftesbury in his *Letter concerning Enthusiasm* (written 1707) declare that "we have few modern writers, who, like Xenophon or Cicero [Caesar?] can write their own Commentaries, and the raw Memoir Writings, and uninformed Pieces of modern Statesmen full of their own interested and private Views, will, in another Age, be of little Service to support their Memory or Name, since already the World begins to sicken with them." Cited by Oldmixon, *A Critical History of England*, 3rd ed., 1727, vol. I, p. 19.

[2] See the observations of Firth, in his introduction to Miss Foxcroft's *Life*, pp. xxx, xxxi. Parts I–IV of de Thou's great work first appeared in 1607–8, but his *Memoirs* were not published till 1620.

[3] In Miss Foxcroft's *Supplement* (1902), pp. 451–524.

reveals the quintessence of his most characteristic personal qualities and, being absolutely sincere, forms a most delightful, as well as a most instructive, piece of writing. When, in 1734, Burnet's family brought out the second volume of his *History*, they opined to substitute for these plain and candid confessions a more regular and elaborate life by the editor, Burnet's youngest son Thomas, on the promise of whose education the father had dilated towards the end of his suppressed sketch.

The changes made by Burnet in transforming what, if it had not been his life's work, had occupied a very considerable share of his attention during the years of his maturity, were, in sum, important. These changes, to a large extent, are open to the inspection of posterity. Besides a long fragment of the original manuscript of the memoirs reaching from 1660 to 1664, we possess smaller fragments concerned with the period from 1679 to 1683, and, again, with that from 1684 to 1696 (from just before the death of Charles II to just before the peace of Ryswyk). Concerning the subsequent period, we have only so much of the memoirs as deals with the years 1708 to 1713; but this section was written with the conception of a more perfect history before the eyes of the author.[1] Nor should it be overlooked that, in 1708, according to the statement of his son, he "thought himself near the end of the history," for which the peace at one time thought likely to follow upon the great victory of Oudenarde (or, rather, upon the full use expected to be made of it) seemed a suitable *terminus*. He, therefore, with a pardonable, and by no means unparalleled, desire not to lose any time in "improving" the most signal occasion of his literary life, wrote a "conclusion" of his history, for which, when he reached the year 1713, and the real end *chartaeque viaeque*, he substituted the short and impressive paragraph with which it actually closes. The "conclusion" of 1708, however, is rightly printed in the editions of his book, to which it would have formed an appropriate epilogue or moral, at whatever point in the narrative of queen Anne's later years it was inserted. For it is really an admonition to those responsible for the guidance of church and state in England to apply the lessons taught by

[1] For an exhaustive statement of the changes introduced by Burnet into his original MS., see Foxcroft, H. C., *Supplement*, etc., introduction and synopsis. For Miss Foxcroft's criticism of the effect of these changes, see her *Life*, pp. 404 ff.

The History, and—in the halcyon days, now seemingly near at hand, of peace and, perhaps, of a lasting political settlement—to do what was possible towards securing a prosperous and a virtuous national future by a series of comprehensive and far-reaching reforms. If this elaborate—but well thought-out and admirably written—"conclusion," as a whole, suggests the charge of a bishop taking leave of his diocese (archidiaconal charges Burnet wished to see abolished), it has the true ring of clear purpose and genuinely liberal feeling, and speaks the mind of a man whose political principles could raise him far above all considerations of party, while his religious aspirations sought the advancement of something wider and higher than the beliefs or interests of any particular sect or church.

Even before the materials for a comparison had been fully surveyed, it was seriously questioned whether Burnet's work did not lose more than it gained by the very drastic revision—amounting, in some passages, to rewriting—to which he subjected his original text; and, in a well-known excursus to his *History of England*,[1] the great historian Ranke argued forcibly, though without having completely surveyed the material, in favour of the superior value, as a historical authority, of the unadulterated memoirs. Without accepting, as more than partially correct, the view that Burnet's motive for revision was not to correct inaccuracies, but to alter what failed to suit views and purposes entertained by him at a later date, we may allow that this revision not only, in many instances (some of which were of considerable significance), deprived his work of the weight of a contemporary authority, but, in many others, altered it for the worse from a literary point of view.[2]

As is pointed out by Burnet's biographer, while the leisure which, at different periods of his life, he was able, or willing, to allow himself left him time for the composition of memoirs, he lacked the opportunity, which de Thou created for himself and which circumstances forced upon Clarendon, for the writing of a great history. Of the actual changes introduced by Burnet, not a few were due to a widening of experience, and others to a

[1] See appendix i, iii, "Burnet's History of his Own Times" in vol. VII of *Englische Geschichte*, etc. (vol. VI of English translation).

[2] So, at the very outset, in the instance dwelt on by Ranke, the "characters" of Charles II and his ministers with which book II of the *History* opens.

desire natural to a right-minded and well-meaning man, such as, at bottom, he was, for softening the asperities of temporary resentment and the vehemence of younger years.   At the same time, however, he had, as he advanced in age, become more of a partisan in the affairs of both church and state.   Yet, in some instances—so in his later, as compared with his earlier, treat-ment of Marlborough—self-interest may have combined with a sense of justice to recast a onesided treatment; in others, as in the removal of unfavourable comments on Portland, towards whom he had never entertained friendly sentiments, he was moved by a generous resentment of the unjust outcry against a most loyal servant of their common master.[1]

When we pass on to consider the design and execution of *The History* as a whole, we may agree that the preface which Burnet wrote in 1702, when setting about the recasting of the work undertaken by him twenty years before, is high-strung, and that the tone of solemn responsibility in which it is indited is not maintained by the spirit of some of the passages of the work which follows.   But the plan of narrating the history of half a century of the national life (his actual work somewhat exceeds this limit)could not but present itself to Burnet's mind, when once more, as it were, contemplating it from the threshold, as a task of high purpose, and he might well entertain a hope that his narrative would "awaken the world to just reflections on their own errors and follies."   It was (as Ranke suggests) as a kind of protest against the reaction confronting him in state and church that he undertook to produce his recast *History*—a protest on behalf of the principle of resistance, which he had himself only gradually adopted, but which had now lost ground, and on behalf of the principle of comprehension, for which even his friends the whigs and their nonconformist *protégés* had become content to substitute that of an extended toleration. He asked the public to accept his book as designed for this end; but, on its appearance, the public was slow to receive it in the spirit with which, when he wrote his preface, there is no diffi-culty in believing him to have been filled.

Its sincerity—that is to say, its veracity of intention as well as of detail—was, from the first, disputed by irreconcilable censors.   It was pronounced to be not only "full of legend and

[1] *Life*, pp. 386–7.

false secret tradition," but, also, to be full of omissions which the author would not have found any difficulty in avoiding. Bolingbroke did not wish it to be left unread, but declared that it must be read as a party pamphlet. Yet there can be little doubt that, though inaccurate by nature, and a victim to the credulity natural to those in whom the desire for information about facts and persons is the least controllable part of their minds, Burnet was neither intentionally unveracious nor essentially untruthful, nor even, by disposition, ungenerous and unfair. What really discredited him, as it has very few other historians of high and honourable intentions and of gifts such as his, was the flaw in his intellect, no doubt deepened by his habits of life—for he was always inquiring, and always writing —which may be described as the weakness of its critical faculty. He had habituated himself to take things for true without inquiring into the evidence for their truth, and thus, when hearsay coincided with his wishes, his foot was sure to find its way into the trap.[1]

By the side of this defect, his partisanship, even had it not been exaggerated by some of his commentators and critics, who were unable to recognise the honesty of purpose which underlay most of his judgments, as well as most of the changes which he introduced into them, is, in itself, of quite secondary importance. And it should be remembered that, though Burnet was not any more successful than was Clarendon in emancipating himself from the influences by which he was surrounded and in accordance with which he shaped his own ecclesiastical and political actions, he did not, as Ranke has well shown, during the reign of Charles II, stand in the actual centre of affairs, or possess the key to the religious and foreign policy of which he observed the unsatisfactory results. His relations with William and Mary became, after a time, intimate at the Hague, and continued so with her after her accession to the throne; but, even in this reign, and much more in that of queen Anne, the part which he played in the history of his times,

---

[1] Of course, his narrative is least trustworthy where, as in the case of the reign of James II, he was at a distance from the scene of action; and his manifest, though nowhere in *The History* explicitly avowed, acceptance of the legend of the supposititious prince of Wales is only an extreme instance of his tendency to believe what he wished.

important though it was, remained only a secondary part; and his life was not, like Clarendon's, merged in the management of the monarchy. At the same time, he knew all the chief men of his age, both English and Scottish, and, as a collector of materials, used his opportunities with unvarying assiduity.

Burnet's style and manner as a historical writer have been criticised with not less asperity than has the substance of his *History;* yet few modern readers will be ungrateful, and, therefore, unjust, enough—for who has not taken delight in at least much of his narrative?—to subscribe to Swift's "I never read so ill a style." It must not be forgotten that, though Clarendon's *Life* was actually written before Burnet's *Memoirs* were first taken in hand, and Clarendon's *History* appeared many years before that of Burnet, he at least began his *Memoirs* without any English model.[1] The comparison with Clarendon is not the less unavoidable, and has been made by a most competent hand—not wholly to the disadvantage of the divine as against the statesman.[2] Although Clarendon's rolling periods are unapproached by Burnet's "jumping" sentences, the realism of the latter gives him the advantage over the somewhat conventional dignity of the former—as Ranke observes, in a different connection, he pleases his readers, though he may fail to convince them of the higher motives of his work. He is an excellent teller of stories—not the least so because he is master of the illustrative method, and never dwells at length on what he introduces incidentally. When, in accordance with the fashion of his age, he makes a supreme effort of style in the drawing of character, he is relatively lacking in finish; but he frequently achieves the effect of a likeness taken from life which Clarendon misses in his more artistically elaborated portraits. Yet the want of order and method which often shows itself in Burnet's arrangement of events likewise interferes with the general effect of some of his characters. The Leibnitian principle *non multa sed multum* was not one of the maxims which guided him in composition, any more than it did in his literary activity at large.

Yet no conclusion could be less correct than the impression that, either in his *History*, or in any other part of his extra-

[1] *Life*, by Foxcroft, H. C., p. 399.
[2] See Firth, C. H., in introduction, *u. s.*, pp. xxxix ff.

ordinarily ample literary output, Burnet's glance was ever more than temporarily diverted from the distinct aims and lofty ideals which he cherished. Any unprejudiced review of his most popular historical work, or of his historical writings in a body, or of the whole of his extant literary productions, including his pulpit deliverances, will lead to a corroboration of the fact, brought out in his "dying speech," as he humorously calls the intended "conclusion" of *The History of My Own Time*, that the pervading purpose of them all was a vindication of freedom under the law as the guiding principle of ecclesiastical and political life. With this ideal, the teaching of the Cambridge Platonists had fascinated his early manhood; it had guided the efforts of the latitudinarian divines of whom, in more ways than one, he had become the most active representative in public life; and it had inspired the view of national political progress which the innumerable and, in part, superfluous, or even objectionable, details of his last historical work had been unable to obscure. And, to this work itself, it had imparted a vitality beyond that of the most entertaining—or even the most scandalous—memoirs.[1]

Among ecclesiastical historians in this period, Burnet has precedence, by right of seniority, over John Strype, whose first appearance as the author of any substantial work, however, dated from after his fiftieth year. His *Memorials of Thomas Cranmer, Archbishop of Canterbury* (1694) was succeeded (1698) by *The Life of the Learned Sir Thomas Smith*, which evenly treats of his services to the welfare of the state and of those to the pronunciation of Greek. Then followed the lives of bishop Aylmer (1701); "the learned Sir John Cheke" (1705); archbishop Grindal (1710); archbishop Parker (1711)—which closes with a fuller attempt at the drawing of character than is usual with the author, perhaps because he was exceptionally impressed by a learning which "though it were universal, yet ran

[1] For a list of the more important controversial writings directed against Burnet's *History of My Own Time*, see bibliography. As to the notes of the earl of Dartmouth, Speaker Onslow, the earl of Hardwicke and Swift, inserted in the Oxford edition of 1823, see Routh's preface to that edition. In varying degree, the retention of them in later editions, in common justice to Burnet, called for curtailment; and Airy, in his edition of books I–III, admitted only such as "seemed to possess real value."

chiefly upon Antiquity"—and archbishop Whitgift (1718).
Strype had now, in his own words, "lived to finish the Lives
and Acts (as far as my Collections will serve me) of the Four
First Holy Archbishops" (in the title-page "Protestant Archbishops") "of Canterbury, those Wise and Painful, Just and
Good Governors of this Reformed Church of England." But,
meanwhile, he had also been at work upon his *magnum opus*,
Annals of the Reformation and Establishment of Religion
(1700–31). The orthodoxy of this work is guaranteed by a sort
of *imprimatur* from the archbishop and bishops of the church of
England, prefixed to vol. II, and commending it, in rather
feminine style, as carrying on "so useful and desirable a Piece
of Church History, so much wanted." As both this work and
the biographies, for the most part, deal with a period later in
date than that covered by Burnet's *History of the Reformation*,
they contain few references to it. The last of Strype's more
important publications is his *Ecclesiastical Memorials, Relating
chiefly to Religion and the Reformation of it*, treating of the
history of the church of England under Henry VIII, Edward
VI, and Mary (3 vols. 1721); the "originals" in the appendixes
to which are particularly full of varied interest. As a historical
writer, he shows the plodding habits, but not always the sure
sagacity, befitting his Dutch descent; and his works, though
the fruit of long and patient research, may, as a whole, be
regarded as compilations rather than compositions; and their
reader has to be prepared to wrestle with appendixes of extraordinary length—averaging not much less than one-third of
the text to which they are attached. But his long and valuable labours mark the steady progress of historical research,
as well as the growth of a love of learning which was to be
among the surest supports of the stability of the church of
England.

A more stirring life and literary activity was that of Jeremy
Collier, to whose combative spirit it is due that he should
already, in a very different connection from that of historical
writing, have appeared on the scene of this work.[1] Born in
1650, he had fulfilled clerical duties of divers kinds before, in

---

[1] See Vol. VIII, Chap. VI, as to his *Short View of the Immorality and Profaneness
of the English Stage* (1698).

1685, he was appointed lecturer at Gray's inn; but, with the revolution of 1688, "the public exercise of his functions became impracticable." In other words, he was henceforth a non-juror. He at once entered into controversy with Burnet, and, in 1692, was for a short time in prison on an accusation of secret correspondence with the Pretender, having scrupulously surrendered in discharge of his bail.[1] When he next came before the public, it was on the occasion of his absolving two Jacobite gentlemen on the scaffold. In his subsequent retreat, he was left unmolested; and in 1697 he quietly put forth his *Essays*, which were published in several editions, and which, divided into four parts, fill three volumes. Many of these *Essays* are in the form, still popular, of dialogues, between Philotimus and Philalethes, and other pairs of speakers. The subjects discussed are partly ethical, partly social and partly a mixture of both, such as *Duelling*, and the well-known *Office of a Chaplain*, which contends that a chaplain in a family is not a servant, and that servility on his part and arrogant treatment on that of the patron are alike to be deprecated. There is some acceptable plain speaking in this as well as in other of the *Essays*—notably in that *Of Lying;* but there is also an occasional lack of urbanity in the way of conveying the truth, or what seems such to the writer. In many instances, the maxims propounded are reinforced by passages translated from the Fathers.

Collier's principal occupation during his years of retirement seems, however, to have been the preparation of his *Historical Dictionary*, based on *Le Grand Dictionnaire historique* of Louis Moréri, which after its first appearance in 1674, went through a large number of editions, and to which Bayle's famous work had originally been intended as a supplement. Of Collier's *Dictionary* the first two volumes appeared in 1701, and the third and fourth, under the respective titles of a *Supplement* and an *Appendix*, in 1705. This was followed by his chief work, *The Ecclesiastical History of Great Britain*, of which the first volume, reaching to the close of the reign of Henry VII, appeared in 1708, and the second, which deals very fully with the reformation and might almost be said to form a running

---

[1] For his chief pamphlets in connection with this and other matters see bibliography.

comment, generally the reverse of friendly, on Burnet's narrative, in 1714. While even Collier's *Historical Dictionary* is held to be of value to closer students of ecclesiastical history, his work which is confined to that subject long maintained its position as a leading authority, though as a matter of course it involved its author, with whom to hold principles was to proclaim them, in a series of controversies with the champions of adverse views. On these it is unnecessary to dwell here; still less can we enter into the subsequent esoteric dissensions between Collier and other non-jurors.[1] His *Ecclesiastical History* itself, massive in conception, and covering a large body of more or less unassimilated materials, does not disdain occasional resort to modern issues, and, while it remains on the whole a trustworthy book of reference, is by no means devoid of interesting and even stimulating passages. Collier lived till 1726, being after the death of Hickes regarded as the leader of the non-jurors.

Of Daniel Neal's *History of the Puritans*, from 1517 to 1548, the first volume appeared in 1732. His reputation, founded on his pastoral work in London, had been enhanced by his *History of New England* (1720), which was very well received in America. The first volume of the work by which he is best known and which is in part founded on the earlier compilations of John Evans, owed much in its account of the Elizabethan period to Strype; it contains a courageous and convincing defence of the policy of Cromwell. Isaac Madox's attack upon it was followed by Zachary Grey's heavier fire against its successors, to which latter Neal left his posthumous editor to reply. His own straightforward attitude and brave spirit well represent the manly nonconformity of his age.

The chief collections of state papers and letters belonging by their date of composition to the period treated in Burnet's *History of My Own Time* were not published till the latter half of the eighteenth century had far advanced, or till an even later date; and will therefore be more conveniently mentioned in a subsequent volume. The above description cannot be applied to the *Letters addressed from London to Sir Joseph Williamson, while Plenipotentiary at the Congress of Cologne in the years*

---

[1] For Collier's chief pamphlets against Burnet and Kennett, and as to the non-jurors' controversy on the usages, see bibliography.

1673 *and* 1674; but, as somewhat nondescript in kind, and as
actually dating from an earlier age, they may be mentioned here
rather than in a later chapter.[1]   While the official despatches of
Sir Leoline Jenkins and of Williamson, the representatives of
England at the congress under the nominal headship of Sunderland (who remained at Paris), are to be read elsewhere, the
gossiping letters written to the junior plenipotentiary by his
friends and dependants in the secretary of state's office (of
whose names the majority appeared in Marvell's *Black List of
Government Pensioners*, printed in Holland in 1677) form a valuable and very amusing addition to the familiar letters of the
age.   "There is not a place in the world so fruitfull in liing
storyes as London," thus writes one of the correspondents of
Williamson; and they all did their best to suit the varied tastes
of the great man, who besides being a prominent statesman and
making a great marriage, became president of the Royal Society
and was a collector of heraldic manuscripts.   He lived till 1701,
having been a trusted diplomatic agent of William III after
serving Charles II as secretary of state.

A composite character, midway between history and
memoirs, belongs to the *Memoirs of James II writ of his own
hand*, in so far as they admit of separation from the editorial
matter in which they are embedded.   Of the original material
the substantial portion, saved by king James at the time of his
catastrophe, is said, after undergoing a long series of strange
adventures, to have been ultimately committed to the flames
at St. Omer, in the days of the great French revolution.   A
biographical work based on them was however put together in
the days and with the sanction of the Old Pretender, and elaborated for publication by order of the Prince Regent (afterwards
king George IV).[2]   To this *Life of James II* the great historian
Ranke's masterhand applied the process of analysis; but the
particular conclusions reached by him cannot be summarised
here.[3]   Suffice it to say that while a French translation of part I
(to 1660), approved by the royal author, had been incorporated

---

[1] They were edited by Christie, W. D., for the Camden Society, 2 vols., 1874.

[2] *The Life of James the Second, King of England*, etc., by Clarke, J. S., 2 vols.,
1816.

[3] See the excursus "On the Autobiographical Memoranda of James II" in vol.
VII of Ranke's *English History*.

into Ramsay's *Vie de Turenne* (2 vols., Paris, 1735), parts II,
to 1685, and III, to 1688 (the latter in a sense supplementary
to Burnet, who was out of England during the reign of James),
were compiled from the king's original memoranda, though
only revised by him so far as 1678. Part IV contains passages
from his memoranda, more especially with regard to the war in
Ireland. James II was a prince whose own notions concerning
his life and actions deserve study. Except in part I, his devotion to the church of his adoption may be said to colour the
whole narrative and to absorb all political principles and moral
convictions he brings into play; an example of this may be
found in his judgment of Clarendon, to whose religious
policy he attributes a large share in his later troubles. The
Memoirs, with the same restriction, can hardly at any time
have amounted to a connected narrative, or have risen to
the level of a history intended to serve the cause of objective
truth.

A place of his own among the political writers of the close of
the seventeenth and beginning of the eighteenth century must
be assigned to Andrew Fletcher of Saltoun. Though his public
life was entirely associated with Scotland and its affairs, his
political speculations took a wider range, and exhibit that cos-
mopolitanism which has for centuries been a distinctive mark
of his nationality. Of his training, in his early years, at the
hand of Burnet, mention has already been made; after this he
travelled and acquired a knowledge of French, as well as of
Italian so far as to compose and publish a treatise in that
tongue. In 1678, he was sent as one of the members for
his native Haddingtonshire to the convention of estates summoned for the purpose of supplying money for the maintenance
of the soldiery employed for the suppression of presbyterian
conventicles; but he joined the opposition to this and other
ecclesiastical measures of the government, incurring thereby
the implacable enmity of James duke of York. In the end he
made his way to Holland, and, though he accompanied Monmouth to England in 1685, did not return to Scotland till the
time of the revolution. The second chapter in his political
career culminated in the Darien expedition, of which he was a
primary promoter; and it was about this time (1698) that he
first appeared as a political writer. *A Discourse of Government*

with relation to Militias, published at Edinburgh in 1698,[1] is thoroughly characteristic of the writer, who, plunging into the midst of the war of pamphlets on the question of standing armies which raged after the peace of Ryswyk, was ready with a complete plan for rendering unnecessary the dangerous expedient of a standing mercenary force. The people must be trained to the use of arms on a carefully planned system but for the purpose of defence only; for the sea is the only empire naturally belonging to Britain. In the same year—clearly in the autumn—Fletcher wrote *Two Discourses on the affairs of Scotland*, shortly after (2nd of July) the Darien expedition had failed. On the fostering of the new colony, the writer declares, depended the whole future of Scotland, cruelly impoverished partly through her own fault, and partly because of the removal of the seat of her government to London. After provision has been made for the colony, thought must be taken of the stricken country at home; and it is in the second of these *Discourses* that Fletcher prescribes the drastic remedy of domestic slavery—especially for the population of the Highlands, for which, it must be observed, he entertained great contempt. A little earlier in the same year was written his Italian discourse on Spanish affairs, apparently suggested by the first Partition Treaty.[2] The *Speech upon the State of the Nation* (1701)—which was probably never delivered—deals with the second of these treatises, as completing the establishment of Bourbon ascendancy—it "is like an alarum bell rung over all Europe. Pray God it may not prove to you a passing-bell." In the heated debates of the Scottish parliament of 1703 Fletcher took a leading part, preparing a bill of Security which would have very narrowly limited the royal authority in Scotland, and, when this was dropped, joining in the refusal of supplies. At least one speech and one pamphlet of this period attributed to him are spurious; but he completed, at the end of 1703, a short piece called *An Account of a Conversation concerning a Right Regulation of Government for the Common Good of Mankind*, which reports, with much vivacity and aptness, "from London" to the marquis of Montrose and other

---

[1] Reprinted in 1755, as well as in the several editions of *The Political Works of Andrew Fletcher*, 1732, etc.

[2] *Discorso delle cose di Spagna, scritto nel mese de Luglio* 1698, Naples, 1698.

Scots lords a dialogue on the relations between England and Scotland, held in the earl of Cromartie's lodgings at Whitehall. Scene, personalities and subject are treated very attractively; the conclusion is that, not an incorporating union, but a federal union is the desideratum for keeping the three kingdoms together. The style of this letter is admirable, and approaches the best English prose style of the age at a time when there was little of performance or even of pretension in Scottish prose.[1] Here is to be found "the famous saying," attributed to "a very wise man," that, "if a man were permitted to make all the ballads, he need not care who should make the laws of a nation."

[1] As to the Scottish prose literature of the age, see Chap. XIII, *post*, and its bibliography.

CHAPTER VIII

Historical and Political Writers

II

BOLINGBROKE

THE historical and political writings of Henry St. John, from 1712 Viscount Bolingbroke, to which we must mainly confine ourselves in the present chapter, were, nearly all of them, composed in the latter, and slightly longer, half of his life which followed on the great collapse of his party at the close of the reign of queen Anne. As to his contributions to philosophical literature, something will be said in the next volume of the present work; in the chief collections of his letters, the public and pragmatic element, for the most part, is so copiously mixed up with the private and personal, that they can hardly be subjected to a literary judgment. This is especially the case with Parke's edition of his *Letters and Correspondence*, which extends over the last four years of the reign of queen Anne and ends with a despondent reference to her death. These letters, on Bolingbroke's sudden flight to France, were secured by the exertions of his under-secretary Thomas Hare, and thus escaped being brought before the House of Commons at his trial in 1715, like some extracts from his correspondence. They are addressed to a large variety of correspondents, of whom lords Strafford (Raby), Orrery, Dartmouth and Shrewsbury, and Matthew Prior, are among the most frequent recipients of letters written in English, and the marquis de Torcy of the much smaller number written in French. They are, of course, invaluable to a student of the peace negotiations and of Bolingbroke's direct share in them;

and in those which adopt a more intimate tone, like the "long scrawl which is only from Harry to Matt, not from the Secretary to the Minister,"[1] there is often a fair amount of malicious wit. Of Bolingbroke's private letters, however, the most pleasing are to be found in the series addressed to his half-sister Henrietta, which are generally written in a natural vein, without a superfluity of the epigrammatic infusion in which the letters of this age abound.[2] Even these, however, on occasion, exhibit Bolingbroke's fatal propensity, when telling the truth, to conceal part of it.

St. John's earliest withdrawal from public life to the consolations of philosophy and literature belongs to the early part of 1708, when he followed Harley out of office. His retirement was carried out with so much pompousness, and so little interfered with his habits of self-indulgence, that it exposed him to much ridicule on the part of his friends, including brutal sarcasm from Swift; and it is not known to have been productive of any compositions in prose or in verse. After his return to public life in 1710, not many weeks before he received the seals as secretary of state (September, 1710), he had, not for the last time in his career, inspired the foundation by the tories of a journal to support them in a vigorous campaign against the whig government. Among the early contributors were Swift, Prior and Robert Freind.

This was *The Examiner* (to be distinguished from other periodicals of that name), of which between thirty and forty numbers appear to have been published up to the spring of 1712. According to the general account,[3] Bolingbroke's first and most important contribution to this journal appeared in no. x, and contained an attack on Marlborough's conduct of the war, with a fierce attack on the duchess. This description, however,

---

[1] Vol. II, p. 41. The replies of Prior (*Henrico colendissimo Matthaeus*) are at least equally vivacious.

[2] See the correspondence, chiefly from manuscript originals, appended to Sichel, W., *Bolingbroke and his Times. The Sequel*, 1902. (Henrietta St. John married Robert Knight, member for Sudbury, afterwards Lord Luxborough. She is also known as the friend and correspondent of Shenstone.) There is no need for referring here to Grimoard's collection, which consists of letters in French, partly originals, partly translations.

[3] See Macknight, T., *The Life of Henry St. John, Viscount Bolingbroke*, pp. 158–9.

does not apply to the number in question; but elsewhere[1] is reprinted what is called "St. John's Letter to *The Examiner*," which inveighs against the whigs, their clubs, their journals, and their literary champions such as "the Hector of Sarum" (Burnet), and speaks of the subjection of the queen "to an arbitrary junto, and to the caprice of an insolent woman." No. XVII of this *Examiner*, it may be added, contains a letter which attacks the duke under the thin disguise of "Crassus," but makes no special attack upon the duchess.

But the five years of office which ensued, the labours, including a journey to France, which resulted in the conclusion of the peace of Utrecht, and the intrigues by which Bolingbroke in vain endeavoured to turn the approaching crisis of the succession to the advantage of the tories left him little time for composition; by the close of March, 1715, he found himself an exile, and, in the following July, in the service of the pretender. It was not till this fatal phase of his career was at an end that he made his first elaborate contribution to political literature. A few months, however, before he wrote the celebrated *Letter to Sir William Wyndham*—the disciple whom he had left at home behind him—he had composed his *Reflections on Exile*, published before the close of 1716, when his hopes of pardon and return had again receded. This effort, founded on Seneca's *Consolatio ad Helviam*, is stuffed with additional quotations from classical and one or two modern sources, and reads almost like a parody of the classicising essay of the period. Although its style has been held to be Ciceronian rather than Senecan,[2] the writer inveighs against "Tully" for unphilosophically lamenting his exile, though, with a characteristic sneer, it is allowed that "his separation from Terentia, whom he repudiated not long afterwards, was perhaps an affliction to him at the time."

A Letter to Sir William Wyndham seems to have been directly provoked by a Jacobite pamphlet entitled *A Letter from Avignon*,[3] which, in its turn, was a product of the rupture between Bolingbroke and the pretender early in 1716, and was

---

[1] In *Somers' Tracts*, vol. XIII, p. 71; also in *The History of His Own Time*, by *Matthew Prior* (ed. Drift, A.), 1740, pp. 306 ff. This letter was answered by *A Letter to Isaac Bickerstaffe, Esq.*, by earl "Cooper," 1710.

[2] Sichel, W., *u.s.*, p. 82.   [3] See Collins, J. Churton, *Bolingbroke*, etc., p. 132.

written in the following year. Its main purpose was to demonstrate, for the benefit of the tories and from the writer's own experience, the suicidal folly of an alliance between them and the Jacobites. But, though the logic of this demonstration is incontrovertible, the historical process by which the experience on which it rests was gained is audaciously misrepresented, and the circumstances in which Bolingbroke offered his services to the pretender are falsified, as are his relations to the tory party and its policy after his fall. It was, not improbably, his knowledge, not only of the truth, but of what others knew of the truth, which prevented him from publishing this famous *Letter* in his lifetime. For few, if any, among his writings equal it in force and effectiveness. Its tone is one of a candour half cynical, half truly English in its straightforwardness. He goes back to the days, in 1710, when the tories returned to power, and when he was himself fain to let Harley have his way, and not to take advantage of his own ascendency in the Commons —who "grow, like hounds, fond of the man who shows them game." The whole account of his rival, though inspired by bitter personal hatred, has the ring of truth. Then follows the skilful analysis of the baffled tory party after queen Anne's death, and the defiant defence of his own conduct—could he resolve "to be obliged to the whimsicals, or to suffer with Oxford?" So he threw in his lot with the Jacobites, and became a member of a court and government which he describes with inimitable contemptuousness—"Fanny Oglethorpe whom you must have seen in England, kept her corner in it, and Olive Trant was the great wheel of our machine." His account of the failure of the contributions made by the pretender's government, and by the pretender himself, to the failure of the 1715 is convincing; less so is that of his own consistency face to face with an inconsistent tory party; while his explanation of the pretender's attitude towards the religious question is transparently ungenerous, however effectively it may clinch his demonstration of the cleavage between tories and Jacobites. But the attention of the reader is held throughout the tract, which excels in both direct invective and insidious sarcasm, and, apart from a few apparent gallicisms near the outset, may be regarded as a masterpiece of lighter English controversial prose.

A decade had nearly passed before Bolingbroke's pen was once more at work as a weapon of political warfare. In 1725, he had returned "two-thirds restored"—safe, that is, in person and estate, but with his attainder still hanging over him and debarring him from participation as a peer in the counsels of the nation. He had found the whig ministry under Walpole and Townshend in the plenitude of power, and the tory party reduced to what seemed hopeless impotence. It was not long before, in alliance with Pulteney, the leader of the discontented whigs, Bolingbroke engaged in a long-sustained and, ultimately, to some extent, successful endeavour to put an end to this condition of things. The assault may be said to have opened, on 5 December, 1726, with the appearance of the first number of *The Craftsman;* although, as a matter of fact, already, on 15 July of that year, Bolingbroke, under the pseudonym "Will, Johnson," had contributed to a sheet called *The Country Gentleman* a homely apologue in derision of Walpole. The minister here appears as coachman to the worthy Caleb D'Anvers at his little country place near the town (in *The Craftsman*, of which D'Anvers was the figurehead, he is usually designated as of Gray's inn); he proves untrustworthy, and ends by breaking his neck when his horses have been scared by an angry rustic populace.[1]

The Craftsman had a much longer, as well as a merrier, life than was reached by most of the political periodicals proper of the early Hanoverian period—*The Englishman, The Examiner* and the rest (it is unnecessary to go back upon earlier sheets of a more mixed kind); for, in one way or another, it lasted for nine or ten years, and, according to Goldsmith,[2] sold much more rapidly than of old had *The Spectator* itself. It was edited by Nicholas Amhurst, a light-hearted Oxonian, who, a few years earlier, had been invited to leave his university for his university's good, and was published by him in conjunction with an enterprising London printer, Richard Francklin. The signa-

---

[1] Printed in vol. 1 of the 1731 edition of *The Craftsman*. See, also, Sichel, W., *u.s.*, pp. 246 ff., where will be found the most recent account of *The Craftsman* and its contributory forces.

[2] See *Life* in *Works*, vol. 1, pp. lix–lx. The circulation of *The Craftsman* is said, at one time, to have exceeded 10,000 copies a week (it was only for a time a bi-weekly publication); but it is not easy to verify such statements. So early as 1737, it was reprinted in an edition which reached 14 volumes.

tures of the contributors were intentionally chosen and inter-
changed so as to mystify the ill- and defy the well-informed
(including Walpole, who employed more than one doughty pen
on the preparation of retorts). Among these contributors
were, in addition to Amhurst (who started the paper under the
name Caleb D'Anvers), Bolingbroke, Pulteney and Pulteney's
cousin David; also, the chief of the opposition wits (in truth,
there were not many wits on the other side), Arbuthnot and
Swift, and, probably, Gay and Pope. Amhurst was, in 1741,
succeeded in the editorship by Thomas Cooke (commonly called
"Hesiod Cooke" from his translation of Hesiod, 1728); and
among the later writers in the journal were Lyttelton and Akenside. Eustace Budgell, formerly a follower of Addison and a
writer in *The Spectator*, as well as a whig official, had, after
(according to his own account) losing a fortune in the South
Sea, turned against Walpole and became a contributor to *The
Craftsman*.

Of Bolingbroke's contributions, with which we are here
chiefly concerned, the bulk is held to belong to the years
1727–31. The first of these, as it seems, appeared in no. 16 of *The
Craftsman* (27 January, 1727), with the title *The First Vision of
Camelick.*[1] Under the thin disguise of an eastern allegory, this
piece is a virulent attack on the arbitrary rule of Walpole, who
is denounced, with extreme malignity, as a vizier of "blunt,
ruffianly malignity . . . his face bronzed over with a glare of
confidence." He tramples on the backs of the parliament
men on his way to the throne; nor is it till his collapse that the
radiant volume of the constitution reappears, while heaven
and earth resound with the cry of liberty, and "the Heart of
the King is glad within him." Among other acknowledged
papers by Bolingbroke in the earlier numbers of *The Craftsman*
are two out of three bearing the signature "John Trot" (afterwards qualified as "yeoman"), of which the earlier[2] contro-
verts, not very frankly, the arguments of *The London Journal*,
then supposed to be under the direction of Benjamin Hoadly
(bishop of Salisbury, and, afterwards, of Winchester[3]), on the
subject of the unwillingness of Walpole's government to declare

---

[1] Reprinted in *Works*, vol. II.   [2] In no. 129, 4 January, 1729.
[3] "The family of the Publicolas are very numerous. . . . I do not presume to
say, for instance, that such a piece was written by Ben, or such a one by Robin."

war against Spain. A later paper, which forms one of a supplementary set printed by Francklin,[1] as *The Craftsman Extraordinary*, discusses the alleged failure of the ministry to obtain anything from that power in the preliminaries of the congress of Cambray, and ends with an adjuration to the bishop to feed "the Flock committed to his Charge," in obedience to the *Apostolical Constitutions*, lib. ii. *c.* 6, cited for his benefit in both Latin and English.

But the most elaborate of Bolingbroke's invectives, though coupled, in this instance, with some historical comments not devoid of interest, is to be found in *Remarks upon the History of England*, which appeared between 5 September, 1730,[2] and 22 May, 1731,[3] with the signature "Humphry Oldcastle." The argument of these letters is carried on in the conversational framework familiar to both Clarendon and Burnet, the main part in the discussion being taken by "an old gentleman," whose views, of course, are Bolingbroke's and who, equally of course, is moved by "the true old English spirit," the direct reverse of "the blind and furious spirit of party." Assuming the existence of a great danger to liberty, and insisting on the need of keeping up that "spirit of liberty" by losing which the Romans lost their freedom itself, the demonstration in the fourth letter reaches English ground. But, though the printer of *The Craftsman*—one can hardly see why[4]—is said to have been arrested on account of the remarks on the later Plantagenets, it was only when dealing with the Lancastrian kings that the writer discovers his purpose by openly attacking those who advocate the dependence of parliament upon government. He has now found his footing. In *Letter* viii, where he solemnly recalls the revival of the spirit of liberty as exemplified in the parliamentary call of Edward II to the throne, he also insinuates a comparison between queen Caroline and queen Elizabeth Woodville! His account of Henry VII (*Letter* ix) may not uncharitably be surmised to have been intended to reflect on George I; and Wolsey, who could not sustain his power save

---

[1] Various pamphlets published about this time by Francklin, in which Bolingbroke may have had a hand, cannot be noticed here.

[2] No. 218.   [3] No. 255. Both are in vol. vii of the 14-volume edition.

[4] Except that the reign of Richard II had long before proved itself a dangerous subject for modern treatment.

by force and corruption (*Letter* x), is, quite manifestly, put forward as the prototype of Walpole. Thus, Humphry Old-castle's public is gradually brought nearer to its own times, and, after being treated to an outburst of wrath against the wicked minister, is instructed how, under Elizabeth, the check on absolutism was the will of the people itself; how her encouragement of commerce and her prudent policy in the earlier part of her reign, together with her abstinence, throughout its course, from the conclusion of unnecessary treaties or unsafe alliances, brought the nation safe through a great crisis of its history (*Letters* xii-xvi). In all this there is some point—and a great deal of sting.

Then, however, there set in the lamentable change. Government itself may be turned into faction. James I, who has been wrongly blamed for not entangling himself more than he did, "and as is done now," in European (German) affairs, yet, being "afraid where no fear was," allowed the British flag, which had waved proudly in the days of queen Elizabeth (queen Anne), to be insulted with impunity. In the reign of Charles I, who came as a party man to the throne, the faction of the court tainted the nation. The claim of James I (like the pretender's) to hereditary right was untenable; the corruption by means of which he tried to govern was unEnglish; and his patronage of popery did nobody good but the puritans (*Letters* xvii–xxii). Under James I, and, still more, under his son and the universally hated minister Buckingham, the policy of the crown was confronted by the spirit of liberty and broken by an unremitting struggle of almost twoscore years. If we look around us now, we see the whole *posse* of ministerial scribblers assembled in augmented numbers—perhaps with augmented pensions—and the insects, albeit they have been dispersed by every flap of *The Craftsman's* pen, gathered again, after their kind, and renewing their din. But the objects of their attack—the gentleman who conscientiously left his friends and party (Pulteney), and another gentleman, who has been accused of ingratitude and of treachery (Bolingbroke)—need not fear the charges heaped upon their heads; and, with a spirited *apologia* for the political conduct of this "other gentleman," this unique *breviarium* of English history comes to a close (*Letters* xxiii–xxiv).

In the autumn of 1732,[1] Bolingbroke's *Remarks upon the History of England* were followed by three papers of similar purport, discussing the policy of the Athenians with a view to the lessons to be drawn thence by a student of English history and politics. In the previous year (1731), in *A Final Answer to the Remarks on The Craftsman's Vindication*[2]—a pamphlet which may be regarded as the climax of the weekly efforts of the scribes in Walpole's pay, though neither it nor Bolingbroke's retort put an end to the inky war of which they formed part— he renewed his self-defence, on the lines followed in the last of his letters in the *Remarks*. So far as his own conduct is concerned, everything really turns on his far from ingenuous assertion, advanced already in the *Letter to Sir William Wyndham*, that neither before nor after his service with the pretender was he a Jacobite. But, as an exercise in the art of invective, delivered as from a high pinnacle of virtue, this diatribe against the "noble pair of brothers" (Robert and Horace Walpole), professing to come from one whose "ambition, whatever may have been said or thought about it, hath been long since dead," must be allowed to have few superiors.

Before adverting to what Goldsmith describes as Bolingbroke's "parting blow" against the object of his concentrated political and personal hatred, it may be convenient to notice the important additions made by Bolingbroke to the political writing by him actually contributed to *The Craftsman*, in the form of certain papers put forth, from January, 1727, onwards, under the title *The Occasional Writer*. Of these, which seem to be four in number, the first, written in a style of mock humility, is inscribed "to the PERSON, to whom alone it can belong," and in whose service, inasmuch as great statesmen set no value upon high literary ability, its composition is professed to have been undertaken. In reality, it is an indictment of Walpole's conduct of foreign affairs, and, more especially, of his alleged subservience to France.[3] Against his wont, Walpole gratified his

---

[1] See vol. VIII of 14-vol. edn., nos. 324–6 (16–30 September). Reprinted in *A Collection of Political Tracts*, printed anonymously in 1748.

[2] Reprinted in *Works*, vol. VI.

[3] The second letter, though with a different turn of irony, carries on the same theme, inveighing against the fatuous pursuit of the ideal of a balance of power. A reference must suffice to Bolingbroke's remarkably luminous pamphlet *The*

adversary by inspiring an angrily contemptuous reply, spurning "the Occasional Writer's" "proffered services"; and this ministerial answer, already noted in a brief postscript to his second paper, is, in the third, disputed "with strict impartiality." In a postscript to a fourth paper, which may or may not be by Bolingbroke, and which is addressed to "his Imperial Majesty" (to whom the writer tenders counsel in a very superior way), the author of the first paper pretends to disclaim the authorship of the third.

The last and most important of the series belonging to this group of Bolingbroke's writings is the celebrated *Dissertation upon Parties*, which appeared in *The Craftsman* in the autumn of 1733.[1] In April of this year, Walpole's virtual abandonment of the Excise bill had severely shaken his authority and encouraged the opposition to fresh efforts. A general election was at hand in 1734; but the prospect of accomplishing the overthrow of the minister was impeded by divisions among his adversaries. In particular, Pulteney and the malcontent whigs disliked the proposed repeal of the Septennial act—a measure on which Bolingbroke was intent and which, fully aware of his authorship of it, Walpole induced the expiring parliament to throw out, in March, 1734.[2] Thus it was in order to bring the long struggle against Walpole to a successful issue, and, with this end, to conciliate the dissatisfied element in the opposition, that *A Dissertation* was composed. Although, beyond a doubt, one of the most notable of its author's polemical efforts, it failed in its immediate purpose; and, instead of Walpole being overthrown, it was Bolingbroke who, early in 1735—the state of his private affairs helping to disconcert him—once more returned to France.

Case of Dunkirk consider'd (1730), which is commended, and from which ample quotations are made, in *The Craftsman*, no. 207 (20 June, 1730). Cf., as to this, Collins, J. Churton, *u.s.*, p. 179.

[1] The series extends from no. 382 (with breaks) to no. 443, from 27 October, 1733, onwards. See vols. XII and XIII of the 14. vol. edition, where many of the letters are signed "O." and the reprint in *Works*, vol. III.

[2] This is the debate, with Walpole's attack upon Bolingbroke, and its supposed consequence, his retirement to France, imaginatively reproduced in "the Opposition Scene in the last century" in Smythe, George A. F. P. Sydney (Lord Strangford) *Historic Fancies* (1844). Bolingbroke comments on the debate in a pathetic speech, in which he apostrophises Liberty as the heritage of the people of the future.

The nineteen letters to Caleb D'Anvers entitled *A Dissertation upon Parties* are preceded by a dedication to Walpole, which denounces the foremost councillor of the reigning sovereign (and of his predecessor) as having gained that position "by wriggling, intriguing, whispering, and bargaining himself into this dangerous post, to which he was not called by the general suffrage, nor perhaps"—here we find just the grain of truth without which no malicious insinuation is complete—"by the deliberate choice of his master himself." Yet, with all the vehemence of the attack, and the wit that enlivens it, its audacity is cheap; for Bolingbroke knew that he was not running any serious personal risk. The interest of the letters into which the *Dissertation* is broken up, therefore, is substantially that of a brilliant dialectical and rhetorical display. The general argument in favour of the maintenance, by all the parties that agreed to it, of the constitution, as finally settled by the revolution of 1688,[1] is skilfully brought home, so to speak, to the consciences of tories and whigs alike; "the chimæra of a prerogative has been removed,"[2] and there is no danger of the House of Commons assuming a preponderance of power,[3] unless the constituent nation co-operates in its own undoing.[4] But liberty, as Machiavelli says, needs a constant renewal of safeguards; and there are new agencies of corruption at work, in the manipulation of the civil list and of the public funds; and it is the duty of all parties to work together against this abuse, directed as it is by the guiltiest of ministers.

Quite apart from the admirable skill with which these letters handle their text, from their lively personal digressions against Walpole[5] and from the historical insight of which, in particular passages,[6] they give proof, the *Dissertation* has the great merit of inner veracity. Whatever we may think of the motive of its composition, or of the effect which it produced or which it failed to produce, Bolingbroke had come to know, by means of an experience the reverse of deceptive, how much was rotten in the party system, in which his own political life had its being.

[1] *Letter* III.   [2] *Letter* IX.   [3] *Letter* XVI.   [4] *Letter* XVIII.

[5] Under *aliases* such as "the bell-wether," and "Pallas the favourite of Agrippina."

[6] Such as that commenting on the effects of the opposition to the Exclusion bill (*Letter* IV) and, more especially, the character of Charles II, probably based upon Temple (*Letter* VII).

This system he was afterwards, though without any real success, to seek to remedy; but his present diagnosis was not devoid of an essential element of truth, and a sense of this pervades the fervour and the flow of his hortatory eloquence.

In the ten or eleven years in which, from his fine and costly estate at Dawley—"Dawley Farm" he, characteristically, preferred to call it—Bolingbroke was influencing the political life of England, his thoughts were also occupied with ambitious literary projects. One of these was a history of his own times, which was to have extended from the peace of the Pyrenees to that of Utrecht, but of which only fragments survive. In the autumn of 1735, by which time he had established himself at Chanteloup, in Touraine, having now for some time alternated between philosophical and historical themes, he not unnaturally bethought himself of applying philosophical treatment to historical labours. The result was a series of *Letters on the Study and Use of History*, addressed by him, in the winter of this year, to Lord Cornbury, Clarendon's great-grandson, afterwards Lord Hyde, a young nobleman of literary tastes and Jacobite leanings, who played a prominent part in Bolingbroke's later literary life. It cannot be doubted that these *Letters*, which are stated to have been of all their author's writings "the most read,"[1] exercised an important influence upon the progress of historical studies and historical literature both in England and in France, where they inspired Voltaire. Bolingbroke, it has been said,[2] was the first to divert English historical inquiry from the dead to the living; perhaps it might be asserted, more broadly, that he was the first English writer to recognise and illustrate the cardinal principle of the continuity of history. But, here again, the muse of history ends as the apologist of a particular chapter of political action. After the first of these eight *Letters* has discussed the motives from which different classes of men engage in the study of history—amusement, desire of display, the love of accumulation for accumulation's sake—the second lays down the time-honoured maxim that history, rightly understood, is philosophy teaching by examples. Although Bolingbroke fails to perceive the radical futility of

[1] Macknight, T., *u.s.*, p. 625.

[2] By Schlosser, cited by Brosch, M., *Lord Bolingbroke und die Whigs und Tories seiner Zeit*, p. 296.

this theory as applied to a science which has its own work to perform, he is too shrewd not to guard himself, as he does in his third *Letter*, against an exaggerated use of his principle. Thus, when he reviews extant historical literature, it is in a sceptical spirit that he treats not only ancient history at large, but Jewish history and Scriptural chronology in particular.[1] "The lying spirit," he says in his fourth *Letter*, "has gone forth from ecclesiastical to other historians." But the historical student is not, on that account, to despair; it is folly to endeavour "to establish universal Pyrrhonism in matters of history, because there are few histories without lies, and none without some mistakes." A critical sifting will leave us still in possession of materials for historical study; the only difficulty, since life is short for the old, and busy for the young, is not to lose time by groping in the dark among them. Abridgments and mere compilations should be eschewed—the ancients are to be read, but modern history, beginning with the era in which a great change was wrought by the concurrence of extraordinary events, is to be studied. From this shallow generalisation, the writer proceeds to a severe judgment as to what English writers have done towards illustrating the division of modern history with which they are more particularly concerned.

"Our nation," he says, "has furnished as ample and as important matter, good and bad, for history, as any nation under the sun; and yet we must yield the palm in writing history most certainly to the Italians and to the French, and I fear even to the Germans. The only two pieces of history we have, in any respect to be compared with the ancient, are the reign of Henry VII, by my Lord Bacon, and the history of our civil wars by your noble ancestor, my Lord Chancellor Clarendon. But we have no general history to be compared with some of other countries; neither have we, which I lament much more, particular histories, except the two I have mentioned, nor writers of memorials, nor collectors of monuments and anecdotes to vie in number or in merit with those that foreign nations can boast. . . ."

Bolingbroke knew very little about the memorials which were either at the disposal of students of the national history or

---

[1] This was the portion of the *Letters* which Lord Hyde in vain sought to prevent Mallet, Bolingbroke's literary executor, from publishing after his death. See Macknight, *u.s.*, pp. 694–7.

awaiting resuscitation; but the truth of his remarks as to the
slow progress of English historical literature to a conception of its
highest and comprehensive purposes is made sufficiently clear
by any consecutive survey of it, such as has been attempted
in these volumes. By way of exemplifying his meaning,
Bolingbroke, in his sixth *Letter*, gives a brief view of the ecclesiastical and of the civil government in Europe in the beginning
of the sixteenth century, and in his two remaining *Letters* carries
on this survey, with far greater fulness, from the treaty of the
Pyrenees to his own day. This portion of the series may be
reckoned among the most effective and enjoyable of Bolingbroke's writings. He alludes, in one of these *Letters*,[1] to his
intention of writing a history of the latter part of the reign of
William III and of the reign of Anne—of which he says more in
a separate *Letter*, apparently addressed to Lord Bathurst.[2]
The two concluding *Letters* of the series are admirably clear and
concise; nor could anything be better, in its way, than the
account of the growth of the power of France from Richelieu
onwards, and the preservation of her preponderance notwithstanding the Triple Alliance. The last *Letter* is instinct with
strong personal feeling, though it maintains a polished calm
and, unlike much of Bolingbroke's political writing, seeks
to convince by argument rather than by eloquence and wit.
He is fair to William III's unsuccessful endeavours to settle
the Spanish succession by peace, and allows that the war was
really unavoidable. The pivot of his argument is that England
did not enter into the war to dispossess Philip, but that the
English government adopted this point of view in 1706 and persisted in it even after the death of the emperor Joseph I. For
economic reasons, it had then become the duty of the British
government to make peace, and those who opposed it—the
emperor and the arrogant whigs—were responsible for England's

---

[1] *Letter* VIII, p. 91 (edn. of 1870).

[2] *A Plan for a General History of Europe*, reprinted in *Works*, vol. IV, which is
of the nature of a quite brief introduction to such a survey, during the sixteenth
and seventeenth centuries, but, of course, extending to the treaties of Utrecht and
Baden and their effects—subjects on which "I think I could speak with some
knowledge." The *History* was to have been a sequence of a sort of political maps,
which Bolingbroke confesses he might not have possessed the ability of constructing; though, characteristically, he has no doubt as to the impartiality with which
he would have performed the task.

not obtaining better terms at Utrecht. The pessimistic conclusion of the *Letter* is more in the author's usual vein, lamenting the condition of the state, composed of "a king without monarchical splendour, a senate of nobles without aristocratic independency, and a senate of commons without democratic freedom," and a general decay of society to match.

About the time when Bolingbroke sketched a plan of European history for Lord Bathurst, a tory peer who was the friend of Congreve, Pope and Sterne, he also composed, for the edification of the same recipient, *A Letter on the True Use of Retirement and Study* (1736). This effort has been very diversely judged; but it can hardly be denied to be a very readable essay on what may be called the philosophy of life, part of which it sees very justly. Though the author nowhere probes human nature very deeply, his diagnosis is keen and his statement of its results forcible without cynicism.

Of greater importance among Bolingbroke's writings is *A Letter on the Spirit of Patriotism*, written by him in 1736, and subsequently addressed to Lord Lyttelton, a rising hope of the opposition. Its theme is one which was to occupy Bolingbroke's mind during the remainder of his political life, and may be regarded as the final position which he had come to occupy, in consequence of the divisions between those with whom he had co-operated, and the failure of the adversaries of Walpole, among whom he was chief, to effect the minister's overthrow. To merge factions in a great national or patriotic party, and, while steadfastly opposing the corrupt existing government, to reform the English system of government itself, was the object to which he now directed the endeavours of public men, and of the rising generation of them in particular. But, while the breadth of this plan gives a certain dignity to the pamphlet in which it is advanced, the praise which has been lavished on its execution has been overdone. If an example of Bolingbroke's best manner is to be found in the last two of the *Letters on the Study and Use of History*, then *A Letter on the Spirit of Patriotism* must surely be regarded as exhibiting only his second-best, a compound of violent invective with more or less turgid declamation. The essay begins with a tirade against Walpole and the whigs, who had at last found out that they had prepared the sway not of a party but of a person, while the tories continued sour, waiting for a messiah that would never come. Then follows a tirade about the true spirit in which opposition should be conducted—the spirit of a patriotism in which there is a satisfaction comparable to that attending on the discoveries of a Newton or a Descartes. That spirit has, in England, been exchanged for a servility more abject than that to be found in France; yet, to check the growing evils in our public life was a task really so easy that it could have been accomplished but for the eagerness of the hunters, intent, lest they should miss their own reward, upon dividing the skin almost before they had taken the beast, and thus postponing the evil day. It is the next generation on whom it remains to set out hopes—a generation which must learn to despise the old differences between Big Endians and Little Endians, the dangers of the church and those of the protestant succession. Neither Demosthenes nor Cicero was an orator only; a definite plan of action has become the sacred duty of a patriotic opposition. All this is clever and acute; but who could describe it as the distilled wisdom of a life nobly devoted to the patriotic action which it approves?

In 1738, by which time Bolingbroke had recognised the futility of hoping for a personal return to power—whatever means he might employ for the attainment of this object—he composed what (with the exception of two smaller pieces) was the last, as it was one of the most notable, of his contributions to political literature—*The Idea of a Patriot King*. It was not published till 1749,[1] when the public situation had greatly changed, when Pelham was at the head of the government, and Lyttelton, to whom, as private secretary of Frederick prince of Wales, this treatise and the *Spirit of Patriotism* had been addressed, was not in opposition, but in office. But it seemed entirely opportune to the public which read and admired it, and it continued to be a sort of symbolic book to the party which set its hopes on Frederick prince of Wales, and, after his death in 1751, with perhaps more show of reason, on his son, afterwards king George III. That monarch himself has been justly described[2] as having "derived the articles of his

---

[1] As to the private impression of 1744, surreptitiously increased by Pope from five or six to fifteen hundred copies, afterwards destroyed by Bolingbroke's orders, see Macknight, *u.s.*, pp. 666-7.   [2] By Churton Collins, *u.s.*, p. 206.

political creed" from Bolingbroke's treatise, which supplied the materials for the political programme of "the King's Friends." Thus, it was not wonderful that *The Patriot King* should continue to be read with an interest never aroused by its predecessor. Nor does the splendour of its eloquence show any falling off from that exemplar. The patriot king, who begins to govern so soon as he begins to reign, and his ministers, selected by him at once as men sure to serve on the same principles as those on which he is prepared to govern—what blessings may not be reckoned upon to flow from these miraculous assumptions!

Of course, the argument has its ironical side or aspect, and, viewed as a satire upon the non-patriot king, and his non-patriotic followers, the essay retained its force so long as it was worth finding fault with George II and the *epigoni* of Walpole. But the historical comment upon the positive value of Bolingbroke's sovereign cure was furnished, not so much by the career of Frederick prince of Wales (of which there is "no more to be said"), as by the history of the earlier years of the reign of George III and of the part played by his "Friends" in English constitutional life. The idea of *The Patriot King* was a fabric of sand, and became a heritage of the winds.[1]

The letter or paper *Of the State of Parties at the Accession of George I*, which, apparently put together to satisfy Lyttelton, was published with the two "patriotic" treatises in 1749, may be unreservedly dismissed as a piece of special pleading neither effective nor adequate. Bolingbroke here takes it upon himself to deny that, during the last four years of queen Anne's reign, there existed any plan for bringing the pretender to the throne. Clearly, he expected the fact of his own correspondence with James, at a time when he was secretary of state under his sister, to be ignored by the reader as it was by the writer. Thus, the charge against George I of having let loose the fury of revenge upon the tories, and goaded men into the rebellion of 1715, instead of accomplishing his succession quietly, as he might have done, falls to the ground, or recoils upon its author.

---

[1] Sichel has directed attention to the reference to Bolingbroke's speculations in the *Historic Fancies*, already cited, of Lord Strangford, at one time a remarkable figure in the "Young England" movement.

Finally, in 1749, Bolingbroke put forth *Some Reflections on the Present State of the Nation, principally with regard to her Trade and her Debts, and on the Causes and Consequences of them*. Although this pamphlet remains a fragment, it would seem as if the main points of the argument were put in the completed portion. After a most unsuccessful and costly war, and after we have participated, "like principal actors," in continental wars and negotiations covering a period of threescore years, it becomes time that public attention should be turned homeward, and especially to the question of national taxes and debts. Since the revolution of 1688, and, more particularly, during the Spanish Succession war, in which the whole weight of expenditure fell on England and Holland, the chief way of meeting it has been that of funding debt (whence the beginning of an era of stock-jobbing), in order to make the fortunes of great numbers depend on the preservation of the new government. The increase of the public debt has been enormous, and has risen since the Hanoverian acquisition of Bremen and Verden became the first link in a chain which has dragged England into new and expensive broils. When, of late, war with Spain became unavoidable, the part we took in it could only end to the advantage of France. We have no Sullys among us; but the public debt must be diminished, and the interest on it reduced; and, though it is necessary to foster the rivalry between Austria and France, and to support the former against the latter, this should be done in accordance with the present interest of England only.

The tone of this pamphlet, though some of the old fire still burns beneath the surface, is, on the whole, calmer and more temperate than is usual with the writer.

It does not form part of our present task to estimate the influence of Bolingbroke upon his contemporaries or upon posterity, except in so far as it was due to his literary qualities. We have not to examine here what there was of intrinsic force in his statesmanship, whether in office or in opposition, or even what there was of inner veracity in his arguments as a political and historical writer—for he knew the value of truth, though he did not love it as much as he hated Walpole. If he is now read, he is read (except by professed historical students) for his style; and, supposing Burke to have had some reason for terming him a "presumptuous and superficial writer,"[1] his style must bear part of the blame. It is Bolingbroke's style as a writer—not as an orator—of which alone posterity is capable of forming an estimate. As a matter of course, the oratorical element in his writings, almost from first to last, is considerable; but though, during his brief public career under queen Anne, he was, beyond a doubt, the most effective speaker in the House of Commons, not a single one of his great speeches has come down to us.

Bolingbroke's style as a writer has the supreme merit—the merit without which all others are, or ought to be, vain—of perfect lucidity. His readers are never left in the slightest doubt as to what he means, or at least as to what he desires them to understand him to mean. And this result he obtains without effort, without any assumption of severe superiority, or any display of overwhelming exuberance. Indeed, his style might almost be called the normal style of English prose, after which even the style of Burke seems to be, in some respects, transnormal. In what measure the lucidity of Bolingbroke as a writer is due to his early and close familiarity with French, it is difficult to decide; at the same time, his style, with hardly an exception worth noting, is perfectly free from gallicisms.

But Bolingbroke's prose is not only clear; it has the strong flow of a river fed from many contributory sources—and yet a flow diversified by currents and eddies of all sorts: movements of anger, scorn and dignified withdrawal into self, of irony and sarcasm, of witty turn or opportune anecdote. We recognise in him the well, if not widely, read man of letters rather than the scholar whose mind has been imbued by his studies; it is the phrases which have commended themselves to his literary

---

[1] See Sichel, W., *u.s.*, pp. 441 ff. It seems unnecessary to examine here the statement that Burke's style was founded on Bolingbroke's; but it may, perhaps, be observed that the clever imitation of Bolingbroke's manner to be found in Burke's first printed work, *A Vindication of Natural Society* (which took in the critics) does not furnish any proof of the assertion. Burke, in his imitation, forgot neither the wide basis from which the argument started, nor the rapid, though varied, treatment of the theme, nor, again, the final touch of personal pathos, and even the ornaments of occasional quotation and illustrative anecdote. The imitation, of course, was intentional, while the higher qualities of Burke's style are not to be sought for in such a composition. But, apart from this, it would not be difficult to point out touches in *A Vindication* which have more in them of Burke than of Bolingbroke.

instinct, and these are what he reproduces or adapts.[1] What he yet lacks has been diversely defined. Yet, if his political writings be compared with those of Burke, or even with those, whatever may be their blemishes, of Milton, the balance must rise in their disfavour. For, notwithstanding the extraordinary elasticity of mind which seconded Bolingbroke's perseverance of purpose, posterity, like his contemporaries, refuses to be persuaded by his political writings, while Burke convinced fervent admirers of the French revolution (such as Gentz) that they were in the wrong, and Milton holds in awe even those who continue to revere the *eikon* which he sought to break.

Down to the earlier half of the eighteenth century, *The Compleat History of England* (1706)—of which the first two volumes contained a series of histories of successive periods and reigns from Milton's *History of Britain* down to Arthur Wilson's *History of King James I*, supplemented by a third volume containing the reigns of Charles I and II, James II, William and Mary (and William), " all new writ by a learned and impartial hand "—had been the only attempt to present a collective view of the national history.[2] That it was accepted as more or less of an authority is shown by the fact that a new edition was published in 1719, and that, so late as 1740, Roger North, of whose contributions to English biographical literature something will be said below, put forth an elaborate criticism of its concluding volume, under the title *Examen, or an Inquiry into the Credit and Veracity of a pretended Complete History*, viz. the supplementary volume aforesaid, of which White Kennett was the author.[3] Kennett, who died as bishop of Peterborough

---

[1] "Montaigne, whom I often quote, as I do Seneca, rather for the smartness of expression than the weight of matter." Bolingbroke, *On the Use of Retirement and Study*, edn. 1870, p. 142.

[2] The *General History of England* by James Tyrrell, grandson of archbishop Ussher and an intimate friend of Locke, which was intended to go down to the reign of William III, was carried no further than the death of Richard II.

[3] This very substantial work, which, besides being, perhaps, the most elaborate criticism ever attempted of a section of an English historical narrative, contains so much important information as to support effectively the author's contention in favour of contemporary history over critical compilation, must primarily be set down as a thoroughly partisan review of what may be allowed to be, in certain respects, a partisan text. Its avowed purpose is "to vindicate the Honour of Charles II and his Happy Reign " from the aspersions cast upon it by the writer

in 1728, after an active literary career (which had begun, or almost begun, by his breaking a lance with Atterbury in the well-known convocation controversy (1701), and of which his *Register and Chronicle, Ecclesiastical and Civil*[1] forms the concluding item), was author of the concluding volume. The character of Charles II which it contains is, no doubt, extremely acrid (it ends with a note on the resemblance of Charles in his outward features, and, to some extent, in other points, to Tiberius); in general, however, the author is temperate in statement, although, in the usual fashion, he inveighs against Cromwell, whose "policy" is margined as "his only piety." For the rest, Kennett was a sound whig, who ventured to answer Sacheverell in a sermon preached before the lord mayor, and who, before he was consecrated bishop, was portrayed as Judas Iscariot in a London church, being a safer object of insult than Burnet.

A rival "complete history" to Kennett's, for a considerable period, was that of Laurence Echard, the "excellency" of which, in the amiable phrase of Roger North,[2] "is coming after a worse." It was conceived on a smaller scale than Kennett's; but, on the other hand, it was the work of a single man. Of his

---

of *The Compleat History;* its author takes the earliest opportunity of announcing that, while the historian must never exceed or fall short of truth, "good" and "bad" are qualities antecedently determined by a standard possessed of an authority superior to that of any reader or writer of history. Thus, he can, at the same time, censure without fear and (so it seems) always in accordance with his own political and religious views. The career of Shaftesbury, the so-called "popish plot," the "sham plots" connected with it, and the transactions of the latter years of Charles II's reign are all effectively reviewed from a standpoint which the critic never finds it necessary to desert, and the king's action is consistently defended in his relation to the whole inner history of his reign. As for the papers found in his strong box after his death—would the evidence as to their authorship be accepted in a court of justice? At the same time, North has some excellent hits at the methods of his author—which are not peculiar to him—especially at his suggestion of possible alternatives (the alternatives which he desires to insinuate) by means of the disjunctive "or," and his leaving the unwary to distinguish unproved deductions from well-warranted facts.—Appended to Montagu North's edition of his father's *Examen* are *Reflections upon some passages in Mr. Le Clerc's Life of Mr. John Locke* by the same hand, in which Shaftesbury and *Ignoramus* once more figure.

[1] Vol. 1 only was published (in 1728); the sequel (reaching to 1679) remains in manuscript in the British Museum, where, also, are many other of Kennett's manuscripts.

[2] *Preface* to *The Life of Francis North, Lord Guilford.*

History of England from the First Entrance of Julius Cæsar, the
first volume, carrying the narrative down to the death of James
I, appeared in 1707; the second and third, which continued it
to "the establishment of King William and Mary," in 1718.
Echard (who, in 1712, was named archdeacon of Stow) was a
strong protestant, as favourable to Cranmer as he was bitter
against Mary I, but he was no friend of dissent, and rather
cynically attributed "the Beginnings of Presbitery" in England
to Cartwright's personal jealousy of a Cambridge rival.[1]
When he comes to the Stewart times, he professes to take great
care to observe "Deference to the Stations and Characters"
of those whose conduct he reviews; but, as he seems to think
that James II might have been forgiven much of his religious
policy had he only kept his word and prefers to let him "fall
gently" because of his two daughters, there must be allowed
to be method in his defence.   The dedication of his second volume to George I sufficiently attests his political "standpoint"
and helps to explain the attacks made on him by Bolingbroke.

It can, however, hardly be denied that the best, and certainly, by far, the most useful, collective history of England in
the earlier half of the century was not an English book at all,
but the French *Histoire d'Angleterre* of Paul de Rapin, sieur de
Thomas, composed in exile at Wesel and published at the
Hague, in eight volumes, in 1724.   A criticism of this work,
which reaches to the death of Charles I, or of its French continuation, to the revolution of 1688, by David Durand (1734),
would be out of place here; but it should be noted that the
whole French *History* was translated by Nicholas Tindal "with
additional notes" in 15 volumes (1723–31).   Thomas Lediard,
author of *The Naval History of England* (2 vols., 1735), and
The Life of John Duke of Marlborough (3-vols., 1736), largely
from original documents, wrote *The History of the Reigns of
William III and Mary, and Anne*, in continuation of Rapin;
and, in 1744–5, his translator, Tindal, published, in folio, *The
Continuation of Mr. Rapin de Thoyras's History of England
from the Revolution to the Accession of King George II*, which was
immediately followed by an octavo edition in 13 volumes, making the whole series amount to 28.[2]   Rapin, in a letter to his

---

[1] Cf. below, as to Oldmixon's censure of Echard's attacks on the dissenters.

[2] It was afterwards further continued by Smollett.

fellow Huguenot Robethon, had humourously described his completed work as "no inconsiderable undertaking for a Gascon"; the indefatigable Tindal survived his historical labours for many years (till 1774). English historical writing owes him a great debt; for, like Rapin himself, whom he introduced to English readers, he provided a solid substructure of well-authenticated and well-arranged facts, together with a narrative free from party bias and written with a single-minded desire to record ascertained truth. It should be added that master and follower alike cite their authorities without ostentation but with perfect clearness, and that the English folios are supplied with an admirable collection of portraits, maps and plans.

From these writers of collective histories we go back slightly in order of time, so as to mention, in conclusion, one or two historical authors of the unmistakable partisan type. Abel Boyer, like Rapin, was a French Huguenot, who settled in England in 1689 and, after several years of strenuous endeavour, gained a long-lived reputation by an Anglo-French and Franco-English dictionary, professing to have been composed for the use of the duke of Gloucester, to whom, in 1692, Boyer had been appointed French tutor. In 1702, when this dictionary was published at the Hague, Boyer also brought out, in English, his *History of William III* (which included that of James II); and, in the following year, he began the yearly publication of *The History of the Reign of Queen Anne digested into annals*, which was preceded by a similar register of political events, notable for the reports of parliamentary debates contained in it, and extending over the years 1713–29. In 1722 appeared his *History of Queen Anne*, of which a second edition, with numerous appendixes, followed in 1735. Boyer was a voluminous producer of books, pamphlets and contributions to journalism, all in the whig interest.[1] Among the pamphlets, one had nearly cost him dear, as it attacked Swift, who, in an often quoted passage of his *Journal to Stella*, vowed vengeance on the "French dog" (a term of abuse to be found already in Froissart). Boyer's *History of Queen Anne* has been found extremely useful,

[1] See bibliography, and cf. the article on Boyer by Espinasse, Francis, in vol. VI of *The Dict. of Nat. Biogr.* (1886). As to Boyer's English translation of the *Mémoires* of Gramont, see *ante*, Vol. VIII, p. 508.

not to say indispensable, by modern historians (by no means
only in the "Annual List of the Deaths of Eminent Persons"
appended to it with short obituary notices—"whoever pretends
to write *Characters* ought," he ventures to think, "to be well
acquainted with those he describes") and shows him capable of
applying the principles of historical writing, as to both matter
and manner, effectively abstracted by him "for his own Instruction, and laid down in his preface."   A continuation of the
work to the death of George I was published in 1747.   English
historical composition was greatly indebted to the infusion of
French lucidity in arrangement and treatment; and, for this
quality, Boyer, too, deserves praise.

Little purpose would be served by entering at length into
the qualities of John Oldmixon as a historical writer.   In *The
Dunciad*,[1] Pope abuses him without, perhaps, very much point;
but, in a note to the passage, he describes him with undeniable
truth as having been "all his life a virulent Party-writer for
hire," who "received his reward in a small place"—the collec-
torship of the port of Bridgwater.   It was not till 1717, or
thereabouts, that Oldmixon obtained this ill and irregularly
paid post—about nine years after he had first exchanged his
efforts as a poet and dramatist for a long series of labours as a
party historian and journalist.   These need not here be examined in detail.   His earliest historical work, *The British Empire
in America* (2 vols., 1708), was at least designed to meet a real
need; *The Secret History of Europe* (4 parts, 1712–5) was a frank
and fierce attack upon the tory government and its subservience
to France.   But the special enmity of the opposition wits he
incurred by his *Essay on Criticism*, prefixed to the third edition
(1727) of *The Critical History of England, Ecclesiastical and Civil*
(2 vols., 1724–6).   The *Essay*, an avowedly and, perhaps, intentionally rambling discourse, supposed to be in the manner of
Montaigne, contains some fair hits at Dryden, Addison, Pope
and others, and keeps up a steady fire of minute criticism
against Echard as a historian.   Of *The Critical History* itself,
the first volume carries on this attack in a sort of running commentary upon previous historians, especially Echard and
Clarendon, in a vein frequently flippant, but by no means without occasional sensible remarks.   Each section ends with a

[1] Bk. II, ll. 283–90.

list of authorities to be studied, so that the book is a curious combination of party pamphlet and school manual. The second volume covers much the same ground, although more particularly devoting itself to ecclesiastical history, and intended to show that the protestant dissenters "have a Claim to our Indulgence and Good-will, as they are Brethren of the Reformation," and that Echard's charges against them of "sedition and enthusiasm" are "groundless and scandalous." From a different point of view, as showing that no literary fashion endures for ever, Oldmixon's remark upon the "affectation of continually drawing characters," especially "when they are arbitrary and are not of the subject," is worth noting. Of *The History of England during the Reigns of the Royal House of Stuart*, the first volume, published in 1729, states at length the charge, already noticed[1] and adverted to in *The Critical History of England*, against the Oxford editors of Clarendon, of having altered his text for party ends. The second volume of the later work (1735) carried on the narrative to the reign of George I, and the third (1739) took it back to the last four Tudor reigns, the whole being written in the spirit of whig constitutionalism. "In the midst of all the infirmities of old age sickness, lameness, and almost blindness," Oldmixon wrote *Memoirs of the Press, Historical and Political, for Thirty Years Past, from* 1710 *to* 1740; but he did not live to see the book, which has much biographical interest, published. He died in 1742; the hardships of his laborious career seem to belie the commonplace that, in a free country, there is nothing like sticking to one's party.

Though also confessedly composed by a partisan—who avows that "he knows not by what influence or means he took very early to the loyal side," and who consistently speaks of its opponents as "the faction against monarchy" or "the faction" pure and simple—Roger North's biographies hold an enduring position in English historical literature. The period with which they deal extends but slightly beyond the reign of Charles II; but the most important of them, *The Life of Francis North, Lord Guilford*, was repeatedly revised, and was not published with the companion *Lives of the Hon. Sir Dudley North and the Hon. and Rev. Dr. John North* till 1740, immediately after the

[1] *Ante*, Vol. VII, p. 500.

author's *Examen*;[1] while Roger North's own *Autobiography* was not generally accessible till 1887, when an edition of it was brought out by Jessopp, who has identified himself with *The Lives of the Norths*.[2]

Roger North, who confesses that he was himself of a timid disposition, gifted neither with readiness of speech nor with the quickness of thought which underlies it, and whose innate modesty is not the least pleasing element in the altruism which ennobled his character, was a true believer in his family. The Norths, he says, "were a numerous flock, and no one scabby sheep in it"; and, though the eldest of the brothers (Lord North and Gray of Rolleston) had "attached himself to the faction," the rest were "in all respects helpful and assistant to each other . . . nor the least favour of difference or feud found amongst them." Roger became the biographer of four of them, including himself. Specially intimate were his relations with the third of the brothers, Francis, who became Lord Guilford and keeper of the great seal. The advancement of Francis in place and prosperity was also that of Roger, whom he associated with himself in every stage of his career, who lodged with him, was a daily guest at his table and, for many years, never failed to see him safe to bed; who, in short, as Roger himself expresses it, was his brother's "shadow." With the frankness which adds both value and charm to his narrative, Roger confesses that his nature at one time rebelled against this dependence; but he never broke through it, and the sincerity with which he judges his brother's character and career is never devoid of piety. Their intimacy enabled the biographer to interpret the laconic notes kept by the successful counsel and eminent judge with a fulness which converts them into so many episodes of legal experience, as well as to expand the "*speculums*" that represented his passing thoughts on the multifarious problems of his public and private life. Thus, Francis North's complex but masculine, though, in more respects than one, not very attractive, character is brought before the reader with all the force of veracity—for he was cautious as well as ambitious, not overscrupulous so long as he kept well within the law (within which he consistently conjured king Charles II to keep); but, at the same time, straightforward in his private and in his public

[1] Cf. *ante*, p. 262, note. [2] See his standard complete edition in 3 vols., 1890.

acts, and content to leave the latter "without any affected lustre or handles to fame if he could avoid them." "No wonder," writes his biographer, with telling irony, "he is so soon forgot."[1] The account of his matrimonial and electioneering operations illustrates the social and political ethics of the age rather than his own. The characters of Lord Guilford's contemporaries in the higher judiciary are drawn with less reticence and extraordinary force—such portraits as those of "Silenus" Saunders and Jeffreys, in their way, are immortal, the latter more especially so because Macaulay's portrait owes to it some of its most telling features; while the finer touches which reveal the biographer's antipathy against Sir Matthew Hale are at least equally to the credit of his artistic skill. By the side of these portraits of legal luminaries may be mentioned the admirable portrait of one whose light was hid behind the backstairs—Will Chiffinch.

To the literary ability of Roger North, the second of these *Lives*, that of Sir Dudley North, the great Turkey merchant, afterwards, at a critical season, appointed sheriff of London by a more than doubtful process dictated by the policy of the court,[2] bears signal witness. This biography depicts, with singular fidelity and force, the career of a young man of family who, virtually, began his mercantile life as supercargo on a ship bound for Archangel, and ended it as treasurer of the Turkey company at Constantinople. The account, derived from him by his brother, of the Turkish system of government (the description of *avanios* or exactions from Christian states

---

[1] Though lord keeper North had the chief share in directing the proceedings against those accused of complicity in the Rye house plot, there is no reason for attributing to him any share in *A True Account of that Horrid Conspiracy against the late King, His Present Majesty and the Government*, drawn up at his suggestion, but composed by Thomas Sprat, bishop of Rochester, and published in 1685. It speaks of Russell's adherence to the doctrine of resistance as "conformable to his Presbyterian education" and of Sidney (sarcastically) as "a stubborn Asserter of the *Good Old Cause*."

[2] An account of these proceedings, from the point of view of those who took the lead in opposing them, will be found in a book based on materials constituting a most valuable addition to the memoir-literature of this period, Papillon, F. W., *Memoirs of Thomas Papillon of London, Merchant* (1623–1702). Thomas Papillon, of distinguished Huguenot descent, was twice an exile—once for joining in an effort to restore Charles I to power, once for his action with regard to the London charter and North's election. He was member for Dover both before and after his second absence from England.

and persons is specially interesting), law and society, is as full of interest as, when first made known, it must have been of novelty; and the personal character of the great merchant—whose eastern notions were not, like his mustachios, suppressed on his return home—is brought out with much affectionate humour. The honours gained by Sir Dudley North after his return nearly involved him in serious trouble after the revolution of 1688: Roger's account of his brother's examination before the House of Commons is one of the best-told episodes in the story. The third of the *Lives*, that of John North, master of Trinity college, Cambridge, has a very different interest; it relates the story of the life of a Cambridge don, first at Jesus, where his younger brother was his pupil but where he grew tired of the "grave, and perhaps empty seniors," then at Trinity lodge, where he was on uneasy terms with the fellows, very unpopular with the undergraduates and "so nice that he never completed anything" in the way of a book. In the end, his intellectual powers decayed with those of his body; through life, his greatest happiness seems to have been the occasional society of his brothers.

Roger, the sixth and youngest of his father's sons, was, as has been observed, born to be the biographer of those among them whose worldly success had outstripped his own. He judged himself humbly, but without hypocrisy—"though not of prime of my rank, yet not contemptible." His tastes were intellectual: mathematics and music had a special attraction for him, and, of amusements, he preferred that of sailing. That he had a genuine literary gift, he seems hardly to have suspected —for he never himself published anything but *A Discourse of Fish and Fish Ponds* (1683); but, during the long evening of his life (from 1690 to 1734), which he spent in his own house at Rougham in Norfolk, after, as a non-juror, he had given up practice at the bar, he wrote the *Lives* of which mention has been made and his own *Autobiography*. The latter breaks off with an account of his long services as trustee under Sir Peter Lely's will, which, like those by him performed under that of his brother Lord Guilford, long occupied most of his leisure. But, though only a fragment, and a repetition, here and there, of what he had already told in the *Lives* of his brothers, it is not the least engaging of his productions, and, occasionally, lifts an unsuspected corner of his inner nature—as in the strange passage concerning a man's right to end his own existence.   In a lighter vein is the comparison—which must amuse readers of *The Rape of the Lock*— of the life of men to a game at ombre.

The merits of Roger North's biographies consist in their transparent candour, combined, as it is, with a shrewdness partly due to experience and partly to an innate insight, and in a naturalness of style which, at the same time, is always that of a well-bred scholar.   He never shrinks from the use of an idiomatic phrase or proverbial turn, still less from that of an apposite anecdote; but they never have the effect of interrupting the pleasant, if somewhat sedate, progress of his narrative. The *"minutiae"* for which he goes out of his way to apologise are, of course, welcome in themselves to readers of later generations; but the effect of each biography, as a whole, is not trifling or petty, and the dignity of the theme—whether it be that of legal eminence, mercantile enterprise, or scholarly calm—is invariably maintained without any apparent effort.   Here and there, although he is constantly referring to the fuller treatment a subject has received in his *Examen*, Roger North becomes lengthy; but the total effect of his *Lives*, as that of all biographies of real excellence, is not less entertaining than it is instructive for those who are open to the appeal of a human life intelligently, truthfully and sympathetically told.

CHAPTER IX

Memoir-Writers, 1715-60

UNDER the first two Georges, English society became consolidated into what Disraeli, with his accustomed iridescence, described as a "Venetian oligarchy." Placemen in, and patriots out of, office flit across the scene. The big county interests of the aristocracy rule, subject to occasional correction from the growing power of finance or the expiring growls of the city mob, and Walpole and Pelham, or their inferiors, pull the strings. The nation, hoping eternally to see corruption extinguished and a new era of virtue and public spirit inaugurated, is, again and again, disappointed. Placemen and patriots cross over, and the game begins anew. But, behind the chief actors in the comedy, may be perceived a slowly gathering knot of observers and note-takers, the chroniclers and memoir-writers of the period. They offer us a unique and fascinating picture of the privileged classes who then presided over the fortunes of the country; and they open a new chapter in literary history. Through them, the eighteenth century is self-portrayed with a vivid insight and picturesqueness probably unrivalled, save in the parallel descriptions of French society from 1648 to 1789.

Lady Mary Wortley Montagu, one must imagine, was a lady of far more masculine understanding and knowledge than most of the classical ladies of whose attainments Johnson thought highly. As a descriptive topographer, she was a keen observer, not superior to the love of gossip, with a quick eye for the telling features of a story or a situation and an easy, effective style. Her manner is one of conscious superiority. She belonged to the great whig aristocracy which ruled England. Her father, Evelyn Pierrepont, was connected with the Evelyns of Wootton, and married Mary Feilding, daughter of the earl of Denbigh, from one of whose brothers Henry Fielding the novelist descended.   Mary was born in May, 1689; a year later, her father became earl of Kingston and, at the whig triumph of 1715, duke of Kingston; she was brought up, carelessly enough, in a library.   One of her girl friends was Anne Wortley Montagu, a granddaughter of the first earl of Sandwich (Pepys's chief), whose father had, on marrying an heiress, taken the name Wortley.   Anne's favourite brother Edward, a most unromantic young man, was strongly attracted by Lady Mary's lucidity of both mind and visage.   A number of letters between them are extant.   The young pair were, unmistakably, in love; but Kingston was inexorable on the subject of settlements and tried to coerce his daughter into another match; whereupon, she eloped with Edward Wortley (August, 1712).   With the whigs' advent to power, the period of narrow means came to an end, and Edward, a relative of Halifax, became M.P. for Westminster and, in 1716, was appointed ambassador to the Porte. In 1717, the couple journeyed to Constantinople, by way of Vienna and Belgrade.   Her most vivid letters were written during this period and remain an imperishable monument of her husband's otherwise undistinguished embassy; for it was upon his successors that devolved the important task of concluding the peace of Passarowitz.   It must not be supposed that we have the letters in their original form.   Moy Thomas came upon a list of letters written by the ambassadress, with notes of their contents.   The published letters correspond but imperfectly to the *précis*, and only two are indexed as copied at length. Of those remaining to us, some that had been copied were reproduced with small alteration; the majority were reconstructed from the diary in which she was accustomed to note the events and thoughts of every day, and from which she had presumably drawn freely for the original correspondence; others, less finished in form, for the most part, have been found and incorporated since.   The substance of many letters hitherto unknown was given as late as 1907 by "George Paston" in her *Lady Mary Wortley Montagu and her Times*.   The *Turkish Letters* (May, 1716–November, 1718), which are the most finished and the most original, were evidently prepared for publication. though they were not actually published until after Lady Mary's death. They were, no doubt, handed round among the writer's private friends. The prefaces are dated 1724-5 and are attributed to Mary Astell; and the early editions include a frontispiece, "Lady M-y W-r-t-l-y M-nt-g-e The Female Traveller, in the Turkish Dress." Lady Mary, in this respect at all events, was a precursor of Lady Hester Stanhope. Besides assuming Turkish attire, she studied the Turkish language, and did her best to disabuse English minds of a vast accumulation of ludicrous prejudice on the score of Ottoman cruelty, luxury and sensuality. It may be added that she gave expression to the common English antipathy of her day (fully brought out by Smollett in the next generation) to Roman catholicism. Her letters still delight by their high power of communicativeness.

In 1739 (after her daughter's elopement with Lord Bute), Lady Mary determined to go abroad for a lengthened residence. The letters of the next two and twenty years of her life, addressed, for the most part, to Lady Bute, are the most natural and, perhaps, the most charming that she ever wrote. She had seen a little of Italy on her return from Pera, by way of Tunis, Genoa and the Mont Cenis. After experiences in Venice, Chambéri and Avignon, she determined, in 1743, to settle at Lovere on Lago d'Iseo, forty miles from Brescia. There, she spent eighteen fairly serene, though solitary, years. Rising at six, after breakfast she worked with her weaving women till nine, inspected poultry, bees and silkworms and, at eleven, allowed herself the pleasure of an hour's reading—all that her eyesight would permit. She dined at twelve, then slept till three, and woke to play whisk with three old priests at a penny a corner, till it was cool enough to set out upon those rides in the mountains which were as delightful as a romance, or to float under her lute-string awning on the river waiting for a fish to bite. "I confess I sometimes wish for a little conversation, but then," she added gaily, "gardening is the next amusement to reading." When the winter came, she found herself obliged to keep the house and wrote to thank Lady Bute for presuming her taste was still undivorced from the gay part of reading—by which she meant novels. These were sent out in cases from England (the beginning of British novel export) and aroused the utmost excitement upon their arrival, as they well might when one single box is reported to have contained *Peregrine Pickle*, *Roderick Random*, *Clarissa Harlowe* and *Pompey the Little*. She set to work at once to read them, and whole letters to her daughter are devoted to discussing the characters and the intrigues of the stories. With her strong and satirical, by this time almost sardonic, understanding, Lady Mary professed a solid Englishwoman's good-natured contempt for the epistolary light wine of Mme. de Sévigné; nevertheless, as she grew older, her letters came more and more to resemble the epistles of that incomparable model, and the resemblance is strengthened by the fact that most of the letters are to her daughter Lady Bute. On 1 January, 1761, her curmudgeon of a husband died, leaving an immense fortune to Lady Bute; and the widow had to return home. She was sick of life. "I am preparing for my last and longest journey and stand on the threshold of this world, my several infirmities like post-horses ready to hurry me away." Horace Walpole saw her again, and repeated his libellous saying about the "she meteor," complaining of her dirtiness, avarice and eccentricity, her cheating "horse and foot," her hideous style of dress. Mrs. (Elizabeth) Montagu refers to her as speaking, acting, dressing like nobody else. Society had unconsciously caught the tone of the venomous master detractor of Twickenham, whose vendetta against Lady Mary is completely explained only by the unhappy combination in him of bad heart and bad health. Everyone in London agreed as to her preserved liveliness and unimpaired faculties; but it soon became known that the intrepid "female traveller" was suffering from cancer; and of this disease she died, in her seventy-fourth year, at her house in Great George street, 21 August, 1762. She was buried in the Grosvenor chapel in South Audley street, where Lord Chesterfield was interred some ten years later. Her letters, collectively regarded and interpreted, form the autobiography of a warm-hearted, but disappointed, unloved and solitary woman.

When Lady Mary died, Walpole reports, in a letter to Mann, that she left twenty-one large MS. volumes, in prose and verse, to her daughter Lady Bute. At least nineteen volumes were actually left to Lady Bute; two, containing the letters during her husband's embassy at Constantinople, had been given to Mr. Sowden of Rotterdam. There were duplicates of these—

and they form the basis of the *Letters* given to the world in two volumes in 1763. The miscellaneous correspondence in Lady Bute's hands, or portions of it, were first edited by James Dallaway (1803). The voluminous diary was always kept under lock and key, and, although Lady Bute often read passages aloud to her daughters and friends, she never trusted it out of her hands, with the exception of the first five or six copybooks, which she once permitted Lady Louisa to peruse alone, on condition that nothing should be transcribed. When she felt her end drawing near, Lady Bute burned the diary (1794), and the eighteenth century lost a document which might have proved of unique interest.

Apart from Lady Mary's *Letters*, her other writings are insignificant and unattractive. They include a translation of the *Enchiridion* of Epictetus, written in 1710, at the time when her marriage was in debate, and submitted to the taste and judgment of her old friend and adviser Gilbert Burnet, bishop of Sarum.[1] Her *Town Eclogues* were written during the period of her friendly intimacy with Pope and owe something to his inspiration, if not to his "correction." They fell by some "mischance" into the hands of Edmund Curll, who published them in 1716 (through his colleague James Roberts), under the title *Court Poems by a Lady of Quality*. Only three, "The Basset-table, An Eclogue," "The Drawing-Room" and "The Toilet," were included in this thin quarto (misdated 1706), "publish'd faithfully, as they were found in a Pocket-Book taken up in Westminster-Hall, the Last Day of the Lord Winton's Tryal," and, upon a perusal at St. James's coffeehouse, "attributed by the General Voice to be the Production of a Lady of Quality." The eclogues numbered six, one for each week-day (1747). Their delicacy and refinement is not conspicuous, and their metrical sprightliness in no way remarkable; their only value, to-day, consists in the little intimate touches that describe the social arcana of the period.

Lady Mary was certainly no poet. Her mind was the reverse of poetical. All that can be said of her heroic verse is that it is generally fluent, often lively and sometimes forcible. She is at the best when, like Gay, she paints the manners of the times in *Town Eclogues*. Her serious satires are far-away

---

[1] The learned prelate's corrections were printed in italics.

echoes of Pope. The prose essays published with her other remains are trite and show that her talent did not easily work in that form. It is to the *Letters*, and to these alone, that she owes her niche in the house of fame. Without being sympathetic or humorous, and with no great store of wit or fancy, she is rich in descriptive faculty, keen perception, good spirits and glorified common-sense. Her style, though correct and perspicuous, is unstudied, natural, flowing, spirited; she never uses an unnecessary word, or a phrase savouring of affectation. At the same time, she meant to write well and was conscious of having succeeded. Before the Bible society letters of George Borrow appeared, it is doubtful if any traveller's letters have proved so generally entertaining, unless we make exception of Smollett's *Letters from France and Italy*, published in 1766.[1] Lady Mary was almost the first to enter the rich mine of eastern manners and colouring. The travellers of the early seventeenth century wrote in an obsolete fashion and employed an antiquated prose. The historians of Turkey, such as Knolles and Rycaut, are full of fabulous detail. She was one of the earliest (long before Pierre Loti) to make a plain tale of the treatment of women in the east (Turkey was far more remote then than Turkestan or Korea are now), and she did not waste her opportunities. Entertaining, however, as Lady Mary was, whether as a discerning traveller or as a writer with a relatively modern style, her fame for a hundred years depended largely, if not mainly, upon the supposed mystery of her life. That the daughter of a duke, the wife of a millionaire and the mother of a man so much talked of as Edward Wortley should be unhappy and should seek refuge abroad in eccentric solitude and isolation from her quality was, to the early eighteenth century, a thing incredible. The malignity of Walpole and the vindictive line of Pope about the lady who "starved a sister" and "denied a debt" stimulated fresh curiosity concerning the cleverest woman of the day.

With the gradual decline of her notoriety and the eclipse, at least in not a few ostensible ways, of her achievement, Lady Mary's writings have received less and less attention, and are now, perhaps, in danger of being as much undervalued as they are generally admitted to have been at one time overrated.

[1] Cf. Vol. X, Chap. ii, *post*.

Fragments of her criticism have survived the general wreck of her descriptive writings, such as the well-known division of the human race into men, women and Herveys, her comparison of Fielding and Steele, with her diagnosis of the happy temperament which forgot everything over a venison pasty and a flask of champagne, and her hearty contempt for Richardson, over whose novels she confessed to sobbing in a most scandalous manner. Her *Constantinople Letters* (of 1763) soon became popular and classical all over Europe. They were reprinted in the successive editions of Lady Mary's *Letters and Works*,[1] of which her great-grand son Lord Wharncliffe's (1837) remained the standard edition till its contents were considerably enriched, but not substantially altered, in that of Moy Thomas (1861). His canon includes twelve letters to Mrs. Hewett, twelve in correspondence with Anne Wortley, thirty-nine with Wortley Montagu, sixty dealing with the embassy of 1716–18, twenty from Pope to Lady Mary, dated 1716–21, fifty-two letters to the countess of Mar 1721–7, twenty-four items of miscellaneous correspondence, and two hundred and seventy-five letters written between 1738 and 1762 to the countesses of Pomfret, Oxford, Bute, Wortley Montagu and others. There are, also, some sixty-four occasional poems and versions besides *Town Eclogues*, the *Enchiridion*, four essays, two of them in French, the second of which, "On a maxim of La Rochefoucauld about marriage," is as humorous as anything Lady Mary ever wrote, besides a rather interesting fragment upon the court of George I at the time of his accession.

One of the most intimate pictures we possess of the court at the beginning of the Brunswick dynasty is the work of another diarist and letter-writer, Mary Clavering, of the Durham family, who married, in 1706, William Cowper, lord and afterwards first earl Cowper. She corresponded with the electoral princess of Hanover, afterwards queen Caroline, whose household she entered in October, 1714, when she began to keep a diary. This extended, originally, to 1720; the last four years of it were, however, all but completely destroyed by the writer in 1722, when her husband was under suspicion of complicity in the Jacobite plot.

[1] See bibliography.

Lady Cowper tells some amusing stories of her mistress, such as that of the snub administered to Robinson, bishop of London:

This day (Dec. 23, 1714) the Bishop of London waited on my mistress and desired Mrs. Howard to go into the Princess and say he thought it his duty to wait upon her, as he was Dean of the Chapel, to satisfy her in any Doubts or Scruples she might have in regard to our Religion and to explain anything to her which she did not comprehend.   She was a little nettled when Mrs. Howard delivered this message to her, and said, "Send him away civilly; though he is very impertinent to suppose that I who refused to be Empress for the sake of the Protestant Religion, don't understand it fully."

The amount of bargaining and backstair dealing revealed in this diary is astonishing; but the notes are too summary to aspire to literary art, and there is little picturing, hardly any descriptive energy. Lady Cowper naturally saw a good deal of the domestic quarrels of the Hanoverian court; but she lets us hear little about them. Very probably, this was the portion destroyed. The mutilated diary was handed down with the other Cowper manuscripts and edited by Spencer Compton in 1864. The Mrs. Howard to whom it refers, Henrietta Hobart, afterwards Mrs. Howard and countess of Suffolk, was, as is well known, adored by the earl of Peterborough and became the mistress of George II.   Her husband anticipated coming events by paying his court with her at Herrenhausen in 1712; and, after she had been appointed bedchamber woman to the princess of Wales, her rooms in St. James's palace became the place of reunion for the little court of the heir apparent. She cultivated the society of men of letters, such as Gay and Arbuthnot, and was the subject of Peterborough's lines "I said to my heart, between sleeping and waking" and of Pope's complimentary verses,

> I knew a thing that's most uncommon
>   (Envy be silent and attend!)
> I knew a reasonable woman,
>   Handsome and witty, yet a friend.

Lady Hervey, Miss Bellenden, Pulteney, Pelham, Pitt, Horace Walpole, Lord Chesterfield, Swift and Young were among her

correspondents; and most of them celebrate her wit and reasonableness. She wrote an often quoted Gulliverian letter to
Swift, which he professed to be unable to understand. George
II built her a house at Marble hill, Twickenham, where her
literary friends professed to act as chamberlains. Though she
lacked sufficient skill for prevailing against queen Caroline, her
conciliatory temper, not less than her position at court, made
her the recipient of many confidences from the *intrigants* about
St. James's. A judicious selection from her correspondence
entitled *Letters to and from Henrietta, countess of Suffolk, and
her second husband, the Hon. George Berkeley from* 1712 *to* 1767
was edited anonymously by the editor of Lord Hervey's
Memoirs (John Wilson Croker), in 1824.

Precursor in chief of Horace Walpole as court gossip, scandal-
monger and memoir-writer was John Lord Hervey, "remorse-
less Hervey of the coffin face and painted cheeks," a miniature
St. Simon at the early Hanoverian court, though, it must be
admitted, a St. Simon rather lacking in the artistic precision
and measured science of his prototype. Lord Hervey's father
and grandfather (Sir Thomas Hervey, son-in-law of Sir Humphrey May, who drew a touching portrait of Charles I's last
hours) were both great letter-writers; and their letters from
1651 to 1731 have now been published, in three volumes. The
MS. diary of John, first earl of Bristol, ranging from 1688 to 1742,
is largely a ledger of payments and expenses; but the letters
furnish an intimate and attractive portrait of a noble family at
the close of the seventeenth, and beginning of the eighteenth,
century. John had a half-brother, Carr Hervey, whose mother
was the earl's first wife; but he was himself the eldest son of the
second countess, a merry lady, who was a correspondent of
Lady Mary Wortley Montagu and lady of the bedchamber to
queen Caroline. Educated at Westminster under Freind, and
at Clare hall, Cambridge, he inherited from both parents,
but especially from his mother, a gift for repartee and a fondness
for riming. After his return from Hanover, in a fine flush of
Hanoverian zeal, he declined hard labour and gravitated
between Ickworth, where he browsed on poetry, and the court
at Richmond. Early in 1720, when a handsome youth of
twenty-four, he secretly married the beauty of the younger

court, Mary Lepell, "Youth's youngest daughter, sweet Lepell," who had charmed all the wits, including Pope. The reciprocal devotion between the Herveys and Lady Mary Wortley Montagu offended both Pope and Horace Walpole, who suspected the ladies of scandal about his paternity. Pope was jealous, with the result that, in the first of his imitations of Horace, addressed to Fortescue, "Lord Fanny" and "Sappho" were generally identified with Hervey and Lady Mary. Hervey had already been attacked in *The Dunciad* and *Bathos*, and he now retaliated. There is no doubt that he had a share (possibly the sole share) in *Verses to the Imitator of Horace* (1732). In *Letters from a nobleman at Hampton Court to a Doctor of Divinity* (1733), he scoffed at Pope's deformity and humble birth. Pope's reply was *A Letter to a noble Lord*, dated November, 1733, and the scathing portrait of Sporus in the *Epistle to Dr. Arbuthnot* (1735). Hervey also quarrelled fiercely with Pulteney over a libel and was very nearly a victim to his adversary's rapier. He also fell out with Frederick, prince of Wales, in the matter of an amour with one of the queen's maids of honour, Anne Vane, who became the prince's mistress. He was thus much exposed on every side to the malice and detraction of declared enemies; and this fact helps to account for the cynicism and venom which overflow in his *Memoirs*. Meanwhile, in 1723, by the death of his brother, he became heir to the earldom of Bristol and assumed the title by which he is remembered.[1] In the new reign, his advancement was assured, inasmuch as, with a strong feeling for self-preservation, he had made sure of all the approaches, and all the backstair exits, of the innermost court.

After a spell of Italian travel, in which he had engaged partly for the sake of his health (which, according to the parental view, had been undermined by that "poisonous plant tea"), he returned in 1729, and, having given in his adherence to the victorious wing of the party in power, was promptly pensioned and appointed vice-chamberlain, with the special purpose of serving as Walpole's agent about the person of queen Caroline, whose closest confidences he shared. Walpole employed his incisive pen to refute the libels contributed to *The Craftsman*

---

[1] In June, 1733, he was called to the House of Lords by writ in virtue of his father's barony.

by Pulteney, whose barbed retorts suggested most of the ugly insinuations which Pope worked up into his scarifying caricature of "Sporus, that mere white curd of ass's milk." After the queen's death in November, 1737, Lord Hervey was admitted to the cabinet as lord privy seal, but, much against his inclination, was thrown out of office by the fall of Walpole. His pamphlets, such as *Miscellaneous Thoughts on the Present Posture of Foreign and Domestic Affairs* and his *Three Speeches on the Gin Act* (1742–3), show that his mental vigour was unimpaired. His health, however, was gradually failing; and he died, in the lifetime of his father, on 5 August, 1743, aged only 46, and was buried in the family tomb at Ickworth. During the last fifteen years of his life, he had been composing his both lifelike and highly polished, but thoroughly cynical, *Memoirs*, which extend from his first coming to court to the death of the queen. The manuscript of these *Memoirs*, entirely in autograph, was left to his sons, by whom it appears that several sheets referring to the more intimate dissensions in the royal family were destroyed. Allusion was made to them by Horace Walpole, who seems to have inspected them in 1759; but Hervey's second son, the third earl, left strict injunctions, in his will, that the *Memoirs* were not to be published until after the death of George III. They appeared, eventually, as *Memoirs of the reign of George the Second*, edited from the original manuscript at Ickworth by John Wilson Croker (1848). They give a wonderfully vivid picture of the court of the second George; but the comedy presented is of the type of classical Roman satire, in which the motive of avarice is overwhelmingly predominant. The *dramatis personae* are the king, the prince, Wilmington, Walpole, Pulteney, Wyndham, Bolingbroke, Chesterfield—and the writer hates them all, sees all their characters at their worst and depicts them with merciless satire. For the queen alone and her daughter the princess Caroline, he had a genuine respect and attachment; indeed, the princess's affection for him was commonly said to be the reason for the close retirement in which she lived after his death.

Apart from the queen and her daughter, Hervey's portraits are all, without exception, of the Spagnoletto school; he systematically blackens. How far his tendency to detraction may have been the result of his epilepsy, of his vegetarian diet, of his habitual cast of thought, or of his literary predilections, it would be impossible to determine. His narrative was never meant to be scrutinised by contemporaries; its confirmation, in many respects, by Horace Walpole's *Memoirs* must be regarded as somewhat ambiguous evidence of accuracy, since it has never yet been tested minutely by any modern critic. The elaborate structure of the periods reveals Hervey as a careful student of the Latin historians of the empire. It must be remembered that he occasionally composed Latin epitaphs and letters. He was a useful patron to Conyers Middleton, who showed his gratitude by dedicating to Hervey his famous *Life of Cicero*. The panegyric earned for its victim the gibe, containing an unkind allusion to Hervey's cadaverous complexion:

> Narcissus, praised with all a parson's power,
> Look'd a white lily sunk beneath a shower.

To whatever cause we may attribute the fact, there can be little doubt that Hervey was a virtuoso in defamatory epithets and studied forms of detraction. Akin to Horace Walpole in rancour, the note-taking Hervey, warmed in the bosom of the court, stung the king and nearly all around him to the full extent of his powers.

"A court," says Lord Rosebery,[1] "is considered fair game by such reptiles. But it is hard to see why princes who after all are human beings should not be allowed to some extent the same sanctity of family life which humbler human beings claim and maintain. Hervey was the intimate associate of the King, the confidential friend of the Queen, the lover of one of their daughters, he was the tame cat of the family circle. He thought it seemly to narrate their secrets in so brutal a fashion that some more decent members of his family tore out and destroyed the coarsest and bitterest passages. What remains is coarse and bitter enough. It shews the King and Queen in a most unfavourable light. But that aspect is fascinating, compared to that in which he presents himself."

Lord Rosebery justly concludes that it is most unwise to attribute literal exactitude or even general veracity to such broken confidences and chronicles, too amusing to be likely to be strictly true, as those of Lord Hervey and his fellow cynic, the "inimitable" Horace.

[1] *Chatham*, p. 197.

Among the less important memoirs of the second quarter of the eighteenth century, before the protagonist of memoir-writing is reached—the great little Horace, whose name, as Sir Leslie Stephen points out, is a synonym for the history of England from 1740 to 1790—a passing mention may be made of the *Memoirs* of Lord Waldegrave and George Bubb Dodington. James, second earl of Waldegrave, a great-grandson of James II, became a favourite with George II, was nominated lord of the bedchamber in 1743 and governor of the prince of Wales, afterwards George III, by whom he was not liked. Though extremely "unlovely" in both address and appearance, Waldegrave, who hated hard work, set up for a man of gallantry and pleasure, and, a few years before his death from small-pox in 1763 (when he was aged only forty-eight), married Walpole's niece, the handsomest woman in England. Waldegrave, though he was prime minister for five days only (8–12 June, 1757), had a close insight into the course of affairs during the period of which he writes (1754–8). The real interest of his *Memoirs* consists in the carefully weighed characters which he draws of the chief actors, and in the strong contrast between these portraits and the sinister silhouettes of the too clever and far from scrupulous Hervey. Thus, in his portrait of George II, Waldegrave insists, as upon the two really salient features in the likeness, on the king's passion for business and his keen knowledge (surpassing that of any of his ministers) of foreign affairs.[1]

Among the Tapers and Tadpoles of the "broad-bottom administration," we are fortunate in possessing a three-quarter length portrait of so typical a fortune-hunter as George Bubb Dodington, who, by a long course of "disagreeable compliances" and grotesque contortions, raised himself to £5000 a year and a peerage as baron Melcombe. He died at Hammersmith, aged seventy, on 28 July, 1762. In the days of his splendour, he sought to become a patron of letters and was accepted as such by Young, Thomson and Fielding, but spurned by Johnson. A diligent student of Tacitus, he compiled a large quantity of political papers and memoranda, which he left to a distant cousin, Henry Penruddocke Wyndham, on condition that those alone should be published which did honour to his memory. Wyndham published the *Diary* in 1784, persuading himself,

[1] Lord Holland edited Lord Waldegrave's *Memoirs* in 1821.

with judicious sophistry, that the phrase in the will formed no barrier to such a proceeding.

The *Diary* presents, perhaps, the most curious illustration in existence of the servile place-hunters of the age, with its unctuous professions of virtuous sentiment and disgust at venality, which serve only to heighten the general effect. It must be said, in Bubb's honour, that he united with Chesterfield and Walpole in trying to save Byng. His *Diary*, though carelessly compiled, contains some curious historical information, especially as to the prince and princess of Wales, during the period which it covers, from 1748 to 1760. In his cynical self-complacency, he becomes almost a humorous artist. But, from a literary point of view, his is a dry light, which few readers of the present day will be specially interested to rekindle.

CHAPTER X

Writers of Burlesque and Translators

AS the seventeenth century drew to its close, there came into being a strange underworld of letters, an *inferno* inhabited by lettered vagabonds, who matched, in scholarship and scurrility, the heroes of Petronius. Beggar students, tavern keepers, idlers from the inns of court, adventurers who had trailed a pike in Holland, flocked thither with spruce young squires who "knew the true manage of the hat," and loungers fresh from the universities. Thus, in the coffee-houses, there grew up a new public, for whose amusement a new literature was invented. The old days of dignity and leisure were passed. The wits of the town wrote, not to please themselves, but to flatter the taste of their patrons, and many of them succeeded so well as to echo in prose or verse the precise accent of the tavern. A familiarity of speech and thought distinguished them all. They were ribald, they were agile, they were fearless. They insolently attacked their great contemporaries. They had, indeed, as little respect for high personages in life or letters as for the English tongue, which they maltreated with light-hearted ribaldry. The slang which they used—and they were all masters in this kind—was not the curious slang of metaphor, such as is enshrined in the pages of Cotgrave's *Dictionary;* rather, it was composed of the catch words which seemed worth a smile when they were heard in the coffee-house, but which instantly lost their savour when they were put in print, and which to-day defy the researches of the archaeologist. As they aimed, one and all at the same mark—popularity—they exhibit in their works no subtle differences. The vanity of individual expression was not for them. They admitted that the booksellers, who paid the

285

piper, had a perfect right to call the tune, and they sang and danced in loyal obedience to the fashion of the moment. They wrote the slippered doggerel, the easy prose, the flippant plays, that were asked of them, and their names might be transposed on many title-pages without any violation of justice or probability.

In spirit and ambition, they were true cockneys. They readily shook off the influences and associations of their childhood. Though Tom Brown went to Christ Church from Shifnal, though Ned Ward was a loyal son of Oxfordshire, though Peter Motteux first saw the light at Rouen, London was their paradise. They saw through her eyes, they spoke with her tongue. Most intimately at home in Will's or Ned Ward's, they dragged their muse, as they would still have called her, down to the level of sawdust and spilled wine. Before all things, and at all times, they were anti-heroic. Their jests never sparkled more brightly than when they were aimed at authority. No poets, living or dead, were sacred in their careless eyes. It seemed to them a legitimate enterprise to ridicule Vergil, or to trick Homer out in the motley garments of the age. Aeneas and Ulysses, esteemed heroes by many generations of men, were for them no better than those who frequented Grub street or took their pleasure in the Mall. And they found in travesty or burlesque an admirable field for the exercise of their untidy talent.

In burlesque, Scarron was their openly acknowledged master. They did not make any attempt to belittle the debt which they owed to *Le Virgile Travesti*. They announced their obligation not merely in their style, but in their titles, and, if this antic form of poetry took some years in crossing the Channel, it flourished with amazing energy after its passage. The success of Scarron himself is a curiosity of literary history. The form was no new thing, when Scarron made it his own. The reverse process, the exaltation of paltry subjects by august treatment, such as was afterwards employed by John Philips[1] in his *Splendid Shilling*, was not unknown to the ancients. The trick of putting the gods and heroes of Greece and Rome into dressing-gowns had been practised in Spain and Italy before Scarron published, in 1648, the first book of his famous

[1] As to John Philips, cf. *ante*, p. 204.

Virgile. But, for France, and, so, for England, Scarron was a
real inventor. The artifice seemed simple enough when it was
discovered. It depended for its triumph upon nothing else
than an obvious contrast. To represent whatever had seemed
sacred to the tradition of the race as trivial and ludicrous was
not a difficult enterprise, while the anachronism which persuaded Vergil to speak of oil-paintings and to quote Corneille
was assured of a laugh. The example of Scarron was quickly
followed. Furetière, Dufresnoy, d'Assoucy hastened to prove
themselves possessed of this new humour. Ovid—curled and
barbered, was sent to pay his addresses to the ladies of the
court with M. de Boufflers. Not even Lucan or Juvenal
escaped the outrage of parody. And the style of the burlesques
matched the irreverence of their thought. It was familiar to
baseness; it flowed with the ease and swiftness of a turbid
stream. In brief, as Boileau said, Parnassus spoke the language of the market, and Apollo, travestied, became a Tabarin.

The enthusiasm which Scarron's experiment aroused made
an easy conquest of courtier and scholar alike. From the
capital, it spread to the provinces, and, though none of his
imitators is worth remembrance, Scarron deserves his meed of
praise. He did an ill thing supremely well. In facility and
suppleness, his *Virgile* has never been surpassed. His humour,
such as it is, is tireless and inexhaustible. Moreover, if he be
happy in his raillery, his work, as French admirers have said,
is not without some value as a piece of criticism. He touches
with a light hand the weakness of the lachrymose hero. He
turns the light of the prevailing "good sense" upon Vergil's
many simplicities, for which few will thank him; and, even in
the very act of burlesque, he pays his victim the compliment of
a scrupulously close adherence to his text.

The fashion was already overpast in France, when Charles
Cotton made his first experiment in English burlesque. In
1664, was published under the title *Scarronides, or Virgil
Travestie*, a mock-poem on the first book of the *Aeneid*. To this,
Cotton added the fourth book six years later, and, presently,
put some of Lucian's dialogues into "English fustian," with the
title *Burlesque upon Burlesque: or the Scoffer Scoff'd*. Of these
experiments in the new craft, no more can be said than that
they were better than the base imitations which speedily fol-

lowed.   Cotton, at any rate, was a man of letters, with a sense
of style and variety, and if he stooped to play the tune which
the tavern-haunters demanded, he played it with some skill
and energy.   He uses the artifices which they all use.   He
mixes ancient and modern inextricably.   He measures the
distance which Aeneas rowed by a familiar standard, "'twixt
Parson's Dock and Billingsgate."   As to Dido's temple, "I
cannot liken any to it," says he, "unless 't be Pancras, if you
know it."   The humour is forced and barren; but those French
critics are in the wrong, who declare that Cotton was content
merely to translate Scarron.   If his theory of burlesque was
Scarron's, the application of it was all his own.

Cotton's success did not long remain unchallenged.   Within
a year, one Monsey of Pembroke hall, Cambridge, gave to the
world his own *Scarronides*, a mock-poem, being the second
and seventh books of Vergil's *Aeneid*, which he dedicated, by
what, no doubt, he thought a great stroke of humour, to "Lady
Ann Dido, Countess of Carthage."   It is a work without character, scrupulously fashioned according to the pattern of the
hour; and a reference to James Hind proves that this author
also has learned the lesson of anachronism.   Then John
Phillips, a true habitant of Grub street, paraphrased, in his
Maronides, the fifth and sixth books of the *Aeneid*.   In a preface, he attempts a timid defence of his temerity.   "I leave
the world to determine," says he, "whether it be not reason
that he that has caused us so often to cry when we were Boys,
ought not to make us laugh as much now we are men."   As
Phillips travestied him, Vergil does not make us laugh, and the
justification fails.   The experiment, in truth, differed little
from the others, save that its author, for the moment a zealous
royalist, put the puritans in hell.   There they all lie, Haselrigge
and Pym, Hugh Peters, the chief of English rogues, Bradshaw,

in a Squarr
Of burning Canvas, lin'd with **Tarr**

and Cromwell himself,

that Devil of a Devil,
Whose Noddle was the Mint of Evil.

The licence which John Phillips allowed himself in his treatment
of Vergil was vastly increased by the author of *The Irish Hudi-*

bras, or Fingallian Prince, who boldly adapted the sixth book of the *Aeneid* to his own time, and turned it to a high encomium of William III, "this present Monarch, England's timely Redeemer, whom Heaven long preserve."

Nor was Vergil the only one of the poets attacked in England with wanton insolence. In 1664, James Scudamore's *Homer à la Mode, A Mock Poem upon the first and second Books of Homer's Iliads*, came upon the town. The version is free from the brutality which disgraced many of its rivals, and gives promise of better things. The promise remained unfulfilled, for the author, who was bred at Christ Church, had but just taken his degree when he was drowned in the Wye, "to the great reluctancy of all those who were acquainted with his pregnant parts." The author of *Homerides: or Homer's First Book Moderniz'd*, who, some fifty years later, essayed Scudamore's task over again, need not awaken our curiosity. He showed a spark of self-knowledge when he called himself Sir Iliad Doggerell, and a complete ignorance of literary fitness, when he regretted that Pope did not give Homer "the English air as well as tongue." Ovid, better suited to the methods of burlesque, did but tempt the makers of travesties to a wilder extravagance. "Naso Scarronomimus," the writer of *Ovidius Exulans*, can scarcely persuade the sorry tit of his humour to move for all his thwackings, and even Alexander Radcliffe, a captain, an inns-of-court-man and a poet, who, in *The Ramble, An Anti-Heroic Poem*, gave proof of a rough vigour and freshness, fails to arouse a laugh by his *Ovid Travestie*. To send Ulysses to Scotland as a volunteer, for the suppression of rebellion, and to leave him loitering at an inn on the homeward road, is an artifice which no literary fashion can justify. In truth, the taste of the dying seventeenth century was not our taste, and we can only wonder at the indiscretion of our ancestors.

Meanwhile, Samuel Butler had discovered in *Hudibras* the real purpose of burlesque.[1] If Scarron had done nothing else than to inspire, at a distance, this work of genius, we should still owe him a debt of gratitude. It was not for Butler to ridicule the ancient mythologies; he saw before his eyes the follies and pretensions of his own time and country awaiting castigation. And so, he turned the travesty magnificently to the uses

[1] Cf. *ante*, Vol. VIII, Chap. II.

of satire.   He employed the artifices of contrast and anachronism beloved by the imitators of Scarron to exhibit in the clear light of absurdity the hypocrisy and meanness of presbyterians. He, too, expressed the high in terms of the low.   His work is the masterpiece of its kind, unique and incomparable.   It is idle to praise its technical perfection.   The resource and ingenuity of the author's rimes, the tireless exuberance of his wit, his easy movement, his bold extravagance are qualities unmatched elsewhere in literature.   Nor does his wisdom lag behind his wit. He concentrates into aphorisms the fruit of his keen observation with so happy a skill that a great part of his work has passed into the possession of all Englishmen.   Thousands quote him with assurance who have never turned the pages of *Hudibras*, who would care not a fig for his fable or his satire, even if they understood them.   And, though he won instant acceptance, he defied imitation.   When he had fashioned his masterpiece, he broke the mould; and, for that very reason, perhaps, he became the prey of the parodists.

There is nothing that looks so easy as perfection, and the coffee-house poets, easily beguiled, thought it no shame to express themselves and their politics in Hudibrastic verse.   If they could not rival the master, they could at least pretend to mimicry in halting octosyllables.   The boldest of them all was Ned Ward, who combined the crafts of publican and poet. Born in Oxfordshire in 1667, he was, says his biographer, "of low extraction and little education."   Whatever his extraction may have been, he cleverly picked up his knowledge of letters as he went along.   He did not scruple to call one of his books *Vulgus Britannicus*, and he believed in the singularity of "an Egyptian Magi."   In his youth, he had travelled in the West Indies, a fact commemorated by Pope, "or shipp'd with Ward to Ape and Monkey Lands."   But he early settled to the professions which suited him best.   His first experiment in innkeeping was made in Moorfields.   He presently moved to Fulwood rents, where he opened a punch-shop and tavern, "but in a genteel way," says Giles Jacob, "and with his wit, humour, and good liquor, has afforded his guests pleasurable entertainment."   Whatever he did was, doubtless, done in a "genteel way," and the guests who found pleasure in his entertainment were, one and all, sound tories and high churchmen.   A big, burly man, he showed a practical faith in his own ale and his own punch, and, while he gossiped at the fireside with his clients, never let a day pass without a verse:

> So Ned, divided, writes and brews,
> To try if darling gain accrues
> More from his Mash-Tub than his Muse.

His mash-tub had the better of it. Not only did it fill his pocket; it did not put him into the pillory. Twice, for his muse's sake, he faced the angry mob at the Royal Exchange and at Charing Cross. "As thick as eggs at Ward in pillory," says Pope; but his humour carried him safely through the vicissitudes of politics, and he died at his tavern, a prosperous potman and scurrile poet, in 1731.

He was a journalist in verse. His *Hudibras Redivivus* is a gazette in rime, which was inspired by the moment, and was published in parts. The ingenious Ward begins his preface with an apology. "Tho' I have made bold," he says, "to borrow a Title from one of the best poems that ever was published in the English Tongue—yet I would not have the world expect me such a wizard as to conjure up the spirit of the inimitable Butler." He need not have been in doubt. He was no wizard, but a pedestrian jogtrot writer of doggerel, whom criticism could not affright nor opposition baulk. Yet his *Hudibras* is a wonderful achievement. Its facile fluent ease marks the versifier who could write two hundred lines standing on one foot. His language is common enough. Neither Brown nor Motteux surpasses him in knowledge of the slang which was heard in the tavern or at the street corner. Had he lived to-day, he might have been an ornament of the sporting press. Living when he did, he supported the cause of church and state in such couplets as jingled in the brain, and tripped readily to the tongue.

For popular government he had a hearty contemp

> For he that will oblige the throng,
> Must ne'er hold one opinion long,
> But turn his doctrine and his creed,
> As often as the Cause has need.

Among those upon whom he poured out his contempt are
"prophet Dan" with "the scoundrel Freedom of his Pen," all
whigs and all dissenters.   He believed, like an eminent statesman, that the one object of the whigs was to make themselves
"masters for life" of England and all that it contained:

> A man of sense, with half an Eye,
> (Says he) may easily descry,
> Thro' all their conscientious Cant,
> What in reality they want;
> Which is, believe me, in a word,
> All that the Kingdom can afford.

Compromise he hated, and impartiality.   He professed a deep
distrust of moderation, which was no better in his eye than a
"modish cant," with which fools disguise "their spite, their
venom, and their lies."   The book is tedious in its facility.
It weighs upon the reader's spirit with the heaviness of all dead
controversies.   Even where he protests against the debtors'
prison, where

> men for poverty alone
> Must wear these doublets made of stone,

he wins your reluctant approval.   He is at his best when he
describes the taverns and shops of the town, their picturesque
signs, and the strange characters who throng the streets, the
campaign wenches and the ale-wives, the lame mumpers and
the disabled seamen.   Here, he spoke with an authority which
none of his colleagues in Grub street could rival.   If he had but
a casual acquaintance with the English tongue, he knew London
and its slang like the tavern keeper that he was.   Whatever
were his shortcomings, his industry was prodigious.   *Vulgus
Britannicus* rivalled his *Hudibras* in dulness and prolixity.
The Republican Procession, in which, among others, he ridicules
Marlborough, "a great Pretender to the trick of State," is
merry only on the title-page.   He poured forth broadsides,
satires, prose and verse with an equal hand.   Impartially, he
sang the praises of a Derby-Ale-House and the New Tunbridge
Wells at Islington.   The love of good living and high principles
breathes in all that he wrote.   The pity is that a sound inspiration found so poor and graceless an expression.   Now and

then, he could sing a song in the true Rabelaisian strain, as in his *Wine and Wisdom: or the Tipling Philosophers:*

> Wise Thales the Father of all
>   The Greek Philosophicall Crew,
> Ere he gaz'd at the Heavens, would call
>   For a chirruping Bottle or two.

In fifty stanzas, he thus extolled what was, assuredly, the more profitable of his two trades, and, for the moment, endowed his doggerel with a rollicking sincerity.

It is, as has been said, by his sketches of London and its streets that Ned Ward saves his Hudibrastic experiments from dulness, and there, in the sights and sounds about him, he found the material best suited to his talent. Whatever disloyalty the hacks of Grub street may have shown to the English language, they were constant in their devotion to the London, which was their world. Ned Ward, in his *London Spy*, and Tom Brown, in his *Amusements Serious and Comical*, have bequeathed to us a picture of the town whose merit is wholly independent of literature. They are the true descendants of Dekker and Nashe, from whom they are separated by less than a century of time. Between them are many centuries of style and thought. The London which Dekker and Nashe describe is enwrapped in an atmosphere of dark mystery and impenetrable gloom. They see the seven deadly sins ever before them, and deplore the iniquity of their city with the solemn eloquence of prophets. Satire is their lightest weapon. They condemn even where they admire. It is in no spirit of flippancy that Dekker denounces the cruelty of this "now once-againe New-reared Troy." Nashe's voice is the voice of a sincerely repentant sinner. "London," he cries, "lay off thy gorgeous attire and cast downe thy selfe before God in contrition and prayer, least hee cast thee downe in his indignation into hell-fire."

Ned Ward and Tom Brown could not look upon the life about them with the grave eyes of their predecessors. It was not for them to be censorious or to hope for better things. If only the city of their habitation were a place of pleasant resort, they cared not for its morals. And they wrote of it in the easy style of the trained reporter. Their temperament in no sense diminishes the value of their sketch. They have shown us a

London infinitely more supple, infinitely commoner and, at the same time, far closer to our own than the London of Dekker and Nashe. The cockney with his nimbler wit and paltrier ideals had intervened, and fixed for all time certain lineaments of the city. No longer is it dominated by gallant or beau or gull. Those who throng the taverns of the time are either impostors, such as Radcliffe paints in *The Ramble*, or mere citizens meanly ambitious of cutting a dash. In brief, it seems perfectly consonant with the prevailing manners that Ned Ward should keep an ale-house, or that Motteux, the translator of Rabelais, should desert literature for the selling of China goods.

The London Spy is, undoubtedly, Ward's masterpiece. After two centuries, it still keeps the fresh stamp of truth. Its design, if design it may be called, is of the simplest. A citizen, who, "after a tedious confinement in a country Hutt," breaking loose from "the scholar's gaol, his study," revisits London. There he meets an old schoolfellow, who shows him the sights, and especially the taverns, of the town. It is a *Gull's Hornbook* of another age, written with a plain simplicity, and with scarce a touch of satire. The two friends range from Billingsgate, where they observe the "oars" and "scullers," who tout by the waterside, and note "the stink of sprats and the unteneable clamours of the wrangling society," to Hummun's Turkish bath. They wander from the Quaker's tavern in Fish lane to that hideous *inferno* the Poultry compter, from the Wits' coffeehouse, where the cockney sketches for his friend a character of the modern poets, to Bartholomew Fair, now stripped of its glory. By the way, they encounter many strange personages, such as the highwayman, who "has good friends in Newgate," and is "well acquainted with the ostlers about Bishopsgate and Smithfield, and gains from them intelligence of what booties go out that are worth attempting." The book is written with a directness and simplicity which command belief, and ends, as in duty bound, with a description of the death and funeral of Dryden, who was the master of them all, and who impressed his laws upon his liege subjects, like the dictator that he was.

Tom Brown followed hard upon the heels of Ned Ward, and, in his *Amusements Serious and Comical Calculated for the Meridian of London*, pictured the London that he saw, with less truth than Ward, and greater wit. London he recognises to be a world by itself, and he imagines "what an Indian would think of such a motley herd of people," thus anticipating Macaulay's imagined New Zealander. He sketches the city, and those whom he and his Indian encounter—the alderman, the usurer, the broker and the rest—with a good-humoured enthusiasm. For him, the playhouse is "an enchanted island." When they walk in the Mall, he persuades his Indian to exclaim, "I never beheld in my life so great a flight of birds." Much of the book is the comedy of the age translated into a light-fingered prose. Tom Brown finds it as hard as Ned Ward finds it to keep away from the taverns and gaming-houses, and, in his exposure of the many rascals who lay in waiting for the unwary traveller, he sets a fashion speedily followed in *The Cheats of London* and a vast library of similar chapbooks. He was, in truth, well fitted by character and training to do the work of Grub street. Educated at Christ Church, he won an instant fame by a pleasant trick of writing Latin verse, and it is said that many pieces were extant of his composition, bearing other names. Even in his youth, his cynic temper preferred money to fame, and no sooner had he left the university for London than he was ready to hire himself out to the highest bidder. Nothing came amiss to his facile brain. To show his touch with the classics, he translated Persius and mimicked Horace. The example of Rabelais was ever before him, and he followed John Phillips in imitating the prognostications of Pantagruel. His epigrams, in Latin or English, are rather coarse than witty. The best of his work is journalism, illuminated always by the light of scholarship. There is no topic so bare that he will not embroider it with tags from the classics. His favourite artifice was to indite letters from the dead to the living, an artifice which gave him the chance to ridicule "Tom" D'Urfey, "Joe" Harris the player, and even the great Dryden himself. The death of "the gallant Dundee" inspired him to imitate Cowley's pindarics, though, as he said himself, he was ill acquainted with that kind of writing, He suffered at once from excessive praise and ill-deserved blame. "Without partiality, we may say," wrote Sam Briscoe, his bookseller, "for satyrical Prose or Verse, Mr. Brown was not inferior to Petronius, Martial, or any other of the witty ancients." These were his models, truly; but his works testify how far he fell short of their performance. On the other hand, a grave injustice was done to him, as it has been to many another, by the thoughtless, who fathered upon him "all the pamphlets good and bad, Lampoons, Trips, *London* Spies, and the like insignificant Trifles." His lively humour won him the name of "Tom Brown the facetious" and the epithet, not wholly complimentary, still clings to him. The enemy, who said of him that "he had less the Spirit of a Gentleman than the rest, and more of a Scholar," spiced his malice with the truth. What, indeed, had a gentleman to make in Grub street? However, with all his faults, Tom Brown was a real man of letters, who, had he not been "too lazy in his temper to write much would have builded himself a better monument." In character, he was careless and independent. He did his best to live by his pen, and, when his pen failed him, he turned pedagogue. At no time would he rely upon the caprices of a patron. "I am one of the first of the Suburban class," he boasted, "that has ventur'd out without making an application to a nobleman's porter, and tiring him out with showing him his master's name." For the rest, he wrote the famous epigram upon Dr. Fell, and died, at last, repentant and absolved. He confessed on his death-bed that he had "complied too much with the Libertinism of the time," and extorted a promise from his bookseller, who speedily went back upon his word, to expunge "all prophane, undecent passages" from his works, when he came to reprint them.

The career of Tom Brown is characteristic of Grub street and of his age. From one—incomparably the best—you may learn all. But, by a curious irony, neither poverty nor the bottle impaired the tireless industry of the hacks. Though the standard of style which they set up for themselves was not a high one, they never feared to put their talent to the test. They fought for causes good or evil with a kind of ferocity. None of them disdained the weapons of the wits. We have seen how Ned Ward expressed his opinions and his prejudices in Hudibrastic verse. The gathered pamphlets of Roger L'Estrange, written, for the most part, in defence of himself and the high church party, would fill a shelf. John Phillips, whom Milton trained for wiser purposes, disgraced himself for ever by selling a hireling pen to Titus Oates. If there is nothing so transient as dead controversy, it must yet be admitted that these writers were artists in their own style. Their skill in invective, their assumption of passionate conviction, their outspoken contempt for the enemy of the moment, cannot but claim our admiration. But in nothing did they display their marvellous energy so clearly as in the task of translation. Here, again, they recall the enterprise of the Elizabethans. They do not challenge comparison with their predecessors. They recognised that each age must look at the classics through its own eyes. They knew, also, that the France and Spain of their time had provided a treasure-house of masterpieces, which their skill and knowledge could unlock. And, when they had taken these masterpieces from their treasure-house, they did not scruple to trick them out in the familiar, parti-coloured style of their own Grub street. It seems, indeed, as though the fashion of translation changed as rapidly as the fashion of hats and coats. Though the *Plutarch* of North and Holland, the *Montaigne* of Florio, the *Seneca* of Lodge were less than a century old, they appeared fantastic, if not unintelligible, to the contemporaries of Dryden. The "several hands," the "persons of quality," who presumed to do again the tasks valiantly performed by their grandsires, aimed less at a splendour of effect than at a uniform neatness. The one licence they permitted themselves, as we shall see, was an incorrigible licence of slang. They thought that their habit of speech was perfectly suited to the heroes and gods of antiquity. They clipped their words in translating the classics, as they clipped them in an insolent pamphlet. They possessed not the smallest sense of propriety, and believed that there was no writer, ancient or modern, whose meaning could not be adequately expressed in their vernacular. Thus, it mattered not who gazed in their mirror; it gave back always the same reflection. Their theory of translation was, of course, the theory of Dryden, who marshalled them for the fray. "The Qualification of a Translator worth reading," said he, "must be a Mastery of the Language he translates out of, and that he translates into; but if a deficiencie be allowed in either, it is in the Original." And it was in the original, were it Latin or Greek, that many of them were deficient. Like the Elizabethans, they, too, sought what help they could find in French versions of their author. Nor was it for them to disobey Dryden's second injunction. "A Trans-

lator," wrote the master, "that would write with any force or
spirit of an Original, must never dwell on the words of an
author." So lightly did they dwell upon their authors'
words, that, in many specimens, it is not easy to distinguish
between translation and burlesque.

By the preferences of these writers we come to know the taste
of the booksellers and of the town. They were not animated
by the spirit of adventure or by the ambition of instructing
kings and nobles in high policy, which moved the Elizabethans. Their sole object was to profit themselves by pleasing
the public. Petronius, to whom they owed a special allegiance,
was easily taught to speak their dialect. The first version we
owe to William Burnaby and another hand. In the second,
Tom Brown, captain Ayloffe and others are said to have given
their aid, though it is not clear what they contributed, and a
comparison of the two by no means justifies the bookseller's
claim that the second is "wholly new." Though much of
Petronius is lost in the process of translation, the work is done
with a sympathy and an energy which we expect from the
authentic descendants of Ascyltus and Eumolpus. Here is no
dwelling on the words of the author. The book may be read
from beginning to end, as though it were an independent and
original romance. The version of Lucian by several eminent
hands displays precisely the same qualities. Deprived of its
atmosphere, it wears the aspect of an English work. The
"eminent hands"—Tom Brown, John Phillips, Walter Moyle
and the rest—handled the English tongue with ease and familiarity, and, if they owed more to the French of d'Ablancourt
than to the Greek of Lucian, they have had no difficulty in
transposing their author into the guise of their own place and
time. The work, done under Dryden's eye, was journey-work,
if you will, and defaced by a tone of commonness. But it has
a character which removes it by many leagues from the crib,
and Dryden, no doubt, speaks truth when he places the translators among "the finer spirits of the age." Walter Moyle
and Sir Henry Sheeres deserve whatever praise he could give
them, but let it not be forgotten that it is the facetious Tom
Brown, whom Dryden could not mention with honour, that
bore the brunt of the work.

John Phillips, whose travesties have already been mentioned,

was eminent among the translators of the time. He took his
share in Englishing Lucian and Plutarch, and the folios to
which he put his name were neither few nor slight. He was
bred in classical learning by his uncle John Milton, whose
influence he early shook off. For many years, he seems to have
gained his livelihood by his pen, and was as versatile as he was
industrious. What Aubrey calls his "jiggish phancy" inspired
him to the making of almanacks, the inditing of satires and
to the conduct of political controversy. A loyal disciple of
Rabelais, he composed a sermon with a passage from *Gargantua*,
for his text, and embraced the doctrine of Pantagruel with a
constant heart. His policy shifted with the convenience of the
hour. He approached Cromwell cap in hand when it suited
him, and afterwards, in a travesty, set the Protector in hell.
He shouted for the king at the restoration, and hailed the
infamous Oates as the saviour of his country. He naturally
incurred the hatred of Anthony à Wood, both for his own sake
and on account of Milton, "that villainous leading incendiary."
But, whatever blots there may have been upon his honour, he
was tireless in industry. He died, so to say, with a pen in his
hand. At seventy years of age, he is described by Dunton as
"a gentleman of good learning, and well born; and will write
you a design off in a very little time, if the gout or claret does
not stop him." For many years, he edited a grave periodical,
The Present State of Europe, and, in the compass and extent of
his translations, he was a near rival to Philemon Holland. To
provide two vast folios in a year is a triumph of persistence, if
no other merit be claimed for it.

And John Phillips's versions are always workmanlike. La
Calprenède's *Pharamond* was once, no doubt, "a fam'd romance," though it is no more likely to find readers to-day than
Madeleine de Scudery's *Almahide, or The Captive Queen;* and
Phillips's task, in Englishing both, was faithfully performed.
His chief lack is a lack of distinction. There is not a page that
most of the other hacks might not have written with equal
ease. For ease is its chief characteristic—ease of phrase, ease
of movement. With the same nonchalance, he Englished
Tavernier's *Voyages in the East*, Ludolphus's *History of Aethio-
pia*, Grelot's *Voyage to Constantinople* and many another forgotten work of travel or fiction. Besides these monuments of

energy, a version of Scarron's *Typhon* seems but the solace of a summer's afternoon.   None of these, as we have said, bears the sole and individual mark of Phillips's talent.   There is one book—his translation of *Don Quixote*—which, for good or evil, is all his own.   Not even Ned Ward, whose inappropriate courage persuaded him to turn the masterpiece of Cervantes into Hudibrastic verse, committed so great an outrage on a noble original as did John Phillips when he made *The History of the most Renowned Don Quixote* English "according to the humour of our Modern Language."   It is difficult to describe this rash experiment.   Imagine *Hamlet* turned into the lingo of the music hall, and fitted with occasional songs and dances, and you will have a faint impression of Phillips's impropriety.   Little as he respected his author, he respected still less the time and place of his incomparable romance.   He has reduced to the level of his own Grub street the style and manner of Cervantes.   His work is less a translation than a travesty.   He has treated *Don Quixote* as Scarron treated the *Aeneid*.   He has composed a debased fantasia of his own upon a well-known and beautiful theme.   In other words, he has employed an imagery as vulgar as the slang of the tavern can make it.   Rosinante, in his eyes, is a "Dover post-horse," the inn keeper is "as true a thief as ever sung psalm at Tyburn."   The fish which Don Quixote has for his supper is "so ill-dress'd as if it had been cook'd in Ram Alley or White-Fryers."   Such humour as anachronism will afford may be found on every page, and, as though it were not enough to create a confusion of time, Phillips never ceases to confound the Spain of the age of Cervantes with the England of his own.   The sail of the windmill throws the knight sprawling, says he, "at the distance of more yards than would have measured Long Megg of Lincoln a gown and petticoat."   He likens the lovers to "young citizens and their wives in an Epsom coach"; in his version, Tolosa masquerades as Betty, "the daughter of a Cobbler in Southwark, that kept a stall under a Chandler's shop in Kent street"; and, by way of a crowning absurdity, the lady tells Don Ferdinand "to read Baxter's *Saints' Everlasting Rest.*"   Now, he merely hints at a false comparison, as when he says that Cardenio held his Lucinda "as the Lobster held the Hair upon Salisbury Plain."   Now, he seems to exhaust his ingenuity in a single passage.

When the inn keeper tells Don Quixote that he, too, had been a knight errant, he boasts, in Phillips's travesty, how

he himself had pursu'd the same Chace of Honour in his youth, travelling through all parts of the World in search of bold Adventures; to which purpose he had left no corner unvisited of the King's Bench Rules, the Skulking Holes of Alsatia, the Academy of the Fleet, the Colledge of Newgate, the Purliews of Turnbull, and Pickt Hatch, the Bordellos of St. Giles's, Banstead-Downs, Newmarket-Heath: . . . not a Publick Bowling Green where he had not exercis'd his heels; nor an Execution-crowd, nor a Hedge-Tavern, where he had not employ'd his pauming, topping, cogging fingers.

This is monumental, but it is not Cervantes. And by how many leagues is it removed from the splendid simplicity of Shelton!

Worse still, the ingenious Phillips makes *Don Quixote* an occasion for setting forth his preferences and his animosities. He packs his pages with modern instances. He drags in Hobbes and the Protector by the heels; nor does he lose a chance of insulting Milton, to whom he owed such scholarship as he possessed. Thus it is that Don Diego di Miranda describes his son's attainments:

he is a great admirer of Horace, Juvenal, and Persius—but as for the modern poets he allows very few to be worth a straw; among the rest he has a particular Peek against Du Bartas, and *Paradise Lost*, which he says has neither Rhime nor Reason.

To defend such a work as Phillips's *Don Quixote* is not easy. There is a flippant irreverence in its jests and gibes which criticism is forced to condemn. No man has a right thus licentiously to transform a masterpiece of literature. The very readiness with which a writer of burlesque can achieve a laugh should warn him that the laugh is not worth achievement. Yet, when all is said that can be said in dispraise, we cannot but acknowledge the supreme skill with which Phillips has performed his task. His zest never flags, his imagery never grows tired. On every page he has a fresh, if perverse, simile. With untiring energy, he illustrates Cervantes from the life of the taverns which he frequented. The vigour and levity of his style are amazing; his understanding of the original is seldom at fault, and, though it may be said that the book should never have been done, it must be added that it is done exceedingly well.   For, if it gives us a very blurred picture of Don Quixote, it presents the clear image of the most flippant, restless and debauched mind of an age which ill understood the punctilio of life or letters.

Peter Motteux, a fitting companion in literature for John Phillips, differed widely from him in blood and breeding.   His youthful steps were not encouraged by a great poet.   Thrown early upon a country whose language he did not understand, he was compelled to make a double conquest, first of a speech which was not his own, and then of the town in which he was an enforced exile.   Born in 1663 at Rouen, he came to England when the edict of Nantes was revoked, and speedily found a place among English men of letters.   So swift a change of nationality is almost without parallel in the history of literature. The author of *Gramont* is no near rival, since he was but four when he was carried to France, and a Frenchman he remained, in all save blood, till the end.   Motteux's achievement was far more wonderful.   He left France at the age of twenty-two, probably with no training either in English or in literature, and, within a few years, he was writing with precisely the same accent as any other haunter of the coffee-houses.   In the preface to his *Rabelais*, he fears that he has "not given his Author the graces of the English language in every place," and protests that he has not followed the example of Lucullus, who wrote a book in Greek and scattered some false Greek in it, to let the world know it was not written by a Greek.   Motteux was not guilty of a similar indiscretion.   What errors may be found in his diction, he assures us, have crept in without his intent.   He need have had no fear, nor have offered his reader any apology. Motteux had many faults.   Gallicism was not among them. He compared himself, proudly enough, with Livius Andronicus, a Greek, and Terence, a Carthaginian, who chose Latin for their tongue, and if he could not vie with them in purity of style, he surpassed them, doubtless, in fluency.   There was no task to which he did not turn a ready hand.   He wrote plays, after the prescribed model, and without the smallest distinction. He furnished the plays of others with doggerel prologues.   He edited *The Gentleman's Journal*, for which *Le Mercure Galant* of his own land served as a model, and was not refused the assistance of the great. Congreve and Prior both condescend to his pages, and, as it was Dryden under whose banner he fought, so it is the influence of Dryden which governs his journal. Frenchman though he was, he differs little enough from his neighbours in Grub street. He might sign their works or they his without much detriment to either side. Nevertheless, he played a part in the literary history of his time. If he won the approval of Dryden and Steele, he was deemed worthy the rancour of Pope, who celebrates him as a bore,

> Talkers I've learned to bear, Motteux I knew,

and, in *The Art of Sinking*, puts him among the eels, "obscene authors that wrap themselves up in their own mud, but are mighty nimble and pert." And then, to prove an astonishing adaptability, Motteux turned an honest tradesman, and sold China and Japan wares "cheap for a quick return." He did not return to the craft of letters, and, after six years of honourable dealing, died a mysterious and shameful death.

Had it not been for his translation of Rabelais, Motteux's name would not have outlived this crowning scandal. His translation gives him a place in history. The work has many faults. It is "nimble and pert," like its author, and Rabelais himself was never for a moment either pert or nimble. A still worse fault is its diffuseness, a fault of which Motteux appears to have been wholly unconscious. His style is as far from the Latin gravity of the original as from the humorous eloquence of Sir Thomas Urquhart. He is able neither to represent the one nor to carry on the tradition of the other. Between him and the knight of Cromarty there is not merely the difference which separates the English of Elizabeth (for Urquhart was a belated Tudor) from the English of Dutch William, but the difference which parts an erudite and curious Scots pedant from the trivial, boisterous frequenter of Will's. Motteux's phrase is simple to tawdriness. He drags Rabelais down to his own level, and in nothing does he prove his lack of taste so clearly as in his use of slang. Now, slang, to the translator of Rabelais, is indispensable. The romance of Pantagruel and Panurge cannot be turned out of its own into any other tongue save by an artist in strange words.   Urquhart was perfectly equipped for the task, because his interest in oddly coloured speech never tired, and because, when he was himself at a loss, he made a liberal use of Cotgrave's *Dictionary*.   Thus it was that his slang had ever a literary flavour; it had already won the freedom of humane letters; the dust of the street corner was not thick upon it.   Motteux's slang was of another kind.   It lacked literary association.   The quickwitted Frenchman had picked it up in the gutter or the tavern; he had caught it fresh minted from the vulgar brains of his friends; and, though it was lively enough to gain an instant laugh, it long since lost its humour. Motteux makes free and frank acknowledgment of the source of his common talk, as he calls it.

"Far be it from me," he writes, "for all this to value myself upon hitting the Words of Cant, in which my drolling Author is so luxuriant, for though such words have stood me in good stead, I scarce can forbear thinking myself unhappy in having insensibly hoarded up so much Gibberish and Billingsgate trash in my memory; nor could I forbear asking myself as an Italian Cardinal said on another account . . . Where the devil didst thou make up all these fripperies?"

He made them up in Grub street; and, when he had contrived them, they were ill suited to his purpose.

The only literary sources from which he gathered his "words of Cant" were the travesties.   He was no better able than John Phillips to escape the anachronisms of Cotton and Radcliffe.   Though he had a finer restraint than the rascal who burlesqued *Don Quixote*, he could not forbear to treat the text of Rabelais with the same kind of wantonness.   His version is full of allusions to his own time, which are wholly out of place in the Englishing of a masterpiece of the sixteenth century, and which to-day no man may understand.   Nothing can be more impertinent than to interrupt the narrative of Rabelais with so foolish a catchword as "his name's Twyford." To translate *maître d'eschole* by "the Busby of the place" is wofully to misunderstand the business of a translator.   Still less excuse has Motteux, when, instead of the simple words "at dawn," he indulges his fancy thus extravagantly: "when day, peeping in the East, made the Sky turn from Black to Red, like a boiling Lobster." The fact that he conveyed the image from *Hudibras*, where it was appropriate, to Rabelais, where it is a tiresome excrescence, does but heighten his sin. On every page, he affronts the reader. He calls Panurge a "sweet babe"; like the journalist that he was, he clips "doctor" into "doc." Worse still, he can find no better equivalent for *c'est tout ung* than "it 's all one to Frank." Thus, he destroys the illusion of Rabelais, and, as though that were not enough, he drags in by the heels all the thievish gibberish that he could pick up in the purlieus of Newgate in Newgate's heyday.

For Roger L'Estrange, the work of translation was but a profitable interlude in a busy, active life. [1] He was by temperament a fighter; by habit, a man of affairs. No man loved the fray better than he; none defended his opinions more bravely. For the principles of an aristocratic toryism, which he advocated fiercely and consistently, he suffered exile and imprisonment. The highest reward, which he obtained for his loyalty to the king, was to be appointed some years after the restoration "surveyor of the imprimery" and one of "the licensers of the press." To the end of his long life, therefore, it was to his pen alone that he could trust, and, though controversy was most to his taste, he fell to translating with the same brisk energy which made him formidable as a pamphleteer. It was for money, of course, that he wrote his many lively versions; he was paid for his *Josephus* at so much a sheet, as he might be paid to-day; but he could prove his preferences by his selection of authors, and a preface always gave him an opportunity of publishing his views. Thus, the face of the controversialist is always seen through the mask of the translator. In his *Colloquies of Erasmus*, for instance, he roundly states that he made choice of this piece and subject for his own sake and not for the readers'. Writing at the time of the popish plot, and with a full consciousness of the suspicion that fell upon him, he makes clear his own position. "Some will have the Translator to be a Papist in Masquerade," says he, "for going so far. Others again will have him to be too much of a Protestant, because he will go no farther: so that he is crushed betwixt the two Extremes, as they hang up Erasmus himself, betwixt Heaven

---

[1] Cf. as to Roger L'Estrange's work as a pamphleteer and journalist, *ante*, pp. 2–4.

and Hell." In his preface to Seneca's *Morals*, he descends from truth itself to his own experience with yet greater clarity. For L'Estrange, though he spoke with another's voice, could still advocate the causes which for him were never lost.

He did his work of translation with the utmost thoroughness. He was the master of many tongues, and when, in Englishing Greek, he used the French version, which lay at his hand, he was very careful to compare the result with the original. But his chiefest qualification for the task was his mastery of his own language. Having spent fifty years in the service of letters, he had turned our English speech into the ready instrument of his thought. Whatever author he translated, he took him not only out of his own tongue, but out of his own land. He made him, for the moment, a true-born Englishman, speaking the slang of the moment with the proper accent of the cockney. As we have said, there are objections to this method. It is inevitable that all works, of whatever time or place, should wear the same aspect, when they have undergone this equalising process. They cannot but lose much of their individual character if they are all brought to walk with the same gait, to use the same gesture. When Nero "looks big upon disaster," and "carries it on at a huffing note," the reader loses sight of Rome and Judaea, and is instantly borne back to Gray's-inn-gate or Little Britain. And the mere fact that L'Estrange set upon all the works which he Englished this very stamp and pattern of his own time, while it increased their momentary popularity, prevents their general acceptance as classics. They are translated not into English, but into the dialect of a particular time and place, and thus, with happy exceptions, they leave the work of interpretation to be done all over again. But L'Estrange's method has one conspicuous merit. It removes all signs of halting uncertainty. You read a version, composed in accord with it, in the confidence that the idiom of the original will never disturb you, that you may judge it not as the tortured expression of a foreign tongue, but as a fresh and independent experiment in style. Pepys, for instance, a critic of quick intelligence, was not blind to the peculiar merit of L'Estrange, thus fortunate in the appreciation of his contemporaries, who saw and approved the end at which he aimed.

In the selection of his originals, L'Estrange displayed a true catholicity. He turned easily from Bona's *Guide to Eternity* to Tully's *Offices*. He took a hand in the translation of Terence and Tacitus, and, by himself, was responsible for *The Visions of Quevedo* and *The Spanish Decameron*. Far better than these are his *Select Colloquies out of Erasmus Roterodamus*. The light touch and merry conceit of the author are qualities after L'Estrange's own heart. The original, moreover, being of a gay irony, was perfectly suited to L'Estrange's licentious method. Here, he could leave the word for the sense with a good heart; and, as Erasmus wrote for all time, looking through the foibles of his friends to the very nature of man, he wore, without difficulty, the garb of an English man of the world. By a hundred happy turns, such as "spoken like a true tarpaulin" for *orationem vere nauticam*, the translator produces the impression of a living book—not the best of living books, truly, for there is sometimes a flippancy of phrase in L'Estrange's version, which is not merely irksome in itself, but wholly unwarranted by the text. However, L'Estrange was no verbal copier "encumbered with so many difficulties at once, that he could never disentangle himself from all." He kept his freedom at the expense of propriety. Even so, he preserved a mean which eluded most of his contemporaries. To compare his *Colloquies* with those done into English by Tom Brown is to measure the distance between the scholar and the bookseller's hack. When Brown put his hand to the *Colloquies*, he showed no respect for Erasmus, little for himself. He declares that he "keeps his Author still in sight"; but he has no scruple in making his version "palatable to the English reader." So, he sprinkles the text with the expletives of the hour, deems no absurdity too bold, and hopes, for instance, to win readers by rendering *nuptias Mortis, opinor, cum Marte*, by "not that of death and the Cobbler, I hope, nor of Bully-Bloody-Bones and Mother Damnable." Thus, he too has produced, not a translation, but a travesty, and is guilty of the same outrage which John Phillips committed upon *Don Quixote*. L'Estrange had many faults; he never sank to the depth of Brown's ineptitude.

The work by which he is best known, and by which he best deserves to be remembered, is his version of Aesop's *Fables*. His language, here also, is the language of talk rather than of literature, yet, for the most part, he observes a strict economy of words, and seldom commits the blunder of making his fables diffuse. "A daw that had a mind to be sparkish," says he; "I had much rather be knabbing of crusts," his Country Mouse declares, "without fear or danger in my own little hole, than be mistress of the whole world with perpetual cares and alarums." In a sensible essay upon fables in general, he asserts that the foundations of knowledge and virtue are laid in childhood, and, presently, with an inapposite humour, makes his fables unfit for a child's comprehension. What child, we wonder, would read further after being confronted by such an opening as this: "In days of old, when Horses spoke Greek and Latin, and Asses made syllogisms"? The fault of taste is doubled when it is committed in defiance of a necessary simplicity. Yet, he sins not always, and his *Aesop*, stripped of its "reflexions," still remains the best that we have. In Seneca's *Morals* and *The Works of Josephus*, he was less happily inspired. In the first place, he challenged comparison with the incomparably better versions of Lodge; in the second, neither Seneca nor Josephus gave the smallest scope for his peculiar humour: when he was most himself, in their case he was furthest from excellence. But, of his *Josephus*, it may, at least, be said that it was a marvellous achievement for a man of eighty-six, beset, as he tells us, by "frequent troubles, and by ill-health." Good or bad, it was a fitting conclusion to a career of rare vigour and energy, the crowning work of one whom Pepys found "a man of fine conversation," and whom even the grave Evelyn pronounced "a person of excellent parts."

Charles Cotton, in his translations, set before himself the same ideal as Roger L'Estrange. He hoped that his versions might have the air of true originals. And certain it is that you may read them without any thought of his texts. Though his style, too, errs, now and again, on the side of the tavern, he sternly avoids the excesses of slang, which soil the works of his contemporaries. Moreover, he made a resolute attempt to keep close to the sense of the authors whom he translated, and, here again, he separated himself rigidly from the custom of his age. His versions are made one and all from the French, and, within the limits of this language, he permitted himself a great latitude of choice. Corneille's *Horace* is among his works, and

Du Vair's *Moral Philosophy of the Stoics*. These he followed by Girard's *History of the Life of the Duke of Espernon*, and the admirable *Commentaries of Blaise de Montluc*. In this last, perhaps, his talent found its worthiest expression. He had a natural sympathy with the original, and he translated it into an English that is both dignified and appropriate. Narrative was in closer accord with his temper than philosophical disquisition, and, though it is by his version of Montaigne's *Essays* that he is principally remembered to-day, his *Commentaries of Montluc* approach more nearly in style and quality to what a translation should be.

In translating Montaigne, Cotton was at a disadvantage, of which he himself was wholly unconscious. He followed in the footsteps of a far greater adept in the difficult art, John Florio. Florio had all the virtues, save accuracy. If his book fails to represent the style of Montaigne, and not infrequently distorts his meaning, it is none the less a piece of living prose. Perhaps, it tells you more of Florio than of Montaigne; but it has that enduring quality, character, and it is unlikely that fashion will ever drive it from the minds of admiring scholars. Cotton's version is of other stuff. Though not always correct, though never close-knit as is the original, it is more easily intelligible than Florio's, and gives, may be, a clearer vision of the French. That, indeed, was Cotton's purpose. "My design," says he, "in attempting this translation was to present my country with a true copy of a very brave original." Both translators use too many words for their purpose, Florio because he delights in the mere sound of them, Cotton, because he had not acquired the gift of concise expression, because he did not always know how to discard the tiresome symbols which encumber his sentences as with pack-thread. Florio, on the one hand, wrote like a fantastic, to whom embroideries were essential, Cotton, on the other, wrote like a country gentleman, who, after a day's fishing, turned an honest penny by the pursuits of scholarship. The one lacks precision, the other distinction, and each man will decide for himself which he prefers.

Charles Cotton, in truth, holds a place apart in the literary history of his time. Though L'Estrange was born to an ancient house in Norfolk, the strife of art and politics, the necessities of his journals had driven him to London and the taverns. Cotton, well as he knew London, remained still faithful to his dale in Derbyshire. In Lamb's phrase, he "smacked of the rough magnanimity of the old English vein." It was in all sincerity that he praised his beloved caves,

> from Dog-star heats,
> And hotter persecution safe retreats

When poverty drove him to do the work of a hack, he did it with what skill and spirit he might. If *The Compleat Gamester* was unworthy his pen, his *Planter's Manual* is a pleasant and practical little treatise. His verses have won the approval of Coleridge and Lamb and Wordsworth, and his lines to his "dear and most worthy Friend, Mr. Isaac Walton" remind us of Horace and his Sabine farm:

> A day without too bright a Beam,
>   A warm, but not a scorching Sun,
> A Southern gale to curl the Stream,
>   And (master) half our work is done.

These four lines are worth the whole of *Scarronides*, and, doubtless, they will be remembered when the translation of Montaigne has faded utterly from the minds of men.

The most industrious and by no means the least distinguished of the translators of his time was captain John Stevens. Who and what he was we know not. There is no record of him or his achievements, save on the title-pages of his many books. There is no doubt that he did a signal service to English letters. It was through his skill and learning that the history of Spain and Spanish literature was made known to his countrymen. His mere industry appals us. He translated nothing save the works of Spaniards, and he accommodated his style to the style of his originals with a variety which no other of his contemporaries could match. Where a light and easy manner was required, as by Quevedo, he knew how to give it, and, when he brought Mariana's *History of Spain* "to speak English," as he said, under the auspices of the earl of Dorset, to whom it is dedicated, he did it with a dignity and eloquence which befit the Muse of history. The one cause of complaint which we have against him is that he could not keep away from Shelton's

Don Quixote, which he "revised and corrected" with a lavish hand. Nor does his excuse better his ill-doing. He declares in a dedication that Cervantes's "successful masterpiece has not prov'd happy in its translators, for though it has been made English twice the versions have neither time been proportionable to the Beauty of the Original." As to Shelton's work, he pronounces it "almost a literal version," and then complains that it is "in such unpolish'd language, and with so many Mistakes, that there seem'd to be nothing left but the outlines and rough Draught of this curious piece." So Stevens took Shelton's masterpiece and amended it, bringing it, it is true, far nearer to the original, and robbing it of what is of far higher worth than accuracy, its style and character.

For the rest, Stevens touched nothing that he did not embellish. Though he did not disdain romance, though we owe to his pen *Pablo de Segovia, the Spanish Sharper*, and a collection of novels, with the title *The Spanish Libertines*, his preference, or the preference of his readers, was for history and travel. Sandoval's *History of Charles V* followed *The Spanish Rule of Trade to the West Indies*, written by Don Joseph de Veitia Linage. He took his share in the English of a series of voyages, published in monthly parts, thus making a link between the old method of publishing and the practice of to-day. So far as we know, he was a translator and a translator only. He seems to have played no part in the life of his time. His dedications, couched in the terms of the loftiest flattery, afford us little clue to his career. Perhaps, as he inscribes his translation of *The Portuguese Asia*, with humble adulation, to Catherine, queen dowager of England, he may have professed the Catholic faith. But, by his works we know him, and by his works alone, and they tell us that he did the journey-work of translation with a sounder scholarship and with a more various style than any of the men of letters, his contemporaries, could boast.

CHAPTER XI

Berkeley and Contemporary Philosophy

THE period of English thought which followed Locke's death was fruitful both in great writers and in important movements. Locke's own influence was felt everywhere. His new way of approaching the subject, his freedom from the traditional technicalities of the schools, and his application of his method to a wide range of human interests, made philosophy count for more with reflective writers generally, and determined the line of thought taken by greater minds. Speculation turned mainly upon three problems—the problem of knowledge, the problem of religion and the problem of morality. The treatment of each problem led to striking developments; and Locke's influence affected them all, though in unequal degrees. The idealism of Berkeley followed directly from his fundamental positions; the leaders of the deists professed themselves his disciples, though they arrived at conclusions different from his; the work of the moralists was less fully determined by his speculations, though his ethical views were, perhaps, seldom far from their minds. In the present chapter, this division of problems will be followed; it will treat, in succession, of the metaphysicians, the deists and the moralists. Most writers, indeed, did not limit their interests to a single problem; and their place here will have to be determined by a view of the permanent importance of their work in different departments. Strict chronological order, also, to some extent, will be sacrificed. In this way, consideration of the writings of Samuel Clarke, for instance—although he was a prominent figure in the whole philosophical movement, and one of the earliest to attain eminence—will be postponed till the last section of the chapter.

I. METAPHYSICIANS

George Berkeley was born at Dysert castle, county Kilkenny, Ireland, on 12 March, 1685, and educated at Kilkenny school and Trinity college, Dublin, which he entered in 1700 and where he remained, first as a scholar, afterwards as fellow and tutor, till January, 1713. These early years are the most remarkable in Berkeley's literary career. He published, anonymously, two mathematical tracts in 1707; his *Essay towards a new theory of vision* appeared in 1709, his *Principles of Human Knowledge, part I*, in 1710; and when, in 1713, he got leave of absence from his college and set out for London, it was "to print his new book"—*Three Dialogues between Hylas and Philonous*—as well as "to make acquaintance with men of merit." These three books reveal the new thought which inspired his life; and the evidence of his *Common-place Book* (discovered and published by Campbell Fraser in 1871) shows that he was barely twenty years of age when this new thought took hold of him. Berkeley was absent from Ireland for eight years, spending his time in London, France and Italy (where, on a second visit, he resided four years). During this period, he did little literary work; he made some progress, indeed, with the second part of his *Principles*, but the MS. was lost in his travels, and the work was never resumed; his Latin treatise *De motu* was written as he was on his way home in 1720, and published in 1721; he collected materials for a natural history of Sicily, but this MS. also was lost; a journal written in Italy, however, and many letters remain to show his appreciation of the beauties of nature and art. His return to England gave a new direction to his energy. The country was in the period of collapse which follows a speculative mania; and Berkeley saw the true cause of the national disaster in the decline of religion, the decay of public spirit and the prevalent corruption of manners. One hundred and forty years later, Mark Pattison described the period as "an age whose poetry was without romance, whose philosophy was without insight, and whose public men were without character."[1] A similar judgment forms the burden of Berkeley's *Essay towards preventing the ruin of Great Britain*, published anonymously in 1721. He returned to

[1] *Essays and Reviews*, 1860, p. 254.

Ireland and to Trinity college later in the same year, and was presented to the deanery of Dromore. The office attracted him because it would give him leisure for reflection and for philanthropic work; but a legal question arose as to the right of presentation, and his hopes received a check. Berkeley is one of the most perfect characters among men of letters; but his perfection was not colourless. He threw himself with energy into the defence of his rights, and at least had the satisfaction of a protracted lawsuit. While the case was still pending, in 1724, he was appointed to a much more valuable preferment—the deanery of Derry. "It is said to be worth £1500 a year," he wrote, "but I do not consider it with a view to enriching myself. I shall be perfectly contented if it facilitates and recommends my scheme of Bermuda." This scheme seems to have taken hold of Berkeley's mind about two years previously; to it he devoted his fortune and ten years of his life. His plan was to found a college in the Bermudas, with the twofold object of "the reformation of manners among the English in our western plantations, and the propagation of the gospel among the American savages." Berkeley spent four years in London in endeavouring to extract a charter and grant of money from a reluctant government and subscriptions from an unbelieving generation; he had to frequent the court and dispute twice a week with Samuel Clarke before queen Caroline, then princess of Wales; he listened to the banter of the wits of the Scriblerus club, and then replied with such eloquence and enthusiasm that they "rose all up together, with earnestness exclaiming, 'Let us set out with him immediately' "; he canvassed every member of parliament with such effect that, in the Commons, there were only two opponents of the vote; even Walpole subscribed to the scheme, though he secretly determined that the government grant of money should never be paid. Bermuda became the fashion, and Berkeley was idolised. But he grudged the waste of time, and, at last—with only a promise from Walpole that the grant would be paid—he set sail from Greenwich in September, 1728, with his newly-married wife. In January, 1729, he landed at Newport, Rhode Island. There he remained for nearly three years, waiting vainly for the government to fulfil its promises. This it never did; he never reached Bermuda, and his college was never founded; but he left his impress upon the early efforts of American philosophy; his interpretation of the material world modified the thinking of Jonathan Edwards, the metaphysician and theologian of New England; and the memory of his visit has been treasured by the American mind. The new world also affected Berkeley's imagination and led to a set of *Verses on the prospect of planting arts and learning in America.* One of his lines—"Westward the course of empire takes its way"—has come to be looked upon as prophetic; but his idea was not geographical; it was that better times would follow better morals, "where nature guides and virtue rules."

Berkeley remained in London for more than two years after his return to England; and a new period of authorship began, during which he joined in the controversies of the age. In *Alciphron, or the Minute Philosopher* (1732), written in the seclusion of his home in Rhode Island, he applied his general principles in defence of religion against the free-thinkers. In 1733 appeared his *Theory of Vision, or Visual Language Vindicated and Explained;* and, in the following year, he published *The Analyst*, in which he criticised the positions of the new mathematics which, in his view, were connected with a materialistic conception of the world. This bold attempt to carry the war into the enemy's country called forth many pamphlets on the other side. In the same year, Berkeley returned to Ireland as bishop of Cloyne; and, henceforth, his literary work was divided between questions of social reform and religious reflection. The reform is represented by *The Querist* (1735), a work full of penetrating remarks; both subjects are combined in *Siris: a Chain of Philosophical Reflexions* (1744), which begins by expounding the medicinal virtues of tar-water and ends in an exposition of idealism in which the Lockean strain has given place to the Platonic. *A Miscellany containing several tracts* was published in October, 1752. Two months earlier he had left Cloyne, that he might spend the remainder of his days at Oxford; and there he died on 14 January, 1753.

When Berkeley launched his idealism upon an unsympathetic world, he had read Descartes and Malebranche and been attracted by the philosophy of Plato; he was also acquainted with the works of the mathematicians and natural philosophers, and suspected a trend to materialism in their theories; but his thought had been formed under the influence of Locke, whose *Essay* found earlier recognition from the academic authorities at Dublin than from those of English universities. At the time when Berkeley entered Trinity college and for ten years afterwards, the provost was Peter Browne, afterwards bishop of Cork, a student and critic of the *Essay*. He had already attracted attention by an *Answer* to Toland (1697). His more original works followed after a long interval—*The Procedure, extent and limits of human understanding*, in 1728, and the work called, for short, *Divine Analogy*, in 1733. These two books are connected with Berkeley's later work, for the theory of our knowledge of God propounded in the former is criticised in one of the dialogues of *Alciphron*, and the criticisms are replied to in Browne's *Divine Analogy*. Browne could not accept Locke's account of knowledge by means of ideas, when it came to be applied to mind. Mind and body, he held, are not known in the same way. We have, indeed, ideas of our mental operations as these are connected with the body; but minds or spirits —whether divine or human—can be known only by analogy. This view, Berkeley, in later life, attacked; but it points to a difficulty in his own theory also—a difficulty which he came to see, without fully resolving it. There is, however, no sufficient evidence for saying that Browne had any direct influence upon Berkeley's early speculation.

Berkeley's theory emerges full-grown, if not fully armed. Even in his *Common-place Book*, there is no hesitation in the references to "my doctrine," "the immaterial hypothesis." Only persons exist: "all other things are not so much existences as manners of the existence of persons." He knows that "a mighty sect of men will oppose me," that he will be called young, an upstart, a pretender, vain; but his confidence is not shaken: "Newton begs his principles; I demonstrate mine." He did not, at first, reveal the whole truth to the world. *An Essay towards a new theory of vision* deals with one point only—the relation between the objects of sight and those of touch. Molyneux had once set the problem to Locke, whether a man born blind, if he recovered his sight, would be able by sight alone to distinguish from one another a cube and a sphere, with which he had been previously acquainted by touch. Molyneux answered his own question in the negative, and Locke expressed agreement with his solution and admiration for the insight which it showed. Berkeley was of one mind with them about the answer to the query, but for a more fundamental reason. If extension be an idea common to sight and touch (as Locke held), then visible squareness must be the same as, or have something in common with, tangible squareness. In virtue of this, the man born blind, so soon as he is made to see, should be able to distinguish between a visible square and a visible circle and to identify this distinction with the distinction between the square and the circle already known by touch. If he is unable to do so, it is because there is nothing in common between the visible object and the tangible. And this is Berkeley's view.

The objects of sight and touch make, if I may so say, two sets of ideas which are widely different from each other. "A man born blind," he says, "being made to see, would at first have no idea of distance by sight: the sun and stars, the remotest objects as well as the nearer, would all seem to be in his eye, or rather in his mind."

A great part of the *Essay* is devoted to an explanation of the apparent immediateness with which the distance of an object is seen. But the essence of the whole consists in two propositions—that the objects (or ideas) of sight have nothing in common with the objects of touch, and that the connection of sight and touch is "arbitrary" and learned by experience only. The connection is arbitrary; but it is regular and constant. What we see suggests to us what we may expect to touch and handle. The whole visible world—as was further enforced in his *Theory of Vision or Visual Language*—consists of a set of signs which, like a language, have for their purpose to convey a meaning; though they neither resemble nor cause that meaning, nor have any necessary connection with it. In using sight to guide our movements, we interpret the language of God.

Some of the details of Berkeley's *Essay* need revision in the light of modern study of the senses. But this does not obscure its merit as one of the most brilliant pieces of psychologic analysis in the English language. A more serious objection to it is that the author pushes too far his war against abstractions. It is true, as he urges, that sight and touch have no common element that can be separated from both and become an independent presentation. Against "abstract ideas" of this sort,

his polemic was fully justified.   But the different senses are not
disconnected either in genesis or in function, and reflection may
discover certain lines of similarity among their processes.
Berkeley decides too quickly that the connection is arbitrary,
because of the striking difference in their contents, and because
one cannot be called cause and another effect; and he argues
too easily from this arbitrary connection to divine volition.
He never gave the same close attention to the conceptual factor
in knowledge as he gave to sense and imagination, and in his
early work the conceptual factor is almost entirely ignored.

The *Essay* did not disclose all that was in Berkeley's mind.
It kept to its topic, the relation of the objects of sight to those
of touch, and it did not question the views commonly held about
the latter.   The full revelation came, a year afterwards, in *A
Treatise concerning the Principles of Human Knowledge*.   This
small volume, more talked about than read at the time—it took
twenty-four years to reach a second edition—is one of the works
which have had a critical influence upon the course of European
thought.   Its importance, in this respect, ranks it with Locke's
Essay and Hume's *Treatise of Human Nature*.   The fresh step
which Berkeley took was short and simple and easy; when
taken, it shows us the whole world from a new point of view.
Locke had said that all the objects of knowledge are ideas, and
he had thus much difficulty—as, indeed, Descartes had had
before him—in defending the reality of the things which he
supposed to be represented by the ideas.   Berkeley solves the
difficulty by denying the distinction.   The ideas *are* the things.
"It is indeed an opinion strangely prevailing amongst men, that
houses, mountains, rivers, and in a word all sensible objects,
have an existence, natural or real, distinct from their being
perceived by the understanding."   But the opinion needs only
to be called in question to show the contradiction it involves;
for these objects are the things we perceive by sense, and we
perceive nothing but our own ideas.   With magnificent confidence, he passes at once to the assertion:

Some truths there are so near and obvious to the mind that a
man need only open his eyes to see them.   Such I take this important one to be, viz. that all the choir of heaven and furniture of the
earth, in a word all those bodies which compose the mighty frame of

the world, have not any subsistence without a mind; that their *being* is to be perceived or known.

As regards material things, therefore, a single phrase expresses Berkeley's thought: "their *esse* is *percipi*." Theirs is a passive, dependent existence. Active, independent existence can belong to minds or persons only. From this position he never wavered, though there is a good deal of difference between his earlier and his later views. He saw that, as the existence of ideas consists in being perceived, so mind must be regarded as perceiving. "Existence . . . is *percipi* or *percipere*" is one of his earliest statements; and, as men may sleep or be rendered unconscious, he is willing, at first, to accept the consequence that "men die or are in a state of annihilation oft in a day." But this solution seemed too dangerous and was soon relinquished, and thus he held it "a plain consequence that the soul always thinks." As there is no material substance, so, also, there can be no material cause. Material things, being our ideas and altogether passive, are related to one another not as cause and effect but only as sign and thing signified. We learn to understand their grouping, and thus one idea suggests others, the like of which have followed it in previous experience; while further experience confirms the anticipation. What we call laws of nature, therefore, are simply a statement of the orderly sequences in which the ideas of the senses occur in our minds. The material substance to which philosophers refer these ideas as their cause is, he labours to prove, an unmeaning and self-contradictory abstraction. Certain ideas—those which we call ideas of imagination—are constructed by the individual mind; but the ideas of sense, or sensible things, though they exist only in the mind, are not caused by my mind or by any other finite mind. There must, therefore, be "an *omnipresent eternal Mind*, which knows and comprehends all things, and exhibits them to our view in such a manner, and according to such rules, as He Himself hath ordained, and are by us termed the *laws of nature*."

Berkeley's works, for the most part, are of the nature of introductions, vindications, and polemics. He explained his new principle and defended it and applied it to current controversies with wonderful resource of argument and beauty of language, and with the power that came from intense conviction. In *Hylas* and in *Alciphron*, he used the dialogue form, with a skill never excelled in English philosophical literature, to bring out the difficulties in his view and to set forth their triumphant solution. But he did not work out his spiritual interpretation of reality into a system. He would answer an objection without following out the bearing of his answer upon other portions of his philosophy. He began, like Locke, by asserting that all the objects of our knowledge are ideas; and he divided ideas into three classes: those of sense, those of mental operations and those of memory or imagination. To which class, then (we may ask), do knowledge of self, of other finite spirits, of God and of the laws of nature belong? The question does not seem to have occurred to Berkeley when, with all the ardour of a discoverer, he wrote his *Principles*. But he raises it in *Hylas*, and says that, in reflection, we have an immediate knowledge of self as an active being and, by inference therefrom, of other finite spirits and of God. This knowledge, as well as our knowledge of laws of nature, is not through ideas, and he calls it *notion*. We have, therefore, not merely ideas of sensible things and of mental operations and of remembered or imagined objects, but, also, notions of spirits and of laws. The terminology was used again when he came to issue the second edition of the *Principles;* but he did not see that it required a modification of the first sentence of that work which declares that *all* the objects of human knowledge are ideas. How idea and notion are related to one another in knowledge, we cannot gather from him. But this is clear: that ideas are inert and fleeting, and that it is through notion that we become acquainted with the permanent active forces of the real universe.

Berkeley stood at a parting of the ways in thought, though he was hardly conscious of their divergence. On the one hand, his principles that all knowledge is of ideas, and that all ideas are of one or other of the three kinds enumerated by him, lead to a view which excludes from knowledge not only material substance, but mind, also, and the reign of law in nature. At times, especially in his *Common-place Book*, he seems on the brink of drawing this conclusion, and thus of anticipating Hume. Afterwards, he sees it only as something to be guarded against. He could not think of the idea as, so to speak, self-supporting. It exists only in so far as it is "in the mind": mind is the true reality, the only agency; ideas exist only in minds, finite or infinite; and the laws of nature are the order in which ideas are produced in us by the infinite Mind. Spiritual agency, spiritual reality, is thus his fundamental thought; and, in *Siris*, the last of his philosophical works, this thought emerges from the midst of reflections on empirical medicine and old-fashioned physiology. No longer dominated by the Lockean heritage of the sensitive origin of knowledge, his idealism is assimilated to the Platonic; the work is full of comments on Neoplatonic writers, ancient and modern; and there is an absence of the simplicity and clearness of his earlier writings; systematic development of his theory is still absent; but there is hardly a page without remarks of pregnant insight, and he is everywhere loyal to the vision of truth with which his career opened.

In 1713, three years after the appearance of Berkeley's *Principles*, Arthur Collier, rector of Langford Magna, near Salisbury, published a work entitled *Clavis Universalis* and professing to be "a demonstration of the non-existence or impossibility of an external world." Collier was born in 1680, and, like Berkeley, seems to have formed his conclusions at an early age: for he says that it was "after a ten years' pause and deliberation" that he decided to put his arguments before the reader. His results are almost identical with Berkeley's; but he arrived at them in a different way. He seems to have been uninfluenced by Locke; Descartes, Malebranche and Norris were his favourite authors; and there was enough, in their writings, to raise the question. Collier writes in a straightforward and simple style; he has none of Berkeley's imagination or eloquence; he does not contend that he has the plain man on his side, nor does he apply his results to current controversy. But he has no less confidence than Berkeley had in the truth of his views; and his arguments are clearly put. Often, they resemble Berkeley's; though greater use is made of traditional metaphysical discussions. Among these, the most notable is the argument from the antinomies of philosophical thought. The external world, conceived as independent of mind, has been held infinite in extent, and also it has been held to be finite; and equally good and conclusive reasons can be given for either alternative. Similarly, it is "both finitely and infinitely divisible." But a thing cannot have two contradictory predicates. External matter, therefore, does not exist.

II. Deists

The first half of the eighteenth century was the period of the deistical controversy in English theology. The writers commonly classed together as deists are Charles Blount, John Toland, Anthony Collins, Matthew Tindal, Thomas Woolston, Thomas Morgan, Thomas Chubb, Peter Annet and Henry Dodwell the younger. Among deists are also reckoned Bolingbroke and the third earl of Shaftesbury, who differed from the rest in paying little attention to the details of theological controversy, and differed from one another in their philosophical interest and importance.

The works of Charles Blount belong to the last quarter of the seventeenth century. He accepted the "five points" of Lord Herbert of Cherbury.[1] This marked him as a deist, and he did not reject the name. In his *Anima Mundi* (1679), he defended the system of natural religion, and, at the same time, emphasised the comparative merits of the heathen religions. His *Great is Diana of the Ephesians* (1680) is an attack on priestcraft. In the same year, he published an English translation of *The two first books of Philostratus, concerning the Life of Apollonius Tyaneus*. On each chapter of this followed "illustrations" by the translator, in which it was easy to find an attack on the Christian miracles and on the doctrine of the divinity of Christ. "Faith," he says, is "like a piece of blank paper whereon you may write as well one miracle as another"; whereas, his own Christianity was founded exclusively on reason. Blount committed suicide in 1693, because he was prevented from marrying his deceased wife's sister. Two years afterwards, his *Miscellaneous Works* (including *The Oracles of Reason*) were published by his disciple Charles Gildon. Gildon defended both the doctrine and the suicide of his master; but, not long after, was himself converted to the orthodox belief by reading Charles Leslie's *Short and Easy Method with the Deists* (1698).

[1] See Vol. IV, p. 337, *ante.*

So far as Blount was concerned, the controversy might have ended here. For, despite his learning and ability, he was something of a free-lance; he could not match himself with his opponents in Christian theology or in biblical learning; his criticism and his own doctrines revealed an outside point of view. There were, however, many sympathisers with his general attitude among wits, and perhaps, also, among scholars: Leslie's reply is a testimony to the prevalence of deism. And, in the year which saw that triumphant reply, there appeared a work by a new author—Toland's *Christianity not mysterious*—with which the controversy entered upon a fresh phase. Within the church, the Roman controversy had died down, and the protestant faith had been firmly established. The time was ripe for the discussion of the content and basis of protestant theology; and the great trinitarian controversy followed. At this point, the chief stimulus to theological thought came, from within the church, indeed, but from outside the ranks of professional theologians. Locke's *Reasonableness of Christianity* appeared in 1695, and marked out the ground to be occupied by almost all controversialists for a long time to come. In his straightforward way, he went to the Scriptures: miracles and prophecy convinced his reason of their authority; the same reason was used for understanding the doctrines they revealed. He did not linger over the former—the external evidences, as they were called, of religion. His interest was in the content of the faith. The same interest dominates the controversies of the first half of the eighteenth century; it was only afterwards that the question of the external evidences came to the front. Throughout the whole century, however, and by both parties, the question was debated in the court of reason. The controversy was not between rationalists and those who distrusted reason. The question was what, on rational grounds, ought to be believed. And, as Clarke and Tillotson and, finally, Butler appealed to reason not less than Locke and Toland and their successors did, so, too, there was another point of agreement between the orthodox and the leaders of the deists. The latter, also, for the most part, and in the earlier stages of the dispute, at any rate, professed to accept the Christian faith. The problem was as to its content: what was its genuine meaning and the scope of its essential doctrines? This much must be borne in mind by anyone who would understand Toland, especially in his earliest and most celebrated work. Toland was born near Londonderry in Ireland in 1670 and died at Putney near London in 1722. His education was varied. He was at school in Ireland, went to the university of Glasgow, took his degree at Edinburgh, afterwards studied at Leyden, and spent some time at Oxford, where he wrote *Christianity not mysterious* (1696). He led a strenuous and varied life, with somewhat uncertain means of livelihood. He was the object of bitter attack by the controversialists opposed to him; and they called in the aid of the civil power. After the publication of his first book, he had to leave Ireland to escape arrest by the Irish parliament, and in England he was for a time in danger of prosecution. He busied himself in political as well as in theological controversy, defended the protestant succession, took part, though unofficially, in important missions, and became known to the electress Sophia and her daughter the queen of Prussia, to whom his *Letters to Serena* (1704) were addressed. He made some influential friends, also, and Leibniz was among his correspondents.

Christianity not mysterious shows the influence of Locke—of his *Essay*, however, rather than of his *Reasonableness of Christianity*, which, published only a year before Toland's book, can hardly have affected its argument. Locke's name is not mentioned by Toland; but Locke's view of knowledge, as consisting in the agreement of ideas, forms the starting-point of his argument and, in the preliminary matter, he often adopts Locke's words. But he is more aggressive in applying his principles. Locke's aim was to show that Christianity was reasonable; Toland's, to demonstrate that nothing contrary to reason, and nothing above reason, can be part of Christian doctrine. There are no mysteries in it. Revelation has unveiled what was formerly mysterious. Whoever reveals anything must do so in words that are intelligible, and the matter must be possible. The things revealed, therefore, are no longer mysteries. This holds, whether the revelation come from God or from man. The only difference between the two cases is that a man may lie, and God can not. Without ideas, neither faith nor knowledge is possible; and, "if by knowledge be meant understanding what is believed, then I stand by it that faith is knowledge."

The ideas may not be adequate; but, in nature as well as in divinity, we have to be content without adequate ideas; even a "spire of grass" is not known in its real essence; we understand only its properties or attributes; and God and the soul are known in the same way.

Toland was a scholar, and boasted acquaintance with more than ten languages. He was also a theologian, and could meet his opponents on their own ground. This interest dominated his literary career; even his political work was in the service of the protestant religion, and his scholarship was chiefly shown in the field of Christian origins. His own theological views went through various modifications. He was brought up a Roman catholic; at the age of sixteen, he became "zealous against popery"; afterwards he was connected with protestant dissenters; when *Christianity not mysterious* was published, he reckoned himself a member of the church of England, his sympathies being with the broad (or, as it was then called, low) church party. When his book was burned at the door of the Irish house of parliament, he may have felt his churchmanship insecure. His later works exhibit its gradual disappearance.

In *Amyntor* (1699), a defence of his *Life of Milton* (1698), he gave, in answer to an opponent, a long list of early apocryphal Christian literature. His interest in researches of this kind was shown afterwards in *Nazarenus; or Jewish, Gentile, and Mahometan Christianity* (1718). His text, in this work, was an Italian manuscript, with Arabic annotations, which he had discovered. He took it for a translation from the Arabic and identified it with the lost Gospel of Barnabas. In both conjectures, later scholarship has shown that he was in error. But his discovery led to some remarkable reflections on the differences between the Jewish and Gentile Christians in the early church. He maintained that the former, who kept the Jewish law themselves, but without enforcing it on the Gentiles, represented "the true original plan of Christianity"; and he declared that he himself took "less exception to the name of Nazarene than to any other." More than a century afterwards, the same distinction as that upon which he laid stress was made fundamental in the explanation of early church history offered by F. C. Baur and his followers.

Among other topics in the *Letters to Serena* was a discussion

of Spinoza, which, perhaps, shows the trend of Toland's speculation.   Leibniz, at any rate, in a letter of 30 April, 1709,
remarks that Toland, in several of his books, refers to the opinion that there is no other eternal being than the universe, but
offers no refutation of this "pernicious" error.   In his reply,
Toland promises an answer to this point in his next; but he does
not seem to have kept his word.   Pantheism, however, was the
doctrine with which he ended, if we may trust the evidence of
Pantheisticon (1720).   This curious piece was issued anonymously, with "Cosmopolis" on the title-page as the place of
publication.   But the author took no pains to conceal his
identity, for the preface is signed "Janus Julius Eoganesius."
Now, Inis Eogain or Inishowen was the place of Toland's birth;
and Janus Julius were the extraordinary names by which he was
christened and known, till a sensible schoolmaster changed
them to John.   The little book, which is written in Latin,
describes the ritual of certain (supposed or real) pantheistic
societies.   It imitates the fashion of a prayer-book, gives the
responses of the congregation and is printed with red rubrics.
As a whole, it is a clever skit, though in the very worst taste.
But Toland had not received any favours from fortune; he
had been harshly attacked by his opponents, even when he
regarded himself as a defender of the Christian faith; and, perhaps, it gave him satisfaction to retaliate bitterly.

Toland thus began as a liberal or rational theologian, and
ended with some form of pantheistic creed.   His writings do
not enable us to trace accurately the steps in this change of
view; but there is no evidence that he ever accepted the cardinal
point of what is commonly called deism—the idea of God as an
external creator who made the world, set it under certain laws,
and then left it alone.[1]   He was a free-thinker rather than a

---

[1] Samuel Clarke (*Being and Attributes of God*, 9th ed., pp. 159 ff.) distinguishes
four classes of Deists: (1) those who "pretend to believe the existence of an eternal,
infinite, independent, intelligent Being; and . . . teach also that this Supreme
Being made the world: though at the same time . . . they fancy God does not at
all concern himself in the government of the world, nor has any regard to, or care
of, what is done therein"; (2) those who, also, admit divine providence in nature;
(3) those who, further, have some notion of the moral perfections of God; (4)
those who, in addition, acknowledge man's duties to God, and see the need for a
future state of rewards and punishments—but all this only "so far as 'tis discov-
erable by the light of nature."

deist. And this, also, describes the position occupied by Anthony Collins, the friend and disciple of Locke, in his best-known work, *A Discourse of Free-thinking, occasioned by the rise and growth of a sect call'd Free-thinkers* (1713). Bentley's brilliant criticism of this book, in his *Remarks upon a late Discourse of Free-thinking,*[1] gained for it an unenviable reputation. The *Remarks* admitted of no answer; but they were more successful in demolishing a free-thinker than in refuting free-thinking; and, perhaps, this was Bentley's sole object in exposing the author's slipshod scholarship. But he was not blind to an ambiguity of which Collins had taken advantage. "Free-thinking" may mean nothing more than the exercise of reason. If this had been all that Collins argued for, there would have been little point in his contention, for both parties claimed that they followed reason. So far, Tillotson would certainly have been with him, and, indeed, Collins claims his support. But he used the term, also, to cover the attitude or doctrines of a "sect of free-thinkers," without any clear account of their position, or any suggestion that the word had more than one meaning. The ambiguity is connected with the duality of the motives which seem to have determined the writings of Collins. One of these was faith in reason—a faith which he had inherited from Locke; the other was a suspicion and dislike of priestcraft. These two motives are indicated by the titles of his earliest works—*Essay concerning the use of Reason* (1707), and *Priest-craft in perfection* (1709). They are combined in *A Discourse of Free-thinking*, in a way which generates more heat than light. Collins held firmly to a belief in God as established by reason; but (though sometimes in guarded language) he was a hostile critic of the Christian creed. His works produced a crowd of controversial literature: his chief later work—*Discourse of the Grounds and Reasons of the Christian Religion* (1724)—having called forth no less than thirty-five replies in two years. He was also the author of a small book called *A Philosophical Inquiry concerning Human Liberty and Necessity* (1715)—an acute and clearly-written argument in favour of the necessitarian solution of the problem.

In some respects—and these, perhaps, the most important—the most significant work of the whole deistical movement was

[1] Cf. Chap. XIII, sec. 1, *post.*

Tindal's *Christianity as Old as the Creation: or, the Gospel, a Republication of the Religion of Nature* (1730). It is no mere defence of the use of reason, nor attack on Christian mysteries. It is a masterly presentation of the prevalent philosophical ideas of the time and a comparison of them with the rational theology which found favour with leaders of the church. "The will of God," said Samuel Clarke, then the most prominent figure in British philosophy and theology, "always determines itself to act according to the eternal reason of things," and "all rational creatures are obliged to govern themselves in all their actions by the same eternal rule of reason." "The religion of the Gospel," said Sherlock, preaching a missionary sermon, "is the true original religion of reason and nature," and its precepts are "declarative of that original religion which was as old as the creation." These extracts Tindal prints on his title-page; and his own aim is to show that "natural religion and external revelation, like two tallies, exactly answer one another, without any other difference between them but as to the manner of their being delivered." Tindal grasps firmly the principles of natural religion, as they were taught by Clarke and Wollaston and other theologians of the day. Reason convinces us of the being and attributes of God, and of the truths of morality; the goodness of God makes it impossible that He should have concealed from any of His creatures what was necessary to their well-being. Christianity, therefore, cannot displace deism, as Clarke held that it could: it can only confirm it. And, as reason suffices to establish the truths of deism, it would seem that Christianity is superfluous. Tindal, however, did not expressly draw this conclusion: he was seventy years of age when he wrote this book, and he retained his fellowship at All Souls, through many changes of government and of personal creed, till his death.

The remaining deistical writers require only the briefest notice. Thomas Woolston was an enthusiast in patriṣtic study, and his enthusiasm seems to have verged on insanity in his later years. He had two passions—"love of the fathers and hatred of the protestant clergy."[1] The latter was intensified by his being deprived of his fellowship at Cambridge; the former led to his allegorical interpretation of scripture. This method

[1] Hunt, J., *Religious Thought in England*, vol. II, p. 40.

he applied to the New Testament miracles, in his series of
Discourses (1727–30), ridiculing the ordinary view of them as
actual events. The historical occurrence of the miracles was
afterwards (1729) defended by Sherlock in *The Trial of the
Witnesses;* and, to this work, Peter Annet replied in *The Resurrection of Jesus examined by a Moral Philosopher* (1744), in
which the expressions are of an open, not to say scandalous,
kind rare in the earlier literature of deism. Thomas Chubb,
an obscure tradesman of Salisbury, with no pretentions to
scholarship or education, published a number of tracts in which
points of the Scriptures were criticised and views similar to
those of Tindal asserted. The same doctrine was stated once
more by Thomas Morgan, a physician, in *The Moral Philosopher*
(1737–41). In the main, he follows Clarke and Tindal; but
he also recalls the investigations of Toland by the prominence
which he gives to the opposition between the Judaising and
the universal factors in early Christianity. *Christianity not
founded on argument*, a pamphlet published in 1742 by Henry
Dodwell (son of the theologian and scholar of the same name),
is one of the latest publications of this school of thought.

Bolingbroke and Shaftesbury stand in a different relation to
the deistical movement from that of the writers already named.
Bolingbroke was not a philosopher, though various occasional
writings of his were collected and published by Mallet as *Philosophical Works* (1752). But he illustrates the way in which the
fundamental doctrines of deism had permeated the thinking of
the men of fashion who played with ideas; and he did much
to confirm this attitude and to extend its influence. Voltaire
regarded his views as significant, and the superficial optimism
of Pope's clear-cut verse, in his *Essay on Man*, was directly due
to Bolingbroke. As a deist, Shaftesbury may have been
coupled with Bolingbroke in the popular mind, and may, also,
have lent inspiration to Pope. But he had a far profounder
view of the problems of thought, which will receive consideration in connection with the group of writers distinguished as
moralists.

The line between deists and churchmen was not always
drawn very clearly. There was a good deal of common ground
in the assumptions of both parties; and there was, besides, a
general ferment of theological thought which disregarded cus-

tomary boundaries. The latter characteristic is exhibited in
the works of William Whiston, mathematician and theologian.
They were related to the controversy, but hardly belong to it.
Whiston was a man of active and original mind, which led him
outside the established church, but in a direction of his own,
different from that of Toland or Tindal. He was opposed to
rationalism, and a believer in prophecy and miracle; but he
came to the conclusion that the Arian heresy represented the
true and primitive Christian creed. His views are fully developed in *Primitive Christianity Revived* (1711–12); but they had
previously become notorious, and had led, in 1710, to his being
deprived of the Cambridge professorship in which he had succeeded Newton. He founded a society to promote the true
faith, as he held it, and composed a revised liturgy for its use;
and he wrote on a variety of topics, not all of them theological.
His translation of Josephus (1737), however, has proved of more
lasting value than his original works. Conyers Middleton, on
the other hand, showed how near a clergyman might come to
the deistical position. He was immersed in the controversy,
and he did something to infuse into it a new historical spirit.
The whole tendency of his contributions, however, was critical
and destructive. He separated himself from most apologists of
the day by denying verbal inspiration; and he examined and
rejected the evidence for the ecclesiastical miracles in a manner
which admitted of wider application. This argument is contained in his most important theological work, entitled *A Free
Inquiry into the Miraculous Powers which are supposed to have
existed in the Christian Church through several successive Ages*
(1748). Of the content of religion, Middleton takes little
account, except as a bulwark of the social order. His work
shows that interest was drifting away from the question of
content, from which it had started, towards the question of
external evidences which suited so well the genius of the later
eighteenth century.

Among the opponents of the deists, the two greatest were
Samuel Clarke and Joseph Butler. Their contributions to the
thought of the period are reserved for discussion in the last
section of this chapter. Of the others, some have been already
referred to; most do not call for more than bibliographical
mention; but one name figures so largely in the controversy as

to require further notice. By his learning, but, still more, by
his mental vigour and resource, William Warburton made an
impression upon his time which is not yet forgotten. He was
born in 1698 and died in 1779. Bred in a solicitor's office, he
took orders without having passed through a university, and,
after other preferments, became bishop of Gloucester in 1759.
He was ready for almost any kind of literary work—controversy
preferred. He wrote *The Alliance between Church and State*
(1736); defended the orthodoxy of Pope's *Essay on Man;* edited
Shakespeare (1747); published a hostile *View of Lord Bolingbroke's Philosophy* (1754), and had the courage to issue *Remarks*
on Hume's *Natural History of Religion* (1757). His most famous
work was *The Divine Legation of Moses demonstrated on the Principles of a Religious Deist* (1737–41). This vast work, which
was never completed, was designed to meet a deistical objection
to the Old Testament scriptures—that the books of Moses
contain no reference to the doctrine of a future life. An objection of this sort does not seem to have been prominent in the
writings of the greater deists; but it suited Warburton's purpose
and enabled him to propound an ingenious paradox. He
agrees that morality needs the support of a belief in a future life
of rewards and punishments; he agrees that Moses did not
appeal to any such belief or teach any such doctrine, although
it was common among ancient authors of other countries. But
just this, he argues, proves the divine legation of the lawgiver.
The laws of nature are an insufficient support for morality;
without the belief in a future life, government cannot be maintained—except by miracle. The absence of the belief among
the Jews is, therefore, taken as a proof that they were under the
immediate providence of God, working by means outside
natural law. The defence of this paradoxical theory gave
Warburton ample scope for displaying his learning and his controversial talent on a great variety of topics, the relevance of
which is not always apparent. Of his learning, Bentley said
that he had a "monstrous appetite and bad digestion." His
ability to get up a case and score a point has been traced to his
legal training; a critic of his own day attributed to the same
source some of the coarser and more violent features of his controversial method. Of insight into history, philosophy or
religion, he does not seem to have had any conspicuous share.

III. Moralists

Samuel Clarke was not a man of original genius; but, by
sheer intellectual power, he came to occupy a leading position
in English philosophy and theology. He touched the higher
thought of the day at almost every point. The new physics,
deism, the trinitarian controversy, biblical and classical study—
all occupied him. Only as to Locke, and the new turn which
Locke gave to many problems, he never defined his position.
He was born in 1675, and died in 1729. In 1697, he published
an annotated Latin translation of the Cartesian Rohault's
Traité de physique, and thereby prepared the way, as he intended to do, for the reception of Newton's works as text-books
at Cambridge; he also translated Newton's *Optics.* In 1699, his
controversies with the deists began, with Toland's *Amyntor* for
a text. In 1704 and 1705, he delivered two courses of Boyle
Lectures, entitled, respectively, *A demonstration of the Being
and Attributes of God,* and *A Discourse concerning the Unchange-
able Obligations of Natural Religion, and the Truth and Certainty
of the Christian Revelation.* He published editions of Cæsar's
Commentaries (1712) and Homer's *Iliad* (1729), as well as many
books of biblical exegesis. His treatise entitled *The Scripture
Doctrine of the Trinity* (1712) brought upon him the accusation
of Arianism, and led to trouble with convocation. In 1715–16,
he was engaged in a controversy with Leibniz, which arose
from a comment of the latter on a remark of Newton's in which
space was spoken of as the *sensorium* of God, branched out into
fundamental questions of metaphysics, and came to an end only
with the death of the German philosopher.

Clarke's Boyle Lectures may be safely reckoned his greatest
work. They contain little that is strikingly new; but the
arrangement of the separate points and the logical consecutive-
ness of the whole are masterly; and they show, nearly always,
an elevation of tone and clearness of phrase which were often
lacking in the controversies of the age. Clarke arranges his
argument in a series of propositions which he first states and
then proceeds to demonstrate; but, otherwise, he did not imitate mathematical method, as Descartes and Spinoza had done.
Nor did he, like Descartes, rely on the purely ontological argument. He argued from existence, not from idea: maintaining

that there must be a self-existent being to account for existing things, and then going on to show the attributes which must belong to this self-existent being. When he has to prove that intelligence and wisdom are among these attributes, he relies expressly on *a posteriori* reasoning. The whole argument—therein resembling Locke's—belongs to the cosmological variety. Clarke's system has been represented as only a less logical Spinozism; but the comparison is superficial. One salient point of resemblance—the view of space as an attribute of God—means something different in the two systems; for Clarke does not identify space with matter. And the method of his argument leaves room for the recognition of freedom and for a distinction of morality from nature, which were impossible for Spinoza.

Clarke's theory of morality has exerted a more permanent influence, and shows more traces of originality, than any of his other doctrines. He had an idea of a moral universe constituted by moral relations, analogous to the physical relations of the physical universe. There are certain "fitnesses of things" over and above their merely physical relations: "there is," he says, "a fitness or suitableness of certain circumstances to certain persons, and an unsuitableness of others, founded in the nature of things and in the qualities of persons, antecedent to will and to all arbitrary or positive appointment whatsoever." Many illustrations are given of these "relations of things"; but their nature is not further explained. "Fitness," "agreement," "suitableness" are the terms by which they are described. They differ, therefore, from the causal relations with which physical science is concerned. They indicate a different aspect—the moral aspect—of reality. But they are known in the same way—by reason. As they are in themselves, so they appear to be to the understanding of all intelligent beings. And, so far as they are intelligent, all reasonable beings guide their conduct by them. God is a free being; but, being rational, it is impossible that He can act against them: He is, therefore, necessarily good. The same relations ought to determine human conduct; but the will of man is deflected by his passions and particular interests, and his understanding is imperfect, so that moral error is possible and common. For this reason, also, the obligation of virtue needs the support of religion.

Clarke thus gave a new reading of an old doctrine.   The view that morality is not arbitrary, but belongs to the order of the universe, had found frequent expression in theories of "the law of nature"; Cudworth, influenced by Platonic idealism, had insisted that the nature or essence of things is immutable, and that good and evil are qualities which belong to that essence; Clarke goes one step further in holding that goodness is a certain congruity of one thing with another—a relation as eternal as is the nature of the things.   But he gave no further definition of this congruity, beyond the description of it by a variety of terms.   That it needed very careful statement became obvious from some of the consequences drawn by his followers.   His views were defended, against the first of a new school of psychological moralists, by John Balguy, in *The Foundation of Moral Goodness* (1727–8).   Still earlier, William Wollaston, in his *Religion of Nature delineated* (1722), had given point to the intellectualism of the moral theory propounded by Clarke. What Clarke had called "fitness" was interpreted by him as an actual existing relation or quality: a wrong act is simply the assertion in conduct of a false proposition.   Thus, "if a man steals a horse and rides away upon him," he does not "consider him as being what he is," namely, another man's horse; and "to deny things to be as they are is the transgression of the great law of our nature, the law of reason."   Bentham's criticism of this is hardly a caricature: "if you were to murder your own father, this would only be a particular way of saying he was not your father."

A more fruitful line of ethical thought was entered upon by Clarke's contemporary, the third earl of Shaftesbury, grandson of the first earl, Locke's patron, and himself educated under Locke's supervision.   He was debarred by weak health from following an active political career, and his life was thus mainly devoted to intellectual interests.   After two or three unhappy years of school life at Winchester, he travelled abroad, chiefly in Italy, with a tutor; in early manhood he resided in Holland; in later life his health drove him to Italy once more.   He was an ardent student of the classics, especially of Plato, Epictetus and Marcus Aurelius, a devotee of liberty in thought and in political affairs, and an amateur of art—at once a philosopher and a *virtuoso*.   His writings were published in three volumes,

entitled *Characteristics of Men, Manners, Opinions, Times*, in
1711; a second edition, carefully revised and enlarged, was
ready at the time of his death in 1713. Several of the treatises
comprised in these volumes had been previously published.
The most important of them, *An Inquiry concerning Virtue, or
Merit*, was surreptitiously printed from an early draft, in 1699,
by Toland—whom he had befriended and financed; *The Moralists, a Philosophical Rhapsody* appeared in 1709; *A Letter concerning Enthusiasm* in 1708; *Sensus Communis: an Essay on the
Freedom of Wit and Humour* in 1709; *Soliloquy: or Advice to an
Author* in 1710. Two of the treatises in later editions were
posthumous: *A Notion of the Historical Draught or Tablature of
the Judgment of Hercules*, 1713, and *Miscellaneous Reflections*,
1714. The style of these works is, nearly always, clear, and it
has the great merit of avoiding traditional technicalities; but it
is over-polished and often artificial—too "genteel," as Lamb
said. Its decorations pleased contemporary taste; but the
rhapsodies of *The Moralists* fall coldly on the modern ear, and
the *virtuoso* has obscured the philosopher.

Shaftesbury was reckoned among the deists, and, perhaps,
not without reason, though his first publication was an introduction to the sermons of Whichcote, the Cambridge Platonist,
and he remained a churchman to the end. His sympathies
were with that spiritual view of the world which is common to
Christianity and to Plato and Marcus Aurelius. He had no
taste for the refinements of theological controversy or for modern religious fanaticisms. He hated, still more, the method of
suppressing the latter by persecution; and this led to his suggestion that they would be better met if their absurdities were
left to ridicule. He never said that ridicule was the test of
truth; but he did regard it as a specific against superstition;
and some of his comments in illustration of this thesis, not
unnaturally, gave offence. He himself, however, was not
without enthusiasms, as is shown by his concern for the good of
his friends and his country and by his devotion to his view of
truth.

For him, the enemy was the selfish theory of conduct, which
he found not in Hobbes only but, also, in a more insinuating form, in Locke. His own ethical writings were intended
to show that the system of man's nature did not point to

selfishness.　There are affections in man which have regard to
his own interest or happiness; but there are also social (or, as
he calls them, natural) affections which are directed to the good
of the species to which he belongs; and he labours to prove that
there is no conflict between the two systems.　But the mind of
man has a still higher reach.　"The natural affection of a
rational creature" will take in the universe, so that he will love
all things that have being in the world: for, in the universal
design of things, "nothing is supernumerary or unnecessary";
"the whole is harmony, the numbers entire, the music perfect."
Further, the mind of man is itself in harmony with the cosmic
order.　Connate in it is a "sense of right and wrong," to which
Shaftesbury gives the name "the moral sense."　And it is for
his doctrine of the moral sense that he is now most often remembered.　In his own century, his writings attained remarkable
popularity: Berkeley (in *Alciphron*) was one of his severest
critics; Leibniz and Diderot were among his warmest admirers.

The doctrine of the moral sense led to immediate development, especially at the hands of Francis Hutcheson.
Hutcheson, a native of Ulster, was educated at the university
of Glasgow, and, in 1729, returned there as professor of moral
philosophy.　Among the more notable British philosophers,
he was the first to occupy a professor's chair; and his lectures
are said by Dugald Stewart

to have contributed very powerfully to diffuse, in Scotland, that
taste for analytical discussion, and that spirit of liberal enquiry, to
which the world is indebted for some of the most valuable productions of the eighteenth century.

Before his appointment as professor, Hutcheson had published
two volumes—*An Inquiry into the Original of our Ideas of
Beauty and Virtue* (1725), and *An Essay on the Nature and Conduct of the Passions and Affections, with Illustrations on the Moral
Sense* (1726)—each containing two treatises.　Text-books on
logic, metaphysics and ethics followed; his *System of Moral
Philosophy* (1755) was published after his death.　The ideas of
Shaftesbury reappear in these works in a somewhat more systematic form and with an increased tendency towards a psychological interpretation of them.　Hutcheson maintained the
disinterestedness of benevolence; he assimilated moral and

aesthetic judgments; he elaborated the doctrine of the moral sense, sometimes speaking of it as merely a new source of pleasure or pain; and he identified virtue with universal benevolence: in the tendency towards general happiness he found the standard of goodness. In this respect, he was, historically, the forerunner of the utilitarians. In his first work, he even used the formula—"the greatest happiness for the greatest numbers"—afterwards, with only a slight verbal change, made famous by Bentham.[1] He anticipated Bentham, also, in the attempt to form a calculus of pleasures and pains.

Hutcheson's first work was described on the title-page as a defence of Shaftesbury against the author of *The Fable of the Bees.* In 1705, Bernard Mandeville, a Dutch physician resident in London, had published a pamphlet of some four hundred lines of doggerel verse entitled *The Grumbling Hive, or Knaves Turn'd Honest.* This was republished as a volume, in 1714, together with "an inquiry into the original of moral virtue" and "remarks" on the original verses, and, again, in 1723, with further additions—the whole bearing the title *The Fable of the Bees; or, Private Vices, Public Benefits.* Mandeville marks a reaction against the too facile optimism which was common with the deists and to which Shaftesbury gave philosophical expression, and against the conventions associated with popular morality. But he did not draw nice distinctions: convention and morality are equally the objects of his satire. He was clever enough to detect the luxury and vice that gather round the industrial system, and perverse enough to mistake them for its foundation. He reverted to Hobbes's selfish theory of human nature, but was without Hobbes's grasp of the principle of order. He looked upon man as a compound of various passions, governed by each as it comes uppermost, and he held that "the moral virtues are the political offspring which flattery begot upon pride." The combination of ability and coarseness with which this view was developed led to many other answers

---

[1] Although Bentham thought and said (*Works*, **x**, 46, 142) that he got the formula from Priestley, it is not to be found in Priestley's works, and was, almost certainly, taken from Beccaria. Beccaria's words (*Dei Delitti e delle Pene*, 1764) were *la massima felicità divisa nel maggior numero*, and these were rendered in the English translation (1767) by "the greatest happiness of the greatest number"— the exact words which Bentham first used in 1776. The dependence of Beccaria on Hutcheson is not established.

than Hutcheson's. Berkeley replied in *Alciphron;* and William Law, as his manner was, went to the heart of the matter in a brilliant pamphlet, *Remarks upon a late book, entituled The Fable of the Bees* (1723).[1] Law also made his mark in the deist controversy by *The Case of Reason* (1731), a reply to Tindal, in which he anticipated the line of argument soon afterwards worked out by Butler.

Joseph Butler, bishop of Durham during the last two years (1750–52) of his life, did not make any contributions to pure metaphysics; but his is the greatest name both in the theological and in the ethical thought of the period. He published two books only—a volume of *Fifteen Sermons* (1726), which (in particular, the first three sermons, entitled "on human nature") express his ethical system, and *The Analogy of Religion, Natural and Revealed, to the Constitution and Course of Nature* (1736). These works are without any pretentions to literary elegance; and it is only in rare passages that the usually sombre style glows with the fire of restrained eloquence. But they are compact of profound thought. The names of other writers are rarely mentioned; but all their arguments have been considered; no difficulties are slurred over, and no opinion is accepted without being probed to the bottom. There is an air of completeness and finality about the reasoning, which needs no grace of diction.

Butler's condensed and weighty argument hardly admits of summary. Yet his view of things as a whole may be expressed in the one word "teleological." Human nature is a system or constitution; the same is true of the world at large; and both point to an end or purpose. This is his guiding idea, suggested by Shaftesbury, to whom due credit is given; and it enables him to rise from a refutation of the selfish theory of Hobbes to the truth that man's nature or constitution is adapted to virtue. The old argument about selfish or disinterested affections is raised to a higher plane. He shows that the characteristic of impulse, or the "particular passions," is to seek an object, not to seek pleasure, while pleasure results from the attainment of the object desired. Human nature, however, is not impulsive merely; there are also reflective principles by which the tendency of impulses is judged and their value appraised. On this

[1] Cf. Chap. XII, p. 347, *post.*

level, selfishness is possible; but self-love is not the only reflective principle of conduct; beside it stands the moral sense, or, as Butler preferred to call it, conscience. The claim to rule, or "superintendency" (a point overlooked by Shaftesbury), is of the very nature of conscience; and, although Butler labours to prove the harmony of the dictates of the two principles, it is to conscience that he assigns ultimate authority. It is true that, in an oft-quoted sentence, he admits

that when we sit down in a cool hour, we can neither justify to ourselves this [*i.e.* moral rectitude] or any other pursuit, till we are convinced that it will be for our happiness, or at least not contrary to it.

But, even if we disregard the "let it be allowed" that introduces the admission, the single sentence is hardly sufficient to justify the assertion that Butler held the authority of self-love to be equal to, or higher than, that of conscience. The passage is, rather, a momentary concession to the selfish spirit of the age; and it has to be interpreted in the light of his frequent assertions of the natural superiority of conscience. "To preside and govern, from the very economy and constitution of man, belongs to it," he says. "Had it strength as it has right, had it power as it has manifest authority, it would absolutely govern the world."

Since the essence of human nature is expressed in this spiritual principle, Butler is able to justify the assertion that man is adapted to virtue. But here his ethics may be said, almost, to stop short. He does not explain further the nature of conscience in relation to reason and will, or derive from it, in any systematic way, the content of morality. He was distrustful of any attempt at a complete philosophy, and resigned to accept probability as the guide of life.

The same fundamental conception and the same limitation reappear in Butler's still more famous work, *The Analogy*. The world is a system—"a scheme in which means are made use of to accomplish ends, and which is carried on by general laws." It is neglect of this truth which makes men think that particular instances of suffering virtue or successful vice are inconsistent with "the wisdom, justice, and goodness of the constitution of nature." In the constitution and government of the world, nature and morality are so closely connected as to form a single scheme, in which "it is highly probable that the first is formed and carried on merely in subserviency to the latter." The imperfections of our knowledge make it impossible to demonstrate this in detail. But grant, as the deists granted, that God is the author of nature, and it can be shown that there is no difficulty in the doctrines of religion, whether natural or revealed, which has not a parallel difficulty in the principle common to both sides in the argument. This is the analogy to the establishment of which in detail Butler's reasonings are directed. They are so exhaustive, so thorough and so candid, that critics of all schools are agreed in regarding his as the final word in a great controversy.

CHAPTER XII

William Law and the Mystics

TO speak of mystical thought in the first half of the eighteenth century in England seems almost a contradiction in terms; for the predominating character of that age, its outlook on life and its mind as expressed in philosophy, religion and literature, was in every way opposed to what is understood by mystical. In literature, shallowness of thought is often found combined with unrivalled clearness of expression; in general outlook, the conception of a mechanical world made by an outside Creator; in religion and philosophy, the practically universal appeal to "rational" evidence as supreme arbiter. In no age, it would seem, have men written so much about religion, while practising it so little. The one quality in Scripture which interests writers and readers alike is its credibility, and the impression gathered by the student of the religious controversies of the day is that Christianity was held to exist, not to be lived, but, like a proposition in Euclid, only to be proved.

This view, however, of the main tendency of the time, though representative, is not complete. There is also an undercurrent of thought of a kind that never quite disappears and that helps to keep the earth green during the somewhat dry and arid seasons when rationalism or materialism gains the upper hand.

This tendency of thought is called mysticism, and it may be described in its widest sense as an attitude of mind founded upon an intuitive or experienced conviction of fundamental unity, of alikeness in all things. All mystical thought springs from this as base. The poet mystic, looking out on the natural world, rejoices in it with a purer joy and studies it with a deeper reverence than other men, because he knows it is not something called "matter" and alien to him, but that it is—as he is—spirit itself made visible. The mystic philosopher, instead of attempting to reason or analyse or deduce, seeks merely to tell of his vision; whereupon, words generally fail him, and he becomes obscure. The religious mystic has for goal the union of himself with God, the actual contact with the Divine Presence, and he conceives this possible because man is "a God though in the germ," and, therefore, can know God through that part of his nature which is akin to Him.

There were many strains of influence which, in the seventeenth century, tended to foster this type of thought in England. The little group of Cambridge Platonists gave new expression to great neo-Platonic ideas, the smouldering embers of which had been fanned to flame in the ardent forge of the Florentine renascence;[1] but, in addition to this older thought, there were not only new influences from without but, also, new conditions within which must be indicated.

A strong vein of mysticism had been kept alive in Amsterdam, whither the first body of exiled separatists had gone in 1593. Elizabeth, thinking to quell independent religious thought at home, had planted nurseries of freedom in Holland, which waxed strong and sent back over seas in the next century a persistent stream of opinion and literature.[2] To this can be traced the root-ideas which animated alike quakers, seekers, Behmenists, anabaptists, familists and numberless other sects which embodied a reaction against forms and ceremonies that, in ceasing to be understood, had become lifeless. They all agreed in deeming it more important to spiritualise this life than to dogmatise about the life to come. They all believed in the "inner light," in the immediate revelation of God within the soul as the supreme and all-important experience. They all held that salvation was the effect of a spiritual principle, a seed quickened invisibly by God, and, consequently, they considered learning useless, or even mischievous, in dealing with the things of the spirit. So far, these various sects were mys-

---

[1] See Vol. VIII, Chap. x.
[2] For an interesting detailed account of this phase of religious life, with full references to original documents, see *Studies in Mystical Religion*, 1909, by Jones, R. M., chaps. xvi and xvii.

tical in thought; though, with the exception of familists, Behmenists and seekers, they cannot unreservedly be classed as mystics. Large numbers of these three sects, however, became "children of light," thus helping to give greater prominence to the strong mystical element in early quakerism.

It only needed the release from the crushing hand of Laud, and the upheaval of the civil war, to set free the religious revival which had long been seething, and to distract England, for a time, with religious excitement. Contemporary writers refer with horror to the swarm of "sects, heresies and schisms" which now came into being,[1] and Milton alone seems to have understood that the turmoil was but the outward sign of a great spiritual awakening.[2] Unhappily, there were few who, with him, could perceive that the "opinion of good men is but knowledge in the making," and that these many sects were but various aspects of one main movement towards freedom and individualism, towards a religion of the heart rather than of the head. The terrible persecutions of the quakers under Charles II[3] tended to withdraw them from active life, and to throw them in the direction of a more personal and introspective religion.[4] It was then that the writings of Antoinette Bourignon, Madame Guyon and Fénelon became popular, and were much read among a certain section of thinkers, while the teachings of Jacob Boehme, whose works had been put into English between the years 1644 and 1692, bore fruit in many ways.[5] Whether directly or indirectly, they permeated the thought of the founders of the Society of Friends,[6] they were widely read

[1] See, for instance, Pagitt's *Heresiography*, 1645, dedication to the lord mayor; or Edwards, who, in his *Gangraena*, 1646, names 176, and, later, 23 more, "errors, heresies, blasphemies."

[2] *Areopagitica*, 1644.

[3] 13,562 Friends suffered imprisonment during the years 1661–97, while 198 were transported overseas and 338 died in prison or of their wounds. See *Inner Life of the Religious Societies of the Commonwealth*, by Barclay, pp. 474–8.

[4] For further observations on early quakerism in its connection with literature, see Vol. VIII, Chap. IV.

[5] Charles I, who, shortly before his death, read Boehme's *Forty Questions*, just then translated into English, much admired it. See a most interesting MS. letter in Latin from Francis Lee to P. Poiret in Dr. Williams's library, C 5. 30.

[6] "Jacob Behmont's Books were the chief books that the Quakers bought, for there is the Principle or Foundation of their Religion." *A Looking Glass for George Fox*, 1667, p. 5. But Boehme was not wholly approved of even among the early quakers; see *Inner Life of the Religious Societies*, p. 479. For the influence of

both in cottage and study[1] and they produced a distinct Behmenite sect.[2]　Their influence can be seen in the writings of Thomas Tryon, John Pordage, George Cheyne, Francis Lee, Jane Lead, Thomas Bromley, Richard Roach and others; in the foundation and transactions of the Philadelphian society; in the gibes of satirists;[3] in forgotten tracts; in the increase of interest in alchemy;[4] in the voluminous MS. commentaries of Freher, or even in Newton's great discovery; for it is almost certain that the idea of the three laws of motion first reached Newton through his eager study of Boehme.

The tracing of this mystical thought, however, during the period under discussion and later, mainly among obscure sects and little-known thinkers, would not form part of a history of English literature, were it not that our greatest prose mystic lived and wrote in the same age.

William Law had a curiously paradoxical career.　After graduating as B.A. and M.A. at Cambridge, in 1708 and 1712, and being, in 1711, ordained and elected fellow of his college (Emmanuel), he refused to take the oaths of allegiance to George I, and thus lost his fellowship and vocation.　Though an ardent high churchman, he was the father of methodism. Though deprived of employment in his church, he wrote the book which, of all others for a century to come, had the most profound and far-reaching influence upon the religious thought of his country.　Though a sincere, and, so he believed, an orthodox Christian, he was the classic exponent of Boehme, a thinker abhorred and mistrusted alike by eighteenth century divines and by Wesleyan leaders.

About the year 1727, Edward Gibbon selected Law as tutor

Boehme on Fox and Winstanley, see *Studies in Mystical Religion*, pp. 494–5; cf., also, Fox's *Journal* for 1648, 8th ed., vol. I, pp. 28–9, with Boehme's *Three Principles*, chap. xx, §§ 39–42; also, life of J. B. in "Law's edition," vol. I, p. xiii, or the *Signatura Rerum*.

[1] See *Way to Divine Knowledge*, Law's *Works*, vol. VII, pp. 84, 85; Byrom's *Journal*, vol. I, part 2, pp. 560, 598; vol. II, part 2, pp. 193, 216, 236, 285, 310–11, 328, 377, 380.

[2] See Richard Baxter's Autobiography, *Reliquiae Baxterianae*, 1696, part I, p. 77.

[3]　　　　　　He Anthroposophus and Floud,
　　　　　　And Jacob Behmen understood.

Hudibras, I, canto I, cf. *A Tale of a Tub*, sect. v, and *Martinus Scriblerus*, end of Chap. I.　　　　　　　　　　　　　　　　　　　　[4] See Aubrey's *Lives*.

for his only son, the father of the historian, and, in 1730, when his pupil went abroad, Law lived on with the elder Gibbon in the "spacious house with gardens and land at Putney," where he was "the much honoured friend and spiritual director of the whole family."[1]

During these years at Putney, Law's reputation as a writer became assured. He was already known as the ablest defender of non-juror principles; the publication of *A Serious Call* in 1729 had brought him renown, and he was revered and consulted by an admiring band of disciples. His later life was spent at his birthplace, King's Cliffe, near Stamford. He settled there in 1737 or 1740, and was joined by Hester Gibbon, the historian's aunt, and Mrs. Hutcheson, a widow with considerable means. This oddly assorted trio gave themselves to a life of retirement and good deeds, the whole being regulated by Law. With a united income of over £3000 a year, they lived in the simplest fashion. They spent large sums in founding schools and almshouses, and in general charity, which took the form of free daily distribution of food, money and clothes, no beggar being turned away from the door, until the countryside became so demoralised with vagrants that the inhabitants protested and the rector preached against these proceedings from the pulpit.[2] The trouble, however, seems to have abated when the three kind-hearted and guileless offenders threatened to leave the parish, and, possibly, it may have caused them to exercise a little discrimination in their giving.

Here, at King's Cliffe, after more than twenty years of residence, passed in the strictest routine of study and good works, Law died, after a short illness, almost in the act of singing a hymn.

Law's writings fall naturally into three divisions, controversial, practical and mystical. His three great controversial works are directed against a curious assortment of opponents: Hoadly, latitudinarian bishop of Bangor, Mandeville, a sceptical pessimist, and Tindal, a deistical optimist. These writers represent three main sections of the religious opinion of the

---

[1] Gibbon's *Memoirs*, ed. Hill, G. B., 1900, p. 24.
[2] See Walton's *Notes*, p. 499. The duty on which Law most insisted was charity; see his defence of indiscriminate giving, in *A Serious Call, Works*, vol. IV, pp. 114–18.

day, and much light is thrown on Law's character and beliefs by the method with which he meets them and turns their own weapons against themselves.

It was a time of theological pamphleteering, and the famous Bangorian controversy is a good specimen of the kind of discussion which abounded in the days of George I. It is, on the whole, good reading, clear, pointed and even witty, and, if compared with similar controversies in the reign of Charles I, presents an admirable object lesson as to the advance made during the intervening years in the writing of English prose.

When queen Anne died, and the claims of the Stewarts were set aside in favour of a parliamentary king from Hanover, the church, committed absolutely to the hereditary, as opposed to the parliamentary, principle, found itself on the horns of a dilemma. High churchmen were forced either to eat their own words, or to refuse to take the oaths of allegiance to the new king and of abjuration to the pretender.[1] Law is a prominent example of this latter and smaller class, the second generation of non-jurors. Feeling naturally ran very high when, in answer to the posthumous papers of George Hickes,[2] the non-juring bishop, who charged the church with schism, Benjamin Hoadly, bishop of Bangor, the king's chaplain, came forward as champion of the crown and church.

Hoadly was an able thinker and writer, and, in his *Preservative against the Principles and Practices of the Non-Jurors*, he attempts to justify the civil power by reducing to a minimum the idea of church authority and even that of creeds. He tells Christians to depend upon Christ alone for their religion, and not upon His ministers, and he urges sincerity as the sole test of truth. On this last point he dwells more fully and exclusively in his famous sermon, *The Nature of the Kingdom of Christ*, preached before the king on 31 March, 1717. Hoadly's pamphlet and sermon raised a cloud of controversy;[3] but by far the

---

[1] For an excellent illustration of the principles and arguments on both sides, compare Law's letter from Cambridge, written to his brother at the time, with that of his future friend Byrom at the same date. Both are quoted by Overton, J. H., *William Law, Nonjuror and Mystic*, 1881, pp. 13–16.

[2] *The Constitution of the Catholick Church, and the Nature and Consequences of Schism.* 1716.

[3] In the course of July, 1717, 74 pamphlets appeared on the subject, and, at one crisis, for a day or two, the business of the city was at a standstill, little was done

ablest answer he received on the part of the non-jurors was
that contained in Law's *Three Letters to theBishop of Bangor*
(1717–19). The bishop never replied to Law, and, indeed,
he gave strong proof of his acuteness by leaving his brilliant
young opponent severely alone.[1]

Law instantly detected that Hoadly's arguments tended to
do away altogether with the conception of the church as a
living spiritual society, and his answer is mainly directed
against the danger of this tendency.[2] He begins by pointing
out that there are no libertines or loose thinkers in England
who are not pleased with the bishop, for they imagine that he
intends to dissolve the church as a society; and, indeed, they
seem to have good grounds for their assumption, since the
bishop leaves neither authorised ministers, nor sacraments, nor
church, and intimates that "if a man be not a Hypocrite, it
matters not what Religion he is of."[3]

Law deals with church authority, and shows that if, as
Hoadly says, regularity of ordination and uninterrupted succession be mere niceties and dreams, there is no difference
between the episcopalian communion and any other lay body
of teachers.[4] He demolishes Hoadly's remarks on the exclusion of the papist succession, and he ends the first letter by
refuting the bishop's definition of prayer, as a "calm, undisturbed address to God,"[5] in a passage which is one of the finest
pleas in our language for the right use of passion, and which
admirably sums up the fundamental difference of outlook
between the mystic and the rationalist temper in the things
of the spirit.

Law's next work, *Remarks on the Fable of the Bees* (1723),
is an answer to Mandeville's poem,[6] the moral of which is that

---

on the Exchange and many shops were shut. See Hoadly's *Works*, vol. II, pp. 385,
429; also Sir Leslie Stephen's *English Thought in the 18th Century*, vol. II, p. 156.

[1] See Hoadly's *Works*, vol. II, pp. 694–5, where he gives his reasons for not
answering Law.

[2] For some of the side issues which were vehemently discussed by other writers
see Leslie Stephen, vol. II, p. 157.

[3] *Works*, vol. I, letter I, pp. 6, 7.   [4] *Ibid,*, pp. 14, 15.

[5] So defined by Hoadly in his sermon *The Nature of the Kingdom or Church of
Christ*, p. 7.

[6] *The Grumbling Hive*, first printed 1705, republished with explanatory notes
under the title *The Fable of the Bees*, 1714.

"private vices are public benefits," and Law, characteristically seizing on the fallacy underlying Mandeville's clever paradoxes, deals with his definition of the nature of man and of virtue in a style at once buoyant, witty and caustic.

The Case of Reason (1731) is Law's answer to the deists, and, more especially, to Tindal's *Christianity as Old as the Creation* (1730). To reply to such arguments as those of Tindal and the deists in general was, to a man of Law's insight and intellect, an easy task. He brings out well the fundamental difference between his and their points of view. Deists saw a universe governed by fixed laws, a scheme of creation which was "plain and perspicuous,"[1] capable of accurate investigation, and they believed in a magnified man God outside the universe, whose nature, methods and aims were, or should be, perfectly clear to the minds of his creatures. Law saw a living universe, wrapped in impenetrable mystery, and believed in a God who was so infinitely greater than man, that, of His nature, or of the reason or fitness of his actions, men can know nothing whatsoever. Why complain of mysteries in revelation, he says, when "no revealed mysteries can more exceed the comprehension of man, than the state of human life itself?"[2]

Tindal asserts that the "fitness of things" must be the sole rule of God's actions. "I readily grant this," says Law, "but what judges are we of the fitness of things?" We can no more judge the divine nature than we can raise ourselves to a state of infinite wisdom; and the rule by which God acts "must in many instances be entirely inconceivable by us . . . and in no instances fully known or perfectly comprehended."[3]

In short, the fundamental assumption of the deists, that human reason is all-sufficient to guide us to truth, is the great error which Law, in his later writings especially, set himself to combat; in his opinion, it is devilish pride, the sin by which the angels fell.[4]

In the further development of his position in *The Case of Reason*, we can see many indications of the future mystic; for the crudely material thought of his opponent seems to have called into expression, for the first time, many of Law's more characteristic beliefs. There is, throughout, a strong sense of

---

[1] *Christianity as Old as the Creation*, p. 20.
[2] *The Case of Reason*, *Works*, vol. II, p. 9.
[3] *Ibid.*, p. 7.
[4] *The Case of Reason*, p. 3.

man's capacity for spiritual development, and a settled belief
that the human mind cannot possibly know anything as it
really is, but can only know things in so far as it is able to
apprehend them through symbol or analogy.   Things supernatural or divine, he says, cannot be revealed to us in their own
nature, for the simple reason that we are not capable of knowing
them.   If an angel were to appear to us, he would have to appear, not as he really is, but in some human bodily form, so that
his appearance might be suited to our capacities.   Thus, with
any supernatural or divine matter, it can only be represented
to us by its likeness to something that we already naturally
know.[1]   This is the way in which revelation teaches us, and it
is only able to teach so much outward knowledge of a great
mystery as human language can represent;[2] reason is impotent
in face of it, and only by the spiritual faculty that exists in us
can the things of the spirit be even dimly apprehended.[3]

Law's practical and ethical works, *A Practical Treatise upon
Christian Perfection* (1726) and *A Serious Call* (1728), have been
more read and are better known than any other of his writings;
moreover, they explain themselves, being independent both of
local controversies and of any special metaphysic.   For these
reasons, comparatively little need be said about them here.
Both treatises are concerned with the practical question of how
to live in accordance with the teachings of Christ, and they
point out with peculiar force that the way consists, not in per-
forming this or that act of devotion or ceremony, but in a new
principle of life, an entire change of temper and of aspiration.

Christian Perfection, though somewhat gloomy and austere
in tone, has much charm and beauty; but it was quite over-
shadowed by the wider popularity of what many consider Law's
greatest work, *A Serious Call*, a book of extraordinary power,
delightful and persuasive style, racy wit and unanswerable
logic.   Never have the inconsistency between Christian pre-
cept and practice been so ruthlessly exposed and the secret
springs of men's hearts so uncompromisingly laid bare.   Never
has the ideal of the Christian life been painted by one who lived
more literally in accordance with every word he preached.
That is the secret of *A Serious Call;* it is written from the heart,
by a man in deep earnest; and in an age distinguished for its

[1] *The Case of Reason*, p. 37.   [2] *Ibid.*, p. 39.   [3] *Ibid.*, pp. 16, 17.

mediocrity and easy-going laxness, Law's lofty ideals acted as an electric current, setting aflame the hearts of all who came under their power.

Few books in English have wielded such an influence. John Wesley himself acknowledged that *A Serious Call* sowed the seed of methodism,[1] and, undoubtedly, next to the Bible, it contributed more than any other book to the spread of evangel-icalism. It made the deepest impression on Wesley himself; he preached after its model;[2] he used it as a text-book for the highest class at Kingswood school; and, a few months before his death, he spoke of it as "a treatise which will hardly be excelled, if it be equalled, in the English tongue, either for beauty of expression or for justice and depth of thought." Charles Wesley, Henry Whitfield, Henry Venn, Thomas Scott, Thomas Adam and James Stillingfleet are among other great methodists and evangelicals who have recorded how profoundly it affected them. But it did not appeal only to this type of mind. Dr. Johnson, who praised it in no measured terms, attributes his first serious thoughts to the reading of it. "I became," he says, "a sort of lax talker against religion, for I did not much think against it; and this lasted till I went to Oxford."[3] When there,

I took up Law's *Serious Call to a Holy Life*, expecting to find it a dull book (as such books generally are) . . . But I found Law quite an over-match for me; and this was the first occasion of my thinking in earnest of religion.

Gibbon[4] and the first Lord Lyttelton (who, taking it up at bed-time, was forced to read it through before he could go to rest),[5] are two among many other diverse characters who felt its force.

Such, very briefly, were Law's views and writings until middle age. Although, before that time, they do not show any marked mystical tendency, yet we know that, from his undergraduateship onwards, Law was a "diligent reader" of mystical books,[6] and when at Cambridge, he wrote a thesis

[1] Sermon CVII, Wesley's *Works*, 11th ed., 1856, vol. VII, p. 194.
[2] Letter to Law of 1738, quoted by Overton, p. 33.
[3] Boswell's *Life of Johnson*, ed. Hill, G. Birkbeck, 1887, vol. I, p. 68, also vol. II, p. 122. [4] Gibbon's *Memoirs*, ed. Hill, G. B., 1900, p. 23.
[5] Byrom's *Journal*, vol. II, part 2, p. 634.
[6] See *Some Animadversions upon Dr. Trapp's late Reply, Works*, vol. VI, p. 319.

entitled *Malebranche, and the Vision of All Things in God.*
There is no question that he was strongly attracted to, and
probably influenced by, Malebranche's view that all true knowledge is but the measure of the extent to which the individual
can participate in the universal life; that, unless we see God in
some measure, we do not see anything; and that it is only by
union with God we are capable of knowing what we do know.[1]
On the other hand, there are points in Malebranche's philosophy—which curiously stops short of its logical conclusion—
quite opposed to Law's later thought: more especially the
belief, which Malebranche shared with Descartes on the one
side and Locke on the other, that body and spirit are separate
and contrary existences; whereas, in Law's view, body and
spirit are but inward and outward expressions of the same
being.[2] Among other mystics studied by Law were Dionysius
the Areopagite, the Belgian and German writers Johannes
Ruysbroek, Johann Tauler, Heinrich Suso and others, and the
seventeenth century quietists, Fénelon, Madame Guyon and
Antoinette Bourignon. The last two were much admired by
Byrom, who loved to recur to them in writing and in talk; but
they were not altogether congenial to Law; they were too
diffuse, sentimental and even hysterical to please his essentially
robust and manly temper. When, however, he was about
forty-six (c. 1733), he came across the work of the seer who
supplied just what he needed, and who set his whole nature
aglow with mystical fervour.

Jacob Boehme (or Behmen, as he has usually been called
in England), the peasant shoemaker of Görlitz, is one of the
most amazing phenomena in an amazing age. He was the son
of a herdsman, and, as a boy, helped his father to tend cattle;
he was taught how to write and read, was apprenticed to a
shoemaker, married the daughter of a butcher and lived quietly
and humbly, troubled only by years of bitter persecution from
his pastor, who stirred up the civil authorities against him.
This was his outer life, sober and hardworking, like that of his
fellow-seer, William Blake, but, like him also, he lived in a glory
of inner illumination, by the light of which he caught glimpses
of mysteries and of splendours which, even in Boehme's broken

---

[1] See *Recherche de la Vérité*, specially livre III, chap. VI, *Que nous voyons toutes choses en Dieu.*　　[2] See *The Spirit of Love, Works*, vol. VIII, pp. 31 and 33.

and faltering syllables, dazzle and blind the ordinary reader. He saw with the eye of his mind into the heart of things, and he wrote down so much of it as he could understand with his reason. He had a quick and supple intelligence, and an intense power of visualising. Everything appears to him as an image, and, with him, a logical process expresses itself in a series of pictures. Although illiterate and untrained, Boehme was in touch with the thought of his time, and the form of his work, at any rate, owes a good deal to it. The older speculative mysticism which rather despised nature, and sought for light from within, coming down from Plotinus through *Meister* Eckhart and Tauler, had, in Germany, been carried on and developed by Caspar von Schwenckfeld and Sebastian Franck; while a revival of the still older practical or "perceptive" mysticism of the east, based on a study of the natural sciences (in which were included astrology, alchemy and magic), had been brought about by Cornelius Agrippa and Paracelsus, both of whom owed much to the Jewish Cabbala. These two mystical traditions, the one starting from within, the other from without, were, to some extent, reconciled into one system by the Lutheran pastor Valentin Weigel, with whose mysticism Boehme has much in common.

The older mystics—eastern and western alike—had laid supreme stress on unity as seen in the nature of God and all things. No one more fully believed in ultimate unity than did Boehme; but he lays peculiar stress on the duality, or, more accurately, the trinity in unity, and the central point of his philosophy is the fundamental postulate that all manifestation necessitates opposition. He asserted the uniformity of law throughout all existence, physical and spiritual, and this law, which applies throughout nature, divine and human alike, is that nothing can reveal itself without resistance, good can only be known through evil, and weakness through strength, just as light is only visible when reflected by a dark body.[1]

Thus, when God, the triune principle, or will under three aspects, desires to become manifest, He divides the will into two, the "yes" and the "no," and so founds an eternal contrast to Himself out of His own hidden nature, in order to enter into

---

[1] "Without contraries is no progression," as Blake puts it in his development of the same thesis in *The Marriage of Heaven and Hell*.

a struggle with it, and, finally, to discipline and assimilate it. The object of all manifested nature is the transforming of the will which says "no" into the will which says "yes," and this is brought about by seven organising spirits or forms. The first three of these bring nature out of the dark element to the point where contact with light is possible. Boehme calls them harshness, attraction and anguish, which, in modern terms, are contraction, expansion and rotation. The first two are in deadly antagonism, and, being forced into collision, form an endless whirl of movement. These two forces, with their resultant effect, are to be found all through manifested nature, within man and without, and are called by different names: good, evil and life; God, the devil and the world; homogeneity, heterogeneity, strain, or the three laws of motion, centripetal and centrifugal force, resulting in rotation. They are the outcome of the "nature" or "no will," and are the basis of all manifestation. They are the "power" of God, apart from the "love," hence, their conflict is terrible. At this point, spirit and nature approach and meet, and, from the shock, a new form is liberated, lightning or fire, which is the fourth moment or essence; in the spark of the lightning, all that is dark, gross and selfish in nature is consumed; the flash brings the rotating wheel of anguish to a standstill, and it becomes a cross. A divine law is accomplished; for all life has a double birth, suffering is the condition of joy and only in going through fire or the Cross can man reach light. With the lightning ends the development of the negative triad, and the evolution of the three higher forms then begins; Boehme calls them light or love, sound and substance; they are of the spirit, and, in them, contraction, expansion and rotation are repeated in a new sense.[1] The first three forms give the stuff or strength of being; the last three manifest the quality of being, good or bad; and evolution can proceed in either direction.

These principles of nature can be looked at in another way. If they are resolved into two sets of three, in the first three the dark principle which Boehme calls fire is manifested, while the last three form the principle of light. These two are

---

[1] Boehme refers to these seven forces in all his writings, but see his *Threefold Life of Man*, chap. I, §§ 23–32; chap. II, §§ 27–36, 73; chap. III, § 1; chap. IV, §§ 5, 12; or *Signatura Rerum*, chap. XIV, §§ 10–15.

eternally distinct, and, whichever is manifested, the other remains hidden. This doctrine of the hidden and manifest is peculiar to Boehme, and lies at the root of his explanation of evil. A spiritual principle becomes manifest by taking on a form or quality. The "dark" or harsh principle in God is not evil in itself when in its right place, *i.e.*, when hidden, and forming the necessary basis for the light or good. But, through the fall of man, the divine order has been transgressed, and the dark side has become manifest and appears to us as evil. Many chemical processes help to give a crude illustration of Boehme's thought. Suppose "water" stands for complete good or reality as God sees it. Of the two different gases, hydrogen (=evil) and oxygen (=good) each is manifested separately, with peculiar qualities of its own, but, when they combine, their original form goes "into hiddenness," and we get a new body "water." Neither of them alone is water, and yet water could not be if either were lacking.

In reading Boehme, it must not be forgotten that he has a living intuition of the eternal forces which lie at the root of all things. He is struggling to express the stupendous world-drama which is ever being enacted, in the universe without and in the soul of man within; and, to this end, he presses into his service symbolical, biblical and alchemical terms, although he fully realises their inadequacy. "I speak thus," he says, "in bodily fashion, for the sake of my readers' lack of understanding." Unless this be remembered, Boehme's work, in common with that of all mystics, is liable to the gravest misunderstanding. He is never weary of explaining that, although he is forced to describe things in a series of images, there is no such thing as historical succession, "for the eternal dwells not in time."[1] He has to speak of the generation of God as though it were an act in time, although to do so is to use "diabolical" (*i.e.*, knowingly untrue) language, for God hath no beginning. Everything he describes is going on always and simultaneously, even as all the qualities he names are in everything which is manifested. "The birth of nature takes place to-day, just as it did in the beginning."

It would be impossible to give here any adequate account of Boehme's vision; but the four fundamental principles which he

[1] *Mysterium Magnum*, part I, chap. VIII.

enunciated and emphasised may be thus summarised: will or desire as the original force; contrast or duality as the condition of all manifestation; the relation of the hidden and the manifest; development as a progressive unfolding of difference, with a final resolution into unity. The practical and ethical result of this living unity of nature is simple. Boehme's philosophy is one which can only be apprehended by living it. Will, or desire, is the root-force in man as it is in nature and in the God-head, and, until this is turned towards the light, any purely historical or intellectual knowledge of these things is as useless as if hydrogen were to study all the qualities of oxygen, expecting thus to become water; whereas, what is needed is the actual union of the elements.

The whole of Boehme's practical teaching, as, also, that of Law, might be summed up in the story told of an Indian sage who was importuned by a young man as to how he could find God. For some time, the sage did not give any answer; but, one evening, he bade the youth come and bathe with him in the river, and, while there, he gripped him suddenly and held his head under the water until he was nearly drowned. When he had released him, the sage asked, "What did you want most when your head was under water?" and the youth replied, "A breath of air." To which the sage answered, "When you want God as you wanted that breath of air you will find Him."

This realisation of the momentous quality of the will is the secret of every religious mystic;[1] the hunger of the soul, as Law calls it,[2] is the first necessity, and all else will follow. Such was the thought of the writer who, spiritually, was closely akin to our two greatest English mystics. William Blake saw visions and spoke a tongue like that of the illuminated cobbler; and of Law, who was not a seer,[3] we learn that, when he first read Boehme's works, they put him into "a perfect sweat." Only those who combine intense mystical aspiration with a clear and imperious intellect can fully realise what the experience must have been.

[1] Cf. St. Augustine, "To will God entirely is to have Him," *The City of Gods* book XI, chap. IV; or Ruysbroek's answer to the priests from Paris who came to consult him on the state of their souls: "You are as you desire to be."

[2] "*Hunger* is *all*, and in all worlds everything lives in it, and by it." See Law's letter to Langcake, 7 September, 1751, printed in Walton's *Notes and Materials*, p. 541. [3] See Law's letter to W. Walker, Byrom's *Journal*, vol. I, part 2, p. 559.

The two most important of Law's mystical treatises are *An Appeal to all that Doubt* (1740), and *The Way to Divine Knowledge* (1752). The first of these should be read by anyone desirous of knowing Law's later thought, for it is a clear and fine exposition of his attitude with regard more especially to the nature of man, the unity of all nature and the quality of fire or desire. The later book is an account of the main principles of Boehme, with a warning as to the right way to apply them, and it was written as an introduction to the new edition of Boehme's works which Law contemplated publishing. Law's later, are but an expansion of his earlier, views; the main difference being that, whereas, in the practical treatises (*Christian Perfection* and *A Serious Call*), he urges certain temper and conduct because it is our duty to obey God, or because it is right or lawful, in his later writings—Boehme having furnished the clue—he adds not only the reason for this conduct being right, but the means of attaining it, by expounding the working of the law itself. The following aspect, then, of Boehme's teaching is that which Law most consistently emphasises.

Man was made out of the breath of God; his soul is a spark of the Deity. It, therefore, cannot die, for it "has the unbeginning unending life of God in it." Man has fallen from his high estate through ignorance and inexperience, through seeking separation, taking the part for the whole, desiring the knowledge of good and evil as separate things. The assertion of self is, thus, the root of all evil; for, so soon as the will of man "turns to itself, and would, as it were, have a sound of its own, it breaks off from the divine harmony, and falls into the misery of its own discord." For it is the state of our will that makes the state of our life. Hence, by "the fall," man's standpoint has been dislocated from the centre to the circumference, and he lives in a false imagination. Every quality is equally good, for there is nothing evil in God, from whom all comes; but evil appears to be through separation. Thus, strength and desire in the divine nature are necessary and magnificent qualities, but when, as in the creature, they are separated from love, they appear as evil. The analogy of the fruit is, in this connection, a favourite one with both Law and Boehme. When a fruit is unripe (*i.e.*, incomplete), it is sour, bitter, astringent, unwholesome; but, when it has been longer exposed to the sun and air, it becomes sweet, luscious and good to eat. Yet it is the same fruit, and the astringent qualities are not lost or destroyed, but transmuted and enriched, and are thus the main cause of its goodness.[1] The only way to pass from this condition of "bitterness" to ripeness, from this false imagination to the true one, is the way of death. We must die to what we are before we can be born anew;[2] we must die to the things of this world to which we cling, and for which we desire and hope, and we must turn towards God. This should be the daily, hourly exercise of the mind, until the whole turn and bent of our spirit "points as constantly to God as the needle touched with the loadstone does to the north."[3] To be alive in God, before you are dead to your own nature, is "a thing as impossible in itself, as for a grain of wheat to be alive before it dies."[4]

The root of all, then, is the will or desire.[5] It is the seed of everything that can grow in us; "it is the only workman in nature, and everything is its work;" it is the true magic power. And this will or desire is always active; every man's life is a continual state of prayer, and, if we are not praying for the things of God, we are praying for something else.[6] For prayer is but the desire of the soul. Our imaginations and desires are, therefore, the greatest realities we have, and we should look closely to what they are.[7]

It is essential to the understanding of Law, as of Boehme, to remember his belief in the reality and actuality of the oneness of nature and of law.[8] Nature is God's great book of revelation, for it is nothing else but God's own outward manifestation of what He inwardly is, and can do. The mysteries of religion, therefore, are no higher, and no deeper than the mysteries of nature.[9] God Himself is subject to this law. There is no question of God's mercy or of His wrath,[10] for it is an eternal principle that we can only receive what we are capable of receiving; and, to ask why one person does not gain any help from the mercy and goodness of God while another does gain

[1] *An Appeal to all that doubt or disbelieve the Truths of the Gospel*, *Works*, vol. VI, pp. 27–8.   [2] *The Spirit of Prayer*, *Works*, vol. VII, p. 24.
[3] *Ibid.*, p. 23.   [4] *Ibid.*, p. 20.
[5] *The Way to Divine Knowledge*, *Works*, vol. VII, pp. 138–9.
[6] See *The Spirit of Prayer*, *Works*, vol. VII, pp. 150–1.
[7] *An Appeal*, *Works*, vol. VI, p. 169.   [8] *Ibid.*, pp. 19–20.
[9] *Ibid.*, pp. 69, 80.   [10] *The Spirit of Prayer*, *Works*, vol. VII, pp. 23, 27.

help is "like asking why the refreshing dew of Heaven does not do that to flint which it does to the vegetable plant?"[1]

Self-denial and mortification of the flesh are not things imposed upon us by the mere will of God: considered in themselves, they have nothing of goodness or holiness; but they have their ground and reason in the nature of the thing, and are as "absolutely necessary to make way for the new birth, as the death of the husk and gross part of the grain is necessary to make way for its vegetable life."[2]

Law's attitude towards learning, which has been somewhat misunderstood, is a part of his belief in the "Light Within," which he shares with all mystical thinkers. In judging of what he says as to the inadequacy of book knowledge and scholarship, it is necessary to call to mind the characteristics of his age and public. When we remember the barren controversies about externals in matters religious which raged all through his lifetime, and the exaltation of the reason as the only means whereby man could know anything of the deeper truths of existence, it is not surprising that, with Law, the pendulum should swing in the opposite direction, and that, with passionate insistence, he should be driven to assert the utter inadequacy of the intellect by itself in all spiritual concerns.[3]

He, says Law, who looks to his reason as the true power and light of his nature, "betrays the same Ignorance of the whole Nature, Power and Office of Reason as if he were to smell with his Eyes, or see with his Nose."[4] All true knowledge, he urges, must come from within, it must be experienced; and, if it were not that man has the divine nature in him, no omnipotence of God could open in him the knowledge of divine things. There cannot be any knowledge of things but where the thing itself is; there cannot be any knowledge "of any unpossessed Matters, for knowledge can only be yours as *Sickness* and *Health* is yours, not conveyed to you by a Hearsay Notion, but the Fruit of your own Perception."[5]

Law, liberal scholar, clear reasoner and finished writer, was

---

[1] *The Way to Divine Knowledge, Works*, vol. VII, p. 60.
[2] *The Spirit of Prayer, Works*, vol. VII, p. 68.   See, also, *ibid.*, pp. 91–2.
[3] See *The Way to Divine Knowledge, Works*, vol. VII, pp. 118–28.
[4] *Ibid*, pp. 50–1.
[5] *Ibid.*, p. 127.

no more an enemy of learning than Ruskin was an enemy of writing and reading because he said that there were very few people in the world who got any good by either.   Their scornful remarks on these subjects often mislead their readers; yet the aim of both writers was not to belittle these things in themselves, but solely to put them in their right place.[1]

Law is among the greatest of English prose writers, and no one ever more truly possessed than he "the splendid and imperishable excellence of sincerity and strength."   Those who least understand his later views, who look upon them as "idle fancies," and on the whole subject of his mystical thought as "a melancholy topic" are constrained to admit, not only that he writes fine and lucid prose in *A Serious Call*, but that, in his mystical treatises, his style becomes mellower and rises to greater heights than in his earlier work.[2]   The reason for this cumulative richness is that the history and development of Law's prose style is the history and development of his character.   As applied to him, Buffon's epigram was strictly true. Sincerity is the keynote of his whole nature, sincerity of thought, of belief, of speech and of life.   Sincerity implies courage, and Law was a brave man, never shirking the logical outcome of his convictions, from the day when he ruined his prospects at Cambridge, to the later years when he suffered his considerable reputation to be eclipsed by his espousal of an uncomprehended and unpopular mysticism.   He had a keen, rather than a profound, intellect, and his thought is lightened by brilliant flashes of wit or of grim satire.   On this side, his was a true eighteenth century mind, logical, sane, practical, with, at the same time, a touch of whimsey, and a tendency to a quite unexpected lack of balance on certain subjects.   Underneath a severe and slightly stiff exterior lay, however, emotion, enthusiasm and great tenderness of feeling.   When he was still a young man, the logical and satirical side was strongest; in later years, this was much tempered by emotion and tenderness.

This description of Law's character might equally serve as a description of his style.   It is strong, sincere, rhythmical, but,

---

[1] See *The Way to Divine Knowledge, Works*, p. 93.

[2] See Bigg, Charles, in his introduction to *A Serious Call*, pp. xxv and xxviii; also, for a view of Law's later thought, Stephen, Leslie, *English Thought in the 18th Century*, vol. II, pp. 405–9.

except under stress of feeling, not especially melodious. A certain stiffness and lack of adaptability, which was characteristic of the man, makes itself felt in his prose, in spite of his free use of italics and capital letters. Law's first object is to be explicit, to convey the precise shade of his meaning, and, for this purpose, he chooses the most homely similes, and is not in the least afraid of repetition, either of words or thoughts. A good instance of his method, and one which illustrates his disregard for iteration, his sarcastic vein and his power of expressing his meaning in a simile, is the parable of the pond in *A Serious Call*, which was versified by Byrom.[1]

Again, if you should see a man that had a large *pond* of *water*, yet living in continual thirst, not suffering himself to drink *half a draught*, for fear of lessening his pond; if you should see him wasting his time and strength, in *fetching more* water to his pond, always *thirsty*, yet always carrying a *bucket* of water in his hand, watching early and late to catch the *drops* of rain, gaping after every cloud, and running greedily into every *mire* and *mud*, in hopes of water, and always studying how to make every *ditch* empty itself into his *pond*. If you should see him grow *grey* and *old* in these anxious labours, and at last end a *careful*, *thirsty* life, by falling into his own *pond*, would you not say, that such a one was not only the author of all his own disquiets, but was foolish enough to be reckoned amongst *idiots* and *madmen?* But yet foolish and absurd as this character is, it does not represent half the follies, and absurd disquiets of the *covetous man*.

Law's use of simile and analogy in argument is characteristic. By means of it, he lights up his position in one flash, or with dexterity lays bare an inconsistency. His use of analogies between natural, and mental and spiritual, processes is frequent, and is applied with power in his later writings, when the oneness of law in the spiritual and natural worlds became the very ground of his philosophy. He had the command of several instruments and could play in different keys. *Remarks upon the Fable of the Bees* (1723), and *The Spirit of Prayer* (1749–50), while exhibiting different sides of the man, are excellent examples of the variety and range of his prose. The earlier work is biting, crisp, brilliant and severely logical, written in pithy

[1] Cf. *The Pond*, in *The Poems of John Byrom* (Chetham Society, 1894), part 1, pp. 196–202.

sentences and short paragraphs, containing a large proportion of words of one syllable, the printed page thus presenting to the eye quite a different appearance from that of his later work. *Remarks* displays to the full Law's peculiar power of illustrating the fallacy of an abstract argument, by embodying it in a concrete example. Mandeville's poem is a vigorous satire in the Hudibrastic vein, and, in Law's answer, it called out the full share of the same quality which he himself possessed. "Though I direct myself to you," he begins, in addressing Mandeville, "I hope it will be no Offence if I sometimes speak as if I was speaking to a Christian." The two assertions of Mandeville which Law is chiefly concerned to refute are that man is only an animal, and morality only an imposture. "According to this Doctrine," he retorts, "to say that a Man is dishonest, is making him just such a Criminal as a Horse that does not dance." This is the kind of unerring homely simile which abounds in Law's writing, and which reminds us of the swift and caustic wit of Mrs. Poyser. Other examples could be cited to illustrate the pungency and raciness of Law's style when he is in the mood for logical refutation. But it is only necessary to glance at the first half page of *The Spirit of Prayer* to appreciate the marked difference in temper and phrasing. The early characteristics are as strong as ever; but, in addition, there is a tolerance, a tender charm, an imaginative quality and a melody of rhythm rarely to be found in the early work. The sentences and phrases are longer, and move to a different measure; and, all through, the treatise is steeped in mystic ardour, and, while possessed of a strength and beauty which Plotinus himself has seldom surpassed, conveys the longing of the soul for union with the Divine.

In *A Serious Call*, Law makes considerable use of his power of character drawing, of which there are indications already in *Christian Perfection*. This style of writing, very popular in the seventeenth century, had long been a favourite method for conveying moral instruction, and Law uses it with great skill. His sketches of Flavia and Miranda, "the heathen and Christian sister" as Gibbon calls them, are two of the best known and most elaborate of his portraits. Law's foolish, inconsistent and selfish characters, such as the woman of fashion, the scholar, the country gentleman or the man of affairs, are more true to

life, and, indeed, more sympathetic to frail humanity, than the
few virtuous characters he has drawn.   This is a key, perhaps,
to the limitations of Law's outlook, and, more especially, of his
influence; for, in his view, a man's work in the world, and his
more mundane characteristics, are as nothing, so that one good
person is precisely like another.   Thus, a pious physician is
acceptable to God as pious, but not at all as a physician. [1]

A Serious Call, as a whole, is a fine example of Law's middle
style, grave, clear and rhythmical, with the strong sarcastic
tendency restrained; not, on the one hand, so brilliant as the
Remarks, nor, on the other, so illumined as *The Spirit of Prayer*.
Yet, it throbs with feeling, and, indeed, as Sir Leslie Stephen—
himself not wholly in sympathy with it—has finely said, its
"power can only be adequately felt by readers who can study it
on their knees."   One can well imagine how repugnant it would
have been to the writer that such a work should be criticised or
appraised from a purely literary point of view; and yet, if
William Law had not been a great literary craftsman, the lofty
teaching of his *Serious Call* would not have influenced, as it has,
entire generations of English-speaking people.

On the whole, the distinguishing and peculiar characteristic
of Law as a prose writer is that, for the most part, he is occupied
with things which can only be experienced emotionally and
spiritually, and that he treats them according to his closely
logical habit of mind.   The result is an unusual combination of
reason and emotion which makes appeal at once to the intellect
and the heart of the reader.

Although Law's spiritual influence in his own generation
was probably more profound than that of any other man of his
day, yet he had curiously few direct followers.   It is easy to see
that he was far too independent a thinker to be acceptable even
to the high churchmen whose cause he espoused, and, though he
was greatly revered by methodists and evangelists, his later
mysticism was wholly abhorrent to them. [2]   The most famous
members of the little band of disciples who visited him at
Putney were the Wesleys, John and Charles, who, two or three
times yearly, used to travel the whole distance from Oxford on

[1] See Bigg's introduction to *A Serious Call*, 1899, p. xxix.
[2] See Overton, chap. XXI, Law's opponents.

foot in order to consult their "oracle."[1]   Later, however, there
was a rupture between them, when Wesley, on his return from
Georgia in 1738, having joined the Moravians, seems suddenly
to have realised, and to have contended, in very forcible language, that, although Law, in his books (*A Christian Perfection*
and *A Serious Call*), put a very high ideal before men, he had,
nevertheless, omitted to emphasise that the only means of
attaining it was through the atonement of Christ.[2]   This was
largely the quarrel of Wesley, as, also, of the later methodists,
with mysticism in general; "under the term mysticism," he
writes from Georgia, "I comprehend those and only those who
slight any of the means of grace."[3]

George Cheyne, fashionable doctor, vegetarian and mystic,
was another of Law's friends at this time; but the most charming and most lovable of his followers was his devoted admirer,
John Byrom.   The relationship between these two men much
resembles that of Johnson and Boswell, and we find the same
outspoken brusqueness, concealing a very real affection, on the
part of the mentor, with the same unswerving devotion and
zealous record of details—even of the frequent snubs received—
on the part of the disciple.   Byrom, in many ways, reminds us
of Goldsmith; he possesses something of the artless simplicity,
the rare and fragrant charm, which is the outcome of a sincere
and tender nature; he has many forgivable foibles and weaknesses, a delightful, because completely natural, style in prose
and a considerable variety of interests and pursuits.   He
travelled abroad and studied medicine, and, though he never
took a medical degree, he was always called Doctor by his
friends; he was an ardent Jacobite, a poet, a mystic and the
inventor of a system of shorthand, by the teaching of which
he increased his income until, in 1740, he succeeded to the
family property near Manchester.

Byrom, though a contemporary of Law at Cambridge,
evidently did not know him personally until 1729, and his first

---

[1] *Works*, vol. IX, Letter IX, p. 123.

[2] For a full account of the relations of Wesley and Law, and the text of their
two famous letters, see Overton, pp. 80–92, and see, also, the account in Byrom's
Journal, vol. II, part I, pp. 268–70.

[3] See Byrom's *Journal*, vol. II, part I, p. 181, and for later methodist views,
The Life of the Rev. Charles Wesley, by Thomas Jackson, 1841, vol. I, pp. 52, 53, 112,
113.

recorded meeting with his hero, as, also, the later ones, form some of the most attractive passages of an entirely delightful and too little known book, *The Private Journal and Literary Remains of John Byrom*. It is from this journal that we gather most of our information about Law at Putney, and from it that, incidentally, we get the fullest light on his character and personality.

On 15 February, 1729, Byrom bought *A Serious Call*, and, on the following 4 March, he and a friend named Mildmay went down in the Fulham coach to Putney to interview the author. This was the beginning of an intimacy which lasted until Law's death, and which was founded on a strong community of tastes in matters of mystical philosophy, and on the unswerving devotion of Byrom to his "master."[1] They met at Cambridge, where Byrom gave shorthand lessons, and Law shepherded his unsatisfactory pupil; at Putney, in Somerset gardens and, later, at King's Cliffe.[2]

Byrom, though scarcely a poet, for he lacked imagination, had an unusual facility for turning everything into rime. He sometimes wrote in very pleasing and graceful vein,[3] and he had an undoubted gift of epigram;[4] but he was particularly fond of making verse paraphrases of prose writings, and especially of those of William Law. His two finest pieces of this kind are *An Epistle to a Gentleman of the Temple* (1749), which versifies Law's *Spirit of Prayer;* and the letter on *Enthusiasm* (1752), founded on the latter part of Law's *Animadversions upon Dr. Trapp's Reply*. This last poem is written with admirable clearness and point; Law's defence of enthusiasm is one of the best things he wrote, and Byrom does full justice to it. "Enthusiasm," meaning, more especially "a misconceit of inspiration,"[5] the laying claim to peculiar divine guidance or

[1]   " O how much better he from whom I draw
        Though deep yet clear his system—'Master Law.'
        Master I call him . . ."   (*Epistle to a Gentleman of the Temple*.)

[2] See, for an example of their conversations, which, in the variety of its topics, and distinctive character of its sentiments, throws much light on Law's thoughts and ideals, that of Saturday, 7 June, 1735.

[3] Especially in his song "Why prithee now" (*Poems*, I, 115), or his early pastoral, "My Time, O ye Muses."

[4] As in the famous lines upon Handel and Bononcini, often attributed to Swift (*Poems*, I, 35), and the Pretender toast (*Poems*, I, 572).

[5] Henry More, *Enthusiasmus Triumphatus*, 1662, § 2.

"inner light," resulting in anything approaching fanaticism or even emotion, was a quality equally abhorred and feared in the eighteenth century by philosophers, divines and methodists, indeed, by everyone except mystics. The first care of every writer and thinker was to clear himself of any suspicion of this "horrid thing."[1] Law's argument, which is to the effect that enthusiasm is but the kindling of the driving desire or will of every intelligent creature, is well summarised by Byrom:—

> Think not that you are no Enthusiast, then!
> All Men are such, as sure as they are Men.
> The Thing itself is not at all to blame
> 'T is in each State of human Life the same,
>
> That which concerns us therefore, is to see
> What Species of Enthusiasts we be.[2]

Byrom hoped that, by turning them into verse, Law's later teachings might reach a larger public,[3] and, in this, Law evidently agreed with him, looking upon him as a valuable ally. Byrom's work certainly did not lack appreciation by his contemporaries; Warburton—who had no cause to love him—thought highly of it, and Wesley, who ascribes to him all the wit and humour of Swift, together with much more learning, says that in his poems are "some of the noblest truths expressed with the utmost energy of language, and the strongest colours of poetry."[4]

Henry Brooke[5] was another writer who was deeply imbued with Boehme's thought, and his expression of it, imbedded in that curious book *The Fool of Quality* (1766–70), reached,

---

[1] Bishop Butler, when talking once to Wesley, exclaimed, "Sir, the pretending to extraordinary revelation or gifts of the Holy Ghost is a horrid thing, a very horrid thing." For an admirable account of "Enthusiasm," see *The English Church in the 18th Century*, by Abbey and Overton, vol. I, chap. IX; also a note by Ward, A. W., in Byrom's *Poems*, vol. II, pt. I, pp. 169–79; and a note by Hill, G. Birkbeck, in Gibbon's *Memoirs*, 1900, p. 22.

[2] Byrom's *Poems*, II, I, pp. 190–1.

[3]   "Since different ways of telling may excite
         In different minds Attention to what 's right,
         And men (I measure by myself) sometimes,
         Averse to Reas'ning, may be taught by Rimes." *Poems*, II, I, 164.

[4] Wesley's *Journal*, Monday, 12 July, 1773.

[5] The uncle of the Henry Brooke of Dublin, who knew Law and greatly admired him.

probably, a larger public than did Law's mystical treatises.[1]
In many ways, Brooke must have been a charming character, original, tender-hearted, overflowing with sentiment, but
entirely incapable of concentration or even continuity of
thought. His book is a brave one, full of high ideals. It is an
extraordinary mixture of schoolboy pranks, romantic adventures, stories—ancient and modern—ethical dialogues, dissertations on mystical philosophy, political economy, the British
constitution, the relation of the sexes, the training of a gentleman and many other topics. Mr. Meekly and Mr. Fenton
(or Clinton) are Brooke's two exponents of a very general and
diluted form of "Behmenism." The existence of the two wills,
the formation of Christ within the soul, the reflection of God's
image in matter as in a mirror, the nature of beauty, of man
and of God, the fall of Lucifer and the angels, and of Adam—
all these things are discussed and explained in mystical language, steeped in emotion and sentiment.[2]

The Fool of Quality found favour with John Wesley, who
reprinted it in 1781, under the title *The History of Henry Earl
of Moreland*. In doing this, he reduced it from five volumes to
two, omitting, as he says in his preface, "a great part of the
mystic Divinity, as it is more philosophical than Scriptural."
He goes on to speak of the book with the highest praise, "I
now venture to recommend the following Treatise as the most
excellent in its kind of any that I have seen, either in the English, or any other language"; its greatest excellence being "that
it continually strikes at the heart. . . . I know not who can
survey it with tearless eyes, unless he has a heart of stone."
Launched thus, with the *imprimatur* of their great leader, it
became favourite reading with generations of devout Wesley-
ans, and, in this form, passed through many editions.[3]

Mystics, unlike other thinkers, scientific or philosophical,

---

[1] Brooke also wrote a large number of plays and poems, two of the latter being
full of mystical thought, *Universal Beauty* (1735–6) and *Redemption* (1772). As
to Brooke's novels cf. Vol. X, Chapter III, *post*.

[2] See *The Fool of Quality*, ed. Baker, E. A., 1906, pp. 30, 31, 33, 39, 133–6, 142,
258–60, 328–30, 336, 367–9, 394.

[3] Wesley's alterations in wording are most instructive and interesting, for he
has not hesitated to alter as well as to omit passages. Cf. Clinton's account of the
nature of man and God in Wesley, ed. of 1781, vol. II, pp. 286–7, with Brooke, 1 vol.
ed. 1906, p. 367.

have little chronological development, since mysticism can neither age nor die. They rarely found schools of thought in their own day. It is, therefore, not surprising that, in spite of various strains of a mystic tendency, the mysticism of Law and his small circle of followers had no marked influence on the main stream of eighteenth century thought. The atmosphere of the age was antagonistic to it, and it remained an undercurrent only, the impulse given by Law in this direction spending itself finally among little-known dreamers and eccentrics.[1]

Later, some of the root-ideas of Boehme returned to England by way of Hegel, Schelling, Jung-Stilling and Friedrich Schlegel, or through Boehme's French disciple, Louis-Claude de Saint-Martin. They influenced Coleridge,[2] and profoundly modified nineteenth century conceptions, thus preparing the way for the better understanding of mystical thought. Blake's prophetic books are only now, after a hundred years, beginning to find readers, and, undoubtedly, Law's *Appeal*, if it were more widely known, would, in the twentieth century, win the response for which it has long been waiting.

---

[1] As, for instance, Francis Okely, or, later, J. P. Greaves and Christopher Walton. There remains, however, to be traced an influence which bore fruit in the nineteenth century. Thomas Erskine of Linlathen was indebted to both Law and Boehme, and he, in his turn, influenced F. D. Maurice and others.

[2] Coleridge also knew both Law and Boehme at first hand; for his appreciation of them see *Biographia Literaria*, chap. IX, *Aids to Reflexion*, conclusion, and notes to Southey's *Life of Wesley*, 3rd ed., 1846, vol. I, p. 476. For his projected work on Boehme, and in connection with his philosophy, see letter to Lady Beaumont, 1810, in *Memorials of Coleorton*, ed. Knight, W., 1887, vol. II, pp. 105-7.

CHAPTER XIII

Scholars and Antiquaries

I. Bentley and Classical Scholarship

A T the end of the seventeenth century, the history of scholarship is illuminated by the great name of Richard Bentley. From 1699, when his *Dissertation on the Epistles of Phalaris* was published, until the end of his long life in 1742, each successive work that came from his pen was expected with impatience and welcomed with enthusiasm by the learned all over Europe, who, by their common use of Latin, were able more easily than now to understand and to communicate with each other.

When Bentley was born in 1662, there were already men in England of great learning. But most of these busied themselves with theology, chronology and patristic study rather than with the classical authors. Five names may be mentioned here. The first of these is John Pearson, successively master of Trinity college, Cambridge, and bishop of Chester. The *Exposition of the Creed* and the *Vindication* of certain epistles attributed to Ignatius of Antioch, have been already treated in an earlier volume.[1] Bentley wrote of him as "the most excellent Bishop Pearson, the very dust of whose writings is gold." John Fell was successively dean of Christ Church and bishop of Oxford. His chief work is a critical edition of the works of Cyprian. The epigram by which his name is chiefly known at the present day was probably written by Tom Brown, while an undergraduate at Christ Church.[2] William Lloyd, bishop of St. Asaph and, later, of Worcester, is famous as one

---

[1] See *ante*, Vol. VIII, pp. 339–340.   [2] As to Fell, cf. *ante*, Vol. VII p. 513.

of the seven bishops. He wrote chiefly on church history and is appealed to by Bentley as "that incomparable historian and chronologer." Henry Dodwell was elected Camden professor of history at Oxford in 1688. The most important of his very numerous works discussed ancient chronology; and Bentley, in his *Phalaris*, while controverting Dodwell's views, constantly refers to his book *De Cyclis*, then in the press, as "that noble work," and to the author as "the very learned Mr. Dodwell." John Moore was bishop of Ely and, as such, became Bentley's judge in 1710. His library, one of the best collections of books and MSS. in Europe, was eventually presented by George I to Cambridge university.

Richard Bentley was born on 27 January, 1662, at Oulton, in Yorkshire, and educated at Wakefield grammar school and St. John's college, Cambridge. He took the degree of B. A. with distinction in 1680 and, after acting for about a year as master of Spalding school, was chosen as tutor to his son by Stillingfleet, then dean of St. Paul's and, from 1689, bishop of Worcester. For six years Bentley was a member of Stillingfleet's household. The dean's library was famous and now forms part of archbishop Marsh's library in Dublin; but one may suppose that these books have never again found a reader so ardent and so apt as Bentley. Johnson once said to Boswell that he had never known a man who studied hard, but that he concluded, from the effects, that some men had done so; and he named Bentley as an example. This may be illustrated by Bentley's own words:

I wrote, before I was twenty-four years of age, a sort of *Hexapla;* a thick volume in quarto, in the first column of which I inserted every word of the Hebrew Bible alphabetically; and, in five other columns, all the various interpretations of those words in the Chaldee, Syriac, Vulgate Latin, Septuagint, and Aquila, Symmachus, and Theodotion, that occur in the whole Bible.

Yet biblical study was only a small part of Bentley's labours.

In 1689, when young Stillingfleet went to Oxford, Bentley went with him and became a member of the university. To him, one of the chief attractions of the place must have been the Bodleian library. Two years later appeared his first published work, the *Epistola ad Millium.*

The Sheldonian press was about to print a manuscript chronicle by a medieval writer named Joannes Malelas; and John Mill, famous for his critical edition of the New Testament, sent the proof-sheets of Malelas to Bentley, on condition that he should contribute something to the book. Of the published book, the last hundred pages are taken up by Bentley's Latin letter. Of the many subjects discussed in the *Epistola*, the chief are the plays of the Attic dramatists and the lexicon of Hesychius. Bentley's *Epistola* gave evidence of a knowledge which embraced all the known writers of antiquity and extended even to the unprinted MSS. of the Oxford libraries. But it showed more than this: Bentley was absolute master of his erudition and could apply it with the nicest precision to solve the problems presented by his author. The Greek texts which he quoted were often so corrupt as to be unintelligible; but, again and again, he restored meaning by emendations as certain as they are wonderful. For such work as this, he had one immense advantage over all his predecessors: he had learnt for himself the laws of Greek metre, which were very imperfectly understood even by such men as Grotius and Casaubon. The whole work bears, in the highest degree, the impress of conscious power. It was soon perceived by the few men in Europe who were competent to judge what Bentley had done that a star of the first magnitude had risen above the horizon.

In 1692, when Robert Boyle, eminent as a natural philosopher, had left money to found a lectureship in defence of the Christian religion, Bentley, who had now been ordained, was chosen as the first lecturer. He delivered eight lectures in two London churches, taking as his subject "A confutation of Atheism." The last three lectures drew arguments from the "origin and frame of the world"; and, for this part of his work, Bentley sought the aid of Isaac Newton, whose *Principia* had been published five years before. Newton sent full replies to Bentley's inquiries and expressed satisfaction that his discoveries should be used as an argument against atheism. Bentley showed great power as a controversialist: his argument, acute and logical, is expressed in a style of remarkable force and vigour. The lectures were printed at once and soon translated into Latin, French, German and Dutch.

Bentley was now a man of mark; and, in 1694, he was

appointed keeper of the royal libraries, with official lodgings in St. James's palace. We learn from one of his letters that a small group of his friends were in the habit of meeting there once or twice a week; their names were John Evelyn, John Locke, Christopher Wren and Isaac Newton.

From his Boyle lectures, he went back to the Greek poets. John George Graevius, professor at Utrecht and the foremost Latin scholar of the day, was about to issue an edition of Callimachus; and Bentley undertook to collect for this work all the fragments of Callimachus extant in Greek literature. Graevius, who had read the *Epistola ad Millium* with the keenest enthusiasm, expected much of Bentley and got even more than he expected. For Bentley discovered twice as many fragments as had been previously known; his metrical knowledge enabled him, in many cases, to correct them where corrupt; and his penetration could often point out the relation of one fragment to another. No such collection of the fragments of a classical author had ever been seen. Until his death in 1703 Graevius remained one of Bentley's heartiest admirers.

The time was now coming when Bentley's friends were to be put to the proof. By no fault of his own, he became involved in a famous controversy, in which he was supposed, by the ignorant, to have had the worst of it, although, in fact, he was completely victorious over his antagonists and, in the course of his reply, also made an immense contribution to the knowledge of antiquity.

The subject of this controversy was the genuineness of certain letters attributed to Phalaris, the half-legendary ruler of Agrigentum, who roasted his enemies in a brazen bull. An idle comparison between ancient and modern learning, begun in France, had spread to England; and Sir William Temple, then eminent as a man of letters, published an essay, in 1690, in which he gave the preference to ancient literature, in general, and praised the letters of Phalaris, in particular, as superior to anything since written of the same kind. Temple's essay having turned attention to Phalaris, a new edition of the letters was published in 1695 by Charles Boyle, then an undergraduate at Christ Church, a grandnephew of Robert Boyle, the founder of the lectures. In his preface, the editor made an insulting reference to Bentley and complained of his discourteous conduct in refusing the use of a MS. of Phalaris kept in the royal library. Bentley wrote at once to Boyle, explaining that there had been a mistake, and that he had intended no discourtesy; but Boyle, acting on the advice of others, refused to make any amends. His reply was practically a defiance to Bentley to do his worst. Bentley was the last man to swallow such an insult, and it was not long before he had an opportunity to say something for himself. His friend, William Wotton, had, in 1694, entered the lists against Sir William Temple in defence of modern learning; and, in 1697, a second edition of his book included an appendix in which Bentley briefly stated his proofs that the letters of Phalaris were spurious, and then gave the true version of the affair of the MS. But he went further: in language of decided asperity, he pointed out errors in Boyle's edition, blaming his teachers for them more than "the young gentleman" himself.

By some of the resident members of Christ Church, this censure was bitterly resented; and it was determined to crush Bentley. The members of this society were numerous and united by an unusually strong corporate feeling, as nearly all of them had been educated at Westminster. Though, in point of learning, they were children compared to Bentley, yet they were formidable antagonists in any controversy at the bar of public opinion. They were wits and men of the world; they had much influence in literary and academic circles; and, though their erudition was meagre, they showed a marvellous dexterity in the use of what they had. The ringleader in the conspiracy against Bentley was Francis Atterbury:[1] of the book, which appeared in 1698 and bore the name of Charles Boyle, he wrote the greater part and revised the whole.

This joint production, to which Boyle seems to have contributed nothing except his name, was read with avidity by a public quite incompetent to judge of the matter in dispute. The book had merits which all could understand: in a polished and pleasant style, it exhausted every art of the controversialist in throwing ridicule on Bentley as a dull pedant without the manners of a gentleman or the taste of a genuine man of letters. Nor was ridicule the only weapon employed: charges of dis-

---

[1] As to Atterbury see the chapter *Divines of the Church of England* in Vol. X, *post.*

honesty, plagiarism and even heterodoxy were scattered up and down its pages. Public opinion, prejudiced in Boyle's favour by his youth and high birth, soon declared decisively against Bentley. It was at this time that Swift, then residing in Sir William Temple's family, ridiculed Bentley in his *Battle of the Books;* and Garth's poem, *The Dispensary*, published in 1699, is chiefly remembered by the foolish couplet in which he expressed his agreement with the prevailing sentiment of polite society:

> So diamonds take a lustre from their foil,
> And to a Bentley 't is we owe a Boyle.

Atterbury and his friends had good reason to suppose that they had crushed Bentley and destroyed not only his reputation for learning but, also, his character.

But it was not easy to crush Bentley. It was about this time that he replied to the condolence of a friend: "Indeed, I am in no pain about the matter; for it is a maxim with me that no man was ever written out of reputation but by himself." He set to work to revise and enlarge what he had already written about Phalaris, and his full reply appeared early in 1699. The *Dissertation* did not instantly convert public opinion to Bentley's side; but competent scholars, not, at that day, a large company, saw at once that Bentley had not only disproved for ever the authenticity of the letters of Phalaris, but had also made large additions to the sum of existing knowledge on every subject which he had occasion to discuss. Nor was it in learning only that Bentley's immense superiority was shown: he was a far more cogent reasoner than his assailants; his language, if sometimes severe, was nowhere scurrilous; and he even came near to beating the Oxford men with their own weapon of ridicule. If he could not rival the rapier thrust of Atterbury, he made uncommonly pretty play with his quarter-staff and brought it down again and again with astonishing precision on the heads of his antagonists.

It is needless here to review the different matters illuminated by Bentley in the course of his discussion. It will be more to the purpose to quote two passages which illustrate his view of language and of literature. Discussing the Greek in which the *Epistles* are written, he says:

Even the Attic of the true Phalaris's age is not there represented, but a more recent idiom and style, that by the whole thread and colour of it betrays itself to be many centuries younger than he. Every living language, like the perspiring bodies of living creatures, is in perpetual motion and alteration; some words go off and become obsolete; others are taken in and by degrees grow into common use; or, the same word is inverted to a new sense and notion, which in tract of time makes as observable a change in the air and features of a language as age makes in the lines and mien of a face. All are sensible of this in their own native tongues, where continual use makes every man a critic. For what Englishman does not think himself able, from the very turn and fashion of the style, to distinguish a fresh English composition from another a hundred years old? Now, there are as real and sensible differences in the several ages of Greek, were there as many that could discern them. But very few are so versed and practised in that language as ever to arrive at that subtilty of taste.

The second extract describes the matter of the *Epistles* and directly contradicts the well-turned sentences in which Temple had expressed his worthless opinion of their unequalled merit:

'It would be endless to prosecute this part and show all the silliness and impertinency in the matter of the *Epistles*. For, take them in the whole bulk, they are a fardle of commonplaces, without any life or spirit from action and circumstance. Do but cast your eye upon Cicero's letters, or any statesman's, as Phalaris was: what lively characters of men there! what descriptions of place! what notifications of time! what peculiarity of circumstances! what multiplicity of designs and events! When you return to these again, you feel, by the emptiness and deadness of them, that you converse with some dreaming pedant with his elbow on his desk, not with an active, ambitious tyrant, with his hand on his sword, commanding a million of subjects.'

In the same year (1699) Bentley received a practical proof of the estimate formed of his character and learning by men who were learned themselves. The two archbishops, with bishops Burnet, Lloyd, Stillingfleet and Moore, had been appointed by king William to act as a commission for filling offices in the gift of the crown; and, by their unanimous vote, Bentley was appointed to the mastership of Trinity college, Cambridge. He was admitted to his new office on 1 February,

1700. It is not the business of this narrative to describe the war which began at once and went on for thirty-eight years between Bentley and the fellows of Trinity college. It is enough to say that Bentley was twice tried for his misdemeanours before judges who cannot be suspected of any bias against him, and twice sentenced to be deprived of his office. In each case, the judge was the bishop of Ely, who had been declared visitor of the college. In 1714, bishop Moore, who had been one of Bentley's electors fourteen years before, died before he could pronounce the judgment which he had written. In 1734, bishop Greene pronounced sentence of deprivation; yet Bentley's ingenuity and pertinacity proved equal even to this emergency, and he remained at Trinity lodge until his death in 1742. But the inscription placed upon his grave in the chapel denies, by its wording, his right to be called master of the college. In his conduct as master, there is much that is inexcusable; but the worst feature is his sordid rapacity. This ugly vice seems alien to his character, which, if proud and overbearing, showed a marked strain of magnanimity in most of the circumstances of his life.

But there is another and a more agreeable side to Bentley's life during these forty-two years. He did much to reform the discipline and promote the studies of the undergraduates. He showed great zeal in encouraging learning; and it is a remarkable proof of the largeness of his mind that he was quite as favourable to other studies as to those in which he had made his own reputation. Thus, the first lectures delivered by Vigani as professor of chemistry (1702) were given in a laboratory (then called an elaboratory) fitted up by Bentley in the rooms now occupied by the bursar at Trinity. For Roger Cotes, Newton's greatest pupil, he built an observatory over the central gate of the college. His urgent pressure induced the reluctant Newton to prepare the second and improved edition of the *Principia*, in 1713; and he himself defrayed the cost of the publication. In 1705, he brought Henry Syke, a learned orientalist, from Utrecht to be Hebrew professor at Cambridge and made him a tutor of Trinity. To Ludolf Küster, a Westphalian scholar then residing in Cambridge, he gave such help as no other man living could have given, for his editions of Suidas and Aristophanes. More than all this,

Bentley set a great example to an academic society by the devotion of his whole life to study. He never went abroad; it seems that, after his marriage in 1701, he never left Cambridge except for London, where he had still an official residence as royal librarian; he took no exercise except a walk in his garden; he never appeared at social gatherings, though he enjoyed the society of a few intimate friends at his own house. The business of his life was to exhaust learning; and he said he should be willing to die at 80, as he should then have read everything worth reading. The books which he published must not be supposed to mark the limits of his study. Thus, he devoted years of labour to Homer and to the text of the Greek Testament; and, though he published nothing in either subject, the manuscript materials which he left have profoundly affected the subsequent study of both. Everything which he wrote for the press was prepared in great haste; and his enemies said, with some appearance of truth, that his main motive for appearing in print was his wish to conciliate public opinion, when one of his many law-suits seemed likely to go against him. He probably regarded his books as an interruption to the more pressing business of study. Still, they are the landmarks of his life; and a short account will be given here of the works published by him after 1700.

The first of these was polemical and appeared at Utrecht in 1710, under the pseudonym Phileleutherus Lipsiensis. A certain John Le Clerc, who, with little real learning of any kind, had contrived to become a considerable figure in European literature, undertook, in an evil hour, to edit the fragments of Menander and Philemon. Of his qualifications for the enterprise, it is enough to say that he knew little of the Greek language and nothing of Greek metre. Bentley wrote out in great haste comments upon 323 of the fragments, exposing the incompetence of the editor and suggesting corrections of his own. He then sent the manuscript to Peter Burmann at Utrecht by the hands of Francis Hare, then serving as chaplain-general to Marlborough's army. Burmann published the notes with a preface of his own. It was at once recognised as Bentley's work and eagerly read: in three weeks, there was not a copy to be had. The unerring sagacity of the critic and the liveliness of the style make it one of the most attractive of Bentley's books.

In 1711 appeared his *Horace*. It was dedicated to Harley, the tory prime minister, of whose powerful aid Bentley was then sorely in need, at a critical stage in his battle with the college. Horace was the first Latin author whom Bentley had edited: till then, his published work had dealt mainly with Greek writers. The object aimed at was a complete revision of the text, and all accessible authorities were used for the purpose; but Bentley relied more upon his power of emendation than upon any MSS. His *Horace* presented over 700 unfamiliar readings; and these novelties, instead of being relegated to the foot of the page, were promoted to the text. All the old power and erudition were shown in the notes in which the editor sought to justify his innovations. The reader who is inclined to reject some change proposed turns to the note and finds it almost impossible to resist the dialectical force of the editor. But there are faults in this work which had not been conspicuous before in Bentley's books—arrogance in asserting his own merits and a tendency to think more of exhibiting his own skill in argument than of discovering what his author really wrote. For the first time, too, he begins to force upon the author his own standards of taste, a fault which betrayed him later into the great literary blunder of his life. The book brought him much praise and as much criticism. The two are pleasantly combined in the language of Atterbury, now dean of Christ Church and on civil terms with Bentley, when he acknowledged the gift of a copy:

I am indebted to you, Sir, for the great pleasure and instruction I have received from that excellent performance; though at the same time I cannot but own to you the uneasyness I felt when I found how many things in Horace there were, which, after thirty years' acquaintance with him, I did not understand.

Bentley's next book was published under his old pseudonym Phileleutherus Lipsiensis; but, this time, the language was English and very racy English too. *A Discourse of Free-thinking*, an anonymous work by Anthony Collins, appeared in 1713, and was instantly followed by a swarm of refutations. But all these were eclipsed by Bentley's *Remarks*. Collins had appealed to antiquity in support of his opinions; but he did not know Greek or Latin well enough to draw the true conclusions from his authors. Here, Bentley was in his element: he lays about him with rare zest and had no difficulty in showing that Collins had undertaken "to interpret the Prophets and Solomon without Hebrew, Plutarch and Zosimus without Greek, and Cicero and Lucan without Latin." He treats the anonymous author unceremoniously enough; but his language does not go beyond what was then thought permissible and even praiseworthy in the mouth of a champion of orthodoxy. To the scholar, the chief interest of this book is to watch Bentley for once interpreting the thought, rather than the language, of the ancients. The mastery with which he extracts the whole meaning and nothing but the meaning from a difficult passage of Lucan (IX. 546-568) shows what he could have done, had he chosen, in this part of a scholar's business.

Of Bentley's edition of Terence, published in 1726, the most remarkable feature is his explanation of a problem which previous editors had declared insoluble. Bentley gave a clear statement of the principles which differentiate the metre of Plautus and Terence from that of Horace and Vergil; and, with this instrument, he was able to correct many corruptions in the text of Terence. All later discussion of this subject starts from the point where Bentley left it.

Manilius was the last Latin poet of whom a revised text was published by Bentley. Early in his career, he had prepared an edition of this poet, but "dearness of paper and the want of good types and some other occasions" prevented its appearance till 1739, when Bentley was seventy-seven years old. The astronomical poem of Manilius is difficult and the text very corrupt. To contemporary critics, the changes which Bentley made in the text seemed to pass all permissible limits. But deeply-seated corruptions cannot be cured by trifling alterations; and more than one competent judge has pronounced that Manilius, rather than Horace or Phalaris, is the chief monument of Bentley's genius.

Of the other work of Bentley's old age, it can only be said that few reputations except his own could have survived it. When the prince regent proposed that Jane Austen should write a romance to glorify the august house of Coburg, she had the good sense to decline the task; it is a pity that Bentley was not equally wise, when queen Caroline expressed her wish that he should edit Milton. The queen may have supposed that he would illustrate Milton's language from Homer and Vergil; but Bentley preferred to revise the text of *Paradise Lost*. It was a task for which he was ill equipped. His turn of mind was prosaic. He thought more of correctness than of poetry, and was quick to find "vitious construction" or "absonous numbers" where Milton rises above the laws of critics. And, though he occasionally quotes from Ariosto and Tasso, from Chaucer and Spenser, he was not really familiar with the poetry and romance which had helped to nourish the youth of Milton.

Starting from the known fact that Milton, being then blind, could not write down his verses or read his proof-sheets, Bentley discovered a large number of what he took to be errors of the amanuensis or of the printer. Next, he invented a hypothesis that some friend, employed by Milton as "editor," abused his trust by inserting in the poem many passages, and some long ones, of his own composition. Bentley professed to correct the misprints and to detect the spurious passages. Further, in very many places he frankly abandons all pretence of recovering Milton's text and corrects the poet himself. The book was published in 1732, shortly before Bentley's second trial before the bishop of Ely. The corrections were printed in the margin in italics; the insertions of the imaginary editor were enclosed between brackets and were also printed in italics; the notes at the foot of the page seek to justify the corrections and excisions.

This strange production cannot be excused on the ground that Bentley was in his dotage. The notes show that his mind was still working with the old vigour. But his undoubted superiority in a different field had apparently persuaded him that he would prove equally successful in an unfamiliar enterprise. He has generally a sort of prosaic logic on his side, and sometimes he has more. A very favourable specimen of his notes will be found on *Paradise Lost*, vi, 332, where Milton speaks of a "stream of nectarous humour" issuing from Satan's wound. Bentley notes that nectar was the drink of the gods; next he shows conclusively that Milton is translating a line in Homer, which says that the blood of the gods is ichor; and he ends by saying that Milton wrote "ichorous humour." This is a notable criticism: if Milton did not write "ichorous," he certainly should have written it.   But Bentley's very next note is typical of the perversity which runs through the whole commentary.   On the line,

And with fierce ensigns pierc'd the deep array[1]

the note is as follows:

Another Blunder again, though not quite so vile as the last. Why are Ensigns, the Colours, called fierce; the tamest things in the whole Battel?   And how could they pierce an Array that are never used for striking?   The Author gave it,

And with fierce *Onset* pierc'd the deep array.

The book was read with amazement; and, while some made fun of the author, others wrote serious refutations.   It is probable, however, that the taste of that age did not resent the outrage as keenly as we might suppose.   It is a remarkable fact that, on the margin of his own copy, Pope signified his approval of many of the new readings, though, in his published poems, he attacked Bentley repeatedly for his treatment of Milton.   Pope's hostility may have been partly inherited from Atterbury and Swift.   He had a grievance of his own as well, if the story be true that Bentley said to him of his translation of Homer: "a pretty poem, Mr. Pope, but you must not call it Homer."   When Bentley was asked, late in life, why Pope assailed him, he said: " I talked against his Homer, and the portentous cub never forgives."

Bentley wrote one piece of English verse which is preserved in Boswell's *Life of Johnson*.   Johnson praised the verses highly on one occasion and recited them "with his usual energy."   He added: "they are the forcible verses of a man of strong mind but not accustomed to write verse; for there is some uncouthness in the expression."   The verses describe the arduous labours and scanty rewards of a scholar's life; and Johnson's praise and his blame are alike just.

Bentley died in Trinity college after a few days' illness on 14 July, 1742.   Four months earlier, Pope had published, in the fourth book of *The Dunciad*, his full-length caricature of the most famous scholar in Europe, now over eighty years old

[1] *Paradise Lost*, Bk. VI, l. 356.

It suited Pope's purpose or his humour to represent Bentley as one of the dullest of men. But the truth is that no greater intellect than his has ever been devoted to the study and elucidation of ancient literature.

Of Bentley's contemporaries at Cambridge and elsewhere, several made a reputation for learning and scholarship; and these will be briefly mentioned here. Of Joseph Wasse, Bentley said: "When I die, Wasse will be the most learned man in England." He was a fellow of Queens' college and edited Sallust, besides preparing material for an edition of Thucydides. John Davies, president of Queens' college and one of Bentley's few intimates, edited many of the philosophical works of Cicero. Conyers Middleton, fellow of Trinity college and protobibliothecarius of the university (1721), bore a prominent part in the warfare against Bentley. During his lifetime, he enjoyed a great reputation as a keen controversialist and the master of an excellent style. Of his numerous works, the chief are his *Life of Cicero*, which brought him much profit, and his *Free Enquiry*, which involved him in prolonged controversy with more orthodox divines. William Warburton, bishop of Gloucester, cannot be called a scholar, in the strict sense of the word: his knowledge of the ancient languages and literature was very small. Yet he had vigour of mind and much miscellaneous reading, so that his chief work, *The Divine Legation*, was regarded by many of his contemporaries as a genuine masterpiece.

The influence of Bentley is clearly seen in the work of three Cambridge scholars who belong to the generation after him.

Jeremiah Markland, fellow of Peterhouse, had some intimacy with Bentley in his studious old age, and devoted his own life to study and retirement. He twice refused to stand for the Greek chair at Cambridge. He edited several Greek plays; but his masterpiece is his edition of the *Silvae* of Statius. It shows great acumen, together with a wide and exact knowledge of the Latin poets; and it still remains the best commentary on this author. John Taylor, fellow of St. John's college, and librarian (1732) of the university, won his reputation by learned editions of portions of the Greek orators. Richard Dawes, fellow of Emmanuel and, afterwards, a schoolmaster at Newcastle, published only one book, his *Miscellanea Critica;* but it marks a distinct advance in Greek scholarship. Though it pleases him to speak slightingly of Bentley, yet it is clear that he had studied Bentley's writings with minute attention; and thus he was enabled to make important discoveries in Greek syntax and Greek metre, which no one would have applauded more heartily than Bentley, had he lived to hear of them.

II. ANTIQUARIES

This summer [1656] came to Oxon "The Antiquities of Warwickshire," &c. written by William Dugdale, and adorn'd with many cuts. This being accounted the best book of its kind that hitherto was made extant, my pen cannot enough describe how A. Wood's tender affections and insatiable desire of knowledg were ravish'd and melted downe by the reading of that book.

It was in these words that Anthony Wood[2] greeted the appearance of a book which represented the firstfruits of a new movement in the study of local history and antiquities. This movement, which becomes noticeable in the seventeenth century, approached the subject from a new standpoint, and, in place of depending upon bald and hackneyed compilations by previous writers, sought to found its history on the study of original documents and records, supplemented by local topographical investigation. With immense industry and untiring patience, "collections" were made from every accessible source. Charters, registers, muniments, genealogies, monumental inscriptions, heraldic achievements, were all made to yield their quota; and if, in the amassing of material, the collectors were sometimes too uncritical of their "originals," or in the maze of detail have lost sight of broader issues, they at least preserved from oblivion a multitude of valuable records and paved the way for the remarkable series of county histories and other kindred works produced in the succeeding century.

The centre of the new school was at Oxford, where, since the opening of its doors in 1602, the library of Sir Thomas Bodley had been rapidly accumulating materials and extending its collections, until it became a great storehouse of sources, and

---

[1] For a list of scholars whose names belong to the history of this period of literature, but are mainly associated with studies other than classical, see the bibliography to this chapter.

[2] *Life and Times of Anthony Wood*, ed. Clark, A., vol. I, p. 209.

served as the nursing-ground of a remarkable group of men, which includes the names of Wood, Hearne, Rawlinson, and Tanner. To these may be added the author of *The Antiquities of Warwickshire*; for, though Sir William Dugdale was not an alumnus of the university, yet, during his sojourn in Oxford, in 1642–6, he fell under the spell of the Bodleian and collected there abundant material for the works he was at that time projecting.

The book which Wood greeted so enthusiastically was not undeserving of the encomium. In its fulness, its method, its reliance upon original sources, and its general accuracy, it was much beyond anything that had hitherto appeared. It set a new standard in topographical history, and inspired succeeding writers to emulate its merits. If, among its author's many works, the *Warwickshire* volume may be esteemed his master-piece, yet the book which, at the present day, most notably maintains Dugdale's fame is *Monasticon Anglicanum*, an account of English monastic houses, consisting, to a large extent, of charters of foundation and other original documents. In this undertaking, he collaborated with Roger Dodsworth, an indefatigable worker who spent his life in the study of genea-logy and ecclesiastical and monastic history, and whose enor-mous manuscript collections now repose in the Bodleian. Wood says of him[1] that "he was a person of wonderful industry, but less judgment, was always collecting and transcribing, but never published anything": a characterisation that would describe equally well many another antiquary whose ambitious schemes have failed of fruition.

The first volume of *Monasticon* appeared in 1655, the year after Dodsworth's death and just seventeen years after the authors began their joint work. The second volume, which was delayed until the sale of the first should produce funds to defray some of the expense, came out in 1661; and, in 1673, Dugdale published a third volume containing *Additamenta* and documents relating to the foundation of cathedral and collegiate churches. The precise share in this work with which the respective authors are to be credited has been, almost from the

[1] *Fasti Oxon.*, ed. Bliss, P., vol. II, p. 24.

first, a subject of controversy; but this is a matter of little moment. Dugdale claimed that a full third of the collection was his, and that the work had wholly rested on his shoulders;[1] and there can be no doubt that, apart from his contributions to the text, the work owes its appearance in print to Dugdale's energy and methodical scholarship. In 1722–3, captain John Stevens, to whom is attributed the English abridgment of *Monasticon* which appeared in 1718, brought out two supplementary volumes to the original work, containing additional charters and the records of the friaries.

By a happy chance, there came into Dugdale's hands, about the year 1656, a large collection of manuscripts and documents relating to St. Paul's cathedral, amounting "to no lesse than ten porters burthens"; and, setting to work upon these, he produced two years later his *History of St. Paul's Cathedral*, and thus preserved a valuable record of the building and monuments that were, within a few years, to be destroyed in the great fire.

The History of Imbanking and Drayning of divers Fenns and Marshes (1662), which was undertaken at the request of Lord Gorges, surveyor-general of the Bedford level, suggests a subject somewhat outside the scope of Dugdale's activities; but his wide acquaintance with manuscript sources and the contents of state archives, aided by a journey through the district in 1657, enabled him to compose a treatise abounding in historical and antiquarian interest. He takes leave to interpret the limits of his subject very widely, and is quite aware of the irrelevancy of his digressions. The isle of Ely gives an opening for narrating at large the life of Saint Audrey (translated from a Cottonian manuscript), and then follows the whole story of the feats of Hereward in defence of the isle against William the conqueror and his knights. It is in this unexpected quarter that the accomplished antiquary reveals himself as an entertaining story-teller.

Dugdale's genius for painstaking research found a thoroughly suitable theme in his *Origines juridiciales* (1666), a historical account of English laws, courts of justice, inns of court, and other cognate matters, in which is embodied much

---

[1] *Life, Diary, and Correspondence of Sir William Dugdale*, ed. Hamper, W., p. 284.

curious information respecting ancient forms and customs
observed therein; while *The Baronage of England*, which he
began during his stay in Oxford and published in 1675–6, is a
monument to his industry. His "church and king" principles
found expression in *A short view of the late troubles in England*,
which appeared anonymously in 1681, though he had not at
first intended to make it public during his lifetime.

In several respects Dugdale was particularly fortunate,
though it must be allowed that this good fortune was worthily
bestowed. Early in his career, he received help and encouragement from influential friends, notably Sir Henry Spelman and
Lord Hatton; and an official position in the College of Arms
secured for him ready access to important collections of manuscripts and records which he used to good purpose. His books
are always methodically arranged, and his text, devoid of superfluous verbiage, is carefully and fully documented by references
to his authorities. In works involving a multitude of details
and covering fields previously little explored, it is not surprising
to find that charges of inaccuracy were levelled at the author;
but, in truth, the wonder is, not that errors may be discovered,
but at the admirable work in which they are embedded. Certain lapses from a critical discernment of the evidences as to the
genuineness of documents were gently pointed out to Dugdale
in a courteous letter[1] from his friend Sir Roger Twysden,
student of constitutional law and upholder of ancient rights and
liberties. Wood, also, says that he sent Dugdale at least sixteen sheets of corrections to *The Baronage*, and he does not
hesitate to repeat other aspersions on Dugdale's accuracy; but
he concludes with this tribute:

Yet however what he hath done, is prodigious . . . and therefore his memory ought to be venerated and had in everlasting remembrance for those things which he hath already published, which
otherwise might have perished and been eternally buried in oblivion.[2]

The most prominent and characteristic name in the Oxford
group is that of Anthony Wood, or Anthony à Wood as, in later
years, he pedantically styled himself. Born in Oxford, in 1632,
he spent, practically, his whole life there, and died, in 1695,

---

[1] Hamper, *u. s.*, p. 335. [2] *Fasti, u. s.*, vol. II , p. 28.

in the house in which he was born. During his undergraduate days, he did not show any particular aptitude for academic studies; but his natural bent towards those antiquarian pursuits which afterwards claimed his whole energies soon declared itself, and at seventeen years of age he had begun to take notes of inscriptions. His graduation as B.A., in 1652, secured for him admission to the Bodleian library, "which he took to be the happiness of his life, and into which he never entred without great veneration."[1] There he browsed at large, and gave himself up to his beloved studies of English history, antiquities, heraldry, and genealogies, with music as his chief recreation.

But it seems to have been Dugdale's *Warwickshire* that gave his studies a special objective. It fired him to attempt a similar work for his own county, and, with this object, he began transcribing the monumental inscriptions and arms in the various churches. As his researches and collections progressed, the scope of his undertaking was enlarged; and, presently, his original idea of preserving a record of extant monuments developed into that of a comprehensive survey which should include the antiquities of the city, a history of the university and colleges, and the biographical records contained in his *Athenae* and *Fasti*. In pursuance of this object, he explored all accessible sources: the manuscripts in the Bodleian, including the collections of John Leland, of which he made much use, the archives of the university, to which he was allowed free access, and the muniments of the several colleges; he also visited London for the purpose of working in the libraries there.

At length, in 1669, the university treatise being completed, the university press offered to publish the work, stipulating that the author should consent to its being translated into Latin "for the honour of the University in forreigne countries." Dr. John Fell, dean of Christ Church,[2] the prime mover in this design, undertook at his own charge the translating and printing. Richard Peers and Richard Reeve were commissioned to make the Latin version, and Fell took the editing into his own hands. His high-handed methods caused the author much heart-burning, and he thus (11 August, 1670) graphically describes the situation:

---

[1] *Life, u. s.*, vol. 1, p. 182.   [2] As to Fell, cf. *ante*, Vol. VII, p. 513.

All the proofs that came from the press went thro the Doctor's hands, which he would correct, alter, or dash out or put in what he pleased, which created a great trouble to the composer and author: but there was no help. He was a great man, and carried all things at his pleasure.

Wood's diary, at this period, contains many complaints about the liberties taken with his book; and for the misdoings of Peers he cannot find words hard enough. But, in spite of his declaration that he would scarce own the book, he was not able to suppress a natural pride in the two handsome volumes which, in 1674, made their appearance under the title *Historia et Antiquitates Universitatis Oxoniensis*. Nevertheless, Wood's dissatisfaction with the Latin version was quite genuine, and, very soon afterwards, he began an English transcription of the whole work, continuing the general history to the year 1660. This recension was not printed in Wood's lifetime; but he bequeathed the manuscript to the university, and it was eventually published by John Gutch in 1786–96.

The other section of Wood's work on Oxford, *Survey of the Antiquities of the City*, or, as it was entitled in Peshall's edition, *The Antient and Present State of the City of Oxford*, was probably begun before the idea of a separate work on the university took definite form, and a considerable portion of it was written between 1661 and 1663. At this point, his interest seems to have been absorbed by the university treatise, and, though he worked on the manuscript to the end of his life, continually revising it and adding fresh notes, the scheme was never actually completed. While a certain lack of form and proportion in the work may, therefore, be disregarded, there can be no question about its value as a minute record and reconstruction of the past, the details of which were industriously garnered from a great variety of sources and carefully collated with personal investigation of the localities.

When pursuing his researches among the university archives, Wood must have come across the papers of Brian Twyne, a diligent Oxford antiquary who had done much pioneer spadework in the same field; but his diaries are curiously reticent on the subject. This silence may have been unintentional; but, as a matter of fact, he drew extensively upon this store; indeed, his latest editor[1] goes so far as to say that "there was no originality in his work, for he merely put into shape Twyne's materials." But, whatever the extent of his indebtedness, no fraudulent motive need be attributed to Wood, for he makes constant reference to Twyne, and, in freely using such materials as came in his way, he was only following the custom of the day.

At the request of the authorities, Wood had written, as an addition to the *Historia*, notices of the lives of Oxford writers, to be appended to the accounts of the respective colleges, and it may have been this task which suggested to him the idea of compiling a counterpart to the history, in the shape of an account of all the writers who had received their education at the university. This undertaking was probably even more akin to his peculiar genius than the *Historia* itself, and for some years he worked energetically at it. He searched registers and all kinds of records, made inquiries far and near, wrote letters innumerable, and received contributions from many friends and correspondents. When *Athenae Oxonienses*, the monumental work upon which his chief fame rests, at length made its appearance, its outspoken criticisms caused no little resentment in various quarters. This reception was, no doubt, anticipated, for the book was issued without the author's name, and, in the preface, endeavours were made to justify "harsh expressions" and "severe reflections," on the ground "that faults ought no more to be conceal'd than virtues, and that, whatever it may be in a painter, it is no excellence in an historian to throw a veil on deformities." But these precautions did not serve to protect the author from the consequences of reckless charges, as he found to his cost. The libel suit which was prosecuted against Wood in the vice-chancellor's court at Oxford for statements reflecting upon Edward Hyde, first earl of Clarendon, ended against him; he was expelled the university, and his book was publicly burned. It has been aptly remarked of Wood that he was "unquestionably one of the most useful of our distinguished writers," and this applies in special measure to *Athenae*. With its wealth of information concerning English authors, it is still of the highest importance, and, in its particular sphere, possibly *The Dictionary of National Biography* is

[1] Andrew Clark, in *Dict. of Nat. Biog.*, vol. LXII, *art.* Wood.

the only work that, in the course of two centuries, has taken a place beside it.

It is hardly possible to consider *Athenae* apart from the personality of the man to whom its existence is due and the impress of whose character it bears. To enormous industry and an insatiable appetite for research, Wood united a naturally ungenerous temperament and asperity of disposition, increased, in later years, by close application to study and the narrowing effects of a too exclusively academic life. Peevish and quarrelsome, disliked and mistrusted, he withdrew more and more from intercourse with his fellows and immersed himself in his self-imposed task. One can picture him in the seclusion of his garret study, penning, with keen satisfaction, severe judgments and spiteful comments upon the lives and achievements of those who did not meet with his approval. He can hardly be acquitted of malice in his animadversions, even if the saying attributed to him concerning his projected third volume of *Athenae* be apocryphal: "When this volume comes out, I 'll make you laugh again." But it must, in fairness, be observed that he did not allow the friction caused by the disposal of Sheldon's manuscripts to warp his estimate of Dugdale, and that he speaks eulogistically of bishop Fell, in spite of his high-handed mode of editing the *Historia*. His claim to a desire for truth must also be conceded to him; but truth was sometimes apt to mean an overscrupulous care lest any weight should be omitted from the adverse scale.

Wood was not only a chronicler of the past, but a recorder, also, of the passing hour, and in his autobiography and diaries we meet him at close quarters. The record is minute, at times even trivial. It embodies much interesting detail of university life; but, except for his youthful reminiscences of the civil war, glimpses of the outside world are few. He notes that Dryden was soundly cudgelled by three men one night near Will's coffee-house in Covent garden; but he seldom gives pictures like that of his meeting with Prynne, who was at that time keeper of the records and had promised to take him to the Tower. Wood, with a soupçon of his accustomed acidity, says[1] that he

---

[1] *Life, u. s.*, vol. II, p. 110.

went precisely at the time appointed, and found Mr. Prynne in his black taffaty-cloak, edg'd with black lace at the bottom. They went to the Tower directly thro the City, then lying in ruins (occasion'd by the grand conflagration that hapned in 1666); but by his meeting with several citizens and prating with them, it was about 10 of the clock before they could come to the same place.

That he is careful to place his own doings in a favourable light is only natural; but he finds pleasure in recording incidents and opinions unfavourable to others, and seems entirely devoid of both sense of humour and the milk of human kindness. We like him better and can forgive him, in a measure, when he tells of his solicitude over Dodsworth's manuscripts, and the pains he took in spreading them out on the leads to dry when they were in danger of perishing from damp. So far as Wood himself is concerned, one is tempted to think it a pity that the autobiography has been preserved, for it leaves the impression that he was a disagreeable person and that, for all his great work, he was a little soul.

Thomas Hearne, too, was a diarist; but his services to literature and learning were of a different nature from those of Wood. From his earliest youth he showed a genius for scholarship, and, shortly after taking his degree at Oxford, was appointed assistant keeper in the Bodleian library, where his energies were devoted to completing the catalogues of the printed books, the manuscripts, and the coins. One of his first essays in publication was, very fitly, commemorative of the founder of the library: *Reliquiae Bodleianae, or Some genuine remains of Sir Thomas Bodley* (1703). Next, as the outcome of his early interest in classical studies, appeared an edition of Pliny's *Epistolae et Panegyricus*, which was followed by other classical texts. *Ductor Historicus, or A short system of Universal History and an introduction to the study of it*, which he brought out in 1704–5, indicated the direction which his activities would soon take. From the original manuscripts in the Bodleian, he published, for the first time, John Leland's *Itinerary* (1710–12) and *Collectanea* (1715)—an undertaking which has indissolubly linked his name with that of the father of English antiquities.

In 1716, Hearne entered upon his important service to

historical study, the production of that admirable collection
of early English chronicle histories which, beginning with
Historia Regum Angliae of John Rous (or Ross), came from the
press in an almost uninterrupted series, down to the *Henry II
and Richard I* of Benedict, abbot of Peterborough, which bears
date 1735, the year of Hearne's death. Hardly less interesting
than the chronicles themselves is the extraordinary gathering
of tractates appended as supplements to the several volumes.
Drawn from a variety of sources, they deal with many curious
and interesting matters, often in no way related to the main
subject of the volume. Among them are a number of manuscript pieces from the collection formed by Thomas Smith, the
learned librarian of the Cottonian library, who had bequeathed
his books and manuscripts to Hearne. The speed with which
these volumes came out hardly admitted of their bearing the
character of critical editions; and, possibly, the wealth of
material which lay ready to his hand and called for publication
operated against deliberate and scholarly work, such as might
have claimed for him the title of historian, in place of the more
modest epitaph of his own choosing—"who studied and preserved antiquities."

Wood made extensive preparations for a third volume of
Athenae, which, in order to avoid interference from censors or
friends, he purposed to have had printed in Holland. But this
scheme he did not live to carry out, and, on his death-bed, he,
"with great ceremony," gave the two manuscript volumes of
this continuation to Thomas Tanner, afterwards bishop of St.
Asaph, "for his sole use, without any restrictions." In so
doing, it is probable that Wood had in view the publication of
this volume by his legatee; but, whether through being occupied
with schemes of his own, or because he did not care to take the
risk of publishing so compromising a work, Tanner took no
steps in the matter.[1]

In the same year, 1695, Tanner, then a young man in his
twenty-second year, brought out the first of his two notable
compilations. *Notitia Monastica*, founded mainly on the

[1] This additional material eventually appeared in the second edition of
Athenae, published, in 1721, by Jacob Tonson, who had acquired the copyright of
the work.

Monasticon of Dodsworth and Dugdale, gives in brief form the foundation, order, dedication, and valuation of the various religious houses in England and Wales, with references to manuscript and printed sources for fuller information. This useful manual, the idea of which was doubtless suggested by the author's own needs, did not allow any scope for original work; but a long preface afforded an opening for noticing the scanty existing literature of the subject, and adding some account of the several orders, with a sketch of the progress of monasticism in England. Tanner's insistence on the value of monastic records in the study of local history and genealogy, and his defence of monks and their learning against the wholesale blackening to which they had been subjected since the dissolution of monasteries, indicates the advance made in the general attitude towards this subject since the days when Camden and Weever had felt it necessary to apologise for making mention of monasteries. At the time of his death, the bishop had nearly completed the transcript of a revised and enlarged edition, and this was brought out by his brother, John Tanner, in 1744.

Tanner's other important work, *Bibliotheca Britannico-Hibernica*, after being in hand for forty years, at length appeared in 1748, under the editorship of David Wilkins, of *Concilia* fame. This book, in which an attempt is made to give an account of all the writers of the three kingdoms down to the beginning of the seventeenth century, long remained the best authority in its own province, and its usefulness is not yet exhausted.

Two of the chief contributors to Wood's *Athenae* were his friends Andrew Allam and John Aubrey. The former of these, though well versed in sectarian controversial writings and highly esteemed by Wood, has left nothing of his own which has found a place in literature. John Aubrey's genial and disinterested but erratic spirit did not lend itself to finished schemes, and it seems to have been his fate that his work should be incorporated in that of others. His *Perambulation of Surrey*, begun in 1673, was, eventually, included in *The Natural History and Antiquities of Surrey*, which Richard Rawlinson published in 1719; and his Wiltshire collections he turned over to Tanner, who was engaged upon the same subject; but the only outcome was the supply of some material for Gibson's edition of Camden.

The chief assistance Aubrey gave to Wood took the form of a series of *Brief Lives* of eminent persons, which, as he said in a characteristic covering letter, had been put in writing "tumultuarily, as they occur'd to my thoughts or as occasionally I had information of them." These much-quoted, haphazard, gossiping notes are full of vivid and intimate touches concerning character, actions, and personal appearance, often freely expressed but always kindly and without malice. In some of the portrait sketches, notably that of Venetia Stanley, he displays the insight of an artist; eyes have an especial attraction for him, and, occasionally, he describes them in words which are in themselves a portrait. His wide acquaintanceship enabled him to write at first hand of many of his contemporaries; and the sketches of men of an earlier generation, such as Shakespeare, Ben Jonson, Ralegh, and Bacon, may be taken to represent reports and anecdotes, more or less authentic, which were in current circulation. The longest and most important of these lives, that of Aubrey's friend Thomas Hobbes, was written at length, to furnish material for Blackburne's Latin biography of the philosopher. The only book which Aubrey himself published, *Miscellanies* (1696), reveals that susceptible side of his character which probably called down upon him Wood's epithets of "credulous" and "magotieheaded." Besides being an entertaining volume of stories, it contains much current folklore concerning omens, ghosts, second-sight and other supernatural beliefs.

Following upon the pioneer labours of Leland, Stow, Camden and Speed, and the early local monographs of Lambarde, Carew and others, progress in the study of local history and topography is marked by William Burton's *Description of Leicester Shire* (1622), and that model for county historians the *Warwickshire* of Dugdale. The second half of the seventeenth century found authors and compilers hard at work and a fever of schemes in the air; but, too often, the collector sank under the burden of his task, and the materials he amassed remained a mere mountain of notes, instead of growing into the fair and monumental edifice planned at the outset. Many of these attempts have survived in manuscript, some have been worked into later and more successful schemes, while others have served as useful quarries; and the few which achieved the distinction of print are of very varying degrees of merit and value.

One of the most extensive of these schemes was that of Robert Plot, at one time secretary to the Royal society and first keeper of the Ashmolean museum, who planned a comprehensive tour through England and Wales for the discovery and recording of antiquities, customs, and natural and artificial curiosities. So ambitious a project was, of course, never realised, but his *Natural History of Oxfordshire* (1677) and *Natural History of Staffordshire* (1686) brought him much credit, though the credulity which they display has not maintained his reputation in a more critical age. Dr. William Stukeley, antiquary and exponent of Druidism, who took an active part in the foundation of the Society of Antiquaries in 1717–8, and acted as its secretary for several years, published some of the results of his antiquarian excursions, in 1724, under the title of *Itinerarium Curiosum*, an account of antiquities and remarkable curiosities in nature or art observed in travels through Great Britain. Alexander Gordon's *Itinerarium Septentrionale* (1726), which dealt chiefly with Roman remains, was the outcome of a similar journey in Scotland and the north of England.

A book which opens with the phrase "England, the better part of the best Island in the World," could hardly fail to secure popularity; but the extraordinary success of Edward Chamberlayne's *Angliae Notitia* was, possibly, due less to this felicitous sentiment than to the practical utility of the work as a convenient handbook to the social and political state of the kingdom. No fewer than nineteen revisions were called for between 1669 and 1702; and, after the author's death in 1703, it continued in vogue in an enlarged form, as *Magnae Britanniae Notitia*, under the editorship of his son, John Chamberlayne. Its success provoked the appearance of a piratical rival, by Guy Miege, under the title *The New State of England;* and this, also, went through several editions.

Among other considerable topographical undertakings of this period was the edition of Camden's *Britannia* (1695) translated and edited by Edmund Gibson, bishop of London, Tanner's friend and fellow-worker, which included contributions by many contemporary antiquaries, and *Magna Britannia et Hibernia antiqua et nova* (1720–31), which, apparently a booksellers' venture, did not claim originality, but was an able compilation edited by Thomas Cox from published sources. Its six volumes contain only English counties.

The notes which Elias Ashmole began collecting in 1667 for *The Antiquities of Berkshire* were not printed till 1719, more than a quarter of a century after his death. Robert Thoroton published his *Antiquities of Nottinghamshire* in 1677, and James Wright's meagre *History and Antiquities of Rutland* came out in 1684. Sir Henry Chauncy's *Historical Antiquities of Hertfordshire* (1700) was followed, on the same plan, by Sir Robert Atkyns's *Ancient and present state of Glocestershire* (1712); but neither of them was a conspicuously meritorious work. Peter Le Neve's great collections for Norfolk antiquities and genealogy served as the groundwork of the *History of Norfolk* which Francis Blomefield began issuing in 1739, in monthly numbers printed at his own private press. After his death, the work was completed in 1775 in an inferior manner. Richard Rawlinson, who had a gift for editing other men's work, and who acted as foster-parent to many orphaned books, designed a parochial history of the county of Oxford, which was to have included Wood's account of the city; and the materials collected both for this work and for his projected continuation of Wood's *Athenae* form part of the immense collection of manuscripts which he bequeathed to the Bodleian library. In addition to printing Aubrey's *Surrey* (1719), Rawlinson also brought out Tristram Risdon's *Survey of Devon* (1714), and fathered separate histories of several cathedral churches, which are not especially valuable.

Individual towns received a due share of attention; among the more successful essays being William Somner's *Canterbury* (1640), Ralph Thoresby's *Leeds* (1715), and Francis Drake's *York* (1736). Stow's *Survey of London*, first published in 1598, had been already several times "augmented," before John Strype once more edited and brought it down to date in 1720. Strype's chief work, however, was in the field of ecclesiastical history and biography; but his books, ill-arranged and uncritical, are distinguished less for their literary value than for the remarkable amount of curious detail which they contain. The diocese of London found a chronicler in Richard Newcourt, who, in 1708–10, published his valuable *Repertorium Ecclesias-*

ticum Parochiale Londinense. Wood's *Oxford* has already been referred to. Thomas Baker, non-juring fellow of St. John's college, Cambridge, added to accurate and wide knowledge the character of unselfish readiness to communicate to others his stores of learning. He made extensive collections towards a history of the university of Cambridge, including an *Athenae Cantabrigienses;* but, with the exception of the admirable history of his college, published, with large additions, by J. E. B. Mayor in 1869, the forty-two folio volumes in Baker's remarkable hand-writing still remain in manuscript. His *Reflections on Learning*, which appeared anonymously in 1700 and went through seven editions, brought him considerable credit at the time, but is now happily forgotten. William Cole, the friend of Horace Walpole, ably followed Baker in the same path, and, though he published nothing, his hundred folio volumes of manuscript collections and transcripts attest his industry, and many contributions from his pen appeared in the works of contemporary writers.

In monastic antiquities, the writings of Dugdale and Tanner stand pre-eminent among the books of this period, as does Dugdale's *St. Paul's* among works devoted to particular ecclesiastical foundations. With these may be mentioned Simon Gunton's *History of the Church of Peterborough* (1686) and James Bentham's *History of Ely Cathedral* (1771). Browne Willis's *History of the Mitred Abbies* (1718), and *Survey of the Cathedrals* were useful, if not particularly accurate, compilations.

Among the more ancient monuments of antiquity, Stonehenge, from the latitude it afforded for ingenious speculation, formed the subject of various theories. Aubrey, in his oftquoted but never printed *Monumenta Britannica*, assigns to it a druidical origin. In 1655, Inigo Jones, in his monograph on the subject, sought to trace a Roman original; while Walter Charleton, in *Chorea Gigantum* (1663), endeavoured to "restore" it to the Danes, and William Stukeley, in 1740, produced his *Stonehenge, a temple restor'd to the British Druids*.

Roman antiquities attracted comparatively small attention, though such books as William Burton's *Commentary on Antoninus, his Itinerary* (1658), and John Horsley's *Britannia Romana* (1732), with the writings of Thomas and Roger Gale,

Nathaniel Salmon, Alexander Gordon, and others, suffice to show that the study was not entirely neglected.

The efforts of archbishop Parker in the sixteenth century to further Old English studies, found a successor, among others, in Sir Henry Spelman, who, besides producing numerous learned works of his own, was ever ready to encourage the studies of others. Neither the short-lived lectureship which he founded at Cambridge, nor Rawlinson's abortive similar project at Oxford more than a century later, succeeded in giving the study an academic status. Nevertheless, the subject did not lack votaries, among whom are to be counted William Somner, whose *Dictionarium Saxonico-Latino-Anglicum* was issued in 1659, Francis Junius, George Hickes, bishop Gibson, editor of the Old English *Chronicle*, William Elstob, and his learned sister Elizabeth, who published a *Homily on the Birthday of St. Gregory* and a *Grammar* of the language.

It is not surprising to find that legal antiquities and the history of various offices of state interested many of the able men who either held office or engaged in the business of law, and the results include some of the most successful essays in the antiquarian literature of the time. Of such was *The History and Antiquities of the Exchequer of the Kings of England* (1711) by Thomas Madox, historiographer royal, whose other works include *Formulare Anglicanum*, a series of ancient charters and documents arranged in chronological sequence from the Norman conquest to the end of the reign of Henry VIII. This book, with its learned introduction, is important as a contribution to the study of diplomatic, a subject long neglected in this country. Elias Ashmole and John Anstis, both members of the College of Arms, each produced a work on the Order of the Garter. The numerous additions to the literature of heraldry comprised, besides writings by Selden, Dugdale, Nisbet, and others, *The Academy of Armory* (1688), by Randle Holme (third of that name), with its extraordinary glossaries of terms used in every conceivable art, trade, and domestic employment.

Two books are noteworthy as ventures into new regions of research that have since become fields of modern activity. Henry Bourne's *Antiquitates Vulgares, or The antiquities of the common people* (1725) foreshadowed the study of local customs and traditions, now called folklore; and the account of English printers and printing which Joseph Ames issued in 1749, under the title of *Typographical Antiquities*, is the foundation stone of the history of printing in England

With the growth of the literature of antiquarian studies consequent upon this increased activity, there arose the need of guides through the labyrinth of existing materials and of working books designed to facilitate research; and, accordingly, such aids begin to appear, though they were not always the outcome of a deliberate intention to furnish the tool-chest of the student of antiquities. Some of these books, such as Tanner's *Bibliotheca Britannica* and *Notitia Monastica*, and the indispensable *Athenae Oxonienses*, have already been mentioned. Sir Henry Spelman's *Glossarium Archaiologicum* represents another class of aids; while Thomas Rymer's *Foedera*, and David Wilkins's *Concilia* (founded on the work of Spelman and Dugdale), though perhaps belonging more properly to the domain of history, may also be noted here. The *English, Scotch, and Irish Historical Libraries* of that industrious but too impetuous antiquary, archbishop William Nicolson, was a new departure which, whatever its shortcomings, continued to be for long after its appearance a useful, and the best existing, conspectus of the literature with which it dealt.

The stores of original sources whence this army of antiquaries quarried material included the various archives of state papers and records, and the chief public and private libraries. A key to the manuscript treasures of the more important libraries, including the extensive collection formed by John Moore, bishop of Ely, was provided, in 1697, by the publication of the *Catalogi Librorum Manuscriptorum Angliae et Hiberniae*, a compilation which has not even yet ceased to be useful, and which must, in its own day, have been invaluable. In this work the editor, Edward Bernard, was assisted by many scholars, including Humfrey Wanley, celebrated for his skill in palaeography and for his catalogue of the Harleian manuscripts, upon which he was at work when overtaken by death.

Of state papers and records the most important depository was the Tower, where, at the beginning of the eighteenth century, something was done towards reducing them to order under the keepership of William Petyt, author, among other works, of *Jus Parliamentarium*, a treatise on the ancient power, jurisdiction, rights, and liberties of parliament. Among public libraries, the Bodleian, with its continuous accession of large and important gifts and bequests, had no rival; and almost every antiquary who essayed original work was indebted to the resources of the Cottonian or the Harleian library.

The former of these two wonderful collections, brought together by Sir Robert Cotton, scholar and antiquary, was justly celebrated as much for the liberality with which the founder and his successors made its riches accessible, as for the extraordinary historical value of its contents, largely composed, as they were, of salvage from the archives and libraries of the dispossessed monasteries. The Harleian library, no less remarkable in its way, was collected by Robert Harley, first earl of Oxford, and his son the second earl, friend of Pope and patron of letters. On the death of the second earl, the printed books (upwards of 20,000 volumes) were purchased by Thomas Osborne, a bookseller who has had fame thrust upon him through having been castigated at the hands of Johnson and satirised by the pen of Pope, but who has a much better claim to being remembered as the publisher of *The Harleian Miscellany* (1744–6). This reprint of a selection of tracts from the Harleian library was edited by William Oldys and Johnson, who also worked together for some time upon a catalogue of the whole collection. Oldys, who deserved a better fate, spent a large part of his life in hack-work, for booksellers. To the edition of Ralegh's *History of the World*, edited by him in 1736, he prefixed an elaborate life of the author, perhaps his most important work. *The British Librarian*, which he issued in six monthly numbers, in 1737, is merely an analytical contents of a selection of books, new and old; but his annotations in copies of various books, especially Langbaine's *Dramatic Poets*,[1] have been largely used by later commentators.

About the year 1572 there had been founded in London, chiefly through the instrumentality of archbishop Parker, a Society of Antiquaries. For nearly twenty years, this society met at the house of Sir Robert Cotton; but, on the accession of

---

[1] As to Langbaine, cf. *ante*, Chap. V.

James I, it was, for some not very apparent reason, suppressed. It seems to have been fully a century later before there was any revival of such reunions; but in 1707 a few persons "curious in their researches in antiquity" arranged to meet weekly for the discussion of such subjects, and, after ten years of these more or less informal meetings, the present Society of Antiquaries was regularly constituted in January, 1717/18, with Peter Le Neve as president, and Dr. Stukeley as secretary. The list of founders included Roger and Samuel Gale, Humfrey Wanley, Browne Willis, and other well-known names. In 1770, the society began to print selections from its papers under the title of *Archaeologia*. This publication formed a convenient repository for minor studies, a function which had previously been performed to some extent by the *Philosophical Transactions*, which the Royal society, instituted in 1660, began to issue five years later.

A period of new activities like that under review is scarcely expected to be productive of definitive work, and few, if any, of the books that have been named in this section attained the degree of exhaustiveness and niceness of accuracy demanded in the present age of work in the same field. Much, however, was done, by collecting data, examining material and making inventorial records, to prepare the way for succeeding workers; and the general results of this period are well summed up in the words of Tanner, which, written in 1695, are applicable with even more force at the close of the time covered by this brief survey.

The advances, that all parts of Learning have within these few years made in England, are very obvious; but the progress is visible in nothing more, than in the illustrations of our own History and Antiquities. To which end we have had our ancient Records and Annals published from the Originals, the Chorographical Description of these Kingdoms very much improved, and some attempts made toward a just body of English History. For those also that are more particularly curious, we have had not only the Histories both Natural and Civil of several Counties, the descriptions of Cities and the Monuments and Antiquities of Cathedral Churches accurately collected; but even the memoirs of private Families, Villages and Houses, compiled and published.[1]

[1] *Notitia Monastica*, preface.

CHAPTER XIV

Scottish Popular Poetry before Burns

DURING a large portion of the sixteenth, and nearly the whole of the seventeenth, century a blight had fallen on secular verse in Scotland; so great a blight that very little of the best and most characteristic verse of the "makaris" would have come down to us but for its preservation in MSS. One or two pieces by Henryson and Dunbar were printed at Edinburgh by Chepman and Myllar in 1508; Henryson's irreproachable *Morall Fables* were printed by Lekprevick at St. Andrews in 1570; but it was in London, and after his death, that even the *Vergil* of Gavin Douglas appeared in 1553 and his *Palice of Honour* in 1579. Lyndsay's poems, printed in London and elsewhere before the reformation, were probably circulated privately in Scotland, where, after the reformation, many editions were published; and they retained their exceptional popularity during the seventeenth century. But, Lyndsay excepted, the old "makaris" were never much known outside the circle of the court or the learned classes; and, though James VI himself wrote verse and patronised Montgomerie and other poets, the old poetic succession virtually perished with the advent of Knox.

Although, however, the age had become inimical to art of every kind, it is very difficult to tell what was the actual effect of the kirk's repressive rule on the manners, morals, habits and ancient predilections of the people, or how far the hymnary of *The Gude and Godly Ballatis*—great as may have been the immediate vogue of the anti-papal portion of it—superseded the old songs which many of them parodied. While the relentless rigidity of the new ecclesiasticism is sufficiently disclosed in its official standards and its enactments, tractates, contemporary histories and session and presbytery records, the actual efficacy of its discipline is another matter. It had to deal with a very stubborn, self-willed and retentive people, and there is at least evidence that the old songs, if their popularity was, for a time, impaired, were by no means killed. Doubtless, many were certain, in any case, to lose their vogue and be gradually forgotten; but there is apparent evidence of the survival in Scotland of some verses which were parodied in *The Gude and Godly Ballatis.* How old are various songs in Ramsay's *Tea-Table Miscellany* (1724, etc.), marked by him as "ancient"—such as *Muirland Willie, Scornfu' Nansie, Maggie's Tocher, My Jocky blyth, Jocky said to Jeany, The Auld Guidman, In January last, John Ochiltree, Todlen Butt and Todlen Ben* and *Jocky met with Jenny fair*—there is no definite means of knowing, though *Fient a crum of thee she faws* is a semi-modernisation of Alexander Scott's *When his Wife Left him*, and may serve as a specimen of the liberties Ramsay took with the songs he termed "ancient." Probably, however, most of them belong to the seventeenth century, and it may be that few are so old as *The Auld Wife ayont the Fire, Jocky Fou and Jenny Fain, Jeany where has thou been* and *Auld Rob Morris*—which Ramsay terms old songs with additions, the addition, sometimes, absorbing all the old song except fragments of stanzas or the chorus—nor so old as others for which he substituted an entirely new song under the old title. Next to Ramsay's—and better in several respects than Ramsay's—is the collection of David Herd, who, having amassed old songs from broadsides, and written down fragments of others from recital, without any attempt to alter or add to them, published a selection of them in 1769, an enlarged edition in two volumes appearing in 1776, and the remainder of the songs in his MSS., edited by Hans Hecht, in 1904. Some of these songs had been utilised by Burns, who sent others, modified by himself, to Johnson's *Scots Musical Museum* (1787–1803): and various old songs, of an improper kind, are preserved with more modern ones in *The Merry Muses*, of the original and authentic edition of which only one or two copies now survive.

From the accession of James VI to the English throne, the rigidity of the kirk's authority was coming to be more and more undermined; and, especially among the better classes, the puritan tendencies, never, in most cases, very deep, began to be greatly modified. It is to this class we evidently owe many of the old songs preserved by Ramsay. None of the old lyrical verse, though it has, and especially to us of a later generation, a popular aspect, is really of popular origin. When closely examined, it gives evidence of some cultured art; though exceedingly outspoken, it is never vulgar; nor is its standpoint that of the people, but similar, as its tone, with a difference, is similar, to that of the "makaris": for example, to that of the author of *The Wife of Auchtermychty* and *Rob's Jok cam to woo our Jenny*, preserved in the Bannatyne MS. But, while also intensely Scottish in tone and tenor, many of these songs are yet, in metre and style, largely modelled upon the forms of English verse, which, from the time of Alexander Scott, had begun to modify the old Scottish dialect and the medieval staves. The language of most of them is only semi-Scots, as is also most of the lyric verse of Scotland from Ramsay onwards.

The relations between English and Scottish popular music and song were, even at an early period, somewhat intimate, and there was a specially close connection between southern Scotland and the north of England, the people on both sides of the Borders being largely of the same race and speaking the same northern dialect of Early English. Chappell, in his *Popular Music of the Olden Time*, and in notes to the earlier volumes of the *Roxburghe Ballads*, Ebsworth, in his notes to the later *Roxburghe* and other ballads, and Furnivall, in introductions to various publications, have pointed out the trespasses of various Scottish editors—such as Ramsay, Thomson (*Orpheus Caledonius* 1725), Oswald (*Scots Airs* 1740) and Stenhouse (Notes to Johnson's *Scots Musical Museum* 1853)—in rapaciously appropriating for Scotland various old popular English tunes and songs; but, on the other hand, the case against the Scottish origin of certain tunes and songs is not so clear as these editors sometimes endeavour to make out; and, in not a few instances, they can be proved to be in error. Several tunes and songs had an international vogue at so early a period that it is really impossible to determine their origin; moreover, the Scottish court, especially during the reign of the five kings of the name of James, was a great centre of all kinds of artistic culture, and probably, through its musicians and bards, exercised

considerable influence on music and song in the north of
England.

That various English tunes are included in the Scottish MS.
collections of the seventeenth century is undeniable: they
merely represent tunes, Scots or English, that came to be popular in Scotland, but a large number, even of the doubtful variety,
may well have been of Scots origin; and, in any case, the titles
of many indicate that they had become wedded to Scottish
words.   Chappell has affirmed that "the religious parodies,
such as *Ane Compendious Booke of Godly and Spirituall Songs*,
are commonly upon English songs and ballads."   Now, when
the book was first published—and, since an edition so early as
1567 survives, there is reason to suppose that it was first published between 1542 and 1546—this was not at all likely, for it
immediately succeeded what may be called the golden age of
old Scottish verse, and, at the date of its publication, Scottish
verse was little, if at all, affected by the new school of English
poetry.   Indeed, English songs, at least those not in the northern dialect, could hardly, before this, have had any popular
vogue in Scotland; but it should be observed that Chappell did
not know of the early date of the book, and supposed it not to
have appeared till 1590.   Thus, after printing the air "Go
from my Window," he adds that, on 4 March, 1587/8, John
Wolfe had licence to print a ballad called "Goe from the window," which "may be the original"; and he then proceeds
gravely to tell us: "It is one of the ballads that were parodied in
Ane Compendious Booke of Godly and Spirituall Songs . . .
printed in Edinburgh in *1590 and 1621*"; whereas, if Wolfe's be
the original English ballad, then "Go from my Window" must
be of Scottish origin—though whether it is or not is uncertain.
Similarly, Chappell was unaware that the compendium was a
much earlier authority for *John come kisse me* than any cited
by him; and the fact that there is an answer to it in Scots in the
same measure—preserved in a Dublin university MS.—favours
the supposition that the original song was in Scots; while an
actual verse of the song may very well be that published by
Herd in 1769 along with the original chorus.   Again, with
regard to *The Wind Blaws Cauld, Hay Now the Day daws* and
The Hunt's Up, it would be easy to point out earlier Scottish
than English references to them.   Later, it is also indisputable

that, while Ramsay and others were indebted to English broadsides for suggestions and, sometimes, for more, various English broadsides are mere travesties, and others reminiscent, or more than reminiscent, of old Scottish songs. Chappell's theory that the original name for the tunes to which some of these ballads were set was "northern"—a synonym, in his opinion, for "rustic"—and that, after the accession of Charles II, such tunes were gradually denominated "Scotch," while it is the only theory consistent with his conclusions, is not in itself a very feasible one, and, besides, the evidence—such as exists—is all against it. Shakespeare likens wooing to a "Scotch jig," "hot and hasty" and "full as fantastical"; Dryden compares Chaucer's tales for their "rude sweetness" to a "Scotch tune"; and Shadwell, in *The Scowrers*, makes Clara describe "a Scotch song" as "more hideous and barbarous than an Irish cronan." No one can credit that the jigs, tunes and songs thus referred to were really not "Scotch" but "northern," or "rustic"; but, unless we interpret "Scotch" in the very special sense that Chappell would attach to it from the time of Charles II in its relation with broadside tunes and ballads, we can arrive at no other conclusion than that tunes and songs recognised to be "Scotch" in the usual sense of that term were well known in London from at least the time of Shakespeare. Moreover, since we find ballads of the early seventeenth century written to tunes which are described as "Scotch," we must suppose that these and subsequent ballad-writers, whether they were under a delusion or not, really supposed that the tunes to which they referred were "Scotch"; and we must assume that the reason for the hypothesis was that they knew them as sung to "Scotch" words. In several instances, also, internal evidence clearly shows the dependence of the Anglo-Scots version on a Scots original. It is very manifest in D'Urfey's *Scotch Wedding*, where "Scotch" can scarcely stand for "rustic," since the piece is merely an amazing version of *The Blythesome Bridal*. Then, what but a Scots original could have suggested ballads with such titles as *Johny's Escape from Bonny Dundee* or *'T was within a Furlong of Edinburgh Town*, or *The Bonny Scotch Lad and the Yielding Lass*, set to the tune of *The Liggan Waters*, *i.e.* Logan Water (an old air well known to Burns, the original words of which are evidently those partly preserved in the

Herd MS. and, with a difference, in *The Merry Muses*); or *The Northern Lass* "to a pleasant Scotch tune called the Broome of Cowden Knowes"; or, indeed, any other broadside ballads concerned with Scottish themes or incidents? Even in cases where a modern Scottish adaptation of an old song may be later than an English broadside on the same theme, we cannot always be certain that it is borrowed from the broadside. Thus, the English broadside *Jenny, Jenny* bears both external and internal evidence of being founded on an old Scots original, whether or not this original was known to Ramsay. Again, Ramsay's *Nanny O* is later than the broadside *Scotch Wooing of Willy and Nanny*, and may have been suggested by it, for it has a very similar chorus; but Chappell has been proved wrong in his statement that the tune to which the broadside is set is English, and the Scots original may well have been, with differences caused by recitation, the version in the Herd MS., *As I came in by Edinburgh town*, a line of which was possibly in the mind of Claverhouse, when he declared his willingness to take "in her smoak" the lady he afterwards married. In some instances where the English broadside may be the original, there is, it must be admitted, a striking superiority in the Scottish version. This is very marked, for example, in *The Jolly Beggar* and *Helen of Kirkconnel;* but, occasionally, as in *Robin's Courtship*, which is merely a Scottish reading of *The Wooing of Robin and Joan*— but not, of course, the work of Herd or any co-conspirator of his, as Ebsworth vehemently supposed—there is deterioration; and, indeed, many vulgar Scottish chapbook songs are mere Scottish perversions of English broadsides.

A lyric in *The Tea-Table Miscellany* of outstanding excellence and entirely Scottish in sentiment and style, *Were na my Heart licht*, was written by Lady Grizel Baillie, who also is known to have written various other songs, though none have been recovered except the mournfully beautiful fragment *The Ewe-buchtin's bonnie*, which may have been suggested by the peril of her father—Patrick Hume, afterwards earl of Marchmont—when in hiding, in 1684, in the vault of Polwarth because of implication in the Rye house plot. Lady Wardlaw is now known to be the author of the ballads *Hardyknute* and *Gilderoy*. *Willie was a Wanton Wag*—suggested by the English *O Willy was so blythe a Lad* in Playford's *Choice Ayres* (1650), but a

sparkling, humorous and original sketch of a Scottish gallant—
was sent by William Hamilton of Gilbertfield to Ramsay's
Tea-Table Miscellany; and the lyrics now mentioned with those
of Ramsay himself, and others consisting of new—and mostly
English—words by "different hands," whose identity, with
few exceptions, cannot now be determined, are the first indication, now visible to us, of the new popular lyrical revival in
Scotland; though mention may here be made of the *Delec-
table New Ballad, intituled Leader-Haughs and Yarrow* (c. 1690),
the work, according to a line of the ballad, of "Minstrel Burn,"
which seems to have set the fashion for later Yarrow ballads
and songs, and was republished by Ramsay in his *Miscellany.*

Meanwhile, the old poetic methods of the "makaris" had
been preserved or revived by Robert Sempill, of Beltrees, Renfrewshire, in his eulogy of the village piper of Kilbarchan,
Habbie Simson. Sempill has also been speculatively credited
with the authorship of *Maggie Lauder*, on account of its mention
of Habbie, but nothing is known of the song previous to its preservation by Herd, and it might just as well have been the work
of Hamilton of Gilbertfield, the scene of whose *Bonnie Heck*,
like that of *Maggie Lauder*, is laid in Fife. More probable is
Sempill's authorship of *The Blythesome Bridal*, which has also
been attributed to his son Francis Sempill, author of a vernacular piece of no great merit, in the French octave, *The Banishment of Povertie*. *The Blythesome Bridal*, though a little rancid
in its humour, is the cleverest of those seventeenth century
pieces with the exception of *Maggie Lauder*. Its portrayal of
the village worthies who went to the bridal, if more cynical
than flattering, is terse and realistic: but the simple, semi-
humorous, semi-pathetic eulogy of the piper was to exercise
a much more pregnant and permanent influence on the future
of Scottish verse. Ramsay, in one of his poetical epistles,
refers to it as "Standard Habbie," and with even greater
reason than it was possible for him to know, though he could
hardly exaggerate what he himself owed to it as an exemplar
for some of his most characteristic verse. It is written in a
six-line stave in *rime couée*, built on two rimes, which can
be traced back to the French troubadours, and was common
in England in the thirteenth, fourteenth and fifteenth centuries.
The stave appears anonymously in the Bannatyne MS., but,

possibly, was introduced into Scotland, not from France, at an early, but from England at a comparatively late, period, for Sir David Lyndsay is the earliest of the "makaris" who is known to have made use of it, though, after him, Montgomerie, Scott and Sir Richard Maitland all had recourse to it. Since it is the stave of one of the *Gude and Godly Ballatis*, and appeared, also, in Sir David Lyndsay's *Pleasant Satyre*, Sempill's knowledge of it is easy to explain; but it had never previously been employed for elegies, and to have recourse to it for this purpose was, on his part, if not an inspiration of genius, at least a very happy thought. If *The Life and Death of Habbie Simson* is but a moderately good achievement, it is hardly exaggeration to affirm that, but for it, the course of Scottish vernacular verse would, in certain almost cardinal respects, have been widely different from what it turned out to be. It set a fashion which was to dominate, in quite a singular way, its whole future. Not only were most future vernacular elegies—beginning with the epitaph of *Sanny Briggs*, the butler of the Sempills and Habbie's nephew, which was either by Robert Sempill or his son Francis—modelled on it, generally down to the adoption of the refrain ending in "dead"; but the stave, which almost writes itself, proved peculiarly adapted for the Scoto-English which had become the prevailing speech in Scotland, and suitable for the expression of almost any variety of sentiment, from homely and familiar humour, the prevailing mood of the vernacular muse, to cutting satire, delicate, tender or highwrought emotion, graphic and impressive description, or moving appeal.

Habbie Simson, already well known as a broadside, was included in Watson's *Choice Collection*, together with an anonymous epitaph in the same stave and manner on the famous traveller William Lithgow, and a variation, *The Last Dying Words of Bonnie Heck*, by William Hamilton of Gilbertfield, on which Ramsay modelled his *Lucky Spence's Last Advice*, and *The Last Speech of a Wretched Miser*, and which, though not in the same stave, suggested Burns's *Death and Dying Words of Poor Mailie*. Hamilton and Ramsay also set another fashion for the use of the stave by utilising it for a series of poetical epistles that passed between them. Other modern pieces in Watson's *Collection* were *The Blythesome Bridal*,

The Banishment of Povertie, The Speech of a Fife Laird and *The Mare of Collington*. The most notable of the old pieces were *Christis Kirk* and Montgomerie's *The Cherrie and the Slae*, both of which had long previously appeared in print;[1] and it is worthy of note that it was in the staves of *Habbie* and these two poems that the most characteristically Scottish non-lyrical verse found expression. The lyrical verse of the revival was not so uniformly Scottish as the other, and much of that which was truly Scottish in tone and method was not so consistently vernacular in its language. In the non-lyrical verse, the influence of the old "makaris" is predominant.

The outstanding figure of the vernacular revival was Allan Ramsay, who was an unknown journeyman wigmaker, when, in 1706, Watson published his *Choice Collection*. The greatness of Ramsay's pioneer work it is difficult for us to appreciate; and, if his early circumstances be considered, a parallel to his strenuous and successful literary career in very unpromising surroundings would be hard to find. Though of gentle descent, he was, through the early deaths of his father (a manager of lead-mines at Leadhills, Lanarkshire) and mother, left wholly dependent on his own exertions for a living. At the age of fourteen, he became apprentice to a wigmaker in Edinburgh, and, in the year after the appearance of Watson's *Collection*, he opened a shop of his own. If we are to credit his own account, in one of his epistles to Hamilton, it was the perusal of the poet's *Bonnie Heck* that "pierced" him with poetic emulation; and his earlier pieces were written in the stave of it and *Habbie*, and were elegiac—some, half-humorous half-pathetic, others, wholly satirical—in aim. They began with an elegy on Maggie Johnstone, who had a small farm and there sold ale to the golfers on Bruntsfield-links, a similar elegy on Lucky Wood, the landlady of a Canongate alehouse, and one on Pat Birnie, the fiddler of Kinghorn in Fife. Almost purely satirical are those on John Cowper or, rather, on his office of kirk-treasurer's man, or tyrant of the cutty-stool, the disreputable Lucky Simpson's *Last Advice* and *The Last Speech of a Wretched Miser*. This series of mock-elegies, with those by Alexander Pennecuick, are unique in Scottish, and, perhaps, in any,

---

[1] Cf., as to these, *ante*, Vol. III, pp. 147 and 153.

literature. From the nature of the subjects, the humour is broader and more incisive than that of their elegiac predecessors in Watson's *Collection*, and some of the more caustically satirical pieces more than foreshadow those of Burns. With other pieces in similar vein, on street characters and incidents, they were sold as halfpenny or penny broadsides, and those now preserved form together a wonderfully realistic representation of some of the outstanding characteristics of a certain phase of Edinburgh life in the eighteenth century.

But, by his two cantos added to *Christis Kirk*, one to an edition which he published in 1716 and the other to a second edition in 1718, Ramsay claimed much more serious attention as a vernacular bard. There was a certain presumption in his thus seeking to link his name with this fine old classic, and the experiment was not justified by the character of his success; for neither was his poetic training nor genius, if genius, as Burns affirmed, he had, akin to that of the author—the supposed royal author—of the ancient poem, nor was the Edinburgh or Scotland of Ramsay's day precisely similar to the rude undisciplined Scotland of the fifteenth century; but, nevertheless, his descriptions have the merit of being graphically and literally representative of the tone and manners of the common people of his own time; and the constant play of humour that pervades them partly atones for their excessive squalidity. In several of his fables and tales, he further showed himself master of a lighter, and, generally, quite irreproachable, vein of comic humour, and *The Monk and the Miller's Wife* is a wonderfully good modern travesty of *The Freiris of Berwick*. Whether or not he had any similar antique original for *The Vision*, his own description of it—as "compylit in Latin by a most lernit clerk in Tyme of our Hairship and oppression, *anno* 1300, and translatit in 1524"—is, manifestly, fictitious. It seems rather to be a kind of Jacobite effusion, voicing the general discontent at the union and its consequences. Written in the stave of *The Cherrie and the Slae*, it also gives evidence of the results of Ramsay's fuller acquaintance with the works of the old "makaris" through the perusal of them in the Bannatyne MS., and, here and there, they seem to have inspired him with the courage to attempt poetic flights rather beyond the common scope of his vernacular muse, although his low comedy genius occasionally plays havoc with his more ambitiously imaginative descriptions.

But Ramsay's crowning poetical achievement is, probably, the pastoral drama entitled *The Gentle Shepherd*. Here, his comic vein is generally restrained within the bounds of propriety, the pervading tone of the poem being lightly humorous. Yet, notwithstanding a certain stilted artificiality borrowed from English eighteenth century models, nature and reality on the whole triumph, and, if he depicts rustic life robbed of its harshness and of many of its more vulgar and grosser features, his idealisation is of a kind quite legitimate in art.

As a lyrist, his actual achievements are a little difficult to appraise, for it is impossible to know precisely how much of the several songs he contributed to *The Miscellany* was his own, how much that of the original author's; but, from what we do know of certain of them, it is plain that he had no claim whatever to gifts as an amender or transformer bearing any distant similarity to those of Burns. In fact, in "purifying" the old songs, he generally transmuted them into very homely and ordinary productions; and, while preserving some of the original spirit of the more humorous among them, the more romantic and emotional appear to have suffered not a little from his lack of ardent feeling and high poetic fancy. This, for example, is very evident in his transmutation of the pathetic ballad of *Bessy Bell and Marie Gray* into a very commonplace semi-sentimental, semi-comic song, as thus:

> Dear Bessy Bell and Mary Gray,
>   Ye unco sair oppress us:
> Our fancies gae between you twae,
>   Ye are sic bonney lasses.

Commonplace, truth to tell, is the dominating note of all his songs, though, in the best of them, *My Peggy is a young thing*, it appears, by some happy chance, in a guise of tender simplicity that completely captivates. He never did anything in lyric verse to compare with it. True, *Lochaber no more* may be instanced as, at least in parts, much superior to this simple ditty; but it is by no means so faultless: indeed, it seems to deteriorate with each succeeding stanza, and the peculiar pathetic beauty that gleams through its defects it may owe to an original

now lost; while it is at least worth mention that, in a note on
Lochaber in Johnson's *Museum*, captain Riddell states: "The
words here given to *Lochaber* were composed by an unfortunate
fugitive on account of being concerned in the affair of 1715";
and, if the song be by Ramsay, he could hardly have hit on
such a theme without some special poetic suggestion. The
more purely English lyrics attained to great vogue in "Mary-
'bone" gardens and similar haunts; and he was one of the most
popular song-writers of his day in England as well as Scotland. His more ambitious English verse cannot be said to
merit much attention. While the mere versification is fluent
and faultless, he has succeeded in aping rather the poetic
offences than the excellences of his eighteenth century models.
Even his satires, when he had recourse to English, almost
lost their sting. His *Scribblers lashed*, for example, is a very
poor imitation of Pope. Again, his elegies on the great,
throughout in stately English, are woefully stilted productions
and compare badly with his robust and animated vernacular
productions, as witness that on Lady Margaret Anstruther,
which begins thus:

> All in her bloom, the graceful fair
> Lucinda leaves this mortal round.

Ramsay's strong devotion to literature and his increasing
poetic repute, combined with the acquaintance he had formed
in the Easy club—access to which he owed, presumably, rather
to his "auld descent" than to his business prosperity, but of
which he was, later, chosen poet-laureate—with various learned
and intellectual Edinburgh citizens, suggested to him, in 1719,
to abandon the wigmaking trade for that of a bookseller. He
also started a circulating library, lending out books at a penny
a night: not the old theological treatises which had hitherto
formed the main intellectual pabulum of the burgher Scot,
but what Wodrow, in a woeful private lament, terms, " all the
villainous, profane and obscene books as printed in London."
Ramsay, certainly, was not squeamish in his tastes; but, by
his courageous defiance of the narrow puritanism of his time,
he effectually removed the old Scottish ban on secular English
literature and did more, perhaps, than any other man to further
the intellectual revival of which, towards the close of the

century, Edinburgh became the centre. Apart from this, by
the publication of his own verse, of *The Tea-Table Miscellany*
(1724-32), and of *The Evergreen* (1724)—a selection of the
verse of the old "makaris" obtained chiefly from the Bannatyne MS.—he disseminated a love of song and verse among
the people, both high and low, which, consummated by the advent of Burns, still remains a marked characteristic of Scotland.
How utterly "the good old bards of Scotland," as Ramsay terms
them, had been forgotten, is witnessed in his introduction to
The Evergreen. Writing of them as if they had belonged to a
remote age or a distant foreign land, he says: "It was intended
that an account of the authors of the following collection should
be given, but not being furnished with such distinct information
as could be wished for that end, at present, the design is delayed," etc. To have been the first to seek to do justice to
these forgotten masters in verse is a sufficient title on Ramsay's
part to the permanent gratitude of his countrymen; but, in
addition, his work as a literary pioneer in the combined capacity of writer, editor, publisher and librarian was, largely
because of the literary dearth of the preceding century in
Scotland, of far greater importance than that of many with
whose literary achievements his own can bear no comparison.

A contemporary and a kind of poetic rival of Ramsay was
Alexander Pennecuick (d. 1730), the thriftless, drunken and
down-at-heel nephew of Dr. Alexander Pennecuik (1652-1722)
of Romanno, author of a *Description of Tweeddale* and other
English verse, published posthumously in 1817. The vernacular verses of the nephew, who is often confounded with
his uncle, appeared, like the early experiments of Ramsay,
as penny broadsides, and, like Ramsay, he also essayed verse
in stilted English, publishing, in 1713, *Britannia Triumphans*,
in 1720, *Streams from Helicon* and, in 1726, *Flowers from Parnassus.* If, in low humour, he is not quite so affluent as Ramsay, he, in *The Merry Wives of Musselburgh at their meeting
together to welcom Meg Dickson after her loup from the Ladder*
(1724), (Meg, a Musselburgh fishwife, had escaped execution
through the breaking of the rope), depicts the incidents of the
semi-grotesque semi-awesome occasion with a grim and graphic
satiric mirth rather beyond him. Other vernacular achievements of Pennecuick are *Rome's Legacy to the Church of Scot-*

land, a satire on the kirk's cutty-stool in heroic couplets, an *Elegy on Robert Forbes*, a kirk-treasurer's man like Ramsay's John Cowper, and *The Presbyterian Pope*, in the form of a dialogue between the kirk-treasurer's man and his female informant, Meg. In his descriptions, Pennecuick shows greater aptitude for individual portraiture and for the realisation of definite scenes than does Ramsay, whose John Cowper might be any kirk-treasurer's man. Pennecuick shows us the "pawky face" of Robert Forbes "keeking thro' close-heads" to catch a brace of lovers in confabulation, or piously shaking his head when he hears the tune of *Chevy Chace*, and, with his "Judas face," repeating preachings and saying grace.

Robert Crawford, son of the laird of Drumsoy, Renfrewshire, contributed a good many songs to *The Miscellany.* His *Bush Aboon Traquair* has one or two excellent lines and semistanzas, the best being, probably, that beginning "That day she smiled and made me glad"; but it evidently owes its repute mainly to its title, and is not by any means so happy an effort as the more vernacular, and really excellent, *Down the Burn Davie;* while *Allan Water* and *Tweedside* are more or less spoiled by the introduction of the current artificialities of the English eighteenth century muse.

Another contributor to *The Miscellany* was William Hamilton of Bangour, whose one notable composition is the imposingly melodious *Braes of Yarrow*, beginning "Busk ye, busk ye, my bony bride," which, written in 1724, and circulated for some time in MS., appeared uninitialled at the close of the second volume of *The Miscellany.* It is probably a kind of fantasia on a fragmentary traditional ballad and may even have been suggested by the anonymous *Rare Willie drowned in Yarrow*, which appeared in the fourth volume of *The Miscellany*, and, consisting of only four stanzas, is by far the finest commemoration of the supposed Yarrow tragedy. If Hamilton wrote both of them, it is all the more regrettable that he mainly confined his poetic efforts to the celebration, in bombastic conventional form, of the charms of fashionable ladies. In 1745, he followed prince Charlie, and he wrote a Jacobite *Ode to the battle of Gladsmuir*, which was set to music by the Edinburgh musician, M'Gibbon.

Sir John Clerk, of Penicuik, is the reputed author of *Merry may the Maid be that Marries the Miller*, which first appeared in 1752 in *The Charmer*, a volume of partly Scots and partly English verse, edited by I. Gair, the first edition of which appeared in 1749. George Halkett, schoolmaster of Rathen, Aberdeenshire, is credited by Peter Buchan with the authorship of *Logie O'Buchan*, which appeared *c.* 1730, in a broadside, and a Jacobite ballad *Wherry Whigs Awa*, included in Hogg's *Jacobite Relics*, but termed by Hogg a confused ballad, the greater part of the twenty copies in his possession being quite different from one another, and visibly "composed at different periods and by different hands." Halkett, it is also supposed, may have been the author of the *Dialogue between the Devil and George II*, which caused the duke of Cumberland, in 1746, to offer a reward of £100 for the author, living or dead. Halkett's *Occasional Poems on Various Subjects*, published in 1727, strongly militate against Buchan's statements, even if *Wherry Whigs Awa*, in the extended fashion printed by Hogg, existed in the time of Halkett. *Logie O'Buchan* may well, however, have been a veiled Jacobite ballad, lamenting the fortunes of the old pretender.

Alexander Ross, a graduate of Aberdeen university, who became schoolmaster at Lochlee in Forfarshire, acquired much fame in the northern counties by his pastoral *Helenore or the Fortunate Shepherdess*, which, with a few of his songs, was published at Aberdeen, in 1768, a revised edition appearing in 1778. Linguistically, it is of special interest as a specimen of the Aberdeenshire dialect; but it is a rather wearisome production, and cannot compare with Ramsay's pastoral, on which it is largely modelled, though the plot is of quite a different and much more romantic character. Its prosy commonplace strikingly contrasts with the wit and vivacity of Ross's songs, such as *The Rock and the Wee Pickle Tow*, *Wooed and Married and a'* and *The Bridal O't*, which, apart from lyric effectiveness, are really admirable sketches of Scottish peasant life in the olden time. Quite the equal, and, indeed, the superior, of Ross, as a song-writer, was John Skinner, episcopalian minister of Longside, Aberdeenshire, the irresistible sprightly cheerfulness of whose *Tullochgorum* so captivated Burns that he pronounced it to be "the best Scots song Scotland ever saw." In much the same vein are *Tune your Fiddle* and *Old Age;* but a much finer achievement than any of these is the *Ewie wi' the Crookit Horn*. Though suggested by the older elegies of Sempill and Hamilton, it is in a different stanza, one of three lines riming together, with a refrain ending in "a" throughout the poem, and it altogether surpasses them in pathetic humour. To it, Burns owed more than the suggestion for *Poor Mailie's Elegy*, following not merely its general drift but partly parodying its expressions, more particularly those in the last stanza, beginning "O all ye bards benorth Kinghorn."

Alexander Geddes, an accomplished catholic priest—who contributed a Scots translation of the first eclogue of Vergil and the first idyll of Theocritus to the transactions of the Scottish Society of Antiquaries and wrote in English *Linton, a Tweedside Pastoral*, and a rimed translation of the first book of *The Iliad*—is one of the few known authors of contemporary Jacobite songs. His *Lewie Gordon*, under the title *The Charming Highlandman*, first appeared in the second edition of *The Scots Nightingale*, 1779: and he is also credited with the inimitably droll *Wee Wifukie*, relating the experiences of a rustic Aberdeenshire dame on her way homewards from the fair, after she had got "a wee bit drappukie." Murdoch M'Lennan, minister of Crathie, Aberdeenshire, narrated the affair of Sheriffmuir in the clever but absolutely impartial *Race of Sheriffmuir*, with the refrain, "and we ran and they ran awa man." John Barclay celebrated the same engagements in the versified *Dialogue betwixt William Lickladle and Thomas Cleancogue*, modelled upon the anonymous ballad of *Killiecrankie;* and a similar ballad, *Tranent Muir*, on the battle of Prestonpans, is attributed to Adam Skirving. Skirving has, also, been usually credited with the authorship of the song *Johnnie Cope;* but a manuscript note by Burns in an interleaved copy of Johnson's *Museum* seems to indicate that the song, as published there, is by Burns: "the air," he says, "was the tune of an old song, of which I have heard some verses, but now only remember the title which was: 'Will ye go to the coals in the morning?'" Two sets are published in Hogg's *Relics*, from Gilchrist's *Collection*.

Dougal Graham, a wandering chapman who followed the army of prince Charlie and afterwards became bellman and town crier of Glasgow, wrote, in doggerel rime, *A full and Par-*

ticular Account of the Rebellion of 1745–6, to the tune of *The Gallant Grahams;* he is credited with a rather witty skit *The Turnpike*, expressing, in Highland Scots, the mingled contempt and wonder with which the roads of general Wade were regarded by the unsophisticated Celt, and his objection to the imposition of tolls; and he wrote and sold various more or less racy and absurd prose chapbooks, as, for example, *The History of Buchhaven*, jocosely imaginary, *Jocky and Maggie's Courtship*, a skit on the cutty-stool, *The Comical Transactions of Lothian Tam*, etc.

Mrs. Cockburn, a relative of Sir Walter Scott, wrote, besides other songs which have not attained to popularity, a version of *The Flowers of the Forest* ("*I have seen the Smiling*"), which appeared in *The Lark* in 1765, and was, as she herself states, sung "at wells"[1] to the old tune. A more vernacular version, "*I've heard them Lilting at the Ewe Milking*"—which includes the first line and the burden of the old song now lost— by Jane Elliot, third daughter of Sir Gilbert Elliot, of Minto, was used by Herd for a version made up from various copies of the old ballad collated; but an authentic copy was obtained by Scott for *The Border Minstrelsy*. Miss Elliot's brother, Sir Gilbert Elliot, was the author of *My Apron Dearie* in Johnson's *Museum*.

Of a considerable number of songs of the eighteenth century, the authorship is either doubtful or quite unknown. *There's nae luck aboot the Hoose* has been attributed both to William Julius Mickle, author of the ballad of *Cumnor Hall*, and to Jean Adams of Greenock, authoress of a book of religious verse; but Burns states that it first came on the streets as a ballad in 1771 or 1772, and it may not be by either of them. Two verses were added to it by James Beattie, author of *The Minstrel*, who confined himself almost wholly to English verse,[2] but wrote a rather clever riming epistle, in the *Habbie Simson* stave, *To Mr. Alexander Ross*, whose "hamely auld-warld muse," he said, had provoked him to ape "in verse and style," our "guid plain country folks." The song *O weel may the Boatie Row* was attributed by Burns to John Ewen, an Aberdeen merchant; but, in any case, it appears to have been suggested by some old fisher chorus.

---

[1] *I.e.*, in watering places.   [2] See, as to Beattie, Vol. X, *post*.

Excellent anonymous songs—all probably, and some certainly, not of earlier date than the eighteenth century—are *Ettrick Banks, Here awa there awa, Saw ye my Father, The Lowlands of Holland, Bess the Gawkie, I had a horse and I had nae mair, Hooly and Fairly, Willie's gane to Melville Castle* and *O'er the Moor amang the Heather* (which Burns said he wrote down from the singing of a disreputable female tramp, Jean Glover, and which, if not largely by Burns, is not all by Jean, and is probably in part founded on an old song).

Towards the later half of the eighteenth century and during it, various anonymous songs, more or less indelicate in tone, found their way into broadsides. Some were preserved by Herd, either from recitation or from print, and several are included, in whole or in part, in his 1769 and 1776 editions; others, too liberal in their humour for general reading, are, with quite unobjectionable songs, included in the limited edition of *Songs from David Herd's Manuscript*, edited by Hans Hecht, 1904. Of these, a few have not appeared at all in other collections, and the others only in a garbled form. Neither the MS. collection of Peter Buchan nor his *Gleanings of Scotch, English and Irish Ballads* (1825), nor Robert Hartley Cromek's *Remains of Nithsdale and Galloway Song* (1810), can be regarded as trustworthy authorities in regard either to texts or sources. Rare copies of broadsides occur containing songs of a certain literary merit and interesting for their glimpses of the characteristics of rustic life in the eighteenth century; but several are not likely ever to be included in collections. Thus, by a careful examination of existing broadsides, much that, for various reasons, deserves preservation might be found; and, in any case, since of certain songs which are known to have first appeared in broadsides no copies in that form exist, not a few songs of some merit are likely to have perished with the broadsides containing them.

For Jacobite songs, the main published authority is still James Hogg's *Jacobite Relics of Scotland*, 1819–21, a work as to which it would be hard to decide whether its merits or its defects are the more intrinsic characteristic. On its preparation, he evidently bestowed immense labour, and he had the co-operation of many enthusiasts, including Scott, in supplying him with copies both in broadsides and manuscript. Indeed, he tells us that he obtained so many copies—of the same ballad and, also, of different ballads—that he actually "grew terrified" when he "heard of a MS. volume of Jacobite songs." His critical notes are, sometimes, inimitable, as, for example, this on *Perfidious Britain:*

I do not always understand what the bard means, but as he seems to have been an ingenious, though passionate writer, I took it for granted that he knew perfectly well himself what he would have been at, so I have not altered a word in the manuscript, which is in the handwriting of an amanuensis of Mr. Scott's, the most incorrect transcriber, perhaps, that ever tried the business;

or the following on *My Laddie:*

This is rather a good song, I am sure the bard who composed it thought it so, and believed that he had produced some of the most sublime verses that had ever been sung from the days of Homer.

The notes also contain much information conveyed in the sprightly and irresponsible manner of which Hogg was a master. Yet, though a diligent, more than clever and, after a fashion, even learned, editor, he is hardly an ideal one. He cannot be trusted; he lacks balance; he has little method; and he allows himself to become the sport of temporary moods, while quite careless in regard to his sources and authorities. As to the actual genuineness of many of the songs, we may judge from his own statement: "I have in no instance puzzled myself in deciding which reading in each song is the most genuine and original, but have constantly taken the one that I thought best"; and this must be further modified by the statement: "I have not always taken the best, but the best verses of each." In fact, Hogg edited the *Jacobite Relics* very much after the fashion in which Scott had edited *The Border Minstrelsy;* and he confesses that, in some instances, he had practically rewritten the song. While, also, he expresses his intention to include only the Jacobite songs which were of Scottish origin, this was a rule which, from the nature of the case, he could not absolutely observe; and, in fact, he broke it whenever he had a mind to do so. Thus, he observes as to *The Devil o'er Stirling:*

This ballad appears from its style to be of English original: the air is decidedly so, but as I got it among a Scots gentleman's MSS and found that it had merit, I did not choose to exclude it on bare suspicion of its illegality.

Of another, *Freedom's Farewell*—surely English—he gravely says, without a word about its nativity, that he inserted it, "on account of its stupendous absurdity"; and various others, as to his authority for which he tells us nothing, he could hardly have believed to be of Scottish authorship.   Further, while his avowed intention was to include only contemporary Jacobite songs, many to which he gave admission were of later origin.   In some instances, he did so owing to imperfect information.   He could not know, for example, that *Ye Jacobites by Name*, which he got from Johnson's *Museum*, was largely the work of Burns.   But he was not particular in his inquiries. Thus, of *It was a' for our Rightfu' King*—which, as he did not know, was partly an arrangement by Burns from non-Jacobite verses, with a suggestion from a semi-Jacobite *Maly Stewart*— he is content to write: "This song is traditionally said to have been written by a Captain Ogilvy related to the house of Inverquharity"; though the tradition could not possibly have been of long standing, and, from the exceptional excellence of the song, was, in itself, very unlikely.   Then, he gives us *Charlie is my Darling* from *The Museum* as "original."   This is so far excusable, in that he did not know any other original, and that it was a "vamp" by Burns; but it was a mistaken, though shrewd, shot at a venture.   *O'er the Water to Charlie*, which is mainly by Burns, he inserted with an additional stanza, doubtless lured, as in the former case, by the excellence of the song. No early printed version of it, in the form in which it appears in *The Museum*, is known to exist, though Hogg, who possessed a copy of the rare *True Loyalist* of 1779, must have known of the two versions in it which have the *Museum* chorus; but he remarks: "I do not know if the last two stanzas have been printed though they have often been sung."   One of the stanzas must have often been sung, having appeared in *The Museum* with the preceding stanzas—about which he says nothing; the other, we must suppose, had never been sung by anyone but Hogg himself, except in the modified form in which it was included in an old traditional non-Jacobite ballad, whence, it would seem, Hogg, consciously or unconsciously, had transferred it. Of *Killiecrankie*, he says: "It is given in Johnson's *Museum*, as an old song, with alterations"; but an additional verse and chorus, of the source of which he tells us nothing, are included in his own version, and, presumably, were written by himself. Similarly, he tells us that he copied *Carle an' the King come* from a certain MS.; but it is identical with the song sent by Burns to Johnson's *Museum*, except for two additional stanzas, by no means harmonising with the older in style. Of *Cock up your Bonnet*, he tells us that there are various sets and that Johnson has left out whatever might be misconstrued; but, evidently, the first part in Johnson was an adaptation by Burns, and Hogg says nothing as to his authority for his additions. In an appendix, he prints *The Chevalier's Lament*, and *Strathallan's Lament*, simply dubbing them "modern," though he ought to have known that they were by Burns; but, of *There'll Never be Peace till Jamie comes Hame*, though he inserted it, he remarks, with admirable discernment: "It is very like Burns," and of *The Lovely Lass of Inverness* he says: "Who can doubt that it is by Burns?" but he could not resist inserting it. Further, he printed *The wee, wee German Lairdie*, to a tune of his own, without any suspicion that the song was modern and by Allan Cunningham.[1] He states that he copied it from Cromek, all but three lines taken from an older collection; but why he should copy from Cromek when he had an older collection he does not explain, and the "collection" must be taken *cum grano salis;* but, though he also includes *The Waes of Scotland*, *Lochmaben Gate* and *Hame, Hame, Hame* from Cromek, he shrewdly remarks in his note to the last: "Sore do I suspect that we are obliged to the same master's hand" (Cunningham's) "for it and the two preceding ones." Of *The Sun rises Bright in France*, he says: "I got some stanzas from Surtees of Mainsforth, but those printed are from Cromek." He was wise in not accepting the stanzas from Surtees; not so wise in inserting those from Cromek; but perfectly correct in his remark: "It is uncertain to what period the song refers"; and he showed a return to discernment when he wrote

[1] See *Notes and Queries*, § 11, vol. III, pp. 286, 354, 430.

of *The Old Man's Lament*—which, however, he inserted—"It is very like what my friend Allan Cunninghame might write at a venture." Last, to name no more, his remark on *Will he no come back again*, which is by Lady Nairn, is merely: "This song was never published till of late years."

Apart from Hogg's translations from the Gaelic, and pieces by known authors, few of either the Scottish or of the English Jacobite songs possess much merit. *Awa Whigs Awa* is, however, picturesquely vigorous, and the various diatribes on king "Geordie" are not lacking in rude wit. *The Whigs of Fife*—which county was notable for its anti-Jacobitism—is characterised by an inordinate strain of abusive vituperation: and *The Piper o' Dundee* abounds in rollicking gaiety. *Wha wadna fecht for Charlie* has spirit and fire; and *The Battle of Falkirk Muir* makes clever, if rather rough, fun of general Hawley. Of the more serious, the best, perhaps, is the unpretending *Bonnie Charlie*, beginning:

> Tho' my fireside, it be but sma'
> And bare and comfortless witha'.

Many of the songs—as is usually the case with political songs—are parodies of the popular ditties of the day; and, since many English songs were popular in Scotland in the eighteenth century, various Jacobite songs of Scottish origin were parodies of English songs and sung to English airs. It is thus not always easy to distinguish between songs of English and songs of Scottish origin, although the context is an assistance to a decision; and, in the case of broadsides, there is usually little difficulty. Some interesting broadsides are included in Ebsworth's *Roxburghe Ballads*, vols. VII and VIII; but a good many are still only to be found in private or public collections. In regard to those in MS. collections, the apprehensions of Hogg were far from groundless: there is an embarrassment, and it is not one of riches. The merit of most is very slight; but an editor of a very patient and laborious temperament might, under the auspices of some learned society, be able to collect a considerable number of more or less interest. As for Hogg's edition, it would be very difficult not to spoil it in any attempt at re-editing.

The succession of the Scottish bards of the revival anterior to Burns closes, as it began, with a signal personality, though it is that of a mere youth. The ill-fated Robert Fergusson died in a madhouse at the early age of twenty-four. At the age of fifteen, while a student at St. Andrews university—where he was more prominent for his pranks than for his scholarly bent —his dawning powers as a vernacular bard were manifested in an elegy, after the *Habbie* fashion, on professor David Gregory, which is really a production of a much keener and subtler wit than that of his early exemplars. The *Elegy on John Hogg late Porter in St. Andrews University*, besides affording us a curious glimpse of a phase of university life that has now vanished, is notable for its facile and rollicking humour; but it is of later date. *The Death of Scots Music*, a whimsical, exaggerated but sincere lament for the demise of M'Gibbon, the Edinburgh musician, is in a more poetic vein than either of the elegies just mentioned. It was, like Ramsay, as the bard of Edinburgh that Fergusson first won fame; but, unlike Ramsay, his main title to fame is in this capacity. Had he lived longer, he might have attained to some ease and freedom in English verse; though, as in the case of Burns, his environment, the cast of his genius, his latent predilection for the vernacular, and the foreign character which, to him as to many Scots of his time, seemed to belong to English speech, militate against this possibility. Be this as it may, in the short career that was to be his, he succeeded, like Burns, in depicting the scenes which he thoroughly knew, and expressing the thoughts and sentiments akin to his circumstances and to the life he led. Unlike Burns, he was, for this reason, an urban, more than a rustic, bard. The influence of a few months spent by him in early manhood with his uncle in the country is revealed in his odes *To the Bee* and *The Gowdspink*, delicately descriptive, humorous and faintly didactic, and in *The Farmer's Ingle*, a picture of a winter evening in a farmhouse kitchen, sketched with perfect insight into the character of the life he depicts and with the full human sympathy essential to true creative art. But it was as the poet of "Auld Reekie, wale of ilka town" that he was to make his mark—not Auld Reekie as represented in its resorts of fashion, but as revealed in its tavern jollifications, street scenes and popular amusements on holidays and at fairs and races. The subject is not great or inspiring, but, such as it is, it is treated with insight and a power of verisimilitude that brings vividly before our imagination the modes and manners of the Edinburgh populace in the eighteenth century. Here, and, indeed, generally, he proved himself, as a vernacular bard, young though he was and short as was his career, superior to Ramsay. Fergusson's wit is not so gross and it is more keenly barbed, his sympathetic appreciation is stronger, his survey is more comprehensive, his vernacular is racier, he has a better sense of style, he is more of a creative artist, and he is decidedly more poetic. He displayed the capacity of the *Habbie* stave for a variety of descriptive narrative as well as for elegies and epistles, and showed a mastery in its use beyond that of his predecessors, though two of his most racily descriptive and humorous pieces, *Leith Races* and *The Hallow Fair*, are in the stave of *Christis Kirk*, with a single refrain ending in "day." Another *Hallow Fair*, modelled on *Let us a' to the Bridal*, signally evinces the hearty merriment which was one of his inborn traits, though ill-health, irksome taskwork, poverty and irregular living clouded it soon with hopeless melancholy. *The Farmer's Ingle* is written in a nine-line stave, formed by adding a line to the old alternatively riming octave; and his other staves are the octosyllabic and heroic couplets, which he also used for English verse. The most notable of his couplet pieces are *Planestanes and Causeway*—an imaginary night dialogue between these two entities, on which Burns modelled his night dialogue between the new and the old *Brigs of Ayr*—the picture of *Auld Reekie*, and *The Bill of Fare*, in which he makes Dr. Samuel Johnson the subject of his satire.

The verse of Fergusson is small in bulk; it lacks maturity of sentiment; here and there it shows patent faults and lapses. But the genuineness, the cleverness, the racy humour and vivid truthfulness of his art are beyond question: and his achievement, so far as concerns the portrayal of the Edinburgh that he knew, has a certain rounded completeness.

CHAPTER XV

Education

TWO parallel lines of interest may be traced in the history of English education from the restoration to the end of George II's reign. One consists of a series of writings by innovators in intention, some of whom were prominent in the world of letters; the other is formed by attempts, only partially successful, to readjust ancient machinery or to create new agents. Thinkers and practical men alike were stimulated by an evident failure of schools and universities to meet the new conditions of life which had arisen during the seventeenth century. Projects of reform took various shapes. Most of them proposed changes in the plan of work which would recognise the existence of contemporary culture and the requirements of the age by introducing "modern" studies; some writers, inspired by Francis Bacon and Comenius, turned to problems of method, for whose solution they looked in a fuller and more accurate knowledge of mental process; a few preached the interest or the duty of the state to instruct all its members. Incidentally, the story exhibits the dependence of education upon national life, and the mischief wrought in the body politic when education is permitted to develop in a partisan atmosphere.

In the seventeenth century, the accepted educational *curriculum* of school and university, as distinct from the professional studies of divinity, law and medicine, was, in effect, the medieval seven liberal arts, but with the balance of studies somewhat changed. Of these, the *quadrivium* (arithmetic so-called, geometry, music, astronomy) belonged to the university; the *trivium* (grammar, logic, rhetoric) was loosely distributed between schoolboys and freshmen, the latter being undistinguishable in modern eyes from the former. Anthony à Wood entered Merton in 1647 at the age of fifteen; Gibbon, more than a century later, was admitted at Magdalen before completing his fifteenth year; Bentley was a subsizar at St. John's college, Cambridge, in 1676, at the age of fourteen. Whether the story be true or not that Milton was birched by his tutor at Cambridge, the following passage from Anthony à Wood seems conclusive that, so late as 1668, the Oxford undergraduates were liable to that punishment. Four scholars of Christ Church having broken some windows, the vice-chancellor "caused them to repair the breaches, sent them into the country for a while, but neither expelled them, nor caused them to be whipt."[1] Ten years later, the vice-chancellor ordered that no undergraduate buy or sell "without the approbation of his tutor" any article whose value exceeded five shillings. The Cambridge undergraduate of the eighteenth century was not a "man" but a "lad," for himself and his companions no less than for his elders. The fact is to be remembered when the reform of university studies in that age is under discussion.

Of the *trivium*, "grammar" meant Latin literature and, more particularly, its necessary preliminary, Latin grammar, the special business of schools. Indeed, the seventeenth century school course may be said to have consisted of Latin, supplemented by Greek; a few schools added Hebrew, fewer still yet another eastern tongue. The underlying theory is thus enunciated by Henry Wotton (*An Essay on the Education of Children*, 1672): "Observe therefore what faculties are strongest in the child and employ and cherish them; now herein it is agreed that memory and what logicians call *simplex apprehensio* are strongest of all." He infers that a child's instruction should begin with Latin, passing to Greek and Hebrew, since in these three languages are to be found "both the fountain of learning as well philology as philosophy and the principal streams and rivers thereof." Wotton's essay is an account of the method which he employed in teaching his son, William (Bentley's comrade in *A Tale of a Tub*), a child who learned to read before he was four years old, began Latin without book at

[1] Clark, A., *Life and Times of Anthony Wood*, vol. II, p. 139.

that age, and at five had already begun Greek and Hebrew. It is not surprising, therefore, that William Wotton took his B.A. degree when thirteen (1679); the surprising thing is that he lived to become the able, judicious and modest collaborator of Bentley in the controversy of ancients and moderns. But his father had always refrained from overburdening the child, and the reformer's note is not entirely absent from his severely classical teaching, for the boy read English daily; "the more gracefully he read English, the more delightfully he read the other languages."

The official round of study and of exercises for degrees remained at both universities what they had been in the later middle ages; this fact reacted upon schools supposed chiefly to prepare for the universities. The medieval conception of the degree was that of a licence to teach; the exercises which led to it were, in effect, trial lessons in disputation or declamation given by novices before other novices and fully accredited teachers, the topics being selected from the Aristotelian metaphysics and natural philosophy, school divinity, or trite literary themes susceptible of rhetorical handling. At Oxford, the Laudian statutes of 1636 had stereotyped these exercises, and had given them an appearance of life which they retained to the close of the commonwealth. Speaking of that period, Anthony à Wood says, "We had then very good exercises in all matters performed in the schools; philosophy disputations in Lent time, frequent in the Greek tongue; coursing very much, ending alwaies in blows."[1] The training manifested itself in much of the controversial divinity of the time; at the Savoy conference (1661), both sides seemed to enjoy wit combats greatly, whole pages of *Reliquiae Baxterianae* being filled with arguments and counter-arguments stated syllogistically. But life and reality went out of these medieval exercises at the restoration, and, though they remained part of the apparatus of both universities, they were regarded throughout the eighteenth century as forms more or less empty, to be gone through perfunctorily, mocked or ignored as the fashion of the moment prompted.

[1] Clark, *op. cit.* vol. 1, p. 300. "Coursing" (a term not confined to English universities) was a fashion of disputation in which a team from one college disputed with a team from another college; the reason for the usual issue will be appreciated.

During the seventeenth century and long afterwards, neither school nor university, as distinct from the educational system of the colleges, took account of that advance in knowledge which university men were very notably assisting; or attempted to adapt, for disciplinary purposes, science, modern languages, history or geography, and the schools neglected mathematics, teaching arithmetic for purely practical ends. Consequently, educational reformers were many.

But the enemies of universities were not confined to those who considered them homes of antiquated knowledge. Throughout the seventeenth century, Oxford and Cambridge were closely associated with the national life, frequently to their material disadvantage, and sometimes to the impairing of their educational functions. Both universities offered an opposition to parliamentary government, which brought upon them the charge of disaffection. Under the commonwealth, a desire for the supersession of universities became evident, which is reflected not only in the writings of such men as Milton, Harrington and Hobbes, but, also, in the fatuous tracts written by obscure scribblers like John Webster.

Apart from the inspiring passages which often occur within its very brief compass, Milton's tractate, *Of Education* (1644), is now chiefly interesting as a criticism of the schools and universities of its time, and as a statement of its author's notions of reforming them.[1] He finds their most patent force in a premature meddling with abstract and formal studies, and a neglect of that concrete knowledge of men and things without which the formal remains empty or barren. He would therefore introduce a plethora of matter into the course, most of it dealing with the objects and processes of nature, but, also, those languages without which he assumed that Englishmen could make little or no advance in the kingdoms of science or of grace. Carried away by the faith in the omnipotence of method which marks most writers on educational reform in his day, Milton sees no insuperable difficulty in communicating, to boys between the ages of twelve and twenty-one, the full round of knowledge and the ability to pursue it in six foreign languages, of which the only modern tongue is Italian. Milton's entire dissatisfaction with educational in-

[1] Cf. *ante*, Vol. VII, pp. 114, 140, 145.

stitutions as then conducted is obvious; it is equally clear that he is wanting in real appreciation of the new philosophy, and in understanding of the method by which the new studies should be conducted. As a consequence, *Of Education* has not exercised any direct influence upon educational practice.

But there is more in the tractate than disparagement of an obsolete system; it is written with a burning indignation against persons and institutions, of which the universities come first. Milton would set up in every city of the kingdom an academy, which, as school and university combined, should conduct the entire course of education "from Lily [*i. e.* from the beginning of school attendance] to the commencing as they term it Master of Art." The only other educational institutions permissible are post-graduate professional colleges of law and physic, a concession, perhaps, in deference to the inns of court and the college of physicians.

The same desire to supersede universities and the same indifference to, or but partial comprehension of, Bacon's teaching, appear in the anonymous Latin book *Nova Solyma* (1648). But the writer has a better notion of what is needed to effect a great educational reform. He plans a national system including state-inspected schools to teach religion and morality, reading, writing and arithmetic, geometry, military drill and handicrafts. A scheme of exhibitions enables poor boys of good capacity to share the liberal and religious education offered by academies, and to follow this in selected cases by a three years' professional study of divinity, law, medicine or state-craft.

Harrington's distrust of the universities as displayed in *The Commonwealth of Oceana* (1656) is based on their predominantly clerical government and on the determination not to permit the intrusion of ecclesiastics into political life. In his utopian polity, for all but a relatively small number of citizens, military service is the great agent of public instruction. Harrington's ideas respecting education are purely formal, except on the administrative side. Oceana has a compulsory system of education, free to the poor and covering the years from nine to fifteen, conducted in state-inspected schools, whose management and course of study are to be everywhere the same. The universities are, mainly, clerical seminaries and custodians of the national religion, but expressly forbidden to take part in public affairs, from which the professional class generally is to be excluded.

In *Leviathan*, Hobbes has some characteristic references[1] to universities, which he elaborated in *Behemoth* (c. 1668), a tract surreptitiously printed in faulty copies, "no book being more commonly sold by booksellers," says William Crooke, the printer of the 1682 edition. According to *Behemoth*, universities encourage speculation concerning politics, government and divinity, and so become hotbeds of civil discord and rebellion.

I despair of any lasting peace till the universities here shall bend and direct their studies . . . to the teaching of absolute obedience to the laws of the king and to his public edicts under the Great Seal of England.

For Latin, Greek and Hebrew, it would be better to substitute French, Dutch and Italian; philosophy and divinity advantage their professors but make mischief and faction in the state; natural philosophy may be studied in the gazettes of Gresham college.

The kind of opposition to learned societies here exhibited by Hobbes became virulent about 1653, when the fanatics in the Barbones parliament anticipated the measures of the French convention of September, 1793, by debating the "propriety of suppressing universities and all schools for learning as unnecessary." The good sense of the majority of the members refused to concur; but a lively war of pamphlets immediately ensued, the most notable champions against the universities being Dell, master of Caius college, and John Webster, "chaplain in the army," and author of *Academiarum Examen* (1654). These obscurantists appear to have been more feared than greater men of a similar way of thinking. Seth Ward, Savilian professor of astronomy, and John Wilkins, warden of Wadham college, men of the highest distinction at Oxford, condescended to traverse the puerilities of Webster's "artless Rapsody," as the author himself styled his tract. The spirit of this rhapsody is revealed in its statement that

[1] See Chap. XXIX.

the end of the Gospel is to discover the wisdom of the world to be mere foolishness. As Ward pointed out, Webster's notion of reform was a combination of the incompatible methods of Bacon and Fludd. Nevertheless, Ward devotes the greater part of his *apologia* (*Vindiciae Academiarum*, 1654) to Webster's *Examen*. Like Hobbes, Webster is mistaken in attributing to the universities a blind devotion to Aristotle; natural science and all new forms of knowledge are welcomed, mathematics has been considerably advanced, chemistry and magnetism are studied, and projects are afoot for establishing a laboratory for chemical, mechanical and optical researches. Those who cry out upon the university exercises in the schools close their eyes to the work done in college halls and in tutors' chambers. Ward's defence curiously anticipates by nearly half a century that made on a similar occasion by John Wallis (the Savilian professor who exposed Hobbes's mathematical pretensions) when writing against Lewis Maidwell's projected academy.[1] Ward's readiness to answer a writer like Webster marks a critical stage in the history of Oxford and Cambridge, whose monopoly, if not existence, was seriously threatened. A project for a northern university, mooted in 1604, was revived in 1642 with Manchester and York as rival claimants for the honour of its seat; in 1652, York petitioned parliament in that sense. The liberal scheme of foundation enjoyed by Gresham college confined its operations to the *quadrivium* and the three learned professions, but it periodically stimulated the thought that London should possess a university; and the notion had been again mooted in 1647. Wilkins, who wrote the preface to Ward's *Vindiciae*, is said to have dissuaded his father-in-law, Oliver Cromwell, from confiscating the rents belonging to the universities in order to pay the army.[2] Even after the restoration, there were reverberations of these movements to destroy Oxford and Cambridge or to establish dangerous rivals. Sprat, in his *History of the Royal Society* (1667), while urging the claims of the new foundation, thought it expedient to explain that its researches could not conflict with the work of schools or of universities, and that the Royal society owed its birth to the labours of university men who had saved the seats of learning from ruin. But, in

---

[1] See *post*, p. 443.   [2] See *Notes and Queries*, 13 Aug., 1881.

July, 1669, Evelyn heard Robert South at Oxford advert in the most public manner to the possible injury which the Society might inflict upon the universities. So late as 1700, Lewis Maidwell's proposal for an academy was viewed with some alarm at Oxford and Cambridge.

But, though drastic reforms or innovations in the universities were undoubtedly contemplated by responsible men during the commonwealth, it would be unjust to represent their authors as hostile to learning or to public education. Throughout its history, the Long parliament gave occasional attention to the latter; through Hartlib, some of its members invited Comenius to London, where he stayed during the months preceding the civil war. The Long parliament initiated the parliamentary subvention for education, voting an annual grant of £20,000 for the stipends of ministers and schoolmasters, and reserving £2000 of it for the better emolument of heads of colleges in the universities. The same body appointed a committee for the advancement of learning, which soon found itself considering many of the plans then current for the extension of schools and the reform of *curriculum*. Finally, Cromwell brought the project of a northern university to a head in 1657 by issuing letters patent for the foundation of a university of Durham; but the scheme did not take material shape.

In the eyes of reformers, seventeenth-century schools were defective in their studies and insufficient in number. Professional opinion occasionally deplored their neglect of the mother tongue; the complaint appears in the writings of prominent schoolmasters like John Brinsley and Charles Hoole. The latter (*New Discovery of the Old Art of teaching Schoole*, 1660) suggested that a school should be placed in every town and populous village to prepare little ones for the grammar school, and, also, for the benefit of those who were too dull or too poor to cultivate scholarship, to teach arithmetic, writing and the reading of English so as "to sweeten their otherwise sour natures." But lay reformers, while desiring to establish schools accessible to the mass of the people, were intent on changes more radical than commonly crossed the minds of schoolmasters. They desired to curtail the time devoted to Latin and Greek, and so find room within the school course for some knowledge of natural objects and phenomena—

"real knowledge," as Locke called it, together with the history and geography of modern times, and the application of mathematics to the practical concerns of daily life. To those who objected that, not under any circumstances, could time be found in which to teach all these things, they answered that the ability to learn could be wellnigh indefinitely increased if teaching followed the natural processes of the child's mind, instead of forcing upon it subjects and modes of study better suited to more mature intelligences.

The Moravian, John Amos Comenius (1592–1671) took a prominent part in familiarising Europe with the idea of national systems of education, covering the whole field from the teaching of infants to the instruction given in universities. His projects form an epitome of contemporary reform; the introduction of modern studies, more especially the mother tongue, the belief in the extraordinary power of method and the search for psychologically grounded principles of teaching are characteristic features of his *Didactica Magna*, whose contents seem to have been well known before its inclusion in his *Opera Didactica Omnia* (1657). Comenius received from Bacon the impulse which made him an ardent believer in method and a tireless advocate of "real" studies pursued inductively. His scheme for a "pansophic" college has a partial prototype in the Solomon's house of Bacon's *New Atlantis* (1627), a state-supported institute for scientific research directed to the "relief of man's estate." Bacon's own purely educational writings are few and of comparatively small importance,[1] but, through Comenius, he affected educational thought, and, in a minor degree educational practice, on the continent, thus anticipating the part played by Locke in the following century.

A more direct, but much less influential, connection between Bacon and the history of English education was established by a small group of reformers who interested themselves in the problem of method, especially in its relation to modern studies of the "useful" kind. Prominent amongst them was Samuel Hartlib, an indefatigable publisher, and sometimes writer, on mechanical invention, trade, agriculture, industry

[1] See *Advancement of Learning*, bk. II *passim*, and *De Augmentis*, bk. VI, chaps. 2, 4.

and protestant re-union. Hartlib instigated the publication of Milton's *Of Education*, of *The Advice of W. P.*, an educational tract by William Petty (1648), and of another *The Reformed School* by John Dury (1649?), who found it advisable to disavow any desire of superseding universities. Hartlib himself wrote a pamphlet[1] advocating a state system of schools, and, in *Macaria* (1642), described the state endowment of research and its administration through boards of agriculture, health, industry, and so forth. Petty's independence of mind was in none of his many projects so completely demonstrated as in his proposed *ergastula literaria*—schools for all children above the age of seven, who should there study "all sensible objects and actions," reading and writing being postponed a little for the purpose. All children should learn drawing, mathematics, bodily exercises and a handicraft; the musical should be taught music, and only those should learn foreign languages who would afterwards make use of them. Petty's notion of school education is nakedly utilitarian; nevertheless, some of his suggestions respecting method are anticipations of Pestalozzi and Froebel.

The flow of reforming schemes was steadily maintained after the restoration. On the eve of the change, John Evelyn sent to Robert Boyle a "proposal for erecting a philosophic mathematic college," to which he did not assign any strictly educational function.[2] But the instruction of boys and of adults was expressly included in Cowley's *A proposition for the Advancement of Experimental Philosophy* (1660/1). Cowley's *Proposition* has already been described.[3] The opening address to the Honourable Society for the Advancement of Experimental Philosophy marks the position attained by the "Invisible College," soon to be incorporated as the Royal society, an incorporation to which this pamphlet gave an impetus. Cowley makes the customary complaints that the universities do not take any account of the advance in scientific knowledge and that schools waste six or seven years "in the learning of words only and that too very imperfectly." His suggestions are chiefly directed towards the endowment of research and

[1] *Considerations tending to the happy accomplishment of England's reformation*, etc., 1647.
[2] *Diary*, III, 3 Sept., 1659.　　　　[3] Vol. VIII, Chap. XVII, *ante*.

of public teaching of an advanced kind, but he has also a scheme for a school, to be taught in turn by two of the sixteen resident fellows of the philosophical college. Here, again, is the familiar combination of school and university. Boys are to be admitted at the age of thirteen, " being already well advanced in the Latine grammar and some authors." No fees may be exacted from any, "though never so rich"; as funds permit, boarding-houses are to receive "such poor men's sons whose good natural parts may promise either use or ornament to the common-wealth," and no differences of political or religious opinion are to be made grounds of exclusion. Had this tolerant attitude become customary, English education would have had a dif-ferent history during the last two centuries. Cowley's school-boys were to study a long list of Latin and Greek authors who had treated of "some parts of Nature"; like Milton, Cowley cannot surrender the scholarly type of education. He wants to repeat his own upbringing at Westminster and Cambridge, and to add the studies of the "men of Gresham"; consequently, he is incapable of scheming a feasible course of instruction calculated to secure his own chief aims.

It is easy to exaggerate the importance of a controversy which, in some of its essential features, is but one more instance of contrary temperaments brooding over "the good old times." But the dispute over the respective merits of ancient and modern learning which raged in France and England during the last decade or so of the seventeenth century shows that modern studies had become self-conscious in both countries; those who followed them were no longer willing to acquiesce in the conventional judgment which elevated all ancient learning into a region apart, and made education an almost superstitious deference of it, while neglect of the newer forms of study was readily tolerated. An early intimation of a different opinion came from Thomas Burnet (*The Theory of the Earth*, 1684) who assumed that there was order and progress in the growth of knowledge, a modest thesis which Temple regarded as a "panegyric" of the moderns. The contrast be-tween the two ages was limited at first to letters, and it was this particular field which, subsequently, displayed the Eng-lish "squabble," as Swift called it. Fontenelle (*Digression sur les Anciens et les Modernes*, 1688) took the reasonable ground that humanity, whether Greek, Latin or French, is, at bottom, much the same, and that differences are due to opportunity, or the want of it, rather than to intrinsic merit or demerit. After Locke, this became the general opinion amongst theorisers on education, English and foreign; differences between man and man were ascribed to the accident of education. Perrault brought the controversy to an acute stage in France. Beginning with adulation of the king (*Le Siècle de Louis le Grand*, 1687), he expanded his theme into a laudation (*Parallèle des Anciens et des Modernes*, 1688) of modern progress in science and the arts: the moderns excel in astronomy, anatomy, painting, sculpture, architecture and music, and may justly compare with the ancients in oratory and poetry. At this point, Sir William Temple (*Essay on Ancient and Modern Learning*, 1690) took up the quarrel, belittled modern science and philosophy, declared that art had been sterile for a century past, and that society was being vulgarised by the pursuit of gain. Temple was so little fitted to criticise the moderns that, in common with many of his contemporaries, he doubted the truth of the discoveries of Copernicus and Harvey; on the other hand, he had little or no Greek. In 1694, William Wotton traversed the assertions of this *Essay* and, in the course of his book, *Reflections upon Ancient and Modern Learning*, stated, with much detail as to names and discoveries, the condition of European, and especially English, science, his general conclusion being that "the extent of knowledge is at this time vastly greater than it was in former ages." Temple's uninstructed championship of the spurious *Letters of Phalaris* and *Fables of Aesop* gave Bentley the occasion in an appendix (*Dissertation on the Epistles of Phalaris*) to Wotton's second edition (1697), to demonstrate the absurdity of the claims made for these two works. This particular "squabble" is now even more outworn than the greater issue of which it is a part; but, in spite of triviality and disingenuousness, it troubled the reading public at that time and long afterwards. The contemporary verdict seems, on the whole, to have gone in favour of Temple and Charles Boyle; it is from the side which was in the wrong that we derive such familiar phrases as "from China to Peru," "sweetness and light," and the misapprehension which traces the renascence to the fall of Constantinople in 1453.

The Phalaris controversy, with the learning and critical acumen of Bentley on the one side and the brilliant pretentiousness of the Christ Church set on the other, is an episode in the perennial feud between the scholar (understood as "pedant") and the man of the world, with the man of letters for ally. The academic pedant, whether as represented by Anthony à Wood or Thomas Hearne, or as caricatured at a later date in *Pompey the Little*, did not commend himself to the man of the world. In the eyes of Temple's friends, Bentley and Wotton were mere index-grubbers and pedantic boors who could not be in the right against a distinguished public man like Temple, or a scion of nobility like Boyle. But, apart from its merits, such as they are, the controversy will always be memorable as the occasion of Temple's *Essay*, Swift's *A Tale of a Tub* and *The Battle of the Books*, and Bentley's initiation of the higher criticism in classical literature.[1]

Under the commonwealth, the superseding of the universities by institutions of a very different kind had been no more than a question for debate; after the restoration, and under stress of political circumstances, this supersession became an actual fact so far as great numbers of dissenters were concerned. Backed, no doubt, by the majority of Englishmen, the church party was determined to render impossible a return of presbyterian or of independent dominance, and, to that end, inflicted the most serious disabilities upon all who refused to conform to the doctrine and practice of the church of England. The act of uniformity and various acts of the same character passed between 1662 and 1672 deliberately extruded dissenters from the schools and universities, whether teachers or pupils. When expounding the bill of 1662 to the lords, sergeant Charlton said that the commons thought it necessary to take care for the upbringing of youth, in view of the great effect of education and, therefore, they attached rather more importance to the conformity of schoolmasters than to that of ministers. The act of 1662 required, on pain of deprivation, unfeigned assent and consent to the book of common prayer, and abjuration of the solemn league and covenant from all masters, fellows and tutors of colleges, from all professors and readers of universities, from all schoolmasters keeping public or pri-

[1] See *ante*, Vol. VIII, Chap. XVIII; Vol. IX, Chaps. IV and XIII, Section I.

vate schools and from every person instructing any youth in any house or private family, as a tutor or schoolmaster. In accordance with ancient ecclesiastical law and custom, all schoolmasters were compelled to seek licence from the Ordinary, and, by the act of 1662, private tutors were put in the same position. Those who presumed to teach without this licence were liable to imprisonment and fine.

An immediate consequence of the act of 1662 was the dismissal of a considerable number of university teachers and other graduates, of whom Singleton, master of Eton, was one, and many of these opened schools for boys or received young men as pupils. Others set up "private academies" which included both school teaching and instruction of a university standard; one of the earliest was carried on by Richard Frankland, whom Cromwell had designed to be vice-chancellor of the university at Durham. In Frankland's case, as in others, the penal laws were not consistently enforced; it is said that in the space of a few years he had three hundred pupils under his tuition at Rathmill, his Yorkshire home. Indeed, the rapid increase of these "academies" in the last thirty years of the seventeenth century shows that some discretion was used as to carrying out the law so far as it was directed against purely educational institutions which were not endowed schools or universities. There were many academies in the provinces, and the northern suburbs of London—Hackney, Stoke Newington, Islington, at that time the recognised names of boarding schools—contained some famous dissenting academies. That kept by Charles Morton, a former fellow of Wadham, at Newington green, was a very considerable establishment; and its head was accordingly prosecuted, and his academy dispersed, while he himself left the country. Morton was one of many who suffered; even those who were permitted to keep their schools or their pupils realised how unstable was their position.

The instruction given by the academies was of different types and standards; but, when they became established institutions, their first care was the education of ministers; dissenting academies supplied their earliest training beyond school age to Samuel Wesley, the elder, to bishop Butler (of *The Analogy*) and to archbishop Secker. But not all the pupils were being educated for the ministry, and this fact was made the ground of a charge, in the circumstances very discreditable to those who preferred it, that the academies diverted men from the universities.

Secker complained that the Latin and Greek which he carried from the Chesterfield free school to Jolly's academy at Attercliffe was lost at the latter place, "for only the old philosophy of the schools was taught there, and that neither ably nor diligently"; like Wesley some years earlier, he thought but poorly of the morals of his fellow-students. In 1710, Secker, then seventeen years old, removed to Bowes's academy in Bishopsgate street, where he learned algebra, geometry, conic sections, read Locke's *Essay* and studied French; Isaac Watts was an inmate of the same house. About 1711, Secker again migrated, this time to an academy kept at Gloucester by a dissenting layman, Samuel Jones.

> There I recovered my almost lost knowledge of Greek and Latin, and added to it that of Hebrew, Chaldee and Syriack. We had also lectures on Dionysius's Geography, a course of lectures preparatory to the critical study of the Bible, and a course of Jewish antiquities, besides logick and mathematics. Here I . . . began a strict correspondence [*i.e.* intimacy] with Mr. Joseph Butler, afterwards Bishop of Durham.[1]

The academy was removed to Tewkesbury, where, says Secker, Jones

> began to relax of his industry, to drink too much ale and small beer and to lose his temper, . . . and most of us fell off from our application and regularity.

Yet, here, Butler wrote his letters to Samuel Clarke, Secker carrying them to a distant post office for concealment's sake, lest his correspondent's youth and real situation should shock the London rector.

Dissenting educators were singled out for especial attack by the framers of that legislation under Anne which culminated in the Schism act of 1714. It would seem that concerted action against the academies was determined upon in the first

---

[1] Secker's unpublished MS. *Memoir.*

years of the queen's reign. The earliest sign was given by the publication of Samuel Wesley's *Letter from a country divine*, 1702, in which he asserted that the academies fostered "the good old Cause," were actively hostile to the church and disloyal to the crown. In the following year, the dedication to the queen of the second part of Clarendon's *History* contained the rhetorical question, repeated more emphatically in the third part, 1704:

What can be the meaning of the several seminaries, and as it were universities, set up in divers parts of the kingdom, by more than ordinary industry, contrary to law, supported by large contributions, where the youth is bred up in principles directly contrary to monarchical and episcopal government?

In 1704, also, Sharp, archbishop of York, moved for an inquiry into the conduct of the academies; in the same year, Defoe, who, like Samuel Wesley, had been educated at Morton's academy, joined in the fray, and Sacheverell at Oxford, in a diatribe against comprehension, raged against illegal "schismatical universities." In 1705, they were denounced in convocation by the Irish clergy.

The struggle had lasting and disastrous effects upon the history of English education; the feeling aroused by it has never since entirely subsided. In the eighteenth century, it sterilised the first promising experiment in popular education, and the triumph of the church was a contributory cause to the apathy which fell upon the universities in the same century. It injured the nation by diverting a large portion of its youth from the main stream of national education into backwaters or into alien rivers. The action of the majority was determined by mixed motives, more political than theological; but, whatever their intentions and whatever their provocation, the churchmen of Anne's day gave birth to a long-lived spirit of faction and contention.

It is true that nothing was taught at the dissenting academies which could not be better learned within the university precincts; but such newer studies as mathematics, French and modern history formed part of the ordinary scheme of work for all their students, and experimental study carried on within the narrow limits of a single building must have entered more intimately into the daily life of the majority of the pupils than was the case at Oxford and Cambridge, where, in fact, study of this kind was not deemed suitable for undergraduates. The academies, therefore, are to be reckoned among the forces which gathered during the eighteenth century to destroy the monopoly held by the ancient *curriculum*.

Discontent with the customary course of studies in school and university had long been exhibited among the classes from which men of affairs were most frequently drawn. Neither school nor university took special note of the changed conditions under which the administrator, courtier, soldier and provincial magnate lived, or adopted any special measures for their benefit. The private tutor was called in to redress the balance, or to take the place of the school. While the ordinary course of those "bred to learning" was from the school to the university, there was an increasing tendency amongst the nobility and the wealthy throughout the seventeenth century to ignore the school in favour of the tutor, who taught his pupil from childhood, accompanied him to the university and acted as guardian on his travels in Europe. The tutor's work, in many cases, ceased when his pupil, either on the conclusion of his university course, or in place of it, entered one of the inns of court. Clement Ellis ascribed the popularity of the inns to the fact that students were there free from the troublesome presence of tutors. They might, or might not, follow the study of law in earnest; to be a member of an inn was deemed a fitting conclusion to an education and a direct introduction into life.

Notably in France, discontent with current educational practice had led to the institution of "academies" where a combination was sought of the medieval knightly arts with modern studies, as we now understand that term; young men learned horsemanship, the practice of arms and of physical exercises generally, modern languages, history, geography and mathematics, particularly in its application to the art of war. These French academies handed on the tradition that the courts of princes and the houses of great nobles were the natural places of education for those who were to spend their lives in the personal service of the sovereign. In Italy, the princely academies had given birth to a literature devoted to "the doctrine of

Courtesy," of which Castiglione's *Il Cortegiano* (1528)[1] may be regarded as the original, and Henry Peacham's *Compleat Gentleman* (1622 and frequently reprinted with additions) the most popular English exemplar.[2] Clarendon gave the subject the benefit of his experience and good sense in two very readable dialogues *Concerning Education* and *Of the Want of Respect due to Age*.[3]

Peacham advises the study of such branches of knowledge as modern history and geography, astronomy, geometry, music, drawing, painting, all with an eye to the needs of the soldier and man of action, for whose benefit physical training in various forms is prescribed. But his typical gentleman is, also, a *virtuoso* interested in "antiquities," and a cultivated man accustomed to sweeten his severer studies by reading poetry, Latin and English; no Greek poet is named. Peacham exhorts his reader to "forget not to speak and write your own [tongue] properly and eloquently," and to read "the best and purest English"; to which end a long list of poets and prosewriters is given, including the names of Chaucer, Spenser and Bacon, but omitting Shakespeare's. The manifold interests of a cultured, travelled Englishman of a later date are well illustrated by the mere mention of topics which Evelyn treated in his various essays; these include forestry, architecture, gardening, "sculptura" (engraving), painting, navigation, agriculture, horticulture and the dressing of salads. The list may be compared with the "manual arts" which Locke thought desirable in a gentleman: gardening, woodwork, metalwork, varnishing, graving, the polishing of glass lenses and the cutting of precious stones (*Some Thoughts concerning Education*).[4]

Higford's *Institution of a Gentleman* (1660) and *The Courtier's Calling* (1675) by "a Person of Honour" are courtesy books which still afford interest to the student of educational history. Jean Gailhard's *The Compleat Gentleman* (1678) and

---

[1] See *ante*, Vol. III, Chap. XIX. [2] See *ante*, Vol. IV, p. 596.
[3] See *ante*, Vol. VII, pp. 250, 500.
[4] Swift, in the preface to *A Tale of a Tub*, announced that it was intended to erect a large academy (to which only wits would be admissible) capable of containing nine thousand seven hundred and forty-three persons, "pretty near the current number of wits in this Island," who were to be distributed over the several schools of the academy, there to study such matters as "Looking-glasses, Swearing, Criticks, Salivation, Hobby-Horses, Poetry, Tops, the Spleen, Gaming."

Stephen Penton's _Guardian's Instruction_, written between 1681 and 1687, and his _New Instructions to the Guardian_ (1694), although dealing with the same theme, take different lines, Gailhard recommending private education and foreign travel with a tutor (he had been a tutor himself), and Penton, sometime principal of St. Edmund hall, Oxford, preferring a university education. Both books appear to have been familiar to Locke when he wrote _Some Thoughts_. The courtesy books proper come to an inglorious termination in such compilations as _The Fine Gentleman_ (1732) of "Mr. Costeker."

Variants of the courtesy books are Francis Osborne's _Advice to a Son_ (6th edition, 1658), _The Gentleman's Calling_ and Clement Ellis's _The Gentile_ (_i. e._ "genteel") _Sinner_ (2nd edition, 1661). Osborne's philosophy of life is that of his friend, Thomas Hobbes; in this popular book[1] he displays much contempt for universities and those long resident in them, and is without any belief whatever in a gentleman's need for "learning" as usually acquired. The other two works are of a sermonising, even ranting type, abounding in generalities, but altogether wanting in the directness of earlier books on the upbringing of a gentleman.

The miscellany of schemes which Defoe styled _An Essay upon Projects_ (1697) includes one for an English academy to "darken the glory" of the Académie Française and "to polish and refine the English tongue," "the noblest and most comprehensive of all the vulgar languages in the world."[2] A second scheme proposes a royal academy for military exercises, which should provide a scientific education for soldiers, and, incidentally, encourage "shooting with a firelock" as a national pastime in the place of "cocking, cricketing and tippling."

The species of academy on the French model, giving instruction in military exercises and in the whole range of modern studies, did not secure a footing amongst English institutions, in spite of numerous attempts to found one in this country. Lewis Maidwell approached parliament, or the government, on four several occasions between 1700 and 1704, with the purpose of obtaining official sanction, a public standing and a state subsidy for such an academy, to be established in his house

[1] See _ante_, Vol. VIII, p. 431.   [2] Cf. _ante_, p. 8.

at Westminster. The details of the project took different shapes at different times, but instruction in navigation was put forward as an aim in all of them. Though nothing came of Maidwell's plan, it aroused opposition from the universities;[1] its absurd scheme of raising funds by a registration fee imposed upon all printed matter showed the author to be no man of business.

During the latter half of the seventeenth and the beginning of the eighteenth century, it became the fashion among wealthy country gentlemen and their imitators to substitute for the school private tuition at home, more especially in the case of eldest sons. As this fashion spread, less care was bestowed on the choice of a tutor, who sometimes became the tool of a too indulgent mother bent upon playing special providence. Swift (*Essay on Modern Education, c.* 1723) makes this charge; Defoe (*Compleat English Gentleman, c.* 1728–9) denies its justice; but it is frequently brought at this time against those who were in well-to-do circumstances. Swift supports the classics, the birch, schools and universities, against private education, coddling and the modern studies. He thinks that the popularity of the army has given the latter their vogue, and that education grew corrupt at the restoration. But, in truth this particular "corruption" was of much earlier growth, and its cause is to be sought in the defects of that mode of education which Swift championed. Defoe[2] represents the eldest sons of wealthy landowners who lived on their estates as growing up in gross ignorance, the learning of schools and universities being regarded as a trade suitable for clergy and others who had to earn an income, but quite unnecessary for gentlemen. Swift (*On the Education of Ladies*) speaks of "the shameful and almost universal neglect of good education among our nobility, gentry and indeed among all others who are born to good estates." The statement is, in effect, reiterated by novelists as well as by professed writers on education. The well-known decline in the number of boys at public schools during the greater part of the eighteenth century to some extent confirms Defoe. In the public mind, the distinction between learning and education was becoming more appreciated, and schools were identified

[1] See *post*, p. 460.					[2] *Op. cit.*

with learning chiefly. "A great part of the learning now in fashion in the schools of Europe . . . a gentleman may in a good measure be unfurnish'd with, without any great disparagement to himself or prejudice to his affairs."[1]

The transition is short from the courtesy books to the reform of education in general. The most notable instance of the passage is afforded by the work just quoted, the greatest of English books of its time which deal with its subject, and the most trenchant condemnation of the mode of education then in favour. The book is the fruit of Locke's experience[2] of tuition, but still more is it the outcome of reading and reflection. His debt to Montaigne is extensive. The general principles of the two writers are very much the same; where Montaigne gives details of procedure, Locke adopts and elaborates them; many passages in his book are but free renderings of the earlier writer's French. Isolated passages, when compared, are not without significance; but the really instructive comparisons are those of general principles, of outlook and attitude. So compared, it is evident that Montaigne is the source of much of *Some Thoughts*. Both writers have chiefly in mind the future man of affairs in whose education learning is much less important than the discipline of judgment and character. Both desire to make their pupils grow in practical wisdom, both employ the same method of action, practice, example, as against the bookish method of the school. The serious business of education, as Locke saw it, was not a matter for children. The training which he would give a child was, primarily, a moral or a quasi-moral one; at that stage, intellectual exercise should be altogether subordinate. So far as knowledge is concerned, it is enough for the child and boy to enjoy a moderate use of the intellectual powers, to avoid unoccupied moments and to get a "little taste" of what industry must perfect at a later period. Childhood, in Locke's view, is that "sleep of reason" to which Rousseau afterwards appealed in justification of the dictum that early education should be purely negative. In spite of mistakes which a better informed psychology has exposed, this conception of childhood gave birth, in due time, to much in modern practice which distinctly

[1] Locke, *Some Thoughts concerning Education*, 1693.
[2] Cf. *ante*, Vol. VIII, p. 395.

benefits the little child; it was also a fruitful conception in eighteenth-century theorising about education in general.

This is not the place to attempt to follow Locke's many prescriptions respecting the course of study, and the method of teaching. He was in sympathy with the innovators of his day who proposed to admit modern studies, and it is evident that he was convinced of the value of the instruction given by French academies to young nobles and gentlemen who resorted to them from all parts of Europe, Britain included. Yet, even in respect of academies, Locke asserts his own point of view, passing lightly over their distinctive arts of riding, fencing, dancing, music, but dwelling at length upon the manual arts, particularly the useful handicrafts, as woodwork and gardening.

The importance of *Some Thoughts* was recognised from the first, as witness the amended and amplified editions which appeared during the author's lifetime. Leibniz valued the book highly. Richardson introduces it into *Pamela* as a suitable present for a young mother. It reached the continent so early as 1695 in Coste's defective French translation, which passed through five editions in fifty years. In 1763, it was translated into Italian, and, in 1787, two German versions appeared. These translations show that there was a greater demand for the work than could be met by the French, a language familiar to the educated all over Europe.

Locke's second contribution to the literature of education is the fragmentary and posthumously published *Of the Conduct of the Understanding*, an addition to the great *Essay* of 1690, and one which Locke put forward as a substitute for the textbooks of logic studied by undergraduates in their first year at the university. *Of the Conduct* and *Some Thoughts* are mutually complementary. Originally, at least, the latter was meant to express Locke's opinions concerning the education of children; *Of the Conduct* is a manual of practice for young men, who are educating themselves. It is in this work that we find the true Locke, independent of the authorities which lie behind *Some Thoughts*, intent mainly upon the problem of building up, confirming, and making continuously operative the essentially rational character of the mind. Locke believes the solution of the problem to be largely independent of schoolmasters and tutors; and every man in proportion to his opportunities is called upon to face the question for himself. This view of the educational process was unlikely to influence those who wrote on, or dealt with, education as customarily understood.

The educated person, as he is drawn in *Of the Conduct*, is one who before all else has learned to think for himself. Convinced that reason will enable him to attain so much of truth as he needs to know, he has habituated himself to its skilful exercise. Mathematics and divinity are named as his appropriate studies; the concluding pages of *Some Thoughts* enable us to add ethics, civil law and constitutional history. A healthy, graceful body and considerable manual skill are desirable possessions for whose attainment the latter book gives many directions. The contrast between Locke's ideal of culture and our own is sufficiently obvious. It is not surprising that he says little of the educational advantage to be got from the study of physical science, though his lifelong interest in research shows this was not an oversight. But of the culture of the human spirit, which literature confers, Locke says nothing, and such cultivation of fine art as he recommends is chiefly for utilitarian ends. The development of the rational is, for him, wellnigh everything: imagination and sentiment are not merely left out, but are more than once referred to as objects of distrust. Locke believed that the "*ancient* authors observed and painted mankind well and [gave] the best light into that kind of knowledge"; but of English writers *Some Thoughts* recommends by name for the pupil's reading, only two, Cudworth and Chillingworth, and neither for "that kind of knowledge."

Locke's significance in the history of education is not to be sought in his expressly pedagogical works. *An Essay concerning Human Understanding* (1690),[1] whence the eighteenth and nineteenth centuries derived their experimental psychology and their rationalist and sceptical philosophies, is, also, the source of its author's great influence upon subsequent educational theory and practice, more especially as these developed in France and Germany. The teaching of *An Essay* respecting the relation of experience to mental develop-

[1] Cf. *ante*, Vol. VIII, pp. 382 ff.

ment is paralleled by the doctrine that formal education is a process which profoundly modifies the minds subjected to it; when philanthropic feeling is added to this doctrine, the desire of making instruction universal is bound to arise. Locke's exposition of mind as itself a development leads straight to the conception that the method of teaching is conditioned, as to nature, material and sequence, by mental development. Hence, the demand so frequently reiterated in eighteenth-century educational theory for the training of the senses, and for modes of instruction, which will make children discover everything for themselves; hence, also, the impatience of authority, the antithesis, sometimes foolishly expressed, between "words" and "things," and an inadequate test of what constitutes usefulness. In short, from *An Essay's* teaching is derived much of the educational theory of Rousseau, La Chalotais, Helvétius, Basedow and their sympathisers, down to Herbert Spencer.

The education of girls above the humblest rank was wholly private. Swift, in a fragmentary essay *On the Education of Ladies*, states the practice thus: "the care of their education is either entirely left to their mothers, or they are sent to boarding-schools, or put into the hands of English or French governesses," "generally the worst that can be gotten for money." The ideal wavered between what was deemed most fitting to the housewife, the devotee or the fine lady severally. Swift says that the common opinion restricted a woman's reading to books of devotion or of domestic management; anything beyond these might "turn the brain." In Law's *Serious Call* (1728) Matilda's daughters read only the Bible and devotional books, but their chief anxiety is to appear "genteel," though they become anaemic and die in consequence. In every case, the ideal carefully avoided any appearance of thoroughness outside the domestic arts. Lady Mary Pierrepoint (1689–1762) (afterwards Lady Mary Wortley Montagu), writing in 1710 to bishop Burnet, complains that "it is looked upon as in a degree criminal to improve our reason, or fancy we have any."

The domestic instruction of girls of course depended for its thoroughness and for its precise scope upon the circumstances of the household and the opinions and capacity of the mother. The results must have differed greatly; but the general level was a low one, especially in those numerous cases where it was thought unnecessary to train the girl as a house-wife though it was not possible to furnish her with highly competent instructors. Swift, in *A letter to a very young lady on her marriage*, declares that not one gentleman's daughter in a thousand can read or understand her own language or "be the judge of the easiest books that are written in it." "They are not so much as taught to spell in their childhood, nor can ever attain to it in their whole lives." Lady Mary Wortley Montagu received lessons in carving in order to take the head of her father's table on public days, occasions on which she dined alone an hour beforehand. She was taught French in childhood and Italian as a young woman of twenty; Latin she studied surreptitiously for two years in her father's library, working five or six hours a day, when it was thought she was reading novels or romances. Elizabeth Elstob, editor of Ael-fric's *Homilies* and author of the earliest Old English grammar, pursued her early education under similar discouraging cir-cumstances.

The medieval distinction between the types of education of the sexes was a distinction of function, and the difference between the education of women and that of men was not greater than the difference between the education of the knight and that of the scholar. But, in the eighteenth century, the difference was regarded as based on capacity. "You can never arrive in point of learning to the perfection of a school-boy," Swift assures a newly-married girl, and he advises that, for some hours daily, she should study English works on history and travel, so that she may prepare to take an intelligent part in conversation. From this platform, it is but a short step, and too often a downward one, to the "accomplishments" of the seventeenth and eighteenth century boarding-school. Here, as in home education, the differences of aim and method were very great. These are at their most ambitious point in *An Essay to revive the antient education of Gentlewomen* (1673) which, in truth, is a thinly-veiled prospectus of a new boarding-school for girls, to be established, or recently established, at Tottenham cross by Mrs. Bathsua Makin, a lady who acquired an extraordinary reputation as "tutress" to Charles I's daugh-ter, Elizabeth.[1] The interest of the essay, probably written by

[1] Princess Elizabeth died at the age of fifteen in 1650.

Mrs. Makin herself, lies in the account of her school. We learn that the things ordinarily taught in girls' schools were "works of all sorts, dancing, music, singing, writing, keeping accompts." Half the time of the new school is to be devoted to these arts, and the remainder to Latin and French, "and those that please may learn Greek and Hebrew, the Italian and Spanish, in all which this gentlewoman hath a competent knowledge." The mixture of aims and indecision as to means are strikingly illustrated in the optional studies, "limning, preserving, pastry and cooking," and in the branches to be taken up by those who remained long at school, astronomy, geography, arithmetic, history. Mrs. Makin was an admirer of Comenius and warmly recommended his plan of teaching Latin and "real" knowledge in association. Experimental philosophy may be substituted for languages in the new school, which has "repositories for visibles," collections of objects, for the purpose.

Swift's proposal for the reform of girls' instruction already alluded to is not unlike that recommended in 1753 by Lady Mary Wortley Montagu for the benefit of her grandchild, the countess of Bute's daughter, except that she adds arithmetic and philosophy, and attaches special importance to needlework, drawing and English poetry. Reformer as she was, she shares the general opinion that scholarly attainments were the affair of the professional man and, accordingly, to be considered derogatory in the owner of a title or of great estates. Lady Mary, therefore, is careful to say that she considers the kind of education which she is advising suited only to those women who will live unmarried and retired lives; and even they should conceal their learning, when acquired, as they would a physical defect.

Mary Astell, the "Madonella" whose "seraphic discourse" and "Protestant nunnery" furnished Swift[1] with topics for coarse satire, was a great admirer of Lady Mary but a reformer on different lines. Her *Serious Proposal to the Ladies* (1694) attracted considerable attention and opposition, partly on account of its suggested conventual education, partly because its author was a known controversialist on the church of England side. Her "religious" were to undertake the education of

[1] *The Tatler*, XXXII, 1709.

girls, instructing them in "solid and useful knowledge," chiefly through the mother tongue. The ladies themselves were to substitute French philosophy and the ancient classics (presumably in translations) for the romances which formed most of the reading of fashionable women. William Law held women's intelligence and capacity in at least as high esteem as he did those of men; but the education which he advised for girls is confined to plain living, and the practice of charity and devotion.

Defoe's *Essay upon Projects* (1697) deprecates the idea of a nunnery and proposes academies which "differ but little from public schools, wherein such ladies as were willing to study should have all the advantages of learning suitable to their genius." He indicates the customary instruction of girls of the middle class.

One would wonder indeed how it should happen that women are conversible at all, since they are only beholding to natural parts for all their knowledge. Their youth is spent to teach them to stitch and sow, or make bawbles; they are taught to read indeed, and perhaps to write their names or so; and that is the heighth of a woman's education.

Defoe's academy "would deny women no sort of learning," but, in particular, it would teach them history, languages, especially French and Italian, music and dancing. This readiness to expand the course of studies appears again in the same author's *Compleat English Gentleman*, where Latin and Greek are said to be not indispensable; but modern studies and, notably, the cultivation of the mother tongue, are described as essential.

The beginning of popular education is an obscure subject, as to which we can with safety make only such general assertions as that rudimentary instruction in the vernacular was first given in response to a commercial, industrial or other distinctly utilitarian demand, and that teachers were private adventurers, frequently women, who carried on their small schools unlicensed. Long before the period under review, children of all ranks but the highest received their earliest schooling in dames' schools. Brinsley (1612) speaks of poor men and women who, by teaching, "make an honest poor living of it, or get somewhat towards helping the same"; at the close of the century, Stephen

Penton refers to "the horn book . . . which brings in the country school dames so many groats a week." Francis Brokesby[1] writes:

There are few country villages where some or other do not get a livelihood by teaching school, so that there are now not many but can write and read unless it have been their own or their parents' fault.

The writer has a doubtful thesis to support, and therefore must not be taken too literally. Shenstone had a much better right to assume the presence of a dame school "in every village mark'd with little spire";[2] but he wrote a whole generation later. In spite of its banter and the prominence assigned to the rod, this burlesque idyll is a tribute of respect to school dames and to the value of their work amidst very unscholastic surroundings. The instruction was usually confined to reading and the memorising of catechism, psalms and scriptural texts; writing was an occasional "extra." Fielding and Smollett throw some light on the country schools of their time. [3]

Schools above this grade taught, or professed to teach, arithmetic, history, geography and, sometimes, the rudiments of Latin; others, of a grade still higher, prepared for Eton and Westminster. Smollett makes Peregrine Pickle (1751) attend a boarding-school kept by a German charlatan who undertook to teach French and Latin and to prepare for these two schools, though, in the end, "Perry" was sent to Winchester.

But, of whatever grade, all these private schools were for persons who could pay a fee; the very poor and the indifferent were not helped by them. In spite of casual attempts of town councils, vestries and private persons to provide instruction, the number of the illiterate and untaught was great and the morals of a large part of the population gave anxiety to

---

[1] *Of Education*, 1701.   [2] *The School-Mistress*, 1742.

[3] Thus, in *Joseph Andrews* (1742) the hero is said to have learned to read "very early," his father paying sixpence a week for the instruction. Tom Jones's henchman had been a village schoolmaster, whose pupils numbered exactly nine, of whom seven were "parish-boys" learning to read and write at the ratepayers' cost; their comrades were the sons of a neighbouring squire, the elder, a boy of seventeen "just entered into syntax," a dunce too old for a more suitable school. Partridge eked out his income by acting as parish clerk and barber, his patron providing a ten pound annuity.

thoughtful men. The increase of pauperism between 1692 and 1699 intensified the evil, and the earliest attempts at amelioration were on economic rather than educational lines. John Bellers came forward with *Proposals for Raising a Colledge of Industry* (1696) which, in fact, consisted of a proprietary workhouse in close association with a farm, by whose means Bellers hoped to eliminate the middleman, solve the puzzle of the unemployed and pay profits to the proprietors. The teaching to be given in the school was to be addressed mainly to reading, writing and handicrafts, children beginning to learn knitting and spinning at four or five years old; the inmates might remain to the age of twenty-four. The scheme secured the approval of William Penn, Thomas Ellwood and other quakers, but it was full of generalities and platitudes, without showing capacity to found a living institution; Cowley was the real author of some of the notions which Bellers presented very nebulously.

In 1697, Locke, then a member of the commission of Trade and Plantations, wrote a memorandum in which he ascribed the increase of pauperism to relaxation of dicipline and corruption of manners. He put forward the more practical portions of Bellers's scheme suggesting the erection at public expense in all parishes of "working schools" for pauper children, between the ages of three and fourteen, who were to learn spinning, knitting or other handicraft, and to be brought to church on Sundays.[1] Half the apprentices of a district should be chosen from these paupers, for whom no premium was to be paid. Locke estimated that the children's labour would pay for their teaching and for a sufficient ration of bread and water-gruel. Defoe (*Of Royall Educacion, c.* 1728) expressed the opinion that "in the manufacturing towns of England, hardly a child above five year old but could get its own bread."

While men like Locke and Bellers addressed themselves chiefly to the economic side of the problem presented by pauperism, others tried to solve it by means of instruction, more particularly through instruction in religion. There was, indeed, a growing uneasiness in religious minds respecting the spiritual condition of the people, not only in these islands but in France and Germany also. Between 1678 and 1698, forty-

[1] Fox Bourne, *Life of John Locke*, vol. II, p. 383.

two "religious societies," chiefly of churchmen, were started in London alone, and similar associations were formed at Oxford, Cambridge, Dublin and elsewhere, the object of all being that deepening of personal piety which, at a later date and on a more extensive scale, became methodism. In the last decade of the seventeenth century "societies for the reformation of manners" endeavoured to effect improvement by setting in force the laws against swearing, drunkenness, street-debauchery and sabbath-breaking; their success was but trifling, and they died out about 1740.

One of the immediate objects of the Society for Promoting Christian Knowledge (founded in 1699) was the institution of schools for instructing poor children between the ages of seven and twelve in reading, writing and the catechism; all boys and some girls were to be taught to cipher, and all girls were to learn sewing, or some other handicraft. The instruction was to be given by a master or mistress, a member of the church of England, licensed by the bishop. A convincing proof of the great popularity of these schools in their earlier period is furnished by the venomous attack upon them made by Bernard Mandeville in his *Essay on Charity, and Charity Schools* (2nd edition, 1723). That habitual paradoxmonger was dead against popular schooling: yet he notes an "enthusiastic passion for charity schools, a kind of distraction the nation hath laboured under for some time," a widespread interest in their fortunes, and a great desire to share in their management. He thought that the money bestowed on them would be better spent upon higher and professional education. If parents are too poor to afford their children the elements of learning "it is impudence in them to aspire any further."

These schools obtained a large measure of support during the reigns of Anne and George I, but, with the accession of George II, there came a check in their increase, and a decline in their efficiency set in, which grew as the century advanced, while an immense field for popular instruction was either unoccupied, or occupied by even humbler schools. Their own defective course and methods of instruction but partly account for the failure of charity schools, which was mainly due to their connection with the church and the supposed Jacobite sympathies of their managers. Responsible persons like archbishop Wake and bishop Boulter, of Bristol, formally warned the authorities of the schools against any appearance of disloyalty.

Charity schools failed to expand, partly because they did not retain the support of the crown, and partly because their managers were too often partisan in their dealings with parents; readers of Fielding will remember why little Joseph Andrews did not receive a charity school education. But these schools played a part in our educational history which makes them memorable. They familiarised men with the idea of a system of popular schools centrally directed, yet very closely associated with the several localities in which the schools were placed; they founded the tradition that the "three R's" are the primary ground of all school work, and they first represented that voluntary system to which English popular education owes much.

Eton and Westminster were commonly accounted the public schools *par excellence* during the first half of the eighteenth century, Winchester taking third place. Rugby's greatness only began with the headmastership of Thomas James (1778–94), while Harrow and Shrewsbury suffered from that instability, or decline in number of pupils, which was general throughout the century at all public schools. The fact is paralleled by the paucity of grammar schools founded under George I and George II. Carlisle gives nineteen schools as founded between 1702 and 1760, of which eight belong to the reign of Anne: scarcely one of the nineteen can lay any claim to importance.

Not in the official plan of studies alone had schools lost touch with the general life of the nation. While domestic manners, comforts and existence generally had become much less austere than they were in the sixteenth century, public schools retained their severity of discipline and roughness of manners. The retention was valued by some as affording a counter-agent to the supposed effeminacy of the times; but it accounts for the unwillingness of many mothers to entrust their boys to boarding-schools. Nor were roughness of manners and frequent floggings the most serious objections to be found in school life. The brutality of an earlier time survived in some of the school sports; at Eton, the "ram-hunt," in its most cruel and cowardly form, was not abolished until 1747. "All that gentleman's misfortunes arose from his being educated at a public-school," said parson Adams, commenting on the down-fall of the dissipated Mr. Wilson.

Schools were understaffed, and it was not possible, there-fore, to fill all the waking hours with a supervised routine which would keep the more audacious spirits out of mischief. "West-minster's bold race" was notorious for its readiness to defy law and order, whether of the school or of the city. "Schemes," or illicit excursions out of bounds, were by no means confined to the hours of daylight, and boys in their 'teens were brought into contact with some of the worst evils of a great city. It was at Westminster that young Qualmsick acquired "a very pretty knowledge of the Town," before he "took lodgings at a University," at the age of seventeen.[1] School discipline was ineffectual to restrain the more reckless boys: Smollett sees no absurdity in making Peregrine Pickle at fourteen "elope" from Winchester, spend some days on a visit and return, to have his escapade winked at, or condoned by the headmaster. Indeed, Perry's private retinue of clerical tutor and footman furnishes a hint as to the way in which laxity on the part of the headmaster might arise.

The growth of tutoring was, also, in itself, one of the reasons for the decline in the number of schoolboys. While William Pitt and his elder brother, Thomas, retained their own domestic tutor at Eton (1719–26), other boys of their rank were educated entirely by tutors and away from schools. The objections to public school education made on grounds of health, or morality, were the more cogent, because boys frequently en-tered the schools very much younger than they do to-day. In 1690, we read of a child of six being admitted to Westmin-ster: Jeremy Bentham went to the same school at that age in 1754. Marbles, hop-scotch, and the "rolling circle" of Gray's Eton *Ode*,[2] tell of boys much younger than the public school-boy of the present time.

So far as the systematic and recognised studies of the schools were concerned, Latin and Greek were the only educational instruments of which every boy could avail himself; presence in "school" meant attendance at a lesson in one of these lan-guages. The spectre schoolmaster of *The Dunciad* declares,

---

[1] *History of Pompey the Little*, pp. 230–2.
[2] Gray was at Eton from 1727 to 1734.

Whate'er the talents or howe'er designed,
We hang *one* jingling padlock on the mind.

But it must not be forgotten that, for boys who passed through
the entire school course, Latin and Greek were literatures, not
"subjects" comparable with one of the studies in a modern
school time-table. Further, much of the time devoted to
classical languages was spent in the active study and exercise
of composition; the old rhetorical training survived from the
sixteenth century and, in spite of its manifest faults, that
training required boys to think about a great variety of topics
of the first importance. Of course, no attempt was made to
teach natural science at any English public school during the
period under review; writing, arithmetic and, at a much later
period, some algebra and geometry received the partial recognition implied in their being taught on half-holidays by teachers
of inferior standing. Modern literature, English and French,
together with accomplishments like drawing, dancing and fencing, were regarded at Eton, and elsewhere, as occupations for
leisure hours only. Boys were expected to give some of their
leisure to private reading, the absence of the highly organised
athleticism of to-day leaving a broad margin of time for the
purpose. Cowper at Westminster (1741–9), in this way, read
with a schoolfellow all the *Iliad* and *Odyssey* in Greek, and
some of Milton's English poems. Peregrine Pickle is represented as learning at Winchester four books of Euclid, some
algebra, trigonometry and surveying, but he learned these
from Jolter, his tutor, and, therefore, apart from the school
studies. The rigour of the classical *curriculum* was a little
relaxed, but only a little, in the preparatory schools of the
London suburbs through which "Westminsters" sometimes
passed to their school.

There is a common consent amongst authorities to the
effect that the years between the restoration and the close
of the reign of George II constituted a period of stagnation,
if not of active decay, in the history of English universities.
Those who fix their attention upon the statutory order of
studies and the terms on which universities then granted degrees are likely to consider this an understatement. To-day,
the underlying supposition is that the degree betokens some

measure of intellectual achievement; it is the conventional certificate of a liberal education and a passport to certain forms of professional employment. But, in the eighteenth century, its chief function was to regularise, in academic society, the position of men who proposed to spend some further years at the university in anticipation of clerical preferment. Intellectual merit alone was not regarded as establishing an unquestionable claim to a place in the academic community, or to the conferment of a degree. Hence, degrees were sometimes refused, or withdrawn, on what would to-day be regarded as irrelevant, or even unfair, grounds. Hence, too, an easy assent to exercises which were mere forms; the eighteenth century sometimes allowed the forms to become farcical.[1]

But, soon after the restoration, it became clear that the medieval system was antiquated beyond any possibility of a useful existence. The scholastic exercises for the B.A. degree comprised disputations, frequenting public lectures, examinations and determinations. At Oxford, the last two could be satisfied by repeating a few catch-phrases in a dubious Latin, often got up beforehand or read from notes, "strings," as they were called. Candidates secured a dispensation for non-attendance at lectures which were not delivered; the examinations of 1716–19, if Amhurst may be believed on the point, could be crammed for in a fortnight. In a similar spirit, the *sex solemnes lectiones* of the statutes for M.A. became, in practice, so many "wall-lectures"—delivered, or professedly delivered, to four walls and to empty benches.

But these statutory courses and exercises fail to give a picture of university education at that date. In the first place, the educational system of the colleges frequently ensured that the forms were not empty. Thus, at St. John's college, Cambridge, in 1694, a candidate for the B.A. degree was examined by two fellows of his college during three days in rhetoric, ethics, physics and astronomy; the three days' examination in the "schools" and "answering questions," exercises before the university at a later stage, were merely

---

[1] Convenient evasions had been found at a still earlier period. In 1675, candidates at Cambridge might put down caution-money as a guarantee that they would go through the statutory exercises; they could get the degree by forfeiting the money.

formal.[1] Bentley, in 1702, introduced written examinations for scholarships and fellowships at Trinity college, and, twelve years later, we read of "a full examination including two days of book-work in classical literature for fellowships at Merton College, Oxford."[2]

Wallis, opposing Maidwell[3] in 1700, maintained that the Oxford tutorial system was an equivalent, and more, of the continental *privata collegia*, or teaching by *Seminar*, which Maidwell had said did not exist in England.[4] It is instructive to find two popular manuals by Cambridge tutors, Waterland's *Advice to a young Student* (1706), and Green's Ἐγκυκλοπαιδεία (1707), recommending the reading of the best English writers as well as books on the new philosophy, in addition to those on the classical, mathematical and philosophical studies of the customary course. At Cambridge, in 1730, Locke's *Essay* and works by English and foreign philosophers and men of science were in use. English essays were regularly prepared for the Oxford tutors at Magdalen, in 1749, and at Hertford, in 1747. Where the tutor was interested in intellectual pursuits and, at the same time, took his tutoring seriously, the extension of the pupil's studies (especially if the latter was responsive) was almost inevitable. That there were such tutors, and that opportunities existed for a wide range of studies at both Oxford and Cambridge between 1660 and 1760, are facts easily demonstrated.

The origin of the Royal society has already been told.[5] Sprat, in his *History of the Royal Society* (1667), while protesting that the new institution is in no sense a rival to the universities, goes on to say that it could not be injurious to them "without horrible ingratitude, seeing that in them it had been principally cherished and revived." In 1659, Robert Boyle brought from Strassburg the chemist, Peter Stael, who taught his science in Oxford at different times between that date and 1670. Though in no sense connected with the university, his classes attracted men of every sort of standing, above the undergraduate. In 1663, Anthony à Wood and John Locke were fellow-members of Stael's "chemical-club." Edward Lhwyd and his

[1] Wordsworth, *Scholae Academicae*, p. 23.
[2] Brodrick, *Memorials of Merton*, p. 130.   [3] See *ante*, p. 443.
[4] *A Letter from a friend of the universities*.   [5] *Ante*, Vol. VIII, Chap. XVII.

Cambridge friend John Ray were only less interested in philology than they were in natural history.

At Cambridge, Bentley is a capital instance of the university teacher whose catholic interest and zeal for knowledge extended beyond his own chosen studies. As first Boyle lecturer (1692), he attempted to confute atheism, not by the authority of the scriptures but by a study of gravitation, physiology and psychology. This sympathy with modern studies was not less characteristic of his mastership of Trinity than was his desperate struggle to maintain his office. In 1704, he made a dwelling and an observatory in the college for one of its fellows, Roger Cotes, the first Plumian professor of astronomy and of experimental philosophy; the fact marks the establishment at Cambridge of the Newtonian school of mathematics. Bentley also fitted up a laboratory for Vigani, who, after lecturing in Cambridge for some years, was made professor of chemistry in 1703. In 1724, Bentley was instrumental in founding the first botany chair in his university, and he favoured a design for drawing up a history of modern geographical discoveries.

Nor were these extra-academic interests confined to the seniors or to the new philosophy. Ambrose Bonwicke (St. John's college, Cambridge, 1710–14) learned French under a private teacher in order to study books "on all sorts of learning published daily in that language." In the same university, René La Butte taught French from 1742, and there, also, Isola taught Gray Italian. At Oxford, in 1741, Magdalen college employed *Magister Fabre, praelector linguae Gallicanae;* a little earlier, Shenstone, Graves and Whistler met in each other's rooms at Pembroke to "sip Florence wine" and to read "plays and poetry, Spectators or Tatlers and other works of lighter digestion." Dr. John Wallis, in 1700, while arguing[1] that Maidwell's projected academy was superfluous, states that instruction was then accessible at Oxford in anatomy, botany, pure and applied mathematics, French, Spanish, Italian, music, dancing, fencing, riding and other manly exercises.

Nor must it be assumed that the universities in their corporate capacity were insensible to the advance of knowledge

[1] In two pamphlets, printed with Maidwell's proposal, in the Oxford Historical Society's *Collectanea*, First Series, 1885.

or of their own responsibility for it. The old curriculum retained its function as an instrument of education, partly because the newer studies had not yet reached that stage of systematisation which is requisite in any branch of knowledge designed to educate. As early as 1683, Oxford found it necessary to open Ashmole's "elaboratory" "for promoting several parts of useful and curious learning," and the study of chemistry was regularly pursued by members of the university under the first "custos," Robert Plot. About the same date, a philosophical society, consisting of a number of distinguished seniors, including heads of houses, was instituted to correspond with the Royal society and with a similar society in Dublin.[1] By the close of the seventeenth century, the Newtonian mathematics began to take possession of the Cambridge schools, not by statutory regulation but simply in recognition of the advance in knowledge.

Between 1702 and 1750, Cambridge founded chairs in chemistry, astronomy and experimental philosophy (Plumian), anatomy, botany, Arabic, geology, astronomy and geometry (Lowndean); and Oxford instituted chairs of poetry, Anglo-Saxon and anatomy. It cannot be said that the regius professorships of modern history, founded in 1724 by George II at both universities, did much to advance the study of modern history during the eighteenth century; still, they are, at least, evidence of goodwill on both sides, though spoiled by vaguely conceived aims and faulty organisation. The work of antiquaries like Anthony à Wood and Thomas Hearne was more to the purpose.

The lethargy which seized upon English university life in the mid-eighteenth century seems to have been less profound at Cambridge, the university which enjoyed a measure of court favour; Oxford was persistently Jacobite down to the death of George II, and, in consequence, forfeited influence and lost opportunties for usefulness. The Cambridge senate house was opened in 1730 and, almost immediately, was made the scene of university examinations, which, from that time, became of a serious character. The chancellor's regulations of 1750, which aimed at stiffening discipline and reducing the expenses of undergraduates, produced a flood of pamphlets

[1] Clark, *Life and Times of Anthony à Wood*, vol. III, pp. 75-8.

which give incidental information on the condition of the university. *The Academic,* one of the best known of these, credits undergraduates with "taste for music and modern languages," and due attention to mathematics, natural philosophy and the ancient languages. The *Remarks on the Academic,* while dissenting from the conclusions of its opponent, agrees with it as to the condition of learning at Cambridge.

Edward Gibbon's impeachment of the Oxford system is well known; he was at Magdalen college (when not elsewhere on "schemes") for fourteen months, in 1752–3, entering from Westminster before he completed his fifteenth year. But his remarks are obviously too prejudiced to be accepted as a plain story of events which happened many years before he wrote his *Memoirs;* Oxford's chief offence was that it was clerical and tory. Still, the charge of idleness which he brings against fellows of colleges had been made as early as 1715 by dean Prideaux, and, in the interval, the circumstances of clerical life at Oxford had not improved. Prideaux in *LVIII Articles for reformation of universities* wanted to enforce ancient discipline throughout academic society, to punish neglectful tutors and to superannuate fellows twenty years after matriculation. A fellow who had not secured a provision for himself at that date was to be removed to a special residence supported by the colleges and named "Drone Hall." The universities were heavily handicapped by a policy which placed so much of their teaching and government in the hands of clerical celibates, whose professional ambition and hopes of "settling in life" frequently centred about a prospective college living.

BIBLIOGRAPHIES

CHAPTER I

DEFOE—THE NEWSPAPER AND THE NOVEL

For the history of English journalism prior to and contemporary with Defoe, see Nichols, J., Literary Anecdotes of the Eighteenth Century, vol. I, pp. 6, 312; vol. IV, pp. 33–97; Hunt, F. Knight, The Fourth Estate, 1850; Andrews, A., History of British Journalism, 1859; Fox Bourne, H. R., English Newspapers, 1887, vol. I, pp. 1–130; Ames, J. Griffith, The English Literary Periodical of Morals and Manners, Mt. Vernon, Ohio, 1904; and the chief authority for the earliest period (to 1666), Williams, J. B., A History of English Journalism to the Foundation of the Gazette, 1908.

For the history of English fiction prior to and contemporary with Defoe, see Dunlop, J. C., History of Prose Fiction, ed. Wilson, H., 1896, vol. II, chaps. IX–XIV; Tuckerman, Bayard, A History of English Prose Fiction, New York, 1882; Raleigh, Sir W., The English Novel, 1894; Cross, W. L., The Development of the English Novel, New York, 1899; Millar, J. H., The Mid-Eighteenth Century, Edinburgh, 1902; and Morgan, Charlotte E., The Rise of the Novel of Manners, Columbia University Studies in English, New York, 1911, which contains a full bibliography

I. SIR ROGER L'ESTRANGE

For L'Estrange's life, see a satisfactory article by Sir Sidney Lee in Dictionary of National Biography, vol. XXXIII. For information as to his writings, see this article; also Watt, R., Bibliotheca Britannica, vol. I, Edinburgh, 1824; Halkett and Laing, Dictionary of Anonymous and Pseudonymous Literature, 4 vols., Edinburgh, 1882–8.

A. *Original Writings*

(1) To a Gentleman, a Member of the Honourable House of Commons [a signed broadside]. July 8, 1646. (2) L'Estrange His Appeale from the Court Martiall to the Parliament, etc. April, 1647. Rptd in Truth and Loyalty Vindicated, pp. 38–45. (3) Lestrange His Vindication to Kent, etc. 1649. (4–23) The Declaration of the City, to the men at Westminster.—The Engagement and Remonstrance of the City of London. December 12, 1659.—The Final Protest, and Sense of the City.—The Resolve of the City. December 23, 1659.—A Free Parliament Proposed by the City to the Nation. Dated Dec. 6, 1659, but apparently combined with a letter To the Honorable the Commissioners of the City of London, for the Liberties and Rights of the English Nation, which is dated Jan. 3, 1659 (*i.e.* 1660). —A Plain Case. January 24, 1659.—To His Excellency, General Monck. A

Letter from the Gentlemen of Devon in Answer to his Lordships of January 23 to them directed from Leicester. D. Jan. 18, 1659.—The Sense of the Army. D. Feb. 2, 1659.—The Citizens Declaration for a Free Parliament (same date).—For his Excellency Generall Monck. D. Feb. 4, 1659.—A Narrative. D., without title, Feb. 12, 1659.—A Word in Season, To General Monck (with his officers, etc.), To the City, and To the Nation. D. February 18, 1659.—A Seasonable Word—Quære for Quære, etc.—No Fool to the Old Fool. D. March 16, 1659.—A Paper against the Faction. D., without title, March 24, 1659.—A Necessary and Seasonable Caution, Concerning Elections; A Sober Answer to a Jugling Pamphlet, Entituled, A Letter Intercepted, etc. D. March 27, 1660.—Treason Arraigned, In Answer to Plain English. 1660.—An Answer to An Alarum to the Armies of England, Scotland and Ireland. D. April 4, 1660. [Nos. 4–23, together in some copies with Nos. 24 and 25, are rptd. in No. 26, L'Estrange His Apology, and in almost every case are said to have been ptd.] (24) No Blinde Guides, In Answer To a seditious Pamphlet of J. Milton's, Intituled Brief Notes upon a late Sermon, etc. April 20, 1660. (25) Physician Cure thy Self: or, an Answer To a Seditious Pamphlet, Entitled Eye-Salve for the English Army, etc. . . . April 23, 1660. (26) L'Estrange His Apology: with A Short View of Some Late and Remarkable Transactions, etc. 1660. (27) An Appeal in the Case Of the late King's Party. 1660. (28) A Plea for a Limited Monarchy, etc. 1660. Rptd. in Harleian Miscellany, vol. 1. 1744. (29) A Caveat to the Cavaliers. . . . Dedicated to the Author [James Howell] of A Cordial for the Cavaliers. 1661. (30) A Modest Plea Both for the Caveat, and The Author of It. With some Notes upon Mr. James Howell, etc. August, 1661. (31) Interest Mistaken, or, The Holy Cheat. . . . By way of Observation upon a Treatise, Entituled, The Interest of England in the Matter of Religion, etc. 1661. (32) The Relaps'd Apostate: or Notes upon A Presbyterian Pamphlet, Entituled, A Petition for Peace, etc. November, 1661. (33) To the Right Hon. Edward Earl of Clarendon, Lord High Chancellor of England: The Humble Apology of Roger L'Estrange. December 3, 1661. (34) State Divinity; or a Supplement to The Relaps'd Apostate, etc. Dec. 4, 1661. (35) A Memento: Directed To all Those That Truly Reverence the Memory of King Charles the Martyr; And as Passionately wish the Honour . . . of his Royall Successour . . . Charles the II. The First Part. April, 1662. New ed. omitting the three last chapters and entitled A Memento treating of the Rise, Progress, and Remedies of Sedition. 1682. (36) Truth and Loyalty Vindicated, From the Reproaches and Clamours of Mr. Edward Bagshaw, etc. June 7, 1662. (37) A Whipp For the Schismaticall Animadverter [Bagshaw] Upon the Bishop of Worcester's Letter, etc. February, 1662. (38) Toleration Discuss'd. 1663. (39) Considerations and Proposals In Order to the Regulation of the Press: together with Diverse Instances of Treasonous, and Seditious Pamphlets, Proving the Necessity thereof. June 3, 1663. (40) The Intelligencer. Published for the satisfaction and information of the people. With Privilege. From Aug. 31, 1663, on Mondays, to January 29, 1666. (41) The Newes. Published for the satisfaction and information of the people. With Privilege. From September 3, 1663, on Thursdays, until January 29, 1666. [Beginning with 1664, these two periodicals were numbered and paged together.] (42) Publick Intelligence. With sole Privilege. [A single number.] Nov. 28, 1665. (43) Publick Advertisements (with Privilege). [One number (?).] June 25, 1666. (44) A Discourse of the Fishery, etc. 1674. (45) The Parallel or, An Account of the Growth of Knavery, Under the Pretext of Arbitrary Government and Popery. With some Observations upon a Pamphlet [by Andrew Marvell], Entitled, An Account of the Growth of Popery, etc. 1677. 3rd ed., 1681, with a new title,

Chapter I

An Account of the Growth of Knavery, under the Pretended Fears of Arbitrary Government, and Popery. With A Parallel betwixt the Reformers of 1677 and those of 1641, etc. (46) Tyranny and Popery Lording it Over the Consciences, Lives, Liberties and Estates both of King and People. 1678. (47) The History of the Plot: Or a Brief and Historical Account of the Charge and Defence of Edward Coleman, Esq. [and 16 others] . . . By Authority. 1679. (48) An Answer to the Appeal [by Charles Blount] from the Country to the City. 1679. (49) The Case Put, Concerning the Succession of his Royal Highness the Duke of York. With Some Observations upon The Political Catechism, And Two or Three Other Seditious Libels. 1679. (50) The Reformed Catholique: or, the True Protestant. 1679. (51) The Free-born Subject: or, the Englishman's Birthright, etc. 1679. (52) Citt and Bumpkin. In a Dialogue over A Pot of Ale, concerning Matters of Religion and Government. 1680. (53) Citt and Bumpkin. The Second Part. Or, a Learned Discourse upon Swearing And Lying, and other Laudable Qualities tending to a Thorow Reformation. 1680. (54) A Seasonable Memorial in some Historical Notes upon the Liberties of the Presse and Pulpit, etc. 1680. (55) A Further Discovery of the Plot, etc. 1680. (56) L'Estrange's Narrative of the Plot. Set Forth for the Edification Of His Majesties Liege People. 1680. (57) The Casuist Uncas'd in a Dialogue Betwixt Richard and Baxter, With a Moderator Between Them For Quietnesse Sake. 1680. (58) Discovery upon Discovery, In Defence of Dr. Oates against B. W's Libellous Vindication of him, in his Additional Discovery; and in Justification of L'Estrange against the same Libell. In a Letter to Doctor Titus Oates. 1680. (59) A Letter to Miles Prance. 1680. (60) L'Estrange's Case In a Civil Dialogue Betwixt 'Zekiel and Ephraim. 1680. (61) A Short Answer to a whole Litter of Libels. 1680. [Some copies read "Libellers."] (62) To the Rev. Dr. Thomas Ken. February 1, 1680. (63) The Character of a Papist in Masquerade; Supported by Authority and Experience. In Answer to the Character of a Popish Successor. 1681. (64) A Reply To the Second Part of the Character of a Popish Successor. 1681. (65) L'Estrange his Appeal Humbly Submitted to the Kings most Excellent Majesty And the Three Estates Assembled in Parliament. 1681. (66) L'Estrange No Papist: In Answer to a Libel Entituled L'Estrange a Papist, etc. In a Letter to a Friend. With Notes and Animadversions upon Miles Prance, Silver-smith, etc. 1681. (67) The Observator, etc. April 13, 1681, to Mar. 19, 1686–87. (68) The Dissenter's Sayings, In Requital for L'Estrange's Sayings. Published in Their Own Words, for the Information of the People. 1681. (69) Dissenters Sayings. The Second Part . . . Dedicated to the Grand-Jury of London, August 29, 1681. 1681. (70) Notes upon Stephen College. Grounded Principally upon his own Declarations and Confessions, etc. 1681. (71) The Reformation Reformed; or a Short History of New-fashioned Christians, etc. 1681. (72) A Word concerning Libels and Libellers, Humbly Presented To the Right Hon. Sir John Moor, Lord-Mayor of London, etc. 1681. (73) The Shammer Shamm'd: In a Plain Discovery, Under Young Tong's Own Hand, of a Designe to Trepann L'Estrange Into a Pretended Subornation against the Popish Plot. 1681. (74) The Accompt clear'd: In Answer to a Libel Intituled A True Account from Chichester, etc. 1682. (75) The Apostate Protestant. A Letter to a Friend, occasioned By the late Reprinting of a Jesuites Book. About Succession to the Crown of England. Pretended to have been written by R. Doleman. July, 1682. (76) Remarks on the Growth and Progress of Non-Conformity, etc. 1682. (77) Considerations upon a Printed Sheet Entituled the Speech Of the Late Lord Russel to the Sheriffs: together With the Paper delivered by Him to Them . . . on July 21, 1683. [Rptd by Clarendon Historical Soc.,

1882.]   (78) The Observator Defended.   By the Author of the Observators, etc
1685.   (79) An Answer to a Letter to a Dissenter [Halifax's], Upon Occasion of
His Majesties Late Gracious Declaration of Indulgence.   1687.   (80–82) A Brief
History of the Times, etc.   3 parts.   1687–8.   (83) A Reply to the Reasons of the
Oxford Clergy against Addressing.   168–.   [Rptd in Scott's Somers Tracts, vol.
IX, 1809.]   (84) Two Cases submitted to Consideration, etc.   1687.

L'Estrange wrote the Notice to the Reader in an edition of Fairfax's Godfrey
of Bulloigne, 1687; and, in 1715, A Key to Hudibras, attributed to him, was
printed in Butler's Posthumous Works.

[L'Estrange has been frequently credited with works which he, probably or
certainly, did not write.]

See, also, Le Breton, A., Le Roman au dix-huitième Siècle, Paris, 1898; Texte,
Joseph, Rousseau et les origines du Cosmopolitisme Littéraire, Paris, 1895;
Warner, G. F., An Unpublished Political Paper by Daniel De Foe, Engl. Hist.
Rev., January, 1907.

B.   *Translations*

(1) The "Visions" of Quevedo.   1667.   (2) Five Love Letters from a [Portu-
guese] Nun to a Cavalier, from the French.   1678.   (3) The Gentleman 'Pothe-
cary; a true Story done out of the French.   1678.   (4) Tully's Offices.   1680.
(5) Cardinal J. Bona's "A Guide to Eternity" (from the Latin).   2nd ed.   1680.
(6) Seneca's Morals by way of Abstract.   5th ed.   1693.   (7) Twenty Select
Colloquies of Erasmus, etc.   1680.   With two additional colloquies, 1689.   (8)
An Apology for the Protestants; Being A full Justification of their Departure from
The Church of Rome. . . . Done out of French into English.   1681.   (9) The
Fables of Aesop and other Eminent Mythologists; with Morals and Reflexions.
1692.   (10) Five Love Letters written by a Cavalier in Answer [to No. (2) above].
1694.   (11) Terence's Comedies made English, etc. [revised by J. Eachard and
L'Estrange].   2nd ed.   1698.   (12) Fables and Storyes Moralized.   Being a
Second Part of the Fables of Aesop and other Eminent Mythologists.   1699.
(13) The Works of Flavius Josephus.   1702.   (14) The Spanish Pole-Cat: or,
the Adventures of Seniora Rufina, etc. [from the Spanish of A. del Castillo Solor-
zano, begun by L'Estrange and finished by Ozell].   1717.   Reissued in 1727 as
Spanish Amusements, etc.

II.   Daniel Defoe

The chief biographies of Defoe are those by Chalmers, George (1790), which
marks the beginning of serious study of the man and his works; Wilson, W. (3 vols.
1830), still valuable, particularly as a history of Defoe's times; Lee, W., in vol. 1
of Life and Newly Discovered Writings of Daniel Defoe (1869), which contains
much new material badly handled and fixes Defoe's bibliography at the point at
which it has stood almost to the present time; Minto, W., in English Men of
Letters (1879), still valuable for the critical acumen displayed; Wright, T. (1894),
which contains new material, but occasionally indulges in extravagant theories.
Other biographers on a larger or a smaller scale, such as Towers, Dr. Hazlitt,
William, the younger, Forster, John, Morley, Henry, and Whitten, W. (1900),
deserve to be mentioned, as well as Stephen, Sir Leslie, and, for a good essay,
Rannie, D. W. (Oxford, 1890).   Cf. also, Lamb, Charles, Works, I, Miscellaneous
Prose, ed. Lucas, E., 1903; Dennis, John, Studies in English Literature, 1883;
York Powell, F., Occasional Writings, ed. Elton, O., 1906.   The most important
recent student of Defoe is Aitken, George A., in his contributions to periodicals

and his introductions to his edition of Defoe's novels. Cf. four articles, chiefly bibliographical, contributed by the present writer to The Nation (New York, 1907–8).

No edition of Defoe's writings has yet been worthy of the name. In 1703 and 1705, he collected some of his tracts and poems, but soon his pen outran the capacity of his contemporaries to identify his work, and there was comparatively little interest in him as a writer from his death to the end of the eighteenth century. In 1810, the edition of the novels with which the name of Scott is connected appeared in 12 vols. Thirty years later, Hazlitt, William, the younger, began an elaborate edition which reached only three volumes. Simultaneously, an edition in 20 vols. was printed at Oxford. This, despite serious defects, remains the only edition giving access to some of the more important miscellaneous books. It is, however, utterly inadequate on the side of Defoe's political writings. There is also an edition in 6 vols. in Bohn's British Classics (1854–5); but the novels and shorter narratives and a few tracts may now be read in the excellent edition of the Romances and Narratives in 16 vols. (1895–6) due to the care of Aitken, G. A. An edition but slightly differing from this in contents was prepared for American readers in 1903 by Maynadier, G. H. (16 vols. New York).

A. *Writings*

[In chronological order, except where otherwise indicated. When ascertainable the actual date of publication is always given, not the date on the title-page.]

A New Discovery of an Old Intreague: A Satyr, etc. 1691.

Ode to the Athenian Society. In Gildon's History of the Athenian Society. 1692.

An Essay upon Projects. 1697. Reissued, 1702.

The Character of the late Dr. Samuel Annesley, by Way of Elegy. 1697.

Some Reflections On a Pamphlet lately Publish'd, Entituled, An Argument Shewing that A Standing Army, etc. 1697.

An Argument Shewing, That a Standing Army, With Consent of Parliament, Is not Inconsistent with a Free Government, etc. 1698.

An Enquiry into the Occasional Conformity of Dissenters in Cases of Preferment. With a Preface to the Lord Mayor. 1698.

> An Enquiry into the Occasional Conformity of Dissenters. With a Preface to Mr. How. 1700. 2nd ed. of the above, with another preface.

A Brief Reply to the History of Standing Armies in England, etc. 1698.

The Poor Man's Plea . . . for a Reformation of Manners, etc. 1698.

Lex Talionis: or, an Enquiry into The Most Proper Ways to Prevent the Persecution of the Protestants in France. 1698.

The Pacificator. A Poem. 1700.

The Two Great Questions Consider'd, etc. 1700.

The Two Great Questions Further Considered, etc. 1700.

The Six distinguishing Characters of a Parliament man, etc. 1701.

The Danger of the Protestant Religion Considered from the Present Prospect of a Religious War in Europe. 1701.

The Free-Holders Plea against Stock-Jobbing Elections of Parliament Men. 1701.

The True-Born Englishman. A Satyr. 1701. First ed. dated 1700.

> Tutchin, John. The Foreigners. A Poem. 1700.

A Letter to Mr. How, etc. 1701.

Considerations upon Corrupt Elections of Members To Serve in Parliament. 1701.

The Villainy of Stock-Jobbers Detected, etc. 1701.

The Succession to the Crown of England, Considered. 1701.

Legion's Address. 1701.

The History of the Kentish Petition. 1701.

The Present State of Jacobitism Considered, etc. 1701.

Reasons against a War with France, etc. 1701.

The Original Power of the Collective Body of the People of England, Examined and Asserted. 1701.

Legion's New Paper, etc. 1702.

The Mock Mourners. A Satyr, By Way of Elegy on King William. 1702.

Reformation of Manners, A Satyr. 1702.

A New Test of the Church of England's Loyalty, etc. 1702.

Good Advice to the Ladies, etc. 1702. [Verse.] Reissued as A Timely Caution; or Good Advice, etc. 1728.

The Spanish Descent. A Poem. 1702.

An Enquiry into Occasional Conformity. Shewing that the Dissenters Are no Way Concern'd in it. 1702. Reissued as An Enquiry into the Occasional Conformity Bill. 1704.

The Shortest Way with the Dissenters: or, Proposals for the Establishment of the Church. 1702.

A Brief Explanation of A late Pamphlet, entitul'd, The shortest Way with the Dissenters. 1703.

　　　　Tutchin, J.　A Dialogue between A Dissenter and the Observator. 1703.

King William's Affection to the Church of England, Examin'd. 1703.

More Reformation. A Satyr upon Himself By the Author of the True Born English-Man. 1703.

A true Collection of the Writings of the Author of the True-Born English-Man. 1703. [This was preceded by a spurious collection.]

The Shortest Way to Peace and Union. 1703.

A Hymn to the Pillory. 1703.

The Case of Dissenters As Affected by the Late Bill Proposed in Parliament, For Preventing Occasional Conformity. 1703.

The Sincerity of the Dissenters Vindicated, From the Scandal of Occasional Conformity, with Some Considerations on a late Book, Entitul'd, Moderation a Vertue. 1703.

An Enquiry into the Case of Mr. Asgil's General Translation, etc. 1703.

A Challenge of Peace, Address'd to the Whole Nation, etc. 1703.

The Liberty of Episcopal Dissenters in Scotland, as it stands by the Laws there, truly Represented. 1703.

Some Remarks On the First Chapter in Dr. Davenant's Essays. 1703. Reissued as Original Right . . . Being an Answer to the first Chapter, etc., 1704.

Peace without Union. By Way of Reply to Sir H[umphrey] M[ackworth]'s Peace at Home. 1703.

The Dissenters Answer to the High-Church Challenge. 1704.

An Essay on the Regulation of the Press. 1704.

A Serious Inquiry into this Grand Question: Whether a Law to prevent the Occasional Conformity of Dissenters would not be Inconsistent with the Act of Toleration, etc. 1704.

The Parallel: or, Persecution of Protestants the Shortest Way to prevent the Growth of Popery in Ireland. 1704.

Royal Religion; Being some Enquiry after the Piety of Princes, etc. 1704.

Moderation Maintain'd, in Defence of a Compassionate Enquiry Into the Causes of the Civil War, etc. In a Sermon Preached . . . by White Kennet, etc. 1704.

The Christianity of the High-Church Consider'd, etc. 1704.

More Short-Ways with the Dissenters. 1704.

The Dissenters Misrepresented and Represented. 1704.

A New Test of the Church of England's Honesty. 1704.

The Storm: or, a Collection Of the most Remarkable Casualties and Disasters which happen'd in the Late Dreadful Tempest, both by Sea and Land. 1704.

An Elegy on the Author of the True-Born-English-Man. With an Essay On the late Storm. 1704.

A Hymn to Victory. 1704.

The Protestant Jesuite Unmask'd, etc. 1704.

Giving Alms no Charity, and Employing the Poor A Grievance to the Nation, etc. 1704.

Queries upon the Bill against Occasional Conformity. 1704.

The Double Welcome. A Poem to the Duke of Marlbro. 1705.

Persecution Anatomiz'd: or, An Answer [to 4 questions]. 1705.

The Consolidator: or, Memoirs of Sundry Transactions from the World in the Moon, etc. 1705.

The Experiment: or, the Shortest Way with the Dissenters Exemplified. Being the Case of Mr. Abraham Gill, etc. 1705. Reissued as The Modesty and Sincerity of those Worthy English Gentlemen, commonly called High Churchmen, etc. 1706.

A Journey to the World in the Moon, etc. 1705.

A Letter from the Man in the Moon, to the Author of The true Born English-man, etc. 1705.

A Second and more strange Journey to the World in the Moon, etc. 1705.

Advice to all Parties. 1705.

The Dyet of Poland. A Satyr. 1705.

The High-Church Legeon: or, the Memorial Examin'd, etc. 1705.

The Ballance: or, A New Test of the High-Fliers of all Sides, etc. 1705.

A Second Volume of the Writings of the Author of the True-Born Englishman, etc. 1705.

Party-Tyranny: or, An Occasional Bill in Miniature; As now Practised in Carolina, etc. 1705.

An Answer to the Lord Haversham's Speech. 1705.

A Hymn to Peace, etc. 1706.

A Reply to a Pamphlet Entituled, the L[or]d H[aversham]'s Vindication of his Speech. 1706.

The Case of Protestant Dissenters in Carolina, etc. 1706.

Remarks on the Bill to Prevent Frauds Committed by Bankrupts, etc. 1706.

Remarks on the Letter to the Author of the State-Memorial. 1706.

An Essay At Removing National Prejudices against a Union with Scotland. 1706.

The same. Part II. 1706.

The same. Part III. Edinburgh, 1706.

A Fourth Essay At Removing National Prejudices, etc. Edinburgh, 1706.

A Fifth Essay At Removing National Prejudices, etc. Edinburgh, 1707.

Two Great Questions Considered . . . Being A Sixth Essay At Removing, etc. Edinburgh, 1707.
Preface to De Laune's Plea for the Non-Conformists, etc. 1706.
> This is said to have been reprinted by Defoe in 1710 as Dr. Sacheverell's Recantation, etc.
A Sermon Preach'd by Mr. Daniel Defoe: On the fitting up of Dr. Burges's late Meeting-House, etc. 1706.
A True Relation of the Apparition of one Mrs. Veal . . . to one Mrs. Bargrave at Canterbury, etc. 1706.
> This tract was often printed with Drelincourt's The Christian's Defence against the Fears of Death.
Jure Divino: A Satyr. In Twelve Books. 1706.
Observations on the Fifth Article of the Treaty of Union, etc. Edinburgh, 1706.
The Vision, A Poem. Edinburgh, 1706. [Erroneously ascribed to the earl of Haddington.]
A Reply to the Scot's Answer, To the British Vision. Edinburgh, 1706.
A Short Letter to the Glasgow-Men. Edinburgh, 1706.
The Rabbler Convicted, etc. Edinburgh, 1706.
Caledonia, A Poem in Honour of Scotland, and the Scots Nation. Edinburgh, 1706.
An Enquiry into the Disposal of the Equivalent. Edinburgh, 1706.
The Dissenters in England Vindicated from some Reflections in a late Pamphlet called Lawful Prejudices, etc. Edinburgh, 1707.
A Short View of the Present State of the Protestant Religion in Britain, etc. Edinburgh, 1707. 2nd ed. as The Dissenters Vindicated; or, a Short View, etc. London, 1707.
A Modest Vindication of the Present Ministry, etc. 1707. [Against lord Haversham.]
A Voice from the South, etc. Edinburgh (?), 1707.
The Trade of Britain Stated, etc. Edinburgh, 1707.
Dyers News Examined as to his Sweddish Memorial against the Review. Edinburgh, 1707.
De Foe's Answer, To Dyers Scandalous News Letter. Edinburgh, 1707.
An Historical Account of The Bitter Sufferings, and Melancholly Circumstances of the Episcopal Church in Scotland, etc. Edinburgh, 1707. Also, same place and date, as Presbyterian Persecution Examined. With an Essay on the Nature and Necessity of Toleration in Scotland.
Reflections on the Prohibition Act, etc. 1708.
Advice to the Electors of Great Britain; occasioned by the intended Invasion from France. 1708.
An Answer to a Paper concerning Mr. De Foe, against his History of the Union. Edinburgh, 1708.
The Scots Narrative Examin'd; or, the Case of the Episcopal Ministers in Scotland Stated, etc. 1709.
The History of the Union of Great Britain. Edinburgh, 1709. As a Collection of Original Papers and Material Transactions, Concerning the late Great Affair of the Union, etc. 1711, 1712.
A Commendatory Sermon Preach'd November the 4th, 1709. Being the Birth-Day of King William of Glorious Memory. 1709.
Advertisement From Daniel De Foe, To Mr. Clark. 1710.
A Letter from Captain Tom to the Mobb, Now Rais'd for Dr. Sacheverell. 1710.

A Speech without Doors. 1710.

Instructions from Rome, In Favour of the Pretender, Inscribed to the most Elevated Don Sacheverellio, etc. 1710.

A New Test of the Sence of the Nation, etc. 1710.

An Essay upon Publick Credit. 1710.

An Essay upon Loans. 1710.

A Word Against a New Election. 1710.

A Supplement to the Faults on Both Sides. 1710.

R[ogue]s on Both Sides. 1711.

Atalantis Major. Edinburgh, 1711.

A Spectator's Address to the Whigs, on the Occasion of the Stabbing Mr. Harley. 1711.

A Letter to the Whigs, etc. 1711. [In part a reprint of the preceding.]

The Secret History of the October Club. Part I. 1711.

The same. Part II. 1711.

The British Visions: or, Isaac Bickerstaff's Twelve Prophecies for the Year 1711. 1711.

The Succession of Spain Consider'd. 1711.

Eleven Opinions about Mr. H[arle]y; with Observations. 1711.

An Essay upon the Trade to Africa. 1711.

The Re-Representation: or, a Modest Search After the Great Plunderers of the Nation. 1711.

A True Account of the Design and Advantages of the South-Sea Trade. 1711.

A Speech for Mr. D[unda]sse Younger of Arnistown. 1711.

An Essay on the South-Sea Trade. 1711.

The True State of the Case between the Government and the Creditors of the Navy. 1711.

Reasons why this Nation Ought to put a Speedy End to this Expensive War. 1711.

The Ballance of Europe: or, an Enquiry into the Respective Dangers Of giving the Spanish Monarchy to the Emperour As well as to King Philip, etc. 1711.

Armageddon: or, the Necessity of Carrying on the War, etc. 1711.

An Essay At a Plain Exposition of that Difficult Phrase A Good Peace. 1711.

Reasons Why a Party Among us, and also among the Confederates, Are obstinately bent against a Treaty of Peace with the French at this time. 1711.

The Felonious Treaty. 1711.

A Defence of the Allies and the Late Ministry: or, Remarks on the Tories New Idol. . . . The Conduct of the Allies, etc. 1711.

An Essay on the History of Parties, and Persecution in Britain. 1711.

No Queen: or, No General. An Argument Proving the Necessity. . . . to Displace the D— of M[arl]borough. 1712.

The Conduct of Parties in England, More especially of those Whigs Who now appear Against the New Ministry, and a Treaty of Peace. 1712.

Plunder and Bribery Further Discover'd, in a Memorial Humbly Offer'd To the British Parliament. 1712.

Peace or Poverty. Being A Serious Vindication of Her Majesty and Her Ministers Consenting to a Treaty for a General Peace. 1712.

No Punishment No Government: and No Danger Even in the Worst Designs. 1712.

The Highland Visions or the Scots New Prophecy: Declaring in Twelve Visions what Strange Things shall come to Pass in the Year 1712. 1712.

Wise as Serpents: Being an Enquiry into the Present Circumstances of the Dissenters, etc. 1712.

The Present State of Parties in Great Britain. 1712.

Reasons against Fighting. 1712.

A Farther Search into the Conduct of the Allies, and the late Ministry, as to Peace and War. 1712.

The Present Negotiations of Peace Vindicated from the Imputation of Trifling. 1712.

The Validity of the Renunciations of Former Powers Enquir'd into, and the Present Renunciation of the Duke of Anjou, Impartially Consider'd, etc. 1712.

An Enquiry into the Danger and Consequences of a War with the Dutch. 1712.

The Justice and Necessity of a War with Holland, In Case the Dutch Do not come into Her Majesty's Measures, Stated and Examined. 1712.

An Enquiry into the Real Interest of Princes in the Persons of their Ambassadors, etc. 1712.

A Seasonable Warning And Caution Against the Insinuations Of Papists and Jacobites In Favour of the Pretender. 1712.

Hannibal at the Gates; or, the Progress of Jacobitism. 1712.

A Strict Enquiry Into the Circumstances of a late Duel [Hamilton and Mohun], With some Account of the Persons Concern'd on Both Sides, etc. 1713.

Reasons against the Succession of the House of Hanover. 1713.

Not[tingh]am Politicks Examined. Being An Answer to . . . Observations upon the State of the Nation. 1713.

The Second-Sighted Highlander . . . Being Ten New Visions for the Year 1713. 1713.

A Brief Account of the Present State of the African Trade. 1713.

And What if the Pretender should come? 1713.

An Answer to a Question That No body thinks of, Viz. But what if the Queen should die? 1713.

An Essay on the Treaty of Commerce with France. 1713.

Union and No Union. Being an Enquiry Into the Grievances of the Scots, etc. 1713.

A General History of Trade, and Especially Consider'd as it Respects the British Commerce, etc. 4 Parts. 1713.

A Letter from a Member of the House of Commons to his Friend in the Country, Relating to the Bill of Commerce, etc. 1713.

Considerations upon the Eighth and Ninth Articles of the Treaty of Commerce and Navigation, etc. 1713.

Memoirs Of Count Tariff, etc. 1713.

Some Thoughts upon the Subject of Commerce with France. 1713.

A Letter To the Dissenters. 1713.

Whigs turn'd Tories, and Hanoverian Tories, From their Avow'd Principles, prov'd Whigs, etc. 1713.

A Letter to the Whigs, Expostulating with Them upon Their Present Conduct. 1714.

The Scots Nation and Union Vindicated; from the Reflections cast on them, in an Infamous Libel. Entitl'd, The Publick Spirit of the Whigs, etc. 1714.

A View of the Real Danger of the Protestant Succession. 1714.

Reasons for Im[peaching] the L[or]d H[igh] T[reasure]r, And some others of the P[resent] M[inistry]. 1714.

A Letter to Mr. Steele, Occasion'd by his Letter to a Member of Parliament, Concerning The Bill for preventing the Growth of Schism. By a Member of the Church of England. 1714.

The Remedy Worse than the Disease: or, Reasons Against Passing the Bill For Preventing the Growth of Schism. 1714.

A Brief Survey of the Legal Liberties of the Dissenters, etc. 1714.

The Weakest go to the Wall, or the Dissenters Sacrific'd by all Parties. 1714.

Advice To the People of Great Britain, with Respect to Two Important Points in their Future Conduct, etc. 1714.

The Secret History of the White-Staff, etc. Part I. 1714.

The same. Part II. 1714.

The same. Part III. 1715.

 The three parts were included in one pamphlet, 1715.

Impeachment, or No Impeachment. 1714.

A Secret History of One Year. 1714.

Strike while the Iron's Hot, or, Now is the Time To Be Happy. 1714.

The Secret History of State Intrigues In the Management of the Scepter, In the late Reign. 1715. Also published as The Secret History of the Scepter, or the Court Intrigues in the Late Reign.

The Secret History of the Secret History of the White Staff, Purse And Mitre. Written by a Person of Honour. 1715.

Memoirs of the Conduct of Her Late Majesty And Her Last Ministry, Relating to the Separate Peace with France. By the Right Honourable the Countess of —. 1715.

Treason Detected, in an Answer to that Traiterous and Malicious Libel, Entitled, English Advice to the Freeholders of England. 1715.

A Reply to a Traiterous Libel, Entituled, English Advice to the Freeholders of England. [By bishop Atterbury?] 1715.

A Letter from a Country Whig, to his Friend in London; Wherein Appears, Who are the Truest Friends To their King and Country. 1715.

A Letter to a Merry Young Gentleman, Intituled, Tho. Burnett, Esq.; In Answer to One writ by him to the Right Honourable the Earl of Halifax, etc. 1715. [Attributed, also, to William Oldisworth.]

Burnet and Bradbury, or the Confederacy of the Press and the Pulpit for the Blood of the Last Ministry. 1715.

A Friendly Epistle By Way of Reproof From one of the People called Quakers, to Thomas Bradbury, A Dealer in many Words. 1715.

An Appeal to Honour and Justice, Tho' it be of His Worst Enemies. By Daniel De Foe. Being A True Account of his Conduct in Publick Affairs. 1715.

Some Reasons Offered by the Late Ministry In Defence of their Administration. 1715.

The Folly and Vanity of Impeaching the Late Ministry Consider'd. 1715.

A Remonstrance from some Country Whigs to a Member of a Secret Committee. 1715.

The Fears of the Pretender Turn'd into the Fears of Debauchery . . . with a Hint to Richard Steele, Esq. 1715.

A Sharp Rebuke From one of the People called Quakers to Henry Sacheverell, The High-Priest of Andrew's Holborn. 1715.

The Family Instructor. In Three Parts. 1715. In Two Parts, vol. II, 1718.

The Second-Sighted Highlander. Being Four Visions of the Eclypse, And something of what may follow. 1715.

Some Methods To supply the Defects Of the late Peace, without entring into a New War. 1715.

A Second Letter from a Country Whig, etc. 1715. [See A Letter from a Country Whig, *ante*.]

Bold Advice: or Proposals For the Entire Rooting out of Jacobitism in Great Britain, etc. 1715.

Some Considerations on the Danger of the Church From her own Clergy, etc. 1715.

An Attempt towards a Coalition of English Protestants . . . To which is added, Reasons for Restraining the Licentiousness of the Pulpit and Press. 1715.

A Seasonable Expostulation with, and Friendly Reproof unto, James Butler, who, by the Men of this World, is Stil'd Duke of O[rmon]d, etc. 1715.

An Account of the Conduct of Robert Earl of Oxford. 1715. Reissued in 1717 as Memoirs of some Transactions during the late Ministry of Robert E. of Oxford.

The History of the Wars, Of his Present Majesty Charles XII. King of Sweden, etc. 1715. Continued in a second edition, 1720.

A Hymn to the Mob. 1715.

An Humble Address to our Soveraign Lord the People. 1715.

An Apology for the Army. In a Short Essay on Fortitude, etc. Written by an Officer. 1715.

An Account of the Great and Generous Actions of James Butler, (Late Duke of Ormond). Dedicated to the Famous University of Oxford. 1715.

A View of the Scots Rebellion, etc. 1715.

The Traiterous and Foolish Manifesto of the Scots Rebels, Examin'd and Expos'd Paragraph by Paragraph. 1715.

A Trumpet Blown in the North, And sounded in the Ears of John Erskine, Call'd by the Men of the World, Duke of Mar. 1715.

A Letter from One Clergy-Man to Another, upon the Subject of the Rebellion. 1715.

A Letter To the Right Hon. Robert Walpole, Esq.; Occasioned by His late Promotion, etc. 1715. Cf. *post.*

An Essay towards Real Moderation. 1716.

Some Thoughts of an Honest Tory In the Country, upon the Late Dispositions of some People to Revolt, etc. 1716.

The Conduct of some People, about Pleading Guilty, etc. 1716.

Some Considerations on a Law for Triennial Parliaments, etc. 1716.

Arguments about the Alteration of Triennial Elections of Parliament. 1716.

The Triennial Act Impartially Stated, etc. 1716.

A True Account Of the Proceedings at Perth, etc. 1716.

    Rptd in vol. II of The Spottiswoode Miscellany (1845), where it is erroneously attributed to the Master of Sinclair.

An Essay upon Buying and Selling of Speeches. 1716.

Some Account of the Two Nights Court at Greenwich. 1716.

A Second Letter to the Right Hon. Robert Walpole, Esq. 1716.

Remarks on the Speeches of William Paul Clerk, and John Hall of Otterburn, Esq.; Executed at Tyburn for Rebellion, the 13th of July, 1716, etc. 1716.

The Layman's Vindication of the Church of England, As well against Mr. Howell's Charge of Schism, As against Dr. Bennett's Pretended Answer to it. 1716.

Secret Memoirs of the New Treaty of Alliance with France. 1716.

Secret Memoirs of a Treasonable Conference at S[omerset] House, For Deposing the Present Ministry, etc. 1716.

Some National Grievances . . . Considered . . . in a Letter to R[obert] W[alpole] Esq. 1717.

An Expostulatory Letter, to the B[ishop] of B[angor] concerning A Book lately publish'd by his Lordship, Entitul'd, A Preservative Against the Principles and Practices of the Nonjurors. 1717.

The Danger of Court Differences: or, the Unhappy Effects of a Motley Ministry: Occasion'd by the Report of Changes at Court. 1717.

The Quarrel of the School-Boys at Athens, As lately Acted at a School near Westminster. 1717.

An Impartial Enquiry into the Conduct Of the Right Honourable Charles Lord Viscount T[ownshend]. 1717.

An Argument Proving that the Design of Employing and Ennobling Foreigners, Is a Treasonable Conspiracy against the Constitution, etc. 1717.

A Curious Little Oration, Deliver'd by Father Andrew, Concerning the Present Great Quarrels That divide the Clergy of France. 1717.

Fair Payment No Spunge, etc. 1717.

What if the Swedes Should Come? With some Thoughts About Keeping The Army on Foot, Whether they Come or not. 1717.

The Repeal of the Act against Occasional Conformity, Consider'd. 1717.

The Question Fairly Stated, Whether Now is not the Time to do Justice to the Friends of the Government, as well as to its Enemies, etc. 1717.

The Danger and Consequences of Disobliging the Clergy consider'd, etc. 1717.

Reaons for a Royal Visitation . . . Shewing The Absolute Necessity of Purging the Universities, and Restoring Discipline to the Church. 1717.

Memoirs of the Church of Scotland, In Four Periods. 1717.

A Farther Argument against Ennobling Foreigners, in Answer To the Two Parts of the State Anatomy, etc. 1717. [By Toland. Cf. An Argument, etc. ante.]

The Conduct of Robert Walpole, Esq., etc. 1717.

The Report Reported: or, the Weakness and Injustice of the Proceedings of the Convocation in their Censure Of Ld. Bp. of Bangor, Examin'd and Expos'd. 1717.

A Short View of the Conduct of the King of Sweden. 1717.

A General Pardon Considered in its Circumstances and Consequences, etc. 1717.

Observations on the Bishop's Answer to Dr. Snape. By a Lover of Truth. 1717.

A Vindication of Dr. Snape, in Answer to Several Libels lately publish'd against him, etc. 1717.

Mr. Benjamin Hoadly. Against The Right Rev. Father in God Benjamin Lord Bishop of Bangor, etc. 1717.

Minutes of the Negotiations of Monsr. Mesnager at the Court of England, Towards the close of the last Reign, etc. 1717.

A Reply to the Remarks upon the Lord Bishop of Bangor's Treatment of the Clergy and Convocation. Said to be Written by Dr. Sherlock. 1717.

A Declaration of Truth to Benjamin Hoadly, One of the High Priests of the Land, and Of the Degree whom Men call Bishops, etc. 1717.

The Old Whig And Modern Whig Revived, in the Present Divisions at Court. 1717.

A Letter to Andrew Snape, etc. 1717.

The Conduct of Christians made the Sport of Infidels. In a Letter From a Turkish Merchant at Amsterdam To the Grand Mufti at Constantinople: On Occasion Of some of our National Follies, but especially of the late scandalous Quarrel among the Clergy. 1717.

Mr. De La Pillonniere's Vindication: being an Answer to the Two School-masters, and their Boy's Tittle Tattle, etc. 1717.

The Case of the War in Italy Stated. 1717.

Memoirs of the Life and Eminent Conduct Of that Learned and Reverend Divine, Daniel Williams, D.D. 1718.

Some Persons Vindicated against the Author of the Defection [Tindal] etc. And that Writer Convicted of Malice and Falshood, R—W—, Esq. 1718.

The Defection Farther Consider'd, wherein the Resigners, As some would have them stil'd, Are really Deserters. 1718.

Considerations on the Present State of Affairs in Great Britain. 1718.

A Vindication of the Press: or, an Essay on the Usefulness of Writing, on Criticism, and the Qualification of Authors, etc. 1718.

Memoirs of Publick Transactions In the Life and Ministry Of his Grace the D. of Shrewsbury, etc. 1718.

A Continuation of Letters Written by a Turkish Spy at Paris, etc. 1718.

A Brief Comment upon His Majestys Speech: Being Reasons for strengthening the Church of England, by taking off the Penal Laws against Dissenters. 1718.

A History of the Last Session of the Present Parliament. With a Correct List of Both Houses. 1718.

A Friendly Rebuke to one Parson Benjamin [Hoadly], Particularly relating to his quarrelling with his own Church, and Vindicating the Dissenters. 1719.

The Life and Strange Surprizing Adventures of Robinson Crusoe, Of York, Mariner. . . . Written by Himself. 1719. Facsimile rpt., ed. Dobson, A., 1883.

The Farther Adventures of Robinson Crusoe: Being the Second and Last Part of his Life, etc. 1719.

Serious Reflections during the Life and Surprising Adventures of Robinson Crusoe: With his Vision of the Angelick World. 1720.

> Among anticipations of Robinson Crusoe may be noted Marivaux, P. C. de, Les Avantures de * * * ou les effets surprenans de la sympathie, 5 vols., 1715; [Tyssot de Patot, S.], Les voyages et aventures de Jacques Massé. 1710.
>
> Cf. Howell, John, Life and Adventures of Alexander Selkirk, Edinburgh, 1829.

The History of the Reign of King George, From the Death of her late Majesty Queen Anne, to the First of August, 1718. 1719.

A Letter to the Dissenters. 1719.

The Anatomy of Exchange-Alley: or, A System of Stock-Jobbing. 1719.

Some Account of the Life, and most Remarkable Actions, of George Henry Baron de Goertz, Privy-Counsellor and Chief Minister of State, to the Late King of Sweden. 1719.

The Just Complaint of the Poor Weavers Truly Represented. 1719.

A Brief State of the Question, Between the Printed and Painted Callicoes and the Woollen and Silk Manufacture. 1719.

The Dumb Philosopher; or, Great Britain's Wonder, containing I. A Faithful and very Surprizing account how Dickory Cronke, a Tinner's Son in the County of Cornwal, was born Dumb, and continued so for 58 Years; and how some Days before he died, he came to his Speech, etc. 1719.

The King of Pirates: Being an Account of the Famous Enterprizes of Captain Avery, The Mock King of Madagascar. 1719.

The Chimera: or, the French Way of Paying National Debts, Laid Open. 1720.

The Trade to India Critically and Calmly consider'd, And prov'd to be destructive to the General Trade of Great Britain, as well as to the Woollen and Silk Manufactures in particular. 1720.

The Case Fairly Stated between the Turky Company and the Italian Merchants. By a Merchant. 1720.

The Compleat Art of Painting. A Poem. Translated from the French of M. Du Fresnoy. By D. F. Gent. 1720.

An Historical Account of the Voyages and Adventures of Sir Walter Raleigh . . . Humbly proposed to the South-Sea Company. 1720, but dated 1719.

The History of the Life and Adventures of Mr. Duncan Campbell, A Gentleman, who, tho' Deaf and Dumb, writes down any Stranger's Name at first Sight; with their future Contingencies of Fortune, etc. 1720. Reissued as The Supernatural Philosopher by Bond, William, 1728.

> It seems clear that Defoe wrote the History; but his work was probably revised by Bond. Defoe also wrote, in 1726, The Friendly Daemon (see *post*), and he may have had some hand in the posthumous Secret Memoirs of 1732.

Memoirs of a Cavalier: or, a Military Journal of The Wars in Germany, and The Wars in England, etc. 1720.

The Life, Adventures, and Pyracies, Of the Famous Captain Singleton. 1720.

A Letter To the Author of the Independent Whig. Wherein The Merits of the Clergy are consider'd, etc. 1720.

A Letter to the Independent Whig Occasioned by his Considerations of the Importance of Gibraltar to the British Empire. 1720.

A True State of Publick Credit; or, a Short View of the Condition of the Nation, with respect to our present Calamities. . . As also Some necessary Observations on the Conduct of the Bank, in this Critical Juncture. 1721.

A Vindication of the Honour and Justice of Parliament Against a most Scandalous Libel, Entituled, The Speech of John A[islabie], Esq. 1721.

Brief Observations on Trade and Manufactures; And particularly of our Mines, and Metals, and the Hard-Ware Works, etc. 1721.

A Collection of Miscellany Letters, Selected out of Mist's Weekly Journal. 2 vols. 1722.

> Defoe contributed to these volumes and probably edited them.

The Fortunes and Misfortunes of the Famous Moll Flanders, etc. Who was Born in Newgate. . . .Twelve Year a Thief, Eight Year a Transported Felon in Virginia. . . . Written from her own Memorandums. 1722.

Due Preparations for the Plague, As well for Soul as Body. 1722.

Religious Courtship: Being Historical Discourses, on the Necessity of Marrying Religious Husbands and Wives only . . . With an Appendix Of the Necessity of taking none but Religious Servants, and a Proposal for the better managing of Servants. 1722.

A Journal of the Plague Year . . . Written by a Citizen, etc. 1722. Ed. Brayley, E. W. 1839.

> Austin, William, (*fl.* 1662). Ἐπιλοίμια ἔπη· or the Anatomy of the Pestilence. A Poem in three parts, describing the deplorable condition of the city of London under its merciless dominion, 1665. 1666.

An History of the Archbishops and Bishops, Who have been Impeach'd and Attainted of High Treason, from William the Conqueror to this time. . . Extracted from the Best Historians, Ancient and Modern. 1722.

An Impartial History of the Life and Actions of Peter Alexowitz, the Present Czar of Muscovy: From his Birth to this Present Time. . . .Written by a British Officer in the Service of the Czar. 1722. Reissued, with additions, as A True, Authentick and Impartial History. . . . The Whole Compil'd from the Russian, High Dutch and French Languages, State Papers, and other Publick Authorities, 1725.

The History and Remarkable Life Of the truly Honourable Colonel Jacque, Commonly Call'd Col. Jack, etc. 1722.

Considerations on Publick Credit. In a Letter to a Member of Parliament. 1724.

The Fortunate Mistress: or, a History of the Life and Vast Variety of Fortunes of Mademoiselle de Beleau, Afterwards Call'd The Countess de Winselsheim, in Germany. Being the Person known by the Name of the Lady Roxana, in the Time of King Charles II. 1724. With a continuation, 1745. Abridged by Noble, F., 1775.

The Great Law of Subordination consider'd; Or, The Insolence and Unsufferable Behaviour of Servants in England duly enquir'd into. . . . In Ten Familiar Letters, etc. 1724. The same year as The Behaviour of Servants in England Inquired into, etc.

A Tour Thro' the whole Island of Great Britain, Divided into Circuits or Journies. Giving a Particular and Diverting Account of Whatever is Curious, etc. Vol. I, 1724; vol. II, 1725; vol. III, 1726. [Defoe's work was much altered in later editions.]

The Royal Progress: or, a Historical View of the Journeys, or Progresses, which several Great Princes have made to visit their Dominions, etc. 1724.

A Narrative of the Proceedings in France, for Discovering and Detecting the Murderers of the English Gentlemen, September 21, 1723, near Calais, etc. 1724.

The History Of the remarkable Life of John Sheppard, Containing A particular Account of his many Robberies and Escapes, etc. 1724.

A New Voyage round the World, by a Course never sailed before, etc. 1724 (dated 1725).

A Narrative Of all the Robberies, Escapes, etc. of John Sheppard; Giving an Exact Description of the Manner of his wonderful Escape from the Castle in Newgate, etc. 1724.

Some farther Account of the Original Disputes in Ireland, about Farthings and Half-pence. In a Discourse with a Quaker of Dublin. 1724. [No place.]

Every-Body's Business, Is No-Body's Business; or Private Abuses, Publick Grievances: Exemplified In the Pride, Insolence and Exorbitant Wages of our Women-Servants, Footmen, etc. . . . By Andrew Moreton, Esq. 1725.

The True and Genuine Account of the Life and Actions of the Late Jonathan Wild. 1725.

The Life of Jonathan Wild, from his Birth to his Death. Containing His Rise and Progress in Roguery . . . By H. D. late Clerk to Justice R—. 1725.

An Account of the Conduct and Proceedings of the late John Gow alias Smith, Captain of the late Pirate, etc. 1725.

The Complete English Tradesman, in Familiar Letters, etc. Vol. I. 1725. 2nd ed. with Appendix. 1726. Vol. II. 1727.

A General History of Discoveries and Improvements, In Useful Arts, Particularly in the Great Branches of Commerce, Navigation, and Plantation, in all Parts of the Known World, etc. 1725–26. Four monthly parts, Oct., Nov., 1725; Feb., Dec.(?), 1726, as The History of the Principal Discoveries and Improvements, In the Several Arts and Sciences, 1727.

A Brief Case of the Distillers, and of the Distilling Trade in England . . . Humbly recommended to the Lords and Commons of Great Britain, in the present Parliament Assembled. 1726.

A Brief Historical Account of the Lives of the Six notorious Street-Robbers, etc. 1726.

An Essay upon Literature: or, an Enquiry into the Antiquity and Original of Letters; Proving That the two Tables, written by the Finger of God in Mount Sinai, was the first Writing in the World; and that all other Alphabets derive from the Hebrew, etc. 1726.

The Political History of the Devil, as well Ancient as Modern: In Two Parts, etc. 1726.

Unparallel'd Cruelty: or, the Tryal of Captain Jeane Of Bristol. Who was convicted at the Old Bailey for the Murder of his Cabbin-Boy, Who he put to Death in the most horrid and barbarous Manner, etc. 1726.

The Friendly Daemon; or, The Generous Apparition. Being a True Narative of a Miraculous Cure newly performed upon. . . . Dr. Duncan Campbell, By a familiar Spirit, that appeared to him in a white surplice, like a Cathedral Singing Boy. 1726.

The Four Years Voyages of Capt. George Roberts; Being a Series of Uncommon Events, Which befell him In a Voyage to the Islands of the Canaries, Cape de Verde, and Barbadoes, etc. 1726.

Mere Nature Delineated; or, a Body without a Soul. Being Observations upon the Young Forester Lately brought to Town from Germany, etc. 1726.

Some Considerations upon Street-Walkers. With A Proposal for Lessening the Present Number of them. In Two Letters to a Member of Parliament. To which is added, A Letter from One of those unhappy Persons, when in Newgate, and who was afterwards executed, for picking a Gentleman's Pocket, to Mrs. — in Great P—ney Street. 1726.

The Protestant Monastery: or, a Complaint against the Brutality of the present Age. Particularly the Pertness and Insolence of our Youth to aged Persons . . . By Andrew Moreton, Esq., etc. 1726.

A System of Magick; or, a History of the Black Art. Being an Historical Account of Mankind's most early Dealing with the Devil, etc. 1726. 2nd ed. as by Andrew Moreton. 1731.

The Evident Approach of a War; And Something of The Necessity of It, In Order to Establish Peace, and Preserve Trade, etc. 1727.

The Evident Advantages to Great Britain and its Allies from the Approaching War, etc. 1727.

Conjugal Lewdness: or, Matrimonial Whoredom. 1727. Reissued the same year as A Treatise Concerning the Use and Abuse of the Marriage Bed, etc.

A Brief Deduction of the Original, Progress, and Immense Greatness of the British Woollen Manufacture, etc. 1727.

An Essay on the History and Reality Of Apparitions, etc. 1727. Reissued 1728 (dated 1729) as The Secrets of the Invisible World Disclos'd: or An Universal History of Apparitions Sacred and Prophane. . . .By Andrew Moreton, Esq.

A New Family Instructor; in Familiar Discourses between a Father and his Children, on the most Essential Points of the Christian Religion. In Two Parts, etc. 1727.

Parochial Tyranny: or, the House-Keeper's Complaint against The insupportable Exactions, and partial Assessments of Select Vestries, etc. 1727.

Some Considerations on the Reasonableness and Necessity of Encreasing and Encouraging the Seamen, etc. 1728.

Augustus Triumphans: or the Way to Make London The Most Flourishing City in the Universe. First by establishing an University where Gentlemen may have Academical Education under the Eye of their Friends, etc. 1728. Abridged as The Generous Projector or a Friendly Proposal to prevent Murder and other enormous Abuses, By erecting an Hospital for Foundlings and Bastard Children, etc., 1730 (dated 1731).

A Plan of the English Commerce. Being a Compleat Prospect of the Trade of this Nation, As well the Home Trade as the Foreign. In three Parts, etc. 1728.

The Memoirs of an English Officer . . . By Capt. George Carleton. 1728. Reissued the same year as The Military Memoirs of Captain George Carleton, etc. Rptd. 1808, with an introduction by Scott, Sir Walter; included in some modern editions of Defoe.

    [Notwithstanding the arguments of Col. A. Parnell, English Historical Review, January 1891, Defoe seems to have had a large share in the composition of this book.]

An Impartial Account Of the late Famous Siege of Gibraltar . . . By an Officer who was at the Taking and Defence of Gibraltar by the Prince Hesse, of Glorious Memory; and served in the Town, during the last Siege. 1728.

Second Thoughts are Best: or, a Further Improvement Of a Late Scheme to prevent Street Robberies. By Andrew Moreton, Esq. 1728.

Street-Robberies, Consider'd: The Reason of their being so Frequent. With Probable Means to Prevent 'em. To which is added, Three Short Treatises. . . . Also a Caution of delivering Goods: With the Relation of several Cheats practiced lately upon the Publick. Written by a Converted Thief, etc. 1728.

Reasons for a War, In Order to Establish the Tranquility and Commerce of Europe. 1729.

An Humble Proposal to the People of England, For the Encrease of their Trade, And Encouragement of their Manufactures . . . By the Author of the Compleat Tradesman. 1729.

An Enquiry Into the Pretensions of Spain to Gibraltar, etc. 1729.

The Advantages of Peace and Commerce; with Some Remarks on the East India Trade. 1729.

Some Objections Humbly offered to the Consideration of the Hon. House of Commons, Relating to the present intended Relief of Prisoners. 1729.

Madagascar: or, Robert Drury's Journal, during Fifteen Years Captivity on that Island . . . Written by Himself, etc. 1729.

    [There is a strong probability that Defoe had a large share in this book.]

The Perjur'd Free Mason Detected; And yet The Honour and Antiquity of the Society of Free Masons Preserv'd and Defended. By a Free Mason. 1730.

An Effectual Scheme, for the immediate Preventing of Street Robberies, etc. 1730. [Dated 1731.]

A Brief State of the Inland or Home Trade of England, etc. 1730.

The Compleat English Gentleman. By Daniel Defoe. Edited for the First Time . . . By Bülbring, K. D. 1890.

Of Royall Educacion. A Fragmentary Treatise By Daniel Defoe. Ed. Bulbring, K. D. 1895.

B. *Periodicals with which Defoe was connected*

A Review of the Affairs of France: and of all Europe, etc. 8 vols. 1705–12. With several changes of name, finally as A Review of the State of the British Nation; with at least one volume and part of another reprinted at Edinburgh.

News from the Moon. A Review of the State of the British Nation, etc., Boston, Mass., 1721, is a curiously belated reprint of the Review for 29 April, 1710, Edinburgh edition.

The Review—a continuation of the above—from 2 August, 1712 to 11 June, 1713.

The London Post. 1704–5. [Defoe was charged, probably with justice, with contributing to this paper.]

The Edinburgh Courant. 1711. [Although Defoe had an interest in this paper, it is not known certainly that he ever wrote for it.]

The Protestant Post Boy. 1711–12.

Mercator: or, Commerce Retrieved, etc. 26 May, 1713—20 July, 1714.

The Monitor. Edited by Defoe. 22 April—7 August, 1714.

The Flying Post and Medley. 27 July—21 August, 1714.

Mercurius Politicus: Being Monthly Observations on the Affairs of Great Britain, etc. May, 1716—December, (?) 1720.

Dormer's News Letter. June, 1716—August, 1718. [No copies of this have been found.]

The Weekly Journal; or Saturday's Post. [Printed by Nathaniel Mist.] 1717–24.

The Wednesday Journal Being an Auxiliary Packet To the Saturday's Post, etc. 25 September–23 October, 1717.

Mercurius Britannicus. 1718–(?).

The Whitehall Evening Post. 1718–(?). 18 September, 1718—June, 1720 (?).

The Daily Post. 4 October, 1719—27 April, 1725 (?).

The Manufacturer: or The British Trade truly Stated. Wherein The Case of the Weavers, and the Wearing of Callicoes, are Consider'd. 30 October, 1719—17 February, 1720 (?).

The Original Weekly Journal [Applebee's]. 25 June, 1720—12 March, 1726.

The Director. 5 October, 1720—16 January, 1720/21 (?).

The Universal Spectator. No. 1, 12 October, 1728. [Ed. by Defoe's son-in-law, Henry Baker.]

Fog's Weekly Journal. 11 January, 1729.

Vols. II and III of Lee's Life and Newly Discovered Writings of Daniel Defoe, 1869, contain selections, for the most part unquestionably authentic, from Defoe's contributions to periodicals during the reign of George I.

Defoe's Letters and Memoranda in print number about two hundred and thirty and are chiefly to be found in vols. IV and V (1897, 1899) of the Fifteenth Report of the Historical MSS. Commission, MSS. of the duke of Portland. Sporadic letters are to be found in other reports of the commission, in Notes and Queries, and in the chief biographies, notably Wright's; but the letters to Harley contained in the Portland MSS. give the best idea of Defoe as a correspondent.

The above list of Defoe's writings does not take account of nearly three hundred books and pamphlets which have been ascribed to him, but for the authenticity of which I cannot vouch with entire confidence. Many of these are almost as much entitled to be received into the accredited list as are most of the items that have been accepted since the time of Chalmers and Wilson; but, for one reason or another, it has seemed best to treat them as plausible ascriptions only and to omit enumerating them here.

It may be added that there is a reason to believe that two inaccessible pamphlets one vouched for by several bibliographers, including Lee, and one by Crossley, will, when found, have to be added to Defoe's practically certain writings. These are The Layman's Sermon upon the Late Storm, 1704, and A Brief Debate upon the Dissolving the late Parliament, 1722.

III. OTHER JOURNALISTS

Cf. bibliography to Vol. VII, Chap. xv.

Amhurst, Nicholas (1697–1742). Terrae Filius. 11 January to 6 July, 1721.
—— The Craftsman. 1726 to 1736. 14 vols. 7131–7. [Under the signature of Caleb d'Anvers.]
  [*Cf.* bibliography to Chap. VIII, *post.*]
Arnall, William (1715?–1741?). The Free Briton. 1730–3.
—— The British Journal. [Under the signature of Francis Walsingham.]
  [Wrote in Walpole's pay against Bolingbroke, Pulteney and The Craftsman.]
Baker, Henry (1698–1774). The Universal Spectator. [*See* under II B, *ante.*]
Boyer, Abel (1667–1729). The Political State of Great Britain. (Monthly.) 38 vols. 1711–29.
—— The Postboy. 1705–9. [On the Whig side.]
—— The True Postboy. 1709. [*See, also,* bibliography to Chap. VIII, *post.*]
Concanen, Matthew (1701–1749). The London Journal. 1700–44. B.M.
  [Probably began 1698.]
—— The Speculatist. 1730. 1725–28. B.M. [This is a collection of letters under the above title, published as a book in 1730.]
—— The Daily Courant. 1702–35. B.M.
  [Wrote against Bolingbroke and the tories.]
Ridpath, George (d. 1726). The Flying Post. 1695–1714. B.M.
Roper, Abel (1665–1726). The Post Boy. 1695–1710. B.M.

Mercurius Latinus. Autore Agricola Candido, Gen. March—October, 1746

CHAPTER II

STEELE AND ADDISON

I. ADDISON

[For a good bibliography of Addison, *see* Selections from the writings of Joseph Addison, edited by Wendell, Barrett and Greenough, Chester Noues. Athenaeum Press Series, n.d.]

A. *Collected Works*

The Works of Joseph Addison, Esq. Collected by Tickell, T. 4 vols. 1721.
The Works of The Late Right Honourable Joseph Addison, Esq. Printed by Baskerville, J. With a Complete Index. 4 vols. Birmingham, 1761.

The Works of the Right Hon. Joseph Addison. A New Edition with Notes. By Hurd, Richard (bp. of Worcester). 6 vols. 1811. New ed. (Bohn's Standard Library.) 6 vols. 1856.

The Works of Joseph Addison, including the whole contents of Bishop Hurd's edition, with letters and other pieces not found in any previous collection; and Macaulay's essay on his life and works. Ed., with critical and explanatory notes, Greene, G. W. 6 vols. New York, 1856.

B. *Particular (including Dramatic) Works*

Addison's most important Latin poems are Sphaeristerium; Machinae Gesticulantes, Anglicè: A puppet-show; Resurrectio delineata ad Altare Col. Magd.; Barometri Descriptio; Insignissimo viro Thomae Burnet (also translated in Mr. Addison's fine ode to Dr. Thomas Burnet on his sacred theory of the earth done into English by the author of a late tale called Coffee, 1727); Praelium inter Pygmaeos et grues commissum. All these appeared in Examen Poeticum Duplex: sive Musarum Anglicanarum Delectus Alter; Cui subjicitur Epigrammatum seu Poematum Minorum Specimen Novum . . . 1698; and in Musarum Anglicanarum Analecta: Sive Poemata quaedam melioris notae, seu hactenus Inedita, seu sparsim Edita. 2 vols. 1699. (Vol. II.)

Translations of Praelium and of Machinae Gesticulantes appeared as Battle of the Pygmies and Cranes and The Puppet-Show, 1716, and were added to 4th edn of Miscellanies in Prose and Verse, 1721. All the above mentioned were rptd with translations in Miscellanea, 1818.

The Fourth Book of Georgics (except the story of Aristeus); the Song for St. Cecilia's Day at Oxford; Story of Salmacis, from the Fourth Book of Ovid's Metamorphoses; An Account of the Greatest English Poets, appeared in The Annual Miscellany: For the Year 1694. Being the Fourth Part of Miscellany Poems. Containing Great Variety of New Translations and Original Copies By the most Eminent Hands, 1694.

The Story of Phaeton, beginning the Second Book of Ovid's Metamorphoses, and Europa's Rape: translated from Ovid, both pieces followed by Notes on the foregoing Story; Milton's Stile imitated, in a Translation of a Story out of the Third Aeneid; The Third Book of Ovid's Metamorphoses, appeared in Poetical Miscellanies: The Fifth Part . . . 1704.

A Letter from Italy to Charles, Lord Halifax. Rptd in Tonson's Miscellany, part v, 1704; separately, 1709. Transl. into Latin Hexameters by Murphy, A. 1799. [Wendell and Greenough suggest 1703 for its date; but *see* Addisoni Epistola, missa ex Italia ad illustrem Dominum Halifax anno 1701.]

The Campaign, A Poem, To His Grace the Duke of Marlborough. By Mr. Addison. 1705. With Latin version Expeditio militaris, by T. G. 1708.

Remarks On Several Parts of Italy in the Years 1701, 1702, 1703. 1705, and many subsequent edns. Rpts: Moore, J. H. in A New . . . Collection of Voyages, vol. II, 1785(?); Mayor, W. F. in General Collection of Voyages and Travels, 1810. French trans. by Misson, F. M.: Remarques sur divers endroits de l'Italie, 1722.

> A Table of all the accurate remarks and surprising Discoveries of the most learned and ingenious Mr. Addison, 1706, [satirical]. *See* Somers, J., A Collection of Scarce and Valuable Tracts, vol. I, 1748, and vol. XII in ed. 1809.

> Le Clerc, J. Observations upon Mr. Addison's Travels through Italy. 1715.

Most of Addison's early work, including translations, was rptd. in Poems on Se eral occasions with a dissertation upon the Roman Poets, 1719; and, with Tentamen de Scriptis Addisonianis, by R. Young, with Engl. trans., in Poems on several Occasions by Mr. Addison, 1724.

Rosamond. An Opera. 1707. With the Opera of Operas: or Tom Thumb the Great, 1743.

  Tickell, T. To Mr. Addison on his opera of Rosamond. In Works of the most celebrated Minor Poets, 1749.

Cato. A Tragedy. As it is Acted at the Theatre-Royal in Drury-Lane, By Her Majesty's Servants. By Mr. Addison. MDCCXIII. Rpts. [without the love scenes] English and Latin, 1764; Bell's British Theatre, vol. III, 1776; ptd. . . . from the prompt book. With remarks by Mrs. Inchbald, 1806; adapted to the stage by J. P. Kemble, 1811.

  Translations: French: Guillemard, G., 1767; de La Bruère, C., 1789; Camarsac, G., 1814. *German:* Gottsched, L. A. V., 1735; anon., 1763; Gottsched J. C. (Louise G.'s husband), produced, 1731, Der Sterbende Cato, for the most part copied from Caton d'Utique by Deschamps, J. (1715), but with ending adapted from Addison's drama. *Italian:* Salvini, A. M., 1715, 1725; Corinteo, P.-A. [*i. e.* Golt, G.], 1776.

  Parodies: Parody on Cato's Soliloquy (act IV, sc. I), 1785, (?); Steere, W. Billing's Gate, 1860.

  Comments and criticisms: Dennis, J., Remarks upon Cato, 1713; The Life and Character of . . . Cato . . Design'd for the Readers of Cato, a Tragedy, 1713; Cato examined: or, animadversions on the fable or plot . . . of the new tragedy of Cato. Dedicated to Joseph Addison, 1713; Mr. Addison turn'd Tory; or, the scene inverted, wherein it is made appear that the Whigs have misunderstood that author in his tragedy call'd Cato . . . to which are added some cursory remarks upon the play itself. By a gentleman of Oxford, 1713. [All four pamphlets were rptd. in one vol. in same year.] The Unfortunate general . . . together with a key or explanation of the new play called Cato, a tragedy, 1713(?). Sewell, G. A., Vindication of the English stage, exemplified in the Cato of Mr. Addison, 1716; Tickell, T., To Mr. Addison on his Tragedy of Cato. In Works of the most celebrated Minor Poets, vol. II, 1749. A parallel betwixt the Tragedy of Cato . . . by Mr. Addison and the Cato of Utica by Mr. Des Champs, 1719.

The Drummer; Or, the Haunted House. A Comedy. As it is Acted at the Theatre-Royal in Drury-Lane. 1716. 2nd edn, with preface by Sir R. Steele, Dedicated to William Congreve. . . occasioned by Mr. Tickell's preface to Addison's Works, 1721. Rptd in Bell's British Theatre, vol. II, 1776. [Plot founded on story of the drummer of Tedworth, recounted in Sadducismus Triumphatus by Glanvil (*see ante*, Vol. VII, Chap. XVI).]

  Translations: French: Destouches, N., 1733; Desgranges, D., 1737. *German:* In Gottsched, J. C., Die deutsche Schaübuhne Bd. 2, 1742; Gottsched, L. A. V., Ein Lustspiel des Herrn Addison nach dem Französischen des Herrn Destouches übersetzt, 1764. *Italian:* anon., 1750.

Dialogues upon the Usefulness of Ancient Medals. [Probably composed 1703-5.] First published in Tickell's ed. of Addison's Works. Vol. I. 1721.

  French trans. in vol. II of De L' Allégorie, ou Traités sur cette matière par Winckelmann, Addison, Sulzer, an VII de la République Françoise. *See, also,* Remarques sur les Dialogues d'Addison by Gibbon, E., rptd. in the above.

originally composed in French at Lausanne. [Miscellaneous Works of Edward Gibbon, 1696. Vol. II—Pièces Détachées.]

Of the Christian Religion. *Ibid.* vol. IV. Rptd. as Evidences of the Christian Religion by Joseph Addison . . . to which are added several discourses against atheism and infidelity and in defence of the Christian Revelation. . . . 1730. Latin trans. by Seigneux de Correvon, G. 1746.

A Discourse On Ancient and Modern Learning. By the late . . . Joseph Addison, Esq.; Now first published from an Original Manuscript. 1739. [Of doubtful authenticity.]

A . . . Collection of the Psalms . . . as imitated . . . by . . . Mr. Addison. 1756.

C. *Essays*

The Tatler. *See under* II. Steele.

The Spectator. Begun 1 March 1711; appeared daily in a series of 555 nos. till 6 Dec. 1712, surviving imposition of stamp duty, 1 Aug., 1712. [*See* No. 445.] Addison contributed 274 papers, all signed by one of the letters of C L I O. In 1714 The Spectator was revived 18 June—29 September, possibly by Budgell (D. N. B.), and Addison contributed 24 papers.

Rptd in seven octavo vols., 1712–13 (*see* Wendell and Greenough, below, on the chronological order of the vols.), vol. VIII being added in 1715. The complete edition, frequently rptd. in eighteenth century, also in British Classics, 1803, vols. V–XII; Chalmers, A., British Essayists, vols. VI–XV, 1817; vols. V–XII, 1823 and 1856; Lynam, R., British Essayists, vols. IV–IX, 1827; Smith, G. G. with introd. essay by Dobson, A., 1897–8; Aitken, G. A. [with introd., notes, etc.], 1898. *See, also,* C[ampbell], J. D., Some portions of Essays. Contributed to the Spectator by . . . Joseph Addison, now first printed from his MS. Note Book, 1864.

Translations: French, 1746. The Spectator inspired what were, virtually, imitations in German *e. g.* Diskurse der Maler, 1721–3; Bodmer and Breitinger, Die Maler der Sitten, Zürich, 1729; both rptd 1746, as Die Maler der Sitten; Neue Beiträge), zum Vergnügen des Verstancles und Witzes (generally called Bremer Beiträge Bremen und Leipzig, 1745–59; Gerstenberg, Der Hypochondrist, 1763; Moser, Justus, Osnabrückische Intelligenzblätter, 1768.

See Milberg E., Die moralischen Wochenschriften des 18 Jhts. Ein Beitrag zur deutschen Literaturgesch. . . Meissen; Kawcynski, M., Studien zur Literurgesch. des XVIII Jhts., Moralische Zeitschriften, Leipzig, 1880; Koch, M., Uber die Beiziehungen der Englischen Literatur zur deutschen in 18 Jht., Leipzig, 1883.

Selections and Commentaries: Arnold, T., Oxford, 1866; Auszug des Englischen Zuschauers, nach einer neuen Uebersetzung, 1782-3; Dobson, A., 1906; Ewald, A. C., 1887; Green, J. R., 1880, last edn 1910 (G.T.S.); Les Beautés du Spectateur . . . en anglais et en français, 1804; Mézières, M. L., Encyclopédie Morale, ou choix des Essais du Spectateur, du Babillard et du Tuteur, 1826; Wendell, B. and Greenough, C. N., 1905 (Athenaeum Press Series), n. d.

Mottos: Mottoes in Five Volumes of The Tatler and to the Two Volumes of Spectators, Latin and English, 1712; The Mottoes to the Spectators, Tatlers, and Guardians, translated into English, 2nd edn., 1737.

Milton Papers: Bodmer, J. J., Critische Abhandlung . . . des Gedichtes J. Milton's von dem verlohrnen Paradiese; der beygefüget ist Joseph Addison's Abhandlung von den Schönheiten in demselben Gedichte, 1740;

Cook, A. S., Criticisms on P. L., 1892; Lille, J. de, Paradise Lost . . . (Remarques d'Addison sur le Paradis Perdu), 1805; Mariottini, F., Critiche di Mr. Addison al P. P., 1894; Morley, H., Criticisms on Milton by J. A., 1886; Paraiso Perdido . . . com o Paraiso Restaurado . . . e as observaçoes de M. Addison sobre o Paraiso Perdido, 1789; Paraiso Perdido . . . coñ notas de Addison, 1882; Rolli, P., Note sopra i dodici libri del Paradiso Perduto, 1742; Scolari, F., Saggio di Critica sul Paradiso Perduto . . . e sulle annotazioni di Giuseppe Addison, 1818.

Ballad Papers: See A Comment upon the history of Tom Thumb, 1711 (in ridicule of Addison's essays on Chevy Chase).

Coverley Papers: Duke, R. E. H., Reflection on the Character and Doings of the Sir Roger le Coverley of Addison, 1900.

See Lillie, C., Original and Genuine Letters sent to the Tatler and Spectator, 1725.

The Medleys for the year 1711. To which are prefixed the five Whig-Examiners. 1712. [The Whig-Examiner was by Addison. The Medley appeared 5 Oct., 1710–27 Nov., 1711, ed. by Maynwaring, A. and Oldmixon, J.]

Addison also contributed 51 pages to The Guardian, two to The Lover (for both of which see *post*), and edited The Freeholder (1st no. 23 Dec., 1715, rptd. in book, 1716), containing among academic and political essays, the papers on The Tory Foxhunter.

D. *Correspondence*

Correspondence of J. Hughes and Mr. Addison, 1773.

Johnson, Brimley. Eighteenth Century Letters, 1897, vol. 1 with introd. by Lane-Poole, S.

Letters by several eminent persons deceased, 1772.

Letters of . . . Mr. Addison and Mr. Pope from 1711–1715, 1735.

Warner, Rebecca. Epistolary curiosities . . . consisting of unpublished letters . . . illustrative of the Herbert family . . . from . . . Joseph Addison, part II, 1818.

E. *Biography, Criticism and* Addisoniana

Addison, Joseph, ou un attique en Angleterre. 1873.

Addison, Joseph, and Sir Andrew Fountaine; or the Romance of a Portrait. [Rptd. from the Athenaeum.] 1858.

Addisoniana. 2 vols. 1803.

Aikin, Lucy. Life of Joseph Addison. 2 vols. 1843. (*See* Macaulay's Essay *below*.)

Ashton, J. Social Life in the Reign of Queen Anne. New edn. 1883.

Beljame, A. Le public et les hommes de lettres en Angleterre au dix-huitième siècle. 1881. [pp. 225–338.]

British Censor, The. 1712. [Poetical satire.]

Contrast, The; or, Addison and Hume; describing their respective feelings and opinions. 1831.

Courthope, W. J. Addison (English Men of Letters). 1884.

D. [Paul, A.]. Addison's influence on the social reform of his age. 1876.

Dobson, A. Side-Walk Studies. 1902.

Drake, N. Essays, Biographical, Critical, and Historical, Illustrative of the Tatler, Spectator, and Guardian. 3 vols. 1805.

Elton, O. The Augustan Ages. Edinburgh, 1899.

General Dictionary. The Life of Addison extracted from . . . to which is prefixed the life of Lancelot Addison. . . his father. 1733.

Gosse, E. W. A History of Eighteenth Century Literature. 1887.

Hazlitt, W. Lectures on the English Comic Writers. Works, vol. VIII. Edd. Waller, A. R. and Glover, A. 1903.

J., G. Memoirs of the Life and Writings of the Right Hon. Joseph Addison, Esq.; with his Character by Sir Richard Steele. 1719.

Johnson, Samuel. Lives of the Most Eminent English Poets. 1779–81; ed. Cunningham, P., 1854; ed. Waugh, A., 1896.

Kippis, A. Addison. In Biographia Britannica. 2nd edn. 1778.

Macaulay, T. B. The Life and Writings of Addison. [Review of Life by Aikin, Lucy.] In Edinburgh Review, July, 1843. [See Hadow, G. E., Essay on Addison by Macaulay and Thackeray, with twelve essays by Addison, 1907.]

Memoirs of the life of . . . Addison, with a particular account of his writings. 1719.

Perry, T. S. English Literature in the Eighteenth Century, pp. 130–82. 1883.

Punchard, C. D. Helps to the study of Addison's Essays. 1898.

Ramsay, A. Richy and Sandy, A Pastoral on the death of Addison. 1720.

Regel, E. Thackeray's Lectures on the English Humourists of the Eighteenth Century, mit bibliographischem Material, litterarischer Einleitung und sachlichen Anmerkungen für Studierende. 1886.

Sande, C. L. E. Die Grundlagen der literarischen Kritik bei Joseph Addison. 1906.

Spence, J. Anecdotes, Observations and Characters of Books and Men. 1820.

Steele, R. Dedicatory Epistle to The Drummer. See ante, sec. B. [Rptd. in Arber's English Garner, VI, 523.]

Swift, J. The Journal to Stella. [See index to edn. by Aitken, G. A. 1901.]

Thackeray, W. M. The History of Henry Esmond, Esq. 1852.

—— The English Humorists of the Eighteenth Century. 1853.

Thomson, Mrs. K. Celebrated Friendships. Vol. I. 1861.

Tickell, T. To the Earl of Warwick on the Death of Mr. Addison. Works, vol. I. 1721.

Tyers, T. An historical Essay on Mr. Addison. 1783.

Vetter, T. Der Spectator als Quelle der Discourse der Maler. 1887.

Young, E. A letter to Mr. Tickell, occasioned by the death of . . . Addison. 1719.

II. STEELE

[For complete bibl. see Aitken, G. A., Life of Richard Steele, vol. II, appendix V, 1889.]

A. *Collected Editions*

[Collections of British essayists and dramatists are mentioned under individual works.]

Dramatic: First three comedies published 1712; Complete plays, with The Christian Hero, 1759. Best modern ed. by Aitken, G. A. (Mermaid Series), 1903.

Political: The Political Writings of Sir Richard Steele, 1715, 1723. Oeuvres Diverses de Mr. Richard Steele, sur les Affaires de la Grande Bretagne. Traduit de l'Anglois, Amsterdam, 1715.

Essays: Nichols, J.: (1) The Lover and Reader; to which are prefixed The

Whig Examiner, and a selection from the Medley of Papers written by the principal authors of The Tatler, Spectator, and Guardian, 1789. (2) The Theatre, . . . The Anti-Theatre; the character of Sir John Edgar; Steele's Case with the Lord Chamberlain; the Crisis of Property, with the Sequel, Two Pasquins, etc., 1791. (3) The Town Talk, the Fish Pool, The Plebeian, The old Whig, The Spinster . . . 1789, 1790.

B. *Particular (including Dramatic) Works*

The Christian Hero: an Argument proving that no Principles but those of Religion are sufficient to make a great man. 1701. [About 20 edns. up to 1820.]

The Funeral; or Grief a-la-Mode. Acted at Drury Lane and published 1701, but dated 1702. [About 20 edns up to 1811.] Modern rpts: Bell's British Theatre, vol. VIII, 1776; vol. XXVII, 1794; The New Engl. Theatre, vol. VII, 1777; Modern British Drama, vol. IV—Comedies, 1811; Aitken, G. A., Dramatic Works of R. Steele (Mermaid Series), 1903.

Translations: French: Les Funérailles, 1749; vol. VIII of Le Théâtre anglois by La Place, P. A. de, 1746–9. *Italian:* Il Funerale, 1742.

See A Comparison between the two stages, with . . . some critical remarks on the Funeral . . . and others, April, 1702 [attributed to Gildon, C.].

The Lying Lover; or, The Ladies Friendship. Acted Dec., 1703, published 1704. 8th edn. 1776. Rpt, Aitken, G. A. (Mermaid Series), 1894.

The Tender Husband; or, The Accomplished Fools. Acted April and published May, 1705. 14th edn. 1799. Rpts: Bell, vol. VIII, 1778; vol. XX, 1791; Mod. Brit. Drama vol. IV—Comedies, 1811; Dibdin's London Theatre, vol. XXVI, 1818; London Stage, vol. III., 1824 and 1826; Jones's Brit. Drama, vol. II, 1824 and 1853; Dick's Standard Plays, no. 139, 1884; Aitken, G. A. (Mermaid Series).

The Englishman's Thanks to the Duke of Marlborough. Jan., 1712. [Signed Scoto-Britannus.]

Letter to Sir Miles Wharton concerning Occasional Peers. March, 1713. [Signed F. Hicks.]

Poetical Miscellanies. Consisting of Original Poems and Translations By the best Hands. Published by Mr. Steele. 1714 (actually Dec., 1713). [Contains two of Steele's productions: To Mr. Congreve, occasion'd by his comedy called The Way of the World and Procession; a Poem on her Majesties Funeral. By a gentleman of the Army, 1695.]

The Importance of Dunkirk consider'd. In defence of the Guardian of August the 7th. In a Letter to the Bailiff of Stockbridge. By Mr. Steele. Sept., 1713. [4 edns the same year.]

French trans.: Réflexions sur l'importance de Dunkerque, 1715.

[Steele had urged the demolition of the fortifications of Dunkirk in no. 128 of the Guardian. The Examiner having retorted by accusing him of disloyalty, Steele replied with the above pamphlet, which Swift met with Importance of the Guardian consider'd.]

The Crisis: Or a Discourse representing, from the most authentic Records, the just causes of the late Happy Revolution . . . With some Seasonable Remarks on the Danger of a Popish Successor. Jan., 1714. 3 more edns same year. Republication of a portion, 1745, as The Wisdom of our Fore Fathers recommended to the present times, shewing the noble stand made by them at the Revolution, and their care to provide against a Popish Succession, and 1746 as Extracts from Sir Richard Steele's Crisis, adapted to the present more dangerous and more important Crisis.

Translations: French: La Crise, London and Amsterdam, both in 1714. *German:* Des Herrn Richard Steele Crisis, 1714; Rpt., Famous Pamphlets [Morley's Universal Lib.], 1886.

[Treats of the Hanoverian Succession. Answered by Swift's Public Spirit of the Whigs, Feb., 1714, which stirred up a formidable paper war, and was the chief cause of Steele's expulsion from the House of Commons, 18 March, 1714.]

Romish Ecclesiastical History of late years. May, 1714.

French trans.: L'Histoire ecclésiastique de Rome. (By Sallengre, A. H. de.)

Letter to a Member of Parliament concerning the Bill for preventing the Growth of Schism, June, 1714. 3 more edns. same year. Answered by Schism destructive of the Government . . . being a defence of the Bill . . . 1714.

The Ladies' Library. Written by a Lady. Published by Mr. Steele. 3 vols. 1714.

French trans.: Janiçon, F. M. La Bibliothèque des Dames, 1717, 1719, 1724 (Amsterdam). *Dutch:* De Boekzaal der Juffers. Uit het Engelsch vertaalt (Amsterdam), 1764.

See Mr. Steele Detected: Or, the poor and oppressed Orphan's Letters . . . Complaining of the great injustice done . . . by the Ladies' Library . . . 1714. [By Meredith, R.]

Mr. Steele's Apology for himself and his Writings. Oct., 1714. [A defence of his political character, containing allusions to his literary works.]

The Court of Honour; or, the laws, rules and ordinances establish'd for the suppression of Duels in France . . . With some observations thereon by Sir Richard Steele. 1720.

The Crisis of Property. An Argument proving that the Annuitants for ninety-nine years, as such, are not in the condition of other subjects of Great Britain, but by compact with the Legislature are exempt from any new direction relating to the said estates. 1 Feb., 1720; 2nd edn. same year. [Answered by Meres, Sir J., The Equity of Parliaments . . . vindicated; and The Crisis of Honesty, both in 1720. On 27 Feb. appeared a sequel by Steele, A Nation a Family.]

Preface to 2nd edn. of The Drummer (*see ante*, sec. I. B), 1721. [Addressed to William Congreve in reply to Tickell's preface to Addison's Works, 1721. Rptd. in Arber's English Garner, vol. VI.]

The State of the Case between the Lord-Chamberlain of His Majesty's Household, and the Governor of the Royal Company of Comedians. With the opinions of Pemberton, Northey and Parker, concerning the Theatre. 1720.

The Conscious Lovers. Acted Nov., 1722. Published in vol. I of Select Collection of English Plays. Edinburgh, 1755. Rpts. by Bell, Mrs. Inchbald, Brit. Theatre, vol. XII, 1808, and Dibdin, and in Modern British Drama and in London Stage. Ed. with notes, introduction, etc. by Aitken, G. A. (Mermaid Series).

Translations: French: Quétant, F. A., Les Amans réservés, Paris, 1778; Vasse, Mme. de, Les Amants généreux. Théâtre Anglois, Paris, 1784. *German:* Ober-Elbe, Geandern von der [*i. e.* Müldener, J. E.], The Conscious Lovers, das ist: Die sich mit einander verstehenden Liebhaber . . . Dresden, 1752.

See, also, Victor, B., An Epistle to Sir Richard Steele, on his play call'd The Conscious Lovers, 1722, and Dennis, J., Remarks on . . . The Conscious Lovers, 1723.

The School of Action and The Gentleman.　Fragments printed by Nichols, 1809, and Aitken, as above.

C.　*Essays*

The Tatler.　By Isaac Bickerstaff, Esq., appeared tri-weekly, 12 April, 1709—2nd Jan., 1711, 271 nos., about 188 by Steele.　Rptd. in 4 vols., 1710-11. About 25 edns. up to 1797.　Re-ed. Nichols, J., with notes, etc., 1786, 1789, 1797; Bisset, R., 1797; Chalmers, A., 1803, 1806, 1808; Sharpe's Brit. Classics, vols. I–IV, 1804, 1815.　Also in Chalmers' and Lynam's Brit. Ess. as above.　Ed. Aitken, G. A., with notes, introduction, etc., 4 vols. 1898-9. [Standard edn.]

　　[Swift's pamphlet, from which Steele borrowed the name, was Predictions for the Year 1708.　Followed by other Predictions, of uncertain authorship.]

　　Translations: French: Le Babillard, 2 vols., Amsterdam, 1723, 1725, 1734-5, 1737 (twice).　*See, also,* Annotations on the Tatler, written originally in French, by Mons. Bournelle, and translated into English by Walter Wagstaffe, Esq. (W. Oldisworth) 1710.　*Dutch:* De Snapper of de britsche Tuchtmeester.　Door den Ridder Richard Steele.　Uit het Engelsch vertaalt door P. le Clerc.　4 vols.　Amsterdam, 1733-52.

　　Selection: Dobson, A., 1896.

　　Mottos: see under Spectator.

The Spectator: *See under* Addison.　Steele contributed 236 papers.

The Guardian.　Appeared daily 12 March—1 Oct., 1713.　175 nos.　2 vols. Dec., 1713 (dated 1714).　[About 26 edns. by 1797.]　Rpts. by Sharpe, Chalmers, Ferguson, Lynam, etc.

　　Translations: French: Le Mentor Moderne, Rouen, 1725, Amsterdam, 1727 and 1728, Bâle, 1737.　*Dutch:* De Guardiaen of de britsche Zedenmeester, Amsterdam, 1723 [incomplete].　*All these* trans. by Van Effen, J. Also by Clercq, P. de, Rotterdam, 3 vols., 1730-1, 1734.　*German:* Der getreue Hofmeister, sorgfältige Vormund und neue Mentor, oder einige Discurse über die Sitten der gegenwärtigen Zeit. . . . Frankfort und Leipzig, 1725; Der Engländische Guardian oder Aufseher, 1749, by Gottsched, L. A. V.

　　Mottos: The Mottoes to the Two Volumes of Guardians, translated into English, 1713.

The Englishman; Being the Sequel to the Guardian.　56 nos., 6 Oct., 1713—11 Feb., 1714; 57th No. appeared 15 Feb., 1714, as The Englishman.　Being the Close of the Paper so called.　Revived 11 July—21 Nov., 1715.

The Lover.　By Marmaduke Myrtle, Gent.　40 nos., 25 Feb.—27 May, 1714. Rpt., Nichols, J., 1789; Harrison's Brit. Classics, vol. VIII, 1797; Lewin, W. (Camelot Series).　1887.

The Reader.　9 nos. 22 April—10 May, 1714; Rpt, Nichols, J., 1789.

Town Talk.　In a Letter to a Lady in the Country.　9 nos., 17 Dec., 1715—13 Feb. 1716.　Rpt, Nichols, J., 1789, 1790.

The Tea-Table.　3 nos., 2 Feb.—March, 1716.

Chit-Chat.　In a Letter to a Lady in the Country.　3 nos., March, 1716.

Plebeian.　To be continued weekly.　4 nos., 14 March—6 April, 1719.　[Started to denounce Lord Sunderland's bill for limiting the power of creating peers. Addison replied in The Old Whig (rptd. by Nichols, J., 1790); also met by The Patrician . . . In answer to the Plebeian.　4 nos., 1719.]

The Theatre.　By Sir John Edgar.　28 nos., 2 Jan.—5 April, 1720.　Rpt., Nichols, J., 1791.

D. *Correspondence*

Letters of . . . Mr. Steele . . . and Mr. Pope. 1735. Nichols, J. The Epistolary Correspondence of Sir Richard Steele . . . with literary and historical
anecdotes. 1787. 2nd edn. [including his familiar letters to his wife and
daughters; to which are prefixed fragments of three Plays. . .]. 1809.
Johnson, B. Eighteenth Century Letters, vol. i. 1897.

E. *Biography, Criticism and Ana*

S e, also, I. E *ante*

Aitken, G. A. Life of Richard Steele. 2 vols. 1889.
Dennis, J. Studies in English Literature. 1883.
Dilke, C. W. Papers of a Critic. 1875.
Dobson, A. A Paladin of Philanthropy. 1899.
—— Eighteenth Century Vignettes. 1892.
—— Richard Steele. (English Writers.) 1888.
Forster, J. Historical and Biographical Essays. **Vol. ii. 1858.**
G[ay], J. The Present State of Wit. 1711.
Hartmann, H. Steele als Dramatiker. Königsberg. 1880.
Hazlitt, W. Lectures on the English Comic Writers. 1819.
[Hoffmann, F.] Two Very Odd Characters tho' the Number be Even. 1714.
John Dennis, the Sheltring Poet's Invitation to Richard Steele, The Secluded
    Party-Writer, and Member; to come and live with him in the Mint . . . 1714.
    (Imitation of Horace's Epp. bk i, ep. i.)
Kawczyński, M. von. I. Einleitung und Verzeichniss der englischen, deutschen,
    französischen . . . moralischen Zeitschriften. II. Über den Tatler. Studien
    zur Literaturgeschichte des xviii^ten Jhts. Leipzig, 1880.
Lacy, J. The Steeleids, or the Tryal of Wit. 1714.
Lewis, L. The Advertisements of the Spectator. With intr. note by Kittredge,
    G. L. 1909.
Montgomery, H. R. Memoirs of the Life and Writings of Sir Richard Steele,
    . . . with his correspondence and notices of his Contemporaries, the Wits
    and Statesmen of Queen Anne's Time. 1865.
Ricken, W. Bemerkungen über Anlage und Erfolg der wichtigsten Zeitschriften
    Steeles und den Einfluss Addisons auf die Entwicklung derselben. 1885.
Swift, J. The First Ode of the Second Book of Horace paraphras'd and addressed
    to Richard St—le. 1714. The Journal to Stella. [*See* index to edn. by
    Aitken, G. A. 1901.]
Toby, Abel's Kinsman. The Character of Richard St—le, Esq. 1713.
Wagstaffe, Dr. W. Miscellaneous Works. 1726.
Ward, A. W. English Dramatic Literature. 2nd edn., 3 vols. 1899. [Vol. iii.]
    For bibliographies of Tickell, Ambrose Philips and Henry Carey *see* bibl. to
Chap. vi. For bibl. of Budgell *see* bibl. to Chap. viii, *post.*

CHAPTER III

POPE

Note. Pope's own methods of publication were so various and intricate,
and the number of books, pamphlets and articles dealing with his life and writings
is so very great, that in no part of this bibliography can more than a selection
be presented.

I. MSS.

The originals and early copies of many of Pope's letters are in existence, an important circumstance, since the correspondence for whose publication he himself was responsible was most elaborately doctored.   The British Museum has the copies which Caryll made of Pope's letters to himself, letters of Pope to Allen, Sir Hans Sloane and Warburton, and letters from some of Pope's correspondents, on the backs of which he wrote his translation of Homer.   Wycherley's letters to Pope and letters of Pope to the earl of Oxford are in the possession of the marquis of Bath at Longleat.   The Bodleian has letters of Pope to Cromwell.   Letters to Martha and Teresa Blount are at Mapledurham.   Letters to lord Bathurst are in the Bathurst collection.   Letters to the earl of Orrery are in the possession of the earl of Cork.   Mr. John Murray has Pope's letters to Broome.   Other letters of Pope and a few books with his autograph notes are preserved.   *See* preface to vol. IX of Courthope's edition.

The MSS. of some of Pope's poems (the Pastorals, An Essay on Man, the Epistle to Arbuthnot, etc.) were given by him to Jonathan Richardson and passed into the Chauncy collection.   The British Museum has the original MSS. of the translations of Homer presented by Mallet, written largely on scraps of paper and the backs of envelopes.

II. COLLECTED EDITIONS
A. *In Pope's Lifetime*

The Works of Mr Alexander Pope.   B. Lintot.   1717.
The Works of Alexander Pope, Esq.   Vol. II.   L. Gilliver.   1735.
The Works of Alexander Pope, Esq.   With explanatory notes and additions never before published.   9 vols.   1735–42.   Vol. II, 1735; vol. I, 1736. [Vols. III–IX.]

B. *Later Collected Editions*

The Works of Alexander Pope.   With his last corrections, additions and improvements, as they were delivered to the Editor a little before his death. . . . Together with the commentaries and notes of Mr. Warburton.   9 vols.   1751. [Warburton's Critical and Philosophical Commentary on Mr. Pope's Essay on Man had been published in 1742.]
Works.   With remarks and illustrations by Wakefield, Gilbert.   Vol. I.   1794.
—— With notes and illustrations by J. Warton and others.   9 vols.   1797.
Works, in verse and prose.   Containing the principal notes of Drs. Warburton and Warton; illustrations and critical and explanatory remarks by Johnson, Wakefield, A. Chalmers . . . and others.   To which are added, now first published, some original letters; with additional observations, and memoirs of the life of the author.   By W. L. Bowles.   10 vols.   1806.
Poetical Works of Alexander Pope, edited by Carruthers, R.   New edn. revised. 2 vols.   1858.
Poetical Works, edited, with notes and introductory memoir, by Ward, A. W. (The Globe Edition.)   1869 ff.
Works.   Edited by Elwin, Whitwell and Courthope, W. J.   New Edition.   Including several hundred unpublished letters, and other new materials.   Collected in part by Croker, J. W.   With Introduction and Notes.   10 vols. 1871–89.

A Supplement to the Works of Alexander Pope, containing such poems, letters, &c., as are omitted in the edition published by Dr. Warburton.   1757.

Additions to the Works of Alexander Pope . . . with many poems and letters of
contemporary writers never before published. 2 vols 1776.

A supplementary volume to the Works of Alexander Pope containing pieces of
poetry, not inserted in Warburton's and Warton's edition; and a collection
of letters, now first published. 1807.

III. POEMS

Pastorals. In Poetical Miscellanies, the sixth part. Tonson. 1709. [A Discourse on Pastoral Poetry was not prefixed to them until the collected vol.
of 1717.]

An Essay on Criticism. 1711.

The Rape of the Lock. In Miscellaneous Poems and Translations. By several
Hands. B. Lintot. 1712. An heroi-comical poem. In five canto's. Written by Mr. Pope. B. Lintot. 1714.

To a Young Lady, with the works of Voiture. In Miscellaneous Poems, etc.
B. Lintot. 1712.

Messiah. A sacred Eclogue, compos'd of several Passages of Isaiah the Prophet.
Written in Imitation of Virgil's Pollio. The Spectator, No. 378. 14 May,
1712.

Windsor Forest. To the Right Honourable George Lord Landsdown. B.
Lintot. 1713.

Ode for Musick (on St. Cecilia's Day). B. Lintot. 1713.

To Mr. Jervas with Dryden's translation of Fresnoy's Art of Painting. In De
Arte Graphica. The Art of Painting . . . translated into English. . . . By
Mr. Dryden. As also a short account of the most eminent painters. . . . By
another hand [i. e. Richard Graham]. 2nd edn. 1716.

Epigrams and the Court Ballad. In The Parson's Daughter. A tale for the use
of pretty girls with small fortunes. To which are added Epigrams, and the
Court Ballad, by Mr. Pope. 1717.

Elegy to the memory of an Unfortunate Lady and Eloisa to Abelard were published for the first time in the Works of 1717, as was also the Epistle following that To a Young Lady (afterwards named as Miss Blount) with the
Works of Voiture, entitled To the Same on her leaving the town after the
Coronation.

To Mr. Addison, occasioned by his Dialogues on Medals. In Tickell's edition
of Addison's Works. 1721.

To the Right Hon. Robert, Earl of Oxford and Earl Mortimer. Dedicatory
Epistle prefixed to Poems on Several Occasions. Written by Dr. Thomas
Parnell . . . and published by Mr. Pope. 1722.

Imitations of English Poets. In Miscellaneous. 1727.
    The Imitation of lord Rochester had appeared in Lintot's Miscellany,
1712.

The Dunciad. An heroic poem. In three books. Dublin; reprinted, London,
for A. Dodd, 1728. The Dunciad Variorum. With the Prolegomena of
Scriblerus. Printed for A. Dod. 1729. The New Dunciad: as it was
found in the year 1741. With the illustrations of Scriblerus and notes variorum. T. Cooper. 1742. The Dunciad, in four books. Printed according to the complete copy found in the year 1742 . . . to which are added
several notes now first publish'd, the Hypercritics of Aristarchus, and his
Dissertation on the Hero of the Poem. M. Cooper. 1743.

The Dying Christian to his Soul. Lewis's Miscellany. 1730.

An Epistle to the Right Honourable Richard Earl of Burlington. Occasion'd

by his publishing   alladio's Designs of the Baths, Arches, Theatres, &c.,
of Ancient Rome.   By Mr. Pope.   L. Gilliver.   1731.   Afterwards called
Of False Taste and finally Of the Use of Riches, the same title as the Epistle
to Bathurst.

Of the Use of Riches, an Epistle to the Right Honourable Allen Lord Bathurst.
L. Gilliver.   1732.

An Epistle to the Right Honourable Richard Lord Visct. Cobham.   (Of the
Knowledge and Characters of men.)   L. Gilliver.   1733.

Of the Characters of Women: an Epistle to a Lady.   L. Gilliver.   1735.

An Essay on Man.   Addressed to a Friend.   Part 1.   J. Wilford.   [1733.]   In
Epistles to a Friend.   Epistle II [1733]; Epistle III [1733]; Epistle IV [1734].

The Universal Prayer.   By the author of the Essay on Man.   1738.

The First Satire of the second book of Horace, imitated in a Dialogue between
Alexander Pope of Twickenham . . . on the one part, and his learned Councel
on the other.   1733.

An Epistle from Mr. Pope to Dr. Arbuthnot.   L. Gilliver.   1734 (published 2
Jan., 1735).
       The earliest version of the character of Addison   finally incorporated
in the Epistle to Arbuthnot) appeared in St. James's Journal, 15 Dec., 1722.
(See Aitken, G. A., The Academy, 9 Feb., 1889.)

Sober Advice from Horace to the Young Gentlemen about Town, as delivered
in his Second Sermon.   Imitated in the Manner of Mr. Pope.   [1734.]

The second Satire of the second book of Horace.   1734 (in an edn. of Sat. II i,
L. Gilliver).

The Sixth Epistle of the First Book of Horace, imitated by Mr. Pope.   Gilliver.
1737.

The first Epistle of the second book of Horace imitated.   T. Cooper.   1737.

The second Epistle of the second book of Horace.   1737.

One Thousand Seven Hundred and Thirty Eight.   A dialogue something like
Horace.   Dial. I, T. Cooper, Dial. II, R. Dodsley.   1738.

Horace, Book I, Epistle VII, Imitated in the manner of Dr. Swift and the latter
part of Book II, Satire VI, were published in 1738 in the octavo edn. of Pope's
Works.

1740.   A Poem.   [This fragment was first printed in Warton's edition.]

Verses upon the late D——ss of M——.   By Mr. P——.   1746.   [A folio sheet
containing the character of Atossa, which had been included in Ep. II in
the edition of the Ethic Epistles left by Pope printed for publication.   This
edn. was suppressed by Bolingbroke's influence and the presentation copies
recalled with the exception, apparently, of one only, now in Brit. Mus.
This sheet, containing the character, was published, it would seem, by Bolingbroke or his agent (see Courthope's Life, p. 347) with an injurious note
mentioning that Pope received £1000 from the duchess to suppress the
lines.]

IV.   POETICAL TRANSLATIONS

The first book of Sta'ius's Thebais.   In Lintot's Miscellany.   1712.

Vertumnus and Pomona.   From the fourteenth book of Ovid's Metamorphoses.
In Lintot's Miscellany.   1712.

Sappho to Phaon.   In Ovid's Epistles translated by several hands.   8th edn.
Tonson.   1712.

The Fable of Dryope.   From the ninth book of Ovid's Metamorphoses.   In the
same.

January and May: or, the Merchant's Tale. **From Chaucer.** In Poetic Miscellanies, the sixth part. Tonson. 1709.

The Wife of Bath, her Prologue. From Chaucer. In Poetical Miscellanies, consisting of original poems and translations. By the best hands. Publish'd by Mr. Steele. 1714.

The Temple of Fame: a vision. B. Lintot. 1715.

The Iliad of Homer (published by Bernard Lintot). Vol. I, 1715; vol. II, 1716; vol. III, 1717; vol. IV, 171 ; vols. V and VI, 1720.

The episode of Sarpedon, from the twelfth and sixteenth books of Homer's Iliad, appeared in Poetic Miscellanies, the sixth part. Tonson. 1709.

The Odyssey of Homer. Vols. –III, 1725; vols. IV, V, 1726.

A translation of the arrival of Ulysses in Ithaca from the 13th Odyssey and of the garden of Alcinous from the 7th app ared in Steele's Miscellany. 1714.

The Satires of Dr. John Donne, versified. Satire II and Satire IV were published in vol. II of Pope's Works, 1735.

The Impertinent, or A Visit to the Court. A Satire. By an Eminent Hand [in great part the same as Satire IV of the above]. 1733.

V. PROSE (*including Letters*)

The Works of Mr. Alexander Pope in Prose. Vol. I, 1737; vol. II, 1741.

The Guardian, No. 4, 16 March, 1713 (Dedications). No. 11 (An elixir that confers an agreeable madness). No. 40 (Pastorals). [Ironical comparison between Ambrose Philips and Pope.] No. 61 (Cruelty to Animals). [Leigh Hunt has emphasised Pope's kindness for animals in his Imaginary Conversations of Pope and Swift.] Nos. 91 and 92 (The Club of little men). No. 173, 29 Sept., 1713 (Gardens).

The Narrative of Dr. Robert Norris, concerning the strange and deplorable Frenzy of Mr. J. Denn—an officer in the Custom-House. 1713.

A Key to the Lock; or a Treatise proving beyond all contradiction the dangerous tendency of a late poem intituled, the Rape of the Lock . . . by Esdras Barnivelt. 1715.

A full and true Account of a horrid and barbarous Revenge by poison, on the body of Mr. Edmund Curll, Bookseller, with a faithful copy of his last Will and Testament. 1716.

Three Hours after Marriage; a comedy. 1717. [Arbuthnot and Pope assisted Gay in writing this.]

Miscellanies [by Pope, Swift, Arbuthnot and Gay]. Vols. I and II, 1727; vol. III, 1728; vol. IV, 1732. [Contains verse as well as prose.]

Familiar Letters written to Henry Cromwell, Esq., by Mr. Pope. In Curll's Miscellanea, in two volumes. Never before published. 1727 (really 1726).

Letters of Mr. Pope and several eminent persons. 2 vols. 1735.

See A Narrative of the method by which Mr. Pope's private letters were procured and published by Edmund Curll, bookseller, 1735.

Letters of Mr. Alexander Pope, and several of his Friends. 1737. [The acknowledged edition, printed for J. Knapton and others.]

The Works of Mr. Alexander Pope, in Prose. Vol. II. 1741. [Printed for Knapton and others. Contains, besides further letters, the Memoirs of Scriblerus and other tracts written by Pope either singly or in conjunction with his friends.]

The Dublin editions of Letters to and from Dr. J. Swift appear to have been published after vol. II mentioned above.

A Collection of Letters, never before printed; written by Alexander Pope and other ingenious gentlemen to the late Aaron Hill. 1751.

Supplemental Volume to the Works of Alexander Pope. 1825. [Containing a considerable addition to his p iv te correspondence.]

The Works of Shakespear . . . collated and corrected by the former editions, by Mr. Pope. Tonson. 1725.

VI. ANNOTATED EDITIONS OF SEPARATE WORKS

Essay on Criticism. Ed., with introduction and notes, West, A. S. Cambridge, 1896. Ed., with introduction and notes, Collins, J. Churton. 1896. Ed., with introduction and notes, Ryland, F. 1900.

Essay on Man. Ed. Pattison, Mark. Oxford, 1869. 2nd edn. 1872.

Satires and Epistles. Ed. Pattison, Mark. Oxford, 1872. 2nd edn. 1874.

The Iliad of Homer. Translated by Alexander Pope, Esq. A new edition, with additional notes, critical and illustrative, by Wakefield, Gilbert. 5 vols. 1806.

The Odyssey of Homer. Translated by Alexander Pope, Esq. A new edition, etc. by Wakefield, Gilbert. 4 vols. 1806.

The Ra e of the Lock. Ed., with introduction and notes, Ryland, F. 1899. The Rape of the Lock and other poems. Ed., with introduction and notes, Parrott, T. M. Boston (U. S. A.), 1906. Illustrated edn. by Beardsley, Aubrey. 1896.

VII. BIOGRAPHY

The early lives of Pope, two anon. in 1744, those under the names of Ayre, W., 1745, Dilworth, W. H., 1759, have no value. Owen Ruffhead's, 1769, has some unpublished letters and material supplied by Warburton.

Carruthers, R. The Life of Alexander Pope, including Extracts from his Correspondence . . . Second edition. 1857.

Courthope, W. J. The Life of Alexander Pope. 1889. Vol. v of Elwin and Courthope's edition of Pope's Works.

Davies, Robert. Pope: Additional Facts concerning his Maternal Ancestry. 1858.

Dilke, Charles Wentworth. The Papers of a Critic. Vol. I. 1875. [Papers rptd. from the Athenaeum and Notes and Queries in which D. had investigated various problems connected with the publication and arrangement of Pope's correspondence, and the facts of his biography.]

Hunter, Joseph. Pope: His Descent and Family Connections. 1857. No. v of Hunter's Critical and Historical Tracts. [See Dilke, C. W., in Athenaeum, 21 Nov., 1857; Papers of a Critic, vol. I, 234.]

Johnson, Samuel. Prefaces, biographical and critical, to the Works of the English Poets. 1779–81. See Hill, G. Birkbeck's edn. of Johnson's Lives, vol. III, Oxford, 1905.

Paston, George (Symonds, Miss E. M.). Mr. Pope: his Life and Times. 2 vols. 1909. [Unpublished letters in the Mapledurham collection and elsewhere are utilised in this work.]

Richardson, Jonathan, the younger. Richardsoniana: or occasional reflections on the moral nature of man . . . with several anecdotes interspersed. 1776.

Spence, Joseph. Anecdotes, Observations, and Characters, of Books and Men. Collected from the Conversation of Mr. Pope, and other Eminent Persons of his time. Now first published . . . by Samuel Weller Singer. 1820. [The edn. published on the same day by Murray with Malone's notes is only a selection.] Rptd. 1858.

Stephen, Sir Leslie. Alexander Pope. English Men of Letters. 1880.

Pope Commemoration, 1888. Loan Museum Catalogue of the books, autographs, paintings and personal relics exhibited in the Town Hall, Twickenham. Edited by Tedder, H. R. (with an introductory poem by Dobson, Austin). (*See* sec. IX, *post.*) 1888.

VIII. CONTEMPORARY CRITICISM, CONTROVERSY AND PERSONALITIES

Addison, Joseph. The Spectator, No. 253, 20 December, 1711. (Notice of An Essay on Criticism.)

Dennis, John. Reflections upon a late rhapsody called An Essay upon Criticism. B. Lintot. [1711.]

Homerides, or, a letter to Mr. Pope occasion'd by his intended translation of Homer by Sir Iliad Doggrel [Thomas Burnet]. 1715.

Mist's Weekly Journal. 1716–28.

Dennis, John. A true character of Mr. Pope. [1717.]

—— Remarks upon Mr. Pope's translation of Homer. With two letters concerning Windsor Forest, and the Temple of Fame. 1717.

Spence, Joseph. An Essay on Pope's Odyssey: in which some particular Beauties and Blemishes of that work are considered. London and Oxford, 1726.

    Spence's chief critical work, Polymetis: or an Enquiry concerning the agreement between the Works of the Roman Poets and the Remains of the Antient Artists, appeared in 1747. As to his Account of Stephen Duck and other lesser publications, *see* Garnett, R., art. Spence, in D. of N. B. vol. LIII.

Theobald, Lewis. Shakespeare Restored: or, a Specimen of the many Errors, as well committed, as unamended by Mr. Pope, in his late Edition of this Poet. . . . 1726.

Dennis, John. Remarks on Mr. Pope's Rape of the Lock. 1728.

Gulliveriana: or, a fourth volume of miscellanies, being a sequel of the three volumes published by Pope and Swift. To which is added, Alexanderiana; or a comparison between the Ecclesiastical and Poetical Pope. 1728. [By Jonathan Smedley, whose name was in consequence substituted in 1729 for Eusden's in Dunciad, II, 291.]

Dennis, John. Remarks upon several passages in the preliminaries to the Dunciad . . . 1729.

One Epistle to Mr. A. Pope, occasion'd by Two Epistles lately published [*i.e.* Two Epistles to Mr. Pope, Concerning the Authors of the Age. 1730. (By Young)]. [Supposed to be by Welsted, Leonard and Smythe, James Moore.]

The Grub-Street Journal. 1730–8.

A Collection of Pieces in verse and prose, which have been publish'd on occasion of the Dunciad. By Mr. Savage. 1732.

An Epistle from a Nobleman to a Doctor of Divinity: in answer to a Latin Letter in verse. Written from H[ampto] n-C[our]t. 1733. [By John lord Hervey.]

Verses addressed to the imitator of the First Satire of the Second Book of Horace. By a Lady. [1733. By lady Mary Wortley Montagu, assisted, probably, by lord Hervey.]

(Mallet, David.) Of Verbal Criticism. An Epistle to Mr. Pope; occasioned by
Theobald's Shakespear and Bentley's Milton. 1733. [In verse.]

Crousaz, J. P. de. Examen de l'Essai de M. Pope. 173 .
—— Commentaire sur la traduction de l'Essai de M. Pope. 1738.

Warburton replied in five letters (afterwards expanded to six) in the
Works of the Learned, 1738, 1739; collected in book form in 1740. Another
letter was afterwards added, and a rearrangement in four letters published
in 1742.

A Letter from Mr. Cibber to Mr. Pope, inquiring into the motives that might induce him in his satyrical works, to be so frequently fond of Mr. Cibber's
name. 1742.

Another occasional Letter from Mr. Cibber to Mr. Pope, Wherein the new hero's
preferment to his throne in the Dunciad seems not to be accepted.
1744.

IX. Later Criticism

A. *General*

Abbott, Edwin. A Concordnace to the Works of Alexander Pope. With
an introduction. 1875. [The introduction deals with Pope's style and
metre.]

Beljame, A. Le Public et les Hommes de Lettres en Angleterre au dix-huitième
siècle (1660–1744). Paris, 1881.

Coleridge, S. T. Biographia Literaria. 1817.

Conington, John. The Poetry of Pope. Oxford Essays. 1858. Rptd. in vol. 1
of his Miscellaneous Works, 1872.

Courthope, W. J. A History of English Poetry, vol. v. 1905.
—— Life in Poetry: Law in Taste, chap. VIII. 1901.

De Quincey, Thomas. Pope. (In Encyclopaedia Britannica, ed. 7.) The
Poetry of Pope. Lord Carlisle on Pope. All these are included in De
Quincey's collected works, ed. Masson, David, vols. IV and XI, 1888–90.

Deetz, Albrecht. Alexander Pope. Ein Beitrag zur Literaturgeschichte des
achtzehnten Jahrhunderts, nebst Proben Pope'scher Dichtungen. Leipzig,
1876.

Dennis, J. Studies in English Literature. 1883.
—— The Age of Pope. 1906.

Dobson, A. Dialogue to the Memory of Mr. Alexander Pope. Collected Poems,
1897 (p. 301).

Elton, O. The Augustan Ages. Edinburgh, 1899.

English Poetry from Dryden to Cowper. The Quarterly Review. July, 1862.

Hazlitt, William. Dryden and Pope. Lectures on the English Poets. 1818.
Collected Works. Edd. Waller, A. R. and Glover, Arnold, 1902–6. (Vol. v,
pp. 68–85.)

Leather, Mary S. Pope as a student of Milton. Englische Studien, vol. xxv,
pp. 398–410. Leipzig, 1898.

Lessing, G. E. Pope ein Metaphysiker! Danzig, 1755. Sämmtliche Schriften
(Lachmann, K. and Maltzahn, W. von), vol. v, pp. 1–35. Leipzig, 1853–7.

Lloyd, Charles [Lamb's friend]. Poetical Essays on the Character of Pope.
1821.

Lochner, Ludwig. Pope's literarische Beziehungen zu seinen Zeitgenossen.
Leipzig, 1910.

Lowell, J. R. Pope. My Study Windows. 1871.

Maack, R. Über Popes Einfluss auf die Idylle und das Lehrgedicht in Deutschland. Hamburg, 1895.

McLean, L. Mary. The riming system of Alexander Pope. Publications of the Modern Language Association of America, vol. VI, pp. 134–58. Baltimore, 1891.

Mead, W. E. The Versification of Pope in its relation to the 17th century. Leipzig, 1889. (Diss.)

Minto, William. Pope. Encyclopaedia Britannica, 11th edn, XXII (1911). [By Minto, W. and Bryant, Margaret.]

Montégut, Émile. Pope. Heures de Lecture d'un Critique: Revue des Deux Mondes. Paris, 1888. Rptd., 1891.

Sainte-Beuve, C. A. Notice of Taine's Histoire de la Littérature anglaise. Nouveaux Lundis, vol. VIII.

Saintsbury, G. A History of English Prosody, vol II. 1908.

Stephen, Sir Leslie. Pope as a Moralist. The Cornhill Magazine. 1873. Rptd. in Hours in a Library, vol. I, 1874.

Taine, H. A. Histoire de la Littérature anglaise. 8th edn. Paris, 1892.

Thoms, W. J. Bibliography of the literature connected with Pope and his quarrels. Notes and Queries, ser. V, vol. XII.

Traill, H. D. Pope. Chambers's Encyclopaedia, vol. VIII. 1908.

Vater, P. Ein Beitrag zur Kenntniss des Dichters und des Philosophen. Halle, 1897. (Diss.)

Wakefield, Gilbert. Observations on Pope. 1796.

Warton, Joseph. An Essay on the genius and writings of Pope. Vol. I, 1756; vol. II, 1782.

Weiser, C. S. Pope's Einfluss auf Byron's Jugenddichtungen. In Anglia, vol. I. Halle, 1878.

Wordsworth, William. Preface and Appendix to Lyrical Ballads. 1798.

B. *On Particular Works or Points*

Arnold, Matthew. On translating Homer. 1861. [Especially Lecture I.]

Bobertag, F. Zu Popes Essay on Criticism. Englische Studien, vol. III, pp. 43–91. Heilbronn, 1880.

—— Zu Pope's Rape of the Lock. Englische Studien, vol. I, pp. 456–80; vol. II, 204–22. Heilbronn, 1877 and 1879.

—— A. Pope's Verhältnis zur Aufklärung des 18 Jahrhunderts. Englische Studien. 1901. [Especially for references to the Essay on Man.]

Lounsbury, Thomas R. The first editors of Shakespeare (Pope and Theobald). 1906.

Mayor, Joseph B. Review of Pattison's ed. of the Essay on Man. Contemporary Review, vol. XIV, pp. 115–24. April, 1870.

Petzet, Erich. Die deutschen Nachahmungen des Popeschen 'Lockenraubes.' Ein Beitrag zur Geschichte des komischen Epos in Deutschland. Zeitschrift für Vergleichende Litteraturgeschichte und Renaissance-Litteratur. N. F. vol. IV, pp. 409–33. Berlin, 1891.

Schade, A. Über das Verhältnis von Pope's January and May und The Wife of Bath, her Prologue zu den entsprechenden Abschnitten von Chaucer's Canterbury Tales. Englische Studien, vol. XXV, 1897, and vol. XXVI, 1899.

Schenk, Theodor. Sir Samuel Garth und seine Stellung zum komischen Epos. Heidelberg, 1900.

Thoms, W. J. Notes on Editions of the Dunciad. n.d. Rptd. from Notes and Queries, ser. I, vols. X and XII.

C. *The Bowles and Byron Controversy*

Bowles, William Lisle. Edition and Memoir of Pope. 10 vols. 1806.

—— The invariable Principles of Poetry: in a letter addressed to Thomas Campbell; occasioned by some critical observations in his specimens of British Poets, particularly relating to the poetical character of Pope. Bath, 1819.

—— A Reply to the charges brought by the Reviewer of Spence's Anecdotes in the Quarterly Review for Oct. 1820 against the last ed. of Pope's works. The Pamphleteer, vol. XVII.

—— Two letters to the Rt. Hon. Lord Byron, in answer to his lordship's letter to **** ****** on the Rev. Wm. L. Bowles's Strictures on the life and writings of Pope: more particularly on the question, whether poetry be more immediately indebted to what is sublime or beautiful in the works of nature, or the works of art. 1821.

—— A Final Appeal to the Literary Public, relative to Pope, in reply to certain observations of Mr. Roscoe in his edition of the Poet's Works. 1825.

—— Lessons in Criticism to W. Roscoe Esq. in answer to his letter to the Rev. W. L. Bowles on the character and poetry of Pope. 1826.

Byron, Lord. Letter to***** ***** [John Murray] on the Rev. W. L. Bowles's strictures on the Life and Writings of Pope. 1821. [A second letter was not published till 1835.] See Appendix III in vol. V of Prothero, R. E.'s edition of Byron's Letters and Journals.

Campbell, Thomas. Specimens of the British Poets; with Biographical and critical Notices, and an Essay on English Poetry. 7 vols. 1819. The Essay and Notices were rptd. in 1848. (As to Pope, see especially pp. 109–17.)

Casson, T. E. W. L. Bowles in Eighteenth Century Literature, in An Oxford Miscellany, Oxford, 1909.

Gilchrist, Octavius Graham. Letter to the Rev. William Lisle Bowles. Stamford, 1820.

Hazlitt, William. Pope, Lord Byron, and Mr. Bowles. The London Magazine. June, 1821. Collected Works, ed. Waller, A. R. and Glover, Arnold, vol. XI, pp. 486–508. 1902–6.

CHAPTER IV

JONATHAN SWIFT

The fullest bibliography of Swift is that by Jackson, W. S., in vol. XII of Bell's edition, 1908. *Cf. also* Lane-Poole, S., in The Bibliographer, November, 1884.

I. COLLECTIONS

Miscellanies in Prose and Verse. 1711. [2nd edn. 1713. This volume, published by Morphew, contains a number of Swift's earlier writings.]

Miscellanies by Dr. Jonathan Swift. 1711. [Unauthorised collection by Curll.]

Miscellaneous Works, Comical and Diverting. By T. R. D. J. S. D. O. P. I. I. In 2 parts. 1720.

Miscellanies in Prose and Verse 4th edn. Dublin, 2721 [1721].

Miscellanies, Written by Jonathan Swift, D.D., Dean of St. Patrick's, Dublin. 4th edn. 1722.

Miscellanea. In Two Volumes. Never before published. 1727.

Miscellanies in Prose and Verse. The First Volume. [The Second Volume.] [The Last Volume.] 3 vols. 1727.

Preface to vol. 1 is signed by Swift and Pope. Vols. 1 and 11 were reprinted in 1728, and vol. 111 in 1733. There was a 2nd edn. in 1733, and
Dublin edns. appeared in 1728–33 and 1732–3.

Miscellanies. The Third Volume. 1732. Other edns: 1732, 1733, 1736, 1738.

Miscellanies. Consisting chiefly of original pieces in Prose and Verse. By
D—n S——t. Never before published in this kingdom. Dublin; rptd.,
London, 1734.

The Works of J. S., D.S.P.D. 4 vols. Dublin, 1735. Other edns.: 6 vols.,
1737; 8 vols., 1746; 20 vols., 1772.

Miscellanies, in Prose and Verse. Volume the Fifth. 1735.

The Poetical Works of J. S., D.D., D.S.P.D. Rptd. from the 2nd Dublin edn.
1736.

Political Tracts. By the Author of Gulliver's Travels. 2 vols. 1738.

The Poetical Works of Dr. Jonathan Swift, Dean of St. Patrick's, Dublin. 2 vols.
[1740?]

Letters to and from Dr. J. Swift, D.S.P.D. From the year 1714 to 1738. Dublin, 1741. Another edn. Dean Swift's Literary Correspondence. 1741.

Miscellanies in Four Volumes. By Dr. Swift, Dr. Arbuthnot, Mr. Pope, and Mr.
Gay. The Fifth Edition corrected. 1747.

A Supplement to the Works of the most celebrated Minor Poets . . . To which
are added, Pieces omitted in the Works of . . . Dean Swift. 1750.

The Works of Dr. Jonathan Swift. 14 vols. 1751.

A Supplement to the Works of Dr. Swift. 1752.

The Works of Jonathan Swift, D.D. Accurately revised in 6 volumes. 4to.
1755. Also 12 vols., 8vo. [The quarto edition was completed by 8 volumes
(including the Letters) published between 1764 and 1779, and the octavo
edition by 13 volumes.]

Satyrische und ernsthafte Schriften, von Dr. Jonathan Swift. 8 vols. Hamburg, 1756.

The Works of Dr. Jonathan Swift. 8 vols. Edinburgh, 1761.

Letters, Written by the late Jonathan Swift, D.D. Dean of St. Patrick's, Dublin;
and Several of his Friends. . . . By John Hawkesworth, LL.D. 3 vols.
1766. A fourth volume appeared in 1768.

Letters 1 and 41 to 65 of the Journal to Stella were first published by
Dr. Hawkesworth in vol. x of Swift's Works, 1766. Letters 2 to 40 were
first published by Swift, Deane, in vol. XII of Swift's Works, 1768. They
were collected in Sheridan's edn., 1784. The most modern annotated edn.
is that by Aitken, G. A., 1901.

Satyrische und ernsthafte Schriften. Preface by Breitenfels, J. von. 8 vols.
Zurich, 1766.

An Appendix to Dr. Swift's Works and Literary Correspondence. Improved
From an Edition printing by Mr. Faulker: And now first published. 1767.

The Works of Dr. Jonathan Swift, Dean of St. Patrick's, Dublin. With The
Author's Life and Character; . . . More complete than any preceding
Edition. 13 vols. Edinburgh, 1768.

The Works of the English Poets. With Prefaces, . . . by Samuel Johnson.
1779. [Vol. XXXIX, Swift's Poems, vol. 1; and vol. XL, Swift's Poems, vol.
II. The Preface is in Prefaces, vol. VIII, 1781.]

The Works of the Rev. Dr. Jonathan Swift, Dean of St. Patrick's, Dublin, Arranged, Revised, and Corrected, with Notes, by Thomas Sheridan, A. M.
17 vols. 1784.

Miscellaneous Pieces, in Prose and Verse. By the Rev. Dr. Jonathan Swift,

Dean of St. Patrick's, Dublin. Not inserted in Mr. Sheridan's edition of the Dean's Works. 1789.

Literary Relics: containing Original Letters from . . . Swift, . . . To which is prefixed, An Inquiry into the Life of Dean Swift. Ed. Berkeley, George-Monck. 1789.

Dean Swift's Tracts on the Repeal of the Test Act. London: Rptd. at the Logographic Press. 1790.

The Sermons of Dr. J. Swift, Dean of St. Patrick's, Dublin. To which is prefixed The Author's Life: together with his Prayer for Stella, his Thoughts, on, and Project for the Advancement of Religion. [1790?]

The Works of the Rev. Jonathan Swift, D.D., Dean of St. Patrick's, Dublin. Arranged by Sheridan, T. New ed. 19 vols. Corrected and revised by Nichols, J. 1801. Other eds.: 24 vols., 1803; 19 vols., 1808.

The Works of Jonathan Swift, D.D., Dean of St. Patrick's, Dublin; Containing Additional Letters, Tracts, and Poems, not hitherto published; with Notes, and A Life of the Author, by Walter Scott, Esq. Edinburgh, 1814. 19 vols. 2nd edn. 1824.

The Poetical Works of Jonathan Swift. [With life by Mitford.] (Aldine Edition.) 1833-4. Other edns.: 1853, 1866.

The Works of Jonathan Swift, D.D. In Two Volumes. With Memoir of the Author, by Thomas Roscoe. 1841.

Swift's humoristische Werke. Aus dem Englischen . . . von Franz Kottenkamp. 3 vols. Stuttgart, 1844.

Opuscules Humoristiques de Swift, traduits pour la première Fois par Léon de Wailly. Paris, 1859.

Selections from the Prose Writings of Jonathan Swift. Ed. Lane-Poole, Stanley. 1884.

Letters and Journals of Jonathan Swift. Sel. and ed., Lane-Poole, S. 1885.

The Tale of a Tub and Other Works by Jonathan Swift. Ed. Morley, H. (Carisbrooke Library.) 1889.

Swift. Selections from his Works. Ed. with life, introductions, and notes. Craik, Sir H. 2 vols. Oxford, 1892-3.

The Prose Works of Jonathan Swift, D.D. With a biographical introduction by Lecky, W. E. H. Ed. Scott, Temple. 12 vols. 1897-1908.

Unpublished Letters of Dean Swift. Ed. Hill, G. Birkbeck. 1899.

Gulliver's Travels and other Works by Jonathan Swift Exactly Rptd. from the First Edition. 1906.

The Poems of Jonathan Swift, D.D. Ed. Browning, W. E. 2 vols. 1910.

Correspondence of Jonathan Swift, D.D. Ed. Ball, F. E. With an introduction by Bernard, J. H. 1910-11.

II. PARTICULAR WORKS

Supplement to the fifth volume of the Athenian Gazette. 1691. [Contains a letter from Swift, and his Ode to the Athenian Society.]

Letters Written by Sir W. Temple, Bart. and other Ministers of State, . . . In Two Volumes. . . . Published by Jonathan Swift Domestick Chaplain to his Excellency the Earl of Berkeley. 1700. [Dedication to William III and Publisher's Epistle to the Reader in vol. 1 are by Swift.]

Miscellanea. The Third Part . . . By the late Sir William Temple, Bar. Published by Jonathan Swift, A. M. 1701. [The Publisher to the Reader is by Swift.]

A Discourse of the Contests and Dissensions between the Nobles and the Commons in Athens and Rome. 1701.

Letters to the King, the Prince of Orange, . . . Being the Third and Last Volume. Published by Jonathan Swift, D.D. 1703. [Preface by Swift.]

A Tale of a Tub. Written for the Universal Improvement of Mankind. . . . To which is added, An Account of a Battle between the Antient and Modern Books in St. James's Library. 1704. 2nd and 3rd edns. 1704. Other edns.: 1705, 1710, 1711, 1724.

    The Battle of the Books. Ed. Guthkelch, A. (King's Classics.) 1908.

Predictions for the Year 1708. Wherein the Month and Day of the Month are set down, the Persons named, and the great Actions and Events of next Year particularly related, as they will come to pass. Written to prevent the People of England from being further impos'd on by vulgar Almanack-makers. By Isaac Bickerstaff Esq. Sold by John Morphew near Stationers Hall. 1708. Several pirated edns. in the same year; also a Dublin edn., and German and Dutch translations.

An Elegy on Mr. Patrige, the Almanack-maker, who Died on the 29th of this Instant March, 1708. 1708. Edinburgh edn. in same year. [Broadside.]

Jack Frenchman's Lamentation, An Excellent New Song. To the Tune of, I 'll tell the Dick, &c. [1708?] Two other edns., one entitled, Jack Frenchman's Defeat: Being an Excellent New Song, to a pleasant Tune.

A Vindication of Isaac Bickerstaff Esq; against What is Objected to Him by Mr. Partridge, in his Almanack for the present Year 1709. By the said Isaac Bickerstaff Esq; 1709.

A Famous Prediction of Merlin, the British Wizard. . . . By T. N. 1709. Edinburgh rpt. in same year. Another edn. 1740.

A Project for the Advancement of Religion, and the Reformation of Manners. By a Person of Quality. 1709. Two other edns. 1709.

A Letter from a Member of the House of Commons in Ireland to a Member of the House of Commons in England, Concerning the Sacramental Test. 1709.

The Tatler. By Isaac Bickerstaff Esq. 1709. [Various papers by Swift.]

Memoirs. Part III. From the Peace concluded 1679. To the Time of the Author's Retirement from Publick Business. By Sir William Temple Baronet. . . . Publish'd by Jonathan Swift, D.D. 1709. [Preface by Swift.]

Poetical Miscellanies. [Commonly known as Dryden's Miscellanies.] The Sixth Part. 1709. [Contains Baucis and Philemon and On Mrs. Biddy Floyd.]

Baucis and Philemon: A Poem On the ever lamented Loss Of the two Yew-Trees . . . . Together with Mrs. Harris's Earnest Petition. By the Author of the Tale of a Tub. 1709. Another pirated edn. by Hills, 1709.

A Meditation upon a Broom-Stick, and Somewhat Beside; of The Same Author's. 1710. Another edn. 1710.

The Virtues of Sid Hamet the Magician's Rod. 1710.

The Examiner. 1710. [Swift's principal contributions are in vol. I.]

The Examiners for the Year 1711. To which is prefix'd, A Letter to the Examiner. 1712.

The Tale of a Nettle. Cambridge, 1710.

A Short Character of His Ex. T. E. of W[harton]. L.L. of I——. With An Account of some smaller Facts. 1711. Another edn. 1715.

The Spectator. 1711. [Swift's contributions were very slight.]

Some Remarks upon a Pamphlet, entitl'd, [A Letter to the Seven Lords of the Committee, appointed to Examine Gregg.] By the Author of the Examiner. 1711.

A New Journey to Paris: Together with some Secret Transactions Between the Fr—h K—g, and an Eng—Gentleman. By the Sieur du Baudrier. Translated from the French. 1711. Second and third edns. 1711.

A Learned Comment upon Dr. Hare's Excellent Sermon Preach'd before the D. of Marlborough, On the Surrender of Bouchain. By an Enemy to Peace. 1711.

An Excellent New Song. Being the Intended Speech of a famous Orator against Peace. [1711.]

The W—ds—r Prophecy. Ptd. in the Year, 1711. [Two edns.]

The Conduct of the Allies, and of the Late Ministry, in Beginning and Carrying on the Present War. 1712 [sic]. The 2nd to the 5th edns. are dated 1711. Other edns. (including Dublin and Edinburgh). 1712.

The Fable of Midas. Ptd. in the Year, 1711. [1712.]

Some Advice Humbly Offer'd to the Members of the October Club, in a Letter from a Person of Honour. 1712.

Some Remarks on the Barrier Treaty, between Her Majesty and the States-General. By the Author of the Conduct of the Allies. 1712. 2nd edn. and Dublin rpt. in same year. Also Spanish trans.

A Proposal for Correcting, Improving and Ascertaining the English Tongue; in a Letter To the Most Honourable Robert Earl of Oxford and Mortimer, Lord High Treasurer of Great Britain. 1712. 2nd edn. in same year.

Some Reasons to Prove, That no Person is obliged by his Principles, as a Whig, To Oppose Her Majesty or her Present Ministry. In a Letter to a Whig-Lord. 1712.

T[o]ll[a]nd's Invitation to Dismal, to Dine with the Calves-Head Club. Imitated from Horace, Epist. 5, Lib. 1. [1712.]

Peace and Dunkirk; Being an Excellent New Song upon the Surrender of Dunkirk to General Hill. 1712.

It 's out at last, or, French Correspondence as clear as the Sun. 1712.

A Dialogue upon Dunkirk, between a Whig and a Tory. 1712.

A Letter from the Pretender, To a Whig-Lord. [1712.]

Remarks on the Bp. of S. Asaph's Preface. Examiner, vol. 11, no. 34. 24 July 1712.

A Letter of Thanks from my Lord W****n to the Lord Bp. of S. Asaph, In the Name of the Kit-Cat-Club. 1712.

An Appendix to the Conduct of the Allies; and Remarks on the Barrier Treaty. Examiner, vol. 111, no. 16. 16 Jan., 1712/13.

Mr. C[olli]ns's Discourse of Free-Thinking, Put into plain English, by way of Abstract, for the Use of the Poor. By a Friend of the Author. 1713.

A Complete Refutation of the Falsehoods alleged against Erasmus Lewis, Esq. Examiner, vol. 111, no. 21. 2 Feb., 1712/13.

The Address of the House of Lords to the Queen. April 9th, 1713. [Ptd. in the Journals of the House of Lords on 10 April.]

Part of the Seventh Epistle of the First Book of Horace imitated: and Address'd to a Noble Peer. 1713. 2nd and 3rd edns. 1713; also a Dublin edn.

The Importance of the Guardian Considered, in a Second Letter to the Bailiff of Stockbridge. By a Friend of Mr. St——le. 1713.

A Preface to the B—p of S—r—m's Introduction To the Third Volume of the History of the Reformation of the Church of England. By Gregory Misosarum. 1713. 2nd edn. 1713. A Dublin edn. in 1714.

The First Ode of the Second Book of Horace Paraphras'd: and Address'd to Richard St—le. Esq. 1713. Another edn. 1714; also a Dublin edn.

The Publick Spirit of the Whigs: Set forth in their Generous Encouragement of the Author of the Crisis: with some Observations on the Seasonableness, Candor, Erudition, and Style of that Treatise. 1714. Several other edns. 1714, some of which omit the passage objected to by the Scots Lords.

John Dennis, the Sheltring Poet's Invitation to Richard Steele, The Secluded Party-Writer, and Member; To come and live with him in the Mint. In Imitation of Horace's Fifth Epistle, Lib. 1. And fit to be Bound up with the Crisis. 1714.

Letters, Poems, and Tales: Amorous, Satyrical, and Gallant. Which passed between Several Persons of Distinction. 1718. (Contains A Decree for Concluding the Treaty between Dr. Swift and Mrs. Long.)

The Works of Sir William Temple, Bart. 2 vols. 1720. (Life by Swift.)

An Elegy On the much lamented Death of Mr. Demar, the Famous rich Man, who died the 6th of this Inst. July 1720.

A Proposal For the universal Use of Irish Manufacture, in Cloaths and Furniture of Houses, &c. Utterly Rejecting and Renouncing Every Thing wearable that comes from England. Dublin, 1720.

The Right of Precedence between Phisicians and Civilians Enquir'd into. Dublin, 1720. Three London edns. in 1720.

The Swearers-Bank: or, Parliamentary Security for Establishing a new Bank in Ireland. Wherein The Medicinal Use of Oaths is considered. (With The Best in Christendom. A Tale.) Written by Dean Swift. Dublin, 1720. A London edn in 1720.

A Letter to a Young Gentleman, Lately enter'd into Holy Orders. By a Person of Quality. Dublin, 1721. Several other London and Dublin edns. in 1721.

A Letter of Advice to a Young Poet; Together With a Proposal for the Encouragement of Poetry in this Kingdom. Dublin, 1721. A London edn. ("By J. Swift.") 1721.

Epilogue, To be spoke at the Theatre-Royal This present Saturday being April the 1st. In the Behalf of the Distressed Weavers. Dublin, [1721]. Another edn.: An Epilogue, As it was spoke by Mr. Griffith At the Theatre-Royal On Saturday the First of April. In the Behalf of the Distressed Weavers. Ptd. on the *verso* of A Prologue, Spoke by Mr. Elrington. Dublin, [1721].

The Bubble: a Poem. 1721.

A Letter to the K[ing] at Arms From a Reputed Esquire One of the Subscribers to the Bank. Dublin, [1721].

The Journal. [Dublin, 1722.]

Some Arguments Against enlarging the Power of Bishops In letting of Leases. With Remarks on some Queries Lately published. Dublin, 1723.

A Letter to the Shop-keepers, Tradesmen, Farmers, and Common-People of Ireland, Concerning the Brass Half-Pence Coined by Mr. Woods, with A Design to have them Pass in this Kingdom. . . . By M. B. Drapier. Dublin, [1724].

A Letter to Mr. Harding the Printer, Upon Occasion of a Paragraph in his News-Paper of Aug. 1st, Relating to Mr. Wood's Half-Pence. By M. B. Drapier. Dublin, [1724].

Some Observations Upon a Paper, Call'd, The Report of the Committee of the Most Honourable the Privy-Council in England, Relating to Wood's Half-pence. By M. B. Drapier. Dublin, [1724].

Another Letter to Mr. Harding the Printer, Upon the Occasion of the Report of the Committee. . . . In Relation to Mr. Wood's Half Pence and Farthings, &c. lately Publish'd. Dublin, [1724].

A Letter to the Whole People of Ireland. By M. B. Drapier. Dublin, [1724].

Seasonable Advic . Since a Bill is preparing for the Grand-Jury, to find against the Printer of the Drapier's last Letter, there are several things . . . before they determine upon it. [n.p.], 1724.

An Excellent New Song upon the Late Grand-Jury. Dublin, 1724.

An Exce[llent New] So[ng] Upon His Grace Our good Lord Archbishop of Dublin. By honest Jo. one of His Grace's Farmers in Fingal. Dublin, 1724.

A Letter To the Right Honourable the Lord Viscount Molesworth. By M. B. Drapier, Author of the Letter to the Shop-keepers, &c. Dublin, [1724].

To the Citizens. (Signed M. B.) Dublin, 1724.

Prometheus, A Poem. Dublin, 1724.

Ireland's Warning, Being an Excellent New Song, upon Woods's Base Half-pence. To the Tune of Packinton's Pound. Dublin, [1724].

A Serious Poem upon William Wood, Brasier, Tinker, Hard-Ware-Man, Coiner, Counterfeiter, Founder and Esquire. Dublin, [1724].

An excellent New Song Upon the Declarations of the several Corporations of the City of Dublin; against Woods's Half-pence. [n.p., 1724.]

Fraud Detected: or, the Hibernian Patriot. Containing, All the Drapier's Letters to the People of Ireland, on Wood's Coinage, &c. Dublin, 1725.

A Poem Upon R—r a Lady's Spaniel. [n. p., 1725.]

The Birth of Manly Virtue, from Callimachus. Dublin, 1725.

A Riddle By Dr. S—t, to My Lady Carteret. [n.p., 1725.]

To his Grace the Arch-Bishop of Dublin, A Poem. Dublin, [1725].

A Young Lady's Complaint for the Stay of Dean Swift in England. Dublin, 1726.

Cadenus and Vanessa. A Poem. Ptd.: and Sold by J. Roberts at the Oxford-Arms in Warwick-Lane, 1726. Other edns.: ptd. for T. Warner, Paternoster Row; and for N. Blandford, Charing Cross; also edns. at Dublin and Edinburgh.

Travels into Several Remote Nations of the World. In Four Parts. By Lemuel Gulliver, First a Surgeon, and then a Captain of several Ships. Vol. I. Printed for Benj. Motte, at the Middle Temple-Gate in Fleet-street. 1726.

Travels into Several Remote Nations of the World. By Captain Lemuel Gulliver. Part III. A Voyage to Laputa, Balnibarbi, Glubbdubdrib, Luggnagg and Japan. Part IV. A Voyage to the Houyhnhnms. Printed for Benjamin Motte, at the Middle-Temple-Gate. 1726.

   Edition A: 8vo, Front., pp. xvi, 148; vi, 164; vi, 155; viii, 199, and six plates. Edition AA: 8vo, Front., pp. xii, 148; vi, 164; vi, 154; viii, 199, and six plates. Edition B: 8vo, Front., pp. xii, 310, 3 leaves between pp. 148 and 149; vi, 353, 4 leaves between pp. 154 and 155. The first issue, edn. A, has the words "Captain Lemuel Gulliver, of Redriff Aetat. suae 58" in the space below the portrait; edn. AA and subsequent issues have these words in the oval around the portrait, and a quotation from Persius in the space below. In A and AA each of the four parts is paged separately, while in B the pagination is continuous through each volume; moreover in A part III ends on p. 155, and in AA and B it ends on p. 154. (N. & Q. Dec. 12, 1885.)

   2nd edn. 1726; 1727.

   Dublin edns in 1726, 1727, 1735. French and Dutch translations in 1727. Other edns.: 1731; 4th edn. corrected, 1742; 5th edn. 1747; with memoir by Saintsbury, G., 1886; ed. Aitken, G. A. (Temple Classics), 1896; with preface by Craik, Sir H., 1894.

   Borkowsky, T. Quellen zu Swift's Gulliver. Anglia, vol. xv, pp. 345–8. Halle, 1893.

The Present Miserable State of Ireland. In a Letter from a Gentleman in Dublin, to his Friend S. R. W. in London. Dublin, [1727?]. Another edn., entitled: The Case Of the Kingdom of Ireland. Taken into Consideration, in a Letter to a Member of Parliament, in the Behalf of Trade, &c. Dublin, [1727].

Helter Skelter, or The Hue and Cry after the Attornies, going to ride the Circuit. [n.p., 1727.]

A Short View of the State of Ireland. Dublin, 1727.

An Answer to a Paper, called A Memorial of the poor Inhabitants, Tradesmen, and Labourers of the Kingdom of Ireland. By the Author of the Short View of the State of Ireland. Dublin, 1728.

The Intelligencer. Numb. I. Saturday. May, 11, To be Continued Weekly. Dublin, 1728. [20 numbers.]

The Intelligencer. . . . Ptd. at Dublin. Rptd. at London, and sold by A. Moor[e]. 1729. [Contains Nos. 1–19.]
No. 19 was rptd. as:
    A Letter from the Revd. J. S. D. S. P. D. to a Country Gentleman in the North of England. Ptd. in the Year 1736.

A Modest Proposal For preventing the Children of Poor People From being a Burthen to their Parents, or the Country, and For making them Beneficial to the Publick. Dublin: Ptd. by S. Harding. 1729. 3rd edn. 1730. Other edns. by Roberts, 1729, and Bickerton, 1730.

The Journal of a Modern Lady. In a Letter to a Person of Quality. By the Author of Cadenus and Vanessa. First Ptd. at Dublin; and now Rptd. at London; for J. Wilford, 1729.

To His Excellency John, Lord Carteret; Lord Lieutenant of Ireland. An Imitation of Horace, Ode IX. Lib. IV. Dublin: Ptd. by James Carson, 1729.

On Paddy's Character of the Intelligencer. [n. p.,1729.]

An Apology to the Lady C[a]r[tere]t. On Her Inviting Dean S[wi]ft To Dinner; . . . Ptd. in the Year 1730.

An Epistle To His Excellency John Lord Carteret Lord Lieutenant of Ireland. [At end] Dublin: Ptd. by George Grierson. [1730.]

An Epistle upon an Epistle From a certain Doctor To a certain great Lord: being a Christmas-Box for D. D——ny. Dublin, 1730.

An Epistle To His Excellency John Lord Carteret, Lord Lieutenant of Ireland. To which is added, an Epistle, upon an Epistle; being A Christmas-Box for Doctor D——ny. Dublin, 1730.

A Libel on D[r] D[elany] and a Certain Great Lord. 1730. Another edn.: A Satire on Dr. D——ny. By Dr. Sw—t. Dublin: And Rptd. at London, for A. Moore. 1730.

To Doctor D—l—y, on the Libels Writ against him. . . . London; rptd., Dublin, 1730.

An Answer to Dr. D——y's Fable of the Pheasant and the Lark. 1730.

An Excellent New Ballad: or, The true En—sh D——n to be hang'd for a R—pe. [1730.]

The Hibernian Patriot: Being a Collection of the Drapier's Letters to the People of Ireland, concerning Mr. Wood's Brass Half-Pence. . . . Ptd. at Dublin. London: Rptd. and Sold by A. Moor[e]. 1730.

A Vindication of his Excellency the Lord C——t, from the Charge Of favouring none but Tories, High-Churchmen and Jacobites. By the Reverend Dr. S——t. 1730. Another edn.: A Vindication of his Ex——y the Lord C——, from The Charge of favouring none but Toryes, High-Churchmen, and Jacobites. Dublin, 1730.

Horace, Book I., Ode XIV., . . . paraphrased and inscribed to Ir[elan]d. Printed in the Year MDCDXXX [sic].

Traulus. Dublin, 1730. [Verses against Lord Allen.]

Memoirs of Capt. John Creichton. Written by Himself. 1731. [The Advertisement To the Reader by Swift.]

The Place of the Damn'd. By J. S. D.D. D.S.P.D. [n. p.], 1731.

A Proposal Humbly offered to the P——t, For the more effectual preventing the further Growth of Popery. . . . By Dr. S——t. To which is added, The Humble Petition of the Weavers. . . . As also two Poems. Dublin; rptd., London, 1731. 2nd edn. 1732.

A Soldier and a Scholar: or the Lady's Judgment Upon those two Characters In the Persons of Captain——and D—n S—t. 1732. Another edn.: The Grand Question debated: Whether Hamilton's Bawn Should be turn'd into a Barrack, or a Malt-house. According to the London Edition, with Notes. Dublin, 1732.

An infallible Scheme to pay the Publick Debt of this Nation in six Months. By D—n S—t. Dublin; rptd., London, for H. Whittridge, 1732.

Considerations upon Two Bills Sent down from the R—— H—— the H ——of L—— To the H——ble H—— of C—— Relating to the Clergy of I*****D. Ptd. for A. Moore. 1732. Another edn., ptd. for Roberts, To which is added, A Proposal for an Act of Parliament, to pay off the Debt of the Nation, . . . By A— P—, Esq. 1732.

An Examination of Certain Abuses, Corruptions, and Enormities in the City of Dublin. Dublin, 1732. Another edn.: City Cries, Instrumental and Vocal: or An Examination of certain Abuses, Corruptions, and Enormities, in London and Dublin. By the Rev. Dr. Swift, D.S.P.D. Dublin; rptd. London, 1732.

The Lady's Dressing Room. To which is added, A Poem on Cutting down the, Old Thorn at Market Hill. By the Rev. Dr. S—t. Ptd. for J. Roberts. 1732. Three Dublin edns. in 1732.

The Advantages propos'd by repealing the Sacramental Test, impartially considered. Dublin, 1732. Another edn.: To which is added, Remarks on . . . Nature and Consequences of the Sacramental Test. Dublin; rptd., London, 1732.

Quæries Wrote by Dr. J. Swift, in the Year 1732. Very proper to be read at this Time by every Member of the Established Church. [1732.]

The Life and Genuine Character of Doctor Swift. Written by Himself. 1733.

On Poetry: A Rapsody. Dublin; rptd. London. 1733. Rptd. Dublin, 1734.

A serious and useful Scheme, to make an Hospital for Incurables, of Universal Benefit to all His Majesty's Subjects. . . . To which is added, A Petition of the Footman in and about Dublin. By a Celebrated Author in Ireland. 1733. Other edns.: 1733, 1734.

The Presbyterians Plea of Merit; In Order to take off the Test, Impartially Examined. Dublin, 1733. Another edn.: London, [1733].

The Correspondent. No. 1 [No. II, . . . No. VI.] Ptd. by James Hoey, 1733.

Ten Reasons for Repealing the Test Act. [1733.]

Some Reasons against the Bill for settling the Tyth of Hemp, Flax, &c. by a Modus. Dublin, MDCCXXIV. [sic; 1734?].

A Beautiful Young Nymph Going to Bed. Written for the Honour of the Fair Sex. . . . To which are added, Strephon and Chloe, and Cassinus and Peter. Dublin; rptd., London, 1734.

An Epistle to a Lady, Who desired the Author to make Verses on Her, in the

Heroick Stile. Also a Poem, Occasion'd by Reading Dr. Young's Satires, called, The Universal Passion. Dublin; rptd., London, 1734.

Reasons Humbly offered to the Parliament of Ireland For Repealing the Sacramental Test, &c. in favour of the Catholics, Otherwise called Roman Catholics, and by their Ill-Willers Papists. [1734?]

Poems on Several Occasions. [By Mrs. Mary Barber.] 1734. [Contains an introductory Letter to John, earl of Orrery, by Swift.]

Speech delivered by Dean Swift to an Assembly of Merchants met at the Guildhall, to draw up a Petition to the Lord Lieutenant on the Lowering of Coin, April 24th, 1736. [Ptd. at beginning of a tract, Reasons why we should not lower the Coins now current in this Kingdom. . . . Dublin.]

A Proposal for giving Badges to the Beggars in all the Parishes of Dublin. By the Dean of St. Patrick's. 1737.

An Imitation of the Sixth Satire of the Second Book of Horace. . . . The first Part done in the Year 1714, By Dr. Swift. The latter Part now first added, And never before Printed. 1738.

The Beasts Confession to the Priest, on Observing how most Men mistake their own Talents. By J. S., D.S.P. Dublin; rptd., London, 1738.

A Complete Collection Of Genteel and Ingenious Conversation, According to the Most Polite Mode and Method Now Used At Court, and in the Best Companies of England. In Three Dialogues. By Simon Wagstaff, Esq. 1738. Dublin edn. 1738.

Verses on the Death of Doctor Swift. Written by Himself: Nov., 1731. 1739. Other edns.: 1739, 1741; Dublin, 1739.

Some Free Thoughts upon the Present State of Affairs. Written in the Year 1714. Dublin, 1741. Two London edns. 1741.

Three Sermons: I. On Mutual Subjection. II. On Conscience. III. On the Trinity. By the Reverend Dr. Swift, Dean of St. Patrick's. 1744. Another edn., with a fourth sermon included in the volume, has The Difficulty of Knowing One's Self at the end. Dublin edns.: 1744, 1760.

Directions to Servants In General; And in particular to The Butler, Cook . . . By the Reverend Dr. Swift, D.S.P.D. 1745. Dublin edn. 1745. 2nd edn. 1746.

The Story of the Injured Lady. Being a true Picture of Scotch Perfidy, Irish Poverty, and English Partiality. With Letters and Poems Never before Printed. By the Rev. Dr. Swift, D.S.P.D. 1746.

Brotherly Love. A Sermon, Preached in St. Patrick's Church; On December 1st, 1717. By Dr. Jonathan Swift, Dean of St. Patrick's, Dublin. 1754. Another edn. Dublin, 1754.

An Essay upon the Life, Writings, and Character, of Dr. Jonathan Swift. . . . By Deane Swift, Esq.; To which is added, That Sketch of Dr. Swift's Life, written by the Doctor himself. 1755.

The History of the Four Last Years of the Queen. By the late onathan Swift, D.D., D.S.P.D. 1758. Another edn.: The History of the Last Session of Parliament, and of the Peace of Utrecht. Written at Windsor in the Year, 1713. By the Rev. Dr. J. Swift, D.S.P.D. Dublin, 1758.

III. Works Attributed to Swift

The Fairy Feast, Written by the Author of A Tale of a Tub, and the Mully of Mountown. 1704. [By Dr. W. King.]

The Swan Tripe-Club in Dublin. A Satyr. Dublin, 1706. A London edn. in same year.

An Answer to Bickerstaff. Some Reflections upon Mr. Bickerstaff's Predictions for the Year MDCCVIII. By a Person of Quality. [1708.]

Squire Bickerstaff Detected; or, the Astrological Impostor Convicted, by John Partridge, Student in Physick and Astrology. [1708.]

A Trip to Dunkirk: Or, A Hue and Cry After the Pretended Prince of Wales. 1708.

Bickerstaff's Almanack: or, a Vindication of the Stars, From all the False Imputations, and Erroneous Assertions, of the late John Partridge, and all other Mistaken Astrologers whatever. By Isaac Bickerstaff, Esq. 1710.

A Complete Key to the Tale of a Tub; With some Account of the Authors. 1710.

A True Narrative Of what pass'd at the Examination Of the Marquis De Guiscard, at the Cock-pit, The 8th of March, 1710–11. 1711. [Revised by Swift.]

The British Visions: or, Isaac Bickerstaff's Twelve Prophecies for the Year 1711. [n.p., 1711.]

The Reasons Which induc'd Her Majesty To Create the Right Honourable Robert Harley, Esq. a Peer of Great-Britain. 1711.

The D. of M——h's Vindication: In Answer to a Pamphlet Lately Publish'd, call'd Bouchain, or a Dialogue between the Medley and the Examiner. 1711. [Revised by Swift.]

Cursory but Curious Observations of Mr. Ab[e]l R[op]er, Upon a late Famous Pamphlet, entituled, Remarks on the Preliminary Articles . . . General Peace. 1711.

A True Relation Of the several Facts and Circumstances Of the intended Riot and Tumult on Queen Elizabeth's Birth-day. 1711. [Revised by Swift.]

Predictions For the Year, 1712. By Isaac Bickerstaff, Esq. in a Letter to the Author of the Oxford Almanack. 1712.

The Dutch Barrier Ours. 1712.

The Story of the St. Alb-ns Ghost, or the Apparition of Mother Haggy. 1712. [Revised by Swift.]

A Fable of the Widow and her Cat. Printed in the Year 1712. [Attributed to Prior.]

The New Way of selling Places at Court. In a Letter from a Small Courtier to a Great Stock-Jobber. 1712. [Revised by Swift.]

An Essay on National Rewards; Being a Proposal for bestowing them on a Plan more durable and respectable. Guardian, No. XCVI. Wednesday 1 July, 1713.

The Character of Richard St—le, Esq.; With some Remarks. By Toby, Abel's Kinsman. 1713.

A Modest Enquiry into the Reasons of the Joy Expressed by a Certain Sett of People, upon the Spreading of a Report of Her Majesty's Death. 1714. [By Mrs. Manley.]

A Letter From the Facetious Doctor Andrew Tripe, at Bath, To the Venerable Nestor Ironside. 1714.

The Conduct of the Purse of Ireland: in a Letter to a Member Of the Late Oxford Convocation. 1714.

An Inquiry into the Miscarriages of the Four Last Years Reign. 1714. [Attributed to C. Povey.]

Essays Divine, Moral, and Political. . . . By the Author of the Tale of a Tub, sometime the Writer of the Examiner, and the Original Inventor of the Band-Box-Plot. 1714.

The Dignity, Use and Abuse of Glass-Bottles. Set forth in A Sermon Preach'd to an Illustrous Assembly. By the Author of the Tale of a Tub. 1715.

Saint Patrick's Purgatory: or, Dr. S——t's Expostulation With his Distressed Friends in the Tower and elsewhere. 1716.

The Narrative of Dr. Robert Norris, Concerning the strange and deplorable Frenzy of Mr. John Denn–An Officer of the Custom·house. 1716. [By Pope.]

God's Revenge against Punning. Shewing the miserable Fates of Persons addicted to this Crying Sin, in Court and Town. 1716. [By Pope.]

Doctor Sw——t's Circular Letter to the Clergy of the Diocese of Dublin; Exhorting them, in the conduct of their lives, to regulate themselves always according to the present Humours of the Times. 1716.

A Full and True Account of a Horrid and Barbarous Revenge by Poison, On the Body of Mr. Edmund Curll, Bookseller; With a faithful Copy of his Last Will and Testament. [1716.] [Attributed to Pope.]

A further Account of the most Deplorable Condition of Mr. Edmund Curll, Bookseller, since his being poison'd on March 28. 1716. [Attributed to Pope.]

A Strange but True Relation how Edmund Curll, of Fleet-street, Stationer, . . . was circumcis'd. [Attributed to Pope.]

A Dedication to a Great Man, Concerning Dedications. 1718. [Attributed to Thomas Gordon.]

Ars Pun-ica, sive Flos Linguarum: The Art of Punning; or, the Flower of Languages; In Seventy-Nine Rules: By the Labour and Industry of Tom Pun-Sibi, (*i e.*) Jonathan Swift, D.D. 1719.

A Letter From the Facetious Dr. Andrew Tripe at Bath, To his Loving Brother The Profound Greshamite, Shewing, That the Scribendi Cacoethes is a Distemper. [1719.]

The Invitation. In imitation of Horace's Epistle to Torquatus. Written by Mr. T—— S—— to D—n S——. Dublin, 1720.

D——n S——t's Prologue to Hyppolitus, Spoken by a Boy of Six Years Old. [1720.]

Duke upon Duke, &c. [1720.]

A Defence of English Commodities. Being an Answer to the Proposal For the Universal Use of Irish Manufactures, and Utterly rejecting and renouncing every Thing that is Wearable that comes from England. . . . Written by Dean Swift. 1720.

The Wonderfull Wonder of Wonders; Being an Accurate Description of the Birth, Education, Manner of Living, Religion, Politicks, Learning, &c. of mine A——se. By Dr. Sw——ft. With a Preface. London: Printed from the Original Copy from Dublin. 1721. Another edn.: London: Printed in the Year 1722.

The Blunderful Blunder of Blunders. Being an Answer to the Wonderful Wonder of Wonders. [1721.] Another edn.: By Dr. Sw——ft. . . . London: Printed from the Original Copies from Dublin. 1721.

Subscribers to the Bank Plac'd according to Their Order and Quality. With Notes and Queries. Dublin, [1721].

A Letter from a Lady in Town to her Friend in the Country, concerning the Bank; or, The List of the Subscribers farther Explained. Dated Dublin, Dec.1, 1721. [In Scott's edn. of Swift, vol. 1, 1814.]

A Supplement to Dean Sw——t's Miscellanies: By the Author. Containing, I. A Letter to the Students of both Universities, . . . II. An Essay upon an Apothecary. III. An Account of a surprizing Apparition. 1723.

Memoirs of the Life of Scriblerus. . . . By D. S——t. Printed from the Original Copy from Dublin. 1723.

To the King's Most Excellent Majesty, The Humble Address of the Knights, Citizens and Burgesses, in Parliament assembled. Dublin, 1723.

A Poem address'd to the Quidnunc's, at St. James's Coffee-House London. Occasion'd by the Death of the Duke of Orleans. 1724.

A New Poem Ascrib'd To the Honble the Gentlemen of the Late Grand-Jury. Dublin, [1724].

The Fifth and Last Letter to the People of Ireland In Reference to Wood and his Brass. Dublin, 1724.

A full and true Account of the solemn Procession to the Gallows, at the Execution of William Wood, Esquire, and Hard-ware-man. 1724.

The Sixth Letter to the Whole People of Ireland. By an Ancient Patriot. Dublin, 1724.

The Drapier Anatomised: A Song. A New Song Sung at the Club at Mr. Taplin's The Sign of the Drapier's Head in Truck-Street. Dublin, 1724.

A Defence of the Conduct of the People of Ireland In their unanimous Refusal of Mr. Wood's Copper-Money. Dublin, [1724].

The True State of the Case, Between the Kingdom of Ireland of the one Part, and Mr. William Wood of the other Part. By a Protestant of Ireland. Dublin, [1724].

Some Considerations on the Attempts Made to Pass Mr. Wood's Brass-Money in Ireland. By a Lover of his Country. Dublin, 1724.

Some Reasons Shewing the Necessity the People of Ireland are under, for continuing to refuse Mr. Wood's Coinage. By the Author of the Considerations. Dublin, 1724. [Dedication signed "D. B."]

Tom Punsibi's Dream. Dublin, 1724-5.

Woods Reviv'd, or, a Short Defence of the Proceedings in Bristol, London, &c. in Reference to the Kingdom of Ireland. [Dublin], 1725.

An Elegy On the Universelly [*sic*] Lamented Death of the Right Honourable Robert Lord Vis. Molesworth, . . . By M. B. 1725.

Enquiries into the principal Causes of the general Poverty of the Common People of Ireland. Dublin, 1725.

Advice to a Son at the University, Design'd for Holy Orders. By a Clergyman. 1725. [Attributed to Rev. T. Curteis.]

The Widows Address To the Rt. Hon. the Lady Carteret. By M. B. Dublin, 1725.

A Letter from D. S——t to D. S——y. [1725.]

A History of Poetry, In a Letter to a Friend, By the Revd. D—— S——t. Dublin, 1726.

It cannot Rain but it Pours: or, London strow'd with Rarities. 1726.

It cannot Rain but it Pours: Or, The First Part of London strow'd with Rarities. . . . N. B. The Second Part of this Book by Mistake of the Printer was published first. 1726.

The Manifesto of Lord Peter. 1726.

The Most Wonderful Wonder That ever appear'd to the Wonder of the British Nation. Being, An Account of the Travels of Mynheer Veteranus, thro' the Woods of Germany: With an Account . . . Written by the Copper-Farthing Dean. 1726.

Travels into several Remote Nations of the World. By Capt. Lemuel Gulliver. Vol. III. 1727.

Memoirs Of the Court of Lilliput. Written by Captain Gulliver. Containing an Account of the Intrigues, and some other particular Transactions of that Nation, omitted in the two Volumes of his Travels. 1727.

Dean Jonathan's Parody on the 4th Chap. of Genesis.   1729.

The Drapier's Advice to the Freemen and Freeholders of the City of Dublin. [Dublin, 1729.]

P[o]em By D—— S——.   On the Scheme Propos'd to the People of Ireland. Humbly Address'd to the Skilfull and Ingenious Mr. Maculla, A Lover of his Country, and of the Publick Good, &c. . . . Dublin. [1729].

Letters upon the Use of Irish Coal. To the Publisher of the Dublin Weekly Journal. [Printed in the issues for 9 and 16 August and 25 October, 1729. Signed S.D.H., M.B.]

A Letter to the People of Ireland. By M. B. Draper [sic]. . . . Dublin, 1729.

The Present State of Ireland Consider'd. . . .   Dublin; rptd., London, 1730.

Some Seasonable Advice to Doctor D—n—y. 1730.

The Colcannen Match: or, the Belly Duel. A Poem. In three Canto's.   1730.

A Brief Account of Mr. John Ginglicutt's Treatise Concerning the Altercation or Scolding of the Ancients. By the Author. Printed for J. Roberts in Warwick-Lane. 1731. [By Arbuthnot.]

An Infallible Scheme To pay the Publick Debt of this Nation In Six Months. Humbly offered to the Consideration of the present P——t. 1731. [Attributed to the Rev. M. Pilkington.]

A Scheme Humbly offer'd, for making R[eligio]n and the C[lerg]y useful. 1731.

A New Simile for the Ladies, with Useful Annotations. Dublin, 1732. [Attributed to Sheridan.]

Chloe Surpriz'd: or, The Second Part of the Lady's Dressing-Room. To which are added, Thoughts upon Reading the Lady's Dressing-Room, and the Gentleman's Study. The former wrote by D—n S—t, the latter by Miss W——. 1732.

An Enquiry whether the Christian Religion is of any Benefit, or only An Useless Commodity to a Trading Nation. 1732.

A Proposal humbly offered to the P—t for the more effectual preventing the further growth of Popery. . . . By Dr. S—t. 1732.

Human Ordure, Botanically Considered. The First Essay, of the Kind, Ever Published in the World. By Dr. S—t. 1733. [Attributed to Dr. Chamberlayne.]

Ub-Bub-A-Boo: or, the Irish-Howl in Heroic Verse. By Dean Swift. 1735.

Bounce to Fop. An Heroick Epistle from a Dog at Twickenham to a Dog at Court. By Dr. S—t. 1736.

A Proposal for erecting a Protestant Nunnery in the City of Dublin. 1736.

Some Proposals for the Revival of Christianity. [Attributed to Rev. P. Skelton.] [Dublin?, 1736.]

A New Proposal For the better Regulation and Improvement of Quadrille. Dublin, 1736. [By Bp. Hort.]

Some Thoughts on the Tillage of Ireland: Humbly Dedicated to the Parliament. . . . . To which is Prefixed, A Letter to the Printer, from the Reverend Doctor Swift. Dublin, 1737.

The Humours of the Age: or, Dean Swift's New Evening-Post. . . . Numb. I. (To be continued Weekly.) [15 October to 21 October, 1738.]

Good Queen Anne Vindicated, and The Ingratitude, Insolence, &c. of her Whig Ministry and the Allies Detected and Exposed. (By that worthy Patriot Dean Swift.) 1748.

A New Project For the Destruction of Printing and Bookselling; for the Benefit of the Learned World. Dublin, 1750.

The Mishap.   A Poem.   Written by the late Rev. J.S. D.D. D.S.P.D.   [1750.]
Some Account of the Irish.   By the late J.S. D.D. D.S.P.D.   1753.

IV. Various (Contemporary)

A Defence of the Reflections upon Ancient and Modern Learning. . . .With
    Observations upon the Tale of a Tub.   By William Wotton, B. D.   1705.
Reflections on Dr. Swift's Letter to the Earl of Oxford, about the English Tongue.
    [1712.]
The British Academy: Being a new-erected Society for the advancement of wit
    and learning.   1712.
The Fable of the Shepherd and his Dog.   1712.
When the Cat's away, the Mice may play.   A Fable.   Humbly inscribed to
    Dr. Swift.   [1712?]
Two Letters concerning the Author of the Examiner.   1713.
An Hue and Cry after Dr. S——t.   1714.
A farther Hue and Cry after Dr. Sw—t.   1714.
The Scots Nation and Union vindicated [by Defoe].   1714.
Dr. S—'s Real Diary.   1715.
A Letter from the Lord V—t B—ke, To the Rev. Dr. S—t.   Written at Calais.
    1715.
A Letter from Aminadab Firebrass Quaker Merchant, to M. B. Drapier.   Dub-
    lin, [1724].
The Drapier demolished and set out in his own proper colours. . . . By William
    Wood Esq.   Dublin, [1724.]
Seasonable Advice to M. B. Drapier.   [1724.]
A Letter from a Lady of Quality to Mr. Harding the Printer.   1724.
An Express from Parnassus.   To the Reverend Dr. Jonathan Swift, Dean of
    St. Patrick's.   [1724.]
A Letter to M. B. Drapier.   Dublin, 1724-5
A Letter from a Friend to the Right Honourable — — — —.   Dublin, 1724.
A Second Letter from a Friend to the Right Honourable — —.   [1725.]
The Donore Ballad.   Dublin, 1724–5.
A Poem to D— S—.   Dublin, 1724–5.
A Second Poem to Dr. Jo—n S—t.   Dublin, 1725.
A Congratulatory Poem on Dean Swift's Return to Town.   Dublin, 1725.
To His Excellency the Lord Carteret, occasioned by seeing The Birth of Manly
    Virtue.   Dublin, 1725.
A Poem inscrib'd to the Author of The Birth of Manly Virtue.   Dublin, 1725.
A Satyr.   Printed in the Year MDCCXXV.
A Letter from a Clergyman to his Friend.   With an Account of the Travels of
    Captain Lemuel Gulliver: And a Character of the Author.   1726.
Several Copies of Verse on Occasion of Mr. Gulliver's Travels.   1727.
Two Lilliputian Odes.   1727.
Gulliveriana: Or a Fourth Volume of Miscellanies.   1728.
A Supplement to the Profound.   1728.
Gulliver decypher'd.   [1728.]   [By Arbuthnot.]
An Epistle to a certain Dean, written originally in Italian.   Dublin, 1730.
A Panegyric on the Reverend D—n S—t.   1730.
The Pheasant and the Lark.   [By Dr. Delany.]   Dublin, 1730.
Poems on several Occasions. . . . By Matthew Pilkington.   Revised by Swift.
    1731.

The Gentleman's Study. In answer to the Lady's Dressing Room. 1732.
An Elegy on Dicky and Dolly. 1732.
A Vindication of the Protestant Dissenters. [1733.]
A Rap at the Rapsody. 1734.
The Dean's Provocation for writing the Lady's Dressing Room. 1734.
A Collection of Welsh Travels. . . . Being a pleasant Relation of D—n S—t's
    journey to that ancient Kingdom. 1738.
An authentic Copy of the Last Will and Testament of the Reverend Dr. Swift,
    Dublin, 1745.
The Last Will and Testament of Jonathan Swift, D.D. Attested by Jo. Wynne,
    Jo. Rochfort, and William Dunkin. Taken out of the Perogative [sic] Court
    of Dublin. Dublin; rptd., London, 1746. A Dublin edn. 1747.

V. Biography and Criticism

Ainger, A. Lectures and Essays. 1905.
Aitken, G. A. Life of Arbuthnot. 1892.
Barrett, J. Essay on the earlier part of the Life of Swift. 1808.
Berkeley, G. M. Literary Relics. 1789.
Bernard, J. H. Introduction to Correspondence of Jonathan Swift. *See* under
    I, above.
Birrell, A. Essays about Men, Women, and Books. 1894.
Caro, Jákob. Lessing und Swift. Jena, 1869.
Collins, J. C. Jonathan Swift, a biographical and critical study. 1893.
Cordelet, Henriette. Swift. Paris, 1907.
Courthope, W. J. Life of Alexander Pope. [Works, vol. v.] 1889.
Craik, Sir H. Life of Jonathan Swift. 1882.
Dilworth, W. H. Life of Jonathan Swift. 1758.
Dobson, A. Eighteenth Century Vignettes. Ser. 2. 1894.
Elton, O. The Augustan Ages. Edinburgh, 1899.
Forster, John. Life of Jonathan Swift. Vol. I. 1875.
Hansen, A. M. En Engelsk Forfattergruppe. Copenhagen, 1892.
Hazlitt, W. The English Poets. Works, vol. II. Edd. Waller, A. R. and Glover,
    A. 1894.
Jeffrey, Lord. Jonathan Swift. 1853.
Johnson, Samuel. Lives of the Poets. 1781.
Kacziány, G. Swift, Jonathan és kora, &c. Budapest, 1901.
King, R. A. Swift in Ireland. 1895.
Lane-Poole, Stanley. Eighteenth Century Letters. 1897.
Lane-Poole, Stanley. Swift and Stella. Fortnightly Review, Feb. 1910.
Lecky, W. E. H. The Leaders of Public Opinion in Ireland. 1861.
Longe, J. S. Martha, Lady Giffard: Life and Letters. 1910.
Mason, W. M. History of St. Patrick's, Dublin. 1819.
Masson, David. Essays, chiefly on English Poets. 1856.
Meyer, R. M. Jonathan Swift und G. C. Lichtenberg. Berlin, 1886.
Moriarty, G. P. Dean Swift and his writings. 1893.
Oliphant, Mrs. Historical Sketches of the Reign of Queen Anne. 1894.
Orrery, John, earl of. Remarks on the Life and Writings of Jonathan Swift.
    1752.
        R. J. [Delany, P.] Observations upon Lord Orrery's Remarks. 1754.
Paul, H. Men and Letters. 1901.
Prevost-Paradol, L. A. Jonathan Swift, sa vie et ses œuvres. 1856.

Reynald, H. Biographie de Jonathan Swift. 1860.

Scott, Sir Walter. Memoirs of Jonathan Swift. (*See* Scott's edn. of Works, sec. I, *ante*.)

Sheridan, T. Life of the Rev. Dr. Jonathan Swift. 1784.

Sichel, Walter. Bolingbroke and his Times. 2 vols. 1901–2.

Simon, P. M. Swift: Étude psychologique et littéraire. 1893.

Smith, Sophie S. Dean Swift. 1910.

Stephen, Sir L. Jonathan Swift. 1882.

Swift, Deane. Essay upon the Life, Writings, and Character of Dr. Jonathan Swift. 1755.

Swiftiana. 2 vols. 1804.

Thackeray, W. M. English Humorists of the Eighteenth Century. 1853.

Ward, A. W. Swift's Love Story in German Literature. Macmillan's Magazine. Feb. 1877.

Wilde, Sir W. The closing years of Dean Swift's Life. 1849.

CHAPTER V

ARBUTHNOT AND LESSER PROSE WRITERS

John Arbuthnot

A. *Collected Works*

The Miscellaneous Works of the late Dr. Arbuthnot. 2 vols. Glasgow, 1751. Other editions, 1751 and 1770 (with a short life of Arbuthnot).

[These volumes contain a number of pieces which are not by Arbuthnot. All the pieces in the collection are mentioned below, and are distinguished by an asterisk.]

The Life and Works of John Arbuthnot. By Aitken, George A. Oxford, 1892.

[This volume includes the pieces marked † below.]

B. *Single Works*

*Of the Laws of Chance. 1692.

Theses Medicae de Secretione Animali. [St. Andrews, 1696.]

*An Examination of Dr. Woodward's Account of the Deluge, &c. With a Comparison between Steno's Philosophy and the Doctor, in the case of Marine Bodies dug out of the Earth. 1697. [Said, by Thomas Hearne, to have been suppressed by the author.]

*An Essay on the usefulness of Mathematical Learning, in a Letter from a Gentleman in the City to his Friend in Oxford. Oxford, 1701. [Dated 25 November, 1700.]

Tables of the Grecian, Roman and Jewish Measures, Weights and Coins, reduced to the English Standard. [1705?]

* †A Sermon preachid to the People at the Mercat Cross of Edinburgh, on the Subject of the Union. Eccles. chap. x., ver. 27. Printed in the year 1706 [Edinburgh].—Dublin [1706]. London, 1707 [Dec., 1706, according to History of the Works of the Learned]: 1745 [?]. With a Preface—reprinted in the Miscellaneous Works—which is attributed to Duncombe, setting forth the advantages which had accrued to Scotland by the Union (Nichols, Lit. Anecdotes, vol. VIII, p. 269).

An Argument for Divine Providence, taken from the constant regularity observed in the Births of both Sexes. [In Philosophical Transactions of the Royal

Society, 1710, vol. XXVII, p. 186, and rptd. in the Abridgment, vol. v, pt. ii, p. 240.]

†Law is a Bottomless Pit, Exemplified in the Case of The Lord Strutt, John Bull, Nicholas Frog, and Lewis Baboon, who spent all they had in a Law-Suit. Printed from a Manuscript found in the Cabinet of the famous Sir Humphrey Polesworth [Feb. 28—March 6]. 1712.

† John Bull in His Senses: Being the Second Part of Law is a Bottomless Pit. [March 13–20] 1712.

†John Bull still in his Senses: Being the Third Part of Law is a Bottomless Pit. [March 15–17] 1712.

† An Appendix to John Bull still in His Senses: or, Law is a Bottomless Pit. [May 8] 1712.

†Lewis Baboon turned Honest and John Bull Politician. Being the Fourth Part of Law is a Bottomless-Pit. Printed from a Manuscript found in the Cabinet of the famous Sir Humphrey Polesworth: And Published (as well as the Three former Parts and Appendix) by the Author of the New Atalantis. [July 31] 1712.

*†The History of John Bull. Edinburgh, 1712. [Law is a Bottomless Pit, exemplified, &c. In three Parts. With the Appendix and a complete Key.] Other editions: 1753 [Le Procès sans Fin]; Glasgow, 1766 [Law is a Bottomless Pit, or the History of John Bull]; 1883 [The English Garner, vol. vi, ed. Edward Arber]; 1889 [Cassell's National Library, ed. Henry Morley, vol. 204].

[The History of John Bull first appeared in 1712, in a series of pamphlets, each of which is described above under its own title: 1. Law is a Bottomless Pit; 2. John Bull in his Senses; 3. John Bull still in his Senses; 4. An Appendix to John Bull still in his Senses; 5. Lewis Baboon turned Honest and John Bull Politician.]

†Proposals for printing a very Curious Discourse, in Two Volumes, in Quarto, en-titled ΨΕΥΔΟΛΟΓΙ'Α ΠΟΛΙΤΙΚΗ' or A Treatise of the Art of Political Lying, with an Abstract of the First Volume of the said Treatise [Oct. 9–16] 1712. —Edinburgh, 1746.

†To the Right Honourable The Mayor and Alderman of the City of London: The Humble Petition of the Colliers, Cooks, Cook-Maids, Blacksmiths, Jack-makers, Brasiers, and others. 1716.

Three Hours after Marriage. A Comedy. [By John Gay.] 1717. [Gay was assisted by Pope and Arbuthnot.]

[In vol. ii, p. 872 of A History of Music, by Sir John Hawkins, 1853, is given a burlesque—taken from Harl. MS. 7316 p. 149, where it is attributed to Arbuthnot—of lines written by Pope for Signora Margarita Durastanti to recite upon her formal retirement from the English operatic stage in 1723. Pope's lines end "Happy soil, adieu, adieu," Arbuthnot's "Bubbles all, adieu, adieu." These lines are also given in the Annual Register for 1775, and in the Additions to Pope's Works, 1776.]

†Reasons humbly offered by the Company exercising the Trade and Mystery of Upholders, against part of the Bill, For the better Viewing, Searching, and Examining Drugs, Medicines, &c. 1724.

The Craftsman. 1726–7. [Probably contained contributions by Arbuthnot.]

Tables of Ancient Coins, Weights and Measures, explained and exemplified in several Dissertations. [Name not given, but prefixed are verses to the King by the author's son, Charles Arbuthnot.] 1727.

Tables of Ancient Coins, &c. 2nd edn. To which is added, An Appendix containing Observations on Dr. Arbuthnot's Dissertations on Coins, Weights and Measures. By Benjamin Langwith, D.D. 1754. Other editions, Utrecht, 1756, Leyden, 1764.

Oratio Anniversaria Harvaeana habita in Theatro Collegii Regalis Medicor. Lond. Die XVIII Octobris A.D. 1727. 1727.

Miscellanies in Prose and Verse. [Preface signed by Swift and Pope.] 3 vols. 1727. [Vol. II contains The History of John Bull and the Art of Political Lying.]—4 vols. 1727–32. [Vol. III contains The Humble Petition of the Colliers, &c., The Essay concerning the Origin of Sciences and It cannot rain but it pours.]

†An Essay of the Learned Martinus Scriblerus concerning the Origin of Sciences. [*See* Miscellanies in Prose and Verse, 1727–32, vol. III.]

†Virgilius Restauratus: seu Martini Scribleri Summi Critici Castigationum in Aeneidem Specimen. [*See* Dunciad, 1729, and Works of Mr. Alexander Pope in Prose, vol. II.]

†Memoirs of the Life, Works and Discoveries of Martinus Scriblerus. [*See* The Works of Mr. Alexander Pope in Prose, vol. II.]

The Dunciad. With Notes Variorum. 1729. [Arbuthnot made contributions to the notes, introductions, &c., including Virgilius Restauratus.]

*†A brief Account of Mr. John Giglicutt's Treatise concerning the Altercation or Scolding of the Ancients. By the Author. [February] 1731.

An Epitaph on Francis Chartres [in The London Magazine, 1732].

An Essay concerning the Nature of Aliments, and the choice of them, according to the different Constitutions of Human Bodies. [May] 1731. 2 vols. 1731, 1732.—[May] 1732. To which is added, Practical Rules of Diet in the various Constitutions and Diseases of Human Bodies. [These Rules were sold separately to perfect the former edition.] Later editions, 1731 [Dublin]; 2 vols. 1735–6; 1744 [in German]; 1751, 1756.

An Essay concerning the Effect of Air on Human Bodies. [July] 1733. Other editions, 1742 [French]; 1753 [Latin]; 1756.

Esther, an Oratorio. [Libretto by Pope and Arbuthnot, with additions by Humphreys. Brit. Mus. Cat.] 1733.

*† ΓΝΩΘΙ ΣΕ' ΑΥΤΟΝ. Know Yourself. A Poem. 1734. [Reprinted in Dodsley's Collection of Poems by several hands. 1748. Vol. I, p. 196.] A Supplement to Dr. Swift's and Mr. Pope's Works now first collected into one Volume. Dublin, 1739.

[The following pieces are ascribed to Arbuthnot in the Table of Contents:—History of John Bull. A Wonderful Prophecy. Memoirs of P. P. The Country Post. Stradling v. Styles. Proposals for Printing the Art of Political Lying. Relation of the Circumcision of E. Curll. God's Revenge against Punning. Petition of the Colliers, &c. The Upholders Reasons. Annus Mirabilis. Essay concerning the origin of Sciences. Virgilius Restauratus. It cannot rain but it pours. True Narrative of what passed in London. Art of Sinking in Poetry. Epitaph on Fr-s Ch-is.]

Works of Mr. Alexander Pope, In Prose. Vol. II. 1741. [Contains Memoirs of Scriblerus, Virgilius Restauratus, and Essay on the Origin of Sciences.] Memoirs of Martinus Scriblerus. Dublin, 1741.

Literary Relics. Edited by Berkeley, George Monck. 1789. [Letters from Berkeley to Arbuthnot, pp. 83-92.]

Letters written by eminent persons in the Seventeenth and Eighteenth Centuries. 3 vols. 1813. [Letters from Arbuthnot to Dr. Charlett, vol. I, pp. 176, 178.]

Works of Jonathan Swift, D.D. Ed. Scott, Sir Walter, Bart. 19 vols. 1824. [Letters to and from Arbuthnot.]

Letters to and from Henrietta Countess of Suffolk. Ed. Croker, J. 2 vols. 1824. [Letters from Arbuthnot.]

An Account of the Rev. John Flamstead. By Baily, F. 1835. [Contains correspondence with Arbuthnot.]

Lives of the Queens of England. By Strickland, Agnes. 12 vols. 1840-8. (Vol. VIII contains Letters to Arbuthnot.)

Works of Alexander Pope. Edd. Elwin, W. and Courthope, W. J. 10 vols. 1871-89. [Letters to and from Arbuthnot.]

Works attributed to Arbuthnot

A Letter from the famous Sir Humphrey Polesworth to the Author of the Examiner: with a Dialogue between Nic Frog, Tom Frog, his brother, and Dick Frog his kinsman. [Printed in the "Examiner" for May 8 to 15, 1712.]

The Story of the St. Alb-ns Ghost, or the Apparition of Mother Haggy. Collected from the best Manuscripts. [Feb. 16-19] 1712.

An Invitation to Peace: or Toby's Preliminaries to Nestor Ironside. 1713.

*The Longitude Examin'd. By Jeremy Thacker, of Beverley, in Yorkshire. 1714.

*†Notes and Memorandums of the Six Days preceding the Death of a late Right Reverend. . . . Containing many remarkable Passages, with an Inscription designed for his Monument. 1715.

*The State Quacks, or the Political Botchers. 1715.

*A Letter to the Reverend Mr. Dean Swift, occasioned by a Satyre said to be written by him, entitled, A Dedication to a Great Man, concerning Dedications, &c. [Signed P. A., Jan. 30, 1718-9.]

*†An Account of the Sickness and Death of Dr. W—dw—d: As also of what appeared upon opening his body. In a letter to a Friend in the Country. By Dr. Technicum. 1719.

*The Life and Adventures of Don Bilioso de L'Estomac. Translated from the original Spanish into French: done from the French into English. With a letter to the College of Physicians. 1719.

*An Epitaph on a Greyhound. (?)

A Letter From the Facetious Dr. Andrew Tripe, at Bath, To his Loving Brother The profound Greshamite [1719]. In "Miscellaneous Works" of Dr. William Wagstaff, 1726.

*A Supplement to Dean Sw—t's Miscellanies: By the Author. Containing I. A Letter to the Students of both Universities, relating to the new Discoveries in Religion and the Sciences, and the principal Inventors of them. II. An Essay upon an Apothecary. III. An Account of a surprising Apparition, Oct. 20, 1722. 1723.

*†The Most Wonderful Wonder, that ever appeared to the Wonder of the British Nation. Being an Account of the Travels of Mynheer Veteranus, through the Woods of Germany: And an account of his taking a most monstrous She Bear, who had nursed up the Wild Boy; &c. Written by the

Copper-Farthing Dean. 1726. [The verses upon William Sutherland given at the end of this tract are claimed for William Meston, in his Poetical Works, 1767.]

†It cannot rain but it pours: Or, London strow'd with Rarities. Being an Account of the arrival of a White Bear at the House of Mr. Ratcliff in Bishopsgate Street: As also of the Faustina, the celebrated Italian Singing-woman: and of the Copper-Farthing Dean from Ireland. And lastly, of the wonderful Wild Man that was nursed in the Woods of Germany by a Wild Beast: &c. 1726.

*The Manifests of Lord Peter (Signed Solomon Andrian). 1726.

*A Learned Dissertation on Dumpling, its Dignity, Antiquity, and Excellence. With a Word upon Pudding, &c. 1726. [By T. Gordon.]

*The Devil to pay at St. James's: or a full and true Account of a most horrid and bloody Battle between Madame Faustina and Madame Cuzzoni, &c. 1727.

*The Masquerade. A Poem Inscrib'd to C—t H—d—g—r. By Lemuel Gulliver, Poet Laureate to the King of Lilliput. [Jan. 30] 1728. [By Henry Fielding.]

*Kiss my a— is no Treason. Or, an Historical and Critical Dissertation upon the Art of Selling Bargains. 1728.

*Gulliver Decypher'd: or Remarks on a late Book, intituled, Travels into Several Remote Nations of the World. By Capt. Lemuel Gulliver, Vindicating the Reverend Dean on whom it is maliciously father'd. With some probable Conjectures concerning the Real Author. 2nd Edn., with a complete Key. [1728?]

*†An Account of the State of Learning in the Empire of Lilliput: together with the History and Character of Bullum the Emperor's Library-Keeper. 1728.

*The Congress of Bees: or, Political Remarks on the Bees swarming at St James's. With a Prognostication on that Occasion from the Smyrna Coffee-house. [Published July 18, 1728, without date.]

*Harmony in an Uproar: A Letter to F——d——k H–d–l Esq: Mr. of the O–a H–e in the Hay-Market, from Hurlothrumbo Johnson, Esq. Composer Extraordinary to all the Theatres in G——t B—t—n excepting that of the Hay-Market. [Dated Feb. 12, 1733.]

*The Freeholder's Political Catechism. 1733. Written by Dr. Arbuthnot. First printed in MDCCXXIII and reprinted in MDCCLXIX.

*†Critical Remarks on Capt. Gulliver's Travels. By Doctor Bantley. Published from the Author's Original MSS. Cambridge, 1735. [Dedication signed "R. B."]

*The History of John Bull, Part III. Containing among other curious Particulars, a Faithful Narrative of the most Secret and Important Transactions of the Worshipful and Ancient Family of the Bulls, from Aug. 1, 1714 to June 11, 1727. By Nathan Polesworth, Sir Humphrey's Nephew, and sole Executor. 1774.

C. *Biography and Criticisms*

Aitken, G. A. Life of Arbuthnot. [In Life and Works, 1892.]
Chesterfield, earl of, Philip Dormer Stanhope, Letters of. Ed. Mahon, Lord. 1845. [Vol. II contains a Character of Dr. Arbuthnot.]
Hansen, A. M. En Engelsk Forfattergruppe. Copenhagen, 1892.
Sichel, W. Bolingbroke and his times. 1902.

Stephen, Sir Leslie.   Art. Arbuthnot, in Dictionary of National Biography, vol. II.
Wentworth Papers, 1883.

See, also, articles in the following Journals:

Asclepiad, April, 1887. [By Sir B. W. Richardson, M. D.]
Athenaeum, 12 March, 1892; 18 June, 1892; 17 June, 1893.
Biographia Britannica. Ed. Kippis. 1778.
Bookman, March, 1892. [Minto, W.]
Cornhill Magazine, vol. XXXIX, 91.
Edinburgh Review, January, 1893.
London Magazine, I, 48, 117: II, 374: VI, 112: X: 364: XX, 96.
Monthly Review, September, 1750. [Notice of Miscellaneous Works.]
Notes and Queries, Ser. I, vol. XII: Ser. III, vols. I, II, VI: Ser. IV, vols. VI, VII:
      Ser. V, vol. XII: Ser. VI, vols. I, VII, VIII.
Quarterly Review, April, 1893.
Retrospective Review, vol. VIII.
Speaker, 27 August, 1892.

D. *Appendix*

A Complete Key to the Three Parts of Law is a Bottomless-Pit, and the Story of
      the St. Alb-ns Ghost. 1712.
Law not a Bottomless Pit: or Arguments against Peace, and some Queries Pro
      and Con. 1712.
A Review of the State of John Bull's Family, ever since the Probate of his Last
      Will and Testament. With some account of the Two Trumpeters, the hire-
      lings of Roger Bold. 1713.
John Bull's Last Will and Testament, as drawn by a Welch Attorney. With a
      Preface to the Ar——p of C——ry. By an Eminent Lawyer of the Temple.
      1713.
A Postscript to John Bull, containing the History of the Crown-Inn, with the
      Death of the Widow, and what happened thereupon. [1714.]
A Continuation of the History of the Crown-Inn, Part II. [1714.]
A Further Continuation of the History of the Crown-Inn, Part III. [1714.]
The Fourth and Last Part of the History of the Crown-Inn. With the character
      of John Bull, and other Novels. Part IV. [1714.]
An Appendix to the History of the Crown Inn. With a Key to the whole. [1714.]
The Present State of the Crown-Inn, for the first Three Years under the New
      Landlord. By the Author of the History of the Crown-Inn. 1717.
A Supplement to the History of the Crown Inn. [1717?]
A Letter to Mr. John Gay concerning his late Farce-entitled A Comedy. By
      Timothy Drub [pseud.]. 1717.
The Confederates. By Joseph Gay [i.e. Capt. Breval]. 1717.
A Complete Key to the New Farce, called Three Hours after Marriage. With
      an Account of the Authors. By E. Parker, Philomath [pseud.]. 1717.
Gulliveriana: Or, a Fourth Volume of Miscellanies. Being a Sequel to the Three
      Volumes published by Pope and Swift. 1728.
Literae de Re Nummaria: in opposition to the Commons Opinion that the Denarii
      Romani were never larger than seven in an ounce: With some Remarks on
      Dr. Arbuthnot's Book and Tables. By the Rev. William Smith, Rector
      of Melsonby, Newcastle-on-Tyne. [July] 1729.

An Epistle to Dr. Arbuthnot. [By Pope.] 1734. [Jan. 1735.]
Observations on Dr. Arbuthnot's Dissertations on Coins, &c. By B. Langwith.
    1747.

COLLEY CIBBER

See bibliography to Vol. VIII, **Chap. VI.**

JOHN DENNIS

A. *Collections*

Miscellanies in Verse and Prose. 1693.
Letters upon several Occasions: Written by and between Mr. Dryden, Mr.
    Wycherley, Mr.——, Mr. Congreve, and Mr. Dennis. Published by Mr.
    Dennis. With a new translation of Select Letters of Monsieur Voiture. 1696.
Miscellany Poems, by Mr. Dennis. With Select Translations of Horace, Juvenal,
    Mons. Boileau's Epistles, Satyrs, and Aesop's Fables in Burlesque Verse.
    To which is added, The Passion of Byblis, with some critical observations on
    Mr. Oldham and his writings. With Letters and Poems. The second
    edition, with large additions. 1697.
A Collection of Divine Hymns and Poems on several Occasions: By the E. of Ros-
    common, Mr. Dryden, Mr. Dennis, Mr. Norris, Mrs. Kath. Phillips,
    Philomela, and others. 1709.
Select Works. Consisting of Plays, Poems, &c. 2 vols. 1718.
Select Works. To which is added, Coriolanus, a tragedy. 2 vols. 1718–21.
Original Letters, Familiar, Moral and Critical. In Two Volumes. 1721.
Miscellaneous Tracts written by Mr. John Dennis in two Volumes. [Only one
    published.] 1727.

B. *Single Works*

For plays, *see* bibliography to Vol. VIII, Chap. VII; and for writtings on the
    condition of the Stage, *see* bibliography to Vol. VIII, Chap. VI, section B,
    where add: The Characters and Conduct of Sir John Edgar, and his three
    Deputy Governours. 1720.
The Characters and Conduct of Sir John Edgar. . . . In a third and fourth letter
    to the knight. 1720.

Poems in Burlesque; with a dedication in Burlesque, to Fleetwood Shepherd,
    Esquire. 1692.
The Passion of Byblis, made English by Mr. Dennis. 1692.
Gentleman's Magazine, or the Monthly Miscellany, 1692–3. [Contains sev-
    eral poems by Dennis.]
The Impartial Critick, or, Some Observations upon a late book entituled A Short
    View of Tragedy, written by Mr. Rymer. 1693.
The Court of Death: A Pindarique Poem dedicated to the Memory of her most
    Sacred Majesty, Queen Mary. 1695.
Remarks on a Book, entitul'd Prince Arthur, an Herioc Poem, with some general
    critical observations, and several new remarks upon Virgil. 1696.
Letters on Milton and Congreve. 1696.
The Nuptials of Britain's Genius and Fame: A Pindarique Poem on the Peace.
    1697.
The Advancement and Reformation of Modern Poetry. A Critical Discourse
    in two Parts. 1701.

The Danger of Priestcraft to Religion and Government. Occasion'd by a Discourse of Mr. Sacheverell's intitul'd The Political Union. 1702.

The Monument: A Poem sacred to the immortal Memory of the best and greatest of Kings, William the Third. 1702.

An Essay on the Navy, on England's advantage and safety prov'd dependant on a formidable and well-disciplined Navy. 1702.

A Proposal for putting a speedy end to the War. 1703.

The Grounds of Criticism in Poetry, contain'd in some new discoveries never made before, requisite for the writing and judging of Poems surely. 1704.

Britannia Triumphans: or the Empire sav'd and Europe deliver'd, by the Success of her Majesty's Forces. A Poem. 1704.

The Battle of Ramillia: or, The Power of Union. A Poem. 1706.

An Essay on the Operas after the Italian Manner, which are about to be establish'd on the English Stage. With some Reflections on the damage which they may bring to the Publick. 1706.

The Muses Mercury. 1707. [Several poems by Dennis.]

Reflections upon a late Rhapsody called An Essay upon Criticism. 1711.

An Essay upon Publick Spirit: being a Satyr in Prose upon the Manners and Luxury of the Times, 1711.

An Essay on the Genius and Writings of Shakspear: with some Letters of Criticism to the Spectator. 1712.

Remarks upon Cato, A Tragedy. 1713.

A Poem upon the Death of Her late Sacred Majesty Queen Anne, and the most happy and most auspicious Accession of his Sacred Majesty King George. 1714.

Priestcraft distinguish'd from Christianity. 1715.

Remarks upon Mr. Pope's translation of Homer: with two Letters concerning Windsor Forest, and The Temple of Fame. 1717.

Julius Caesar acquitted, and his Murderers condemn'd, In a Letter to a Friend. 1722.

A Defence of Sir Foppling Flutter, a Comedy. Written by Sir George Etheridge. 1722.

A Short Essay towards an English Prosody. [In second edition of Greenwood's Essay towards a practical English Grammar.] 1722.

Remarks on a Play call'd The Conscious Lovers, a Comedy. 1723.

Vice and Luxury Public Mischiefs: or Remarks on a Book intitul'd The Fable of the Bees, or Private Vices Public Benefits. 1724.

Letters against Mr. Pope at Large. (See Daily Journal, 11 May, 1728.)

The Faith and Duties of Christians. Written originally in Latin by the late Rev. Thomas Burnet. Translated into English by Mr. Dennis. [1728?]

Remarks on Mr. Pope's Rape of the Lock. In several Letters to a Friend. With a Preface, occasion'd by the late Treatise on the Profound and the Dunciad. 1728.

Remarks upon several Passages in the Preliminaries to the Dunciad, both in the Quarto and in the duodecimo edition, and upon several passages in Pope's Preface to his Translation of Homer's Iliad. 1729.

A Treatise concerning the State of Departed Souls. . . . Written originally in Latin by the late Rev. Dr. Thomas Burnet. Translated into English by Mr. Dennis.

C. *Doubtful Works*

A True Character of Mr. Pope. [1717.]

A Compleat Collection of all the Verses, Essays, Letters and 'Advertisements, which have been occasioned by the publication in three Volumes of Miscellanies, by Pope and Company. 1728.

D. *Authorities*

John Dennis. His Life and Criticism. By Paul, H. G. New York, 1911.
Dictionary of National Biography. Art. by Roberts, William.
Life of Richard Steele. By Aitken, G. A. 1889.
Works of Alexander Pope. Edd. Elwin and Courthope. 1871–89.
Retrospective Review. Vol. I. Art. by Talfourd, Sir T. N.

E. *Adversaria*

The Justice of the Peace: or, A Vindication of the Peace from several late pamphlets, written by Mr. Congreve, Dennis, &c. 1697.
The New Association ... Occasion'd by a late pamphlet entitul'd The Danger of Priestcraft. [By Charles Leslie.] 1702.
The Narrative of Dr. R. Norris, concerning the frenzy of Mr. J. Denn—. [By Pope.] [1713.]
The Critical Specimen. 1715.
A Critick no Wit: Or, Remarks on Mr. Dennis's late Play, called, The Invader of his Country. In a letter from a School-Boy to the Author. 1720.
An Answer to a whimsical Pamphlet call'd, The character of Sir John Edgar, &c. 1720.
A free consideration and confutation of Sir John Edgar. By Sir Andrew Artlove. (Applebee's Journal, 1720. Rptd. in The Theatre, &c., 1791.)
The Life of Mr. John Dennis, the renowned Critick. Not written by Mr. Curll. 1734.

THOMAS EDWARDS

A Supplement to Mr. Warburton's edition of Shakespear, being the Canons of Criticism, and Glossary, collected from the notes in that celebrated work. 1747.
The Canons of Criticism, and Glossary, being a Supplement to Mr. Warburton's edition of Shakespear, collected from the notes in that celebrated work, and proper to be Bound up with it. 1748. [Often reprinted.]
An Account of the Trial of the Letter ϒ alias Y. [Published with a design of settling the orthography of our language.] 1753.
Free and Candid Thoughts on the Doctrine of Predestination. 1761.
Sonnets by Edwards are in Dodsley's Collection, and in the last editions of the "Canons of Criticism." Letters will be found in vol. III of Richardson's "Correspondence." Akenside wrote an Ode to Edwards on his controversy with Warburton.

CHARLES GILDON

History of the Athenian Society. 1691.
The Postboy robbed of his Mail, or, the Pacquet broke open, consisting of 500 letters to Persons of several Qualities. 1692.
Nuncius Infernalis: or, a new Account from below. In two dialogues. 1692.
A Letter to Mr. D'Urfey, occasioned by his play called The Marriage Hater Matched. 1692.

Miscellany Poems upon several Occasions, 1692.
Miscellaneous Letters and Essays . . . in prose and verse . . . by several ladies and gentlemen. 1694.
Miscellaneous Works of the Deist, Charles Blount. 1695.
Lives and Characters of the English Dramatick Poets. [*See* Langbaine, *post.*] 1699.
Examen Miscellaneum. 1702.
A Comparison of the Two Stages. 1702.
The Deists' Manual, or a rational enquiry into the Christian Religion. 1705.
The Life of Mr. Thomas Betterton. 1710.
A New Rehearsal: or, Bays the Younger, containing an examen of Mr. Rowe's plays, and a word or two on Mr. Pope's "Rape of the Lock." 1714.
The Complete Art of Poetry. 2 vol. 1817.
The Life and Adventures of Mr. D—— De F——, of London, Hosier. 1719.
The Laws of Poetry as laid down by. . . Buckingham, . . . Roscommon and . . . Lansdown, explained and illustrated. 1721.

Plays

The Roman Bride's Revenge. 1697.
Phaetan, or the Fatal Divorce. 1698.
Measure for Measure. [Adapted from Shakespeare.] 1700.
Love's Victim. 1701.
The Patriot, or the Italian Conspiracy. 1703.

ZACHARY GREY

A Vindication of the Church of England. 1720.
Presbyterian Prejudice displayed. 1722.
A Pair of Clean Shoes for a Dirty Baronet, or an answer to Sir Richard Cox. 1722.
The Knight of Dumbleton foiled at his own weapon. 1723.
A Century of Presbyterian Preachers. 1723.
A Letter of Thanks to Mr. Benjamin Bennet. 1723.
A Caveat against Mr. Benjamin Bennet. 1724.
A Defence of our Critical and Modern Historians against the frivolous cant of a late pretender to Critical History. [Oldmixon.] 1724.
A Looking-Glass for Schismaticks. 1725.
The Ministry of the Dissenters proved to be null and void. 1725.
The Spirit of Infidelity detected. 1736.
English Presbyterian Eloquence. 1736.
Examination of Dr. Chandler's "History of Persecution." 1736.
The True Picture of Quakerism. 1736.
A Caveat against the Dissenters. 1736.
An impartial Examination of Mr. Daniel Neal's "History of the Puritans." 1736.
An Examination of the 14th Chapter of Sir Isaac Newton's "Observations upon Daniel." 1736.
An Attempt towards the Character of Charles I. 1738.
The Schismatics delineated. By Philalethes Cantabrigiensis. 1739.
A Vindication of the Government of the Church of England. 1740.
The Quakers and Methodists compared. 1740.
A Review of Mr. Daniel Neal's "History of the Puritans." 1744.

Hudibras, in three Parts, written in the time of the late Civil Wars, corrected and amended, with large annotations and a preface; adorned with a new set of cuts. [Edited by Grey, Z.] 2 vols. 1744.

A Serious Address to Lay Methodists. 1745.

A Word or two of Advice to William Warburton, a dealer in many words. By a Friend. With an Appendix containing a taste of William's spirit of railing. 1746.

Remarks upon a late Edition of Shakespeare . . . to which is prefixed a Defence of the late Sir Thomas Hanmer, Bart., addressed to the Rev. Mr. Warburton. [1748?]

A Free and familiar Letter to that great refiner of Pope and Shakespeare, the Rev. Mr. W. Warburton. 1750.

Critical, Historical, and Explanatory Notes upon Hudibras, by way of Supplement to the two editions published in 1744 and 1745. 1752.

Critical, Historical, and Explanatory Notes on Shakespeare. 1754.

Memoirs of the Life and Writings of T. Baker, from the papers of Zachary Grey. . . . By R. Masters. 1784.

BENJAMIN HEATH

An Essay towards a demonstrative proof of the Divine Existence, Unity, and Attributes. 1740.

Notae sive Lectiones ad . . . Aeschyli, Sophoclis, Euripidis quae supersunt dramata deperditorumque reliquiae. 1762.

The Case of the County of Devon with respect to the consequences of the new Excise Duty on Cyder and Perry. 1763.

A Revisal of Shakespeare's Text, wherein the alterations introduced into it by the more modern editors and critics are particularly considered. [Anon.] 1765.

Annotations illustrative of the Plays of Shakespeare, by Johnson, Stevens, Malone, Heath, &c. 1819.

JOHN HUGHES

The Triumph of Peace, a Poem. 1698.

The Court of Neptune. 1699.

The House of Nassau, a Pindaric Ode. 1702.

An Ode in praise of Music. 1703.

A complete History of England. 3 vols. [Hughes collected materials, and translated a Life of Queen Mary in vol. II.] 1706.

Advices from Parnassus. . . . All translated from the Italian by several Hands. Revised and corrected by Mr. Hughes. 1706.

Fontenelle's Dialogues of the Dead . . . with two original Dialogues. 1708.

Calypso and Telemachus, an Opera. 1712.

An Ode to the Creator of the World. 1713.

The Lay Monk. [With Sir R. Blackmore.] 1713–14. [Republished in 1714 as the "Lay Monastery."]

The Works of Mr. Edmund Spenser. . . . With a glossary explaining the old and obscure words. 6 vols. 1715.

Apollo and Daphne: A Masque. 1716.

An Ode for the birthday of Her Royal Highness the Princess of Wales. 1716.

A Layman's Thoughts on the late treatment of the Bishop of Bangor. 1717.

Charon, or The Ferry-Boat. A Vision. Dedicated to the Swiss Count —— [J. J. Heidegger.] 1719.

The Ecstacy: An Ode. 1720.

The Siege of Damascus: A Tragedy. 1720.

Letters of Abelard and Heloise. . . . Extracted chiefly from Monsieur Bayle. Translated from the French. 1722.

Poems on Several Occasions, with some select Essays in Prose. Ed. Duncombe, W. 2 vols. 1735.

> [Hughes's Poems are in the ordinary collections, including Johnson's (with a Life).]

The Complicated Guilt of the late Rebellion. 1745. [Written in 1716.]

Letters by several eminent Persons deceased, ed. by Rev. John Duncombe. [Contains Hughes's correspondence, some new pieces, and the original plan of the "Siege of Damascus."] 1773.

WILLIAM KING, D.C.L.

A. *Collected Works*

Miscellanies, in Prose and Verse. [1705.]

Remains of Dr. William King. [Ed. Brown, J.] 1732.

Posthumous Works of Dr. William King. Ed. Browne, Joseph, M.D. 1734.

The Original Works of William King, LL.D., with historical notes, and memoirs of the Author. [By John Nichols.] 3 vols. 1776.

B. *Single Works*

Reflections upon Mons. Varillas's History of Heresy. [With Edward Hannes.] 1688.

A Dialogue showing the Way to Modern Preferment. [1690.]

Animadversions on a pretended Account of Denmark. 1694.

A Journey to London in the year 1698. After the ingenious method of that made by Dr. Martin Lister to Paris in the same year. Written originally in French, by Monsieur Sorbière, and newly translated into English. 1698.

A short Account of Dr. Bentley's Humanity and Justice. 1699.

Dialogues of the Dead, relating to the present controversy concerning the Epistles of Phalaris. 1699.

The Furmetary. A very innocent and harmless Poem. 1699.

The Transactioner, with some of his Philosophical Fancies, in two Dialogues. 1700.

Molly of Mountown. 1704.

The Fairy Feast. Written by the Author of A Tale of a Tub. [This is the same piece as "Orpheus and Euridice."] 1704.

The Art of Cookery, in imitation of Horace's Art of Poetry: with some Letters to Dr. Lister and others, occasioned principally by the title of a book published by the Doctor, being the works of Apicius Caelius, concerning the Soups and Sauces of the Ancients. [1708.]

The Art of Love: In Imitation of Ovid de Arte Amandi. 1709.

Useful Transactions in Philosophy and other sorts of Learning, to be continued monthly, as they sell. [3 parts.] 1709.

A friendly Letter from honest Tom Boggy to the Rev. Mr. Goddard, Canon of Windsor. 1710.

A second Letter to Mr. Goddard, occasioned by the late Panegyric given him by the Review. 1710.

A Vindication of the Rev. Dr. Sacheverell. 1711.

Mr. Bisset's Recantation. 1711.

An Answer to a second scandalous Book that Mr. Bisset is now writing. 1711.

Historical Account of the Heathen Gods and Heroes. 1711. [Fourth edn., 1727.]

Rufinus, or an Historical Essay on the favourite Ministry under Theodosius and his son Arcadius. 1711.

Useful Miscellanies, Part the First. 1712.

Britain's Palladium, or Lord Bolingbroke's Welcome from France. 1712.

Apple Pye. [Printed in The Northern Atlantis.] 1713.

An Essay on Civil Government. 1776.

C. *Appendix*

A Letter to Dr. W. King, occasioned by his Art of Cookery. [An attack.] 1708.

A Pindarick Ode to the memory of Dr. William King. [A eulogy.] 1712.

GERARD LANGBAINE

The Hunter: A discourse of Horsemanship. Oxford, 1685.

Momus Triumphans, or the Plagiaries of the English Stage exposed. 1688.

A new Catalogue of English Plays. 1688.

An Account of the English Dramatic Poets, or some observations and remarks on the lives and writings of all those that have published either comedies, tragedies, tragicomedies, pastorals, masques, interludes, farces, or operas, in the English Tongue. Oxford, 1691.

The Lives and Characters of the English Dramatick Poets: First began by Mr. Langbain, improved and continued down to this time by a careful Hand. [Gildon.] 1699.

JAMES PUCKLE (1667?–1724)

The Club, or A Dialogue between Father and Son, *in vino veritas*. 1711. New edns., 1834 and 1890.

THOMAS RYMER

See bibliographies to Vol. VIII, Chapters VI B and VII, also to Chapters VII and VIII of the present volume.

JOHN UPTON

Epicteti quae supersunt dissertationes ab Arriano collectae. . . . Recensuit notisque illustravit J. Uptonus. 1739. [Another edition, 2 vols. 1744. Upton's notes were used by Schweighäuser in his edition of 1799–1800.]

Critical Observations on Shakespeare. 1746. [Second edition, 1748.]

A new Canto of Spenser's "Fairie Queene." [? by Upton.] 1747.

A letter concerning a new Edition of Spenser's "Fairie Queene." To Gilbert West, Esq. 1751.

Spenser's "Fairie Queene" . . . With a glossary and notes by John Upton. 1758. [In An impartial Estimate of the Reverend Mr. Upton's Notes on the Fairy Queen, 1759, Upton is charged with copying from Wharton without acknowledgment.]

CHAPTER VI

LESSER VERSE WRITERS

I. General

A. *Collections*

The principal works of the writers treated in this Chapter will be found in the following Collections of British Poets:

The Poets of Great Britain from Chaucer to Churchill. (Bell's edn.) 109 vols. Edinburgh, 1777–92.

The Works of the English Poets: With prefaces biographical and critical by Johnson, S. 68 vols. 1779–81.

The Works of the British Poets. Ed. Anderson, R. 14 vols. Edinburgh, 1793–1807.

The Works of the British Poets. Ed. Park, T. 48 vols. 1805–9.

The Works of the English Poets from Chaucer to Cowper including the series ed., with prefaces biographical and critical, by Dr. Samuel Johnson, and the most approved translations. With additional lives by Alex. Chalmers. 21 vols. 1810.

B. *Biography and Criticism*

Beljame, A. Le public et les hommes de lettres en Angleterre au 18 siècle, 1660–1744. Paris, 1881.

Cibber, Theophilus. The Lives of the Poets of Great Britain and Ireland. 5 vols. 1753.

Courthope, W. J. A history of English Poetry. Vol. v. 1905.

Elton, O. The Augustan Ages. Edinburgh, 1899.

Gosse, E. A history of eighteenth century literature. 1889.

Hettner, H. J. T. Literaturgeschichte d. 18. Jahrhunderts. 3rd edn. Vol. i. Gesch. der englischen Literatur, 1660–70. Brunswick, 1872.

Johnson, S. The Lives of the English Poets. Ed. Hill, G. Birkbeck. 3 vols. Oxford, 1905.

Pope, Alexander. Works. Edd. Elwin, W. and Courthope, W. J. 10 vols. 1871–89.

Rémusat, C. F. M. de. L'Angleterre au 18me siècle. New edn. 2 vols. Paris, 1865.

Saintsbury, G. A history of Criticism. Vol. ii. Edinburgh, 1902.

—— A history of English Prosody. Vol. ii. 1908.

Spence, Joseph. Anecdotes, observations, and characters of books and men. Ed. Singer, S. W. 2nd edn. 1858.

Ward, T. H. The English Poets. Selections with critical introductions by various authors, and a general introduction by Arnold, Matthew. 2nd edn. Vol. iii. 1884.

II. Particular Writers
Section (i)

JOHN GAY

(1) *Collected editions*

Poems. 1720, 1727, 1752.
Works. 4 vols. Dublin, 1770.

Poetical, dramatic, and miscellaneous works, with Johnson's life. 6 vols. 1793.
Poetical works. Ed. Underhill, J. (The Muses Library.)   2 vols. 1893.

(2) *Poems published separately*

Wine, a poem. 1708.
Rural Sports, a Georgic inscribed to Mr. Pope. 1713.
     Translated in part into Italian verse by Ercolani, C. 1886.
The Fan, a poem in three books. 1713.
The Shepherd's Week. In six pastorals. 1714.
A Letter to a lady, occasioned by the arrival of Her Royal Highness the Princess
     of Wales. 1714.
A Journey to Exeter. 1715.
Trivia, or the art of walking the streets of London. 1716.
An Epistle to the Duchess of Marlborough. 1722.
Fables. 1727, 4th edn. 1733, 1736.
—— 2nd series. 1738.
Fables complete. 1750, 1762, 1779 (with Bewick's cuts), 1793, 1796 (with life by
     Coxe, W.), 1816, 1854 (with memoir by Owen, O. F.), 1882 (ed. Dobson, A.,
     with a bibliography). Trans. into French, 1759, 1811, 1857, etc.; into
     Italian, 1767, 1773; into Latin, by Anstey, C., 1798.
Gay's Chair. Poems, never before printed, by J. Gay; with a sketch of his
     life from the manuscripts of Butler, J. Ed. Lee, H. 1820.

(3) *Plays published separately*

The Mohocks. A tragi-comical farce. 1712.
The Wife of Bath. A comedy. 1713. Republished, 1730.
The What d'ye call it. A tragi-comi-pastoral farce. 1715, 3rd edn. 1716. (Con-
     tains 'T was when the seas were roaring.)
Three Hours after Marriage. A comedy. (By Pope, Gay and Arbuthnot.)
     1717.
The Captives. A tragedy. 1724.
The Beggar's Opera. 1728, 4th edn. 1735, 7th edn. 1754. Ed. Macleod, G. H.
     1905.
Polly. An opera. Being the second part of The Beggar's Opera. 1729.
     These two ed., with introd. and notes, by Sarrazin, G., Weimar, 1898.
Acis and Galatea. An English pastoral opera. 1732.
Achilles. An opera. 1733.
The Distressed Wife. A comedy. 1743, 2nd edn. 1750.
The Rehearsal at Goatham. 1754.

(4) *Biography and Criticism*

See, *also*, subsections (1) and (2), *ante.*

Coxe, W. Life of Gay. 2nd edn. 1797.
Bruce, J. D. Some unpublished translations from Ariosto, by John Gay. Rptd.
     from Archiv für das Studium der neueren Sprachen etc. Vol. cxxiii.
     Brunswick, 1910.
Hazlitt, W. On Swift, Young, Gray, Collins, etc. Lectures on the English
     Poets, Works, edd. Waller, A. R. and Glover, A. Vol. v. 1902.

THOMAS PARNELL

Poems on severall occasions. (Ed. by Alexander Pope.) 1722, 1726. 6th edn. Dublin, 1735. With a life by Oliver Goldsmith. 1770.

Posthumous Works. 1758.

Poetical works. Ed. Mitford, J. (Aldine edn.) 1833.

Poetical works. Ed. Aitken, G. A. 1894.

Essay on the different styles of Poetry. 1713.

On the life, writings, and learning of Homer. Prefixed to Pope's translation of the Iliad. 1715.

Homer's Battle of the Frogs and the Mice [translated]. With the Remarks of Zoilus. To which is prefix'd the Life of the said Zoilus. 1717.

AMBROSE PHILIPS

Pastorals, epistles, odes and other poems. 1748, 1765.

The Distrest Mother. A tragedy as it is acted at the Theatre Royal in Drury Lane, by Her Majesty's Servants. 1712.

The Briton. A tragedy as it is acted at the Theatre Royal in Drury Lane by His Majesty's Servants. 1722.

Humfrey, Duke of Gloucester. A Tragedy, as it is acted at the Theatre Royal in Drury Lane, by His Majesty's servants. 1723.

These three plays collected. 1725.

JOHN POMFRET

Poems on several occasions. 1699, 2nd edn. 1702, 10th edn. 1736.

The Choice. 1700.

A Prospect of Death, an ode. [1700.]

Reason, a poem. 1700.

MATTHEW PRIOR

(1) *Collected Works*

Miscellaneous Works. Ed. Drift, A. 2 vols. 1740.

The Writings of Matthew Prior. (Poems on Several Occasions.—Dialogues of the Dead, and other works in prose and verse.) Ed. Waller, A. R. 2 vols. Cambridge, 1905–7.

(2) *Collected Poems*

Miscellany Poems. Ed. Dryden, John. 6 parts. 1684–1709 (and later edns.)

Poems on Affairs of State. . . . Written by the greatest wits. 1697. As to Prior's contributions to these two collections, cf. Waller's edn., *ante.*

Poems on Several Occasions. 1707 (unauthorised edn.), 1709 (first authorised edn.) 1713, 1717.

A Second Collection of Poems on Several Occasions. 1716 (unauthorised).

Poems on Several Occasions. Folio. 1718. Frequently rptd. Trans. into German, 1783. Solomon on the Vanity of the World was trans. into Latin by Dobson, W., Oxford, 1734–6; and Alma by Martin, T., Salisbury, 1763.

A New Miscellany of Original Poems, by Mr. Prior, Mr. Pope, etc. 1720.

A Supplement to Mr. Prior's Poems. 1722.

A New Collection of Poems on Several Occasions. 1725.

Poetical Works. With explanatory notes and memoirs of the author. Ed.
    Evans, T. 2 vols. 1779.
—— With a memoir by Mitford, J. (Aldine poets.) 2 vols. 1835, 1866. New
    edn. revised, with a memoir by Johnson, R. B. 2 vols. 1892.
—— With a memoir by Gilfillan, G. Edinburgh, 1858.
Selected Poems. With introduction and notes by Dobson, A. 1889.

(3) *Separately published works*

The Hind and the Panther transvers'd to the story of the Country-Mouse and
    the City-Mouse. 1687, 1709. (By Prior and Charles Montague.)
An Ode in imitation of the Second Ode of the Third Book of Horace. 1692.
An English Ballad: In answer to Mr. Despreaux's Pindarique Ode on the Taking
    of Namure. 1695.
To the King. An Ode on His Majesty's arrival in Holland. 1695.
Carmen Saeculare for the year 1700. To the King. 1700. Latin trans. by
    Dibben, T. 1701.
A Letter to Monsieur Boileau Depreaux [*sic*]. 1704.
Prologue spoken at Court before the Queen, on Her Majesty's birth-day, 1704.
    1704.
An Ode, humbly inscrib'd to the Queen. On the glorious success of Her Majesty's
    arms. 1706.
Pallas and Venus. 1706.
Horace, Lib. I, Epist. IX imitated. To the Right Honourable Mr. Harley.
    [1711.]
Two Imitations of Chaucer. I. Susannah and the Two Elders. II. Erle
    Robert's Mice. 1712.
The Dove, a poem. 1717.
The Female Phaeton. [1718?]
Verses spoke to the Lady Henrietta-Cavendish Holles Harley, in the Library
    of St. John's College, Cambridge, November the 9th, An. 1719. 1720.
Prologue to The Orphan. Represented by some of the Westminster-Scholars
    at Hickford's Dancing-Room, the 2d of February, 1720. 1720.
The Conversation, a tale. 1720.
Colin's Mistakes. Written in imitation of Spenser's style. 1721.
Down-Hall, a poem. 1723.
The Turtle and the Sparrow. A poem. 1723.
Lyric Poems; being twenty-four Songs (never before printed) by the late Mat-
    thew Prior, Esq. Set to Music by several Eminent Masters. 1741.

NOTE. It should be remembered that many poems by Prior were published
as broadsides, and that several poems attributed to him cannot be said with
certainty to be his. For a brief list of these, *see* Waller's edn., *ante*, vol. II, p. 408.

(4) *Biography and Criticism*

Aitken, G. A. Matthew Prior. Contemporary Review. May, 1890.
Bolingbroke, H. St. John, Viscount. Letters and correspondence. 2 vols.
    1798.
Dartmouth. The MSS. of the Earl of Dartmouth. (Hist. Manuscripts Com-
    mission.) 1887, etc.
Dobson, A. Matthew Prior. New Princeton Review. Vol. VI. July, 1888.
Longleat. Calendar of the MSS. of the Marquis of Bath, reserved at Longleat.
    1904, etc.

Memoirs of Matthew Prior, with a copy of his will. 1722.

Roberts, W. Prior as a Book Collector. Athenaeum, 19 June, 1897.

Sichel, W. Matthew Prior. Quarterly Review. Oct., 1899.

Taylor, W. Was Matthew Prior a Dorsetshire man? Longman's Magazine.
   Oct., 1884.

Thackeray, W. M. Prior, Gay, and Pope. Lectures on the English Humourists.
   Works. Biographical edn. Vol. VII. 1898.

Wukadinović, S. Prior in Deutschland. Grazer Studien zur deut. Philologie
   IV. Graz, 1895.

THOMAS TICKELL

Oxford. 1707.

A Poem to his Excellency the Lord Privy-Seal on the Prospect of Peace. 1713.
   3rd edn. 1713.

The First Book of Homer's Iliad. Trans. by Mr. Tickell. 1715.

An Epistle from a Lady in England to a Gentleman at Avignon. 1717. 4th
   edn. 1717.

An Ode occasioned by Earl Stanhope's Voyage to France. 1718.

An Ode inscribed to the Earl of Sunderland at Windsor. 1720.

Works of Joseph Addison. Ed. Thomas Tickell. 4 vols. 1721. (Contains
   Tickell's To Mr. Addison on his opera of Rosamond and To the Earl of
   Warwick on the death of Mr. Addison.)

To Sir Godfrey Kneller at his Country Seat. 1722.

Kensington Gardens. 1722.

On Her Majesty's rebuilding the Lodgings of the Black Prince and Henry V at
   Queen's College, Oxford. 1733.

ANNE FINCH, COUNTESS OF WINCHILSEA

The Poems of Anne Countess of Winchilsea, edited by Myra Reynolds. (With
   Bibliography.) Chicago, 1903.

Miscellany poems, written by a lady. 1713.

Dowden, E. Essays, Modern and Elizabethan. 1910.

Gosse, E. Gossip in a Library. 1891.

Reynolds, Myra. The Treatment of Nature in English Poetry between Pope
   and Wordsworth. 1909.

Walpole, H. Catalogue of Royal and Noble Authors. Ed. Park, T. Vol. IV.
   1806.

A. T. B.
T. S.

Section (ii)

MARY BARBER (1690?–1757)

Poems on Several Occasions. 1734.

SIR RICHARD BLACKMORE

Prince Arthur, an heroick poem in ten books. 1695.

King Arthur, an heroick poem in ten books. 1697.

Eliza, an epic poem in ten books. 1705.

The Nature of Man, a poem in three books. 1711.

Creation, a philosophical poem demonstrating the existence and providence of
   God. 1712.

Redemption, a divine poem.   1722.
Alfred, an epic poem in twelve books.   1723.

JAMES BRAMSTON

The Art of Politicks; in imitation of Horace's Art of Poetry.   1729.
The Man of Taste, occasioned by an Epistle of Mr. Pope's on that subject.   1733.

HENRY BROOKE

See bibliographies to Chap. XII, and to Vol. X, Chap. III, *post.*

WILLIAM BROOME

Poems on several occasions.   1727, 2nd edn. 1739.
    As to his and Fenton's relations with Pope and his share in the translation of the Odyssey, *see* Pope's Correspondence, in Works, vol. VIII, edd. Elwin and Courthope.

ISAAC HAWKINS BROWNE

Poems upon various subjects, Latin and English.   Ed. by his Son.   1768.

HENRY CAREY

Poems.   1713, 1720, 1729.
Chrononhotonthologos.   1734.
Dramatic works.   1743.

ROBERT DODSLEY

A Muse in livery, or the Footman's Miscellany.   1732.
Beauty, or the Art of Charming, a poem.   1735.
The Toyshop, a dramatic satire.   1735.
Trifles.   1745.
The Oeconomy of Human Life.   1751.
Public Virtue, a poem in three books.   1753.

A Collection of Poems by several hands.   Ed. Dodsley, R.   6 vols.   1748–58.
    Frequently rptd.   Revised and continued by Pearch.   10 vols.   1775.
        Courtney, W. P.   Dodsley's Collection of Poetry, its contents and contributors.   Privately printed.   1910.
A Select Collection of Old Plays.   Ed. Dodsley, R.   12 vols.   1744.   Revised by J. P. Collier.   12 vols.   1825-7.   Ed. Hazlitt, W. C.   15 vols.   1874–6.

Straus, R. S.   Robert Dodsley, Poet, Publisher, and Playwright.   [With a full bibliography.]   1910.

STEPHEN DUCK

Poems on several subjects written by Stephen Duck, lately a poor thresher in a barn in the county of Wilts . . . which were publickly read . . . to Her Majesty.   With a life.   1730, 9th edn. 1733.
Truth and Falsehood.   A fable.   1734.
Poems on several occasions.   With an account of the author by Spence, J.   1736.
The Vision.   A poem on the death of Queen Caroline.   1737.

RICHARD DUKE

Poems upon several subjects.   1717.

LAURENCE EUSDEN

A Letter to Mr. Addison on the King's Accession to the throne. 1714.
Verses at the last Publick Commencement at Cambridge. 1714.
A Poem to Her Royal Highness on the birth of the Prince. 1718.

ELIJAH FENTON

Oxford and Cambridge Miscellany Poems. [1709.]
An Epistle to Mr. Southerne. 1711.
Poems on several occasions. 1717.
Mariamne, a tragedy. 1723.
    See also under William Broome, *ante*.

SIR SAMUEL GARTH

The Dispensary. 1699, 3rd edn. 1699, 4th edn. 1700 9th edn. 1726, 10th edn.
   1741.
Claremont. 1715.
Ovid's Metamorphoses in English verse. 1717.

Schenk, T. Sir Samuel Garth und seine Stellung zum komischen Epos. Anglis-
   tische Forschungen. Heidelberg, 1900.

ANTHONY HAMMOND

A New Miscellany of original poems, translations, and imitations . . . published
   by A. H[ammond]. 1720.

JAMES HAMMOND

Love Elegies. Written in the year 1732. With preface by the E. of C[hester-
   fiel]d. 1743. Rptd. by Park, T., 1805 and by Dyer, G., 1818.

WILLIAM HARRISON (1685–1713)

Woodstock Park. Ptd. in Dodsley's Collection. [Editor of The Tatler, January
   —May, 1711.]

AARON HILL

Works. 4 vols. 1753. 2nd edn. 1754.
Dramatic works. 2 vols. 1760.
Elfrid, or the Fair Inconstant. 1710. Re-written as Athelwold. 1732.
The Creation. 1720.

JOHN HUGHES

See Vol. VIII, bibliography to Chap. **VII.**

HILDEBRAND JACOB

Works. 1735.
Chiron to Achilles, a poem. 1732.
The Nest of Plays. 1738.

WILLIAM KING

See bibliography to Chap. **v,** *ante.*

GEORGE GRANVILLE, LORD LANSDOWNE

Poems upon several occasions. 1712.
            See also Vol. VIII, bibliography to Chap. VII.

DAVID LEWIS

Miscellaneous Poems by several hands [including poems by Lewis, who edited the collection]. 1726. 2nd series. 1730.
Philip of Macedon, a tragedy. 1727.

DAVID MALLET

Works. 3 vols. 1759.
William and Margaret. [1723.]
Eurydice, a tragedy. 1731.
Mustapha, a tragedy. 1739.
Alfred, a masque [with Thomson]. 1740. New edn. 1751.
Amyntor and Theodora, or the Hermit. A poem in three cantos. 1747.
Britannia. 1755.
Edwin and Emma. 1760.

JOHN PHILIPS

Works. 1712, 1720.
The Splendid Shilling. 1705.
Blenheim. A poem. 1705.
Cerealia. An imitation of Milton. 1706.
Cyder. A poem. 1708.
Pastorals. 1710.

CHRISTOPHER PITT

A Poem on the death of the late Earl Stanhope. 1721.
Vida's Art of Poetry, translated into English Verse. 1725.
An Essay on Virgil's Aeneid, being a translation of the first book. 1728.
Virgil's Aeneid translated. 2 vols. 1740.

RICHARD SAVAGE

Works. 2 vols. 1775.
Sir Thomas Overbury, a tragedy. 1724.
The Bastard. 1728.
The Wanderer. 1729.
Various poems. 1761.

Markower, S. V. Richard Savage, a mystery in biography. [With a useful bibliography.] 1909.

EDMUND SMITH

Works, with a life. 4th edn. 1729.
Phaedra and Hippolitus, a tragedy. [1709.]
A Poem on the death of Mr. John Philips. [1710.]

GEORGE STEPNEY

An Epistle to Charles Montague, Esq. on His Majesty's voyage to Holland. 1691.
A Poem dedicated to the blessed memory of her late gracious Majesty Queen Mary. 1695.

Joseph Trapp

Abramule, or Love and Empire, a tragedy. 1704.
Praelectiones poeticae. 1711–15. Eng. trans. 1742.
Peace. A Poem inscribed to Lord Bolingbroke. 1713.
Aeneis of Virgil translated. 2 vols. 1718–20.
Thoughts upon the Four Last Things: Death, Judgment, Heaven, Hell. A Poem. 1734–5.

William Walsh

Works in prose and verse. 1736.
A funeral elegy on the death of the Queen. 1695.

Isaac Watts

Horae Lyricae. 1706.
Hymns. 1707.
Divine Songs for Children. 1715. Divine and Moral Songs for Children. 10th edn. 1729.
Psalms of David. 1719.

Leonard Welsted

Works. Ed. Nichols, J. 1787.
Epistles, Odes, etc. written on several subjects. 1724.
Oikographia. 1725.

Gilbert West

The Institution of the Order of the Garter. 1742.
The Odes of Pindar, with several other pieces translated. 1749.
Education. 1751.

Thomas Wharton, first Marquis of Wharton, (1648–1715)

Lilli Burlers, Bullen-a-la. 1688. [Set to music by Purcell.]

Thomas Yalden

Ode for St. Cecilia's Day. 1693.
On the Conquest of Namur. 1695.
The Temple of Fame. 1700.

A. T. B.

CHAPTERS VII AND VIII

HISTORICAL AND POLITICAL WRITERS

I. Gilbert Burnet

A. *Works*

For a complete bibliography, by Foxcroft, H. C., of Burnet's published works, with a statement of its sources, see Appendix II to A Life of Gilbert Burnet, by Clarke, T. E. S. (Scotland) and Foxcroft, H. C. (England). Cambridge, 1907.

A Discourse on the Memory of . . . Sir Robert Fletcher of Saltoun. Written by a Gentleman of his Acquaintance. Edinburgh, 1665.
A modest and free Conference betwixt a Conformist and a Nonconformist about the present distempers of Scotland. In six Dialogues. By a Lover of Peace. n. p., 1669.

A Vindication of . . . the Church and State in Scotland. In four Conferences. Wherein the answer to the Dialogues betwixt the Conformist and the Nonconformist is examined. Glasgow, 1673.

The Mystery of Iniquity unveiled. 1613.

The Memoirs of the Lives and Actions of James and William Dukes of Hamilton and Castleherald. . . . In which an account is given of the rise and progress of the Civil Wars of Scotland and other great Transactions. . . . 1677. (Ptd. as Part II of the History of the Church and State of Scotland. Rptd. Oxford, 1852.)

The History of the Reformation of the Church of England. (Vol. I.) The First Part of the Progress made in it during the Reign of Henry VIII. 1679. (Vol. II.) The Second Part. Of the Progress made in it till the Settlement of it in the beginning of Queen Elizabeth's Reign. 1681. The Third Part (Suppl.) with reissue of Parts I and II. 1715. New edn., revised by Pocock, N. 7 vols. Oxford, 1875.

> The Abridgement of the History of the Reformation of the Church of England. 1682.
>
> Reflections on Mr. Varillas's History of the Revolutions that have happened in Europe in matters of Religion, and more particularly in his ninth book that relates to England. 1686; in which year also appeared a French trans. by Le Clerc, Jean.
>
> A defence of the Reflections on . . . Mr. Varillas's History of Heresies. Being a reply to his answer. Amsterdam, 1687.
>
> A continuation of Reflections on Mr. Varillas's History of Heresies, particularly . . . his third and fourth Issues. 1687.
>
> Reflections on the Relations of the English Reformation, lately ptd. at Oxford. Part I. 1688. [By Obadiah Walker.]
>
> Reflections on the Oxford Theses Relating to the English Reformation. Part II. Amsterdam, 1688.
>
> Le Grand, J. Histoire du divorce de Henri VIII, avec réfutation des deux premiers livres de l'Hist. de Burnet. Paris, 1688.
>
> A Letter to Mr. Therenot containing a Censure of M. le Grand's History of K. Henry the Eighth's Divorce. 1688.
>
> A Censure of M. de Meaux's History of the Variations of the Protestant Churches: Together with some further Reflections on M. le Grand. 1688.
>
> Wharton, H. Specimen of Errors . . . in History of the Reformation by Burnet. 1693.
>
> A Letter writ . . . to the . . . Bishop of Cov[entry] and Litchfield concerning a Book [on the History of the Reformation] by Anthony Harmer. 1693.

Some Passages of the Life and Death of . . . John Earl of Rochester who died 26 July, 1680. 1680 (and many later editions, and German and French translations).

The Life and Death of Sir Matthew Hale . . . Sometime Lord Chief Justice of his Majesties Court of King's Bench. 1682 (and many later editions, and a French translation by Dumesnil, L. Amsterdam, 1688).

The History of the Rights of Princes in the disposing of Ecclesiastical Benefices and Church-lands relating chiefly to the . . . Regale. . . . 1682.

An Answer to the Animadversions on the Rights of Princes. . . . 1682.

A letter writ by the last Assembly-General of the Clergy of France to the Protestants inviting them to return to their Communion. . . . Translated
. . . and examined. 1683.

Utopia. Written in Latin by Sir Thomas More, Chancellor of England. Translated into English. 1684 (and later editions).

The Life of William Bedell, Bishop of Kilmore in Ireland. 1685 (with a French
translation by Dumesnil, L. Amsterdam, 1687).

A letter containing some remarks on the two papers writ by his late Majesty
King Charles II concerning religion. n. d. (1686 and later editions with
French and German translations.)

Some Letters; containing an account of what seemed most remarkable in Swit_
zerland, Italy, etc. . . . to T. H. R[obert] B[oyle]. 1686 (and many later
editions, incl. several French translations and one German).

> Supplements to Dr. Burnet's Letters . . . being Further Remarks . . .
> written by a Nobleman and communicated to the Author. . . .
> 1687.
> Three Letters concerning the present State of Italy. . . . Being a
> Supplement to Dr. Burnet's Letters. n. p., 1688.
> Animadversions upon the Reflections upon Dr. B[urnet]'s Travels.
> 1688.

Some Reflections on His Majesty's Proclamation for 12 February, 168⅞, for
a Toleration in Scotland. [1687.]

A letter containing some Reflections on His Majesty's Declaration for Liberty
of Conscience dated 4 April, 1687. [1687.]

Reasons against the Repealing the Acts of Parliament concerning the Test.
Humbly offered to. . . the Members of both Houses, at their meeting on 28
April, 1687.

A Relation of the Death of the Primitive Persecutors. Written originally in
Latin by L. C. F. Lactantius. Englished by G. B., to which he hath made
a large Preface concerning Persecution. Amsterdam, 1687.

Reflections on a late Pamphlet entitled Parliamentum Pacificum. Amsterdam,
1688.

Dr. Burnet's Vindication of Himself from the Calumnies [of] Parliamentum
Pacificum. [1688.]

An Enquiry into the measures of submission to the Supreme Authority; and
of the grounds upon which it may be lawful or necessary for Subjects to
defend their Religion, Lives and Liberties. n. p., (1688).

A Review of the Reflections on the Prince of Orange's Declaration. n. p., (1688).

Reflections on a Paper entituled, his Majesty's Reasons for withdrawing himself
from Rochester. Published by Authority. 1689.

An Enquiry into the present state of Affairs, and in particular, Whether we owe
Allegiance to the King in these Circumstances? And whether we are bound
to treat with Him and call Him back again or not? Published by Authority.
1689.

A pastoral Letter to the clergy of his Diocese concerning the Oaths of Allegiance
and Supremacy to K. William and Q. Mary. 1689.

A Discourse of the Pastoral Care. 1692.

An Essay on the Memory of the late Queen. 1695.

An Exposition of the Thirty-Nine Articles of the Church of England. 1699.
[Frequently reprinted.]

Reflections on a Book entitled [The Rights, Powers and Privileges of an English Convocation, Stated and Vindicated]. 1700.

Speech in the House of Lords, upon the Bill against Occasional Conformity [1 December, 1703]. 1704.

Speech in the House of Lords upon the first Article of the Impeachment of Dr. Henry Sacheverell [16 March, 1710]. 1710.

Two Discourses to Lord Russell. (1683.) First publ. in Some Sermons . . . and an Essay towards a new book of Homilies. 1713.

The History of my Own Time. Vol. I. 1724. (Dutch trans. 1725. French trans. 1725 and 1727.) Vol. II. With the author's Life by the Editor. 1734. Whole work. 3 vols. 1735. French trans. 2 vols. 1735. Ed. Routh, M. J. 7 vols. Oxford, 1823. Vols. I and II. Ed. Airy, O. Oxford, 1897, etc.

    Braddon, L. Burnet's Late History charged with Partiality. 1725.

    Cockburn, John. A specimen of some free and impartial remarks on public affairs and particular persons, esp. relating to Scotland, occasioned by Dr. Burnet's History of his own times. n. d.

Journal of Lord Russell's last week. First published in General Dictionary, vol. VIII, 1739; afterwards in Lord (John) Russell, Life of William Lord Russell, 1819 (and later editions).

Thoughts on Education. 1761. [Written 1668.]

Memorial offered to Princess Sophia containing a delineation of the constitution and policy of England. 1815.

    A Supplement to Burnet's History of My own Time; derived from his Original Memoirs, his Autobiography, his Letters to Admiral Herbert, and his Private Meditations. All hitherto unpublished. Ed. Foxcroft, H. C. Oxford, 1902.

Letters to George Savile, Lord Halifax. Ed. Foxcroft, H. C. In Camden Miscellany, vol. XI. 1907.

    Some Unpublished Letters of George Savile, Lord Halifax, to Gilbert Burnet. Ed. Poole, Dorothy Lane. In English Historical Review, p. 703, July, 1911. [Partly answers to the above.]

B. *Biography and Criticism*

Clarke, T. E. S. and Foxcroft, H. C. A Life of Gilbert Burnet. (Scotland, by Clarke; England, by Miss Foxcroft.) With an Introduction by Firth, C. H. Cambridge, 1907. [The standard biography of Burnet.]

II. HENRY ST. JOHN, VISCOUNT BOLINGBROKE

A. *Collected Works and Letters.*

Works, published by David Mallet. 5 vols. 1754. 11 vols. 1786. 8 vols, 1809. 4 vols. Philadelphia, 1841.

Letters and Correspondence, Public and Private, of Henry St. John Viscount Bolingbroke, during the time he was Secretary of State to Queen Anne. with State Papers. . . . By Clarke, Gilbert. 2 vols. 1798.

Lettres Historiques, Politiques, Philosophiques et Particulières de H. St. John, Vic. Bolingbroke, depuis 1710 jusqu'à 1736. 3 vols. Paris, 1808. [Partly originals, partly translations.]

B. *Periodicals*

The Examiner. [By Bolingbroke, and others.] 1710, etc.

The Craftsman. By Caleb D'Anvers. 14 vols. 1731-7. [A collected reprint.
First number 5 December, 1726.]
The Occasional Writer. [By Bolingbroke.] 1727.

C. *Separate Works*

A Dissertation upon Parties. 1735. [Originally appeared in The Craftsman.]
The Idea of a Patriot King. 1749.
Letter on the Spirit of Patriotism. 1749, 1752.
Reflections on Exile. 1752.
Of the True Use of Retirement and Study. 1752.
Letters on the Study and Use of History. 1752.
Some Reflections on the State of the Nation. 1752.
A Letter to Sir W. Wyndham. 1753.

D. *Biographical and Critical Writings*

Brosch, M. Lord Bolingbroke und die Whigs und Tories seiner Zeit. Frankfort.
1883. (Chap. 8: Bolingbroke als Schriftsteller.)
Collins, J. Churton. Bolingbroke, a Historical Study. 1886.
Cooke, G. W. Memoirs of Bolingbroke. 2 vols. 1835.
Harrop, R. Bolingbroke. (Statesmen Series.) 1884.
Hassall, A. The life of Viscount Bolingbroke. 1889.
Macknight, T. The Life of Henry St. John, Viscount Bolingbroke. 1863.
Rémusat, C. de. L'Angleterre au XVIIIᵐᵉ siècle. 2 vols. Paris, 1856.
Sichel, W. Bolingbroke and his times. (The Sequel.) 1901-2.

III. OTHER WRITERS

Nicholas Amhurst

Poems on Several Occasions. 1720.
Terrae Filius. 1721.
Contributions to The Craftsman (1726-36).

William Pulteney, Earl of Bath

Contributions to The Craftsman (1727-9 chiefly).

Abel Boyer

The History of King William III. 1702.
The History of the Reigns of Queen Anne, King George I and King George II.
27 Parts, digested into Annals. 1703-29.
The Political State of Great Britain. 60 vols. 1711-40.
The History of Queen Anne. 1722. (2nd edn., with numerous Appendices.
1735.)
The Theater of Honour and Nobility. 1729.

Eustace Budgell (1686-1737)

Contributions to The Spectator (1711-14); The Craftsman (1731-7); The Bee
(1733-5).
A Letter to a Friend in the Country. 1721.
A Letter to Mr. Law on his Arrival in England. [1721.]
Memoirs of the Lives and Characters of the Illustrious Family of the Boyles,
particularly Charles Earl of Orrery. 1737.

William Carstares (1649–1715)

State Papers and Letters, addressed to William Carstares, confidential Secretary to King William during the whole of his Reign. To which is prefixed his Life. Ed. McCormick, Joseph. Edinburgh, 1774. [Of very great importance, since Carstares, in conjunction with Portland and the Dalrymples, virtually directed the Scottish policy of William III.]

    Story, R. H. William Carstares, a Character and Career of the Revolutionary Epoch (1649–1715). 1874.

Jeremy Collier

Essays upon Several Moral Subjects. 4 parts in 3 vols. 1697–1709.
The Great Historical, Geographical, Genealogical and Poetical Dictionary. Collected from Historians, especially L. Morery. 2nd edn., revised to 1688. 2 vols. 1701–21.
Reasons for Restoring some Prayers and Directions as they stand in the Communion Service of the First English Reformed Liturgy. . . . 1717.
An Ecclesiastical History of Great Britain, chiefly of England, with a brief Account of the Affairs of Religion in Ireland. Ed. Lathbury, T. 9 vols. 1852.

    See also bibliography to Vol. VIII., Chap. vi.

George Mackenzie, Earl of Cromartie (1630–1714)

Historical Account of the Conspiracy of the Earl of Gowrie. . . . 1713.
A Vindication of the Reformation of the Church of Scotland, with some account of the Records. Scots Magazine. 1802.

William Dampier (1652–1715)

Voyages. 4 vols., containing A New Voyage round the World, 1697. Voyages and Descriptions. 2 vols. 1699. A Voyage to New Holland. Part i, 3 vols., 1703; part ii, 3 vols., 1709.

Laurence Echard

The History of England from the first entrance of Julius Caesar and the Romans to the end of the reign of James I. 1707. Vols. ii and iii: to the Establishment of King William and Queen Mary. 1718. Vol. iv, consisting of explanations and amendments, as well as new and curious additions . . . together with some apologies and vindications. 1720.

Andrew Fletcher of Saltoun

The Political Works of. 1732. (Later editions 1737, 1749 and 1798.)

A Discourse of Government with relation to Militias. Edinburgh, 1698. (Rptd. in Works.)
Two Discourses concerning the Affairs of Scotland; written in the year 1698. Edinburgh, 1698. (Rptd. in Works.)
Discorso delle cose di Spagna, scritto nel mese di Luglio, 1698. "Napoli" [Edinburgh], 1698. (Rptd. in Works.)
A Speech upon the State of the Nation, in April, 1701. n. p., n. d. (Rptd. in Works.)

An Account of a Conversation concerning a Right Regulation of Government for the Common Good of Mankind. In a letter to the Marquis of Montrose, &c. 1704. (Rptd. in Works.)

> Ormond, G. W. T. Fletcher of Saltoun. (Famous Scots Series.) Edinburgh and London. 1897.
> Scott Macfie, R. A. Bibliography of Andrew Fletcher of Saltoun. Edinburgh, 1901.

James II

Clarke, J. S. The Life of James the Second. Collected out of Memoirs of James II writ of his own hand. 2 vols. 1816.

> Quadriennium Jacobi, or The History of the Reign of King James II from his first Coming to the Crown to his Desertion. 1689. [Vehement against the policy of James, including the indictment of Oates.]

White Kennett (bishop of Peterborough)

A Compleat History of England; with the Lives of all the Kings and Queens thereof. Vol. III. (Charles I to William III.) 1706. New edn. 1719. (As to Roger North's Examen see under Roger North, below.)

A Register and Chronicle, Ecclesiastic and Civil; containing Matters of Fact delivered in the words of the most authentick Books, Papers and Records. . . . from the Restauration of King Charles II. Vol. I (to 1662). 1728.

John Ker of Kersland (1673–1726)

Memoirs; with account of the Ostend Company. 3 parts in 2 vols. 1726–7.

Robert Knox (1640?–1720)

An Historical Relation of the Island of Ceylon in the East Indies. 1681.

David Lloyd (1635–1692)

The Statesmen and Favourites of England since the Reformation. 1665.

Memories of the Lives, Actions, Sufferings and Deaths of those . . . that suffered . . . for the Protestant Religion and . . . Allegiance to their Soveraigne. . . . 1668.

George Lockhart (1673–1731)

Memoirs of the Affairs of Scotland from Queen Anne's Accession to the Commencement of the Union, 1707. 1714.

Papers on the Affairs of Scotland. 2 vols. 1817. [Very valuable for the history of the Jacobite movement, from the Jacobite side.]

Sir George Mackenzie (1636–1691)

Collected Works. Ed. with Life, by Ruddiman, Thos. 2 vols. Edinburgh, 1716–22.

Memoirs of the Affairs of Scotland. Edinburgh, 1822.

John Macky (d. 1726)

Memoirs of the Secret Services of John Macky Esq., during the reigns of King William, Queen Anne and King George the First. 1733.

John Churchill, first Duke of Marlborough (1650–1722)

Letters and Despatches, from 1702 to 1712. Ed. Mackay, General Sir G. 5
vols. 1845.

Robert, First Viscount Molesworth (1656–1723)

An Account of Denmark. 1692.

Daniel Neal

A History of New England. 1720.
The History of the Puritans; or Protestant Nonconformists; from the Reformation in 1517 to the Revolution in 1688; comprising an Account of their
Principles: their attempts for a further reformation in the Church; their
sufferings; and the Lives and Characters of their most considerable Divines.
Vol. I, 1732; vol. II, 1733; vol. III, 1736; vol. IV, 1738. Ed. Toulmin, J.,
with Life of the author. 5 vols. 1797. (Rptd. 1822.)

    Maddox, Isaac, Bishop of Worcester. A Vindication of the Doctrine,
        Discipline, and Worship of the Church of England . . . from . . .
        Mr. Neal's first Volume of the History of the Puritans. 1733.
A Review of the Principal Facts objected to in the first Volume of the History
of the Puritans. 1734.

    Grey, Zachary. An Impartial Examination of the Second Volume of
        [the same]. 1736. [And later publications.]

Roger North

A Discourse of Fish and Fish Ponds. 1713.
Examen: or, An Enquiry into the Credit and Veracity of a Pretended Complete
History; shewing the perverse and wicked Design of it, and the many Falsi-
ties and Abuses of Truth contained in it. Together with some Memoirs
occasionally inserted. All tending to Vindicate the Honour of the late
King Charles II, and his Happy Reign, from the intended Aspersions of that
Foul Pen. 1740.
Life of the Rt. Hon. Francis North, Baron of Guilford. 1742.
Life of the Hon. Sir Dudley North and of the Hon. and Rev. Dr. John North,
1744. New edn. of the Lives of the Norths. Ed. by Jessopp, A. 3 vols.
1890.
Discourse on the study of the Laws. 1824.
Memoirs of Musick. Ed. by Rimbault, E. F. 1846.
Autobiography. Ed. by Jessopp, A. 1887.

John Oldmixon

The Secret History of Europe, in Four Parts compleat. Consisting of the most
private affairs, transacted by all Parties for 50 Years past. . . . With
a large Appendix, containing Original Papers. . . . 1712–15.
The Critical History of England Ecclesiastical and Civil: wherein the Errors of
the Monkish Writers, and others before the Reformation, are expos'd and
corrected. As also are the Deficiency and Partiality of the Historians, And
particular Notice is taken of The History of the Grand Rebellion, And Mr.
Echards History of England. . . . To which is added, An Essay on Criticism; as it regards Design, Thought and Expression, in Prose and Verse.
2 vols. 1724–6.

The History of England during the Reigns of the Royal House of Stuart, 1730.
Vol. II: during the Reigns of King William and Queen Mary, Queen Anne,
King George I. 1735. Vol. III: during the Reigns of Henry VIII, Edward
VI, Queen Mary, Queen Elizabeth. 1739.

Humphrey Prideaux (1648–1724)

The true nature of Imposture fully display'd in the life of Mahomet. 1697.
French translation. 1698.
The Old and New Testament connected in the History of the Jews. 2 vols·
1716–18. French transl. 2 vols. Amsterdam. 1722. German transl.
2 vols. 1726.
Letters to John Ellis. Ed. Thompson, E. M. Camden Soc. 1875.

Paul de Rapin de Thoyras (1661–1725)

Histoire d' Angleterre. Continued by Durand, D. 13 vols. 1724–36. Trans.
and continued by Tindal, N. 4 vols. 1743–7.

Henry Sidney, Earl of Romney

Diary of the Times of Charles the Second, including his correspondence with the
Countess of Sunderland and other distinguished persons of the English
Court: to which are added, Letters illustrative of the Times of James II
and William III. Ed. Blencowe, R. W. 2 vols. 1843.

Sir Paul Rycaut (1628–1700)

The Present State of the Ottoman Empire. 1668.
A History of the Turkish Empire. 1679.

Thomas Rymer

Foedera, Conventiones, Literae et cujuscunque generis Acta Publica, inter Reges
Angliae, et alios quosvis Imperatores, Reges, Pontifices, Principes vel Com-
munitates. 20 vols., 1704–35. (Vol. XVI (1715) was prepared, chiefly from
Rymer's materials, by Sanderson, Robert, who also brought out vol. XVII
(1717), and three supplemental volumes (XVIII–XX). The index and syl-
labus of Rymer's manuscript materials, printed by Sanderson in vol. XVII,
are extant in Brit. Mus.) 2nd edn., emendata studio Georgii Holmes, 20 vols.
(vols. XVIII–XX duplicate of preceding), 1727–35. Foedera etc. (abrégé
historique by Le Clerc and Rapin, P.), 10 vols. The Hague, 1739–45 [the
best typographically and with some new documents]. New edn., 1066–1383.
4 vols. in 7 parts, Record Publ., 1816–69. [The best so far as it goes.] Syl-
labus, in English, of Foedera by Hardy, Sir T. D., Record Publ. 3 vols.,
1869–85. Acta Regia, from the French abridgment of Rapin, trans. by
Whatley, Stephen. 4 vols. 8vo. 1725–7, one fo. 1732.
    See also bibl. to Vol. VIII, Chap. VI B and Chap. VII, ante.

Thomas Sprat, bishop of Rochester (1635–1713)

A True Account and Declaration of the horrid Conspiracy against the late King,
His present Majesty, and the Government. 2 parts in one vol. 1685.
[Part II contains copies of informations, etc.]

Sir John Dalrymple, first Earl of Stair (1648–1707) and John Dalrymple, second Earl of Stair (1693–1747)

Annals and Correspondence of the Viscount and the First and Second Earls of Stair. By Graham, J. M. 2 vols. Edinburgh and London. 1875.

John Strype

Memorials of Thomas Cranmer. 1694. New edn. Eccl. Hist. Soc., 3 vols. in 4. Oxford. 1848–54.

The Life of the learned Sir Thomas Smith, Kt., Doctor of the Civil Law, Principal Secretary of State to King Edward the Sixth and Queen Elizabeth. 1698.

Historical Collections of the Life and Acts of John Aylmer, Bishop of London. 1701.

The Life of Sir John Cheke. 1705.

The Life and Actions of Edmund Grindal, Archbishop of Canterbury, 1710.

The Life and Acts of Matthew Parker, the First Archbishop of Canterbury in the Reign of Queen Elizabeth. . . . 1711.

The Life and Acts of . . . John Whitgift, D.D., the Third and Last Lord Archbishop of Canterbury in the Reign of Queen Elizabeth. 1718.

Ecclesiastical Memorials, Relating chiefly to Religion and the Reformation of it, and the Emergencies of the Church of England, under King Henry VIII, King Edward VI and Queen Mary. 3 vols. (with appendix to each vol.). 1721.

Annals of the Reformation and Establishment of Religion, and other various Occurrences in the Church of England, during the First Twelve Years of Queen Elizabeth's Happy Reign. (With Appendix and Repository.) 3 vols. 1721. 2nd edn. 3 vols. 1725–8.

All the above works were rptd. in 19 vols., Oxford, 1812–24; followed by General Index to the Historical and Biographical Works of John Strype, by Laurence, R. F. 2 vols. 1828.

Sydney Family

Letters and Memorials of State, in the Reigns of Queen Mary, Queen Elizabeth, King James, King Charles the First, Part of the Reign of King Charles II, and Oliver's Usurpation, written and collected by Sir Henry Sydney, Sir Philip Sydney . . . Philip Lord Viscount Lisle, and his Brother Colonel Algernon Sydney . . . Ed. Collins, Arthur. 2 vols. 1746.

Sir Joseph Williamson

Letters addressed from London to Sir Joseph Williamson, while Plenipotentiary at the Congress of Cologne in the years 1673 and 1674. Ed. Christie, W. D. Camden Society. 2 vols. 1874.

Miscellanea Aulica, or a Collection of State Treatises. Ed. Brown, T. 1702.

CHAPTER IX
MEMOIR-WRITERS, 1715–60

JOHN HERVEY, FIRST EARL OF BRISTOL

Letter-Books of John Hervey, First Earl of Bristol. With Sir Thomas Hervey's

Letters during courtship and Poems during widowhood. 1651–1750. 3 vols. Wells, 1894.

Diary, with extracts from his book of expenses, 1688–1742. Wells, 1894.

MARY, COUNTESS COWPER

Diary, 1714–20. Ed. Cowper, Spencer. 1864. 2nd edn. 1865.

JOHN, LORD HERVEY

Observations on the writings of the Craftsman. (With a Sequel.) 1730.

Remarks on the Craftsman's vindication of his two honble patrons. 1731.

Verses to the Imitator of Horace [Pope]. [In conjunction with Lady Mary Wortley Montagu.] 1733.

Letters from a Nobleman at Hampton Court to a Doctor of Divinity. 1733.

The conduct of the Opposition and the tendency of modern patriotism review'd and examin'd. 1734.

Ancient and modern liberty stated and compar'd. 1734.

Miscellaneous thoughts on the present posture both of our foreign and domestic affairs. 1742.

Letters between Lord Hervey and Dr. Middleton concerning the Roman Senate. Publ. by Knowles, T. 1778.

Memoirs of the reign of George the Second from his accession to the death of Queen Caroline. Ed. Croker, J. W. 3 vols. 1848. Another edn. 3 vols. 1884.

GEORGE BUBB DODINGTON, LORD MELCOMBE

Diary, 1748–9—1761. Ed. Wyndham, H. P. Salisbury, 1784, 3rd edn. 1785. Another edn. 1823.

LADY MARY WORTLEY MONTAGU

(1) *Letters and Works*

Letters of Right Hon.'Lady M . . . y W. . . y M . . . e written during her Travels in Europe, Asia, and Africa to persons of distinction, men of letters, &c. in different parts of Europe. 3 vols. 1763. [Published surreptitiously. An additional volume, probably spurious, appeared in 1767.] Other edns., 1778, 1784, 1789.

Works, including her Correspondence, Poems and Essays. Published, by permission of the Earl of Bute, from her genuine papers. [Edited, with a Memoir of the Author, by Dallaway, James.] 5 vols. 1803. Another edn. 1817.
French translations of the Letters appeared in 1805 by Garnier, G. and in 1822 by Mme. Dufrénoy.

Letters and Works. Edited by her great-grandson, Lord Wharncliffe. [With an appendix.] 3 vols. 1837.

Letters from the Levant. Ed. St. John, J. A. 1838.

Letters and Works, with additions and corrections derived from the original manuscripts, illustrative notes, and a new memoir by W. Moy Thomas. Anecdotes by Lady Louisa Stuart. 2 vols. 1861. Another edn. 1887.

Select passages from her letters. [Arranged to give a continuous account of her life.] Ed. Ropes, A. R. 1892.

Letters and Works. Edited by her great-grandson Lord Wharncliffe. With a memoir by W. Moy Thomas. Introductory Anecdotes by Lady Louisa Stuart. 2 vols. 1893.

(2) *Poems*

Town Eclogues (first published piratically as Court Poems, and misdated 1706). 1716. Republished by R. Dodsley. 1747.
Poetical Works. Ed. Reed, I. 1768.

(3) *Biography and Criticism*

Aitken, G. A. The Life and Works of John Arbuthnot. 1892.
Bagehot, W. Lady Mary Wortley Montagu. National Review. January, 1862. Rptd. in Literary Studies, ed. Hutton, R. H. New edn., vol. II, 1905.
Chesterfield, P. D. S., 4th Earl of. Letters. Edd. Strachey, C. and Calthrop, A. 2 vols. 1901. [For the character of Lord Bute.]
Dilke, C. W. Lady Mary Wortley Montagu. Papers of a Critic. Vol. I. 1875.
Hunter, J. South Yorkshire. [Vol. II contains an account of the family of Wortley-Montagu, with memoir and letters.] 1831.
Lady Mary Wortley Montagu. Temple Bar, vol. XCVIII. 1893.
The Letters and Works of Lady Mary Wortley Montagu. Quarterly Review. February, 1837.
The Letters and Works of Lady Mary Wortley Montagu. Quarterly Review. Oct., 1897.
McIlquham, H. Lady Mary Wortley Montagu and Mary Astell. Westminster Review, vol. CLI. 1899.
Marinoni, L. Lady Montagu Wortley prima della sua venuta alle rive del Sebino. Studio storico biografico. 1903.
Nichols, J. Literary Anecdotes of the 18th century. 9 vols. 1812–15.
"Paston, George." Lady Mary Wortley Montagu and her times. 1907.
Pope, A. Works. Edd. Elwin, W. and Courthope, W. J. [Vol. IX contains Lady Mary's correspondence with Pope.] 1886.
Spence, J. Anecdotes, observations, and characters of books and men. Ed. Singer, S. W. 1820. 2nd edn. 1858.
Stanhope, Philip Henry, 5th Earl. Italian Memoir by Lady Mary Wortley Montagu. Miscellanies. 2nd ser. 1872.
Tallentyre, S. G. The Great Letter-Writers. II. Lady Mary Wortley Montagu. Longman's Magazine, vol. XXXIII. 1899.
Walpole, H. Letters. Ed. Toynbee, Mrs. Paget. 16 vols. Oxford, 1903–5.

"GEORGE PSALMANAZAR" (1679?–1763)

Memoirs of * * * commonly known by the name of George Psalmanazar. 1764.
    An Historical and Geographical Description of Formosa, an Island subject to the Emperor of Japan. 1704.

HENRIETTA HOWARD, COUNTESS OF SUFFOLK

Letters to and from Henrietta, Countess of Suffolk, and her second husband the Hon. George Berkeley, 1712–1767. Ed. Croker, J. W. 2 vols. 1824.

JAMES, SECOND EARL WALDEGRAVE

Memoirs from 1754 to 1758. 1821.
    Quarterly Review, July, 1821. (Review.)

T. S.
A. T. B.

CHAPTER X

WRITERS OF BURLESQUE AND TRANSLATORS

Brown, Tom, of Shifnal. Amusements Serious and Comical, Calculated for the Meridian of London. 1700.

—— A Collection of all the Dialogues written by Mr: one of them Entituled Democratici Vapulantes, Being a Dialogue between Julian, and others. Never before Printed. 1704.

—— A Collection of all the Dialogues, To which are added, His Translations & Imitations of several Odes of Horace, of Martial's Epigrams Etc. 1704.

—— The Works of. Serious & Comical. In Prose & Verse. In Four Volumes. Fifth Edition. 1720.

—— The Beauties of. To which is prefixed A Life of the Author by C. H. Wilson. 1808.

He translated:

 Scarron. The Whole Comical Works of, Translated by Mr. Thos. Brown, Mr. Savage & others. III Edition. 1712.

 —— The Comical Romance, & other Tales by Scarron. Done into English by Tom Brown of Shifnal, John Savage, and others with an introduction by J. J. Jusserand. 1892.

He also collaborated in translating Petronius (*see* Burnaby, J.) and Lucian (*see* Phillips, J.).

 Memoirs Relating to the late Famous Mr. Tho. Brown. With a Catalogue of his Library. 1704.

Burnaby, J. The Satyr of Titus Petronius. With its Fragments, recorded at Belgrade. Made English by Mr. Burnaby of the Middle-Temple, and another Hand. 1694.

—— Petronius, Arbiter Titus, The Satyrical Works of. Together with his Life & Character written by Mons. St. Evremond; Made English by Mr. Wilson. Mr. Burnaby, Mr. Blount, Mr. Thos. Brown, Captain Ayloff and several others. 1708.

Colvil, S. Mock Poem, or Whiggs Supplication. 1681.

—— Mr. Samuel Colvil's Prophecy anent the Union, as contained in his Scots Hudibras. 1707.

Cotton, Charles. The Compleat Gamester. 1674.

—— The Planters Manual; being instructions for planting all sorts of fruit trees. 1675.

—— The Wonders of the Peak. 1685.

—— Poems on Several Occasions. 1689.

He translated:

 Du Vair, G., The Morall Philosophy of the Stoicks, 1664; Girard, G., History of the Life of the Duke d'Espernon, 1670; Corneille, Horace, 1671; Lasseran-Massencone, B. de, Commentaries, 1674; Montaigne, Michel de, Essays of, 1685; Pontis, L. de, Memoirs of, 1694.

Dixon, R. Canidia or the Witches. 1683.

D'Urfey (Thos.). Collin's Walk through London and Westminster, a Poem in Burlesque. 1690.

—— Butler's Ghost or Hudibras the fourth part. 1682.

Head, Richard (1637?–86?). The English Rogue. (Part I.) 1665. [Parts II–IV, published in 1671, were not by Head.]

?Johnson, Charles (*fl.* 1724–36). A General History of the Robberies and Murders of the most notorious Pyrates. 1724. [Perhaps a pseudonym.]

? Johnson, Charles. A General History of the Lives and Adventures of the most famous Highwaymen. 1734.

?Lucas, Theophilus (*fl.* 1714). Memoirs of the Lives, Intrigues and Comical Adventures of the most famous Gamesters and celebrated Sharpers in the reigns of Charles II, James II, William III and Queen Anne. 1714. [Perhaps a pseudonym.]

Meston, William. Phaethon . . . burlesqu'd. 1720.

—— The Knight. 1723.

—— The Poetical Works of. 1767.

(Midgley, Robert (1653–1733), editor.) Letters writ by a Turkish Spy . . . from 1637 to 1682. 8 vols. 1687–93.

Monsey, R. Scarronides: or Virgile Travestie, A Mock-Poem. Being The Second Book of Virgils Æneis, Translated into English Burlesq. 1665.

Mottley, John (Jenkins, Elijah). Joe Miller's Jests. 1739.

Phillips, John. Typhon: or the Gyants War with The Gods, translated from Scarron. 1665.

—— Maronides or Virgil Travestie Being a new Paraphrase upon the Fifth Book of Virgils Æneids in Burlesque Verse. 1672.

—— D. R. A Satyr against Satyrs: or St. Peter's Vision transubstantiated. 1680.

He translated:

Casas, Bartolomé de las. The Tears of the Indians: Being an Historical & True Account of the Cruel Massacres and Slaughters of above Twenty Millions of innocent People. Written in Spanish by Casas, an Eye-Witness of these Things; And made English. 1655.

Scudery, Georges de. Almahide, An Excellent New Romance, Never before in English . . . Written in French by the Accurate Pen of Monsieur de Scudery, Governor of Nostre Dame. Done in English. 1677.

La Calprenède, G. de C. de. Pharamond, or the History of France. A fam'd Romance in Twelve Parts. 1677.

Grelot, W. J. A late Voyage to Constantinople. Made English. 1683.

Plutarch. Morals, translated by J. Phillips and other hands. 1684.

Cervantes. The History of the most Renowned Don Quixote of Mancha: and his Trusty Squire Sancho Pancha, Now made English according to the Humour of our Modern Language, by J. P. 1687.

Lucian of Samosata. Works. Translated by J. Phillips and other hands. 1711.

Lives of Edward and John Phillips by Godwin, J. 1815.

Pope, Walter (d. 1714). Memoirs of M. Du Vall. 1670.

—— Life of Seth Ward. 1697.

Radcliffe, Alexander. Bacchinalia Caelestia: a Poem in praise of Punch. 1680.

—— Ovid Travestie, a burlesque upon Ovid's Epistles. 1680.

—— The Ramble: An Anti-Heroick Poem. Together with Some Terrestrial Hymns and Carnal Ejaculations. 1682.

Scudamore, James. Homer à la Mode. 1664.

Stevens, Captain John, Translated:

Faria y Sousa, Manuel de. The Portuguese Asia: or the History of the Discovery & Conquest of India by the Portuguese. Written in Spanish. 1695.

Faria y Sousa, Emanuel de. The History of Portugal . . . Written in

Spanish by. Translated & Continued down to the present year. 1698.

Mariana, John de. The General History of Spain. From the first peopling of it by Tubal, till the Death of King Ferdinand. . . . Written in Spanish. The Whole Translated. 1699.

Veitia Linage, Joseph de. The Spanish Rule of Trade to the West-Indies. Written in Spanish by. Made English. 1702.

Sandoval, D. F. Prudencio de. The History of Charles Vth Emperor and King of Spain, the Great Hero of the House of Austria. . . . Written in Spanish. 1703.

Cervantes Saavedra, Michael de. The History of the most Ingenious Knight Don Quixote de la Mancha. Written in Spanish by. Formerly made English by Thomas Shelton; now Revis'd, corrected, & partly new Translated from the Original. 2nd Edition. 1706.

Cieza, Peter de. The Seventeen Years Travels of, Through the Mighty Kingdom of Peru, and the large Provinces of Cartagena & Popagan in South America. Translated from the Spanish. 1709.

Teixeira, Antony. The History of Persia Containing the Lives and Memorable Actions of its Kings, etc. The Persian History written in Arabick by Mirkond, a famous Eastern Author . . . translated into Spanish by Antony Teixeira who lived several years in Persia & India: & now render'd into English. 1715.

Herrera, Antonio de. The General History of the Vast Continent & Islands of America commonly call'd The West Indies, from The First Discovery thereof. In 24 vols. 1725.

Ward, Edward (commonly known as Ned). The Miracles Performed by Money; A Poem. 1692.

—— A Dialogue between Bow-Steeple Dragon and the Exchange Grasshopper. 1698.

—— Modern Religion & Ancient Loyalty. A Duologue. 1699.

—— Modern Religion & Ancient Loyalty. 1699.

—— The Sots' Paradise: or the Humours of a Derby Ale-House: With a Satyr upon the Ale. 1700.

—— A Step to the Bath: With a Character of the Place. 1700.

—— The Insinuating Bawd: and The Repenting Harlot! Written by a Whore at Tunbridge, & Dedicated to a Bawd at the Bath. 1700.

—— A Step to Stir-Bitch-Fair: with Remarks upon the University of Cambridge. 1700.

—— The Dancing School. With the Adventures of the Easter Holy-Days. 1700.

—— A Frolic to Horn-Fair, with a walk from Cuckold's Point thro' Deptford and Greenwich. 1700.

—— A Walk to Islington with a Description of New Tunbridge-Wells & Sadler's Musick House. 1701.

—— The Poet's Ramble after Riches: with Reflections Upon a Country Corporation. Also the Author's Lamentation in the Time of Adversity. 1701.

—— All Men Mad: or England a Great Bedlam. 1704.

—— The London Spy Compleate in eighteen parts. 1704-6.

—— The Secret History of the Calves-Head Club, Complt. or, The Republican Unmask'd. 6th Edition. 1706.

—— The London Terraefilius, or the Satyrical Reformer. 1707.

—— The Forgiving Husband, & Adulteress Wife: or, A Seasonable Present to the Unhappy Pair in Fenchurch Street. 1708.

Ward, Edward. Hudibras Redivivus: or, a Burlesque Poem on The Times. 1708.
—— The Rambling Fuddle-Caps: or a Tavern-Struggle for a Kiss. 1709.
—— Mars stript of his Armour: or the Army Display'd in all its true Colours. 1709.
—— Nuptial Dialogues & Debates; or a useful prospect of the felicities & discomforts of a marry'd life. 1710.
—— Vulgus Britannicus or, the British Hudibrass. 1710.
—— The Life & Adventures of Don Quixote de la Mancha, translated into Hudibrastic Verse. 1711.
—— The history of the Grand Rebellion, digested into Verse. 3 vols. 1713.
—— The Republican Procession; or the Tumultuous Cavalcade. A Merry Poem. The Second Edition. 1714.
—— The Field-Spy. 1714.
—— The Hudibrastick Brewer: or a Preposterous Union Between Malt & Meter. A Satyr upon the suppos'd Author of the Republican Procession; or, The Tumultuous Cavalcade. 1714.
—— The Field-Spy or The Walking Observator. A Poem. 1714.
—— A Collection of Historical & State Poems. 1717.
—— The Tipling Philosophers. A Lyrick Poem. 1719.
—— The Delights of the Bottle or the Compleat Vintner. A Merry Poem. By the author of the Cavalcade. 1720.
—— Durgen, or a plain satyr upon a pompous Satyrist. 1729.

Anonymous Burlesques

B. M. Typhon: or the Wars of the Gods and Giants. A Burlesque Poem in Imitation of Mons. Scarron. 1704.
The Irish Hudibras or Fuigallian Prince, taken from the Sixth Book of Virgil's Ænaeids, and adapted to the Present Times. 1689.
Naso Scarronomimus. Ovidius Exalaus, or Ovid Travestie. 1673.
Pendragon; or the Carpet Knight His Kalendar. 1698.
The Woeful Treaty: or the Unhappy Peace. An Ode in the Measure of the celebrated Song of Chevy-Chase. 1716.

CHAPTER XI

BERKELEY AND CONTEMPORARY PHILOSOPHY

I. General Authorities and Divinity

Bagehot, W. Bp. Butler in Estimates of some Englishmen and Scotchmen. 1858.
Elton, O. The Augustan Ages. Edinburgh, 1899.
Farrar, A. S. Critical History of Free Thought. 1862.
Hunt, J. Religious Thought in England. 1870–2.
Lechler, G. V. Geschichte des englischen Deismus. Stuttgart, 1841.
Leland, J. View of the Principal Deistical Writers. 1754–6.
Lyon, G. L'idéalisme en Angleterre au XVIIIᵉ siècle. 1888.
Millar, J. H. The Mid-Eighteenth Century. Edinburgh, 1902.
Pattison, M. In Essays and Reviews. 1860.
Robertson, J. M. Short History of Free Thought. 1906.
Stephen, Sir Leslie. English Thought in the Eighteenth Century. 2 vols. 1876.

II. George Berkeley

Arithmetica absque Algebra aut Euclide demonstrata. Dublin, 1707.

Miscellanea Mathematica. Dublin, 1707.

An Essay towards a New Theory of Vision. Dublin, 1709.

A Treatise concerning the Principles of Human Knowledge. Part 1. Dublin, 1710. (2nd edn., with "Part 1" omitted from title, London, 1734.)

Passive Obedience: or, The Christian Doctrine of not resisting the Supreme Power, proved and vindicated, upon the Principles of the Law of Nature. 1712.

Three Dialogues between Hylas and Philonous. 1713.

De motu: sive de motus principio et natura, et de causa communicationis motuum. 1721.

An Essay towards preventing the ruin of Great Britain. 1721.

A Proposal for the better supplying of Churches in our Foreign Plantations and for converting the savage Americans to Christianity, by a College to be erected in the Summer Islands, otherwise called the Isles of Bermuda. 1725.

Alciphron, or the Minute Philosopher. 1732.

The Theory of Vision, or Visual Language . . . vindicated and explained. 1733.

The Analyst, or, A Discourse addressed to an infidel mathematician. 1734.

A Defence of Free-Thinking in Mathematics. 1735.

The Querist (three parts, Dublin, 1735, 1736, 1737; published together in revised form, 1750).

Siris, a chain of Philosophical Reflexions and Inquiries concerning the virtues of Tar-water and divers other subjects connected together and arising one from another. 1744.

Farther Thoughts on Tar-water (published in his Miscellany, 1752).

Collected Works

Editions appeared in 1784, 1820, 1837, 1843, 1871, 1897–8, 1901. The standard edition is that by Fraser, A. Cambbell, 4 vols., Oxford, 1871, revised, 1901. This is the first really complete edition, and contains the Commonplace Book, formerly unknown. Fraser has also published Selections from Berkeley, 1874 (frequently re-edited) and Berkeley (in Blackwood's Phil. Classics), 1881. In these and in the 1901 edition of the Works copious bibliographical references will be found. On the text of the Commonplace Book, see Lorenz, T., in Mind, N. S., vol. XIII, and in Archiv für Ges. d. Phil., vol. XVIII. See, also, Balfour, A. J., biogr. introduction to edition by Sampson, G., vol. I, 1897; Tyler, M. C. Three Men of Letters. (On G. B. and his American visit.) New York, 1895.

III. Other Writers

Vincent Alsop (d. 1703)

Antisozzo. [Against Bp. Sherlock.] 1675.

Duty and Interest united in praise and prayer for Kings. 1695.

God in the Mount. Sermon. 1696.

A Confutation of some of the Errors of D. Williams. 1698.

Peter Annet (1693–1769)

The Resurrection of Jesus considered. 3rd edn. 1744.

A Collection of the Tracts of a certain Free Enquirer. 1739–45.

John Balguy (1686–1748)

A Letter to a Deist concerning the Beauty and Excellency of Moral Virtue. 1726.
The Foundation of Moral Goodness. 1727. Part II, 1728.
A Collection of Tracts, Moral and Theological [containing the above and others].
  1734.
Essay on Redemption. 1741.

Andrew Baxter (1686–1750)

Enquiry into the nature of the Human Soul, wherein the Immateriality of the
  Soul is evinced from the principles of Reason and Philosophy. [1733.]

Richard Bentley

Matter and Motion cannot think; or, a Confutation of Atheism from the faculties of the Soul. 1692.
Remarks upon a late Discourse of Free-thinking. By Phileleutherus Lipsiensis.
  1713.
    See, also, bibliography to Chap. XIII, sec. I, post.

Charles Blount

Anima Mundi. 1679.
Great is Diana of the Ephesians. 1680.
The Two First Books of Philostratus concerning the Life of Apollonius Tyaneus.
  1680.
Miscellaneous Works, with preface by Charles Gildon. 1695.

Henry St. John, Viscount Bolingbroke

Philosophical Works. Ed. Mallet, D. 1754.
    See, also, bibliography to Chaps. VII and VIII, sec. III, ante.

Peter Browne (d. 1735)

Letter in answer to a Book entitled Christianity not Mysterious. 1699.
Procedure, Extent, and Limits of the Human Understanding. 1728.
Things Divine and Supernatural conceived by Analogy with Things Natural
  and Human. 1733.

Joseph Butler

Fifteen Sermons preached at the Chapel of the Rolls Court. 1726.
The Analogy of Religion, Natural and Revealed, to the Constitution and Course
  of Nature. 1736.
Works. Ed. Halifax, S., Oxford, 1849; Gladstone, W. E., Oxford, 1896; Bernard,
  J. H., 1900.

Thomas Chubb (1679–1747)

The Supremacy of the Father asserted. 1715.
A Discourse concerning Reason. 1731.
The True Gospel of Jesus Christ. 1739.
Posthumous Works. 1748.

John Clarke (d. 1730)

An Examination of the [Wollaston's] Notion of Moral Good and Evil. 1725.

The Foundation of Morality in theory and practice. York [1730]. [A criticism of Samuel Clarke.]

An Examination of what has been advanced relating to Moral Obligation. 1730.

An Examination of the Sketch or Plan of an Answer [by C. Middleton] to a Book entitled Christianity as old as the Creation. 1734.

John Clarke (dean of Salisbury) (1682–1757)

An Enquiry into the Cause and Origin of Evil. (Boyle Lecture, 1720.) [Defended the views of his brother, Samuel Clarke.]

Joseph Clarke (d. 1749)

Treatise of Space [a criticism of Samuel Clarke]. 1733.

A further examination of Dr. Clarke's Notions of Space. 1734.

Samuel Clarke

Some Reflections on that part of a book called Amyntor, or a Defence of Milton's Life, which relates to the Writings of the Primitive Fathers, and the Canon of the New Testament. 1699.

A Discourse concerning the Being and Attributes of God, the Obligations of Natural Religion, and the Truth and Certainty of the Christian Revelation. 1705, 1706. [Two courses of Boyle lectures, 1704 and 1705.]

A Letter to Mr. Dodwell, wherein all the arguments in his Epistolary Discourse are particularly answered. 1706.

The Scripture Doctrine of the Trinity. 1712.

A Collection of Papers which passed between the late learned Mr. Leibnitz and Dr. Clarke (to which are added Remarks upon a book entitled A Philosophical Enquiry concerning Human Liberty). 1717.

A Letter to Benjamin Hoadly, F.R.S., occasioned by the controversy relating to the proportion of Velocity and Force in Bodies in Motion. (Phil. Trans. No. 401.) 1728.

Cf. Le Rossignol, J. E., Ethical Philosophy of S. Clarke, Leipzig, 1892; Leroy, G. von, Die phil. Probleme in dem Briefwechsel zw. Leibniz und Clarke. Giessen, 1893.

Arthur Collier

Clavis Universalis: or, a New Inquiry after Truth. Being a Demonstration of the Non-Existence, or Impossibility, of an External World. 1713. (Rptd., Edinburgh, 1836 (with letters to Clarke, etc.); in Parr's Metaphysical Tracts, 1837: Chicago, 1909.)

A Specimen of True Philosophy; in a Discourse on Genesis, the first chapter and the first verse. Sarum, 1730. (Rptd. in Parr's Metaphysical Tracts, 1837.)

Logology, or a Treatise on the Logos or Word of God, in seven sermons on John, i. 1, 2, 3, 14. 1732.

Anthony Collins

Essay concerning the use of Reason in propositions the evidence whereof depends on Human Testimony. 1707.

Priestcraft in Perfection. 1709.

Vindication of the Divine Attributes. 1710.

A Discourse of Free-thinking, occasioned by the Rise and Growth of a Sect called Free-thinkers. 1713.

Inquiry concerning Human Liberty. 1715.
A Discourse of the Grounds and Reasons of the Christian Religion. 1724.
Scheme of Literal Prophecy considered. 1727.
Liberty and Necessity. 1729.

Richard Cumberland (the elder, bishop of Peterborough) (1631–1718)

De legibus Naturae. 1672.
A Brief Disquisition of the Law of Nature. 1692. (Abridged translation by
Tyrrell, J., of Cumberland's De Legibus Naturæ Disquisitio Philosophica.)

William Derham (1657–1735)

Physico-Theology (Boyle lectures). 1713.
Astro-Theology. 1715.
Christo-Theology. 1730.

Henry Dodwell (the elder) (1641–1711)

An Epistolary Discourse proving from the Scriptures and the first Fathers that
the Soul is a principle naturally mortal, but immortalized actually by the
pleasure of God. 1706.
A Preliminary Defence of the Epistolary Discourse. 1707.
The Natural Mortality of Human Souls clearly demonstrated. 1708.

Henry Dodwell (the younger)

Christianity not founded on argument. 1742.

James Hervey (1714–1758)

Collected Works. 6 vols. Edinburgh, 1769. 6 vols. Pontefract, 1805. 6 vols.
1825.
Meditations and Contemplations. 2 pts. 1746–7.
Theron and Aspasio, or a series of dialogues and letters upon the most important
and interesting subjects. 3 vols. 1755.

Benjamin Hoadly (1676–1761)

Works. 3 vols. 1773.
The Reasonableness of Conformity to the Church of England. 1703.
A Persuasive to Lay-Conformity. 1704.
A Defence of the reasonableness of Conformity. 1705.
A Preservative against the principles and practices of the Non-jurors. 1716.
The nature of the Kingdom or Church of Christ. 1717.
An Answer to the Representation drawn up by the Committee of the Lower House
of Convocation. 1718.

Francis Hutcheson

An Inquiry into the Original of our Ideas of Beauty and Virtue, in two treatises.
1725.
An Essay on the Nature and Conduct of the Passions and Affections, with Il-
lustrations on the Moral Sense. 1728. (French trans., Amsterdam, 1749;
German trans., Frankfort, 1762.)
Philosophiæ moralis institutio compendiaria. Glasgow, 1742. (English trans.,
Glasgow, 1747.)

Metaphysicæ Synopsis. Glasgow, 1742.
A System of Moral Philosophy. Glasgow, 1755.
Logicæ Compendium. Glasgow, 1756.
    Cf. Fowler, T., Shaftesbury and Hutcheson, 1882; Scott, **W. R.**, Francis Hutcheson, Cambridge, 1900.

John Jackson (1686–1763)

The Existence and Unity of God proved from his Nature and Attributes [a defence of Clarke]. 1734.

Samuel Johnson (1649–1703)

Works. 1710. 2nd edn. 1713.
Julian the Apostate. 1682.
An Humble and hearty Address to all the English Protestants in the present army. 1686.
Julian's Arts to undermine and extirpate Christianity. 1689.
An Argument proving that the abrogation of K. James from the regal throne was according to the Constitution. 1692.

Nathaniel Lardner (1684–1768)

Works, with life by A. Kippis. 11 vols. 1788. New edn. 10 vols. 1838.
The Credibility of the Gospel history. 17 vols. 1727–57.
A large collection of ancient Jewish and Heathen testimonies to the truth of the Christian Revelation. 4 vols. 1764–7.

Edmund Law (1703–1787)

An Essay on the Origin of Evil. By [Abp.] W. King. Translated from the Latin, with notes. 1731.
Inquiry into the Ideas of Space, Time, Immensity and Eternity. Cambridge, 1734.

William Law (1686–1761)

Remarks upon a late Book entituled the Fable of the Bees. 1723.
The Case of Reason, or Natural Religion, fairly and fully stated. 1732.
    See, also, bibliography to Chap. XII, *post.*

John Leland (1691–1766)

The Divine Authority of the Old and New Testament asserted. 2 vols. 1739–40.
Remarks on [H. Dodwell's] Christianity not founded on Argument. 1744.
A Defence of Christianity. 2nd edn. 1753.
The Advantage and Necessity of the Christian Revelation. 2 vols. 1764.

Charles Leslie (1650–1722)

Theological works. 2 vols. 1721. 7 vols. Oxford, 1832.
The Snake in the Grass. 1696.
A Short and Easy method with the Deists. 1698. 5th edn. 1712.

Bernard Mandeville

Treatise of the Hypochondriack and Hysterick Passions. 1711.

The Fable of the Bees; or Private Vices, Public Benefits. 1714. (With An
Essay on Charity and Charity Schools, and A Search into the Nature of
Society, 1723.)
Free Thoughts on Religion. 1720.
The Origin of Honour, and the Usefulness of Christianity in War. 1732.

Cf. Sakmann, P., Mandeville und die Bienenfabel-Controverse. Freiburg
i/B., 1897.

John Mill (1645–1707)

Novum Testamentum cum lectionibus variantibus J. Millii. **1707.**

Thomas Morgan (d. 1743)

Philosophical Principles of Medicine. 1725.
A Collection of Tracts. 1726.
The Moral Philosopher. In a Dialogue between Philalethes a Christian Deist,
and Theophanes a Christian Jew. 1737.
—— Vol. ii. Being a farther Vindication of Moral Truth and Reason. 1739.
—— Vol. iii. Superstition and Tyranny inconsistent with Theocracy. 1740.

Anthony Astley Cooper, third Earl of Shaftesbury

Characteristics of Men, Manners, Opinions, Times, 1711; 2nd edn., 1713. (New
reprint by J. M. Robertson, 1900; French trans., 1769; German trans.,
1776–9.)
Letters to a Young Man at the University. 1716.

Cf. Brown, J., Essays on The Characteristics, 1751; Gi'zycki, G. v., Die
Phil. Shaftesbury's, Berlin, 1876; Zart, G., Einfluss d. engl. Phil. seit Bacon
auf die deutsche Phil. d. 18ten Jahrhunderts, Berlin, 1881; Fowler, T., Shaftesbury and Hutcheson, 1882; Rand, B., Life, Letters, and Philosophical Regimen
of Shaftesbury, 1900 [contains much material formerly unpublished].

Thomas Sherlock (1678–1761)

Works. Ed. Hughes, T. S. 5 vols. 1830.
The Use and Intent of Prophecy. 1725.
The Tryal of the Witnesses of the Resurrection of Jesus Christ. 1729. 16th
edn. 1807.
Discourses at the Temple Church. 4 vols. 1754–8. Vol. v. Oxford, 1797.

Matthew Tindal

Essay of Obedience to the Supreme Powers. 1694.
Essay on the Power of the Magistrate and the Rights of Mankind in Matters
of Religion. 1697.
The Liberty of the Press. 1698.
The Rights of the Christian Church. 1706.
Four Discourses on Obedience, Laws of Nations, Power of the Magistrate and
Liberty of the Press. 1709.
A Defence of the Rights of the Christian Church. 2nd edn. 1709. [Burned
by order of the House of Commons, 1710.]
Christianity as old as the Creation; or the Gospel a Republication of the Religion
of Nature. 1730. (German trans., 1741.)

John Toland

Christianity not mysterious.   1696.
Life of Milton.   1698.
Amyntor, or a Defence of Milton's Life.   1699.
The Art of Governing by Parties.   1701.
Anglia Libera.   1701.
Vindicius Liberius.   1702.
Letters to Serena.   1704.
An Account of the Courts of Prussia and Hanover.   1705.
Adeisidæmon.   The Hague, 1709.
Origines Judaicæ.   The Hague, 1709.
Nazarenus, or Jewish, Gentile and Mahometan Christianity.   1718.
Tetradymus.   1720.
Pantheisticon, sive Formula celebrandæ Sodalitatis Socraticæ.   1720.
A Collection of Several Pieces of Mr. John Toland (with life by Des Maizeaux).
     1726.

> *Cf.* Berthold, G., Johann Toland und der Monismus der Gegenwart.   1876.

William Wake (1657–1737)

Sermons.   1690.
The Genuine Epistles of the Apostolic Fathers. . . .   Transl. with discussions
     by W. Wake.   1693.
Principles of the Christian religion.   1699.
The State of the Church and Clergy of England.   1703.

William Warburton (*bishop of Gloucester*)

Works.   Ed. Hurd, R. (bishop of Worcester).   7 vols.   1788.
The Alliance between Church and State.   1736.   10th edn. 1846.
The Divine Legation of Moses demonstrated on the principles of a Religious
     Deist.   In six books.   2 vols.   1738–41.   9th edn. 1765 (as vols III–V in
     continuation of the 2 vols. of the 4th edn. of the first part).
A Commentary on Mr. Pope's Essay on Man.   1739.   Remodelled as A Critical
     and Philosophical Commentary on Mr. Pope's Essay. . . .   1742.
The Works of Shakespear . . . with Comments and Notes by Mr. Pope and Mr.
     Warburton.   8 vols.   1747.
A Letter to the Editor of the Letters on the Spirit of Patriotism.   1749.
A View of Lord Bolingbroke's Philosophy in four Letters to a Friend.   1754–5.
The Doctrine of Grace, or the Office and Operation of the Holy Spirit vindicated
     from the Insults of Infidelity and the Abuses of Fanaticism.   2 vols.   1762.

Daniel Waterland (1683–1740)

Collected works, with life by W. van Mildert.   12 vols.   Oxford, 1823–8.
A Vindication of Christ's divinity.   1719.   A Second Vindication.   1723.   A
     Farther Vindication.   1724.
A Critical History of the Athanasian Creed.   1723.

William Whiston (1667–1752)

A New theory of the Earth.   1696.
A Short View of the Chronology of the Old Testament.   Camb. 1702.
The Accomplishment of Scripture prophecies.   Camb. 1708.

Primitive Christianity revived.　5 vols.　1711–12.
Historical memoirs of the life and writings of Dr. Samuel Clarke.　1730.
The Works of Josephus translated.　1737.
Memoirs of the life and writings of Mr. Whiston, written by himself.　2 vols.
　　1749–50.

William Wollaston (1660–1724)

The Religion of Nature Delineated.　1722.
　　Cf. Drechsler, Ueber Wollaston's Moralphil.　Erlangen, 1802.

Thomas Woolston

The Old Apology for the Truth of the Christian Religion . . . revived　1705.
The Moderator between an Infidel and an Apostate.　1725.
Discourses.　1727–9.

CHAPTER XII

WILLIAM LAW AND THE MYSTICS

I. WILLIAM LAW

A. *Collected Works*

Works.　9 vols.　Printed for J. Richardson, 1753–76.　[All references have been
　　given to this edition, as it is the one usually in libraries.]　Ed. Morgan, G. B.
　　Privately ptd. for Moreton, G. (i. e. Morgan, G. B.), Setley, Brockenhurst,
　　New Forest, Hampshire, 1892–3.

B. *Separate Works*

A Sermon Preach'd at Hazelingfield, . . . On Tuesday, July 7, 1713. . . . By
　　W. Law, M. A.　[Not reprinted in the collected editions of Law's works.]
The Bishop of Bangor's late Sermon and his Letter to Dr. Snape in Defence of
　　it, Answer'd. . . .　1717.
A Second Letter to the Bishop of Bangor. . . .　1717.
A Reply to the Bishop of Bangor's Answer to the Representation of the Com-
　　mittee of Convocation. . . .　1719.
Remarks upon A Late Book, Entituled, The Fable of the Bees. . . .　1724.
The Absolute Unlawfulness of the Stage-Entertainment Fully Demonstrated
　　. . 1726.
A Practical Treatise upon Christian Perfection. . . .　1726.
A Serious Call to a Devout and Holy Life.　Adapted to the State and Condition
　　of All Orders of Christians. . . .　1729.
The Case of Reason, or Natural Religion, Fairly and Fully Stated.　In Answer
　　to a Book, Entitul'd Christianity as old as the Creation. . . .　1731.
A Demonstration of the Gross and Fundamental Errors Of a late Book, called
　　A Plain Account of the Nature and End of the Sacrament of the Lord's
　　Supper, &c. . . .　1737.
The Grounds and Reasons of Christian Regeneration, or, the New-Birth. . . .
　　1739.
An Earnest and Serious Answer to Dr. Trapp's Discourse of the Folly, Sin, and
　　Danger, of being Righteous over-much. . . .　1740.

An Appeal to all that Doubt, or Disbelieve The Truths of the Gospel. . . . To
which are added, Some Animadversions upon Dr. Trapp's Late Reply. . . .
1740.
The Spirit of Prayer; or, The Soul rising out of the Vanity of Time, into the
Riches of Eternity. In Two Parts. Part I. 1749. Part II. 1750.
The Way to Divine Knowledge. . . . 1752.
The Spirit of Love. Part the First. 1752. The Second Part. 1754.
A Short but Sufficient Confutation of . . . Warburton's Projected Defence (As
he calls it) of Christianity, in his Divine Legation of Moses. . . . 1757.
Of Justification by Faith and Works. A Dialogue between A Methodist and
A Churchman. . . . 1760.
A Collection of Letters. . . . 1760. [In which is included (pp. 141–62) a tract
called Christian Piety, freed from The many Delusions of Modern En-
thusiasts. . . . By Philalethes, 2nd edn., 1756.]
An Humble, Earnest, and Affectionate Address to the Clergy. . . . 1761.
Letters to a Lady inclined to enter into the Communion of the Church of Rome.
. . . 1779.
    [These were written in 1731–2, to Miss Dodwell, daughter of Henry
Dodwell, the nonjuror, but were not published until 1779. They are therefore not in the collected edition of the Works, 1762. *See* Morgan's edition,
1892–3.]
    [Three more letters written by Law [to Langcake?] in 1749, 1750, and 1753,
were printed in]
A Serious and Affectionate Address to All Orders of Men. . . . Bath: . . . 1781.

C. *Modern Reprints of Single Works (Selected List)*

Remarks on the Fable of the Bees, with an Introduction by Maurice, F. D.
Cambridge, 1844.
A Serious Call. Ed. Overton, J. H. 1898. Ed. Bigg, C. 1899.
Liberal and Mystical Writings of William Law. Edd. Scott Palmer, W. and
Du Bose, W. P. 1908.

D. *Unpublished MSS.*

The Walton Collection in Dr. Williams's Library, Gordon Square, W. C. [This
is a unique and valuable collection, made by Christopher Walton (1809–77),
an ardent admirer of Law and Boehme. It consists (*a*) of MSS., (*b*) of printed
books. The MSS. are principally: unpublished MSS. and letters of Law
(*see* 1146. I. I. 75; II. 10, II. 11); letters written to Law by various people;
Freher's writings and drawings, of which there are duplicates in the B. M.
(*see* under Freher, below); copies of Freher's works in Law's handwriting;
Dr. Francis Lee's MSS. (*see* under Lee, below); a mass of Walton's own
MSS., preparatory to his projected work on Law, Boehme, Freher, Lee and
other mystics. The printed books are a valuable collection of mystical
writings, of the seventeenth and eighteenth centuries principally.]

E. *Controversial Works answered by Law or connected*
with his Writings

(1) *Bangorian Controversy.*

Hickes, George. The Constitution of the Catholick Church, and the Nature
and Consequences of Schism. . . . 1716.

Hoadly, Benjamin (bp. of Bangor and of Winchester). A Preservative against
    the Principles and Practices of the Nonjurors. . . . 1716.
—— The Nature of the Kingdom, or Church, of Christ. . . . 1717.
—— An Answer to the Representation drawn up by the Committee of the Lower-
    House of Convocation. . . . 1718.
—— A Plain Account of the Nature and End of the Sacrament of the Lord's-
    Supper. . . . 1735.
—— The Works of Benjamin Hoadly, D.D. 3 vols. . . . 1773.
Philanagnostes Criticus. An Account of the Pamphlets in the Bangorian Con-
    troversy (1719). Hoadly's Works, vol. II, pp. 381–401.
Prat, D. A review of the writers in the controversy with the Bishop of Bangor.
    . . . 1717.
        For further literature on this subject, see B. M. catalogue, under Hoadly,
    also under Gilbert Burnet, Thomas Pyle, John Jackson and A. Snape; and
    cf. Figgis, J. Neville, Hoadly and the Bangorian Controversy, The Guardian,
    11 Oct., 1905, p. 1679.

(2) *Attack on the Stage.*

Dennis, John. The Stage Defended, . . . Occasion'd by Mr. Law's late
    Pamphlet against Stage-Entertainments. . . . 1726.
Law Outlaw'd: Or, A Short Reply to Mr. Law's Long Declamation against
    the Stage. . . . 1726.

(3) *Reply to Mandeville.*

Mandeville, Bernard de. The Fable of the Bees: or, Private Vices Publick
    Benefits. . . . 1714.
[The poem was first printed in 1705, in a 6d. pamphlet, under the title The
Grumbling Hive; or Knaves turn'd Honest.]

(4) *The Deist Controversy.*

[Tindal, Matthew.] Christianity as old as the Creation. Vol. I. 1730. [The
    second volume was destroyed in MS. by bp. Gibson, to whom it had been
    bequeathed.]

(5) *Answer to Dr. Trapp.*

Trapp, Joseph. The Nature, Folly, Sin, and Danger of being Righteous over-
    much; with a particular view to the Doctrines and Practices of certain
    Modern Enthusiasts. 3rd edn. . . . 1739.

(6) *Warburton.*

Warburton, William (bp. of Gloucester). The Divine Legation of Moses. . . .
    2 vols. 1738–41.
—— The Works of William Warburton. 7 vols. . . . 1788. [For Warburton's
    remarks about Law, see specially The Doctrine of Grace, Works, vol. IV,
    pp. 565, 624, 626, 699-707.]
Payne, John. A Letter occasioned by the Lord Bishop of Gloucester's Doctrine
    of Grace. . . . 1763.
Hartley, Thomas. A Short Defence of the Mystical Writers; against some
    Reflections in a late Work, intitled The Doctrine of Grace; [appended to]
    Paradise Restored. . . . 1764.
Horne, George (bp. of Norwich). Cautions to the Readers of Mr. Law. (c. 1750?)
    [Printed in Appendix to] Memoirs of George Horne, . . . by William Jones.
    . . . 1795, pp. 198–204.
—— A Letter to a Lady on the Subject of Jacob Behmen's Writings. April 8,
    1758. [In Appendix, *ibid.* pp. 205-21, see, also, *ibid.* pp. 73-4.]

F. *Biographical and Critical Works*

A Letter to Mr. Law; Occasion'd by reading his Treatise on Christian Perfection:
By a Lover of Mankind. . . . 1728.

A Short Account of the two charitable Foundations at Kings-Cliffe, Stamford.
1755.

Article on Law in Chalmers's Biographical Dictionary, vol. xx, 1815.

Four Letters on Law and his works (by W. Hamilton Reid, Z. Cozens, "Ouranius"
and "Theophilus") in The Gentleman's Magazine, Nov. 1800, pp.
1038–41.

[Langcake, Thomas.] A Serious and Affectionate Address to all orders of Men
. . . in which are earnestly recommended the Works of . . . . William
Law. . . . Bath . . . 1781.

[Moreton, G.] Memorials of the Birthplace and Residence of . . . Law at
King's Cliffe. . . . Guildford, 1895.

Overton, J. H. The Nonjurors, their lives, principles and writings. 1902.

—— William Law, Nonjuror and Mystic. 1881.

Tighe, Richard. A Short account of the Life and Writings of . . . Law. . . .
1813.

[Walton, Christopher.] Notes and Materials for an adequate Biography of
. . . Law. . . . 1854.

[A mine of information in all that relates to Law and Boehme, as well as
to many other mystics, principally of the eighteenth century. The part
more directly relating to Law will be found imbedded in a footnote, which
runs from p. 334 to p. 628.]

II. FOLLOWERS OF LAW

A. *John Byrom*

An Epistle to a gentleman of the Temple. . . . 1749.

Enthusiasm; a Poetical Essay. 1751.

Miscellaneous Poems. 2 vols. Manchester. 1773. Rptd. at Leeds, 1814.
Francis Okely collected and printed those of Byrom's poems which are
paraphrased from Law, under the title:

Seasonably Alarming and Humiliating . . . Truths . . . in a Metrical Version
of certain select passages taken from the works of . . . William Law. . . .
1774.

The Private Journal and Literary Remains of John Byrom. Ed. Parkinson,
R. 4 vols. Chetham Society. 1854–7.

The Poems of John Byrom. Ed. Ward, A. W. 2 vols. Chetham Society.
Manchester, 1894–5. [A third volume is about to appear.]

A Catalogue of the Library of the late John Byrom. . . . 1848. [Contains a
valuable list of contemporary and earlier mystical and theological books,
tracts and pamphlets.]

Stephen, Sir Leslie. John Byrom. Studies of a Bibliographer, vol. I. 1898.

B. *Henry Brooke*

The Fool of Quality; or the History of Henry Earl of Moreland. In four volumes. . . . 1766. Vol. v, 1770. Ed. Kingsley, Charles. 2 vols. 1859.
Rpt. in one vol. Routledge, 1906. [All references are given to this latter edn.]

The History of Henry, Earl of Moreland. 1781. [Abridged and edited by John Wesley.]
Poetical Works. 3rd edn. 4 vols. Dublin, 1792. [With life of Brooke.]

Brooke, Richard Sinclair. Article on Henry Brooke in Dublin University Magazine, Feb., 1852.

III. OTHER ENGLISH MYSTICS AND FOLLOWERS OF BOEHME IN THE SEVENTEENTH AND EIGHTEENTH CENTURIES

A. *Thomas Bromley* (d. 1691)

The Way to the Sabbath of Rest, or the Soul's Progress in the work of the New-Birth. . . . 1710. [First published *c.* 1678?, a 2nd edn. in 1692.]

B. *George Cheyne* (1671–1743)

Philosophical Principles of Natural Religion. . . . 1705; 2nd edn., corrected and enlarged. . . . 1715.
Dr. Cheyne's own Account of Himself and of his writings. . . . 1743.

C. *Jane Lead* (1623–1704)

[For list of works, published between 1681 and 1704, *see* D. of N. B. *See, also*, art in British Quarterly Review, vol. LVIII, pp. 181–7.]

D. *Francis Lee* (1661–1719)

ΑΠΟΛΕΙΠΟΜΕΝΑ, or, Dissertations. 2 vols. . . . 1752.
[A paraphrase or enlargement of Boehme's Supersensual Life, printed in "Law's edn." of Boehme, and said by the editors to be by Law, vol. IV, 1781, *q. v.*, below. The MS. of this, in Lee's writing, is in Dr. Williams's library, II. 8.]
The Last Hours of Jane Lead, by an Eye and Ear Witness. [No English edn. of this is now to be found, although a German translation of it was published at Amsterdam. A MS. re-translation into English is in Dr. Williams's library, C. 5. 30.]
Mystical poems [in Jane Lead's works]. These are almost certainly by Lee. See Notes and Queries, Ser. IV, vol. XII, p. 381.

For many other books by Lee published anonymously, *see* Dictionary of National Biography, vol. XXXII.
Unpublished MSS. from his hand are preserved in Dr. Williams's library, C. 5, 30, II. 8, II. 6.
Secretan, C. F. Memoirs of the Life and Times of the pious Robert Nelson. 1860 [pp. 69–71, and chap. III].
[Though Law had little sympathy with the "Philadelphians" (*see below*) of which society Lee was a member, he was deeply interested in Lee's writings. He obtained Lee's MSS. about 1740, and copied out many of them, and the MSS. were found among Law's papers after his death. Walton procured them from Miss Gibbon's successors, and deposited them in Dr. Williams's library, where they now are. *See* Walton's Notes, pp. 225, 505. For an account of Lee, *see* Overton's William Law, pp. 408–10, as well as Lee's Dissertations, and Secretan's Life of Nelson.]

E. *Morgan Llwyd* (1619–1659)

[A Welsh puritan divine and mystic writer, who, during the civil war, was with the Parliamentary forces in England, probably as chaplain. He must undoubtedly have known Boehme, and he wrote many books in Welsh which are full of Boehme's philosophy; more especially:]

Llyfr y tri Aderyn (Book of the Three Birds). 1653. Rptd. by Dent, MCM. Ed. Owen Jones. 1889.

An English translation of the above by Parry, L. J., was published in the Transactions of the National Eisteddfod of Wales, Llandudno, 1896, pp. 195 ff.

[One book in English is attributed to Llwyd:]

Lazarus and his Sisters Discoursing of Paradise: . . . 1655. [A MS. copy of this in Francis Lee's writing was found among Law's papers, and is now in Dr. Williams's library.]

For an account of Morgan Llwyd and his writings, with extracts from the Three Birds, *see* Palmer, A. N., A History of the Older Nonconformity of Wrexham and its Neighbourhood, Wrexham, 1888.

For a fine appreciation of him by a contemporary, *see* A Winding Sheet for Mr. Baxter's Dead . . . being an Apology for several ministers. . . . 1685.

F. *Philadelphian Society* (1697–1703)

Propositions . . . extracted from the Reasons for the Foundation . . . of a Philadelphian Society. . . . 1697.

The State of the Philadelphian Society. . . . 1697. [By Philadelphus, *i. e.* Francis Lee.]

Theosophical Transactions of the Philadelphian Society. Nos. 1–5. . . . 1697.

See a good article on the Philadelphian Society in The Dawn (London), Dec., 1862, pp. 236–42.

[This society, founded in 1697, and dissolved in 1703, was formed in order "to cultivate spiritual and practical piety, founded on the study of Jacob Behmen." Its principal members were Mrs. Jane Lead; Dr. Francis Lee, *q. v.*, and Thomas Bromley. For Law's views on it see Animadversions, Works, VI, p. 313, and Walton's Notes, p. 370, also letter to Langcake, *ibid.* pp. 45–6. See also correspondence of Henry Dodwell and Francis Lee, 1698–9, in Walton's Notes, pp. 188–232.]

G. *Richard Roach* (1662–1730)

The Great Crisis. . . . 1725. [Published 1726.] [Interesting for an account of contemporary mystics, the Philadelphian Society, etc.]

The Imperial Standard of Messiah Triumphant. . . . [1727.]

H. *Thomas Tryon* (1634–1703)

The Way to Health. . . . 1691. Tryon's Letters. . . . 1700. The Knowledge of a Man's Self. . . . 1703. Some Memoirs of the Life of Mr. Tho. Tryon [mostly by himself]. 1705. And other works.

Gordon, Alex. A Pythagorean of the seventeenth century. [A paper.] 1871.

[Tryon is an interesting person, a student of Pythagoras and of Boehme. He was read by Byrom (Journal, vol. I, pt. 2, p. 615), and was doubtless known to Law.]

IV. Foreign Influences

A. *Jacob Boehme* (1575–1624)

[Although Boehme wrote some 32 works, only one small volume, Weg zu Christo (= (13), (14), (15) in list below), was published during his lifetime. His MSS. went to Holland, and were printed one by one at Amsterdam, principally by Heinrich Beets, a Dutch merchant, between the years 1633–76. Beets's editions date from 1656–77. Three of his works, Christ's Testaments, the Book of Prayer, and 177 Theosophic Questions, were also printed at Dresden, 1641, 1642. The first collected edition of Boehme was edited by Gichtel, J. G., Amsterdam, 1682. His works—which must have been circulated in MS.—were translated into English, by John Sparrow, John Ellistone, Humphrey Blunden and Charles and Durand Hotham, and published in London between the years 1645–62. Some of his books have rather long titles, and, in the various lists given of them, are not always called by the same name, nor are the same treatises always published together, which is confusing. Below is given a complete list of his works in the order in which he wrote them, followed by the titles of the English translations. For the best account of Boehme's writings, see Hamberger's Jacob Böhme, 1844.]

(1) Collected Editions

German.

Des Gottseeligen Hoch Erleuchteten Jacob Böhmens Teutonici Philosophi Alle Theosophische Wercken. [Ed. Gichtel, J. G.] Amsterdam, 1682 and 1715.

Theosophia revelata. Das ist: Alle göttliche Schriften . . . J. Böhmens. Anbey mit . . . J. G. Gichtels . . . Summarien . . . ausgezieret. 7 vols. Amsterdam, 1730–1. [This is the best and fullest edn. of Boehme.]

Jakob Böhme's sämmtliche Werke herausgegeben von K. W. Schiebler. 7 vols. Leipzig, 1831–46.

English.

[There is no complete English edition of Boehme's works, although the various translations published between 1644–62 make up a complete edition, with several works duplicated. The 4 vols. 4to of 1764–81, generally called "Law's edition," contain only 17 out of Boehme's 32 works. This edition was not edited by Law, but by his friends George Ward and Thomas Langcake, who published it after Law's death, at the cost of Mrs. Hutcheson. They rptd. it in the main, with some few alterations, from the earlier English editions by Sparrow. Below is the title of this edition, and its contents.]

The works of Jacob Behmen, The Teutonic Theosopher. Volume I containing, I The Aurora. II The Three Principles. To which is prefixed, The Life of the Author. With Figures, illustrating his Principles, left by the Reverend William Law, M. A. 1764. [Vol. III. 1772. Vol. IV. 1781.]

On pp. v–vi of vol. I there is A Dialogue between Zelotes, Alphabetus, Rusticus and Theophilus, almost certainly by Law.

Altogether, the following works are printed in this edition (see complete list): vol. I, (1), (2); vol. II, (3), (4), (5), (31); vol. III, (19), (20); vol. IV, (9), (17), (13), (14), (15), (21), (24), (10), (23).

A complete reprint of Boehme's works in English is now in hand, ed. by Barker, C. J., the first two volumes of which, The Threefold Life of Man, and The Three Principles, have already been published.

(2) Complete list of Jacob Boehme's Works in the order in which he wrote them

(1) 1612. The Aurora [unfinished]. With Notes added by his own hand, in 1620. (2) 1619. The Three Principles of the Divine Essence. With an Appendix Concerning the Threefold Life of Man. (3) 1620. The Threefold Life of Man. (4) 1620. Answers to Forty Questions Concerning the Soul, proposed by Dr. Balthasar Walter. With an Appendix Concerning the Soul and its Image, and of the Turba. (5) 1620. The Treatise of the Incarnation; in 3 parts. (i) Of the Incarnation of Jesus Christ. (ii) Of the Suffering, Dying, Death, and Resurrection of Christ. (iii) Of the Tree of Faith. (6) 1620. A Book of the Great Six Points. Also a small book of other Six Points. (7) 1620. Of the Earthly and of the Heavenly Mystery. (8) 1620. Of the Last Times. [2 Epistles to P[aul] K[eym], included in (32) i.] (9) 1621. De Signatura Rerum. (10) 1621. Of the Four Complexions. (11) 1621. Two Apologies to Balthasar Tylcken: (i) for the Aurora, (ii) for Predestination and the Incarnation. (12) 1621. Considerations upon Esaiah Stiefel's Book concerning the Threefold State of Man, and the New Birth. (13) 1622. A Book of True Repentance. (14) 1622. A Book of True Resignation. (15) 1622. A Book of Regeneration. (16) 1622. The Apology in answer to Esaiah Stiefel concerning Perfection. (17) 1623. A Book of Predestination and Election. (18) 1623. A Short Compendium of Repentance. (19) 1623. Mysterium Magnum. (20) 1623. A Table of the Divine Manifestation, or an Exposition of the Threefold World. (21) 1624. The Super-sensual [or super-rational] life. (22) 1624. Of Divine Contemplation or Vision [unfinished]. (23) 1624. Of Christ's Testaments, viz.: Baptism and the Supper. (24) 1624. A Dialogue between an enlightened and unenlightened Soul [or the Discourse of Illumination]. (25) 1624. An Apology in Answer to Gregory Richter [*i. e.* for the Books of True Repentance and True Resignation]. (26) 1624. 177 Theosophic Questions, with answers to 13 of them [unfinished]. (27) 1624. An Epitome of the Mysterium Magnum. (28) 1624. The Holy Week or a Prayer Book [unfinished]. (29) 1624. A Table of the Three Principles. (30) 1624. A Book of the Last Judgment [lost]. (31) 1624. The Clavis. (32) 1618–24. Sixty-two Theosophic Epistles. (i) 35 Epistles. (ii) 25 Epistles. (iii) 2 other Epistles (nos. 7 and 20 in German edn.), one forefixed to The Super-sensual Life (21), the other forms the Preface to the second Apology to B. Tylcken (11).

(3) English Translations

(For corresponding numbers *see* IV, A, (2), *ante*.)

Two Theosophicall Epistles: . . . Whereunto is added, A Dialogue between an Enlightened and a Distressed Soule. . . . 1645. Epistles 1 and 10 of (32) i and (24).

XL Questions concerning the Soule. Propounded by Dr. Balthasar Walter. And Answered, By Jacob Behmen. . . . 1647 [reissue slightly altered in] 1665. [Translated by Sparrow.] (4).

The Clavis, or Key, or, An Exposition of some principall Matters, and words in the writings of Jacob Behmen. . . . 1647. (31).

The Second Booke. Concerning The Three Principles of The Divine Essence. . . . 1648. [With] An Appendix or . . . Description of the Threefold Life in Man. [Translated by Sparrow, with preface by him.] (2).

The Way to Christ Discovered. . . . 1648, and 1654. (13), (14), (15), Epistle
1 of (32) iii, (21), (24), (18), chap. xv of (3) and Epistle 32 of (32) i, are all
included here. [Translated by Blunden.]

The Fourth Epistle. A Letter to Paul Keym: Being An answer to him concerning Our Last Times. . . . The Fifth Epistle. Another Letter to Paul
Keym. . . . 1649. [Translated by Sparrow.] Epistles 4 and 5 in (32) i.

The Epistles of Jacob Behmen. . . . 1649. [35 Epistles translated by Ellistone.] (32) i.

The High and Deep Searching Out of The Threefold Life of Man through [or
according to] The Three Principles. . . . Englished by J. Sparrow. . . .
1650. (3).

Signatura Rerum: . . . 1651. [Translated by Ellistone.] (9).

Of Christs Testaments, viz.: Baptisme and the Supper. Englished by John
Sparrow. . . . 1652. (23).

A Consideration Upon the Book of Esaias Stiefel of the Threefold State of Man
and his New Birth. . . . 1653. (12).

Mysterium Magnum or An Exposition of the First Book of Moses called Genesis.
. . . 1654. Fol. [Trans. Ellistone and Sparrow.] (19) and (27).

The Tree of Christian Faith. . . . MDCXLIV (1654?). iii of (5).

Four Tables of Divine Revelation. . . . Englished by H. B. . . . 1654. Fol.
[The first of these Tables is (20), the second, third and fourth are (29).]

A Consolatory Treatise of the Four Complexions. . . . 1654. [Preface by
Ch. Hotham.] (10).

Jacob Behme's Table, Of the Divine Manifestation. Or An Exposition of The
Threefold World. . . . 1655. [Sparrow.] (20).

Concerning the Election of Grace. . . . 1655. [With] An Appendix To the
Book of Election. [Preface by Sparrow.] (17).

Aurora. That is, the Day-Spring. . . . By Jacob Behme. . . . 1656. [Pre-
face by Sparrow.] (1).

The Fifth Book of the Authour. . . . 1659. [Preface by Sparrow.] (5).

Several Treatises of Jacob Behme. . . . Englished by John Sparrow. . . . 1661.
(6), (26), (7), (28), (22), (29), letter 6 of (32) i, re-translated.

The Remainder of Books written By Jacob Behme. Englished by John Sparrow.
. . . 1662. (32) iii and (11), (10), (12), (16), (25), (32), ii.

The Way to Christ Discovered. . . . Manchester. . . . 1752. [A reprint by
Byrom of Blunden's edn., 1648.]

The Way to Christ . . . also . . . the Four Complexions. Bath, 1775. [With
preface; a different translation from H. Blunden's, 1648 and 1654.]

(4) Biographical and Critical

[The earliest (and best) life of Boehme is that written by his friend Abraham
von Franckenberg, in the printed editions always dated 1651, but written by
Franckenberg (in Latin) in 1637. It reached Amsterdam, and was translated
into German as early as 1638—and probably was circulated in MS. (see a letter
from "E. H." from Görlitz, 21 Feb., 1669, printed by Francis Okely, in his Memoirs of J. B., 1780, p. 122). It is printed in many editions of Boehme's works,
as, for instance, in the Forty Questions, pub. 1665 in London, or in German,
in the 1682 edition, Amsterdam, and it forms the basis of all the other lives,
such as the earliest English one below, or that prefixed to "Law's edition."
For a collection (translated into English) of all documents giving firsthand information as to Boehme's life and work, see Francis Okely's Memoirs, 1780,
below.]

Anderdon. J. One Blow at Babel in those of the People called Behmenites. Whose Foundation is . . . upon their own Carnal Conceptions, begotten in their Imaginations upon Jacob Behmen's Writings. . . . 1662.

Boutroux, E. Le Philosophe allemand Jacob Boehme. Paris, Alcan, 1888.

Brockhaus' Konversations-Lexikon. Leipzig, 1892. New edn. 1901. Article, Böhme.

Deussen, Paul. Jakob Böhme. Über sein Leben und seine Philosophie. Kiel, 1897.

Ederheimer, E. Jakob Böhme und die Romantiker. [Heidelberg, 1904.] [J. B.'s influence on Tieck and Novalis.]

Fechner, H. A. Jakob Böhme, sein Leben und seine Schriften, in Neues Lausitzches Magazin, vol. XXXIII, pp. 313–446. Görlitz, 1857. [Reviewed in Saturday Review, 12 July, 1873.]

Hamberger, Julius. Die Lehre des deutschen Philosophen Jakob Böhme. . . . Munich, 1844.

Harless, G. C. A. von. Jakob Böhme und die Alchymisten. . . . Berlin, 1870.

Hartmann, F. The Life and Doctrines of . . . Jacob Boehme, 1891.

Hotham, Charles. Ad Philosophiam Teutonicam Manuductio. . . . 1648. Translated under title: Introduction to the Teutonick Philosophie. Being a Determination concerning the Original of the Soul. . . . By C. Hotham, one of the Fellows of Peter-House. . . . 1650. [Hotham later (1654) translated the Four Complexions.]

Hotham, Durand. The Life of Jacob Behmen, written by Durand Hotham, Esquire, Novemb., 1653. . . . 1654.

    As to Charles Hotham and his brother, *see* Mullinger, J. Bass, The University of Cambridge, vol. III, p. 418.

Life, The, of one Jacob Boehmen: Who although he were a Very Meane man, yet wrote the most Wonderful deepe Knowledge in Naturall and Divine Things That any hath been knowne to doe since the Apostles Times. . . . 1644.

Martensen, H. L. Jacob Boehme: his life and teaching . . . translated from the Danish by T. Rhys Evans. 1885. [Reviewed in Saturday Review, 26 June, 1886, pp. 895–6.]

Mecurius Teutonicus. . . . Being Divers Prophetical Passages . . . Gathered out of the mysticall Writings of . . . Behmen. . . . 1649 and 1656.

[More, Henry.] Philosophiæ Teutonicæ Censura. 1670.

Okely, Francis. Memoirs of the Life, Death, Burial and Wonderful Writings of Jacob Behmen. . . . Northampton, 1780.

Penny, Mrs. A. J. An Introduction to the Study of Jacob Boehme's writings. New York, 1901. [Essays collected from Light and Life, Nov., Dec., 1885, and Feb., 1887, and from Light, and printed privately by Grace Shaw Duff. Most valuable for serious study, but unfortunately not in the B. M.]

Poiret, Pierre. Petri Poiret Bibliotheca Mysticorum selecta. . . . Amsterdam, 1708. [Jacob Boehme, pp. 162–76, 186.]

P[ordage], J. A Treatise of Eternal Nature with Her seven Essential Forms, . . . J. P. M.D. . . . 1681. [An account of Boehme's philosophy by Dr. Pordage, bound up with "Theologia Mystica. . . . By J. P. M.D. . . . 1683," and not separately catalogued in B. M.]

Taylor, E. J. Behmen's Theosophick philosophy unfolded. 1691.

Theological and Practical Divinity: with Extracts of several Treatises written by Jacob Behmen. . . . Published By a Gentleman retired from Business. . . . 1769.

Theological and Practical Divinity: A Compendious View Of the Grounds of the
Teutonick Philosophy. With considerations, by way of Enquiry into the
. . . writings of Jacob Behmen. . . . Published by a Gentleman retired
from Business. . . . 1770.

Walton, C. Notes and Materials. . . . 1854. [*See* under Law.]

Whyte, A. Jacob Behmen: An Appreciation. Edinburgh, 1894.

[Articles on Boehme, of great value, are]

Allen, G. W. A Master Mystic. An Introduction to the teaching of Jacob
Boehme, in the Theosophical Review, 1904–5, vol. XXXV, pp. 202, 321, 420,
and vol. XXXVI, p. 160.

—— A Series of "Excerpts from Boehme" with comments, in The Seeker, ed.
Allen, G. W., Nov., 1906, Aug., Nov., 1907, May, Aug., Nov., 1908, Feb.,
May, Aug., Nov., 1909 (in progress).

[The influence of Boehme on Sir Isaac Newton is an interesting point
which cannot be developed here. Law definitely asserts that Newton owed
a debt to Boehme. *See* Some Animadversions upon Dr. Trapp's Reply,
Works, vol. VI, pp. 314–15, The Spirit of Love, Works, vol. VIII, p. 38, and
letter to Dr. Cheyne, printed in Walton's Notes, p. 46, note. *See, also*,
Walton's Notes, p. 408, note, and 416, note; the Athenæum, 26 Jan., 1867,
p. 127, and Overton's William Law, p. 189.]

B. *Other Writers*
Antoinette Bourignon (1616–1680)
(1) Works

Toutes les œuvres de Mlle. Anthoinette Bourignon. 19 vols. Amsterdam,
1679–84 and 1686. [Ed. by Poiret, Pierre.]

[Mademoiselle Bourignon knew Boehme's works, and had met admirers of
him in Amsterdam; she enumerates him with Tauler, à Kempis and Engelbrecht
in her list of inspired and illuminated men. Her works were translated into
English (in 1699, 1703, 1707, 1708, etc.) and much read, more especially in Scotland.]

(2) Biographical and Critical

Gordon, Alex. The Fortunes of a Flemish Mystic. A paper read before the
Liverpool Literary and Philosophical Society, 4 March, 1872.

La vie de Damlle. Antoinette Bourignon. Amsterdam, 1683. [By Poiret,
Pierre, translated by Dr. Garden into English, in 1696. *See below.* Poiret
also wrote an apologetic Mémoire of her in the Nouvelles de la rép. des lettres,
1685, and defended her against V. L. von Seckendorf, 1686.]

Linde, Antonius von der. Antoinette Bourignon, das Licht der Welt. Leiden,
1895. [This gives a very full account of her life and work, and of the people
closely connected with her, also a full list of her writings on pp. 261–4, and
of early lives and later accounts of her.]

Macewen, Alex. R. Antoinette Bourignon, Quietist. 1910.

Select Lives of Foreigners, eminent in piety. 2nd edn. Bristol, 1796.

The Light of the World: A most True Relation of a Pilgrimess, M. Antonia
Bourignon, Travelling towards Eternity, To which is added A Preface to
the English Reader. 1696. [Preface by George Garden, an Aberdeen
minister (1650–78) who warmly espoused Mlle. Bourignon's views, and was,
in consequence, in 1701, deposed by the General Assembly for teaching her

"damnable errors." His chief opponent was Dr. Cockburn, Episcopalian minister of Aberdeen, who wrote Bourignianism Detected. Garden replied to this as well as to Leslie's Preface to The Snake in the Grass, in his Apology for M. Bourignon, 1699. His nephew, Garden, J., also a mystic, was later a friend of Byrom; see Journal, vol. I, pt. 2, pp. 519–20 and vol. II, pt. I, pp. 128–30.]

(3) The Bourignon Controversy

Cockburn, John. Bourignianism Detected: or the Delusions and Errors of Antonia Bourignon, and her Growing Sect. 1698.
—— A Letter from John Cockburn, D.D. To his Friend in London. 1698.
[Leslie, Charles.] The Snake in the Grass. Third Edition. . . . 1698.
[Garden, Dr. George.] An Apology for M. Antonia Bourignon, in Four Parts. 1699.
White, George. Advertisement anent the reading of the books of Antonia Bourignon. Aberdeen, 1700.
[Barclay, Robert.] A Modest and Serious Address to the well meaning Followers of Ant. Bourignon. 1708.
Hog, James. Notes about the Spirit's Operations. . . . Edinburgh, 1709.

[In 1771 the ordination formula was drawn up by General Assembly of the Free Kirk of Scotland, embracing a renunciation of Bourignian errors, which remained until in 1844 "Erastian" was substituted.]

Dionysius Andreas Freher (1649–1728)

A large quantity of MS. writings (duplicates in B. M. and Dr. Williams's library), some few in Freher's hand, but mostly copied by his friend Leuchter. They are commentaries on and expositions of Boehme, and were much prized by Law, who himself copied out a number of them. Freher also left many symbolical drawings, illustrating Boehme, which are very interesting. Some of these were specially chosen out by Law, and were reproduced in the edition of Boehme's works (1764–81) which appeared after Law's death.

For some account of Freher by himself, *see* Walton's Notes and Materials, p. 141, note; and, of his writings, with copious extracts from them, *ibid.* pp. 258–491., and for a list of the MSS., *see* Walton, pp. 679–84, or Appendix B. to Barker's reprint of Boehme's Threefold Life of Man, 1909. There are 27 vols. of Freher's MSS. in the B. M. [Add. MSS. 5767–5794].

Madame Guyon (1648–1717)

(1) Works

Lettres Chrétiennes et Spirituelles (Madame Guyon et Fénelon), à Londres (Lyons), 1767–8. 5 vols. [Ed. by Dutoit, J. P., and really published at Lyons.]
["Lettres Spirituelles" in] Le Directeur Mistique, ou Les Œuvres Spirituelles De Mons. Bertot, . . . Directeur de Mad^e Guion. [4 vols.] A Cologne. . . . 1726.
Opuscules Spirituels De Madame J. M. B. de la Mothe Guion. A Cologne. . . . 1704.
Recueil de Divers Traitez De Theologie Mystique qui entrent dans la Célèbre Dispute du Quietisme qui s'agite présentement en France. Contenant I. Le Moyen court et très facile de faire Oraison: II. L'Explication du Cantique des Cantiques. Cologne. . . . 1699.

Vie de Madame J. M. B. de La Mothe Guion, écrite par elle-même. . . . Cologne, 1720. [Ed. by Poiret, P.]

(2) Biographical and Critical

Allen, T. T. Autobiography of Madame Guyon. 2 vols. . . . 1897.

Guerrier, L. Madame Guyon, sa vie, sa doctrine, et son influence. Orleans, 1881.

Life, The, of Lady Guion. . . . Bristol. . . . 1772.

Masson, M. Fénelon et Madame Guyon, Documents nouveaux et inédits. . . . Paris, 1907.

Matter, M. Le Mysticisme en France au Temps de Fénelon. Paris, 1865.

Quakerism A la-Mode: or a History of Quietism, Particularly that of the Lord Archbishop of Cambray and Madam Guyone. Containing An Account of her Life, her Prophecies and Visions. . . . 1698.

Upham, T. C. Life . . . of Madame Guyon. 2nd edn. 1905.

Nicolas Malebranche (1638–1715)

De La Recherche de la Vérité. . . . A Paris, chez André Pralard. 2 vols. 1674. 3rd vol. 1678. [Two English translations appeared in 1694.]

V. Later Influence of Law and Boehme

Samuel Taylor Coleridge (1772–1834)

[See note 2 to p. 367, ante.]

Thomas Erskine of Linlathen (1788–1870)

Letters of Thomas Erskine. Ed. Hanna, W. Edinburgh. 2nd edn. 1878.

Henderson, H. F. Erskine of Linlathen, selections and biography. Edinburgh, 1899. [See specially, pp. 26, 27, 67.]

Louis Claude De Saint-Martin (1743–1803)

[St. Martin visited London in 1787, where he became acquainted with Law's writings which profoundly impressed him. He apparently did not read Boehme until 1792, but was from that time onwards his devoted student and admirer and called him le prince des Philosophes divins. He translated several of Boehme's works into French.]

(1) Works

[For complete list, see bibliographies by Matter, M., and Waite, A. E.; see below.]

De l'Esprit des Choses. . . . Paris, 1800. [St. Martin describes this as a preparatory introduction to the works of Boehme.]

Le Ministère de l'Homme-esprit. Paris, 1802. [Translated into English by Penny, E. B., 1864. Contains, pp. 21–8, a masterly summary of Boehme's philosophy.]

Œuvres Posthumes de St. Martin. 2 vols. Tours, 1807.

La Correspondance Inédite de L. C. de Saint-Martin, dit le Philosophe Inconnu, et Kirchberger, Baron de Liebistorf . . . du 22 mai, 1792, jusqu'au 7 novembre 1797. . . . Amsterdam. Paris [printed], 1862. [Translated into English, under the title:]

Mystical Philosophy and Spirit Manifestations. Selections from the . . . Correspondence between L. C. de Saint-Martin . . . and . . . Baron de Liebistorf. . . . Translated by E. B. Penny. . . . Exeter, 1863.

(2) Biographical and Critical

Caro, E. Du Mysticisme au xviiie siècle. Essai sur la vie et la doctrine de Saint-Martin. Paris, 1852.

Franck, A. Le Philosophie Mystique en France à la Fin du xviiie siècle. Paris, 1866.

Gence, J. B. M. Notice Biographique sur Louis Claude de Saint-Martin. Paris, 1824. [*See* specially extract in Walton's Notes, pp. 492–626.]

Matter, M. Saint-Martin, le Philosophe Inconnu. . . . Paris, 1862. 2nd edn. 1864.

Moreau, L. Le Philosophe Inconnu, Réflexions sur les Idées de L. C. de S. Martin. . . . Paris, 1850.

Waite, A. E. The Life of Louis Claude de Saint-Martin . . . and the substance of his transcendental doctrine. 1901.

VI. Later Influence of Boehme in Germany in Early Nineteenth Century, returning thence to England

[*See*, on this, Hamberger's preface to his Jacob Boehme, and Hoffmann's book on Baader below.]

Baader, F. X. v. Sämmtliche Werke, 16 vols. Leipzig, 1851–60. [Specially] Vorlesungen über speculative Dogmatik. Fermenta Cognitionis. Gesammelten philosophischen Aufsatz.

    [Baader is an exponent and follower of Boehme.]

Hegel, G. W. F. (1770–1831). [Account of Boehme's philosophy in] Geschichte der Philosophie, vol. iii, Werke, Berlin, 1836, vol. xv, pp. 296–327.

Hoffmann, F. Franz v. Baader in seinem Verhältniss zu Hegel und Schelling. Leipzig, 1850.

Schelling, F. W. J. (1775–1854). [His later philosophy, specially] Philosophische Untersuchungen über das Wesen der menschlichen Freiheit. 1809.

—— Denkmal der Schrift . . . des Herrn F. H. Jacobi. 1812.

    [*See* Schopenhauer's remarks on Schelling's debt to Boehme, in Handschriftlichen Nachlass, Leipzig, 1864, p. 261.]

Schlegel, K. W. F. v. (1774–1829). Vorlesungen über die Philosophie des Lebens. 1828. [Much in it is owing to Boehme.]

    [Interesting notices of Boehme in] Vorlesungen aus den Jahren 1804–6, vol. i, pp. 424–9. Geschichte der alten und neuen Literatur, 1815, vol. ii, pp. 223–5.

VII. General History and Criticism

Abbey, C. J. The English Church and its Bishops; 1700–1800. 2 vols. 1887.

—— and Overton, J. H. The English Church in the Eighteenth Century. 2 vols. 1878.

Barclay, R. The Inner Life of the Religious Societies of the Commonwealth. 1876.

Baxter, Richard. Reliquiae Baxterianae, or Mr. Richard Baxter's Narrative of the most memorable passages of his Life and Times. . . . 1696.

Blunt, J. H. Dictionary of Sects, Heresies, Ecclesiastical Parties and Schools of religious thought. 1874.

De la Croix, Henri. Études d'histoire et de psychologie du Mysticisme. Paris, 1908.

Fox, George. A Journal, or Historical Account of the life, travels, Sufferings . . . of . . . George Fox. . . . 2 vols. 1694–8. Ed. from the MSS. by Penny, Norman, with introd. by Harvey, T. E. 2 vols. Cambridge, 1911.

Gichtel, Johann Georg. Theosophia Practica. 3rd edn. Leyden, 1722. [See Index vol. for Boehme, Lead and other mystics.]

Inge, W. R. Christian Mysticism. (Bampton Lectures.) 1899.

—— Studies in the English Mystics. (St. Margaret's Lectures.) 1899.

Jones, Rufus M. Studies in Mystical Religion. 1909.

Julian, John. A Dictionary of Hymnology. Revised edn. 1907. [Short accounts of A. Bourignon, Mme. Guyon, Byrom, etc.]

Lecky, W. E. H. A History of England in the Eighteenth Century. Vols. I and II. 3rd edn. 1883–90.

Marsden, J. B. History of Christian Churches and Sects. 2 vols. 1856.

Overton, J. H. The Nonjurors, their lives, principles and writings. 1902.

—— and Relton, F. The English Church from the accession of George I to the end of the eighteenth century (1714–1800). 1906. [Vol. VII in A History of the English Church, ed. Hunt, W.]

Pattison, Mark. Tendencies of Religious Thought in England [in] Essays and Reviews, 1860. Essays of Mark Pattison, Oxford. . . . 1889, vol. II, pp. 42–118.

Perry, G. G. The Student's English Church History. Vols. II and III. 1878. 1887.

Récejac, E. Essai sur les fondements de la connaissance mystique. Paris, 1897. [Eng. translation by Upton, S. C., 1899.]

Sewel, William. The History of the Rise, Increase and Progress of the . . . Quakers. 1722.

Skeats, H. S. A History of the Free Churches of England. 1894.

Southey, Robert. The Life of Wesley, 3rd edn., with notes by . . . S. T. Coleridge. . . . 1846. 2 vols.

Stephen, Sir Leslie. History of English Thought in the eighteenth century. 2 vols. 1876.

Underhill, Evelyn. Mysticism. 1911.

Vaughan, R. A. Hours with the Mystics. 2 vols. 1860.

Wedgwood, Julia. John Wesley, and the Evangelical Reaction of the Eighteenth Century. 1870.

Wesley, John. Works. 14 vols. 1829.

Woodward, Josiah. An Account of the Rise and Progress of the Religious Societies, In the City of London . . . the 3rd edn. enlarged. . . . 1701.

CHAPTER XIII

SCHOLARS AND ANTIQUARIES

I. RICHARD BENTLEY

A complete Bibliography of the works of Richard Bentley and of all the literature called forth by his acts or by his writings, by A. T. Bartholomew and J. W. Clark, was published at Cambridge in 1908.

A. *Collected Works and Correspondence*

Works. Vols. 1–3. Ed. Dyce, A. No more appeared. They contain the Dissertations upon the Epistles of Phalaris, etc.; Epistola ad J. Millium; Sermons at Boyle's Lecture and his other Sermons; Remarks upon a Discourse of Free-Thinking; Proposals for printing the Greek Testament, etc. 1836–8.

Richardi Bentleii et doctorum virorum Epistolae. Ed. Burney, C. 1807, 1825.

Epistolae Bentleii, Graevii, etc. Ed. Kraft, F. G. Altona, 1831.

The Correspondence of Richard Bentley. Ed. Wordsworth, Chr. 2 vols. 1842.

B. *Separate Works and Editions*

Epistola ad Joannem Millium [on Malelas]. Published as an Appendix to Mill's edition of the Historia Chronica of Malelas. Oxford. 1691.

The Folly of Atheism. Boyle Lecture, I. 1692.

Matter and Motion cannot Think. Boyle Lecture, II. 1692.

A Confutation of Atheism from the Structure and Origin of Humane Bodies. 3 parts. (Boyle Lectures, III, IV, V.) 1692.

A Confutation of Atheism from the Origin and Frame of the World. 3 parts (Boyle Lectures, VI, VII, VIII.) 1692–3.

> Four Letters from Sir Isaac Newton, containing some arguments in proof of a Deity. 1692–3. Ptd. 1756.

> Bentley's Sermons on the Confutation of Atheism were collected and rptd. 1699, 1724, 1735, 1809. They were translated into Latin (Berlin, 1696), German (1715), French, and Dutch.

Of Revelation and the Messias. Sermon . . . 5 July, 1696. 1696.

Callimachi Fragmenta a Richardo Bentleio collecta.—R. Bentleii Animadversiones in nonnulla Hymnorum Callimachi loca. Published in edition by Graevius, J. G. Utrecht, 1697.

A Proposal for building a Royal Library. 1697. Rptd. in Bartholomew and Clark, pp. 93 ff.

> Temple, Sir W. Upon Ancient and Modern Learning. (Miscellanea, vol. II.) 1690. [Extols the writings of Phalaris and Aesop.]

> Wotton, W. Reflections upon Ancient and Modern Learning. 1694. [Answers Sir W. Temple.]

> Phalaridis Agrigentinorum Tyranni Epistolae. Rec. Boyle, C. Oxford, 1695. 1718. [The preface insults Bentley.]

Dissertation upon the Epistles of Phalaris, Themistocles, Socrates, Euripides, and Others; and the Fables of Æsop. Ptd. with the 2nd edn. of Wotton, W., Reflections upon Ancient and Modern Learning. 1697.

> Dr. Bentley's Dissertations on the Epistles of Phalaris and the Fables of Aesop examin'd by the Hon. C. Boyle. [Chiefly the work of Atterbury.] 1698.

A Dissertation upon the Epistles of Phalaris. With an Answer to the Objections of the Hon. Charles Boyle. 1699. Rptd. 1777, 1816, 1817, 1874, 1883. Transl. into Latin, 1777, into German, 1857.

Emendationes ad Ciceronis Tusculanas. Ptd. in edition by Davies, J. Cambridge, 1709.

Emendationes in Menandri et Philemonis Reliquias ex nupera editione Joannis Clerici. Auctore Phileleuthero Lipsiensi. Utrecht, 1710. Cambridge, 1713.

The Present State of Trinity College in Cambridge, in a Letter from Dr. Bentley to the Bishop of Ely. 1710.

> For a complete view of the literature of Bentley's Trinity college controversies see Bartholomew and Clark, pp. 60–74.

Q. Horatius Flaccus ex recensione et cum notis R. Bentleii. Cambridge, 1711. Amsterdam, 1713, 1728.

Q. Horatius Flaccus ad nuperam Richardi Bentleii editionem accurate expressus. Notas Addidit Thomas Bentleius. Cambridge, 1713.

Remarks upon a late Discourse of Free-Thinking [by Anthony Collins]. In a Letter to F[rancis] H[are] D.D. By Phileleutherus Lipsiensis. 1713.

A Sermon upon Popery. . . . 5 November, 1715. Cambridge, 1715.

A Sermon preached before King George. . . . 3 Feb. 1716/17. 1717.

Two Letters to Dr. Bentley concerning his intended edition of the Greek Testament. Together with the Doctor's Answer. 1717.

Proposals to print a new edition of the Greek Testament. [1720.]

> Remarks upon the Proposals. By Middleton, Conyers. 1721.

Dr. Bentley's Proposals to print a new edition of the Greek Testament. With a full answer to all the Remarks [of Middleton, Conyers]. 1721.

> Some Farther Remarks upon the Proposals. By Middleton, Conyers. 1721.

A Reply to a Copy of Verses made in Imitation of Book III, Ode 2 of Horace. Ptd. in The Grove, 1721, and in Monk's Life of Bentley, ed. 2, vol. II, pp. 173–4. [Bentley's only extant English verses.]

Publii Terentii Comoediae, Phaedri Fabulae Aesopiae, Publii Syri et aliorum veterum Sententiae, ex recensione R. Bentleii. Cambridge, 1726. Amsterdam, 1727.

The Case of Trinity College in Cambridge. Whether the Crown or the Bishop of Ely be the General Visitor. 1729.

Milton's Paradise Lost. A New Edition by Richard Bentley. 1732.

M. Manilii Astronomicon, ex recensione R. Bentleii. 1739.

M. Annaei Lucani Pharsalia cum notis Hugonis Grotii et R. Bentleii. Ed. Cumberland, Richard. Strawberry-Hill, 1760.

C. *Biography and Criticism*

Beeching, H. C. Francis Atterbury. 1909.

De Quincey, Thomas. Essay on Bentley. Ptd. as a review of Monk's Life in Blackwood's Edinburgh Magazine, vol. XXVIII, 1830. Rptd. in Works, 1854, etc. (vol. VII).

Jebb, Sir R. C. Bentley. (English Men of Letters.) 1882, 1902. German trans. 1885.

Maehly, J. Richard Bentley. Leipzig, 1868.

Monk, J. H. Life of Richard Bentley. 1830. 2nd edn., 2 vols. 1833.

Nicoll, H. J. Great Scholars. Buchanan, Bentley, Porson, Parr, and others. Edinburgh, 1880, 1884.

Sandys, Sir J. E. History of Classical Scholarship, vol. II, chap. XXIV, pp. 401 ff. Cambridge, 1908.

II. Other Classical Scholars

Robert Ainsworth (1660–1743)

The most natural and easie way of institution; containing proposals for making a domestic education less chargeable to parents and more easie and beneficial to children. 1698.

Thesaurus linguae Latinae compendiarius; or a compendious dictionary of the Latin tongue designed principally for the use of the British nations. **1736.** With additions by Beatson, B. W. Revised by Ellis, W. 1829.

William Baxter (1650–1723)

De analogia, sive arte Latinae linguae commentariolus. 1679.
Anacreontis Carmina. Ed. Baxter, W. 1695.
Q. Horatii Flacci Eclogae. Ed. Baxter, W. 1701.
Glossarium antiquitatum Britannicarum. 1719. 2nd edn. **1733.**
Opera posthuma. Ed. Williams, M. 1726.

Vincent Bourne (1695–1747)

Carmina Comitialia Cantabrigiensia. 1721.
Poematia, Latine partim reddita, partim scripta. 1734. 5th edn. **1764.** 8th edn. Oxford, 1808.
Miscellaneous Poems. **1772.**
Poetical Works. 2 vols. Oxford, 1808. Another edn. Oxford, 1838.

Thomas Cooke (1703–1756)

The Poems of Moschus and Bion translated. 1724.
The Works of Hesiod translated. 2 vols. 1728. Rptd. in Chalmers's English Poets, 1810 ff.
Terence's Comedys translated (with the text). 3 vols. 1734.
Plautus's Amphitruo translated. 1746.
[Editor of The Craftsman from 1741.]

Thomas Creech (1659–1700)

T. Lucretius Carus his six books de natura rerum done into English verse. 1682.
The Odes, Satyrs, and Epistles of Horace done into English. 1684.
Idylliums of Theocritus done into English. 1684.
T. Lucretii Cari de rerum natura libri VI, quibus interpretationem et notas addidit T. Creech. 1695.
The five books of M. Manilius done into English verse. 1697.

John Davies, President of Queen's College

Ciceronis Tusculanae. Ed. Davies, J. Cambridge, 1709.
—— De natura Deorum. Ed. Davies, J. Cambridge, 1718.
—— De divinatione et de fato. Ed. Davies, J. Cambridge, **1721.**
—— Academica. Ed. Davies, J. Cambridge, 1725.
—— De legibus. Ed. Davies, J. Cambridge, 1727.
—— De finibus. Ed. Davies, J. Cambridge, 1728.

Richard Dawes

Miscellanea Critica. Cambridge, 1745.

Henry Dodwell

De veteribus Graecorum Romanorumque cyclis. Oxford, 1701.
Exercitationes duae: prima de aetate Phalaridis, secunda de aetate Pythagorae Philosophi. 1704.
        See, also, ante, Vol. VIII (Chap. XII, bibl.).

John Fell

Cypriani Opera.   Ed. Fell, J.   Oxford, 1682.
> See, also, ante, Vol. VII, p. 513.

John King (1696–1728)

Euripidis Hecuba, Orestes et Phoenissae.   Cambridge, 1726.   Another edn. 1748.

Adam Littleton (1627–1694)

Linguae Latinae liber dictionarius quadripartitus.   A Latine dictionary in four parts.   1673.   Also 1678, 1685, 1695, 1723, 6th edn. 1735.

William Lloyd

Chronological account of the life of Pythagoras.   1699.

Jeremiah Markland

Euripidis Supplices.   1763.
—— Iphigenia in Aulide.   1771.
—— Iphigenia in Tauride.   1771.
> These three editions were rptd. by Gaisford, T., Oxford, 1811.

Statii Silvae.   Ed. Markland, J.   1728.   Rptd. 1827.
—— Opera ex recensione J. Gronovii.   Notae J. Marklandi.   Mannheim, 1782.

Conyers Middleton

Works.   4 vols.   1752.
Life of Cicero.   2 vols.   1741.
Free Enquiry into . . . Miraculous Powers.   1749.
> As to his collisions with Bentley, see sec. I B, ante.

John Ozell (d. 1743)

The Iliad of Homer, done from the French.   5 vols.   1712, 1734.
> For a catalogue of Ozell's translations see D. of N. B. vol. XLIII, 1895.

Zachary Pearce (1690–1774)

Longinus: De sublimitate commentarius.   Gr. et Lat.   1724.   9th edn.   1806.
Cicero: Dialogi tres de oratore.   Cambridge, 1716.   2nd edn.   1732.
—— De officiis libri tres.   1745.   3rd edn.   Cambridge, 1777.

John Potter (1674?–1747)

Archaeologia Graeca.   2 vols.   Oxford, 1697–9.   9th edn.   1775.
Lycophron.   Alexandra.   Ed. Potter, J.   Oxford, 1697.

Thomas Robinson, D.D.

Hesiodi Ascraei quae supersunt, Gr. et Lat. cum notis variorum.   Oxford, 1737.

Sir Henry Sheeres (d. 1710)

The History of Polybius translated.   1693.
The Works of Lucian translated.   1711.

Joseph Spence

See bibliography to Chap. III, sec. VII and sec. VIII, *ante.*

John Taylor

Lysiae Orationes . . . Rec. Taylor, J.   1739.
Demosthenis et Aeschinis Opera. Ed. Taylor, J. 2 vols. Cambridge,
  1748–57.

John Walker (1692?–1741)

M. T. Ciceronis de natura Deorum libri III. Ed. Davisius, J. Accedunt emendationes J. Walkeri. Cambridge, 1718.

Joseph Wasse

Sallustii quae extant . . . rec. J. Wasse. 1710.
Thucydidis De bello Peloponnesiaco. Rec. J. Wasse. Amsterdam, 1731.

David Watson (1710–1756)

The Odes, Epodes, and Carmen Seculare of Horace translated into English prose.
  With the text. 1741.
A clear and compendious history of the Gods and Goddesses and their contempo-
  raries. 1752.

A. T. B.

III. Oriental, Modern and Other Scholars

Aldrich, Henry (1647–1710). Artis logicae compendium. Oxford, 1691. Many
  times rptd., including four edns. by Mansel, H. L., Oxford, 1852–62.
Bedford, Arthur (1668–1745). Animadversions on Sir I. Newton's . . . Chronology of Ancient Kingdoms Amended. 1728.
—— Scripture Chronology demonstrated by Astronomical Considerations. 1741.
Beveridge, William (1637–1708). De linguarum orientalium, praesertim He-
  braicae, Chaldaicae, Syriacae, Arabicae, et Samaritanae praestantia, neces-
  sitate, et utilitate quam et theologis praestant et philosophis. 1658.
—— Grammatica linguae Domini nostri Jesu Christi, sive grammatica Syriaca
  tribus libris tradita. 1658.
—— Institutionum chronologicarum libri duo. 1669.
—— Συνοδικόν, sive pandectae canonum SS. apostolorum, et conciliorum ab
  ecclesia Graeca receptorum. Oxford, 1672.
—— Codex canonum ecclesiae primitivae vindicatus ac illustratus. 1678.
—— Private thoughts upon religion. 1709. Often rptd.
—— Theological works. 12 vols. Oxford, 1842–8.
Blount, Thomas (1618–1679). The academie of eloquence, containing a com-
  pleat English rhetorique . . . digested into an easie and methodical way
  to speak and write fluently. 1654. Several times rptd.
—— Glossographia, or a dictionary interpreting all such hard words . . . now
  used in our refined English tongue. 1656. Often rptd.
—— Boscobel, or the history of his Sacred Majesties most miraculous preser-
  vation after the battle of Worcester, 3 Sept., 1651. 1660. Often rptd.
—— A law dictionary. 1670.
—— Fragmenta antiquitatis: Antient tenures of land, and jocular customs of
  some mannors. 1679.
Bysshe, Edward (*fl.* 1712). The art of English poetry. 1702. 8th edn. 1737.

Bysshe, Edward. The memorable things of Socrates, written by Xenophon. Translated in English. 1712.

Cockeram, Henry (*fl.* 1650). The English dictionarie, or an interpreter of hard English words. 1623. 12th edn. 1670.

Cotgrave, Randle (d. 1634?). A dictionarie of the French and English tongues. 1611. Several times rptd.

Derham, William (1657–1735). Physico-Theology. (Boyle lectures.) 1713.

Hyde, Thomas (1636–1703). Historia religionis veterum Persarum. Oxford, 1700.

—— Syntagma dissertationum. Ed. Sharpe, G. 2 vols. Oxford, 1767.

Jervas, Charles (1675?–1739). The life and exploits of the ingenious gentleman Don Quixote de la Mancha. Translated from the original Spanish. 2 vols. 1742. Many subsequent edns.; one of the latest and best is that by Fitzmaurice-Kelly, J., 2 vols., Oxford, 1907.

Knight, Samuel (1675–1746). The life of Dr. John Colet . . . founder of St. Paul's School: with some account of that foundation. 1724. Another edn., 1823.

—— The life of Erasmus, more particularly that part of it which he spent in England. Cambridge, 1726.

Locker, John (1693–1760). Letters and remains of the Lord Chancellor Bacon. collected by R. Stephens. Ed. Locker, J. 1734.

—— The works of Francis Bacon. Ed. Birch, T., from the collections of Stephens, R. and Locker, J. 5 vols. 1765.

—— The life of Charles XII, King of Sweden. Translated from Voltaire. 1731. [The last two books only.]

Maittaire, Michael (1668–1747). Graecae linguae dialecti. 1706.

—— Stephanorum historia, vitas ipsorum ac libros complectens. 2 vols. 1709.

—— Historia typographorum aliquot Parisiensium, vitas et libros complectens. 2 vols. 1717.

—— Annales typographici. 3 vols. The Hague and Amsterdam, 1719–26.

—— Senilia sive poetica aliquot in argumentis varii generis tentamina. 1742.

Marsham, Sir John (1602–1685). Diatriba chronologica. 1649.

—— Chronicus Canon Ægyptiacus, Ebraicus, Graecus, et disquisitiones. 1672.

Pococke, Edward, the elder (1604–1691). Specimen historiae Arabum, sive . . . de origine et moribus Arabum succincta narratio. Oxford, 1650.

—— Porta Mosis, sive dissertationes aliquot . . . Arabice . . . et Latine edita. 1655.

—— Theological works. Ed. Twells, L. 2 vols. 1740.

Pococke, Edward, the younger (1648–1727). Philosophus Autodidactus, sive epistola Abi Jaafar Ebn Tophail . . . ex Arabica in linguam Latinam versa. Oxford, 1671. An English trans. from the Latin version was published in 1674.

Sale, George (1697?–1736). The Koran . . . translated into English immediately from the original Arabic . . . To which is prefixed a preliminary discourse. 1734. This has been many times rptd., and remains the standard English version.

Sale also wrote the articles relating to oriental history in Bayle's General Dictionary, 1734–41.

Smith, Thomas (1638–1710). Diatriba de Chaldaicis Paraphrastis, eorumque versionibus, ex utraque Talmude ac scriptis Rabbinorum concinnata. Oxford, 1662.

—— Syntagma de druidum moribus ac institutis. 1664.

Smith, Thomas. Remarks upon the manners, religion, and government of the Turks; together with a survey of the seven churches of Asia, and a brief description of Constantinople. 1678. A trans. of Epistolae duae, 1672, and Epistolae quatuor, 1674.

—— Catalogus librorum manuscriptorum bibliothecae Cottonianae. Oxford, 1696.

—— Vitae quorundam eruditissimorum et illustrium virorum (J. Ussher, J. Cosin, H. Briggs, J. Bainbridge, J. Greaves, Sir Peter Young, Pat. Young, J. Dee). 1707.

Ward, John (1679?–1758). De Asse et partibus ejus commentarius. 1719.

—— The lives of the professors of Gresham College, to which is prefixed the life of the founder, Sir Thomas Gresham. 1740.

Wotton, William (1666–1727). Reflections upon ancient and modern learning. 1694.

—— The history of Rome from the death of Antoninus Pius to the death of Severus Alexander. 1701.

—— Miscellaneous discourses relating to the traditions and usages of the Scribes and Pharisees. 2 vols. 1710.

—— A discourse concerning the confusion of languages at Babel. 1730.

IV. ANTIQUARIES

A. *General*

Anderson, J. P. The book of British topography. 1881.

Archaeologia, vol. I. 1770. For history of the Society of Antiquaries. (*See, also*, Nichols's Lit. Anecdotes, vol. VI.)

Biographia Britannica. 6 vols. 1747–66.

Gough, R. British topography. 2 vols. 1780.

—— Catalogue of books relating to British topography, bequeathed to the Bodleian Library by R. Gough. Oxford, 1814.

Macray, W. D. Annals of the Bodleian Library. 2nd edn. Oxford, 1890.

Malcolm, J. P. Lives of topographers and antiquaries who have written concerning the antiquities of England. 1815.

Nichols, J. Literary anecdotes of the eighteenth century. 9 vols. 1812–15.

Rawlinson, R. The English topographer. (Anon.) 1720.

Upcott, W. A bibliographical account of the principal works relating to English topography. 3 vols. 1818.

Wood, A. Athenae Oxonienses and Fasti. Ed. Bliss, P. 6 vols. 1813–20.

For references to further authorities and for fuller bibliographies the Dictionary of National Biography should be consulted. Manuscript collections of several of the writers named below are in the British Museum or the Bodleian library: see the various published catalogues of manuscripts in these libraries.

B. *Particular Writers*

Abingdon *or* Habington, Thomas (1560–1647). The antiquities of the cathedral church of Worcester: to which are added . . . Chichester and Lichfield. [Ed. Rawlinson, R.] 1717.

Ames, Joseph. Typographical antiquities; being a historical account of printing in England . . . to the year 1600: with an appendix concerning printing in Scotland and Ireland. 1749. New and enlarged edn., by Herbert,

W., 3 vols., 1785–90. Another edn., by Dibdin, T. F., vols. I–IV, 1810–19 (not completed).

Anstis, John. The Register of the Order of the Garter, . . . usually called the Black Book. 2 vols. 1724.

Archaeologia: or miscellaneous tracts, relating to antiquity. Published by the Society of Antiquaries of London. 1770 ff. (In progress.)

Ashmole, Elias. The institution, laws, and ceremonies of the most noble Order of the Garter. 1672. New edn. (The History of the . . . Order of the Garter), with continuation by Walker, T. 1715.

—— The antiquities of Berkshire. 3 vols. 1719.

Memoirs of the life of . . . Elias Ashmole, drawn up by himself by way of diary. . . . Publish'd by C. Burman. 1717.

Atkyns, Sir Robert. The ancient and present state of Glocestershire. 1712. 2nd edn. 1768.

Aubrey, John. Miscellanies: viz. i. Day-fatality. ii. Local-fatality. iii. Ostenta. iv. Omens. v. Dreams. vi. Apparitions. vii. Voices. viii. Impulses. ix. Knockings. x. Blows invisible. xi. Prophecies. xii. Marvels. xiii. Magic. xiv. Transportation in the air. xv. Visions in a beril, or speculum. xvi. Converse with angels and spirits. xvii. Corpse candles in Wales. xviii. Oracles. xix. Ecstasies. xx. Glances of love and envy. xxi. Second-sighted persons. 1696.

—— The natural history and antiquities of the county of Surrey. Begun in the year 1673 by John Aubrey, Esq., F. S. A., and continued to the present time. [Ed. Rawlinson, R.] 5 vols. 1718–19.

—— The natural history of Wiltshire. Edited and elucidated by notes, by J. Britton. Wiltshire Topographical Society. 1847.

—— Wiltshire. The topographical collections of John Aubrey. Corrected and enlarged by Jackson, J. E. Wiltshire Archaeological and Natural History Society. 1862.

A portion of this work was privately printed, in 2 parts, by Sir Thomas Phillips, under the titles: Aubrey's Collections for Wilts, pt. I, 1821; An essay towards the description of the North Division of Wiltshire, 1838.

The Introduction was printed in Miscellanies on several curious subjects, 1714.

—— Lives of eminent persons. In vol. II of Letters written by eminent persons . . . and Lives of eminent men by John Aubrey. 1813. A fuller, and better, ed. by Clark, A., from the author's MSS. 2 vols. Oxford, 1898.

—— Remaines of Gentilisme and Judaisme. Ed. Britton, J. (Folklore Society.) 1881.

Memoir of John Aubrey . . . and an account of his works. By Britton, J. Wiltshire Topographical Society. 1845. See, also, an article on Aubrey by Masson, D., in British Quarterly Review, vol. XXIV, pp. 153–82. 1856.

Baker, Thomas. Reflections upon learning, wherein is shewn the insufficiency thereof, in its several particulars, in order to evince the usefulness and necessity of revelation. By a Gentleman. 1700. 8th edn. 1756.

—— The funeral sermon of Margaret Countess of Richmond and Derby, by John Fisher. Ed., with preface, by Baker, T. 1708.

—— History of the College of St. John the Evangelist, Cambridge. Ed. Mayor, J. E. B. 2 vols. Cambridge, 1869.

Memoirs of the life and writings of . . . Thomas Baker . . . from the papers of Dr. Zachary Grey, with a catalogue of his MS. collections. By Masters, Robert. Cambridge, 1784.

Baker's manuscript collections are contained in 42 folio volumes. The first 23 of these are in the British Museum, and the remainder in the University library, Cambridge. An Index to the Baker Manuscripts, by Four Members of the Cambridge Antiquarian Society, was published at Cambridge in 1848.

Bentham, James. The history and antiquities of the conventual and cathedral church of Ely. 2 vols. 1771.

Bernard, Edward. Catalogi librorum manuscriptorum Angliae et Hiberniae in unum collecti, cum indice alphabetico. Oxford, 1697.

Bibliotheca topographica Britannica. Ed. Nichols, J. 8 vols. 1780–90. [Contains many pieces of this period from both manuscript and printed sources.]

Blomefield, Francis. An essay towards a topographical history of the county of Norfolk. 5 vols. Fersfield, Norwich and Lynn, 1739–75. Continued from p. 678 of vol. III, by Parkin, C. Another edn. 11 vols. 1805–10.

—— Collectanea Cantabrigiensia; or, Collections relating to Cambridge. Norwich, 1750.

Borlase, William (1695–1772). Observations on the antiquities, historical and monumental, of the county of Cornwall. Oxford, 1754.

—— The natural history of Cornwall. Oxford, 1758.

Bourne, Henry. Antiquitates vulgares; or, the antiquities of the common people. Newcastle, 1725. [Incorporated by Brand, John, in his Observations on popular antiquities. 1777.]

—— The history of Newcastle upon Tyne. Newcastle, 1736.

Bridges, John (1666–1724). The history and antiquities of Northamptonshire. Ed. Whalley, P. 2 vols. Oxford, 1791.

Broughton, Richard (d.1634). Monastichon Britannicum: or, a historicall narration of the first founding and flourishing state of the antient monasteries . . . of Great Brittaine. 1655.

Burton, William (1575–1645). The description of Leicester Shire. (1622.)

Burton, William (1609–1657). Commentary on Antoninus, his itinerary . . . so far as it concerneth Britain. 1658.

Carter, Matthew (fl. 1660). Honor redivivus; or, an analysis of honor and armory. 1655.

Chamberlayne, Edward. Angliae notitia: or, the present state of England; together with divers reflections upon the antient state thereof. 1669. 38th edn. 1755. 21st (1704) and later edns. ed. by Chamberlayne, John; 22nd (1708) and later edns. entitled Magnae Britanniae notitia.

Charleton, Walter. Chorea gigantum; or, the most famous antiquity of Great Britain, vulgarly called Stone-Heng, standing on Salisbury Plain, restored to the Danes. 1663.

Chauncy, Sir Henry. The historical antiquities of Hertfordshire. 1700. Another edn. 1826.

Cole, William. Cole's manuscript collections, consisting of nearly 100 volumes, are in the British Museum.

Index to the contents of the Cole MSS. in the British Museum. By Gray, G. J. Cambridge, 1912.

Dart, John (d. 1730). The history and antiquities of the cathedral church of Canterbury and the once-adjoining monastery. 1726.

Dart, John. Westmonasterium, or the history and antiquaries of the abbey church of St. Peter's, Westminster. 2 vols. 1742.

Dodsworth, Roger. Monasticum Anglicanum. *See* Dugdale.

Drake, Francis. Eboracum: or, the history and antiquities of the city of York . . . together with the history of the cathedral church, and the lives of the archbishops of that see. 1736.

Ducarel, Andrew Coltee (1713–1785). A tour through Normandy, described in a letter to a friend. (Anon.) 1754.

—— A series of above two hundred Anglo-Gallic or Norman and Aquitain coins of the antient kings of England; exhibited in sixteen copper-plates. 1757.

—— Anglo-Norman antiquities considered, in a tour through part of Normandy. 1767.

    For a full list of Ducarel's numerous writings *see* D. of N. B.

Dugdale, Sir William. Monasticon Anglicanum. 3 vols. 1655–73. Vols. I and II bear the names of Dodsworth and Dugdale; vol. III, that of Dudgale alone. The first volume was reprinted, with large additions, in 1682. For supplement *see* Stevens, J. A new edn., "enriched with a large accession of materials now first printed," by Caley, J., Ellis, H., and Bandinel, B. 6 vols. 1817–30. Rptd. 1846. Two English abridgments have been published, one by Wright, J., 1693; the other, and better edn., 1718, is attributed to Stevens, J.

—— The antiquities of Warwickshire illustrated; from records, leiger books, manuscripts, charters, evidences, tombes, and armes. 1656. 2nd edn., by Thomas, W. 2 vols. 1730.

—— The history of St. Paul's cathedral in London . . . extracted out of originall charters, records, leiger books, and other manuscripts. 1658. 2nd edn., by Maynard, E. 1716. 3rd, and best, edn., with a continuation by Ellis, H. 1818.

—— The history of imbanking and drayning of divers fenns and marshes, both in foreign parts and in this kingdom. 1662. 2nd edn., by Cole, C. N. 1772. The original manuscript collections for this work are in the British Museum (Harl. 5011).

—— Origines juridiciales, or historical memorials of the English laws, courts of justice, forms of tryall, punishment in cases criminal, law writers, law books, grants and settlements of estates, degree of serjeant, Innes of Court and chancery. Also a Chronologie of the lord chancelors and keepers of the great seal, lord treasurers. . . . 1666.

—— The Baronage of England, or an historical account of . . . our English nobility. 2 vols. 1675–6.

—— A short view of the late trouble in England . . . to which is added a perfect narrative of the treaty at Uxbridge in an. 1644. Oxford, 1681.

—— The antient usage in bearing of such ensigns of honour as are commonly call'd arms. With a catalogue of the present nobility. Oxford, 1682. Another edn., ed. Banks, T. C. 1811.

—— A perfect copy of all summons of the nobility to the Great Councils and Parliaments of this realm. 1685.

    Some of Dugdale's visitations as Norroy King of Arms have been published by the Chetham and Surtees Societies.

    The life, diary, and correspondence of Sir William Dugdale. . . . Ed. Hamper, W. 1827.

Elstob, Elizabeth. An English-Saxon homily on the birthday of St. Gregory . . . translated into modern English. 1709.

Elstob, Elizabeth. The rudiments of grammar for the English-Saxon tongue. . . .
  With an apology for the study of northern antiquities. 1715.
Erdeswicke, Sampson (*fl.* 1603). A survey of Staffordshire; containing the an-
  tiquities of that county. [Ed. Rawlinson, R.] 1717.
Fulman, William (1632–1688). Academiae Oxoniensis notitia. 1665. Another
  edn. 1675.
Gale, Roger and Samuel. Reliquiae Galeanae; or miscellaneous pieces by the
  late learned brothers Roger and Samuel Gale. In Nichols's Bibliotheca
  Topographica Britannica, vol. III, 1790.
Gale, Samuel. The history and antiquities of the cathedral church of Winchester
  . . . begun by Henry late Earl of Clarendon, and continued to this time by
  S. Gale. 1715.
Gale, Thomas. Historiae Anglicanae scriptores quinque . . . nunc primum in
  lucem editi. Historiae Britannicae, Saxonicae, Anglo-Danicae scriptores
  xv. ex vetustis codd. MSS. editi opera T. G. Vols. II and III of Rerum
  Anglicarum scriptorum veterum. Oxford, 1687–91.
—— Antonini iter Britanniarum, commentariis illustratum. Ed. Gale, R.
  1709.
Gibson, Edmund. Chronicon Saxonicum, ex MSS. codicibus nunc primum
  integrum edidit, ac Latinum fecit. Oxford, 1692.
—— Camden's Britannia, newly translated into English: with large additions
  and improvements. 1695.
—— Codex juris ecclesiastici Anglicani: or, the statutes, constitutions, canons,
  rubricks and articles of the Church of England, methodically digested under
  their proper heads. 2 vols. 1713.
Gordon, Alexander. Itinerarium septentrionale: or, a journey thro' most of
  the counties of Scotland, and those in the north of England. 1726.
Gunton, Simon. The history of the church of Peterburgh. 1686.
Harleian Miscellany (The): a collection of scarce, curious, and entertaining
  pamphlets and tracts . . . in the late Earl of Oxford's library. Ed. Oldys,
  W. 8 vols. 1744–6. Another edn. 10 vols. 1808–13.
Harris, John (1667?–1719). The history of Kent. Vol. I. 1719. (No more
  published.)
Hearne, Thomas. A complete list of Hearne's publications, including the pieces
  added as appendixes to the various volumes, will be found at the end of his
  autobiography (*see below*) published in 1772.
  The more important are (in chronological order):
    Reliquiae Bodleianae: or some genuine remains of Sir Thomas Bodley.
      1703.
    Plinii epistolae et panegyricus. Oxford, 1703.
    Eutropii breviarium historiae Romanae. Oxford, 1703.
    Ductor historicus: or, a short system of universal history, and an intro-
      duction to the study of it. 2 vols. 1704–5.
    Justini historiarum ex Trogo Pompeio libri xliv. Oxford, 1705.
    Livii historiarum ab urbe condita libri qui supersunt. 6 vols. Oxford, 1708.
    The life of Ælfred the Great, by Sir John Spelman. With consider-
      able additions. Oxford, 1709.
    The Itinerary of John Leland the antiquary. 9 vols. Oxford, 1710–12.
    Henrici Dodwelli de parma equestri Woodwardiana dissertatio. Oxford,
      1713. Suppressed by the University authorities.
    Joannis Lelandi antiquarii de rebus Britannicis collectanea. 6 vols.
      Oxford, 1715.

Acta Apostolorum Graeco-Latine, e codice Laudiano. Oxford, 1715.

Joannis Rossi antiquarii Warwicensis historia regum Angliae. Oxford, 1716.

Titi Livii Foro-Juliensis vita Henrici quinti, regis Angliae. Oxford, 1716.

Aluredi Beverlacensis annales. Oxford, 1716.

Gulielmi Roperi vita D. Thomae Mori, lingua Anglicana contexta. (Oxford,) 1716.

Gulielmi Camdeni annales rerum Anglicarum et Hibernicarum regnante Elizabetha. 3 vols. (Oxford,) 1717.

Gulielmi Neubrigensis historia, sive chronica rerum anglicarum. 3 vols. Oxford, 1719.

Thomae Sprotti chronica. Oxford, 1719.

A collection of curious discourses written by eminent antiquaries upon several heads in our English antiquities. Oxford, 1720. Another edn., enlarged. 2 vols. 1771.

Textus Roffensis. Oxford, 1720.

Roberti de Avesbury historia de mirabilibus gestis Edvardi III. Oxford, 1720.

Johannis de Fordun Scotichronicon. 5 vols. Oxford, 1722.

The history and antiquities of Glastonbury. Oxford, 1722.

Hemingi chartularium ecclesiae Wigorniensis. 2 vols. Oxford, 1723.

Robert of Glocester's chronicle. 2 vols. Oxford, 1724.

Peter Langtoft's chronicle (as illustrated and improv'd by Robert of Brunne). 2 vols. Oxford, 1725.

Joannis Glastoniensis chronica, sive historia de rebus Glastoniensibus. 2 vols. Oxford, 1726.

Adami de Domerham de rebus gestis Glastoniensibus. 2 vols. Oxford, 1727.

Thomae de Elmham vita et gesta Henrici Quinti. Oxford, 1727.

Liber Niger Scaccarii. 2 vols. Oxford, 1728.

Historia vitae et regni Ricardi II, a monacho quodam de Evesham consignata. Oxford, 1729.

Johannis de Trokelowe annales Edvardi II. Oxford, 1729.

Thomae Caii vindiciae antiquitatis Academiae Oxoniensis. 2 vols. Oxford, 1730.

Walteri Hemingford historia de rebus gestis Edvardi I, Edvardi II, et Edvardi III. 2 vols. Oxford, 1731.

Duo rerum Anglicarum scriptores veteres, viz., Thomas Otterbourne et Johannes Whethamstede, ab origine gentis Britannicae usque ad Edvardum IV. 2 vols. Oxford, 1732.

Chronicon sive annales prioratus de Dunstaple. 2 vols. Oxford, 1733.

Benedictus Abbas Petroburgensis de vita et gestis Henrici II et Ricardi I. 2 vols. Oxford, 1735.

Hearne's autobiographical sketch was published in The Lives of Leland, Hearne, and Wood (ed. by Huddesford, W.), Oxford, 1772. In 1736 an attack on the character and works of Hearne was issued by Curll, the bookseller, under the title of Impartial memorials of the life and writings of Thomas Hearne, by Several Hands. His Collectanea or diaries (contained in 145 volumes), together with his other manuscripts, were bequeathed by Rawlinson, R., to the Bodleian library. Some extracts from the diaries were published by Bliss, P., under the title of Reliquiae Hearnianae, 2 vols.,

Oxford, 1857; and an enlarged edition was issued in 3 vols. in 1869. The Oxford Historical Society has undertaken a practically complete edition, entitled Remarks and Collections of Thomas Hearne; the eight volumes already published (1885–1907), under the editorship of Doble, C. E., Rannie, D. W., and others, cover the period 1705–25.

Hickes, George. Institutiones grammaticae Anglo-Saxonicae et Moeso-Gothicae. Oxford, 1689.

—— Linguarum vett. septentrionalium thesaurus grammatico-criticus et archaeologicus. 2 vols. Oxford, 1703–5.

Holme, Randle. The academy of armory, or, a storehouse of armory and blazon: containing the several variety of created beings, and how born in coats of arms . . . with the instruments used in all trades and sciences, together with their terms of art. Chester, 1688. The second volume was printed, for the first time, by the Roxburghe Club, in 1905.

Horsley, John. Britannia Romana; or the Roman antiquities of Britain. 1732.

Jeake, Samuel (1623–1690). Charters of the Cinque Ports, two ancient towns, and their members. Translated into English, with annotations. 1728.

Jones, Inigo. The most notable antiquity of Great Britain, vulgarly called Stone-Heng, on Salisbury Plain, restored by I. J. 1655.

Junius, Franciscus. Gothicum glossarium, quo Argentei codicis vocabula explicantur atque illustrantur. Dort, 1665.

—— Etymologicum Anglicanum . . . edidit Edwardus Lye. Praemittuntur vita auctoris et grammatica Anglo-Saxonica. Oxford, 1743.

Kennett, White (bishop of Peterborough). Parochial antiquities, attempted in the history of Ambrosden, and other adjacent parts, in the counties of Oxford and Bucks. Oxford, 1695. Another edn., enlarged, by Bandinel, B. 1818. See, also, bibliography to Chaps. VII and VIII, ante.

Kilbourne, Richard (1605–1678). A topographie, or survey of the county of Kent, with . . . historicall, and other matters touching the same. 1659.

King, Daniel (d. 1664?). The vale-royall of England, or, the county-palatine of Chester illustrated. . . . Performed by William Smith and William Webb. Published by Mr. Daniel King. 1656.

Langbaine, Gerard, the elder (1609–1658). The foundation of the Universitie of Oxford; with a catalogue of the principall founders and speciall benefactors of all the Colledges. 1651.

Le Neve, John. Fasti ecclesiae Anglicanae: or, an essay towards deducing a regular succession of all the principal dignitaries in each cathedral, collegiate church, or chapel . . . in . . . England and Wales. 1716. New edn., with continuation, by Hardy, T. D. 1854.

—— Monumenta Anglicana; being inscriptions on the monuments of eminent persons deceased in or since the year 1600 (to the end of 1718). 5 vols. 1717–19.

Letters written by eminent persons in the seventeenth and eighteenth centuries: to which are added, Hearne's journeys to Reading and to Whaddon Hall . . . and Lives of eminent men, by John Aubrey. 2 vols. (in 3 parts). 1813.

Lewis, John (1675–1747). The history and antiquities of the Isle of Tenet, in Kent. 1723.

—— The history and antiquities of the abbey and church of Favresham in Kent. 1727.

—— A dissertation on the antiquity and use of seals in England. (Anon.) 1740.

Lewis wrote numerous other works, including a life of Caxton and a history of the Translations of the Bible into English. *See* list in D. of N. B. and in British Museum Catalogue.

Leycester, Sir Peter (1614–1678). Historical antiquities, in two books. The first treating in general of Great-Brettain and Ireland; the second containing particular remarks concerning Cheshire. 1673.

Lhuyd, Edward (1660–1709). Archaeologia Britannica, giving some account . . . of the languages, histories and customs of the original inhabitants of Great Britain. Vol. 1, Glossography. Oxford, 1707. (No more published.)

Lisle, William (1569?–1637). A Saxon treatise concerning the Old and New Testaments . . . by Ælfricus Abbas . . . now first published (with a translation). 1623.

—— The Faire Aethiopian. 1631. A rhymed version of Heliodorus.

—— Divers ancient monuments in the Saxon tongue. 1638.

Madox, Thomas. Formulare Anglicanum: or, a collection of ancient charters and instruments of divers kinds . . . from the Norman Conquest to the end of the reign of King Henry the VIII. 1702.

—— The history and antiquities of the exchequer of the kings of England. . . taken from the records. 1711.

—— Firma Burgi: or, an historical essay concerning the cities, towns and boroughs of England, taken from records. 1726.

—— Baronia Anglica: an history of land-honours and baronies, and of tenure in capite, verified by records. 1736.

Magna Britannia et Hibernia, antiqua & nova. Or, a new survey of Great Britain . . . collected and composed by an impartial Hand [Thomas Cox]. 6 vols. 1720–31. [Contains only the English counties.]

Maitland, William (1693?–1757). The history of London, from its foundation by the Romans to the present time. 1739. Many later edns.

—— The history of Edinburgh, from its foundation to the present time. 1753.

—— The history and antiquities of Scotland. 2 vols. 1757.

Miege, Guy. The new state of England. 1691. Continued as The present state of Great Britain. 1707. 11th edn. 1748.

Miscellanies on several curious subjects, now first publish'd from their respective originals. [Ed. Rawlinson, R.] 1714.

Morant, Philip (1700–1770). The history and antiquities of . . . Colchester. 1748.

—— The history and antiquities of the county of Essex. 2 vols. 1768.

Morgan, Sylvanus (1620–1693). The sphere of gentry; deduced from the principles of nature; an historical and genealogical work of arms and blazon. 1661.

—— Armilogia sive ars chromocritica, the language of arms by the colours and metals. 1666.

Newcourt, Richard. Repertorium ecclesiasticum parochiale Londinense: an ecclesiastical parochial history of the diocese of London. 2 vols. 1708–10.

Nicholson, William. Leges marchiarum, or border laws . . . of England and Scotland . . . from the reign of Henry III to the union of the two crowns . . . with . . . an appendix of charters and records. 1705.

—— The English historical library, or a short view and character of most of the writers . . . which may be serviceable to the undertakers of a general history of this kingdom. 3 pts. 1696–9.

—— The Scottish historical library. 1702.

—— The Irish historical library. 1724.

These three were published together in 1736, and again in 1776, under the title of The English, Scotch and Irish historical libraries.

Nisbet, Alexander. An essay on additional figures and marks of cadency, shewing the ancient and modern practice of differencing descendants in this and other nations. Edinburgh, 1702.

—— An essay on the ancient and modern use of armories, and an explanation of the terms of blazonry. Edinburgh, 1718.

—— A system of heraldry, speculative and practical, with the true art of blazon . . . illustrated with examples of armorial figures and atchievements of the most considerable sirnames and families in Scotland. 2 vols. Edinburgh, 1722–42.

Oldys, William. The life of Sir Walter Raleigh. Prefixed to Raleigh's History of the World. 2 vols. 1736.

—— The British Librarian, exhibiting a compendious review or abstract of our most scarce, useful and valuable books. 6 nos. (Jan.–June 1737). 1738.

—— Catalogus bibliothecae Harleianae in locos communes distributus, cum indice auctorum. (By Johnson, S., Maittaire, M. and Oldys, W.) 5 vols. 1743–5.

See, also, Harleian Miscellany.

Palmer, Samuel (d. 1732). The general history of printing, from its first invention in the city of Mentz . . . particularly its introduction, rise and progress here in England. 1732.

Parker, Richard (1572–1629). Σκελετὸς Cantabrigiensis, sive collegiorum umbratilis delineatio. Published by Hearne in vol. v of Leland's Collectanea. Oxford, 1715.

Parkinson, Anthony (1667–1728). Collectanea Anglo-Minoritica; or, A collection of the antiquities of the English Franciscans, or . . . Grey Friers. With an appendix concerning the English nuns of the Order of St. Clare. 1726.

Pearson, John (bishop of Chester). See bibliography to Vol. VIII, Chap. xii, pp. 518, 519.

Peck, Francis (1692–1743). Academia tertia Anglicana; or, the antiquarian annals of Stanford in Lincoln, Rutland, and Northampton Shires. 1727.

—— Desiderata curiosa . . . memoirs, letters, wills and epitaphs . . . all now first published from the original MSS. 2 vols. 1732.

Petyt, William. The antient rights of the Commons of England asserted; or, a discourse proving . . . that the Commons of England were ever an essential part of Parliament. 1680.

—— Jus Parliamentarium: or, The antient power, jurisdiction, rights and liberties of . . . Parliament, revived and asserted. 1739.

Philosophical Transactions of the Royal Society. 1665 ff. (In progress.)

Pits, John (1560–1616). Relationes historicae de rebus Anglicis, sive de illustribus Britanniae scriptoribus. Paris, 1619.

Plot, Robert. The natural history of Oxfordshire, being an essay toward the natural history of England. Oxford, 1677.

—— The natural history of Staffordshire. Oxford, 1686.

Rawlinson, Richard. The life of Mr. Anthony Wood, historiographer of the most famous University of Oxford. (Anon.) 1711.

—— The history and antiquities of the cathedral church of Rochester. 1717.

—— The history and antiquities of the city and cathedral church of Hereford. 1717.

—— Epistolae Abaelardi et Heloisae, cum codd. MSS. collatae. 1718.

Rawlinson, Richard. The history and antiquities of the cathedral church of Salisury, and the abbey church of Bath. 1719.

—— The English topographer; or, an historical account of all the pieces . . . relating to the antiquities, natural history, or topographical description of any part of England. By an impartial hand. 1720.

—— A new method of studying history. Originally written in French by Lenglet du Fresnoy, and translated . . . by R. Rawlinson. 2 vols. 1728.
    See, also, Abingdon, Aubrey (Surrey), Erdeswicke, Miscellanies, Risdon.

Risdon, Tristram. The chorographical description, or survey, of the county of Devon; with the city and county of Exeter. (Ed. Rawlinson, R.) 2 vols. 1714. Another, and better, edn. 1811.

Rymer, Thomas. *See* bibliogrpahy to Chaps. VII and VIII, *ante.*

Salmon, Nathaniel. Roman stations in Britain. 1726.

—— A survey of the Roman antiquities in some midland counties of England. 1726.

—— The history of Hertfordshire; describing the county, and its antient monuments, particularly the Roman. 1728.

Salmon, Nathaniel. A new survey of England wherein the defects of Camden are supplied . . . the Roman military ways traced and the stations settled. 11 pts. 1728–9.

—— Antiquities of Surrey . . . with some account of the present state and natural history of the county. 1736.

—— The history and antiquities of Essex. 1740. [Not completed.]

Savage, Henry (1604?–1672). Balliofergus: or, a commentary upon the foundation, founders, and affaires of Balliol Colledge. Oxford, 1668.

Sibbald, Sir Robert. *See* bibliography to Chap. XIV, sec. B, II, *post.*

Smith, Thomas. *See* section III, *ante.*

Somner, William. The antiquities of Canterbury. 1640. 2nd edn., revised and enlarged, by Battely, N. 1703.

—— Dictionarium Saxonico-Latino-Anglicum. Accesserunt Ælfrici abbatis grammatica Latino-Saxonica, cum glossario suo ejusdem generis. Oxford, 1659.

—— A treatise of gavelkind, both name and thing. 1660.

—— A treatise of the Roman ports and forts in Kent. Publish'd by James Brome. . . . To which is prefixt the life of Mr. Somner [by bp. Kennett]. Oxford, 1693.

Spelman, Sir Henry. De non temerandis ecclesiis; a tract of the rights and respects due unto churches. 1613. Many times rptd.

—— Archaeologus. In modum glossarii ad rem antiquam posteriorem continentis Latino-barbara, peregrina, obsoleta et novatae significationis vocabula. (Part I only.) 1626. The complete work, ed. by Dugdale, W., was issued in 1664 under the title Glossarium archaeologicum.

—— Concilia, decreta, leges, constitutiones, in re ecclesiarum orbis Britannici. Vol. I (to 1066). 1639. Vol. II, ed. Dugdale, W. 1664.

—— De sepultura. 1641.

—— A protestant's account of his orthodox holding in matters of religion at this present indifference in the Church. (Anon.) Cambridge, 1642. Rptd. in Somers's Tracts, ed. Scott, vol. IV, p. 32.

—— Tithes too hot to be touched. Ed. Stephens, J. 1646. Reissued in 1647, as The larger treatise on tithes.

—— Aspilogia. Ed. Biss, E. 1654.

—— Villare Anglicum; or a view of the townes of England. By Spelman and Dodsworth, R. 1656.

Spelman, Sir Henry. The history and fate of sacrilege, discover'd by examples. 1698. An abridgment in French was published in 1698, and a German translation in 1878.

—— Reliquiae Spelmannianae. The posthumous works of Sir Henry Spelman, relating to the laws and antiquities of England. With the life of the Author. Ed. Gibson, E. Oxford, 1698.

—— The English works of Sir Henry Spelman . . . together with his post‐humous works relating to the laws and antiquities of England; and the life of the author. Ed. Gibson, E. 1723.

Stevens, John. The history of the antient abbeys, monasteries, hospitals, cathe‐dral and collegiate churches. Being two additional volumes to Sir William Dugdale's Monasticon Anglicanum. 2 vols. 1722–3.

The 1718 English abridgment of the Monasticon is also attributed to Stevens.

—— Monasticon Hibernicum; or The monastical history of Ireland. 1722.

—— A new Spanish and English dictionary. 1706.

Stevens also published an English version of Bede's Ecclesiastical His‐tory, and a number of translations from the Spanish and Portuguese.

Strype, John. A survey of the cities of London and Westminster . . . by John Stow . . . brought down from the year 1683 to the present time. 2 vols. 1720. See, also, bibliography to Chaps. VII and VIII, ante.

Stukeley, William. Itinerarium curiosum, or an account of the antiquitys and remarkable curiositys in nature or art, observ'd in travels thro' Great Brit‐tan. Centuria I. 1724. 2nd edn. (the complete work). 2 vols. 1776.

—— Stonehenge, a temple restor'd to the British Druids. 1740.

—— Abury, a temple of the British Druids, with some others, described. 1743.

—— An account of Richard of Cirencester, with his antient map of Roman Brit‐tain, and the itinerary thereof. 1757. (The work attributed to Richard of Cirencester, and dealt with in this book, was a forgery by Charles Bertram.)

Tanner, Thomas. Notitia monastica, or a short history of the religious houses in England and Wales. Oxford, 1695. 2nd edn., enlarged, ed. by Tanner, J. 1744. Rptd., with additions, by Nasmith, J., 1787.

—— Bibliotheca Britannico-Hibernica: sive, de scriptoribus, qui in Anglia, Scotia, et Hibernia ad saeculi XVII initium floruerunt . . . commentarius. 1748.

Thomas, William (1670–1738). A survey of the cathedral-church of Worcester; with an account of the bishops thereof. 1736.

Thoresby, Ralph. Ducatus Leodiensis; or the topography of the . . . town and parish of Leedes, and parts adjacent. . . . With the pedigrees of many of the nobility and gentry. 1715. 2nd edn., by Whitaker, T. D. 1816.

—— Vicaria Leodiensis: or, the history of the church of Leedes. 1724.

—— Diary, 1677–1724. Ed. Hunter, J. 2 vols. 1830.

Thoroton, Robert. The antiquities of Nottinghamshire. 1677. 2nd edn., by Throsby, J. 3 vols. 1790.

Thorpe, John (1682–1750). Registrum Roffense: or a collection of ancient records . . . illustrating the ecclesiastical history and antiquities of the diocese and cathedral church of Rochester. 1769.

Twyne, Brian. Antiquitatis Academiae Oxoniensis apologia. Oxford, 1608. Reissued, 1620.

Twysden, Sir Roger. The commoners liberty: or, the Englishman's birthright (Anon.) 1648.

Twysden, Sir Roger. Historiae Anglicanae scriptores x. 1652.

—— An historical vindication of the Church of England in point of schism, as it stands separated from the Roman, and was reformed I Elizabeth. 1657.

Warburton, John (1682–1759). Vallum Romanum: or the history and antiquities of the Roman wall, commonly called the Picts' wall. 1753.

—— William (bishop of Gloucester). *See* bibliography to Chap. xi, *ante.*

Webb, John (1611–1672). A vindication of Stone-Heng restored. 1665.

Weever, John. Ancient funerall monuments within . . . Great Britaine, Ireland, and the islands adjacent. 1631.

Wilkins, David. Concilia Magnae Britanniae et Hiberniae, a Synodo Verolamiensi, A. D. 446, ad Londinensem, A. D. 1717. 4 vols. 1737. [Founded on the work of Spelman and Dugdale, and in its turn formed the basis of Haddan and Stubbs's Councils and Ecclesiastical Documents.]

—— Leges Anglo-Saxonicae ecclesiasticae et civiles. 1721.

Willis, Browne. Notitia parliamentaria: or, an history of the counties, cities and boroughs, in England and Wales. 3 vols. 1716–50.

—— An history of the mitred parliamentary abbies, and conventual cathedral churches. 2 vols. 1718–19.

—— A survey of the cathedral church of St. David's. 1717.

—— A survey of the cathedral church of Llandaff. 1719.

—— A survey of the cathedral church of St. Asaph. 1720.

—— A survey of the cathedral church of Bangor. 1721.

—— A survey of the cathedrals . . . with an exact account of all the churches and chapels in each diocese. . . . 3 vols. 1727–30.

—— The history and antiquities of the town, hundred, and deanery of Buckingham. 1755.

Wood, Anthony. Historia et antiquitates Universitatis Oxoniensis. 2 vols. Oxford, 1674.

—— The history and antiquities of the University of Oxford. Now first published in English, from the original MS. in the Bodleian Library, by John Gutch. 3 pts. Oxford, 1792–6.

—— The history and antiquities of the Colleges and Halls in the University of Oxford. Now first published in English from the original manuscript in the Bodleian Library, with a continuation to the present time, by J. Gutch. Oxford, 1786–90.

—— Athenae Oxonienses. An exact history of all the writers and bishops who have had their education in the University of Oxford from 1500 to 1690; to which are added the Fasti or Annals of the said University. 2 vols. 1691–2. 2nd edn. 2 vols. 1721. [With corrections and additions. *See* D. of N. B., vol. lxii, p. 352.] 3rd (and best) edn. Ed. Bliss, P. 6 vols, 1813–20. [Embodies the corrections and additions of Tanner, Kennett. Baker, Wanley, and others. The prefatory matter includes the more important pieces relative to Wood's life and writings.]

    A new edn., also under the editorship of Bliss, was projected by the Ecclesiastical History Society; but only the first volume, containing Wood's autobiography, was issued (1848).

—— Modius Salium, a collection of such pieces of humour as prevail'd at Oxford in the time of Mr. Anthony à Wood. Collected by himself, and publish'd from his original manuscript. Oxford, 1751.

—— Survey of the antiquities of the City of Oxford. Ed. by Clark, A. 3 vols. Oxford Historical Society. 1889–99.

    A garbled and inaccurate edn., with additions, by Peshall, Sir J., was

published in 1773, under the title of The antient and present state of the
City of Oxford.

Wood, Anthony.   Autobiography (1632–72).   This was first published by Hearne
    in his edition of Thomae Caii Vindiciae Antiquitatis Academiae Oxoniensis
    (Oxford, 1730).   Rptd., with additions from Wood's diaries continuing the
    narrative to the date of Wood's death, by Huddesford, W., in 1772, both
    separately and as vol. ii of The Lives of Leland, Hearne and Wood; and
    included, in its extended form, in vol i of Bliss's edition of Athenae (1813),
    and in vol. i of his projected edition of Athenae in 1848.   [All these have been
    superseded by]

—— The Life and Times of Anthony Wood, antiquary of Oxford, 1632–1695,
    described by himself: collected from his diaries and other papers by Andrew
    Clark.   5 vols.   Oxford Historical Society, 1891–1900.   [The introduction
    contains a full account of Wood's manuscripts, which are now in the Bod-
    leian library.]

Wright, James.   The history and antiquities of the county of Rutland.   1684.

                                                              H. G. A.

CHAPTER XIV

SCOTTISH LITERATURE FROM 1603 TO 1786

(1) *General*

BIBLIOGRAPHY AND GENERAL WORKS OF REFERENCE

Aldis, H. G.   A list of books printed in Scotland before 1700.   Edinburgh Biblio-
    graphical Society, 1904.

Couper, W. J.   The Edinburgh Periodical Press, 1642–1800.   2 vols.   Stirling,
    1908.

Darien.   For bibliography of the Darien colony *see* A bibliography of printed
    documents and books relating to the . . . Darien Company, by Scott, J.,
    and Johnston, G. P.   2 pts.   (Edinburgh Bibliographical Society, 1904–6.)

Graham, H. G.   Scottish men of letters in the eighteenth century.   1901.

Irving, D.   Lives of Scotish writers.   2 vols.   Edinburgh, 1839.

—— The history of Scotish poetry.   Edinburgh, 1861.

Millar, J. H.   A literary history of Scotland.   1903.

Terry, C. S.   A catalogue of the publications of Scottish historical and kindred
    clubs and societies.   Glasgow, 1909.

Walker, H.   Three centuries of Scottish literature.   2 vols.   Glasgow, 1893.

A. THEOLOGY AND RELIGIOUS CONTROVERSY

I. (1603–1660)

Adamson, John (d. 1653).   Dioptra gloriae divinae: seu enarratio Psalmi xix,
    et in eundem meditationes.   Edinburgh, 1637.

Balcanquhall, Walter (1586?–1645).   *See* bibliography to Vol. VII, Chaps. viii
    and ix, p. 491, *ante*.

Baron, Robert (1593?–1639).   Philosophia theologiae ancillans.   St. Andrews,
    1621.

—— Disputatio theologica, de formali objecto fidei.   Aberdeen, 1627.

—— Disputatio theologica, de vero discrimine peccati mortalis et venialis.   Aber-
    deen, 1633.

Baron, Robert. Metaphysica generalis . . . opus postumum. Leyden, 1657.

Binning, Hugh (1627–1653). The common principles of Christian religion clearly proved. Glasgow, 1659.

—— The sinner's sanctuary . . . being xl Sermons. Edinburgh, 1670.

—— Works. Edinburgh, 1735.

Boyd, Robert (1578–1627). Hecatombe Christiana, hymnus ἑκατόνστροφος ad Christum servatorem. Edinburgh, 1627. Translated by Mure, Sir Wm. as A Spirituall Hymne, Edinburgh, 1628.

—— In Epistolam Pauli Apostoli ad Ephesios praelectiones supra cc. 1652.

Boyd, Zachary (1585?–1653). The last battell of the soule in death, carefulle digested for the comfort of the sicke. Edinburgh, 1628. Another edn., with an account of the author and his works, by Neil, G. Glasgow, 1831.

—— The balme of Gilead prepared for the sicke. Edinburgh, 1629.

—— A clear form of catechising. Glasgow, 1639.

—— Four letters of comforts for the deaths of the Earle of Haddingtoun and of the Lord Boyd. Glasgow, 1640.

—— 1. Crosses, 2. Comforts, 3. Counsels, needfull to bee considered, and carefully to be laid up in the hearts of the godly, in these boysterous broiles and bloody times. Glasgow, 1643.

—— The garden of Zion: wherein the life and death of godly and wicked men in scriptures are to be seene. 2 vols. Glasgow, 1644. In verse.

—— The psalmes of David in meeter. Third edn. Glasgow, 1646.

Bruce, Robert (1559–1631). Sermons preached in the kirk of Edinburgh. Edinburgh, 1591.

—— The way to true peace and rest; delivered at Edinborough in xvi sermons. 1617.

—— Sermons. Ed. Cunningham, W. Wodrow Society, 1843.

Corbet, John (1603–1641). The ungirding of the Scottish armour: or an answer to the informations for defensive arms against the Kings Majestie . . . drawn up at Edinburgh. Dublin, 1639.

Dickson, David (1583–1663). True Christian love. To be sung with any of the common tunes of the Psalms. Edinburgh, 1634.

—— A short explanation of the Epistle of Paul to the Hebrewes. Aberdeen, 1635.

—— Expositio analytica omnium apostolicarum epistolarum. Glasgow, 1645.

—— A brief exposition of the evangel of Jesus Christ according to Matthew. Glasgow, 1647.

—— A brief explication of the . . . Psalms. 3 pts. 1653–5.

—— Therapeutica sacra: seu de curandis casibus conscientiae circa regenerationem per foederum divinorum prudentem applicationem libri tres. 1656.

—— Select practical writings. Edinburgh, 1845.

Douglas, William (fl. 1660). Academiarum vindiciae, in quibus novantium praejudicia contra academias etiam reformatas averruncantur, eorundem que institutio recta proponitur. Aberdeen, 1659.

—— The stable trueths of the kirk require a sutable behaviour. Holden forth by way of a sermon. Aberdeen, 1660.

Durham, James (1622–1658). A commentarie upon the Book of the Revelation Edinburgh, 1658.

—— The dying man's testament to the Church of Scotland; or, a treatise concerning scandal. Edinburgh, 1659.

—— Clavis Cantici; or, an exposition of the Song of Solomon. Edinburgh, 1668.

Durham, James. The law unsealed: or a practical exposition of the ten commandments. 2nd edn. Glasgow, 1676.

—— The blessednesse of the death of those that die in the Lord . . . discoursed in seven very searching, but very sweet sermons. 1681.

—— The great corruption of subtile self; discovered, and driven from its lurking holes. . . . In seven sermons. Edinburgh, 1686.

—— Christ crucified: or the marrow of the Gospel evidently holden forth in lxxii sermons on the whole 53 chapter of Isaiah. 3rd edn. Edinburgh, 1700.

Fergusson, James (1621–1667). A brief exposition of the Epistles of Paul to the Philippians and Colossians. Edinburgh, 1656.

—— A brief exposition of the Epistles of Paul to the Galatians and Ephesians. Edinburgh, 1659.

—— A brief exposition of the . . . Epistles of Paul to the Thessalonians. Glasgow, 1675.

—— A brief relation of the errors of toleration, Erastianism, independency and separation. Edinburgh, 1692.

Forbes, John (1593–1648). Irenicum amatoribus veritatis et pacis in ecclesia Scoticana. Aberdeen, 1629.

—— Gemitus ecclesiae Scoticanae, sive tractatus de sacrilegio. Aberdeen, 1631.

—— A peaceable warning to the subjects in Scotland. Aberdeen, 1638.

—— Opera omnia. 2 vols. Amsterdam, 1702–3.

Forbes, Patrick (1564–1635). An exquisite commentarie upon the Revelation of Saint John. 1613.

—— Eubulus; or a dialogue, wherein a rugged Romish ryme (inscrybed Catholicke questions to the protestant) is confuted and the Questions thereof answered. Aberdeen, 1627.

   Funerals of a Right Reverend Father in God, Patrick Forbes of Corse, Bishop of Aberdeen. Aberdeen, 1635. (Contains Latin verses by the chief Scottish scholars of the day.)

Gillespie, George (1613–1648). A dispute against the English-Popish ceremonies, obtruded upon the Church of Scotland. 1637.

—— Certaine brief observations and antiquaeries: on Master Prin his Twelve questions about church-government. 1644.

—— Wholesome severity reconciled with Christian liberty. Or, the true resolution of a present controversie concerning liberty of conscience. 1645.

—— Aaron's rod blossoming, or the divine ordinance of church government vindicated. 1646.

—— An usefull case of conscience discussed and resolved, concerning associations and confederacies with idolaters, infidels, hereticks, or any other known enemies of truth and godlinesse. Edinburgh, 1649.

—— A treatise of miscellany questions: wherein many usefull questions and cases of conscience are discussed and resolved. Edinburgh, 1649.

—— Works, now first collected. With memoir of his life and writings, by Hetherington, W. M. 2 vols. Edinburgh, 1846.

   Gillespie also engaged in a pamphleteering controversy with Thomas Coleman, an opponent in the Westminster Assembly.

Gray, Andrew (1633–1656). The mystery of faith opened up. Glasgow, 1659.

—— Directions and instigations to the duty of prayer. Glasgow, 1669.

—— Great and precious promises. Edinburgh, 1669.

—— The spiritual warfare; or, some sermons concerning the nature of mortification. Edinburgh, 1671.

Gray, Andrew. Whole works. Glasgow, 1762.

Guild, William (1586–1657). Levi his complaint: or, the moane of the poor ministrie. Edinburgh, 1617.

—— Moses unvailed; or, those figures which served unto the patterne and shaddow of heavenly things, pointing out the Messiah Christ Jesus, briefly explained. 1620.

—— Issachars asse braying under a double burden; or, the uniting of churches. Aberdeen, 1622.

—— The old Roman Catholik, as at first he was taught by Paul; in opposition to the new Roman Catholik, as of latter he is taught by the pope. Aberdeen, 1649.

Henderson, Alexander (1583?–1646). The government and order of the Church of Scotland. Edinburgh, 1641.

—— Sermons, prayers, and pulpit addresses. Ed. Martin, R. T. 1867.

Maxwell, John. (1590?–1647). Sacro-sancta regum majestas: or, the sacred and royall prerogative of Christian kings. Oxford, 1644. (This was answered by Samuel Rutherford in Lex Rex. 1644.)

—— The burthen of Issachar: or, the tyrannicall power and practises of the presbyteriall government in Scotland. 1646.

Rutherford, Samuel (1600–1661). Exercitationes apologeticae pro divina gratis. 1636.

—— A peaceable and temperate plea for Paul's presbytery in Scotland. 1642.

—— Lex, Rex; the law and the prince. A dispute for the just prerogative of king and people. 1644. (Written chiefly as a reply to Maxwell's Sacrosancta regum majestas, Oxford, 1644; it was burned by the common hangman at the Restoration.)

—— The divine right of church government and excommunication. 1646.

—— Disputatio scholastica de divina providentia. Edinburgh, 1649.

—— A free disputation against pretended liberty of conscience. 1649.

—— The covenant of life opened; or a treatise of the covenant of grace. Edinburgh, 1655.

—— Joshua redivivus, or Mr. Rutherfoord's letters; now published for the use of all the people of God. 1664. Many times rptd.

Sempill, Sir James (1566–1625). Sacrilege sacredly handled, that is according to Scripture onely; for the use of all churches in generall, but more especially for those of North Britaine. 1619.

—— A picktooth for the Pope, or the packman's paternoster, set down in a dialogue betwixt a packman and a priest. (In verse.) Edinburgh (1630 c.). Often rptd.

Struther, William (fl. 1633). Christian observations and resolutions; or, the daylie practise of the renewed man. 2 pts. Edinburgh, 1628–9.

—— A looking glasse for princes and people. Edinburgh, 1632.

—— A looking glasse for princes and popes; or, a vindication of the sacred authoritie of princes from the anti-Christian usurpation of the popes. Edinburgh, 1632.

—— True happiness, or King David's choice. Edinburgh, 1633.

Symson, Archibald (1564?–1628). Christes testament unfolded: or, seaven godlie and learned sermons on our Lords seaven last words. Edinburgh, 1620.

—— Heptameron, the seven dayes: that is, meditations and prayers, upon the worke of the Lords creation. St. Andrews, 1621.

—— Samsons seaven lockes of haire: allegorically expounded, and compared to the seaven spirituall vertues. St. Andrews, 1621.

Symson, Archibald. Hieroglyphica animalium . . . quae in scripturis sacris inveniuntur. 4 pts. Edinburgh, 1622–4.

—— A sacred septenarie, or, a godly and fruitful exposition of the seven psalmes of repentance. 1623.

II. (1660–1707)

Annand, William (1633–1689). Pater noster, our Father: or, the Lord's Prayer explained. Edinburgh, 1670.

Barclay, Robert. *See* bibliography to Vol. VIII, Chap. IV, p. 471, *ante.*

Bell, Thomas (*fl.* 1672). Roma restituta; sive antiquitatum Romanarum compendium absolutum. Glasgow, 1672.

—— Grapes in the wilderness; or, the solid grounds of sweet consolation. 1680.

—— Nehemiah the Tirshatha; or, the character of a good commissioner. Edinburgh, 1692.

Brown, John (1610?–1679). An apologeticall relation of the particular sufferings of the faithful ministers and professours of the Church of Scotland since August, 1660. 1665.

—— Christ, the way, and the truth, and the life. Rotterdam, 1677.

—— Quakerisme the pathway to paganisme; or, a view of the Quakers religion. Edinburgh, 1678.

—— The history of the Indulgence . . . together with a demonstration of the unlawfulness thereof. 1678.

Clark, James (d. 1724). Memento mori, or a word in season to the healthful, sick, and dying, fit for this calamitous time. Edinburgh, 1699.

—— Presbyterial government of the Church of Scotland, methodically described. Edinburgh, 1701.

—— A new years-gift or the Christians pocket-book. Being a bundle of familiar exhortations to the practice of piety. Edinburgh, 1703.

—— A just reprimand to Daniel Defoe. Edinburgh, n. d.

Clark's other works include several separate sermons.

Forrester, Thomas (1635?–1706). The hierarchical bishop's claim to a divine right tried at the Scripture-bar. Edinburgh, 1699.

And other controversial tracts.

Geddes, William (1600?–1694). The saint's recreation, third part, upon the estate of grace. Edinburgh, 1683.

Guthrie, William (1620–1665). A short treatise of the Christians great interest. Edinburgh, 1659.

—— Two sermons preached at Finnick, the 17 day of August, 1662. 1680.

—— Crumbs of comfort; or, grace in its various degrees. 1681.

Honyman, Andrew (d. 1676). The seasonable case of submission to the church-government, as now re-established by law, briefly stated and determined. Edinburgh, 1662.

—— A survey of the insolent and infamous libel entitled Naphtali [by Sir James Stewart]. 2 pts. 1668–9.

Jameson, William (*fl.* 1689–1720). Verus Patroclus; or, the weapons of Quakerism the weakness of Quakerism. Edinburgh, 1689.

—— The summ of the episcopal controversy, as it is pleaded from the holy Scriptures. . . . Edinburgh, 1712.

—— Spicilegia antiquitatum Ægypti, atque vicinarum gentium. Glasgow, 1720.

And other anti-episcopalian tractates.

Keith, George (1639?–1716). Help in time of need, from the God of Help . . .
    Writ by George Keith, prisoner for the Truth in Aberdeen. (Aberdeen) 1665.
—— The deism of William Penn and his brethren . . . exposed. 1699.
—— The standard of the Quakers examined; or, an answer to the Apology of
    Robert Barclay. 1702.
—— A journal of travels from New-Hampshire to Caratuck, on the continent
    of North America. 1706.
        And many other Quaker treatises. (See Smith, Joseph. A descriptive
    Catalogue of Friends' Books. Vol. II. 1867.)
Leighton, Robert (1611–1684). See Vol. VIII, p. 518.
Livingstone, John (1603–1672). A brief historical relation of Mr. John Living-
    ston, minister of the Gospel . . . written by himself in Holland, during
    his banishment. 1727.
McWard, Robert (1633?–1687). The case of the accommodation lately pro-
    posed by the bishop of Dunblane. 1671.
—— The English ballance, weighing the reasons of Englands present conjunction
    with France, against the Dutch. 1672.
—— The poor man's cup of cold water. 1678.
—— The banders disbanded. 1681.
Monro, Alexander. A letter . . . giving an account of all the treatises that have
    been publish'd, with relation to the present persecution of the Church of
    Scotland. 1692.
—— (d. 1715?). An apology for the Church of Scotland. 1693.
—— Sermons preached upon several occasions. 1693.
—— An enquiry into the new opinions, chiefly propagated by the presbyterians
    of Scotland. 1696.
Naphtali. See Stewart, Sir James.
Rule, Gilbert (1629?–1701). A vindication of the Church of Scotland.   1691.
—— A second vindication of the Church of Scotland. Edinburgh, 1691.
—— A just . . . reproof of a pamphlet, called, The Scotch presbyterian elo-
    quence. Edinburgh, 1693.
        And other anti-episcopalian tracts.
Sage, John (1652–1711). An account of the late establishment of presbyterian
    government by the Parliament of Scotland anno 1690. 1693.
—— The principles of the Cyprianic age, with regard to episcopal power and
    jurisdiction, asserted. 1695.
—— The fundamental character of presbytery, as it hath been lately established
    in the kingdom of Scotland, examin'd and disprov'd. 1695.
—— Works, with memoir. Ed. by Shand, C. F. 3 vols. Spottiswoode Society,
    1844–6.
Scougal, Henry (1650–1678). The life of God in the soul of man (or the nature
    and excellency of the Christian religion). 1677. Often rptd.
Shields, Alexander (1660?–1700). A hind let loose, or an historical representation
    of the testimonies of the Church of Scotland for the interest of Christ. 1687.
—— A true and faithful relation of the sufferings of . . . Mr. Alexander Shields
    . . . written with his own hand. 1715.
Stewart, Sir James (d. 1713). Naphtali; or, the wrestlings of the Church of
    Scotland for the kingdom of Christ . . . from the beginning of the Refor-
    mation of religion until the year 1667. 1667.
Webster, James (1658?–1720). A discourse demonstrating that the government
    of the church, which is of divine right, is fixed, and not ambulatory. Edin-
    burgh, 1704.

Webster, James. Three poems, Mahanaim, or strivings with a Saviour . . . Peniel, or the combatant triumphing . . . and The triumph consummat, or the state of glory. 1706.

—— Lawful prejudices against an incorporating union with England. Edinburgh, 1707. (Answered in Defoe's The dissenters in England Vindicated. Edinburgh, 1707.)

Young, Robert (*fl.* 1663). A description of the first ten persecutions in the primitive church. Glasgow, 1660.

—— A breviary of the later persecutions of the professors of the gospel. Glasgow, 1663.

III. (1707–1786)

Anderson, George (1676?–1756). The use and abuse of diversions: a sermon on Luke xix. 13. With an appendix shewing that the stage in particular is an unchristian diversion. Edinburgh, 1733.

—— An analysis of the moral and religious sentiments contained in the writings of Sopho [Lord Kames] and David Hume. Edinburgh, 1755.

—— A remonstrance against Lord Viscount Bolingbroke's philosophical religion, Edinburgh, 1756.

Blackwell, Thomas (1660?–1728). Schema sacrum; or, a sacred scheme of natural and revealed religion. Edinburgh, 1710.

—— Ratio sacra; or, an appeal unto the rational world, about the reasonableness of revealed religion. Edinburgh, 1710.

Boston, Thomas (1676–1732). Human nature in its fourfold state. Edinburgh. 1720. Often rptd.

—— The sovereignty and wisdom of God displayed in the afflictions of men. (The crook in the lot.) Edinburgh, 1737. Often rptd.

—— Memoirs. Written by himself, and addressed to his children. Edinburgh, 1776.

—— Works. Ed. McMillan, S. 12 vols. Aberdeen, 1848–52.

Brown, John (1722–1787). An historical account of the rise and progress of the Secession. 1766.

—— A dictionary of the Holy Bible. Edinburgh, 1769.

—— A general history of the Christian church. 2 vols. Edinburgh, 1771.

—— The self-interpreting Bible. . . With explanatory contents, parallel Scriptures, large notes and practical observations. 2 vols. Edinburgh, 1778.

Calder, Robert (1658–1723). The lawfulness and expediency of set forms of prayer, maintain'd. 1706.

—— An answer to Mr. James Hog at Carnock, his Letter to a gentleman [*see below*]. Edinburgh, 1710.

—— Miscellany numbers; relating to the controversies about the Book of common prayer, episcopal government, the power of the Church in ordaining rites and ceremonies, etc. Edinburgh, 1713.

Calder, who, as an episcopalian minister, suffered much persecution, was, also, the reputed author of The Scotch Presbyterian Eloquence; or, the foolishness of their teaching discovered from their books, sermons and prayers. 1692.

Campbell, Archibald (1691–1756). An enquiry into the original of moral virtue, wherein it is shewn (against the author of the Fable of the bees, etc.) that virtue is founded in the nature of things . . . With some reflections on a late book [by F. Hutcheson] intitled, An enquiry into the original of our ideas of beauty and virtue. Edinburgh, 1733.

This work had previously been issued in 1728, in his own name, by Alexander Innes, to whom Campbell had entrusted it for publication.

Campbell, Archibald. The necessity of revelation: or, an enquiry into the extent of human powers with respect to matters of religion. 1739.

—— The authenticity of the Gospel history justified. 2 vols. Edinburgh, 1759.

Erskine, Ebenezer (1680–1754). The sovereignty of Zion's king; in some discourses. Edinburgh, 1739.

—— Sermons and discourses. 4 vols. Glasgow, 1762.

Erskine, Ralph (1685–1752). Faith no fancy: or, a treatise of mental images. Edinburgh, 1745.

—— Gospel sonnets, or spiritual songs. Edinburgh, 1726. 25th edn. 1797. (First published, as Gospel Canticles, in 1720.)

—— Scripture songs, selected from the Old and New Testament. Glasgow, 1754.

—— Sermons and other practical works. 2 vols. Glasgow, 1765. Another edn. 7 vols. 1863.

Glas, John (1695–1773). The testimony of the King of Martyrs concerning his kingdom. Edinburgh, 1727.

—— Works. 5 vols. Dundee, 1782–3.

Hadow, James (1670?–1764). A survey of the case of the episcopal clergy, and of those of the episcopal persuasion. Edinburgh, 1703.

—— The antinomianism of the Marrow of Modern Divinity detected. Edinburgh, 1721. Answered by James Hog (see below).

Hog, James (1658?–1734). A letter to a gentleman, in which the unlawfulness of imposing forms of prayer, and other acts of worship is plainly demonstrated. Edinburgh, 1710. Answered by Robert Calder (see above).

—— The controversie concerning the Marrow of Modern Divinity considered in several familiar dialogues. 2 pts. (Edinburgh.) 1721–2.

—— The scope and substance of the Marrow of Modern Divinity . . . explained and vindicated. Edinburgh, 1722. Written to confute James Hadow's Antinomianism (see above).

—— A letter, wherein the Scriptural grounds and warrants for the reformation of churches by way of covenant, are succinctly considered and cleared. Edinburgh, 1727.

—— Memoirs of the public life of James Hogg . . . Written by himself. Edinburgh, 1798.

Hog, who was the leader of the "Marrow men" in the Church of Scotland, published a number of other works, chiefly of a controversial nature.

Howie, John (1735–1793). Biographia Scoticana; or, a brief historical account of the lives, characters, and memorable transactions of the most eminent Scots worthies. 1774. 2nd edn., enlarged, 2 pts. Glasgow, 1781–2.

Walker, Patrick (d. 1745). Some remarkable passages of the life and death of Mr. Alexander Peden, late minister of the Gospel at Glenluce. 1724.

—— Some remarkable passages of the life and death of . . . Mr. John Semple, Mr. John Welwood, Mr. Richard Cameron. . . . Edinburgh, 1727.

—— Some remarkable passages in the life and death of . . . Mr. Daniel Cargill . . . Edinburgh, 1732.

—— Six saints of the covenant. Ed. by Fleming, D. Hay. 2 vols. 1901. (A collected edn. of the three preceding works.)

Willison, John (1680–1750). A treatise concerning the sanctifying of the Lord's day. Edinburgh, 1716.

—— An apology for the Church of Scotland, against the accusations of prelatists and Jacobites. Edinburgh, 1719.

—— A defence of national churches, and particularly of the national constitution of the Church of Scotland. Edinburgh, 1729.

—— Practical works. With an essay on his life and times by Hetherington, W. M. Glasgow (1846).

Witherspoon, John (1723–1794). Ecclesiastical characteristics; or, the arcana of church policy. Glasgow, 1753.

—— Essay on the connection between the doctrine of justification by the imputed righteousness of Christ, and holiness of life. Glasgow, 1756.

—— A serious enquiry into the nature and effects of the stage. Glasgow, 1757. (Called forth by the production of Home's Douglas on the Edinburgh stage in the previous year.)

—— Sinners sitting in the seat of the scornful. 1762.

—— Works. 9 vols. Edinburgh, 1804–5.

B. History and Antiquities

I. (1603–1660)

Baillie, Robert (1599–1662). *See* Vol. VII, p. 511, *ante*.

Baillie, Sir William, of Lamington (*fl.* 1648). *See* Vol. VII, p. 511, *ante*.

Blair, Robert (1593–1666). *See* Vol. VII, p. 511, *ante*.

Calderwood, David (1575–1650). *See* Vol. VII, p. 504, *ante*.

Craig, Sir Thomas (1538–1608). Jus feudale. 1655.

—— Scotland's sovereignty asserted . . . against those who maintain that Scotland is a feu, or fee-liege of England. Translated from the Latin by Ridpath, G. 1695.

—— The right of succession to the kingdom of England. (Translated into English by Gatherer, J.) 1703.

  Sir Thomas Craig also wrote various complimentary Latin poems addressed to royal personages.

Crawfurd, Thomas (d. 1662). History of the University of Edinburgh from 1580 to 1646. Edinburgh, 1808.

Gordon, James (1615?–1686). History of Scots affairs, from 1637 to 1641. Ed. by Robertson, J., and Grub, G. 3 vols. Spalding Club, 1841.

Hume, David, of Godscroft (1560?–1630). Poemata omnia. Paris, 1639.

—— The history of the houses of Douglas and Angus. Edinburgh, 1644.

  Reissued in 1648 as, A generall history of Scotland. An earlier edition was printed, but apparently not published, about 1630.

—— De familia Humia Wedderburnensi liber. Ed. by Miller, J. Abbotsford Club, 1839.

Johnston, Robert (1567–1639). The history of Scotland during the minority of King James VI. Done into English by T. M. 1648.

—— Historia rerum Britannicarum, ut et multarum Gallicarum, Belgicarum et Germanicarum, ab anno 1572–1628. Amsterdam, 1655.

Melville, Sir James, of Halhill (1535–1617). *See* Vol. III, p. 572, *ante*.

Melville, James (1556–1614). *See* Vol. III, p. 572, *ante*.

Monteith, Robert (*fl.* 1621–1660). Histoire des troubles de la Grand Bretagne (1633–1649). Paris, 1661.

Monteith, Robert. The history of the troubles of Great Britain, containing a particular account of the most remarkable passages in Scotland from 1633 to 1650. Trans. by Ogilvie, James. 1735.

Row, John (1586–1646). The history of the kirk in Scotland, from the year 1558 to August 1637. With a continuation to July 1639, by his son John Row. Ed. by Laing, D. Wodrow Society, 1842. Also edited for the Maitland Club in the same year. (This history, though printed for the first time in 1842, circulated widely in manuscript in the seventeenth century.)

Scot, Sir John, of Scotstarvet (1585–1670). The staggering state of the Scots statesmen, for one hundred years, viz. from 1550 to 1650. Edinburgh, 1754.

    Delitiae Poetarum Scotorum (1637), edited by Johnston, A., was published under the auspices of Sir John Scot, who was a liberal patron of letters.

Simson, Patrick (1556–1618). A short compend of the historie of the first ten persecutions moved against Christians. 5 pts. Edinburgh, 1613–16.

Spalding, John (*fl.* 1650). History of the troubles and memorable transactions in Scotland from the year 1625 to 1645. 2 vols. Aberdeen, 1792.

    Also edited for the Bannatyne Club, 1828–9, and the Spalding Club, 1850–1.

Spottiswode, John (1565–1639). *See* Vol. VII, p. 504, *ante.*

Wishart, George (1599–1671). De rebus auspiciis serenissimi et potentissimi Caroli . . . sub imperio illustrissimi Jacobi Montisrosarum Marchionis . . . anno 1644 et duobus sequentibus praeclare gestis, commentarius. 1647.

—— The history of the King's Majesties affairs in Scotland, under the conduct of . . . James Marques of Montrose . . . 1644–46. 1648. A translation of the preceding. It was reprinted, with a continuation, in 1652, under the title of Montrose redivivus.

    A second translation, with the title A complete history of the wars in Scotland; under . . . Montrose, was published in 1720; and a third, entitled Memoirs of the . . . Marquis of Montrose, appeared in 1756. An excellent critical edition of the complete Latin text, with a new translation, was brought out by Murdoch, A. D., and Simpson, H. F. M., in 1893.

II. (1660–1707)

Brodie, Alexander (1617–1680). The diary of Alexander Brodie of Brodie, Esq., who was one of the senators of the College of Justice . . . Taken from his own manuscript. Edinburgh, 1740.

Burnet, Gilbert (1643–1715). *See* Vol. VIII, pp. 516, 517, and the present vol., pp. 537–540, *ante.*

Cockburn, John (1652–1729). An historical relation of the General Assembly held at Edinburgh . . . in the year 1690. 2 pts. 1691.

—— A short history of the Revolution in Scotland. 1712.

—— A specimen of some free and impartial remarks on publick affairs and particular persons, especially relating to Scotland; occasion'd by Dr. Burnet's History of his own times. n. d.

Cromarty, George Mackenzie, Earl of (1630–1714). A vindication of Robert III, king of Scotland, from the imputation of bastardy. Edinburgh, 1695.

—— An historical account of the conspiracies by the Earls of Gowry and Robert Logan of Restalrig against King James VI. Edinburgh, 1713.

    Mackenzie also wrote several tracts on the Union, of which he was an advocate and supporter.

Dalrymple, Sir James (*fl.* 1714). A second edition of Camden's description of Scotland. Edinburgh, 1695.

—— Collections concerning the Scottish history, preceding the death of King David the First, in the year 1153. Edinburgh, 1705.

Guthry, Henry (1600?–1676). *See* Vol. VII, p. 512.

Irvine, Christopher (*fl.* 1638–1685). Historia Scoticae nomenclatura Latino-vernacula. Edinburgh, 1682.

Irvine also published Medicina magnetica (1656), and Bellum grammaticale: ad exemplar Mri A. Humii . . . editum (1658). The latter seems to have been identical, in both title and subject, with a play by Spense printed at Oxford in 1635, but performed there as early as 1592.

Jaffray, Alexander (1614–1673). Diary of Alexander Jaffray, provost of Aberdeen. 1833.

Kirkton, James (1620?–1699). The secret and true history of the Church of Scotland from the restoration to the year 1678. Ed. by Sharpe, C. K. Edinburgh, 1817.

Lamont, John (*fl.* 1671). The chronicle of Fife; being the diary of John Lamont of Newton, from 1649 to 1672. Ed. by Kinloch, G. R. Maitland Club, 1830.

Law, Robert (d. 1690?). Memorialls; or the memorable things that fell out within this island of Brittain from 1638–1684. Ed. by Sharpe, C. K. Edinburgh, 1818.

Mackenzie, Sir George (1636–1691). Aretina; or, the serious romance. Edinburgh, 1660.

—— Religio stoici; with a friendly addresse to the phanaticks of all sects and sorts. Edinburgh, 1663.

—— A moral essay, preferring solitude to public employment. Edinburgh, 1665.

—— Moral gallantry. Edinburgh, 1667.

—— A moral paradox, maintaining that it is much easier to be vertuous than vitious. Edinburgh, 1667.

—— Observations upon the laws and customs of nations as to precedency. Edinburgh, 1680.

—— Jus regium; or, the just and solid foundations of monarchy. Edinburgh, 1684.

—— Defence of the antiquity of the Royal line of Scotland. Edinburgh, 1685.

—— The moral history of frugality with its opposite vices. Edinburgh, 1691.

—— Vindication of the government in Scotland during the reign of Charles II. 1691.

—— Memoirs of the affairs of Scotland from the restoration of King Charles II. Edinburgh, 1822.

—— Works. 2 vols. Edinburgh, 1716–22.

Mackenzie also wrote on heraldry, and published several important treatises on legal subjects.

Nicoll, John (*fl.* 1660). A diary of public transactions and other occurrences, chiefly in Scotland, from January, 1650, to June, 1667. Ed. by Laing, D. Bannatyne Club, 1836.

Scott, Walter (1614?–1694?). A true history of several honourable families of the name of Scot. Edinburgh, 1688.

Sibbald, Sir Robert (1641–1712). An account of the Scotish atlas, or the description of Scotland ancient and modern. Edinburgh, 1683.

—— Scotia illustrata, sive prodromus historiae naturalis. Edinburgh, 1684.

Sibbald, Sir Robert. Memoria Balfouriani, sive historia rerum pro literis promovendis gestarum à clarissimis fratribus Balfouriis D. D. Jacobo . . . et D. D. Andrea. Edinburgh, 1699.

—— Commentarius in vitam Georgii Buchanani, ab ipsomet scriptam. Edinburgh, 1703.

—— The liberty and independency of the kingdom and church of Scotland, asserted from antient records. Edinburgh, 1703.

—— Historical enquiries, concerning the Roman monuments and antiquities in the north-part of Britain called Scotland. Edinburgh, 1707.

—— An account of the writers . . . which treat of the description of North Britain called Scotland. Edinburgh, 1710.

—— The history . . . of the sheriffdoms of Fife and Kinross. Edinburgh, 1710.

—— The history . . . of the sheriffdoms of Linlithgow and Stirling. Edinburgh, 1711.

—— Commentarius in Julii Agricolae expeditiones. Edinburgh, 1711.

—— Portus, coloniae, et castella Romana, ad Bodotriam et ad Tuam; or conjectures concerning the Roman ports, colonies, and forts on the Friths of Forth and Tay. Edinburgh, 1711.

—— The description of the isles of Orkney and Zetland. Edinburgh, 1711.

—— Autobiography. Printed in Maidment's Analecta Scotica. Vol. 1. Edinburgh, 1834.

III. (1707–1786)

Abercromby, Patrick (1656–1716?). The martial achievements of the Scots nation. Being an account of . . . such Scotsmen as have signaliz'd themselves by the sword. 2 vols. Edinburgh, 1711–15.

Anderson, James (1662–1728). An historical essay shewing that the crown and kingdom of Scotland is imperial and independent. Edinburgh, 1705.

—— Collections relating to the history of Mary Queen of Scots. 4 vols. Edinburgh, 1727–8.

—— Selectus diplomatum et numismatum Scotiae thesaurus. Edinburgh, 1739.

Blackwell, Thomas (1701–1757). An enquiry into the life and writings of Homer. 1735.

—— Memoirs of the court of Augustus. 3 vols. Edinburgh and London, 1753–63.

Clerk, Sir John (1684–1755). Dissertatio de monumentis quibusdam Romanis, in boreali Magnae Britanniae parte detectis, anno. 1731. Edinburgh, 1750.

—— Historical view of the forms and powers of the Court of Exchequer in Scotland. Edinburgh, 1820.

Dalrymple, Sir David, Lord Hailes (1726–1792). Memorials and letters relating to the history of Britain in the reign of James the First (and Charles the First). 2 vols. Glasgow, 1762–6.

—— Historical memorials concerning the provincial councils of the Scottish clergy. Edinburgh, 1769.

—— An examination of some of the arguments for the high antiquity of Regiam Majestatem; and an enquiry into the authenticity of Leges Malcolmi. Edinburgh, 1769.

—— Ancient Scottish poems published from the MS. of George Bannatyne. Edinburgh, 1770.

—— Remarks on the history of Scotland. Edinburgh, 1773.

Dalrymple, Sir David. Annals of Scotland. 2 vols. Edinburgh, 1776–9.
See also bibl. to Vol. X, Chap. XII, *post*.

Dalrymple, Sir John (1726–1810.) An essay towards a general history of feudal property in Great Britain. 1757.

—— Memoirs of Great Britain and Ireland (1681–1692). 2 vols. 1771–3. *See also* bibl. to Vol. X, Chap. XII, *post*.

Fountainhall, Lord. *See* Lauder, Sir John.

Gordon, Alexander (d. 1752). The history of Peter the Great, emperor of Russia. 2 vols. Aberdeen, 1755.

Gordon, Alexander (1692?–1754?). *See* bibl. to Chap. XIII, p. 585, *ante*.

Gordon, William (*fl.* 1726). The history of the . . . family of Gordon . . . together with the history of the most remarkable transactions in Scotland . . . to the year 1690. 2 vols. Edinburgh, 1726–7.

Guthrie, William (1708–1770). A general history of Scotland. 10 vols. 1767–8.

Hailes, Lord. *See* Dalrymple, Sir David.

Innes, Thomas (1662–1744). A critical essay on the ancient inhabitants of . . . Scotland. 2 vols. 1729.

—— The civil and ecclesiastical history of Scotland. Ed. by Grub, G. Spalding Club, 1853.

Lauder, Sir John, Lord Fountainhall (1646–1722). The decisions of the Lords of Council and Session from 1678 to 1712. 2 vols. Edinburgh, 1759–61.

—— Chronological notes of Scottish affairs from 1680 till 1701. Edinburgh. 1822.

—— Historical observes of memorable occurrents in church and state, from October, 1680, to April, 1686. Bannatyne Club, 1840.

—— Historical notices of Scotish affairs, selected from the manuscripts of Sir John Lauder (1661–1688). 2 vols. Bannatyne Club, 1848.

Mackenzie, George (1669–1725). Lives and characters of the most eminent writers of the Scots nation. 3 vols. Edinburgh, 1708–22. [A portentous and entirely untrustworthy work.]

Millar, John (1735–1801). Observations concerning the distinction of ranks in society. 1771.

—— Historical view of the English government . . . to the accession of the House of Stewart. 1787. Another edn., extended to the Revolution in 1688. 4 vols. 1803.

Nisbet, Alexander (1657–1725). *See* bibl. to Chap. XIII, p. 589, *ante*.

Ridpath, George (1717?–1772). The Border history of England and Scotland. 1776.

Robertson, William (1721–1793). *See* bibl. to Vol. X, Chap. XII, *post*.

Wallace, James (*fl.* 1684–1724). A history of the kingdom of Scotland. Dublin, 1724.

Wodrow, Robert (1679–1734). The history of the sufferings of the Church of Scotland, from the Restauration to the Revolution. 2 vols. Edinburgh, 1721–2.

—— Analecta; or, materials for a history of remarkable providences, mostly relating to Scotch ministers and christians. 4 vols. Maitland Club, 1842–3.

—— Collections upon the lives of the reformers and most eminent ministers of the Church of Scotland. 2 vols. Maitland Club, 1834–45.

—— Selections from Wodrow's Biographical Collections. Ed. Lippe, R. New Spalding Club, 1890.

—— Correspondence. Ed. by McCrie, T. 3 vols. Wodrow Society, 1842–3. Extensive collections of Wodrow's papers, a large portion of which is still unpublished, are in the Advocates' Library, Edinburgh, and the Library of the University of Glasgow.

C. POETRY (INCLUDING DRAMATIC)

See also part (2) below.

A book of Scotish pasquils, 1568–1715. (Ed. Maidment, J.) Edinburgh, 1868.
Scotish elegiac verses, 1629–1729. (Ed. Maidment, J.) Edinburgh, 1842.
Various pieces of fugitive Scotish poetry; principally of the seventeenth century. (Ed. Laing, D.) 2 series. 1825–53.
Delitiae Poetarum Scotorum. (Ed. Johnston, A.) 2 vols. Amsterdam, 1637,
Musa Latina Aberdonensis. Ed. Geddes, Sir W. D. and Leask, W. K. 3 vols. New Spalding Club. 1892–1910.
Scottish Poetry of the Seventeenth Century. Abbotsford Series, ed. Eyre-Todd. G. Glasgow, 1895.
Scottish Poetry of the Eighteenth Century. Abbotsford Series. 2 vols. Glasgow, 1896.

I. (1603–1660)

Adamson, Henry (d. 1639). The muses threnodie . . . containing varietie of pleasant poeticall descriptions . . . with the most remarkable antiquities of Scotland. Edinburgh, 1638.
Adamson, John (d. 1653). The muses welcome to the high and mightie Prince James . . . at his M. happie return to . . . Scotland. (Ed. by Adamson.) Edinburgh, 1618. (A collection of complimentary poems addressed to James I, on the occasion of his revisiting Scotland in 1617.)
Alexander, Sir William, Earl of Stirling (1567?–1640). The tragedie of Darius. Edinburgh, 1603.
—— Aurora: containing the first fancies of the authors youth. 1604.
—— The monarchicke tragedies: Croesus, Darius, the Alexandraean, Julius Caesar. 1607.
—— Doomes-day, or the great day of the Lords judgement. Edinburgh, 1614
—— Recreations with the Muses. 1637. (A collection of his poems.)
—— Poetical works. 3 vols. Glasgow, 1870–2.
　　See also bibl. to Vol. V, Chap. XIII, *ante.*
Ayton, Sir Robert (1570–1638). *See* Vol. VII, p. 467, *ante.*
Barclay, John (1582–1621). *See* Vol. IV, p. 567, *ante.*
Craig, Alexander, of Rosecraig (1567?–1627). Poetical essayes. 1604.
—— Amorose songes. 1606.
—— Poetical recreations. Edinburgh, 1609.
—— The pilgrime and the heremite. Aberdeen, 1631.
—— Poetical works . . . Now first collected. Hunterian Club. Glasgow, 1873.
Culross, Lady (Elizabeth Melville), (*fl.* 1603). Ane godlie dreame, compylit in Scottish meter. Edinburgh, 1603.
　　This popular poem of which at least nine editions appeared in the 17th century has been reprinted in the Scottish Text Society's edn. of Alex. Hume's poems.
Drummond, William, of Hawthornden (1585–1649). *See* Vol. IV, p. 480.
Gardyne, Alexander (1585?–1634?). A garden of grave and godlie flowres. Edinburgh, 1609.
—— The theatre of Scottish kings. Edinburgh, 1709.
　　Both were rptd. by the Abbotsford Club in 1845.

Gordon, Patrick (*fl.* 1614–1650). Neptunus Britannicus. 1614. (On the death of Prince Henry, etc.)

—— The famous historye of Penardo and Laissa . . . in heroik verse. Dort, 1615.

—— The famous historie of the renouned and valiant Prince Robert, surnamed the Bruce, king of Scotland . . . in heroik verse. Dort, 1615.

Grahame, Simion (1570?–1614). The passionate sparke of a relenting minde. 1604.

—— The anatomie of humors. Edinburgh, 1609.

    Both were rptd. by the Bannatyne Club, in 1830.

Hume, Anna (*fl.* 1644). The triumphs of love, chastitie, death; translated out of Petrarch. Edinburgh, 1644.

    Anna Hume also superintended the publication of her father's (David Hume) History of Douglas and Angus.

Johnston, Arthur (1587–1641). Epigrammata. Aberdeen, 1632.

—— Parerga. Aberdeen, 1632.

—— Poemata omnia. Middelburg, 1642.

    Vols. I and II of Musa Latina Aberdonensis (New Spalding Club, 1892–5) contain all Johnston's secular poems. Johnston also edited the wellknown collection Delitiae Poetarum Scotorum (*see above*).

Lauder, George (*fl.* 1677). The Scottish souldier. Edinburgh, 1629.

——.Wight. Edinburgh, 1629.

    Both reprinted by Boswell, A., in Frondes Caducae, 1818. *See, also,* other pieces in Laing's Fugitive Scottish Poetry. 1853.

Lithgow, William (1582–1645?). The totall discourse of the rare adventures and painfull peregrinations of long nineteene yeares. 1614.

—— The pilgrimes farewell to his native countrey of Scotland. Edinburgh, 1618.

—— Scotlands welcome to her native sonne and sovereigne lord, King Charles. Edinburgh (1633).

—— A true and experimentall discourse, upon the . . . last siege of Breda. 1637.

—— The gushing teares of godly sorrow; containing the causes, conditions, and remedies of sinne. Edinburgh, 1640.

—— A true experimentall and exact relation [of the] . . . siege of Newcastle. Edinburgh, 1645. Rptd. in Somers's Tracts, vol. V.

—— The poetical remains of William Lithgow . . . now first collected. Ed. Maidment, J. Edinburgh, 1863.

Melville, Andrew (1545–1622). Poemata. (In Delitiae Poetarum Scotorum. Ed. Johnston, A. Amsterdam, 1637.)

Melville, Elizabeth. *See* Culross, Lady.

Montrose, James Graham, Marquis of (1612–1650). Poems. Printed in Watson's Choice Collection of . . . Scots Poems, 1711, and Mark Napier's Montrose and the Covenanters, 1838.

Mure, Sir William, of Rowallan (1594–1657). A spirituall hymne. Edinburgh, 1628.

—— The true crucifixe for true catholickes. Edinburgh, 1629.

—— The cry of blood and of a broken covenant. Edinburgh, 1650. (On the execution of Charles I.)

—— The history and descent of the House of Rowallane. Glasgow, 1825.

—— Works. Ed. Tough, W. 2 vols. Scottish Text Society, 1898. (Mure's Dido and Aeneas is printed for the first time in this edn.)

Murray, Sir David, of Gorthy (1567–1629). The tragicall death of Sophonisba.
    1611.
—— Poems. Ed. Kinnear, T. Bannatyne Club, 1823.
Philotus: quhair in we may persave the greit inconveniences that fallis out in the
    mariage betweene age and youth. Edinburgh, 1603. Rptd. for the Ban-
    natyne Club, 1835. Rptd. in Pinkerton's Scottish Poems, vol. III. (An
    anonymous comedy, the plot of which is taken from a tale by Barnaby
    Rich.)
Ramsay, Andrew (1574–1659). Miscellanea et epigrammata sacra. Edin-
    burgh, 1633.
—— Poemata sacra. Edinburgh, 1633.
—— A warning to come out of Babylon, in a sermon. Edinburgh, 1638.
Sempill. The poems of the Sempills of Beltrees, now first collected, with . . .
    biographical notices . . . by James Paterson. Edinburgh, 1849.
Stirling, Earl of. *See* Alexander, Sir William.

II. (1660–1707)

Clark, William (*fl.* 1685). Marciano, or the discovery; a tragicomedy. Edin-
    burgh, 1663.
—— The grand tryal; or, poetical exercitations upon the Book of Job. Edin-
    burgh, 1685.
Cleland, William (1661?–1689). A collection of several poems and verses, com-
    posed upon various occasions. 1697.
Colvill, Samuel (*fl.* 1681). Mock poem, or whiggs supplication. 1681. Often
    rptd.
Livingstone, Michael (*fl.* 1680). Albion's congratulatory; or, a poem, upon . . .
    Prince James Duke of Albany and York, his return into Scotland. Edin-
    burgh, 1680.
—— Patronus redux: or, our protector is return'd safe again. An historicall
    poem [on the Earl of Callander]. Edinburgh, 1682.
Paterson, Ninian (*fl.* 1688). Epigrammatum libri octo cum aliquot Psalmorum
    Davidis paraphrasi poetica. Edinburgh, 1678.
       Paterson was also the author of a number of funeral elegies, of inferior
    merit, which were issued as broadsides.

III. (1707–1786)

Armstrong, John (1709–1779). *See* bibl. to Vol. X, Chap. VII, *post.*
Beattie, James (1735–1803). *See ib.*
Blacklock, Thomas (1721–1791). Poems on several occasions. Glasgow, 1746.
—— The Graham: an heroic ballad, in four cantos. 1774.
Blair, Robert (1699–1746). *See* bibl. to Vol. X, Chap. VII, *post.*
Bruce, Michael (1746–1767). Poems on several occasions. Edinburgh, 1770.
—— Works. Ed. Grosart, A. B. Edinburgh, 1865. Another edn., ed. Stephen
    W. Paisley, 1895. *See, also,* Logan, John, *below.*
Colvill, Robert (d. 1788). Eidyllia; or miscellaneous poems . . . With a hint
    to the British poets. Edinburgh, 1757.
—— The Caledonians: a poem. Edinburgh, 1779.
—— Savannah, a poem in two cantos. 2nd edn. 1780.
—— The downfall of the Roman confederacy, or, the ever memorable 12th of
    April, 1782. A heroic poem, in three cantos. Edinburgh, 1788.
—— Poetical works. 1789.

Douglas, Francis (1710?–1790?). Rural love, a tale in the Scottish dialect. Aberdeen, 1750.

—— The birth-day; with a few strictures on the times; a poem in three cantos. By a farmer. Glasgow, 1782.

See, also, sec. E, Jacobite Literature.

Falconer, William (1732–1767). *See* bibl. to Vol. X, Chap. VII, *post.*

Hamilton, William of Bangour (1704–1754). *See* part (2), *post.*

Harvey, John (*fl.* 1729). A collection of miscellany poems and letters, comical and serious. Edinburgh, 1726.

—— The life of Robert Bruce, king of Scots: a poem. Edinburgh, 1729.

This was remodelled and reissued, without the author's name, as The Bruciad. 1769.

Home, John (1722–1808). Douglas: a tragedy. Edinburgh, 1757.

The stir caused by the production of this popular piece led to Home's resignation of his ministerial charge at Athelstaneford. None of his subsequent tragedies (Agis, 1758; The siege of Aquileia, 1760; The fatal discovery, 1769; Alonzo, 1773; Alfred, 1778) met with conspicuous success. For his history of the Rebellion of 1745, *see* sec. E, *below.* His collected works were ed. by Mackenzie, H., 3 vols., 1822.

See, also, Carlyle, Alexander, in sec. D, *below.*

Lauder, William (d. 1771). Poetarum Scotorum musae sacra. Edinburgh, 1739.

—— An essay on Milton's use and imitation of the moderns in his Paradise Lost. 1750. This unconvincing attempt to convict Milton cf plagiarism first appeared in the Gentleman's Magazine, 1747.

—— A letter to the Rev. Mr. Douglas, occasioned by his vindication of Milton. 1751. (A confession of, and apology for, his literary forgery.)

Logan, John (1748–1788). Poems. 1781.

—— Runnamede, a tragedy. 1783.

Logan's action as editor of the poems of Michael Bruce (*see above*) led to a controversy, which centred chiefly round the Ode to the Cuckoo, and is remarkable more for its longevity than its importance.

Macpherson, James (1736–1796). *See* bibl. to Vol. X, Chap. X, *post.*

Mallet, David (1705?–1765). *See* bibl. to Chap. VI, *ante.*

Thomson, James (1700–1748). *See* bibl. to Vol. X, Chap. V, *post.*

Wilkie, William (1721–1772). The Epigoniad, a poem. Edinburgh, 1757.

—— Fables (in verse). 1768.

Wilson, John (1720–1789). The Earl of Douglas, a dramatic essay. 1760.

—— Clyde, a poem. 1764.

D. Miscellaneous

I. (1603–1660)

Barclay, William (1570?–1630?). Nepenthes; or the vertues of tabacco. Edinburgh, 1614.

—— Callirhoe, the nymph of Aberdene. Edinburgh, 1615.

—— The nature . . . of the new found well at Kinghorne. Edinburgh, 1618.

—— Sylvae tres. Edinburgh, 1619.

Dempster, Thomas (1579?–1625). *See* Vol. VII, pp. 358, 543.

Hume, Alexander (*fl.* 1612). A diduction of the true and catholik meaning of our Saviour his words, This is my bodie, in the institution of his laste supper. Edinburgh, 1602.

Hume, Alexander. Grammatica nova. Edinburgh, 1612.
—— Prima elementa grammatica. Edinburgh, 1612.
—— Of the orthographie and congruitie of the Britan tongue. Ed. Wheatley, H. B. Early English Text Society. 1865.
James VI, King of Scotland (1566–1625). The essayes of a prentise in the divine art of poesie. Edinburgh, 1584.
—— His Majesties poeticall exercises at vacant houres. Edinburgh, 1591.
—— Daemonologie. Edinburgh, 1597.
—— The true lawe of free monarchies. Edinburgh, 1598.
—— Basilikon doron. Edinburgh, 1599.
—— A counter blaste to tobacco. 1604.
—— Workes. 1616.
Makluire, John (fl. 1630). The buckler of bodilie health, whereby health may be defended, and sicknesse repelled. Edinburgh, 1630.
—— Sanitatis semita. Edinburgh, 1630.
Napier, John, of Merchiston (1550–1617). See Vol. IV, p. 577.
Row, John (1598?–1672?). Hebraeae linguae institutiones . . . Χιλιάς Hebraica: seu, vocabularium continens praecipuas radices linguae Hebraeae, numero 1000. 2 pts. Glasgow, 1644.
    In 1646 the General Assembly of the Church of Scotland recommended to general use this work, which was the first of its kind printed in Scotland.
—— Εὐχαριστία Βασιλική. Ad illustrissimum monarchum Carolum II . . . carmen. Aberdeen, 1660.
Urquhart, Sir Thomas (1611–1660). See Vol. VII, pp. 520, 521.
Wedderburn, David (1580–1646). In obitu summae spei Principis Henrici. Edinburgh, 1612.
—— A short introduction to grammar. Aberdeen (1632).
—— Institutiones grammaticae. Editio secunda. Aberdeen, 1633.
—— Meditationum campestrium, seu epigrammaton moralium centuriae duae. Aberdeen, 1643. Centuria tertia. Aberdeen, 1644.
—— Perseus enucleatus, sive commentarius . . . in Persium. Amsterdam, 1662.

II. (1660–1707)

Balfour, Sir Andrew (1630–1694). Letters writ to a friend: containing excellent directions and advices for travelling thro' France and Italy. Edinburgh, 1700.
Brown, Andrew (fl. 1700). A vindicatory schedule, concerning the new cure of fevers. Edinburgh, 1691.
—— Bellum medicinale; or, the papers written in defence of Dr. Brown, his publication of the new cure of fevers. Edinburgh, 1699.
—— The character of the true public spirit, especially with relation to the ill condition of a nation, thro' the prevalency of the privat spirit, selfish and sinister designs. 1702.
—— An essay on the new project for a land mint. Edinburgh, 1705.
—— A scheme proposing a new touch-stone for the due trial of a proper union betwixt Scotland and England. Edinburgh, 1706.
Crawford, David (1665–1726). Courtship à-la-mode; a comedy. 1700.
—— Ovidius Britannicus: or, love epistles in imitation of Ovid. 1703.
—— Love at first sight; a comedy. (1704.)
—— Memoirs of the affairs of Scotland; containing a full and impartial account of the revolution in that kingdom begun in 1567. 1706.

Donaldson, James (*fl.* 1713). Husbandry anatomized, or, an enquiry into the present manner of teiling and manuring the ground in Scotland. Edinburgh, 1696.

—— A pick-tooth for swearers; or, a looking-glass for atheists and prophane persons. Edinburgh, 1698. (In verse.)

—— The undoubted art of thriving. Edinburgh, 1700.

—— Considerations in relation to trade considered, and a short view of our present trade and taxes, compared with what these taxes may amount to after the Union, &c., reviewed. 1706.

—— A letter from Mr. Reason, to the high and mighty Prince the Mob. 1706. (Concerning the Union.)

Fletcher, Andrew, of Saltoun (1655–1716). *See* bibl. to Chaps. VII and VIII, sec. III, *ante.*

Kirk, Robert (1641?–1692). Psalma Dhaibhidh an meadrachd, do reir an phroimhchanamain. Edinburgh, 1684. (The first complete translation of the Scottish metrical psalms into Gaelic.)

—— An essay of the nature and actions of the subterranean (and, for the most part), invisible people, heretofoir going under the name of elves, faunes, and fairies, or the lyke, among the low-country Scots . . . (1691). Edinburgh, 1815. Another edn., under its alternative title A Secret Commonwealth, was published by Lang, A., in 1893.

Law, John, of Lauriston (1671–1729). Proposals and reasons for constituting a council of trade. Edinburgh, 1701.

—— Money and trade considered, with a proposal for supplying the nation with money. Edinburgh, 1705.

—— Oeuvres . . . contenant les principes sur le numéraire, le commerce, le crédit et les banques. Paris, 1790.

Mackaile, Matthew (*fl.* 1657–1696). Fons Moffetensis: seu descriptio topographico-spagyrica fontium mineralium Moffetensium. Edinburgh, 1659. An English version was published, also at Edinburgh, in 1664.

—— The diversitie of salts and spirits maintained . . . Together with a new system of the order and gradation, in the worlds creation. Aberdeen, 1683.

—— Terrae prodromus theoricus. Containing a short account of Moses Philosophizans. Or, the old (yet new) and true Scripture theory of the earth. Aberdeen, 1691.

Mylne, Robert (1643–1747). A Book of Scottish Pasquils, ed. Maidment, J., from a collection by Mylne, R. jun. 1827. [His collections were largely used in Crawford, G., History of the Shire of Renfrew.]

Pitcairne, Archibald (1652–1713). Dissertatio de legibus historiae naturalis. Edinburgh, 1696. (An attack on Sir Robert Sibbald's Scotia Illustrata.)

—— The Assembly; a comedy. By a Scots gentleman. 1722.

—— Babell; a satirical poem on the proceedings of the General Assembly in the year 1692. Maitland Club, 1830.

—— Selecta poemata Archibaldi Pitcarnii (et aliorum). Edinburgh, 1727.

 Pitcairne also published several medical dissertations in Latin, which were gathered together under the title of Dissertationes medicae (Rotterdam, 1701), and an English translation was afterwards issued as "The whole works." 3rd edn. 1740.

 A satire upon Pitcairne appeared in 1695 under the title of Apollo Mathematicus, according to the principles of Dr. Pitcairne. This tract, which was attributed to Dr. Edward Eyzat, led to a lively controversy in which Dr. Charles Oliphant, Dr. Andrew Brown, and Dr. George Hepburn took part.

An account of the life and writings of the celebrated Dr. Archibald Pitcairne. By Charles Webster. Edinburgh, 1781.

Sinclair, George (d. 1696). Satan's invisible world discovered; or, a choice collection of modern relations, proving evidently . . . that there are devils, witches, and apparitions. Edinburgh, 1685.

Sinclair, who was professor of natural philosophy at Glasgow, also published works on natural philosophy and mathematics.

Stair, James Dalrymple, Viscount (1619–1695). The institutions of the law of Scotland. Edinburgh, 1681. Second edn., much enlarged. Edinburgh, 1693.

—— Physiologia nova experimentalis, in qua generales notiones Aristotelis, Epicuri, et Cartesii supplentur, errores deteguntur et emendantur. Leyden, 1686.

—— A vindication of the divine perfections, illustrating the glory of God in them by reason and revelation. 1695.

Wallace, James (d. 1688). An account of the islands of Orkney. To which is added, an essay concerning the Thule of the ancients. Edinburgh, 1693.

III. (1707–1786)

Anderson, James (1739–1808). Essays relating to agriculture and rural affairs Edinburgh, 1775.

—— The interest of Great Britain with regard to her American colonies considered. 1782.

—— An account of the present state of the Hebrides and western coasts of Scotland. Edinburgh, 1785.

—— The Bee, or literary weekly intelligencer. 18 vols. Edinburgh, 1791–4.

—— Recreations in agriculture, natural history, arts, and miscellaneous literature. 6 vols. 1799–1802.

Bell, John (1691–1780). Travels from St. Petersburg in Russia, to diverse parts of Asia. 2 vols. Glasgow, 1763.

Blair, Hugh (1718–1800). A critical dissertation on the poems of Ossian. 1763.

—— Lectures on rhetoric and belles lettres. 2 vols. 1783.

—— Sermons. 5 vols. Edinburgh, 1771–1801.

See, also, bibl. to Vol. X, Chap. x, post.

Burnett, James. See Monboddo, Lord, below.

Callender, John (d. 1789). Terra australis cognita; or, voyages to the Terra Australis, or southern hemisphere, during the sixteenth, seventeenth and eighteenth centuries. 3 vols. Edinburgh, 1766–8.

—— An essay towards a literal English version of the New Testament in the Epistle of the Apostle Paul directed to the Ephesians. Glasgow, 1779.

——Two ancient Scottish poems: The gaberlunzie-man, and Christ's kirk on the green. With notes and observations. Edinburgh, 1782.

Campbell, George (1719–1796). A dissertation on miracles; containing an examination of the principles advanced by David Hume. Edinburgh, 1762.

—— The philosophy of rhetoric. 2 vols. 1776.

—— The four Gospels, translated from the Greek, with preliminary dissertations. 2 vols. 1789.

—— Lectures on ecclesiastical history. Ed. by Keith, G. S. 2 vols. 1800.

Carlyle, Alexander (1722–1805). An argument to prove that the tragedy of

Douglas ought to be publickly burnt by the hands of the hangman. Edinburgh, 1757. (A satirical tract in defence of Home's Douglas.)

Carlyle, Alexander. Plain reasons for removing a certain Great Man [Wm. Pitt] from his M——y's presence and councils for ever. By O. M. Haberdasher. 1759.

—— The question relating to a Scots militia considered. Edinburgh, 1760.

—— Autobiography. Ed. by Burton, J. H. Edinburgh, 1860.

Cunningham, Alexander (1655?–1730). Q. Horatii Flacci poemata: ex antiquis codd. et certis observationibus emendavit. 1721.

—— Animadversiones in R. Bentleii notas et emendationes ad Q. Horatium Flaccum. 1721.

—— P. Virgilii Maronis Bucolica, Georgica, et Aeneis. Ex recensione Alexandri Cuningamii. Edinburgh, 1743.

—— Phaedri Augusti Liberti fabularum Aesopiarum libri quinque. Ex recensione Alexandri Cuninghamii Scoti. Edinburgh, 1757.

Edinburgh Review (The). Nos 1 and 2. Edinburgh, 1755–6. (No more published.)

Ferguson, Adam (1723–1816). The history of the proceedings in the case of Margaret, commonly called Peg, only lawful sister to John Bull, Esq. 1761. (A tract on the militia question.)

—— An essay on the history of civil society. 1766.

—— Institutes of moral philosophy. Edinburgh, 1769.

—— The history of the progress and termination of the Roman Republic. 3 vols. 1783.

—— Principles of moral and political science. 2 vols. Edinburgh, 1792.

    See, also, bibl. to Vol. X, Chap. XIII, *post*.

Home, Henry, Lord Kames (1696–1782). Essays upon several subjects concerning British antiquities. Edinburgh, 1747.

—— Essays on the principles of morality and natural religion. Edinburgh, 1751. (Written in opposition to Hume.)

—— Elements of criticism. 3 vols. Edinburgh, 1762. 7th edn. 1788.

—— Sketches of the history of man. 2 vols. Edinburgh, 1774.

—— The gentleman farmer; being an attempt to improve agriculture, by subjecting it to the test of rational principles. Edinburgh, 1776.

    Lord Kames was also the author of several important works on legal subjects.

    Memoirs of the life and writings of Henry Home of Kames. By A. F. Tytler. 2 vols. Edinburgh, 1807.

Kames, Lord. *See* Home, Henry.

Logan, George (1678–1755). A treatise on government; shewing that the right of the kings of Scotland to the crown was not strictly and absolutely hereditary: against the earl of Cromarty, Sir George Mackenzie, Mr. John Sage, and Mr. Thomas Ruddiman. Edinburgh, 1746.

—— A second treatise on government. Edinburgh, 1747.

    These were followed by other controversial tracts to the same purpose.

Mackenzie, Henry (1745–1831). *See* bibl. to Vol. X, Chap. III, *post*.

Monboddo, James Burnett, Lord (1714–1799). Of the origin and progress of language. 6 vols. Edinburgh, 1773–92.

—— Antient metaphysics; or, the science of universals. 6 vols. Edinburgh, 1779–99.

Moor, James (1712–1779). Essays, read to a Literary Society, at their weekly meetings, within the College of Glasgow. Glasgow, 1759.

—— On the end of tragedy, according to Aristotle. Glasgow, 1763.

Moor, James. On the praepositions of the Greek language. Glasgow, 1766. Moor was also the author of a Greek grammar which went through numerous editions, and he assisted in the production of many of the editions of the classics for which the Foulis press at Glasgow is celebrated at this period.

Reid, Thomas (1710–1796). *See* bibl. to Vol. X, Chap. XIV, *post*.

Ruddiman, Thomas (1674–1757). Rudiments of the Latin tongue. Edinburgh, 1714. Numerous subsequent editions.

—— Grammaticae Latinae institutiones. 2 vols. Edinburgh, 1725–31.

—— A vindication of Mr. George Buchanan's paraphrase of the Book of Psalms from the objections rais'd by W. Benson. Edinburgh, 1745.

—— An answer to the Rev. George Logan's late Treatise on Government: in which . . . the ancient constitution of the crown and kingdom of Scotland, and the hereditary succession of its monarchs are asserted and vindicated. Edinburgh, 1747.

—— A dissertation concerning the competition for the crown of Scotland, betwixt Lord Robert Bruce and Lord John Baliol, in the year 1291. Edinburgh, 1748. (Another answer to Logan and other writers.)

—— G. Buchanani opera omnia . . . nunc primum in unum collecta . . . Curante T. Ruddimanno. 2 vols. Edinburgh, 1715.

In addition to this important undertaking, Ruddiman edited or assisted in the production of many works, including an edition of Gavin Douglas's Virgil (1710).

The life of Thomas Ruddiman. By George Chalmers. 1794.

Scots Magazine (The), containing a general view of the religion, politicks, entertainment, &c., in Great Britain, and a succinct account of publick affairs. No. 1. January, 1739. Edinburgh, 1739.

This monthly periodical, which aspired to fill, in Scotland, the place which the Gentleman's Magazine occupied in England, pursued a successful course down to 1794, when it commenced a new series and at the same time entered upon a more chequered career.

Smith, Adam (1723–1790). *See* bibl. to Vol. X, Chap. XIV, *post*.

Smollett, Tobias George (1721–1771). *See* bibl. to Vol. X, Chap II, *post*.

Wallace, Robert (1697–1771). A dissertation on the numbers of mankind in antient and modern times. Edinburgh, 1753.

—— Various prospects of mankind, nature, and providence. 1761.

Weekly Magazine, or Edinburgh Amusement. Edinburgh, 1768–84.

Known as "Ruddiman's Weekly," and notable for its editor's ingenious but unsuccessful attempts to circumvent the stamp duty. Many of Robert Fergusson's poems appeared in this magazine.

Williamson, Peter (1730–1799). French and Indian cruelty exemplified in the life . . . of P. W. York, 1757.

—— Travels . . . amongst the . . . savage Indians in America. Edinburgh, 1768.

Williamson also conducted in Edinburgh the two short-lived periodicals, The Scots Spy (1776), and The New Scots Spy (1777).

E. JACOBITE LITERATURE

The following is a selection only from the voluminous literature of the subject, with special reference to the risings of 1715 and 1745. For fuller lists see Terry, C. S., The Rising of 1745 (1903), and the Historical Catalogue of the Scottish Exhibition held at Glasgow in 1911. The poetry called forth by the Stewart

cause will be found in Hogg's Jacobite relics of Scotland (1819–21), and Mackay's
Jacobite songs and ballads of Scotland (1861).

Account, an, of the late Scotch invasion, with true copies of authentick papers.
1709.

Albemarle papers, the: being the correspondence of William Anne, second Earl
of Albemarle, Commander-in-chief in Scotland 1746–47. Ed. Terry, C. S.
2 vols. New Spalding Club, 1902.

Alexis: or, The young adventurer. A novel. 1746.

Arbuthnot, Archibald. Memoirs of the remarkable life and surprising adventures
of Miss Jenny Cameron. 1746. (The whole work, including the name of
the author, is fictitious.)

—— The life, adventures, and many and great vicissitudes of fortune of Simon
Lord Lovat. 1746. (Also fictitious.)

Ascanius: or, The young adventurer. (By Griffiths, Ralph.) 1746.

Book, the, of the Chronicles of William, Duke of Cumberland. Edinburgh,
1746. One of a series of Biblical parodies. Others were:

    The Book of the Lamentations of Charles the son of James. Edinburgh,
    1746.

    The Book of the Lamentations of Simon Prince of the Tribe of Lovat.
    1746.

    The Acts of the Rebels, by James Ray. 2nd edn. Newcastle-on-Tyne,
    1746.

Boyse, Samuel (1708–1749). An impartial history of the late Rebellion in 1745.
Reading, 1748.

Burton, John (1710–1771). A genuine and true journal of the most miraculous
escape of the young Chevalier from the battle of Culloden to his landing
in France . . . By an Englishman. 1749.

Cameron, Archibald. An historical account of the life, actions, and conduct
of Dr. Archibald Cameron. 1753.

Cameron, Jenny. The life of Miss Jenny Cameron, the reputed mistress of the
deputy Pretender. 1746. [Fictitious.]

Chronicle, the, of Charles the young man. n. d.

Compleat history of the late Rebellion. 1716.

Doddridge, Philip (1702–1751). Some remarkable passages in the life of the
honourable Col. James Gardiner. Edinburgh, 1747.

Douglas, Francis (1710?–1790?). The history of the Rebellion in 1745 and 1746;
extracted from the Scots Magazine. Aberdeen, 1755.

    Douglas also founded, in 1750, a Jacobite journal called The Aberdeen
Intelligencer.

Enquiry, an, into the causes of the late Rebellion and the proper methods for
preventing the like misfortune for the future. 1746.

Faithful register, a, of the late Rebellion: or, An impartial account of the im-
peachments, trials, speeches, etc. of all who have suffered for the cause of
the Pretender in Great Britain. 1718.

Female rebels, the: being some remarkable incidents of the lives . . . of the
titular Duke and Duchess of Perth, the Lord and Lady Ogilvie, and of Miss
Florence McDonald. Edinburgh, 1747. [Fictitious.]

Forbes, Robert (1708–1775). A plain authentick and faithful narrative of the
several passages of the Young Chevalier from the battle of Culloden to his
embarkation for France. By Philalethes. 1765.

—— The Lyon in Mourning. Ed. Paton, H. 3 vols. Scottish History
Society 1895–6.

Full collection, a, of all poems upon Charles Prince of Wales published since his arrival in Edinburgh. (Edinburgh) 1745.

Full collection, a, of all the proclamations and orders published by the authority of Charles Prince of Wales since his arrival in Edinburgh. 2 pts. Edinburgh and Glasgow, 1745–6.

Graham, Dougal (1724–1779). An impartial history of the rise, progress, and extinction of the late Rebellion in Britain in the years 1745 and 1746. 1746. (This popular metrical history by the Glasgow bellman was often reprinted.)

Henderson, Andrew (*fl.* 1734–1775). The history of the Rebellion, 1745 and 1746. Edinburgh, 1748. Another edn., London, 1753, is practically a new work. *See, also,* Young Chevalier.

Historical papers relating to the Jacobite period, 1699–1750. Ed. Allardyce, J. 2 vols. New Spalding Club, 1895–6.

History of the conspiracies, trials, and dying speeches of all those who have suffered on account of the House of Stuart from the Revolution down to the commencement of the last Rebellion. 1747.

Home, John (1722–1808). The history of the Rebellion in the year 1745. 1802.

Hughes Michael (*fl.* 1746). A plain narrative or journal of the late Rebellion . . . till the full and glorious defeat at Culloden. 1746.

Leslie, Charles (1650–1722). Gallienus redivivus: or murther will out, etc., being a true account of the De-Witting of Glencoe, Gaffney, etc. Edinburgh, 1695.

Letter, a, touching the late Rebellion and what means led to it; and of the Pretender's title. By Philalethes. 1717.

Lovat, Lord. Genuine memoirs of the Life of Lord Fraser of Lovat. 1746.

—— Memoirs of the life of Lord Lovat. 1746.

—— Memoirs of the life of Simon Fraser, Lord Lovat. Edinburgh, 1767. *See, also,* Arbuthnot, *above.*

Macky, John (d. 1726). *See* bibl. to Chaps. VII and VIII, p. 543, *ante.*

Macpherson, James. The history of the present Rebellion in Scotland . . . Taken from the relation of Mr. James Macpherson. 1745. (Of doubtful authenticity.)

Marchant, John. The history of the present Rebellion. 1746.

Memoirs of John Duke of Melfort; being an account of the secret intrigues of the Chevalier de S. George, particularly relating to the present times. 1714.

Memoirs of the Chevalier de St. George. 1712.

Memoirs of the Lord Viscount of Dundee, the Highland Clans, and the massacre of Glenco; with an account of Dundee's officers after they went to France. By an officer of the army. 1711.

Memoirs of the lives and families of the Lords Kilmarnock, Cromartie, and Balmerino. 1746.

Murray, John, of Broughton. Genuine memoirs of John Murray, late secretary to the Young Pretender. 1747. (Untrustworthy.)

—— Particulars of the secret history of Murray of Broughton. 1766.

—— Memorials of John Murray of Broughton. Ed. Bell, R. F. Scottish History Society, 1898.

Oracle, the, of Avignon: or, a new and true account of all the great actions and most remarkable occurrences of the life of the Pretender . . . Being a comico-prosaico-poetical essay on the actions of this hero, by B—— H——, his poet-laureat. 1723.

Particular account, a, of the battle of Culloden, April 16, 1746. In a letter from an officer of the Highland army, to his friend at London. 1749. (By Lord George Murray.)

Patten, Robert (*fl.* 1717). The history of the late Rebellion. 1717.

Philip, James (*fl.* 1691). The Grameid, an heroic poem descriptive of the campaign of Viscount Dundee in 1689. Ed. Murdoch, A. D. Scottish History Society, 1888.

Philips, John (*fl.* 1617). The Earl of Mar marr'd, with the humours of Jockey the Highlander. A tragi-comical farce. 1715.

—— The Pretender's flight: or, a mock coronation, with the humours of the facetious Harry Saint John. A tragi-comical farce. Being the sequel of The Earl of Mar marr'd. 1716.

Plain, a, authentick and faithful narrative of the several passages of the Young Chevalier from the battle of Culloden to his embarkation for France. 1750.

Rae, Peter (1671–1748). A history of the late Rebellion. Dumfries, 1718.

Ray, James (*fl.* 1745). A complete history of the Rebellion. York, 1749.

Secret History, the, of Colonel Hoocke's negociations in Scotland in 1707. Edinburgh, 1760.

Secret history, the, of the Chevalier de St. George, being an impartial account of his birth and pretences to the Crown of England. 1714.

Serious address, a, to the people of Great Britain, in which certain consequences of the present Rebellion are fully demonstrated. 1745.

Short and true narrative, a, of the Rebellion in 1745. Edinburgh, 1779.

Sinclair, John, Master of Sinclair (1683–1750). Memoirs of the insurrection in Scotland in 1715. Abbotsford Club, 1858.

Towneley MSS., the. English Jacobite Ballads . . . from MSS. at Towneley Hall. Ed., with notes etc., Grosart, A. B. 1877.

True account, a, of the behaviour and conduct of Archibald Stewart, Esq., late Lord Provost of Edinburgh. 1748. (Ascribed to David Hume.)

True account, a, of the proceedings at Perth; the debates in the secret council there; with the reasons and causes of the suddain breaking up of the Rebellion. Written by a Rebel. 1716.

Wanderer, the: or, the surprizing escape. A narrative founded on true facts. 1747.

Young Chevalier, the: or, a genuine narrative of all that befell that unfortunate adventurer from his fatal defeat to his final escape. (1746 *c.*)
(By Andrew Henderson.)

Young Juba: or, the history of the Young Chevalier from his birth to his escape from Scotland after the battle of Culloden. 1748.

H. G. A.

(2)

SCOTTISH POPULAR POETRY BEFORE BURNS

See also part (1) C *above*

I. TEXTS

Albyn's Anthology. Ed. Campbell, A. 2 vols. 1816–18.

Buchan, Peter. Ancient Ballads and Songs of the North of Scotland. 2 vols. Edinburgh, 1828. New edn. 1875. [Very untrustworthy.]

Caw, G. Poetical Museum. Hawick, 1784.

Chambers, Robert. Miscellany of Popular Scottish Songs. Edinburgh, 1841·
—— Popular Rhymes of Scotland. Edinburgh, 1826. 3rd edn. 1851. New
    edn. 1870.
—— Scottish Songs. 1829.
—— Songs of Scotland Prior to Burns. With the tunes. Edinburgh and Lon-
    don. 1880.
Charmer, the. 1749. 2nd edn. in 2 vols. 1752. 3rd, 1765. 4th, 1782.
Crawford, Robert (d. 1733). Tweedside and other songs in Allan Ramsay's
    Tea Table Miscellany (*see below*).
Cromek, R. H. Select Scottish Songs Ancient and Modern. 2 vols. 1810.
—— Remains of Nithsdale and Galloway song. 1810. Rptd., Paisley, 1880.
    [Both works are untrustworthy and contain forgeries by Cunningham,
    Allan].
Cunningham, Allan. Songs of Scotland. 4 vols. Edinburgh. 1825.
Dixon, W. M. Edinburgh Book of Scottish Verse. Edinburgh. 1910.
Douglas, Sir George. The Book of Scottish Poetry. 1910.
Fergusson, Robert. Poems by Robert Fergusson. Edinburgh, 1773·
—— Poems on Various Subjects with Life by Ruddiman T. Edinburgh, 1779.
    3rd edn. 1785. Numerous other edns., including Perth, 1789, Paisley,
    1796, and St. Andrews, 1800.
—— Works, with Life by Peterkin. 1809.
—— Poems, with Life by Bannington, F. 1809. Edn. in 2 vols. with engravings
    by Bewick. Alnwick, 1814.
—— Poems, with Life. Philadelphia, 1815.
    Also edns., with Life, by Gray, James, Edinburgh, 1821, and Chambers,
    Robert, Edinburgh, 1840. The most satisfactory edn. is Works of Robert
    Fergusson, ed. A. B. G. [A. B. Grosart], 1851.
Goldfinch, the; or New Modern Songster. Edinburgh, 1777. 2nd enlarged
    edn. 1782.
Graham, Dougal (1724–1779). A full, particular and true Account of the Re-
    bellion in the year 1745-6. [In rhyme.] 1746. Numerous later edns.
—— Collected Writings with Essay on Chapbook Literature by Maꞃgregor, G.
    2 vols. 1883.
Hamilton, William, of Bangour (1704–1754). Poems on Several Occasions.
    Glasgow, 1748, 1749. 2nd edn. Glasgow, 1758. Edinburgh, 1760, 1790.
—— Poems. Chiswick. 1822.
—— Poems and Songs. Ed. Paterson, James. Edinburgh, 1850.
Hamilton, William, of Gilbertfield (1665?–1751). *See* Ramsay, Allan, *below*.
Herd, David (1732–1810). Ancient and Modern Scottish Poems. 1769. 2nd
    (enlarged) edn. in 2 vols. Edinburgh, 1776. [Both published anonymously.]
    Rptd., 2 vols., Glasgow, 1869. Unauthorised edn. with additions and omis-
    sions. 2 vols. Edinburgh, 1791.
—— Songs from David Herd's Manuscript, edn. with Introduction and notes
    by Hecht, Hans. Edinburgh, 1904.
Hogg, James. Jacobite Relics of Scotland. 2 vols. 1819–21. Rptd., Paisley,
    1874.
Johnson, James (d. 1811). The Scots Musical Museum. 5 vols. 1787–1803.
    Rptd., 6 vols., Edinburgh, 1833, and 4 vols., *ib.* 1853, with Notes by Sten-
    house, William; Laing, David; and Sharpe, C. K.
Lark, the. 1740.
Lark, the. Vol. 1. Edinburgh, 1765. (No more published.)
Loyal Songs, Collection of. Edinburgh, 1744·

Loyal Songs. [n. p.], 1750.

Loyalist, the True, or the Chevaliers Favourite. [Rare.] [n. p.], 1779.

Mackay, Charles. Jacobite Songs and Ballads of Scotland, 1688–1746. 1861.

Macquoid, G. S. Jacobite Songs. 1888.

Maidment, James. Scottish Ballads and Songs. Edinburgh, 1859, 1868.

—— A Book of Scottish Pasquils. Edinburgh, 1868.

—— A Packet of Pestilent Pasquils. Edinburgh, 1868.

Merry Muses, the. [Surreptitiously printed. Original and unaltered edition.]

Meston, William (1688?–1745). The Knight of the Kirk. 1723. [Imitation of Hudibras.]

Musical Miscellany, the. Ed. Smith, A. Perth, 1786.

Musical Repository, the. Glasgow, 1799. Edinburgh, 1802.

Pennecuick, Alexander. A Collection of Scots Poems on several occasions, by the late Alexander Pennecuik and others. Edinburgh, 1756, rptd. Glasgow. 1787.

Ramsay, Allan. Christis Kirk on the Green, with additional canto by Ramsay, Edinburgh, 1716. 2nd edn., *ib.* 1718, with two cantos.

—— Patie and Roger. Edinburgh, 1718.

—— Poems. Edinburgh, 1721. New edn. with additions. Edinburgh, 1728; London, 1731; Dublin, 1733.

—— Jeannie and Maggie. Edinburgh, 1723.

    Combined in the Gentle Shepherd, 1725, 10th edn., 1750, edn. illustrated by Allan, David, published by R. and T. Foulis, Glasgow, 1788. Many subsequent editions.

—— The Evergreen. (Mainly from the Bannatyne MSS.) 2 vols. Edinburgh, 1724–7. 2nd edn. 1761.

—— The Tea Table Miscellany (containing old Scottish Songs, English Songs, Songs by Ramsay and various contemporaries, and rereadings of Scots Songs by Ramsay). 4 vols. 1724–5–7–32. Frequently rptd.; 2 vols., Glasgow, 1871.

—— Works. Ed. Chalmers, George. 2 vols. Edinburgh, 1800. 3 vols., Edinburgh, 1848; 2 vols., Paisley, 1877. (Contains Seven Familiar Epistles which passed between Lieutenant Hamilton and the author.)

Ritson, Joseph (1752–1803). Scottish Songs. Edinburgh, 1794. Rptd., Glasgow, 1869.

Ross, Alexander (1699–1784). Helenore, or The Fortunate Shepherdess; also Songs and Forbes' Ajax. 1768. Frequently rptd.

—— Works. Ed. Longmuir, J. Edinburgh, 1866.

Scots Minstrelsie. A National Monument of Scottish Song. Ed. and arranged by Greig, John. 6 vols. Edinburgh, 1893.

Scots Poems ancient and Modern, A choice collection of. Printed by Ruddiman Walter. Edinburgh, 1776.

Skinner, John (1721–1807). Amusement of Leisure Hours. Edinburgh, 1801.

—— Songs and Poems with life by Reid, G. Peterhead, 1859.

Thomson, William (*fl.* 1725). Orpheus Caledonius. 1725–6. 2nd enlarged edn. 2 vols. 1733.

Universal Laughter, The, or Museum of Mirth. Illustrated by George and Robert Cruikshank. 3 vols. 1825–6–8.

Watson, James (d. 1722). Choice Collection of Comic and Serious Scots Poems both Ancient and Modern. 3 pts. 1706–9–11. Rptd. Glasgow, 1869.

II. CRITICAL AND HISTORICAL WRITINGS

Borthwich, J. D.   History of Scottish Song.   Montreal, 1874.

Brown, Colin.   Introduction to The Thistle.   A Miscellany of Scottish Songs. Glasgow, 1884.

Burns, Robert.   Notes on Scottish Songs.   Ed. Dick, James C.   1908.

Chappell, William.   Old English Popular Music.   New edn., by Wooldridge H. Ellis.   2 vols.   London and New York, 1893.

Dauney, William.   Ancient Scottish Melodies.   (Bannatyne Club.)   Edinburgh, 1839.

Douglas, Sir George, Baronet.   Scottish Poetry: Drummond of Hawthornden to Fergusson.   Glasgow, 1911.

Glen, J.   Early Scottish Melodies.   Edinburgh, 1900.

Graham, G. F.   Popular Songs of Scotland with Melodies.   1884.

Henderson, T. F.   Scottish Vernacular Literature.   1898.   2nd edn. 1900.   3rd 1910.

Irving, David.   History of Scotish Poetry.   Ed. Carlyle, Dr. John.   Edinburgh, 1861.

—— Lives of Scotish Poets.   2 vols.   Edinburgh, 1804.   2nd edn.   1810.

Masson, D.   Edinburgh Sketches and Memories.   1902.

Millar, J. H.   A Literary History of Scotland.   1903.

Miller, Frank.   The poets of Dumfriesshire.   Glasgow, 1910.

Ross, J. D.   The Book of Scottish Poems, Ancient and Modern.   2 vols.   Paisley, 1882.

Veitch, John.   History and Poetry of the Scottish Border.   Edinburgh, 1878. 2 vols.   1893.

Walker, Hugh.   Three Centuries of Scottish Literature.   2 vols.   Glasgow, 1893.

CHAPTER XV

EDUCATION

I. EDUCATIONAL TREATISES, ESSAYS AND TRACTS

A. *Writings on Education*

Ainsworth, Robert (1660–1743).   The most natural and easie way of Institution; containing proposals for making a domestic education less chargeable to parents, and more easie and beneficial to children.   1698.

—— Thesaurus linguae Latinae compendiarius.   1736.   Ed., with additions, by B. W. Beatson and W. Ellis.   1840.

Brinsley, J.   Ludus Literarius or the Grammar Schoole, shewing how to proceede from the first entrance into learning to the highest perfection required in the grammar schooles, etc.   1612.

B., F. [Brokesby, Francis].   Of Education with respect to Grammar Schools and the Universities; concluding with directions to young students in the Universities.   1701.

Budgell, Eustace.   Spectator, Nos. 307, 313, 337, 353.

Clarke, John.   An Essay upon the Education of Youth in Grammar Schools. 1720.   2nd edn. with very large additions.   1730.

Comenius [Komensky], John Amos.   Opera Didactica Omnia.   Amsterdam, 1657.

Common Errors, The, in the Education of Children and their consequences, with the methods to remedy them, etc.   1744.

Dury, John. The Reformed School. n. d. [1649?].

"Gentleman," "A" (Thos. Baker). Reflection upon Learning, etc. 2nd edn. 1700.

Guardian, The. Nos. 62, 72, 94, 105, 155.

Hoole, Charles. A new discovery of the old art of teaching schoole, etc. 1660.

Keatinge, M. W. The Great Didactic of John Amos Comenius. 1896.

Law, William. A Serious Call to a Devout and Holy Life. Adapted to the State and Condition of all Orders of Christians. [1728.] 10th edn. 1772. [Chaps. XVIII–XIX on education of boys and girls respectively.]

Locke, John. The Works of. 3 vols. [Thoughts and Conduct in vol. III.] 1714.

—— Some Thoughts concerning Education. 1693. Ed. Quick, R. H. Cambridge, 1898.

—— Locke's Conduct of the Understanding. Ed. Fowler, T. Oxford, 1890. *See also* bibliography to Vol. VIII, Chap. XIV, *ante.*

"Lover of her Sex" [Astell, Mary]. A Serious Proposal to the ladies for the advancement of their true and great interest. 1694. 4th edn. with an added 2nd part. 1697.

[Makin, Mrs. Bathsua?.] An Essay to Revive the antient Education of Gentlewomen in Religion, Manners, Arts and Tongues, with an Answer to the Objections against this Way of Education. 1673.

[Milton, John.] Of Education. To Master Samuel Hartlib. 1644. Ed. Browning, O. Cambridge, 1895.

Newton, Richard. University Education. 1726.

Osborn, Francis. Advice to a Son, or Directions for your better Conduct through the various and most important Encounters of this Life, etc. [1656 D. of N.B.] 6th edn. Oxford, 1658.

[Petty, William.] The Advice of W. P. to Mr. S. Hartlib for the advancement of some particular parts of learning. 1648.

Steele, Richard. Tatler, Nos. 63, 173, 234, 252.

—— Spectator, Nos. 157, 168, 230, 294, 330, 430.

—— Guardian, Nos. 72, 94.

Swift, Jonathan. Works, vol. IX, An Essay on Modern Education. Of the Education of Ladies. Ed. Scott, Sir Walter. 19 vols. 1883.

Tatler, The, Nos. 63, 173, 197, 234, 252, 253.

[Walker, Obadiah.] Of Education especially of Young Gentlemen. In Two Parts. Oxford, 1673.

Wase, Christopher. Considerations concerning Free Schools as settled in England. Oxford, 1678.

Wotton, Henry. An Essay on the Education of Children in the First Rudiments of Learning, together with a Narrative of what knowledge William Wotton, a child six years of age, had attained unto upon the improvement of those rudiments in the Latin, Greek, and Hebrew Tongues. 1753. [Written, 1672.]

B. *Courtesy Books*

Costeker, J. L. The Fine Gentleman, or the Complete Education of a Young Nobleman. 1732.

Defoe, Daniel. The Compleat English Gentleman. Ed. Bülbring, K., with introduction and notes. 1890.

Ellis, Clement. The Gentile Sinner, or England's Brave Gentleman characteriz'd in a Letter to a Friend, both as he is and as he should be. 2nd edn. Oxford, 1661.

Gailhard, J. The Compleat Gentleman, or Directions for the Education of Youth as to their Breeding at Home and Travelling Abroad. In Two Treatises, by J. Gailhard, who hath been Tutor abroad to several of the Nobility and Gentry. 1678.

Gentleman's Calling, The. 1667. [Preface dated 1659.]

Higford, William. The Institution of a Gentleman. In Three Parts. 1660.

Peacham, Henry. The Compleat Gentleman Fashioning him absolute in the most necessary and commendable qualities concerning Minde, or Bodie, that may be required in a Noble Gentleman. 1622.

—— Rpt. of 1634 edn. with introduction by Gordon, G. S. Oxford, 1906.

[Penton, Stephen.] The Guardian's Instruction, or the Gentleman's Romance. Written for the Diversion and Service of the Gentry. 1688. Rpt. with introduction by Sturmer, H. H. 1897.

—— New Instructions to the Guardian, etc. 1694.

"Person of Honour, A." The Courtier's Calling; shewing the ways of making a Fortune and the Art of Living at Court according to the Maxims of Policy and Morality. In Two Parts, the First concerning Noblemen, the Second concerning Gentlemen. 1675.

C. *Projects and Utopias*

Bellers, John. Proposals for raising a Colledge of Industry of all useful Trades and Husbandry with profit for the Rich, a Plentiful Living for the Poor, and a Good Education for Youth, which will be Advantage to the Government by an Increase of the People and their Riches. 1696.

Cowley, A. A proposition for the advancement of experimental philosophy. 1660/1.

—— Cowley's Essays. Ed. Lumby, J. R. Cambridge, 1887. Ed. Waller, A. R. Cambridge, 1906.

D. F. [Defoe, Daniel]. An Essay upon Projects. 1697.

Harrington, James. The Commonwealth of Oceana. 1656. Ed. Morley, H. 1887.

Hartlib, Samuel. A description of the famous Kingdom of Macaria. 1641.

Maidwell, Mr. [Lewis]. An Essay upon the necessity and excellency of education. With an [account of erecting the Royal Mathematical Schole Recommended by His Royal Highness, Lord High Admiral of England etc., upon a Report from the Navy Board. Declaring amongst other advantages to the Nation the particular services of such a Foundation to the Royal Navy of England, in Its several capacitys. 1705.

Novae Solymae—Libri Sex. [Anon.] 1648. Trans. by Begley, Walter under title: Nova Solyma. The Ideal City, or Jerusalem Regained, etc. 2 vols. 1902.

II. Controversial Works

A. *Pamphlets and Sermons*

Ayliffe, J. The Case of Dr. Ayliffe at Oxford. 1716.

Boreman, Robert. Παιδεία θρίαμβος, the triumph of learning and of truth, an answer to four queries: Need of Universities? etc., 1653. Harl. Miscellany, vol. 1, p. 505. 1808.

Chandler, S. Doing good recommended, and An Answer to Essay on Charity Schools. 1728.

Charity Schools, An Account of, lately erected in England, Wales, and Ireland. 6th edn. (Annual Publication.) 1707.

Charity Mathematical School, An Account of the, in Hatton Garden Founded Anno Domini 1715, etc. 1749.

D. D. [Defoe, Daniel]. More Short Ways with the Dissenters. 1704.

Dell, William. The Tryal of Spirits . . . whereunto is added . . . The right Reformation of Learning, Schools and Universities, according to the State of the Gospel, and the light that shines therein, etc. 1653.

—— The Stumbling Stone, etc. 1653.

Green, John. The Academic, or a Disputation on the State of the University of Cambridge and the Propriety of the Regulations made in it on the 11th of May and the 26th day of June 1750. 1750.

     Remarks on the Academic. 1751.

Hall, Thomas. Vindiciae Literarum, the Schools Guarded, etc. 1654.

Hendley, W. A Defence of the Charity Schools wherein the many false, scandalous and malicious objections of those advocates for ignorance and irreligion, the authors of the Fable of the Bees, and Cato's Letter in the British Journal, June 15, 1723, are fully and distinctly answer'd, etc. 1725.

[Hobbes, Thomas. Leviathan or the Matter, Forme and Power of a Commonwealth, Ecclesiastical and Civil. 1651. Rptd., ed. Waller, A. R. (Cambridge English Classics.) Cambridge, 1904.]

—— Tracts of Mr. Thos. Hobbs of Malmesbury. I. Behemoth, the History of the Causes of the Civil Wars of England from 1640 to 1660. 1682.

—— English Works of Thomas Hobbes. Ed. Molesworth, Sir William. 11 vols. 1839–46. [Behemoth in vol. VI.]

Mandeville, Bernard. See bibliography to Chap. XI, ante.

Newton, R. Rules and Statutes for the Government of Hertford College, in the University of Oxford, with observations on particular parts of them, shewing the Reasonableness thereof. 1714.

[Owen, James, of Shrewsbury.] Moderation still a Virtue, in Answer to several bitter Pamphlets . . . with A Defence of the Private Academies against Mr. Sacheverell's misrepresentations of 'em. 1704.

[Palmer, Samuel.] A Defence of the Dissenters' Education in their Private Academies in Answer to Mr. W——y's disingenuous and Un-Christian Reflections upon 'em. 1703.

—— A Vindication of the Learning, Loyalty, Morals and most Christian Behaviour of the Dissenters towards the Church of England. In answer to Mr. Wesley's Defence of his letter concerning the Dissenter's Education in their Private Academies, and to Mr. Sacheverel's Injurious Reflections upon them. 1705.

Sacheverell, Henry. The Nature and Mischief of Prejudice and Partiality stated in a sermon preach'd at St. Mary's in Oxford at the Assizes held there, March 9th, 170¾. 2nd edn. Oxford, 1704.

—— The Communication of Sin. A Sermon preach'd at the Assizes held at Derby, August 15th, 1709. 1709.

Sedgwick, Joseph. Ἐπισκόπου Διδακτικός, learning's Necessity to an able minister of the Gospel. 1653.

—— A Sermon preached at St. Marie's in the University of Cambridge, May 1st, 1653 . . . Together with an Appendix, wherein Mr. Del's Stumbling-stone is briefly repli'd into.   And a fuller Discourse of the use of Universities and Learning, etc.   1653.

Talbott, James.   The Christian School Master, or the Duty of those who are employ'd in the Publick Instruction of Children, especially in Charity Schools.   1707.

H. D. [Ward, Seth].   Preface by N. S. [Wilkins, John].   Vindiciae Academiarum, containing some brief Animadversions upon Mr. Webster's Book stil'd The Examination of Academies, Together with an Appendix concerning what M. Hobbs and M. Dell have published on this Argument.   Oxford, 1654.

Waterhous[e], Edward.   An humble Apologie for Learning and Learned Men. 1652/3.

Webster, John [Chaplain in the Army].   Academiarum Examen, wherein is discussed and examined the Matter, Method, and Customs of Academick and Scholastic Learning and the insufficiency thereof discovered and laid open; and also some expedient proposed for the Reforming of Schools and the perfecting and promoting of all kind of Science, etc.   1654.

[Wesley, Samuel, the Elder.]   A Letter from a Country Divine to his friend in London concerning the Education of Dissenters in their Private Academies, in several parts of this Nation.   1702.   [Written in 1693.]

—— A Defence of a Letter concerning the education of Dissenters in their Private Academies: with a more full and satisfactory account of the same, and of their morals and behaviour towards the Church of England.   Being an Answer to the Defence of Dissenters' Education.   1704.

—— A Reply to Mr. Palmer's Vindication of the Learning, Loyalty, Morals, and most Christian Behaviour of the Dissenters towards the Church of England.   1707.

Willis, Richard.   A Sermon Preach'd in the Parish Church of St. Andrews, Holborn.   1704.   ["Account of Charity Schools," appended.]

Wilson, Thos.   (Bp. of Sodor and Man).   The True Christian Method of Educating the Children both of the Poor and Rich, etc.   1724.

B.   *Ancients v. Moderns Controversy*

See, also, bibliographies to Chaps. IV and XIII, sec. I B, *ante.*

Bentley, Richard.   A Dissertation upon the Epistles of Phalaris.   1699.

B., C. [Boyle, Charles].   Phalaridis Epistolae.   Ex MSS. recensuit C. B. Oxford, 1695.

—— Dr. Bentley's dissertations on the Epistles of Phalaris, etc., examin'd.   1698.

Burnet, Thomas.   The Theory of the Earth, containing an account of the original of the Earth, and of all the general changes which it hath already undergone, or is to undergo till the consummation of all things.   1684.

—— Telluris Theoria Sacra—Orbis Nostri Originem et Mutationes Generales, quas aut jam subiit aut olim subiturus est, complectens.   2 vols.   1681–9.

Fontenelle, Bernard Le Bovier de.   Oeuvres diverses, etc.   Amsterdam, 1701. [Vol. III contains, Une Digression sur les Anciens et les Modernes.]

Perrault, Charles.   Parallèle des anciens et des modernes en ce qui regarde les arts et les sciences.   Dialogues.   4 vols.   Paris, 1688.

Swift, Jonathan.   A Tale of a Tub, written for the universal improvement of mankind: To which is added An Account of a Battel between the antient and modern books in St. James's Library.   1704.

Swift, Jonathan. A Discourse concerning the mechanical operation of the Spirit, in a letter to a Friend. 1704.

—— The Battle of the Books; with selections from the literature of the Phalaris controversy. Ed. Guthkelch, A. 1908.

Temple, Sir William. Miscellanea, Part II [containing, "Essay on Ancient and Modern Learning"]. 1690.

—— Essays on Ancient and Modern Learning, and Poetry. Ed. Spingarn, J. E. Oxford, 1909.

Wotton, William. Reflections upon Ancient and Modern Learning. 1694.

—— (with Richard Bentley). Reflections upon ancient and modern Learning. with a dissertation upon the Epistles of Phalaris, etc. 2nd edn. of preceding. 1697.

—— A Defense of the Reflections upon Ancient and Modern Learning, with observations upon The (sic) Tale of a Tub. 1705.

III. Historical and Critical Works

Act of Uniformity. Documents relating to the Settlement of the Church of England by the Act of Uniformity of 1662. 1862.

Adamson, J. W. Pioneers of Modern Education, 1600–1700. Cambridge, 1905.

Allen, W. O., and McClure, E. Two Hundred Years: the History of the Society for Promoting Christian Knowledge. 1898.

Ayliffe, J. The Antient and Present State of the University of Oxford. 2 vols. 1714.

Baker, Thomas. History of the College of St. John the Evangelist, Cambridge. Ed. Mayor, J. E. B. Cambridge, 1869.

Brodrick, G. C. A History of the University of Oxford. 2nd edn. 1891.

—— Memorials of Merton College. Oxford Hist. Soc. Oxford, 1885.

Carlisle, Nicholas. A Concise Description of the Endowed Grammar Schools in England and Wales. 2 vols. 1818.

Clark, Andrew. The Life and Times of Anthony Wood, Antiquary of Oxford, 1632–1695, described by Himself. Oxford Hist. Soc. 5 vols. Oxford, 1891–1900.

Cooper, C. H. Annals of Cambridge. 5 vols. Cambridge, 1842–1908.

Godley, A. D. Oxford in the Eighteenth Century. 1908.

Laurie, S. S. John Amos Comenius, Bishop of the Moravians. Cambridge, 1887.

Leach, Arthur F. A History of Winchester College. 1899.

—— Educational Charters and Documents, 598–1909. Cambridge, 1911.

Lyte, H. C. Maxwell. A History of Eton College. 4th edn. 1911.

McDonnell, M. F. J. A History of St. Paul's School. 1909.

Montmorency, J. E. G. de. State Intervention in English Education. Cambridge, 1902.

Mullinger, J. B. A History of the University of Cambridge, vols. I–III. 1886–1911.

Oxford Historical Society's Publications. Collectanea. First Series. 1885. Second Series. 1890. Third Series. Oxford, 1896.

Sandys, Sir J. E. A History of Classical Scholarship. 3 vols. Cambridge, 1903–8.

Sargeant, John. Annals of Westminster School. 1898.

Sprat, Thomas (Bp. of Rochester). The History of the Royal Society of London for the Improving of Natural Knowledge. 1667.

Ward, John. The Lives of the Professors of Gresham College. 2 vols. 1740.

Watson, Foster. The English Grammar Schools to 1660; their curriculum and practice. Cambridge, 1908.

—— The Beginnings of the teaching of modern subjects in England. 1909.

—— The Education of the Early Nonconformists. In Gentleman's Magazine, vol. CCXCI, Sept., 1901.

—— Unlicensed Nonconformist Schoolmasters, 1662, and onwards. In Gentleman's Magazine, vol. CCXCIII, Sept., 1902.

—— Schoolmaster Followers of Bacon and Comenius. In Gentleman's Magazine, vol. CCXCV, Nov., 1903.

Wordsworth, Christopher. Scholae Academicae: Some Account of the Studies at the English Universities in the Eighteenth Century. Cambridge, 1877.

<h3 style="text-align:center">IV. MEMOIRS AND ANA</h3>

A., N. [Amhurst, Nicholas]. Terrae Filius, or the Secret History of the University of Oxford, in several Essays, to which are added Remarks upon a late Book entitled University Education, by Newton, R., D.D., Principal of Hart Hall. 1726.

Aubrey, J. Letters written by eminent persons in the seventeenth and eighteenth centuries. 2 vols. (vol. II in 2 parts). 1813.

Bourne, H. R. Fox. The Life of John Locke. 2 vols. 1876.

(Bristow, W.) The genuine account of the life and writings of Eugene Aram. . . . To which are added the remarkable defence he made on his trial . . . his Plan for a Lexicon, some pieces of poetry etc. [1759.]

Calamy, Edmund. An Abridgment of Mr. Baxter's History of his Life and Times. 1702.

—— An Historical Account of My own Life. Ed. Rutt, J. T. 2 vols. 1829.

[Coventry, Francis.] The History of Pompey the Little: or the Life and Adventures of a Lap-Dog. 1751.

Cumberland, Richard. Memoirs of Richard Cumberland, written by Himself. 1806–7.

Evelyn, John. Diary and Correspondence of John Evelyn, F. R. S. Ed. Bray, W. 4 vols. 1902.

Gibbon, Edward. The Memoirs of the Life of Edward Gibbon with various observations and excursions by himself. Ed. Hill, G. Birkbeck. 1900.

Hearne, Thomas. Reliquiae Hearnianae: The Remains of Thomas Hearne, M.A.. of Edmund Hall. Being Extracts from his MS. Diaries, Collected with a Few Notes by Philip Bliss. 3 vols. 1869.

Jebb, Sir R. C. Richard Bentley. 1882.

Kettlewell, John. Compleat Works of. To which is prefix'd the Life of the Author, with an Appendix of several original papers. 2 vols. 1719.

Mason, William. Isis: an Elegy. 1749.

Mayor, J. E. B. (ed.). Life of Ambrose Bonwicke by his Father, 1729. Cambridge, 1870.

—— Life of Ambrose Bonwicke (the Elder). Cambridge, 1870.

—— Cambridge under Queen Anne. Illustrated by Memoirs of Ambrose Bonwicke (1729) and Diaries of Francis Burman (1710) and Z. C. von Uffenbach (1712). Ed., with notes by Mayor, J. E. B., with preface by James, M. R. Cambridge, 1911.

Monk, James Henry. The Life of Richard Bentley. 2nd edn. 2 vols. 1833.

Montagu, Lady Mary Wortley. The Letters and Works. Ed. Wharncliffe, Lord, and Thomas, W. M. 2 vols. 1887.

Quiller Couch, L. M. (ed.). Reminiscences of Oxford by Oxford Men, 1559–1850. Oxford Hist. Soc. Oxford, 1892.

Shenstone, William. Poems. Vol. XIII in The Works of the English Poets from Chaucer to Cowper. 1810.

—— The School-Mistress; a poem in imitation of Spenser. 1742.

Tyerman, L. Life and Times of the Reverend Samuel Wesley, M.A., Rector of Epworth. 2 vols. 1866.

Warton, Thomas. The Progress of Discontent. 1746. In Poetical Works of Thos. Warton. Ed. Mant, Richard. 2 vols. Oxford, 1802.

—— The Triumph of Isis, a Poem occasioned by Isis, an Elegy. n. d. [1749].

Wordsworth, Christopher. Social Life at the English Universities in the Eighteenth Century. Cambridge, 1874.

Unpublished

Archbishop Secker's Diary. In the MSS. Collections of the Archbishop's Library, at Lambeth.

TABLE OF PRINCIPAL DATES

1692 Rymer's *Short View of Tragedy* (dated 1693).

1692–3 Bentley's Boyle Lectures on *The Folly and Unreasonableness of Atheism*.

1693 Locke's *Some Thoughts concerning Education*.

1694 Bank of England established.

1694 Leslie's *Short and easy method with the Deists*.

1694 Strype's *Memorials of Cranmer*.

1694 Wotton's *Reflections upon Ancient and Modern Learning*.

1694–1702 William III.

1695 Blackmore's *Prince Arthur*.

1695 Tanner's *Notitia monastica*.

1695 *The Flying Post* (Whig) begins to appear.

1695 *The Post Boy* (Tory) begins to appear.

1696 Aubrey's *Miscellanies*.

1696 Toland's *Christianity not mysterious*.

1697 Peace of Ryswyk.

1697 Collier's *Essays*.

1697 Defoe's *Essay upon Projects*.

1698 Andrew Fletcher's *Discourse of Government with relation to Militias*.

1698 Granville's *Heroick Love*.

1698 Ward's *London Spy* begins to appear.

1699 Society for Promoting Christian Knowledge founded.

1699 Bentley's *Dissertation on the Epistles of Phalaris*.

1699 Garth's *Dispensary*.

1699 William King's *Dialogues of the Dead*.

1700 Death of Dryden.

1700 Pomfret's *Choice*.

1700–31 Strype's *Annals of the Reformation*.

1701 Act of Settlement.

1701 Defoe's *The True-Born Englishman*.

1701 John Philips's *Splendid Shilling*.

1701 Steele's *Christian Hero*.

1702 Defoe's *Shortest Way with the Dissenters*.

1702 *The Daily Courant* (first daily paper founded.)

1702–14 Anne.

1703 Death of Pepys.

1703 Defoe's *Hymn to the Pillory*.

1703 Steele's *Lying Lover*.

1703? Henry Brooke born (d. 1783.)

1704 Death of Locke.

1704 Battle of Blenheim.

1704 Addison's *Campaign*.

1704 Dennis's *Grounds of Criticism in Poetry*.

1704 Swift's *A Tale of a Tub* and *The Battle of the Books* (written about 1697).

1704 Defoe establishes *The Review*, which is carried on till 1713.

1704–5 Samuel Clarke's Boyle Lectures.

1704–35 Rymer's *Foedera*.

1706 Death of Evelyn.

1706 Act of Succession.

1706 Union with Scotland.

1707 Echard's *History of England*, vol. i.

1707 Prior's *Poems on Several Occasions* (unauthorised ed.).

1708 Collier's *Ecclesiastical History*, vol. i.

1708 Motteux's translation of Rabelais (begun by Urquhart).

1708 John Philips's *Cyder*.

1708 Swift's *Sentiments of a Church of England man; Argument against abolishing Christianity; Predictions of Isaac Bickerstaff;* and *Account of Partridge's Death*.

1709 Defoe's *History of the Union of Great Britain*.

1709 Berkeley's *Essay towards a new theory of vision*.

1709 Pope's *Pastorals* appear in Tonson's *Miscellany*.

1709 Prior's *Poems on Several Occasions*.

1709 Rowe's edition of Shakespeare.

1709 *The Tatler* begins to appear.

1710 Trial of Sacheverell. Tory Ministry.

1710 Berkeley's *Principles of Human Knowledge*.

1710 Ambrose Philips's *Pastorals*.

1710 Swift's *City Shower* and *Baucis and Philemon*.

1710–12 Hearne's edition of Leland's *Itinerary*.

1711 Bentley's edition of Horace.

1711 Pope's *Essay on Criticism*.

1711 Occasional Conformity Act.

1711 Shaftesbury's *Characteristics*.

1711 Swift's *Conduct of the Allies*.

1711 2 January. Last number of *The Tatler*.

1711 First number of *The Spectator*, March 1.

1712 Arbuthnot's *Art of Political Lying*.

1712 Blackmore's *Creation*.

1712 Clarke's *Scripture Doctrine of the Trinity*.

1712 Dennis's *Essay on . . . Shakespeare*.

1712 Ambrose Philips's *Distressed Mother*.

1712 Pope's *The Rape of the Lock* published in Lintot's *Miscellany*.

1712 Whiston's *Primitive Christianity revived*.

1712 Last number of *The Spectator* appears, December 6.

1712 *The Examiner* established.

1712–13 Arbuthnot's *History of John Bull*.

1713 Treaty of Utrecht.

1713 Addison's *Cato*.

1713 Anthony Collins's *Discourse of Free-Thinking*.

1713 Bentley's *Remarks on a late Discourse of Free-Thinking*.

1713 Berkeley's *Three Dialogues*.

1713 Arthur Collier's *Clavis Universalis*.

1713 Gay's *Rural Sports*.

1713 Pope's *Windsor Forest* and *Ode on Saint Cecilia's Day*.

1713 Swift's *Cadenus and Vanessa*.

1713 Lady Winchilsea's *Poems*.

1714 Gay's *Shepherd's Week*.

1714 Schism Act.

1714–27 George I.

1715 Jacobite rising.

1715 Gay's *Trivia*.

1715 Pope's edition of Homer's *Iliad*, vol. I, appears. (Vol. II, 1716; vol. III, 1717; vol. IV, 1718; vols. V, VI, 1720.)

1715 Tickell's translation of Homer's *Iliad.*, Book I.

c. 1715 Carey's *Sally in our Alley*.

1716 Septennial Act.

1716 Hearne begins publication of a series of English chronicle histories.

1717 Sittings of Convention close.

1717 Hoadly's *Preservative against the principles and practices of the nonjurors* and *Sermon on the nature of Christ's Kingdom*.

1717 Pope's *Works*.

1717–19 Law's *Three Letters to the Bishop of Bangor*.

1718 Society of Antiquaries instituted.

1718 Prior's *Poems on Several Occasions*.

1719 Defoe's *Robinson Crusoe*.

1720 South Sea Bubble.

1720 Defoe's *Memoirs of a Cavalier* and *Captain Singleton*.

1721–42 Sir Robert Walpole in power.

1721 Parnell's *Poems on Several Occasions*.

1721 Death of Prior.

1721 Ramsay's *Poems*.

1721 Strype's *Ecclesiastical Memorials*.

1722 Defoe's *Journal of the Plague Year*, *Moll Flanders*, *Colonel Jacque*.

1722 Steele's *Conscious Lovers*.

1723 Mallet's *William and Margaret*.

1723 Mandeville's *Fable of the Bees* and Law's *Remarks* upon it.

1724 "Atterbury's plot."

1724 Burnet's *History of my own time* (vol. II, 1734).

1724 Defoe's *Roxana*.

1724 Ramsay's *Tea-Table Miscellany*; and *The Evergreen*.

1724 Swift's *Drapier's Letters*.

1725 Pope's edition of Shakespeare.

1725 Pope's translation of Homer's *Odyssey* (Vols. I–III) appears.

1725 Ramsay's *Gentle Shepherd*.

1726 Bentley's edition of Terence.

1726 Butler's *Sermons*.

1726 Swift's *Gulliver's Travels*.

1726 First number of *The Craftsman* appears, 5 December.

1727 Death of Newton.

INDEX

[Ff. after an entry implies that there are references to the same subject on at least two immediately succeeding pages.]

A Selection from the
Catalogue of

G. P. PUTNAM'S SONS

❦

Complete Catalogue sent
on application